FEMINISMS AND **WOMANISMS**

D1334220

FEMINISMS AND WOMANISMS

A Women's Studies Reader

Edited by Althea Prince and Susan Silva-Wayne
with the assistance of Christian Vernon

Women's Press
Toronto

Feminisms and Womanisms: A Women's Studies Reader
Edited by Althea Prince and Susan Silva-Wayne
1004640134
First published in 2004 by
Women's Press, an imprint of Canadian Scholars' Press Inc.
180 Bloor Street West, Suite 801
Toronto, Ontario
M5S 2V6

www.womenspress.ca

Canadian Scholars' Press/Women's Press gratefully acknowledges financial support for our publishing activities from the Government of Canada through the Book Publishing Industry Development Program (BPIDP).

National Library of Canada Cataloguing in Publication

Feminisms and womanisms : a women's studies reader / edited by Althea Prince and Susan Silva-Wayne with the assistance of Christian Vernon.

Includes bibliographical references.
ISBN 0-88961-411-3

1. Feminism. I. Prince, Althea. II. Silva-Wayne, Susan.

HQ1111.F456 2004   305.42   C2004-902724-7

Cover design by Slava Jericeric/Design Point www.designpoint.com
Text design and layout by Brad Horning

04   05   06   07   08   5   4   3   2   1

Printed and bound in Canada by AGMV Marquis Imprimeur Inc.

Canada

For our sisters,

Emily
Enid
Gloria
Jennette
Judith
Maria
Olive

TABLE OF CONTENTS

SECTION TWO
DIVERSITY

Anne Fausto-Sterling
The Five Sexes, Revisited
-133-

Ruth Frankenberg
Growing up White: Feminism, Racism,
and the Social Geography of Childhood
-139-

Yvonne Bobb-Smith
Caribbean Feminism versus Canadian Feminism
-167-

Amita Handa
Modest and Modern: Women As Markers of the Indian Nation State
-171-

Makeda Silvera
Man Royals and Sodomites: Some Thoughts on
the Invisibility of Afro-Caribbean Lesbians
-179-

SECTION THREE
SOCIALIZATION AND GENDER ROLES

Lois Gould
X—A Fabulous Child's Story
-189-

Naomi Wolf
Nakedness: Pride and Shame
-197-

Andrea O'Reilly
Mothers, Daughters, and Feminism Today:
Empowerment, Agency, Narrative, and Motherline
-207-

SECTION FIVE
WORK

SECTION SIX
THE CLASSROOM

SECTION SEVEN
POPULAR CULTURE

SECTION NINE
GLOBALISM

Sojourner Truth
1797–1883

[Speech written for May 28–29, 1851]

[Speech given at the Women's Rights Convention in Akron, Ohio, in 1852]

"Well, children, where there is so much racket there must be something out of kilter. I think that 'twixt the negroes of the South and the women of the North, all talking about rights, the white men will be in a fix pretty soon. But what's all this here talking about?

That man over there says that women need to be helped into carriages and lifted over ditches, and to have the best place everywhere. Nobody ever helps me into carriages, or over mud-puddles, or gives me any best place! And ain't I a woman? Look at me! Look at my arm! I could have ploughed and planted, and gathered into barns, and no man could head me! And ain't I a woman? I could work as much and eat as much as a man—when I could get it—and bear the lash as well! And ain't I a woman? I have borne thirteen children, and seen them most all sold off to slavery, and when I cried out with my mother's grief, none but Jesus heard me! And ain't I a woman?

Then they talk about this thing in the head; what's this they call it? [Intellect, somebody whispers] ... That's it, honey. What's that got to do with women's rights or negros' rights? If my cup won't hold but a pint, and yours holds a quart, wouldn't you be mean not to let me have my little half measure-full?

Then that little man in black there, he says women can't have as much rights as men, 'cause Christ wasn't a woman! Where did your Christ come from? Where did your Christ come from? From *God and a woman! Man had nothing to do with Him.

If the first woman God ever made was strong enough to turn the world upside down all alone, these women together ought to be able to turn it back, and get it right side up again! And now they is asking to do it, the men better let them.

Obliged to you for hearing me, and now old Sojourner ain't got nothing more to say."

*****

Acknowledgements

W̲e gratefully acknowledge the mission and history of Women's Press, which encouraged the publication of this collection. We also thank our colleagues at CSPI/Women's Press for their suggestions and contributions that make this the comprehensive book that it is.

For their review of the manuscript and their excellent suggestions that led to new directions, we thank the following scholars: Maureen Fitzgerald, Jean Golden, and Viviane Namaste.

Feminisms and Womanisms[1]

Introduction

Here, we have gathered what we consider to be lucid and interesting voices in feminist discourse. We selected the writers, topics, and structure of the reader in a specific philosophical and chronological way, in order to reflect the shifts and developments in the women's movement and those in corresponding feminist discourse and theory.

The first section of *Feminisms and Womanisms*, "Foundation," includes the history of feminist thought upon which subsequent generations of philosophers and pragmatists based their discourse and actions. The challenges, deviations, and dreams of these early feminists served as a road map for Second Wave feminists, and it is, in our view, a logical opening to the reader.

The first set of essays by Meg Luxton, Sharon Donna McIvor, L. Pauline Rankin, and Jill Vickers represents three streams of Canadian feminist thought: First Nations, English, and French. The following essays by Emma Goldman, Simone de Beauvoir, Betty Friedan, Germaine Greer, and Gloria Steinem challenge the accepted notion of women's roles and the role expectations that dominate women's lives. These early works also explore love, marriage, work, and gender relations, presenting challenges to the myths surrounding personal development, happiness, success, and security.

There is much discussion in the scholarship to suggest that mainstream feminism focused (and still focuses) on male domination while exercising White privilege through the exclusion of First Nations, Black, Hispanic, and other marginalized women from the discourse and the formally organized movement.[2]

Alice Walker, with her introduction of "womanism," presents an inclusive and new language with which to claim space in the praxis and discourse of the feminist movement. The placement of the bell hooks essay after Walker's is incisive in that it dissects the nature of feminism as a transformational politic for society as a whole.

Samantha Sacks answers the question "Why are you a feminist?" As a young woman who has engaged in women's studies and feminist action, her personal journey is a useful precursor to that of Anne-Marie Kinahan's scholarly critique of the feminist backlash that poses as a post-feminist movement.

The next section, "Diversity," contains the writing of five scholars whose work we selected because of the micro and macro focus on diversity. Anne Fausto-Sterling's groundbreaking piece on the five sexes challenges mainstream society's notions of gender and sexual diversity. Ruth Frankenberg offers an honest and open account of her experience with the social construction of whiteness, feminism, and racism.

Both Yvonne Bobb-Smith and Amita Handa report on their research studies into identity and the transcendence struggles of Caribbean and South Asian women in North America's White patriarchy. Makeda Silvera's article illuminates the impact of homophobia on African Caribbean lesbians' sense of *place* in society.

In the "Diversity" section we saw a demonstration of the all-pervasive way in which people's experiences are socially determined. Moving from "Diversity" into "Socialization and Gender Roles" is a logical next step in the reader. The initial gender roles, the early sexual identities, the familial relationships, romantic ideals, and social role expectations all stem from where people are socially located. We chose the work of writers who explore these issues in new and interesting ways. The range of their voices is impressive in terms of theory, life experience, and focus. The first set of writings are: Lois Gould's socialization fable; Naomi Wolf's essay on nakedness, pride, and shame; Andrea O'Reilly's theoretical essay on the mother-daughter relationship; and Michelle Hammer's further exploration of the psychological connection with the mother line. The section closes with the comedic, feminist voice of Margaret Cho, who revisits her youthful, romantic notions about intimacy; and Patricia Payette's narrative about the accommodations she makes between "feminist wife" and "political engagement."

The next section deals with "Identity, Body, and Health." These are areas that have had feminists' attention from as early as Sojourner Truth's dramatic courtroom speech about race, gender roles, and womanhood, and Emma Goldman's untenable position in her essay on the question of motherhood and its impact on women's creative and productive energies.

All of the writing in this section takes a stance of resistance on issues of identity, body, and health. It includes: Mariko Tamaki's edgy and humorous take on body image; Kathleen LeBesco's "fat and fabulous" resistance to the oppression of the construction of female body ideals; Kim Anderson's critique of the social construction of a negative, First Nation's identity; Julie Glaser's essay on eating disorder; Inga Muscio reclaiming woman's body as a liberating process; Nancy Graham dealing with issues of women's mental health; and Carolyn Egan and Linda Gardner chronicling the effects of racism on the reproductive freedom of women of colour. The section closes with essays by Susan Sontag, Clarissa Pinkola-Estés, and Margaret Cruikshank that provide feminist responses to society's oppression of women as they age.

The next two sections of *Feminisms and Womanisms*, "Work" and "The Classroom," focus on women in the work environment. First, the "Work" section examines the issues with which women have struggled and continue to struggle in the market economy and work environment. The work of Jan Borowy, Shelly Gordon, and Gayle Lebans exposes the poor working conditions for homeworkers, and chronicles one campaign to obtain a living wage. This is followed by an essay by Pat Armstrong and Hugh Armstrong, who offer a feminist, Marxist analysis of women's position in the political economy.

For some women, work includes the personal vulnerability of being in the sex trade. Chris Bruckert's study of the world of the professional stripper brings a scholarly analysis to voices that are usually silenced.

The work environment can include both racial and sexual harassment. Himani Bannerji presents a case study of one such experience by a woman for whom she was called upon to act as an advocate. This troubling case is a dramatic conclusion to this section.

The feminist agenda has always included attention to critical pedagogies that empower women, allow them agency, and enhance their intellectual development. As sites for the development and growth of feminist consciousness, women's studies classrooms have not been free from pedagogical issues requiring feminist intervention. Linda Briskin opens the way for new approaches to women's studies as she advocates intersections between social theory and social action as the basis for women's studies programs. An essay by Vivanne Namaste and Georgia Sitara offers a pedagogical method for including transgender issues in the women's studies curriculum. The section closes with Jean Bobby Noble's theoretical framework for questioning the normative precepts of the heterosexual classroom.

We have included the section on "Popular Culture" to encourage the reader's exploration of the work of feminist artists. We selected the writing of cultural workers who have created poetry, song, and cultural criticism. This section includes the work of Janice Accoose on the literature of First Nations women; Motion in feminist hip-hop *rhymez*; Adrienne Rich on being a feminist poet; Margaret Atwood on the shift to feminism in Adrienne Rich's work; Catherine MacKinnon's essay on pornography in popular culture; Audre Lorde on the body erotic; and Angela Davis on women in jazz.

The theory and discourse of the women's movement have been driven by women's social action. The next set of essays in the section on "Praxis—Social Change" presents examples of women's collective action, organized around social issues such as housing, safety, disAbilities, same-sex marriage, environmental justice, and woman abuse.

Harriet Rosenberg recounts the celebrated case of the "housewife activists" who brought to light the environmental waste hazards affecting their community, the Love Canal.

Diane Driedger, Nita Israelite, and Kim Swartz contribute historical and contemporary accounts of disAbled women's struggle for access to services and life opportunities. Joanne Cohen and Beverly Smith focus on the quest of same-sex couples for equal rights.

Women in Quebec have a long and noble history of social activism. We opened the reader with Meg Luxton's detailed discussion of their engagement in feminist action. The case study "2000 Good Reasons to March" looks at the collective action of the Fédération des femmes du Québec. It recounts the powerful activism of women in Quebec that resulted in their being heard, and having their demands reflected in a number of institutional changes that would impact women's lives. The study highlights the vigilance of feminist activists in Quebec when they set about demanding changes in the law to protect women.

This section closes with two essays on women's physical and psychological safety. First, an essay by Tammy C. Landau traces changes in the criminal justice system that affect women in the arena of "woman abuse." The section closes with Cornelia Sollfrank's essay on hacking and cyberfeminism.

The final section of *Feminisms and Womanisms*, "Globalism," is futuristic in its analyses of and prognostications for ecofeminism, trans-nationalism, and globalism. The essays by Lee-Anne Broadhead, Naila Kabeer, Maria Mies, and Vandana Shiva contribute to a deeper understanding of the gendered dimension in the quest for global justice.

Notes

1.   See Alice Walker's essay titled "Womanist."
2.   See essays by Alice Walker, Kim Anderson, bell hooks, and Meg Luxton for discussion of this.

SECTION ONE

FOUNDATIONS

Feminism As a Class Act:
Working-Class Feminism and
the Women's Movement in Canada

Meg Luxton

In 1996 the Canadian Labour Congress (CLC) and the National Action Committee on the Status of Women (NAC) organized a national women's march against poverty.[1] With the slogan "For Bread and Roses, for Jobs and Justice," caravans left both the west and east coasts on 14 May, following the CLC convention in Vancouver. The marchers travelled for a month, visiting over 90 communities and participating in events involving about 50,000 women. They met in Ottawa on 15 June for the largest women's demonstration in Canadian history and NAC's annual general meeting.[2]

This alliance of the main national union organization and the largest national organization of the autonomous women's movement was based on demands focused specifically on the situations of working-class and poor women. The demands explicitly linked struggles for both women's equality and anti-racism with working-class struggles for more equitable distributions of wealth and access to resources. As NAC President Sunera Thobani declared, "women's dreams of equality can never be realized in a society polarized between the 'haves' and the 'have-nots,' where the poorer regions of the country are marginalized, racism grows, and the most vulnerable members of our community are abandoned."[3]

In this essay, I argue that the political links between the labour movement and the women's movement, represented by this march, with its explicit focus on working-class and poor women's issues, came about because of the existence of a union-based, working-class feminism that has been a key player in the women's movement, the labour movement, and the left since the late 1960s and early 1970s. It has become popular in recent years to assert that the women's movement of the 1960s and 1970s was largely middle class and that its politics reflected the concerns and interests of such women.[4] I think this argument is incorrect in the Canadian context and I suggest that such beliefs are part of a larger pattern in which both working-class women and their organizing efforts, and left-wing or socialist feminism, get written out of, or "hidden from history."[5]

In her study of women auto workers, Pam Sugiman has demonstrated the existence of "working-class feminism":

> Contrary to the popular belief that the North American women's movement was an exclusively middle-class development, the experiences of female auto workers suggest that a distinct "feminist trade unionism" emerged in the 1960s.[6]

The feminism Sugiman identifies was not unique to auto workers. In this essay, I argue, against the formulation that the women's movement was middle class and focused on reforming the state, that working-class and socialist feminist activists developed a strong feminist presence in the labour movement and a significant working-class orientation in the women's movement.[7] I document some of the dynamics in the development of the women's movement in the 1960s and 1970s that created an environment in which a union-based, working-class feminism found a space and became an important political player. That presence has shaped the subsequent development of the women's movement in Canada. The 1996 march was one expression of that politics.

The Context for Feminist Organizing in Canada

The 1996 alliance between the CLC as a federation of member unions and NAC as a coalition of groups from the autonomous women's movement, and the organization of the March as a series of events in different communities, illustrated some of the aspects of feminist organizing particular to Canada. Any efforts to build national or pan-Canadian, extra-parliamentary political organizations confront two difficulties specific to the national situation that shape their politics and organizational structures. First, Canada's relatively small population, spread out over a large geographic area, and its federated state structure mean that organizing typically occurs at a local or regional level, reflecting regional differences based on local and diverse economies, provincial or territorial and municipal legislation, and linguistic, racialized, ethnic, or national cultures, and patterns of settlement. The political differences that hamper building pan-Canadian movements are compounded by the logistical difficulties and financial costs imposed by the physical distances.

Second, the dynamics of Quebec as a distinct nation, inside and subordinated to the rest of Canada and particularly the Canadian state, has generated two significantly different political currents: francophone feminists in Quebec and what gets awkwardly called the feminist movement "in the rest of Canada." Co-operation and collaboration between these two movements has been difficult and uneven. The colonization of aboriginal or indigenous peoples and their efforts to resist and to assert claims for self-determination have generated a number of aboriginal women's groups allied together in a Native Women's movement autonomous from but with links to the other currents of the women's movement.[8]

Thus federally, there are at least three distinct women's movements: the movement in the rest of Canada, the francophone movement in Quebec, and the movements of First Nations women.[9] As immigrant women, women of colour, and women who for reasons of language, ethnicity, national origin, or skin colour are subject to racism began to organize, they challenged especially the movement in the rest of Canada for failing to deal with racism, and to a certain extent formed another current. As a result, as Hamilton and Barrett note, "A belief in undivided sisterhood was never very marketable in Canada."[10] Both strategically and organizationally, feminism in Canada has tended toward a politics of solidarity based on coalitions that recognize different constituencies. That dynamic created a space and legitimacy for union-based, working-class feminism.[11]

The important position of working-class women as part of the revitalization of the women's movement in the rest of Canada in the 1960s was stimulated by at least three distinct, though clearly related developments: the increased education and labour market participation of women through the 1960s and 1970s and the related growing strength of working-class women in the labour movement; the organizational practices of the autonomous women's movement, especially as developed in the Nation Action Committee on the Status of Women (NAC), a national coalition of women's groups; and the socialist feminist politics that developed as part of the early women's liberation movement. These created a political terrain in which union feminism was able to grow, providing a significant base for the larger women's movement and transmitting basic feminist perspectives into the wider society.

Women in the Labour Force: Challenges to the Unions

During the 1960s, as the college and university sector expanded, the proportion of women and students from working-class families attending universities and colleges increased. While the growing numbers of women with post-secondary education meant that the disparities between women have increased over the last 40 years, with a small number of elite women earning significantly higher incomes than the majority, it has also produced a layer of professional women who to varying degrees have used their skills to advance women—staffing women's medical and legal clinics, challenging school curricula by developing anti-sexist and anti-racist pedagogies, taking feminist politics into the formal political arenas, and working for women in both the labour movement and the autonomous women's movement.[12]

As the women's movement grew, young women students confronted the deeply entrenched sexism in the universities and colleges. Developing increasingly sophisticated critiques of the traditions of formal knowledge, in the early 1970s they created Women's Studies as the academic wing of the women's movement.[13] Informed by the progressive politics of the student movement and the growth of left-wing organizations, some women combined a left-wing women's liberation politics and a concern for working-class issues with a developing socialist feminist theorizing to produce a body of research on working-class women,

and to a lesser extent on aboriginal and black women, women of colour, immigrant women, and other minority groups.[14] As Women's Studies became institutionalized, its explicit links to the activist women's movement were often weakened or lost, but it remains a source of scholarship which includes important work on and for, and sometimes by, working-class women and unions.[15]

The 1960s also marked a significant change in women's labour force participation. While the actual number of women in the labour force, and the percentage of women compared to men, both steadily increased throughout the century, they increased dramatically between 1960 and 1980. In 1961, almost 30 percent of women were in the paid labour force and they were about 30 percent of the total labour force. By 1981 more than 50 percent of women, including married women, were in the paid labour force and women were increasingly in the labour force even when they had young children.[16]

Despite the dramatic changes in women's levels of education, and their increased numbers in paid employment, the labour force in the 1960s was significantly sex segregated and women's earnings remained considerably lower than men's.[17] In many workplaces women confronted sexist discrimination and harassment. More than men, women also had to juggle the often conflicting demands of both their paid employment and domestic, family, and community responsibilities, especially for child care. Thus, as increasing numbers of women were in paid labour for longer periods of their lives, and especially when their children were young, they confronted the sexism of the sexual division of labour, and inequalities and discrimination in the paid work force. Feminism offered many of them a framework that made sense of their experiences as women and a politics that made struggles for change seem possible.[18]

The labour movement in the early 1960s, based mainly in male-dominated occupations, was organizationally overwhelmingly male. In 1962 women were only 16.4 percent of all union members, although they were about 30 percent of the total paid labour force.[19] Politically the labour movement's positions on women were more contradictory. Through the first half of the 20th century, the labour movement as a whole had been conflicted about ways of responding to women workers. From the beginning, some unions and many individual activists fought for women's rights as workers and as union members. Particularly those unions with a socialist orientation or with significant numbers of their members affiliated with the Communist or Socialist parties had explicit policies supporting equality for all oppressed peoples and often took strong positions supporting women workers.[20] The majority of unions, however, reflecting the prevailing sexism of the times, had not given particular support to women workers.[21] Analyzing the labour movement's response to women in the period from 1881 to 1921, Julie White argues:

> Unions were faced with the reality that single women were a small and transient contingent of the labour force, while the vast majority of married women were dependent upon their men's wages. Confronted with the employers' use of cheap female labour to undercut men's wages, and unable to move beyond the ideology of women's domestic nature, most often unions failed to organize women workers and turned instead to protective legislation and the idea of the family wage to deal with the "problem" of the working woman.[22]

By the early 1960s most unions either continued the practices White describes or, especially in workplaces with significant numbers of women, conceived of the women as "workers" just like men, ignoring gender differences.[23] Women workers themselves often shared that perspective.[24] But when apparently gender-neutral policies and practices ignore gender differences, "issues are shaped according to men's lives, men's visions, and men's needs."[25] Some of the more politically progressive unions began to address women's issues explicitly. In 1964, for example, the United Auto Workers held its first conference for women workers and called for full equality.[26]

As more and more women were in the labour force, and as the labour movement began organizing new sectors such as the public service where there were large numbers of women, the conflict intensified between sexist gender-neutral practices and the working lives of many union members, especially women. Sugiman describes as "labour's dilemma" this ambivalent relationship between the labour movement and wage earning women:

> When women workers make demands in the industry and in their union, they uncover the masculine biases. When women try to rewrite the agenda, some men resist. There is conflict and struggle. We can see the gender politics of the union.[27]

Between 1965 and 1975 the number of employed women in Canada increased by 79 percent; the number of women union members increased by 144 percent.[28] The proportion of union members who were women increased from 16 percent in 1962 to nearly 40 percent in the 1990s.[29] Inevitably the gender politics of the labour movement became more visible.[30]

Feminism and Unions: Working-Class Feminism

More and more women confronted both the pressures of their paid employment, increasingly combined with domestic labour and child care, and the gender politics of the labour movement, which rarely addressed the specific concerns of women. As they articulated their concerns, and fought in the workplace and in the unions for better conditions for women, they fueled the developing women's movement. In that re-emerging feminism of the late 1960s and early 1970s, many of them found a discourse that offered a critique of their daily lives and possibilities for change. While only a small core became activists in both the labour movement and the women's movement, feminist ideas became widespread:

> While only a minority of women were activists, others were not untouched by the politics of the women's movement. "Union-wise" feminists had educated their sisters in various ways and degrees. Even women who clung to conventional beliefs and arrangements modified their strategies and filtered them through new ideas. In many women, elements of feminism coexisted (uneasily) with patriarchal ideologies.[31]

Not surprisingly, working-class women focused most of their energy on trying to force employers to pay them fair wages and ensure them job security and safe working conditions. The viciousness of employer resistance revealed how important women's low wages and unregulated working conditions were, and are, to the process of capital accumulation and profit-making. For example, in the Fleck strike in Ontario in 1978, 120 workers, mostly immigrant women, were out for six months trying to get a first contract. Women's liberation groups supported the workers who eventually won but only after weeks of police harassment, including arrests and beatings. The police bill came to about two million dollars (about $16,000 per striker!). As the plant owner was related to the then Ontario Attorney General, the strikers and their supporters came to recognize that the socialist feminist argument about the links between capital and the state had some legitimacy.[32] Heather Jon Maroney's analysis of the impact of that strike on the women workers shows how their self-organization in struggle fostered a more general working-class feminist analysis:

> Militant strike action by women is also an objective challenge to their economic exploitation, their individuation into the illusory privacy of the family, and the ideological construction of women as passive dependents protected by men which is at the core of women's place in the contemporary capitalist sexual division of labour. At Fleck, the strikers explicitly articulated this challenge .... The lesson that they confirmed was that, given the right political conditions, self-organization in struggle will radicalize, mobilize and broaden feminist consciousness and action.[33]

As their numbers grew, union women challenged the sexist structures and organizational cultures of their unions and worked to get unions to adopt positions that would directly affect women. A number of individual women, with years of union organizing experience behind them, were well positioned in existing union organizations to raise such issues. Activists such as Madelaine Parent, of the Canadian Textile and Chemical Union and one of the founders of the Canadian Confederation of Unions, Evelyn Armstrong of the United Electrical Workers, and Grace Hartman from the Canadian Union of Public Employees led the fights inside the labour movement by strengthening their ties with the women's movement.

The 1970s in particular was a period of women's organizing activities in unions. For example, at the 1970 United Auto Workers convention, union women called for "full equality now."[34] The fight for affirmative action started with struggles to get women hired into so-called non-traditional jobs or all-male preserves at workplaces such as Stelco and Inco or in the trades; such initiatives demanded union support for challenges to employers.[35] Union women formed organizations to help them fight inside the labour movement to improve women's situations; for example, in March 1976 Organized Working Women (OWW) was formed in Ontario, with Evelyn Armstrong as its first president, with a membership restricted to women already in unions, while in September 1979 Saskatchewan Working Women (SWW) formed with its membership open to all women who agreed with its objectives. Frustrated by the lack of support for women in the existing unions and outraged by the failure of the union movement to organize in predominantly female workplaces, a group of socialist feminists in 1972 formed an independent union in BC, the Service, Office and Retail Workers' Union of Canada (SORWUC).[36] Unable to sustain their efforts in the face of employers' hostility and the reluctance of the union movement to support them, they collapsed after a few years, but their initiative prodded the union movement to pay more attention to predominantly female sectors of the labour force.[37]

Responding to increasing pressures from their members, unions began to take up union women's issues.[38] They held conferences, educationals, and training programmes. Many unions from locals to national organizations developed women's committees or caucuses intended to help women identify their concerns, develop the strategies and tactics to advance their issues, and strengthen their capacities to intervene in the male-dominated culture of the union. In 1965 the Ontario Federation of Labour set up its first women's committee, which was chaired by Grace Hartman, then a vice-president of CUPE. In 1966 that committee organized a conference on Women and Work.[39] In 1976 the CLC held its first conference for women union activists. Unions developed new structures and new positions. In 1977 the Ontario Public Service Employees

Union hired its first full-time equal opportunity co-ordinator. Recognizing their failure to get women into leadership positions, some bodies developed affirmative action measures. In 1984, for example, the CLC designated a minimum of six women vice-presidents. They recognized that when competent women leaders are visible, more women are likely to participate and more men and women are able to accept women in leadership positions. Even more important were the positions unions adopted both in contract negotiations on, for example, maternity and parental leave or same-sex spousal benefits, and in union policies such as providing child care at conventions. Finally, unions were also part of, and supported the activities and organizations of, the women's movement. They co-sponsored specific activities such as International Women's Day demonstrations and joined coalitions to work on campaigns such as those for employment and pay equity, access to abortions, and quality child care.

Such efforts publicly recognized that discrimination against women existed, and identified it as a problem. They also went some way toward improving the situation. What they illustrate is the extent to which women pushed for a new gender politics more favourable to women both inside the unions, and, through their unions, in the women's movement. However, having women in leadership does not necessarily mean that those women are concerned with women's issues and union-organized women's caucuses may easily become just another unit of the existing union structure. If progressive union leaderships promote demands that many members do not actively support, contract negotiations on these issues are likely to founder and it does women little good if their issues are the first to be dropped in negotiations. Only if enough members are mobilized and committed to struggling around particular concerns are those issues likely to remain on the agenda with any likelihood of long-term success. So, what is more important is the extent to which women workers themselves are mobilized in their particular workplaces and throughout their unions. In the period from the late 1960s through the 1970s, a majority of women workers supported basic feminist equality demands. A minority of activists also supported more explicit socialist feminist demands. In combination they generated a union perspective on feminism that developed by the end of the 1970s into a distinct and important current of working-class feminism in the women's movement. Pam Sugiman describes this process among women in the United Auto Workers Union (UAW):

> A core group of women with years of active involvement in the UAW fervently threw itself into the contemporary feminist debate. These women became the driving force behind the fight for women's rights in the auto plants.[40]

Some of them also became a driving force for working-class issues in the autonomous women's movement.

Coalition Politics: NAC and Unions

In the period between the ebb of the first wave of feminism in the 1920s and its revitalization in the 1960s, a range of women's organizations continued to provide services for and work on behalf of women. Some, such as the National Council of Women of Canada (NCWC) (founded in 1893), the Canadian Federation of Business and Professional Women's Clubs (BPW) (founded 1930), and the Canadian Negro Women's Association (founded in 1951) involved women in national politics. Many others were local, focused on neighbourhoods or municipalities such as the Association of Women Electors, which from 1937 to 1986 monitored Toronto municipal affairs.[41] Some, such as the various groups associated with the Communist and Socialist parties, or the Voice of Women formed in 1960 to work for peace, were tied to international politics. While the groups were often dispersed and disparate, they were also sometimes loosely linked both by organizational connections and through personal ties among members.

In the period when there was no mass mobilization of women, the most prominent organizations were those able to attract public attention, often because although they lobbied various levels of government on behalf of women, they requested reforms rather than dramatic changes. Typically such groups were organized nationally with provincial or territorial and local chapters.[42] Their national (and sometimes provincial or territorial) leaderships were often very active; the chapters were more or less active, usually at a very local level. The leaders of these organizations were typically part of the same class as federal politicians and often had personal ties to them.[43] They were usually white, English-speaking, and of Anglo or European backgrounds, either professional women concerned with improving their own circumstances or wives of professional men who had the time, energy, and resources to take up social and political issues.[44] A similar layer of white French-speaking Quebecoises played a similar role in Quebec politics. A very few of them were also associated with the anglophone national organizations.[45]

While most of these groups focused on particular issues at any one time, their overall project was to take apart the structures of discriminatory laws and exclusionary social practices that maintained women's inequality as compared to men. Their goal was to ensure for women the same rights and opportunities available to men. That formulation did not question the systemic inequalities between men, so class and race inequalities were rarely addressed. Groups such as the National Council of Jewish Women or the Canadian Negro Women's Association, formed specifically to address the concerns of racialized women, like Communist and Socialist groups addressing the issues of working-class and poor women, were the exception. Most of the large national women's groups had no serious critique of capitalism as a socio-political economic system based on the exploitation by the owners of wealth of working people whose labour produces that wealth. Rather, they wanted reforms that would enable women to compete like men in the labour market, in politics, and in society as a whole for access to wealth, power, and other resources. They believed that by informing and educating politicians about the issues, they could convince them to introduce new policies to improve the situation of women. Thus, one of their main strategies for change was lobbying politicians and attempting to educate people about the issues to ensure wider support for their lobbying.[46]

The national executives were also linked both to other national organizations and to comparable organizations internationally. One of the key links was provided by the United Nations' Status of Women Commission where women from different countries met to compare their situations, and from which they could pressure their governments to investigate and improve the situation of women. Many national organizations such as the NCWC, BPW, and the YWCA were part of international federations that had formal status as participants in UN agencies and members of their organizations served as Canadian representatives.[47] Laura Sabia, an activist in the Canadian Federation of University Women, said of her meetings in the late 1950s and early 1960s with women's delegations from various countries:

> They were all doing the same damn thing. The question of abortion was in every country. That's why it became a very dominant question. Everybody was looking at it. And the property laws were all the same. They all had different kinds of property laws, but they all wanted something better than they were having. The women were not getting a fair deal. My knowledge first came from the United Nations.

Their international experiences convinced many of these women of the universality of women's issues and of the importance of working co-operatively. They also meant that such women were strategically positioned to act quickly and effectively as catalysts for the newly re-emerging women's movement of the 1960s.

This "second wave" involved major political and cultural shifts in the way women understood themselves and their place in society. Existing women's groups grew and expanded their range of activities as new women joined. New organizations such as the BC Indian Homemakers' Association (formed in 1960), and new federations of groups such as the Fédération des femmes du Québec (formed in 1966) were established. Small radical activist groupings came together briefly over particular events or actions and hundreds of individual women began speaking out publicly.

In this climate, the leaders of the large national women's groups saw the possibility for new ways of organizing. In 1966, Laura Sabia, then president of the Canadian Federation of University Women, realized that most of the national women's organizations were lobbying the federal government about the same issues:

> Everybody was writing briefs to the government in those days. We wanted poverty law, law reform on divorce ... abortion .... So every one of these organizations ... was sending briefs to the government. And there was a common thread .... We were all asking for the same damn thing.

She realized that by lobbying separately, they diffused their impact on the government and on each other: "Every year ... the government would receive women's organizations—one by one—separate so they didn't talk to each other."

Assuming that they would be more effective if they co-operated, she wrote to 35 national English-language organizations, inviting them to send representatives to a meeting in Toronto.[48] "So they all came to the meeting and we batted back and forth what to do and I showed them how all the resolutions were the same, we all wanted the same things and why don't we do it as a group?" They formed a coalition of 32 groups called the Committee for the Equality of Women in Canada (CEWC). Christine Bennett of the United Steelworkers of America was the first union representative on CEWC. She was replaced after a few months by Grace Hartman as chair of the OFL women's committee, who then worked to persuade the organized labour movement to support CEWC.[49] The CLC voted to support CEWC and named Hartman as the CLC representative. CEWC also worked with Thérèse Casgrain, Monique Bégin, and others to forge links with Quebec women's groups, particularly with the newly formed Fédération des femmes du Québec. As the members of these groups clarified the basis for their collaboration, they decided to demand a Royal Commission on the Status of Women.[50]

Formed in 1967, the Commission toured the country, holding public meetings and inviting written briefs. It acted as a catalyst, providing a focus for many women who mobilized their groups or formed new ones to make presentations. It also created a space for women in mixed organizations to push for attention to women's issues. Grace Hartman worked hard to ensure that both CUPE and the CLC made presentations to the Commission so that union women's issues were clearly on the agenda of both the (often reluctant) union federations and the Commission. According to Susan Crean, while the CLC submission was cautious, the three union women attending its presentation made sure in the question period that the Commissioners heard their more radical positions, especially on abortion. The CUPE presentation was more forthcoming about the reasons why union women were also involved in the autonomous women's movement:

We differ from other labour organizations which state that the labour movement is in the forefront of all organizations striving for equality of women. CUPE does not feel that the labour movement does enough to fight discrimination against working women .... The majority of female workers who fight for true equality do so without the wholehearted support of their fellow trade unionists, male and female.[51]

When the Commission filed its Report of the Royal Commission on the Status of Women in 1970, it provided a thoughtful and critical examination of the situation of women in Canada and made 167 recommendations. While the more conservative women thought the document went a bit too far and left-wing and women's liberation activists criticized it for not going far enough, most of the women who had participated considered the process a productive one. The challenge was to pressure the government to implement the Report's recommendations.

The member groups of the Committee for Equality for Women in Canada continued with their various activities, including lobbying the federal government and monitoring its response to the Report, but CEWC itself was inactive until Sabia called a meeting in 1971 where she urged member groups to remember that "only in joint action can we be sure that the Report will not gather dust on some Parliamentary shelf."[52] CEWC decided to reform itself as The National Ad Hoc Action Committee on the Status of Women (NAC) with the specific goal of ensuring the implementation of the Royal Commission's recommendations.[53] Frustrated by the lack of response, NAC organized a national conference in 1972 in Toronto called "Strategy for Change" to discuss how to get action on the recommendations of the Report. About 800 women attended.[54] Sabia recalls the power of bringing such a variety of women together:

It brought everybody together. It was just incredible. You had the prim ladies from the local Council of Women, the Councils of Women. You know, those women who legitimately did an awful lot of good work, but did it in the way the government wanted them to do it—nice manner, nice ladies. Then you had the other group who were the Trotskyites and who were just as bold as you could probably do ... they came and screamed and yelled and just did about everything .... They had never come across these women before .... So in essence, we all learned from each other.[55]

The conference affirmed the importance of monitoring the federal government's treatment of women's issues and lobbying for further improvements and confirmed NAC as a national organization to serve "as an educational and communications link for women in Canada who are striving to improve their status and to change the traditional attitudes and habits of prejudice towards women." Intended to "not duplicate nor supersede established organization," NAC also reaffirmed the coalition structure as a way of ensuring that specific groups could continue to focus primarily on their own concerns while uniting to monitor and lobby government.[56] As president, Sabia repeatedly affirmed the importance of bringing together women from very different perspectives:[57]

> ... but if you don't go after those women ... the ones who were so anti-establishment ... those are the women who worked, they're the ones who kicked the asses, and if you can't work with them, and the polite ones are polite and that's fine and it's great to have them on board, but we need the others too.[58]

Despite Sabia's enthusiasm about learning from "everybody" and her willingness to work with both the conservative members from mainstream organizations and more radical grassroots women, the conference was severely criticized for its lack of militancy by a radical caucus formed by about 60 participants, including activists such as labour militant Madelaine Parent and socialists from Toronto Women's Liberation.[59] One of the radical caucus members explained their concerns:

> There was nothing wrong with the Royal Commission recommendations. We were prepared to support any call to have them implemented. But we wanted much more; we wanted the conference to come out loud and clear in support of way more radical positions, like an end to capitalism and for workers' control—not something those bourgeois ladies were prepared to discuss.[60]

NAC's leadership and its subsequent positions, at least in the first few years, confirmed its position primarily as a voice for liberal feminism:[61] "For the first few years of its existence, NAC's executive committee members tended to represent either the established women's groups or the growing number of Status of Women committees."[62]

The existence of NAC as an increasingly large and highly visible organization since then has been both a strength and a problem for the women's movement in Canada. While its organizational form and lobbying tactics have kept feminist concerns on the national political agenda, its visibility has encouraged some commentators, especially in the media, to erroneously equate it with the women's movement as if its organizational positions are shared by its member groups (which they often are not) and as if it includes the whole of the women's movement (which it never has). This assumption in turn leads to the claim that the women's movement was largely middle class and concerned primarily with state reform. As a result, the rest of the women's movement, and particularly its working class and left wing, are often ignored. Instead, the argument is made that the agenda of the women's movement demands an expansion of the social welfare system and greater government receptivity to women's issues.[63] Liberal feminism does have that strategy; for left-wing feminism it is only a tactic. Of course demands must be made of the state, but real change will only come from the mass mobilization of women challenging capital.[64]

Despite NAC's predominantly middle-class reformist leadership in the first decade, and especially the strong representation of federal Liberal women, the organization included both the original radical caucus and groups of union and working-class women.[65] Key individual union activists such as Madelaine Parent and Laurel Ritchie, from the Canadian Confederation of Unions, held prominent positions in NAC and so ensured union issues were always on the agenda. Grace Hartman was treasurer for its first three years. NAC's coalition politics meant it remained committed to alliances with unions and working-class feminists. Quite deliberately, as a signal that it was open to working-class and union issues, in 1974, NAC chose as its second president Grace Hartman, at that time the secretary-treasurer of the Canadian Union of Public Employees (CUPE):

> She (Grace Hartman) came from Labour and it was a good thing to have a woman in Labour take on that kind of thing because some of the women in the Labour movement were very suspicious of those of us who were not part of the labour movement or those of us who lived 'rich on the hog', so to speak. you know, that's what they thought, we were these ladies that really didn't know anything about the labour force. So we sort of planned that Grace Hartman would be the Chairman and she was a good chairman. [66]

The impact of union women on NAC's policies was reflected in the organization's 1974 opposition to wage and price controls, despite the strong presence of Liberal party members. Union women's involvement in NAC gave the organization access to resources that few other women's groups could offer. The Federation of Women Teachers' Associations of Ontario, for example, provided office space, support, and handled publicity and public relations for NAC for years.[67] Union locals and federations have been members; individuals periodically serve as union representatives on the executive and important union issues such as pay and employment equity, health and safety concerns, and basic union concerns, such as the right to strike, typically won NAC support. As NAC took up such issues, it gained a qualified legitimacy from more radical women, especially those coming out of the women's liberation movement and socialist feminists:

> As socialist feminists we support the goal of working together for changes in our lives and in society and we have been active in NAC for a number of years .... We also understand that sexism, racism, hetrosexism [sic] and class oppression are very much integrated, and maintained, by the economic and political structures under which we live. The lives of working-class women, women of colour, immigrant women and lesbians are affected by all of these oppressions, and our analysis and methods of work must reflect this.[68]

NAC's membership increased from the original 31 groups in 1972 to 120 groups in 1977, to 458 groups in 1986 of which 36 were from the labour movement.[69] In 1996 there were over 600 member groups. The presence of working-class and union women acted to remind everyone that winning rights for elite women does little to advance women's equality generally. Kay Macpherson, then vice-president of NAC, quoted approvingly Grace Hartman, who said:

> I often think of a woman standing on the cold hard cement of a fish packing plant, ankle deep in slime, working eight hours a day for poverty-level wages, and of women in "bucket shop" factories, large and small offices, banks, restaurants and hundreds of other places of work where unions have either been unable or have not tried to organize. What is more important to these women: the fact that a woman is head of Statistics Canada, or that they are fighting to have free child care provided by the employer?[70]

This alliance kept union issues on the agenda for other women's organizations and strengthened union women's ability to carry feminist politics back to their unions. It also insured that a class analysis was presented in NAC debates:

> Leftist-feminist ideas were also reflected in the News [The NAC newsletter]. The struggles by unionists such as Grace Hartman and Madelaine Parent to win collective-bargaining objectives for working-class women were reported throughout the period [1972-1978]. Class aspects of issues such as abortion were highlighted.[71]

A sensitivity to class and a commitment to reducing class inequalities remained central to NAC's positions. Its 1992 Review of the Situation of Women in Canada:

> ... shows that the lives of most women are getting more difficult, while at the same time more barriers protect a smaller number of women who have access to increasing proportions of the wealth ... the goal of feminism was never to create situation [sic] where a privileged few women have the freedom to have it all when the majority of women are falling further towards poverty.[72]

The development of working-class feminism and the strength of socialist feminism in the wider women's movement were also fueled by the particular way the women's liberation movement and socialist feminist politics evolved in Canada. Reciprocally, the growth of that left-wing feminism was fueled by the strength of working-class feminism in the unions and in the autonomous women's movement.

The Women's Liberation Movement, Socialist Feminism, and Working-Class Women

During the 1960s, a wave of radical political protest swept much of Europe and North America. Inspired by the revolutionary, democratic, anti-imperialist movements, and struggles for national liberation and socialism in much of Latin America, Africa, and Asia, it demanded liberation—freedom from oppression—and developed critiques of the systems of power, institutions, and agents that oppressed. Central to it was an analysis of the United States both as an imperialist war-mongering power internationally, particularly in Vietnam, and as a society based on racism. Protest movements coalesced around the anti-racist civil rights movement and later the Black Power movement in the United States, the international peace movement fighting the militarism of the Cold War, and especially the threat of nuclear war. They also led to the rise of the New Left with its reworking of the older left-wing communist politics, and an international student and youth movement challenging existing social conventions and morality. All these movements challenged prevailing formal knowledge through a rediscovery of Marxism, communist history, and a focus on the oppressed peoples of the world. Women activists applied their critique of oppression and their vision of liberation to their own situations and developed the women's liberation movement as part of the second wave of the women's movement.[73]

In Canada, the women's liberation movement developed in the context of the growth of the New Left and particularly a new alliance of the populist social democratic, federal political party, the Co-operative Commonwealth Federation (CCF) with the unions in the New Democratic Party. Canadian radical protest movements were also specifically influenced by a Canadian nationalist movement opposed to American domination of Canada, which, fueled by the anti-Vietnam war protests, developed a critique of imperialism and sometimes, a larger critique of capitalism.[74] The women's liberation movement was also tied to the important political protests in the 1960s generated by the rise of Native rights organizations, the 1963 formation of the Front de liberation du Québec demanding political and economic independence and self-determination for Quebec, and the activism of anti-poverty groups demanding redistribution of wealth.[75] All of these movements questioned the legitimacy of capitalism and, in calling for social transformation, created a (limited) receptivity to socialist politics within the radical protest movements. "Canadian women more uniformly developed an analysis of their oppression based on a class notion of society .... The Marxist perspective has since been central to the development of the Canadian women's liberation movement."[76]

Canadian socialist politics were dominated neither by the trade unions nor by the Communist Party as in Britain or Europe,[77] nor marginalized and demonized as in the United States.[78] Instead, a place for a modest form of socialism in the mainstream of Canadian politics was carved out by the existence of the New Democratic Party, a federal political party formed from an alliance of the older Co-operative Commonwealth Federation (CCF) and

the organized labour movement. The CCF, with its base in rural agricultural communities and populist workers' and farmers' co-operatives, had a tradition of communal democracy and hostility to big business, especially the banks. Farm women's organizations and women in rural communities had played central roles in the CCF since its founding in 1920. Some of that support for populist movements, coalitions, and women's equality was retained in the early years of the NDP. More generally, extra-parliamentary socialist politics retained a degree of legitimacy that proved important to the development of socialist feminist currents in the women's movement.

The New Left emerged in organizations such as the Student Union for Peace Action (SUPA), the Company of Young Canadians (CYC), later in the Waffle, a left-wing caucus eventually expelled from the NDP, and various Marxist and Leninist organizations associated with international Trotskyist, Maoist, and anarchist movements such as Red Morning, Rising Up Angry, The International Socialists, and The Revolutionary Marxist Group.[79] The growth of these left-wing Marxist-Leninist communist and socialist organizations, while always numerically small, offered a sophisticated political analysis and energetic political organizers and militants in most cities. A significant number of key women activists developed their political analysis of socialism and women's liberation and learned their organizing skills in New Left groups. They took those lessons into the unions and the autonomous women's movement. In fact, many of the key organizers of the 1996 Women's March had been activists in New Left organizations 20 years previously.[80]

The women's liberation movement that emerged from this particular political conjuncture, in the late 1960s, was on the one hand part of a widespread, international movement with shared critiques, similar strategies, and common visions. On the other hand, organizationally it tended to appear as tiny local groups that came together for a period of time after which the members dispersed to other groups. Sheila Rowbotham describes the political orientation common to women's liberation internationally:

> The early women's liberation movements of the late 1960s and early 1970s rejected those approaches to emancipation associated with the liberal project of modernizing capitalism and with state socialism, both of which sought simply to bring women into the public sphere on equal terms with men without regard for domestic life. They were also critical of welfare reformism which took the existing sexual division of labour for granted. They aimed instead to transform social relationships as a whole at work and at home. Though radical feminists emphasized male domination (or patriarchy) as the key, and socialist feminists believed that oppressive relations of race and class were equally important, they shared a utopian faith in the possibility of changing individuals and society.[81]

Women's liberation groups sprang up in many places across the country. As a movement, it encompassed a number of different currents, especially radical feminism, lesbian feminism, and Marxist or socialist feminism. Its activists formed women's caucuses in New Left and other protest groups. They set up consciousness-raising groups, study circles, and published newsletters and journals as part of a process of developing an analysis of women's oppression and strategies for winning liberation.

Less concerned about developing enduring organizations and institutional forms, they relied on informal networks between individuals and small groups. They were quick to public action on specific issues, organizing demonstrations, street theatre, and other ways of making their politics known.[82] They also set up collectives to provide services to women and strengthen the public face of the women's liberation movement. Often these were also intended to prefigure new liberatory ways of organizing society. Communal and co-operative housing efforts, and worker co-ops such as bookstores and community centres attempted to develop alternative structures to oppressive sexual, marital, and familial relations, and to exploitative capitalist businesses. Parent and worker run co-operative daycare centres experimented in ways of raising children more collectively.[83] The Canadian Women's Educational Press began publishing in 1972 as an explicitly socialist feminist publishing house to provide materials rejected by mainstream publishers.[84] Women's liberation activists set up shelters for women recovering from men's violence and participated in building a national reproductive rights movement that was eventually at least able to decriminalize abortion and make access to birth control and abortion more available.

Local organizing efforts frequently generated heated disputes and splits based on their differences, but a strong socialist feminist politic developed that continues to shape the women's movement.[85] Central to that politic was a class analysis that understood the struggle "for the liberation of women as part of the liberation of all human beings," or as Rosemary Brown put it: "Until all of us have made it, none of us have made it."[86]

That orientation encouraged socialist feminists to concentrate their organizing initiatives on issues that concerned the majority of women—jobs and decent working conditions, pay equity, child care, access to birth control and abortion, and an end to forced sterilizations. Where NAC focused on lobbying the government to improve women's situation through federal legislation and policy initiatives, most socialist feminist initiatives assumed the state was both capitalist and patriarchal and therefore hostile to women's concerns. Strategically, socialist feminism aimed to enable and empower women to act on their own behalf politically rather than relying on leaders.[87] Seeking to build coalitions that would generate mass, militant actions such as demonstrations, rallies, and public meetings, specific socialist feminist groups tried to ally not only with other feminists and with anti-racist and lesbian and gay activists, but also with other organizations such as anti-imperialist solidarity groups and aboriginal groups. As unions constituted the largest organized group of working-class women, and as some of the key activists of the women's liberation movement were also active in the unions, the labour movement was an obvious ally.

Such interactions forged links of understanding between working-class women and other activists in the women's movement. In Ontario, for example, a whole range of strikes in the late 1970s and early 1980s, where women workers and women's issues were central—Fleck, Radio Shack, Fotomat, Irwin Toy, Bell Canada, and Blue Cross—brought union women into the women's movement and reminded the rest of the women's movement about the importance of working-class feminism. Just as the Fleck strike had played an important part in developing feminist consciousness among the strikers, in turn, some of the women's liberation activists who had joined the Fleck strikers on the line had their commitment to a socialist politics reaffirmed. A member of a Toronto socialist feminist Fleck support group described her appreciation of the strikers:

> Those women were amazing. I learned so much walking with them—their courage, their strength, were so inspiring. They are mostly immigrants, they struggle with English, they face racism every day and they work in the most appalling conditions imaginable for shitty pay. They reminded me that our struggle is absolutely worth it. If even just one employer can get away with treating workers like this, then all employers will be tempted. The only way we can win liberation for women is by fighting with women like these Fleck women.[88]

Such ties were mobilized effectively during the 1984–1985 Eatons strike. In an effort to get a first contract, employees at six stores in Ontario went out on strike in November 1984. The CLC called for a boycott of Eatons; NAC immediately supported it. After two organizers from the Retail and Wholesale Department Store Union (RWDSU) attended an OWW conference in early 1985, union women and women's liberation activists formed a Women's Strike Support Coalition, which met regularly throughout the rest of the strike, organizing strike support carol singers during the Christmas season, special women's pickets, and a fund-raising concert. The striking Eaton's workers were cheered when they spoke at the Toronto International Women's Day rally on 9 March 1985 and the march itself detoured through the flagship store at the Eaton's Centre, plastering "Boycott Eaton's" throughout the store. The striking women and the women organizers from RWDSU were clear that the support from the women's movement was very important in helping them stick out the long strike through the winter. The next year, the Women's Committee of the Labour Council of Metropolitan Toronto held a labour breakfast to celebrate IWD.[89]

Conclusions

Alliances between liberal feminists, women's liberation activists, union feminists, and working-class women have never been easy. Such moments of unity and mutual support as the Fleck strike are infrequent and the tensions between the various segments of the women's movement are frequent and painful. The homophobia and conservatism of aspects of working-class feminism were revealed for example in 1979 during the organizing for International Women's Day (IWD) in Toronto when Organized Working Women proposed that abortion and lesbian issues be dropped for fear of offending and alienating union women.[90] Several years later, however, when Bell Workers were on strike, Toronto IWD marchers, many of whom had previously done solidarity picketing, carried small bells to symbolize the strike and the march included the Bell office in its demonstration. A Bell worker at the IWD rally was shocked at the presence of lesbians who were also demanding support for their issues, in particular, custody rights for lesbian mothers. She was taken to task by her co-striker, who explained that as "they've supported us on our line; so we support them on theirs."[91]

In her discussion of women auto workers, Sugiman notes that, while some auto workers became women's liberation activists, the majority "... moved carefully and somewhat ambivalently between conventional womanhood, patriarchal unionism, and a working-class feminism or feminist unionism."[92] The same could probably be said for many working-class union women. However, because the working-class feminism they developed was able to find spaces in the political configuration of the women's movement, it helped to keep a space for a more radical socialist feminism, which continues to play a key role in the contemporary women's movement. The 1996 Women's March was no anomaly; it was a logical outcome of 30 years of coalition politics in which women in the labour movement and socialist feminists worked long and hard to forge an alliance with each other and with the rest of the autonomous women's movement, which kept working-class women's issues and left-wing politics alive even in an era of neo-liberal attacks and misogynist backlash.[93]

I want to thank Thelma McCormack for encouraging me to write this essay. Amanda Glasbeek, Kate Bezanson, and Alice de Wolff all read the first draft and gave me helpful comments that led to substantial revisions. Five anonymous reviewers for *Labour/Le Travail* also gave me helpful feedback. *Labour/Le Travail* editor Bryan Palmer offered support and encouragement and impressive patience. Heather Jon Maroney and I have worked together politically and academically throughout the period covered in this essay. Her influence on my thinking is profound. While I accept full responsibility for the argument in this essay, I couldn't have written it without the collective effort of the women's movement and the specific help of my friends and colleagues.

Notes

1. The inspiration for this march came from the 1995 march of women in Quebec who left Montreal, Longueil, and Rivière-du-Loup on 26 May and marched over 200 kilometres to Quebec City where on 4 June they presented the government with a series of demands intended to alleviate women's poverty, such as access to jobs, higher education, equal pay, and services for immigrant women. Buoyed by the success of that march, Quebec women took to the Fourth International United Nations and NGO Conferences on Women at Beijing in August/September 1995 a proposal for an international women's march in 2000. In Montreal, on 18 October 1998, 140 women from 65 countries adopted a platform of demands for the World March of Women in the Year 2000. On International Women's Day, 8 March 2000, women's groups in over 150 countries launched the World March, which terminated at the United Nations on 17 October 2000. The Bread and Roses March of 1996 was part of this ongoing initiative.

2. Judy Rebick and Kike Roach, *Politically Speaking* (Vancouver 1996), 33–34. The Canadian Labour Congress produced a video of this march called "For Bread and Roses, for Jobs and Justice: The Women's March against Poverty," 1996.

3. National Action Committee on the Status of Women (NAC) and the Canadian Labour Congress (CLC) "Women to

March: For Bread and Roses, for Jobs and Justice," Press Release, Toronto, 8 March 1996.

4. Janine Brodie, *Politics on the Margins: Restructuring and the Canadian Women's Movement* (Halifax 1995), 10.

5. Sheila Rowbotham, *Hidden from History: Rediscovering Women in History from the 17th Century to the Present* (New York 1974).

6. Pam Sugiman, *Labour's Dilemma: The Gender Politics of Auto Workers in Canada, 1937–1979* (Toronto 1994), 156.

7. The other charge has been that the women's movement, composed predominantly of white women, has been unwilling and unable to deal with racism. That is a related but different history to the study of class dynamics and I have not taken it up here. At present there is no adequate analysis of racism in the women's movement, just as there is no systematic analysis of the relations among the various women's movements, particularly among aboriginal women, francophone women outside of and in Quebec, and women in the rest of Canada. Working on this essay has reinforced my frustration that so little of the history of the last 30 years of the women's movement has been written up. There are some provocative insights emerging in the USA as women's liberation activists challenge the presentation of their history. Patricia Romney documents a group of 50 women of colour based in New York and Oakland, California, who—along with other Black activists in the 1960s and 1970s—became the forgotten women in subsequent rewritings of women's liberation as exclusively white. See Patricia Romney, unpublished notes prepared for Roundable Discussion "Writing about a Visionary Movement in the 'Get Real' World of the '90s: The History of Women's Liberation in the United States," 10th Berkshire Women's Conference, State University of North Carolina, June 1996, cited in Lynne Segal, *Why Feminism?* (New York 1999), 10.

In this essay I do not deal with the women's movements in Quebec or of aboriginal women. I focus exclusively on the women's movement in the rest of Canada and many of my examples are drawn from Ontario, or Toronto, because that is where I was located and so I have knowledge about and evidence for such activities. Alice de Wolff has pointed out that women from the west (or anywhere else) would have a somewhat different take on this history.

8. Kathleen Jamieson, "Multiple Jeopardy: The Evolution of a Native Women's Movement, *Atlantis* 4 (1979), 157–177, esp. 161.

9. Jill Vickers, Pauline Rankin, and Christine Appelle, *Politics As If Women Mattered: A Political Analysis of the National Action Committee on the Status of Women* (Toronto 1993), 18.

10. Roberta Hamilton and Michèle Barrett, eds., *The Politics of Diversity: Feminism, Marxism and Canadian Society* (London 1986), 4.

11. Heather Jon Maroney, "Feminism at Work," in Heather Jon Maroney and Meg Luxton, eds., *Feminism and Political Economy: Women's Work, Women's Struggles* (Toronto 1987), 86–87.

12. Sherrill MacLean, *Invisible Women: The Women Who Run Canada* (Toronto 1992), 75.

13. Alison Prentice, Paula Bourne, Gail Cuthbert Brandt, Beth Light, Wendy Mitchinson, and Naomi Black, *Canadian Women: A History*, second edition (Toronto 1996), 426.

14. See, for example, Himani Bannerji, "Introducing Racism: Notes towards an Anti-Racist Feminism," *Resources for Feminist Research* 16 (1987), 10–12; Dionne Brand, "Black Women in Toronto: Gender, Race and Class," *Fireweed* (Summer/Fall 1984), 26–43; Patricia Monture-Angus, *Thunder in My Soul: A Mohawk Woman Speaks* (Halifax 1996); Rosemary Brown, *Being Brown* (Toronto 1989) and the articles and the works discussed in Hamilton and Barrett, *The Politics of Diversity*.

15. See, for example, Linda Briskin and Lynda Yanz, eds., *Union Sisters: Women in the Labour Movement* (Toronto 1983); Linda Briskin and Pat McDermott, eds., *Women Challenging Unions: Feminism, Democracy and Militancy* (Toronto 1993); Charlene Gannage, *Double Day, Double Bind: Women Garment Workers* (Toronto 1986); Meg Luxton, *More Than a Labour of Love: Three Generations of Women's Work in the Home* (Toronto 1980); Meg

Luxton and June Corman, "Getting to Work: The Women Back into Stelco Campaign," *Labour/Le Travail* (1991), 149–185.

16. Statistics Canada, "Historical Labour Force Statistics," Catalogue number 71-201 (Ottawa 1995); Statistics Canada, "Labour Force Annual Averages," Catalogue number 71-220-XPB (Ottawa 1996), B-8.

17. This continues to be the case. A study by Statistics Canada of 20 million tax returns for 1995 found that women earned on average 58 percent of what men earned; that for every 10 men earning $100,000 or more, only one woman earned that much, and women were the majority of the 25 per cent of the population earning less than $10,000 (CBC Radio, "The World at Six," 14 July 1997).

18. See, for example, Workers' Unity, "Salt of the Earth: Two for the Price of One," Workers' Unity Voice of the UAW Rank and File (Windsor 1971) in Corrective Collective #6, *Women Unite!* (Toronto 1972).

19. Julie White, *Sisters and Solidarity: Women and Unions in Canada* (Toronto 1993), 56.

20. Joan Sangster, *Dreams of Equality: Women on the Canadian Left* (Toronto 1989); Julie Guard, "The Woman Question in the Canadian UE," Ph.D. thesis, University of Toronto, 1994.

21. For an example from the early 1970s of a women's liberation activist's critique of the way unions and union men treated women workers, see Jean Rands, "Toward an Organization of Working Women," in Corrective Collective #6, *Women Unite!* (Toronto 1972), 141–148.

22. White, *Sisters and Solidarity*, 43.

23. Renée Geoffroy, *Attitude of Union Workers to Women in Industry, Studies of the Royal Commission on the Status of Women in Canada* 9 (Ottawa 1971).

24. Ester Reiter, "First Class Workers Don't Want Second Class Wages: The Lanark Strike in Dunnville, Ontario," in Joy Parr, ed., *A Diversity of Women: Ontario, 1945–1980* (Toronto 1995), 168–199.

25. Sugiman, *Labour's Dilemma*, 10.

26. Pam Sugiman, "Unionism and Feminism in the Canadian Auto Workers Union, 1961–1992," in Linda Briskin and

Patricia McDermott, eds., *Women Challenging Unions* (Toronto 1993), 172–188.

27. Sugiman, *Labour's Dilemma*, 10.

28. Ontario Women's Bureau, *Women and Labour Unions* (Toronto 1977).

29. White, *Sisters and Solidarity*, 56.

30. Canadian Union of Public Employees, *The Status of Women in CUPE: la Situation de la femme dans le SCFP* (Ottawa 1971).

31. Sugiman, *Labour's Dilemma*, 184.

32. Nancy Adamson, Linda Briskin, and Margaret McPhail, *Feminist Organizing for Change: The Contemporary Women's Movement in Canada* (Toronto 1988), 139.

33. Maroney, "Feminism at Work," 94.

34. Sugiman, *Labour's Dilemma*, 181.

35. Jennifer Penny, ed., *Hard Earned Wages: Women Fighting for Better Work* (Toronto 1983); Luxton and Corman, "Getting to Work."

36. Jackie Ainsworth et. al., "Getting Organized: In the Feminist Unions," in Maureen FitzGerald, Connie Guberman, and Margie Wolfe, eds., *Still Ain't Satisfied* (Toronto 1982), 132–140.

37. Bank Book Collective, *An Account to Settle: The Story of the United Bank Workers* (SORWUC) (Vancouver 1979).

38. White, *Sisters and Solidarity*.

39. Susan Crean, *Grace Hartman: A Woman for Her Time* (Vancouver 1995), 68.

40. Sugiman, *Labour's Dilemma*, 151.

41. Kay Macpherson, *When in Doubt, Do Both: The Times of My Life* (Toronto 1994), 79.

42. Some of these organizations (followed by their founding date) include: The Women's Christian Temperance Union (first Canadian local formed in Picton, Ontario), 1874; The National Council of Women of Canada, 1893; National Council of Jewish Women, 1893; The Nation Young Women's Christian Association, 1894; Federated Women's Institutes of Canada, 1919; Canadian Federation of University Women, 1919; Canadian Federation of Business and professional Women's Clubs, 1930; Congress of Canadian Women, 1950; Canadian Negro Women's

Association, 1951; Voice of Women, 1960; Planned Parenthood of Canada, 1961. The separate organizations of Jewish and Negro or Afro-Canadian women indicate both their discomfort in the predominantly Christian or white groups and their recognition that their particular concerns warranted separate organizations.

43. For example, as children, Madelaine Parent and Laura Sabia attended the same convent school in Montreal (Macpherson, *When in Doubt*, 153). Laura Sabia, founding president first of the Committee for Equality and then of NAC, was a neighbour of Judy La Marsh, the only woman in the Pearson cabinet when the demand for a Royal Commission on the Status of Women was presented. La Marsh and Sabia consulted regularly on strategies to get the Cabinet to agree to the Commission. Later, Sabia's son married Pearson's granddaughter. Ursula Franklin, founder of the Voice of Women, was a professor at the University of Toronto.

44. Laura Sabia, a university-educated women, was married to a doctor. She had paid domestic workers who helped run her household and she described how the enforced boredom of her life as an upper middle-class housewife led to her involvement in politics (Sabia interview, 14 January 1988, 43). In *When in Doubt, Do Both*, Kay Macpherson describes how middle-class wives of professional men got active in politics in the 1950s and 1960s in organizations such as the Association of Women Electors and the Voice of Women. Muriel Duckworth's biography makes the same point. Some of the quotes in the rest of the text come from interviews I conducted. Where that is the case, the name or, if confidentiality was requested, an ID number, the date of the interview, and, where available, the page number of the transcript, are cited in the text. Copies of the interviews are available on request. The interview with Laura Sabia was also conducted by Shelagh Wilkinson, Women's Studies, York University, Toronto on 14 January 1988.

45. Examples of such women include Réjane Colas who headed several Quebec women's organizations and Thérèse Casgrain who had been a leader in the struggle for suffrage (won in 1940 about 20 years later than the rest of Canada). Micheline Dumont, Michèle Jean, Marie Lavigne, and Jennifer Stoddart, *Québec Women: A History*, translated by Roger Gannon and Rosalind Gill (Toronto 1987).

46. The history of many of these groups remains to be written. Some important examples include: N.E.S. Grifiths, *The Spendid Vision: Centennial History of the National Council of Women of Canada, 1893–1993* (Ottawa 1993); Ethel Vineberg, *The History of the National Council of Jewish Women of Canada* (Montreal 1967).

47. Some Canadian groups affiliated to international organizations, such as The National Council of Women of Canada, had observer status to the UN Commission from its inception. Canada officially became a member in 1958.

48. The meeting on 3 May 1966 was held at the University Women's Club on St. George Street in Toronto (where Sabia was a member). Fifty women representing 32 organizations attended. These included groups such as The National Council of Women, the YWCA, Business and Professional Women's Clubs, Zontas, Imperial Order of the Daughters of the Empire (IODE), The Federation of Women Teachers' Associations of Ontario, Voice of Women, and the Catholic Women's League.

49. Crean, *Grace Hartman*, 79.

50. Cerise Morris, "'Determination and Thoroughness': The Movement for the Royal Commission on the Status of Women in Canada," *Atlantis* 5 (Spring 1980), 1–21.

51. Crean, *Grace Hartman*, 83–84.

52. Canadian Women's Movement Archives, CEW papers, Correspondence, 6 January 1971.

53. The group later dropped the ad hoc from its name.

54. The conference was held 7–9 April 1972. The groups attending included: Canadian Federation of Business and Professional Women; Canadian Federation of University Women; Canadian Home Economics Association; Canadian Union of Public Employees; Catholic Women's League of Canada; Federated Women's Institute of Canada; Federation of Labour (Ontario); Federation of Women Teachers Association of Ontario; National Chapter of Canada-IODE; National Council of Jewish Women; New

Feminists; Toronto Women's Liberation Movement; YWCA; National Voice of Women; Single Parents' Association; the Association for the Repeal of the Abortion Law; and the Ontario Committee on the Status of Women. Many women attended as individuals. Many left-wing activists ignored it as "too reformist," a perception that was confirmed when some women from Trotskyist groups were prevented from speaking.

55. Interview with Laura Sabia, 14 January 1988, 60.

56. *Status of Women News* (Summer 1973), cover.

57. She also worked hard to find ongoing bases of unity even in the face of profound political disagreements. As an active Roman Catholic she tried to persuade the Catholic Women's League to remain in NAC after NAC took a position in support of women's rights to have abortions. She reports:

> I was the Chairman and I had to say to them, "Well, everyone here wants us to keep on the issue of abortion. We've all voted on it. Now you are the only group that says no. Would you like to work with us on other subjects and we won't ask you for any other opinions on abortion?"

The Catholic Women's League left.

58. Interview with Laura Sabia, 14 January 1988, 23.

59. Macpherson, *When in Doubt*, 153; Vickers, Rankin, and Appelle, *Politics as If Women Mattered*, 74–75.

60. From an interview conducted in December 1999 with someone who had participated in the Strategies for Change conference. She has preferred to remain anonymous.

61. The relationship between NAC and socialist feminism warrants further study. During the 1970s, some socialist feminists dismissed NAC as "liberal feminist" and reformist, and therefore chose not to work with NAC. For example, talking about lesbian efforts to be included in mainstream women's organizations in the early to mid 1970s, Ross ignores the Committee for Equality and NAC: "Unlike the BCFW (British Columbia Federation of Women) or the national Organization of Women in the United States, there was no centralized, broad-based feminist organization in Ontario within which Toronto lesbians might agitate for the inclusion of a lesbian platform." See Becki Ross, *The House That Jill Built: A Lesbian Nation in Formation* (Toronto 1995), 30. However, others decided to work in NAC to try to influence its politics.

62. Macpherson, *When in Doubt*, 156.

63. Brodie, *Politics on the Margins, Restructuring and the Women's Movement*, 44.

64. Adamson, Briskin, and McPhail, *Feminist Organizing for Change*.

65. Vickers, Rankin, and Appelle, *Politics As If Women Mattered*, 85.

66. Interview with Laura Sabia, 14 January 1988, 57.

67. Macpherson, *When in Doubt*, 155.

68. IWD, "Editorial," *International Women's Day Newsletter* (Toronto May 1986), 3.

69. Vickers, Rankin, and Appelle, *Politics as If Women Mattered*, 77, 162.

70. Kay Macpherson, "Doing It Ourselves," *Canadian Forum* (September 1975), 41.

71. Vickers, Rankin, and Appelle, *Politics As If Women Mattered*, 77.

72. Alice de Wolff, *Review of the Situation of Women in Canada* (Toronto 1992), 1–2.

73. Sheila Rowbotham, *Women, Resistance and Revolution* (London 1972).

74. Although Canadian nationalism and its critique of American imperialism was widespread in English Canada, it was much harder to advance a critique of imperialism generally, and specifically of English Canadian imperialism in relation to Quebec and aboriginal peoples. Support from English Canadians for Quebec and aboriginal anti-imperialist struggles for self-determination was hard to mobilize.

75. Vern Harper, *Following the Red Path: The Native People's Caravan* (Toronto 1979); Myrna Kostash, *Long Way from Home: The Story of the Sixties Generation in Canada* (Toronto 1980).

76. Corrective Collective #6, *Women Unite!* (Toronto 1972), 10.

77. Sheila Rowbotham, "Introduction: Mapping the Women's

Movement," in Monica Threlfall, ed., *Mapping the Women's Movement* (London 1996), 7.

78. Rachel Blau DuPlessis and Ann Snitow, eds., *The Feminist Memoir Project: Voices from Women's Liberation* (New York 1998).

79. Kostash, *Long Way from Home.*

80. One of the reviewers of this essay asked for specific examples. I was involved in many of the activities and organizations discussed in this essay, so can name a range of such women. However, I do not have their permission to do so and unless they have explicitly identified themselves in print, I am unwilling to "out" them. Thinking through this issue made me realize how little of the early women's liberation movement, left-wing, and socialist movement history of this period is actually in print. More historical work needs to be done.

81. Rowbotham, "Introduction," in Thelfall, ed., *Mapping the Women's Movement*, 13.

82. Adamson, Briskin, and McPhail, *Feminist Organizing for Change*, 42–61; Ross, *The House That Jill Built*, 23–40.

83. Meg Luxton and Heather Jon Maroney, "Begetting Babies, Raising Children: The Politics of Parenting," in Jos Roberts and Jesse Vorst, eds., *The Crisis in Socialist Theory, Strategy and Practice* (Winnipeg 1992), 161–198.

84. Corrective Collective #6, *Women Unite!*

85. Carolyn Egan, Linda Lee Gardner, and Judy Vashti Persaud, "The Politics of Transformation: Struggles with Race, Class, and Sexuality in the March 8th Coalition," in Frank Cunningham, Sue Findlay, Marlene Kadar, Alan Lennon, and Ed Silva, eds., *Social Movements, Social Change:* *The Politics and Practice of Organizing* (Toronto 1988), 20–47; Charnie Guetell, *Marxism and Feminism* (Toronto 1974); Hamilton and Barrett, eds., *The Politics of Diversity*; Heather Jon Maroney and Meg Luxton, eds., *Feminism and Political Economy: Women's Work, Women's Struggles* (Toronto 1987).

86. First quote is by Rowbotham, *Women, Resistance and Revolution*, 11; Brown, *Being Brown*.

87. IWD, "Editorial," *International Women's Day Newsletter* (Toronto May 1986), 3.

88. Interview #17, 15 February 1980.

89. Egan, Gardner, and Persaud, "The Politics of Transformation," 30–31.

90. Nadja, "Women's Liberation" RWL/LOR Pan Canadian Pre Convention Discussion Paper, 2 (April 1979), 12.

91. Personal field notes, International Women's Day. Heather Jon Maroney reports a similar conversation between Fleck workers about alliances with lesbians at another IWD (Maroney, "Feminism at Work," 97).

92. Sugiman, *Labour's Dilemma*, 202.

93. Four years later, as they celebrated the start of the International Women's March 2000 at the May 2000 NAC annual general meeting, outgoing NAC president, Joan Grant-Cummings, declared: "NAC would not have survived without the feminists in the labour movement." Nancy Riche, vice-president of the CLC, replied: "The labour movement is part of NAC."

Self-Government
and Aboriginal Women

Sharon Donna McIvor

The eagles of war
whose wings lent you glory
they were nothing but
carrion crows;
push'd the wrens from
their nest
stole their eggs
chang'd their story[1]

Aboriginal peoples, collectively and individually, have the inherent right to self-government and the right to self-determination. In plain language, women and men have the collective and individual right to govern themselves, their land, people, and resources. This is a right that accrues to all human beings living a social existence among other human beings. The right to self-government is an individual right, exercised when individuals decide to live as a group and be governed by rules of social, moral, political, and cultural behaviour upon which they agree.

Collective and individual rights are inherent, protected in, but not created by, the Canadian *Constitution*. They are rights that have existed since people existed, and the right of self-government is one of them. It is foundational and fundamental, and cannot be taken away from

individuals or groups in society. There has been a misunderstanding of the concept of self-government rights, as was seen in the Charlottetown process, where Aboriginal women were not allowed to be equal participants in defining their constitutional place in Canadian and Aboriginal society.

In the constitutional process leading to the development of the Charlottetown accord, there was a notion that Aboriginal women advocated individual rights to protect gender equality, and that the predominantly male Aboriginal leadership advocated collective rights. This is a false dichotomy. Collective and individual rights coexist in domestic and international law, as do the rights of self-government and self-determination.[2] Self-determination relates to the "self," to the individual, and collectively may refer to a group of individuals who share fundamental traits like race, language, culture, tradition, and values.

In examining the meaning of the inherent right to self-government, it is important to remember that women and men had and retain traditional political, social, economic, and cultural roles, responsibilities, and rights within Aboriginal societies. These roles, responsibilities, and rights are protected within the inherent right to self-government. The traditional roles of women are protected in section 35(1) of the *Constitution*, and their rights in section 35(4). Aboriginal women and men share the same desire for self-government, although their visions may differ.[3]

The scope and content of the inherent right to Aboriginal self-government have yet to be set out in the *Constitution* and Canadian legal framework. All governments and male Aboriginal leaders have been reluctant to commit principles to paper that will govern the implementation of the right to self-government. There has been an absence of trust by governments and Aboriginal peoples.[4]

Gender Equality and Self-Government

The inherent right brings forward the recognition and affirmation of the participatory right to self-government of Aboriginal women that they enjoyed under traditional matriarchies. The inherent right to self-government recognizes and affirms matriarchal governments. Women's right to participate politically, socially, culturally, and militarily is part of the custom and tradition recognized and affirmed within the existing right to Aboriginal self-government in section 35(1) of the *Constitution*.

This balance between women and men's participation in government-making is also inherent. Indian, Inuit, and Metis women have individual rights that abridge the collective rights.[5] This includes restoring the gender relations that existed between Aboriginal women and men since time immemorial. Restoring this gender balance requires throwing aside women's obedience and men's sexual powers over women, eradicating patriarchy, and returning harmony to human relations in the home and in communities.[6] The American Indian case law is clear that rights exist even if they are not practiced, or if they are suppressed.

To deny Aboriginal women their participatory rights because Canadian laws expelled women from the communities and denied them their traditional rights would run completely contrary to the willingness of all parties to recognize the inherent right to self-government. It would recognize only the patriarchal interpretation of the inherent right while blatantly denying the traditional, political roles of women. I reject the assumption that the recognition of women's gender rights abridging collective rights is a purely European idea. Much of the literature on individual rights shows clearly that the liberal tradition of individual rights emanates from North American Indian philosophies.

This modern-day quest by Aboriginal women to be involved in decision-making which affects their future, and that of their children, reflects their immediate past. Kathleen Jamieson described the situation of Indian women plainly: "one thing is clear—that to be born poor, an Indian and a female is to be a member of the most disadvantaged minority in Canada today, a citizen minus. It is to be victimised, and utterly powerless, and to be, by government decree, without legal recourse of any kind."[7]

Women's Rights as "Existing" Aboriginal Rights

As with other "existing" Aboriginal rights, Aboriginal women's civil and political rights are foundational and do not derive from documents or treaties.[8] The right of women to establish and maintain their civic and political role within the context of Aboriginal self-government has always existed. The regulation of women's political rights through successive Indian Acts did not extinguish their fundamental civil and political rights. Even if the suppression of women's rights was so oppressive it led to their banishment from Aboriginal communities, this, in itself, did not lead to extinguishment of their rights. There is no "extinguishment by regulation" in the Aboriginal field.[9] Even though it is regulated, an Aboriginal right continues to exist.[10]

Are Aboriginal women's civil and political rights part of the existing Aboriginal and treaty rights? These rights are part of the inherent right to self-government, of customary laws of Aboriginal people. As such, civil and political rights of Aboriginal women are now recognized as part of the common law. "Such practices or forms of social organisation do not require the imprimatur of state action to qualify as rights."[11] Self-government is central to Aboriginal nationhood, culture, and existence. The civil and political rights of women are central to traditional, matriarchal, and equalitarian forms of government. If Aboriginal self-government is central to the existence of Aboriginal nations, the ability to determine civil and political rights of members must also be central to exercising the right of Aboriginal self-government, which includes self-defining the roles of women.[12]

Fundamental human rights, like civil and political rights of Aboriginal women, can never be extinguished, and these rights existed in some form in 1982. The distinction between the *Indian Act* civil and political rights of Aboriginal women and their inherent rights lies in the regulation of women's rights. The questionable aspect of Aboriginal women's civil and political rights arose in the period from 1982 to 1985 when the *Indian Act* was amended to end sex discrimination against Indian women. After the passage of Bill C-31, *An Act to Amend the Indian Act*, the Government of Canada reinstated Indian women and their children to their communities and ended legislated sex discrimination. The legislation effectively restored the civil and political rights of Indian women who regained their Band membership and right to vote. The *Constitution Act, 1982* did not revive Aboriginal women's civil and political rights, but did confirm their existence.[13]

The *Sparrow* decision makes it clear that Aboriginal women's civil and political rights were not frozen in their regulated form. The Supreme Court ruled that "an existing aboriginal right cannot be read so as to incorporate the specific manner in which it was regulated before 1982.

The notion of freezing existing rights would incorporate into the Constitution a crazy patchwork of regulations."[14] The Supreme Court agreed with Brian Slattery that "existing" means "unextinguished" instead of "exercisable at a certain time in history."[15] The Court held that the term "existing" must be interpreted flexibly to permit its evolution over time.[16] Using the Court's interpretation, the civil and political rights of Aboriginal women were affirmed in their contemporary form "rather than in their primeval simplicity and vigour."[17] Aboriginal women's rights were not frozen in time in their regulated form, but were affirmed as amended in 1985, with sex discrimination removed.[18]

In the *Sparrow* case, the government attempted to prove that the right of Musqueam Indians to fish in the Fraser River had been extinguished by regulation. The Court disagreed with this position.[19] Similarly, the civil and political rights of Aboriginal women have been regulated to the point where they have been denied participation in elections of *Indian Act* Chiefs and Councillors. When Indian women married non-Indians they were banished from their communities and their legal right to be an "Indian" was stripped from them. This directly affected 12,000 Indian women. In 1985, these women and approximately 40,000 descendants were restored to their previous Indian status and Band membership. It would be absurd to use the "patchwork" of regulation approach to examine the existence of Aboriginal women's civil and political rights. The Court's approach is correct; in *Sparrow*, it held "that the right is controlled in great detail by the regulations does not mean that the right is thereby extinguished."[20] Thus, if a right is not extinguished, it exists.

Prior to the 1985 amendments to the *Indian Act*, Parliament made it clear in law that Indian women who intermarried with non-Indian men lost their civil and political rights within their communities. In this context, the *Lavell* decision of the Supreme Court of Canada agreed that parliamentary supremacy gave parliamentarians the right to determine who had Indian status. The Court refused to use the Canadian *Bill of Rights* to strike down the offensive sections of the *Indian Act*, and refused to recognize that it discriminated on the basis of sex against Indian women. After the 1985 amendments to the *Indian Act*, it was equally clear that Parliament intended to restore status and Band membership to women who lost those rights. The legislation was retroactive. Even if an Indian woman had lost status forty years earlier than 1985, she could have that status restored. If she had since died, she could still have her status restored. In either case, her descendants could apply to have Indian status and Band membership. The legislation also restored control of Band membership and regulation of Indian lands to *Indian Act* governments.

The *Sparrow* decision held that there must be "clear and plain" intention on the part of the government where it intends to extinguish Aboriginal and treaty rights. The Court also held that in "the context of aboriginal rights, it could be argued that before 1982, an aboriginal right was automatically extinguished to the extent that it was inconsistent with a statute."[21] On this point, Aboriginal women would have had to overcome this argument, had Bill C-31 not reinstated them and attempted to end sex discrimination against Indian women. After the 1985 amendments to the *Indian Act*, Parliament's clear and plain intention was restorative of rights that had been regulated.[22] In *Sparrow*, the Court noted that Justice Hall in *Calder* held that, "the onus of proving that the Sovereign intended to extinguish the Indian title lies on the respondent and that intention must be 'clear and plain.'"[23]

The scope of modern-day Aboriginal women's civil and political rights will be determined in the context of the inherent right of self-government. Over the past few years, Aboriginal women's groups like the Native Women's Association of Canada have fought for participatory rights. They demand participation in the policy and legislative processes defining, developing, and interpreting their forms of Aboriginal government. This includes defining who is a member of the "group" or members of the "collective." Bill C-31, *An Act to Amend the Indian Act*, restored women and their descendants to the "base group," Band, or Tribe that will exercise the right of self-government.

Some Aboriginal leaders and governments will look to the nature of Aboriginal women's civil and political rights and believe that the manner in which the rights were regulated will determine the scope of the rights. The Court in *Sparrow* rejected that approach. Aboriginal women, themselves, must be part of the process of delineating their civil and political rights. The Court also held that, "Government policy can, however, regulate the exercise of that right, but such regulation must be in keeping with section 35(1)."[24] Aboriginal women can use section 35(1) to negotiate the definition of their modern civil and political rights. If legislated forms of Aboriginal self-government will involve provincial governments as well as the federal government, the *Sparrow* decision makes it clear that Aboriginal rights are protected from provincial legislative power.[25]

At least since 1867, Parliament has relied on section 91(24) of the *Constitution Act, 1867* to pass laws governing Indians and lands reserved for Indians. Until 1985, when the *Charter of Rights and Freedoms* came into effect, Parliament was recognized as having the power to pass laws under section 91(24) whose effect was to discriminate against Indian women based on sex. The effect of section 35(1) upon section 91(24) powers has not yet been determined. I would argue, however, that section 35(1) has established new rules where courts can question sovereign claims made by the Crown.[26] It diminishes parliamentary supremacy. For Aboriginal women, it means they must be consulted by governments that intend to discriminate against them on the basis of sex. Such discrimination is no longer allowed under section 15 of the *Charter*. It means Parliament cannot establish new rules in the *Indian Act* in the future that discriminate on the basis of sex.

The Supreme Court of Canada held in *Sparrow* that section 35(1) was to be interpreted in a purposive way.[27] "When the purposes of the affirmation of aboriginal rights are considered, it is clear that a generous, liberal interpretation of the words in the constitutional provision is demanded."[28] Section 35(1) recognized and affirmed existing Aboriginal and treaty rights including civil and political rights of Aboriginal women. Evidently, women as well as men comprise members of First Nations and First Peoples of Canada. In 1983, Aboriginal women were successful in lobbying federal and provincial governments, and Aboriginal leaders, to have section 35(4) added to the *Constitution Act, 1982*. Section 35(4) affirmed that Aboriginal and treaty rights were guaranteed equally to men and women. This, to women, was a double confirmation of their rights. The section did not create new rights, but confirmed that women's rights are contained in section 35(1).[29]

The Supreme Court of Canada has also held that Aboriginal and treaty rights should be interpreted while taking into account Aboriginal history and tradition.[30] In interpreting Aboriginal women's civil and political rights as Aboriginal and treaty rights under section 35(1), the Court must consider the historic roles of women within their traditional as well as contemporary Aboriginal societies. Part of the history of Aboriginal women is one of an oppressive state government that has attempted to deny women their civil, political, and property rights within their communities. Rather than suppressing the civil, political, and property rights of Aboriginal women, it is argued that the federal government has an active responsibility to respect and protect the rights of Aboriginal women. The federal fiduciary trust responsibility may also require the Government of Canada to protect the civil and political roles of Aboriginal women within their societies. The Supreme Court of Canada reconfirmed the *Guerin* trust in *Sparrow* and decided the "government has the responsibility to act in a fiduciary capacity with respect to aboriginal peoples.

The relationship between the government and aboriginals is trust-like, rather than adversarial, and contemporary recognition and affirmation of aboriginal rights must be defined in light of this historic relationship."[31]

The Court found that section 35(1) was not subject to section 1 of the *Charter of Rights and Freedoms*. Under section 52, federal and provincial laws which conflict with Aboriginal and treaty rights under section 35(1) would be of no force and effect. This view was rejected in *Sparrow*.[32] The Court held the legislation would be valid if it met the test for justifying an interference with a right recognized and affirmed under section 35(1).

Women's Fundamental Rights

The fundamental human rights of Aboriginal women—including civil and political rights—form part of the inherent right to Aboriginal self-government in section 35(1) of the *Constitution Act, 1982*.[33] The Supreme Court of Canada has determined in *Sparrow* that certain Aboriginal and treaty rights may be regulated.[34] Even if Aboriginal women's civil and political rights were regulated since 1867 by removal of women from Indian lands for intermarrying with non-Indians,[35] this was rectified by the 1985 amendments to the *Indian Act*.[36] One of the purposes of the legislation was to remove sex discrimination from the *Indian Act*[37] and bring the legislation in line with the *Charter of Rights and Freedoms*.[38] Civil and political rights are fundamental human rights that cannot be extinguished, even if the exercise of those rights is denied.

The civil and political rights of Aboriginal women differ according to culture and Tribal traditions, although most Aboriginal societies were matriarchal and matrilineal, including hunting and gathering societies. The rights of women were not written in the treaties, but they are rights which women have exercised since the formation of their Indigenous societies. They are rights women had upon contact with non-Aboriginal settlers and, in some cases, these rights were suppressed by non-Aboriginal laws. This is a form of regulation that has been removed with respect to political rights. Civil and property rights are the subject of sex discrimination in the current *Indian Act* and still need to be challenged under the *Charter*.

International law dictates the recognition of fundamental civil and political rights of Aboriginal women in the documents: *International Covenant on Civil and Political Rights*; *Elimination of All Forms of Discrimination against Women*; and *Universal Declaration of Human Rights*. The *Charter of Rights and Freedoms* provides for governments to respect the civil and political rights of all women, including Aboriginal women. Human rights codes of the provinces and territories also call for the adherence to fundamental human rights without discrimination based on race or sex. The *Calder* decision recognized that Aboriginal persons can rely on Aboriginal and treaty rights as binding on the Government of Canada.

Thus, three events have occurred in constitutional history that lead to the conclusion that Aboriginal women's civil and political rights are "existing" Aboriginal and treaty rights. In 1982, the *Constitution Act* recognized gender equality in sections 15 and 28, and existing Aboriginal and treaty rights. In 1983, all First Ministers and Aboriginal representatives endorsed the inclusion of section 35(4) in the *Constitution Act, 1982* to recognize that men and women equally enjoy Aboriginal and treaty rights. In 1985, Parliament passed amendments to the *Indian Act* purportedly to eradicate sex discrimination against Indian women. The *Sparrow* decision ends the federal theory that Aboriginal rights have been extinguished by regulations. Just as the Aboriginal right to fish was not extinguished by specific fisheries' legislation, so, too, the *Indian Act* has not extinguished female civil and political rights. There can be no extinguishment by regulation of Aboriginal women's civil, political, and property rights.[39]

The Primacy of Women's Rights

The struggle for equality for Native women is continuing today .... Our goal is to enjoy our place in society as did our mothers and grandmothers in their day.[40]

The Battle of Rights

It is useful to examine the primacy of Aboriginal women's rights as fundamental rights in the context of the Aboriginal community or collective.[41] Aboriginal women have struggled to have their "first generation" rights recognized. "First generation" rights include civil and political rights, which are fundamental to human beings.[42] Aboriginal men's organizations have always actively sought to suppress Indian women's struggle for sexual equality, claiming it interfered with their struggle for collective rights.[43] "Group rights" are described by Blaustein and Tenney as "fourth generation" rights that include "indigenous" rights. They include "the special rights of indigenous peoples—rights based on race, language and ethnicity, and rights that flow from membership in a particular tribe or caste. This is well illustrated by Article 27 of the *International Covenant on Civil and Political Rights*."[44] That battle has been described as women's rights versus Indian rights.[45]

Are Aboriginal and treaty rights collective or individual rights? Are these rights transportable with the individual? For example, do they move with the individual from the reserve to the city? The courts have attempted to answer this question in the context of linguistic rights guaranteed under the *Charter of Rights and Freedoms* to French-language speakers. In the case of language rights guaranteed under sections 16 to 23 of the *Charter*, the right invoked is collective, not individual. These rights require a critical mass of persons entitled to the right in order to invoke the right. However, where there is a French school that will not admit a child of a French-speaker, the right is individual.[46] Thus, the simple answer is that Aboriginal and treaty rights are both collective and individual rights, exercisable by both the collective and individuals.

Sub-Committee on Indian Women and the Indian Act

The battle lines between individual and group rights were drawn in 1982 before the Sub-Committee on Indian Women and the Indian Act.[47] The National Indian Brotherhood wanted immediate control of Band membership.[48] It was prepared to act with no resolution over reinstatement of men and women who had lost their rights under the *Indian Act*. While the Assembly of First Nations advocated control of membership and indicated that men and women would then decide the form of self-government and membership criteria, only those then in group the would make such decisions. The 100,000 disenfranchised Indians who eventually registered under Bill C-31, *An Act to Amend the Indian Act*, were not intended to have any voice in determining membership criteria or the form self-government would take in their former communities. The Assembly of First Nations asked legislators to remember that collective rights, including the right to determine membership, was also protected in international human rights instruments. The organization stated that many of the international standards which Canada signed support First Nations' rights, and that the nationhood of First Nations is based on culture.[49] The Chiefs of the Assembly of First Nations supported equality for Indian women provided that the government paid for that equality; they claimed they did not want to harm the collective that was already living in poverty.[50]

Indian women were equally clear that they wanted reinstatement before the recognition of Indian self-government and a legislated end to sex discrimination in the *Indian Act*.[51] The Native Women's Association of Canada insisted that the women and their descendants

be reinstated first, so that collectively with men and women on reserves, they would decide membership criteria and the form of self-government. The Native Women's Association of Canada claimed "discrimination on the basis of sex goes against international covenants which Canada has signed. It is therefore within the realm of human rights protection."[52] In a parliamentary submission, the Native Women's Association of Canada asked that legislators remember Indian women have paid psychologically, economically, socially, culturally, and politically because of state sex discrimination, and women have been denied millions of dollars in government programs, services, and lands.

The Commissioner of the Canadian Human Rights Commission noted to the legislators in 1982 that Canada had been found in violation of Article 27 of the *International Covenant on Civil and Political Rights*.[53] He also noted that Canada had acceded to the *United Nations Convention on the Elimination of All Forms of Discrimination against Women*.[54] The Supreme Court of Canada has not anticipated the changing world of women's rights. The Court was, however, instrumental in inspiring women, including Aboriginal women, to take political action to achieve sexual equality.

At the time of the "Indian Women and the Indian Act" hearings, the *Charter of Rights and Freedoms* was not available to Indian women. The battle for the *Charter* was related to the defeat of women's struggle for equality in the Supreme Court of Canada. Canadian Indian women, like their female counterparts in the United States, had little or no domestic redress for gender bias in Band or Tribal rules. Neither group had the opportunity to bring their Nation to task for gender-based discrimination under the *Convention on the Elimination of All Forms of Discrimination against Women*. While it is evident that Canadian Indian women can still pursue domestic remedies, it is not clear whether United States Tribal women have similar options as I point out later.

Individual Rights in the Context of Collective Rights

Where collective and individual rights conflict, group rights accede to individual rights. There ought to be a hierarchy of rights in which individual rights prevail. For example, first generation rights of women—civil and political rights—ought to predominate over fourth-generation rights of Aboriginal collectivities.

In *Thomas* v. *Norris*, the British Columbia Supreme Court dealt with the civil rights of an Aboriginal man and gave his rights priority over group rights of his Aboriginal Nation.[55] This case questions whether group rights to traditional spiritual practices ought to yield to individual charter rights to security of the person. The facts of *Thomas* are that Mr. Thomas was seized against his will and forced to take part in an Indian spiritual dancing ceremony. During the ceremony he was assaulted, beaten, and forced to dance. The ceremony is a tradition and practice of a number of West Coast Indian Tribes. Part of the practice is to seize persons against their will and initiate them into the ceremony. The Court ruled against the Indian Tribe and held that Mr. Thomas had been assaulted, battered, and imprisoned.[56] That decision is not favoured by proponents of collective rights.[57] One author found the Court's decision to be "culturally vulgar."[58]

The British Columbia Supreme Court in *Thomas* considered the conflict between an Indian individual's common-law right not to be assaulted in the context of an Aboriginal community's practice to induct individuals into traditional spiritual practices.[59] The facts accepted by the judge included recognizing that the defendant had been assaulted, battered, and falsely imprisoned without consent. Section 25 of the *Constitution Act, 1982* was not invoked because the litigation was between private parties.[60] The judge also held that spirit dancing of the Coast Salish people was not proven to be an "existing" Aboriginal right protected by sections 35 and 52 of the *Constitution Act, 1982*.[61]

The defendants—those who grabbed the plaintiff—asked the Court to consider the question: "Are the individual rights of aboriginal persons subject to the collective rights of the aboriginal nation to which he belongs?"[62] The judge concluded that "the assumed aboriginal right ... is not absolute and the Supreme Court of Canada affirmed this in *Sparrow*. Like most freedoms or rights it is, and must be, limited by laws, both civil and criminal, which protect those who may be injured by the exercise of that practice."[63] Judge Hood found that Aboriginal rights are abridged by criminal and civil laws where they are in conflict.[64] This interpretation, however, has yet to be decided by a higher court, whether there is an abridgement of an existing Aboriginal right without an explicit reference in legislation. There is no law against spirit dancing as practiced by the Coast Salish Indians since time immemorial. The author noted that certain Acts were extended to Indians prior to Confederation that may have impacted adversely upon Aboriginal jurisdiction over civil matters arising in this case.[65] Judge Hood decided that the plaintiff's civil rights could not be subjected to the collective rights "of the aboriginal nation to which he belongs."[66]

Aboriginal Women's "Group" Rights

The other difficulty encountered by Aboriginal women is the severability of collective rights into group rights. It is rare for collective rights to be discussed in terms of rights based on class or gender.[67] The exception may be gender rights of Aboriginal women that are guaranteed by section 35(4) of the *Constitution Act, 1982*. Under that section, Aboriginal and treaty rights are guaranteed equally to male and female persons. Section 35(4) is evidence that collective Aboriginal and treaty rights may be enjoyed by two groups within the Aboriginal community: men and women. This section has not been considered by the courts.

Two other sections of the *Constitution* make it evident that women, as a group, enjoy rights and freedoms: section 15 and 28. Section 15 provides that men and women, as individuals and groups, have the right to be equal under and before the law, and the right to enjoy the benefits of the law in Canadian society. Section 28 guarantees men and women, as individuals and groups, the right to equally enjoy *Charter* rights and freedoms. It would seem, then, that collective rights are severable into group rights, and that women are a prime beneficiary of this severability. The same applies to men— the group most likely to litigate under section 15.

In attempting to resolve the matter of concurrent group and individual rights, it may be important to consider the distinction made by the Royal Commission on Aboriginal Peoples between the right and the *exercise* of the right. A proper interpretation of the *Thomas* decision may be that the group had a collective right, but the manner in which it was exercised conflicted with Canadian law on assault, battery, and false imprisonment.[68] The *Thomas* decision may explain, in part, Aboriginal women's fears that their individual rights could be obliterated by collective rights.[69] Thomas Isaac suggested:

> The importance of the *Thomas* decision, is further evidence which supports the claims made by some Aboriginal women and their representative associations that any constitutional recognition of an inherent right of Aboriginal self-government must be subject to the *Charter* and its sexual equality provisions. Aboriginal women's organisations have stated that the constitutionalization of an inherent right of Aboriginal self-government may have the effect of curtailing their individual rights as women.

The author noted that the Quebec Native Women's Association wanted both collective and individual rights recognized, and for that reason they wanted the Canadian *Charter of Rights and Freedoms* to apply to Aboriginal governments. The Native Women's Association of Canada, as a national umbrella group, also asked that the *Charter* apply to Aboriginal governments. Not only must the individual have rights, but she must have the freedom to exercise those rights.[70]

Should "collective" rights take precedence over women's rights individually or as a group? One theory is that collective rights are protected by the *Charter*.[71] These collective rights are intended to protect minority groups from the majority.[72] Do individuals within the minority group have individual rights? What about women's rights within the collective? One court decided individual rights should not take a subservient role. Placing the collective above the individual is akin to living in a totalitarian state, the court found. Every individual has a right to enjoy his or her rights to the fullest without having such rights eroded by collective rights.[73]

The collective, the group, and individuals in the group all claim the right of self-definition. The Aboriginal group claims the right to define its own membership; women claim the right to define themselves as Indigenous first, women second.[74] Evidently some Indian Tribes and Metis groups will exclude certain members on the basis of sex. In the United States, Tribes may define their own membership, but programs and services will be offered only to those whom the government recognizes as quarter-blood Indians.[75] In Canada, membership is decided by Indian Bands and Metis associations, but the federal government will only recognize persons who meet the *Indian Act* criteria for status and Band membership. The group finds it repugnant to have an outside force, like legislation, determine who is a member of the group.[76]

The United States and Aboriginal Rights

Like the *Lavell* case in Canada, the *Santa Clara Pueblo* case in the United States froze the efforts of Tribal women to have their individual right to sexual equality endorsed by the courts. Mrs. Martinez, a member of the Santa Clara Pueblo before her marriage, married a non-Pueblo man and was struck from the membership list. Her children would not be entitled to membership because of her marriage. Pueblo men could marry non-Pueblo women and not suffer the same fate. Mrs. Martinez claimed sex discrimination in the Pueblo membership rules and went to court arguing that this discrimination was contrary to federal law, namely the *Indian Civil Rights Act of 1978*.[77] The statute was passed by the United States Congress to protect individuals like Mrs. Martinez from human rights abuses not available to them under the Articles of Confederation. The Articles do not apply because Tribes had existed long before the coming into being of the American *Constitution*. The court found in the Martinez case that it was without jurisdiction. This left Mrs. Martinez in a legal limbo with no recourse to regain her Tribal membership. In considering the right of individuals against the rights of the Tribe, the Supreme Court ruled that *habeas corpus* was the only mechanism for judicial review.[78] This decision has left Native women in the United States virtually paralyzed within a system that subordinates women's right to collective rights at the Tribal level. Carla Christofferson argued that there is a need to expand the *Indian Civil Rights Act of 1978* to protect women's Tribal rights in the United States.

One Native American woman has stated: "My only crime is being born a female. I want the same rights as men—the right to vote for a chief and the right to live on the reservation." Women who are discriminated against because of gender-biased Tribal membership codes suffer both financially and psychologically. They no longer receive federal Indian benefits, such as annuities from the Tribe, access to education and health programs, and housing. Moreover, they suffer the loss of their cultural identity, because they lose the right to live on the reservation with their family and friends.[79]

American Native women are in a different constitutional position than Aboriginal women in Canada, particularly "Indian women." In Canada, the state established the criteria for who is an "Indian" and the state is subject to the Canadian *Charter of Rights and Freedoms*, a constitutional document. Tribes in the United States are not subject to the *Constitution* and their Articles. Some members of Congress and the U.S. Senate believed that this could be overcome by passing the *Indian Civil Rights Act of 1978*. This legislation, while granting human and civil rights to American Indians, cannot be imposed upon United States Tribes without their concurrence. Gender-biased Tribal membership codes can, therefore, withstand constitutional challenges based on sex discrimination. Gender-biased Band membership codes in Canada are not likely to withstand a *Charter* challenge because of sections 15, 28, and 35(4), and the inherent rights of women contained in section 35(1). Because of this difference, at least one author argued there is a need for gender-specific protection in the United States to protect Tribal women from Tribal sex bias to ensure they have the same protection as other women.[80]

Canadian Aboriginal women have justiciable rights to sexual equality within the collective. It has been suggested that group rights are not justiciable because such rights are inherently political.[81] Language rights are group rights in Canada and they are justiciable and are exercised by individuals. Women also have group rights under sections 15, 28, and 35(4), and these rights are justiciable.

The adjudication of collective or group rights will require that the exercise of the right be considered in a cultural context. Because of the variety of Aboriginal cultures across the country, it may be that particularization is required in adjudication.[82] Which court ought to adjudicate cultural matters where a conflict arises between the Aboriginal community and its members? One author has proposed a national human rights panel composed of appointees from the Assembly of First Nations, the Congress of Aboriginal Peoples, and the Native Women's

Association of Canada.[83] Such a suggestion is likely to meet with substantial resistance from Aboriginal communities that want the centre of power and jurisdiction to remain at the local level.

Aboriginal Collectives as "Legal Fictions"

Aboriginal collectivities, where they are created by Parliament, are "legal fictions" having little foundation in reality. The lands reserved for Indians were selected by non-Indian settlers and do not represent "Indian lands." The entire province of British Columbia is under claim by 27 Tribal groups living in 197 communities carved out of the territory in 1911. The people living in those communities are also a legal fiction having been defined by a non-Indian government in such a way as to diminish the actual number of persons entitled to live on Indian lands. Because *Indian Act* Indians and *Indian Act* governments are legal fictions created by federal law, since 1850, Parliament has arbitrarily decided who was an Indian in Canada for purposes of benefitting from programs and services and for determining who would live on Indian reserve lands. Until 1985, Parliament allowed non-Indian women who married Indian men to become Indians. The law also stated that Indian women who married non-Indians were no longer deemed Indians. The *Indian Act* and its regulations do not allow off-reserve Indians to vote for Chief and Band Councillors, thus disenfranchising over 300,000 Indians from democratically exercising their rights to determine their own political leadership. The *Indian Act* community is a fictitious body, "composed of the individual persons who are considered as constituting ... its members.'"[84]

Conclusion

The flaw in the debate between collective and individual rights in the Aboriginal community is the creation of a legal fiction by government that the Aboriginal collective is an entity in itself. When parliamentary supremacy went unchecked by the *Charter*, it could declare Indians to be non-Indians, and vice-versa. It created an artificial group of "Indians" who qualified for programs and services under the *Indian Act*.

The individual has legal rights. The community has collective rights exercisable by individuals or by a collection of entitled individuals. For example, the determination of membership and control of land and assets are collective rights of the Aboriginal community. The distinction that needs to be made if Aboriginal women are to exercise their equality rights is that all community members share in these rights: they cannot be limited just to members of the artificially created "community" as set out in the *Indian Act*. Where collective rights are violated, the wrong accrues to the individual members of the collective. "In this sense, aboriginal rights are personal in that their violation affects the individual Band members' enjoyment of those rights."[85]

Today, Aboriginal Peoples embark upon a road less travelled in government-Aboriginal relations. There is a lot of brush on the road. There is our oppressive past and there is our murky present. In 1992, we heard governments—federal and provincial—state that they recognize the "inherent right" of self-government as contained in section 35(1) of the *Constitution Act, 1982*. They did not explain the meaning of these words. As Aboriginal leaders we accepted their words as if they had meaning.

We have heard the federal Minister of Indian Affairs and Northern Development state that he is dismantling the Department, and devolving its programs and services to the Indian Bands. This process has been going on for over twenty years. Political accords have been signed between ministers and Aboriginal leaders on Indian programs and services; on gaming; on land claims; and on a plethora of services. In this context, it is left to us, as men and women of Aboriginal Nations, to determine the government agenda. As women of Aboriginal Nations we have to be concerned about the impact of these activities upon women and future generations. National, provincial, and local women's groups must be involved in the day-to-day negotiations on implementing self-government rights. Historically, women have been excluded from the national, regional, Tribal, and Band government organizations. Thus a conscious effort must be made to include women and their organizations.[86]

As women of Aboriginal Nations, as Metis women, and as Inuit women, we have the freedom to exercise our right to self-government and self-determination within our Nations. In November 1994, plans were announced for governing bodies for the territory of Nunavut that will be carved out of the present Northwest Territories. The territory will be almost exclusively Inuit. The new government, it was announced, would have equal representation from Inuit women and Inuit men, but when put to a referendum, it was defeated.

As a group of Aboriginal women in the organized movement, since 1971, we had a vision. It is a simple vision where we see ourselves united with our own people, on our own lands, determining our forms of government, deciding rules for membership in our Nations, and deciding who will live on our lands. That is the vision. We see ourselves home, among our own people—that place from which our mother, our aunts, our sisters, and our grandmothers were banished by law. We see ourselves back there. When the road is lonely and dark, and we are cold from the reception we receive when we speak of our right to participate, of our right to be at negotiating tables, and of our right to vote in our communities, that is the vision that sustains us.

Notes

1. Song by Aboriginal singer, Buffy Ste. Marie.
2. Lillianne Ernestine Krosenbrink-Gelissen, *Sexual Equality as an Aboriginal Right: The Native Women's Association of Canada and the Constitutional Process on Aboriginal Matters, 1982–1987* (Saarbrucken, Germany: Verlag Breitenback Publishers, 1991), 7:

    In statements to the United Nations, Canadian government representatives have explained that they refuse to recognize the Indigenous peoples as "peoples" because under international law "peoples" have a right to self-determination— a right they do not want to recognize for Indigenous peoples, because Canada claims that Indigenous peoples would use this right to seek independence. Canada claims that, at the level of international law, it will recognize Indigenous rights only as individual rights. This effort to deny the reality of the Indigenous peoples as "peoples"

    in order to avoid the obvious consequence in international law, may well prove to be counterproductive to Canada's interests. And it reminds us of the "Person's Case" *Edwards v. Attorney-General of Canada* (1929) P.C., Canada's infamous refusal to refer to its female citizens as "persons" to avoid the effects of a law which gave "persons" the right to be appointed to the Senate.

3. Canada, Department of Justice, *Federal Issues Document on Violence Against Women* (Ottawa: Department of Justice, May 1994), 7.
4. Christos Sirross, Minister of Natural Resources and Minister Responsible for Native Affairs, "Notes for a Speech to the Federal-Provincial-Territorial Meeting of Ministers Responsible for Native Affairs and Leaders of the National Aboriginal Organizations," Quebec City, 17 May 1994, 3: "When we adopt this approach, we often realize that the

difficulties stem from the fear we have of each other, and that this fear is rooted in our mutual ignorance."

5. Ibid.

6. Krosenbrink-Gelissen, *supra*, 44. "Moreover, the missionaries made serious efforts to change Indian gender relations. Women's obedience and men's sexual rights over women were gradually imposed in the Indian systems."

7. Kathleen Jamieson, *Indian Women and the Law in Canada: Citizens Minus* (Ottawa: Department of Indian Affairs and Northern Development, 1978), 9.

8. *R.* v. *Sparrow* (1990), 70 D.L.R. (4th) 385 (S.C.C.), 390.

9. Ibid., 391.

10. Ibid.

11. Michael Asch and Patrick Macklem, "Aboriginal Rights and Canadian Sovereignty: An Essay on *R.* v. *Sparrow*," *Alberta Law Review*, vol. 29, no. 2 (1991), 506.

12. Ibid., 505.

13. *Sparrow, supra*, 395.

14. Ibid., 396.

15. Ibid. See Brian Slattery, "Understanding Aboriginal Rights," *Canadian Bar Review*, vol. 66 (1987), 781–2; Kent McNeil, "The Constitutional Rights of Aboriginal Peoples of Canada," *Supreme Court Law Review*, vol. 4 (1982), 258; William Pentney, "The Rights of the Aboriginal Peoples of Canada in the Constitution Act, 1982, Part II, Section 35: The Substantive Guarantee," *University of British Columbia Law Review*, vol. 22 (1987), 207.

16. Ibid., 397.

17. Ibid.

18. Ibid.

19. Ibid., 400.

20. Ibid.

21. Ibid., 401.

22. Ibid.

23. *Calder* v. *A-G. B.C.* (1973), 34 D.L.R. (3d) 145, at 216.

24. *Sparrow, supra*, 401.

25. Ibid., 406.

26. Ibid, citing Professor Noel Lyon, "An Essay on Constitutional Interpretation," *Osgoode Hall Law Journal*, vol. 26 (1988), 100, "the context of 1982 is surely enough to tell us that this is not just a codification of the case law on aboriginal rights that had accumulated by 1982. Section 35 calls for a just settlement for aboriginal peoples. It renounces the old rules of the game under which the Crown established courts of law and denied those courts the authority to question sovereign claims made by the Crown."

27. Ibid., 407.

28. Ibid.

29. *Nowegijick* v. *The Queen* (1983), 144 D.L.R. (3d) 193, at 198.

30. *Sparrow, supra*, 408, citing *R.* v. *Agawa* (1988), 43 C.C.C. (3d) 266, 28 O.A.C. 201, 215–6: "The second principle … emphasized the importance of Indian History and traditions as well as the perceived effect of a treaty at the time of its execution. He also cautioned against determining Indian rights in a vacuum. The honour of the Crown is involved in the interpretation of Indian treaties, as a consequence, fairness to the Indians is a governing consideration …. This view is reflected in recent judicial decisions which have emphasized the responsibility of government to protect the rights of Indians arising from the special trust relationship created by history, treaties and legislation: see *Guerin* v. *The Queen* (1984), 13 D.L.R. (4th) 321."

31. Ibid.

32. Ibid., 409.

33. *Constitution Act, 1982*, 35(1): "The existing aboriginal and treaty rights of the aboriginal peoples of Canada are hereby recognized and affirmed."

34. *R.* v. *Sparrow* (1990), 70 D.L.R. (4th) 385 (S.C.C.).

35. John Leslie and Ron Macguire, *The Historical Development of the Indian Act* (Ottawa: Department of Indian and Northern Affairs Canada, 1979), 25. An Act of 1851, 14–15 Victoria, c. 59, was the first to exclude white men married to Indian women from being "legal Indians," but white women married to Indian men and their children would henceforth be "Indians." At page 55, the authors reported that the *Act* of 1869 "was the first Canadian statute governing status of native women after marriage to non-Indians, or to Indians of other bands." The 1876 *Act*

disenfranchised illegitimate children, Indians who lived continuously outside Canada for five years, and half-breeds.

36. Bill C-31, *An Act to Amend the Indian Act*, R.S.C. 1985, c. 32 (1st Supp. 1985).

37. *Indian Act*, R.S.C. 1970, c. 1-6, s. 12 (1)(b).

38. Part I of the *Constitution Act, 1982*, being Schedule B to the *Canada Act, 1982* (U.K.), 1982, c. 11.

39. W.I.C. Binnie, "The Sparrow Doctrine: Beginning of the End or End of the Beginning?" *Queen's Law Journal*, vol. 15 (1992), 226. "In fact, extinguishment by regulation has for many years been a premise of the federal Indian claims policy. If the doctrine has 'no merit,' which is certainly the view for the time being of the Supreme Court of Canada, then a substantial chunk of the governmental defences against Aboriginal rights claims across Canada ... may collapse."

40. Verna Kirkness, "Emerging Native Women," *Canadian Journal of Women and the Law*, vol. 2 (1987–88), 415.

41. I use the term "collective" to identify the Tribal group to which women belong; for example, an Interior Salish woman belongs to an Interior Salish Tribe, a Sioux woman belongs to the Sioux Nation. In Canada, the legislature created artificial groups known as Indian "Bands." A community or collective includes an Indian Band.

42. Albert P. Blaustein and Carol Tenney, "Understanding 'Rights' and Bills of Rights," *University of Richmond Law Review*, vol. 25, no. 3 (1991), 414. The authors coined civil and political rights as "first generation rights" and I adopt their terminology.

43. I refer to Aboriginal men's organizations mentioned in the case *Native Women's Association of Canada* v. *Canada* (1992), 95 D.L.R. (4th) 106 (F.C.A.).

44. Blaustein and Tenney, *supra*, 415.

45. Sally M. Weaver, "Indian Women, Marriage and Legal Status," in *Marriage and Divorce in Canada*, ed. K. Kishwaran (Toronto: McGraw-Hill Ryerson, 1978), 18.

46. Michael McDonald, "Should Communities Have Rights? Reflections on Liberal Individualism," *Canadian Journal of Law and Jurisprudence*, vol. 4, no. 2 (1991), 245 (hereinafter "Communities").

47. Canada, Parliament of Canada, Standing Committee on Indian Affairs and Northern Development, *Report of the Sub-Committee on Indian Women and the Indian Act*, Chair, Keith Penner (Ottawa: Queen's Printer, 1982) Issue 58 (hereinafter "Report on Indian Women").

48. The National Indian Brotherhood in 1994 is now called the Assembly of First Nations. I use the name "Assembly of First Nations."

49. *Report on Indian Women*.

50. Ibid., 17.

51. Ibid., 19.

The Assembly of First Nations said that by concentrating upon the discrimination in the *Indian Act* against individual women, there was a danger that remedies might be damaging to internationally recognized collective rights. "Under international standards the collective rights under civil and political rights is recognized ... all we are saying is that if you deal with the individual right in isolation of the collective right, part of the collective right for men and women to form their own government and to determine their own policy on citizenship questions, that is part of the civil and political rights issue that we are talking about under international standards. So you are taking away from it. By dealing with the one issue on a sex basis, you are discriminating against all Indians, never mind women, under those standards you are citing to me now." The Assembly of First Nations felt that the problem of discrimination against Indian women in the *Indian Act* was a symptom of the non-recognition of the collective rights of the Indian community, which include the right of the men and women together to decide their own form of government.

52. Ibid.

53. Ibid., 18.

54. *Declaration on Elimination of Discrimination Against Women*, Art. 5, 1967 U.N.Y.B. 518, U.N. Doc. A/6716/ 1967. The United Nations declared that "women shall have the same rights as men to acquire, change or retain their nationality" and that "marriage to an alien shall not automatically affect the nationality of the wife either by rendering her stateless or by forcing on her nationality of

her husband." *Declaration on Human Rights*, 1948 3 Y.B. Int'l L. Comm'n 15, U.N. Doc. A/811/1948.

55. *Thomas v. Norris*, 1992 2 C.N.L.R. 139 (B.C.S.C.).

56. Thomas Isaac, "Individual Versus Collective Rights: Aboriginal People and the Significance of *Thomas v. Norris*," *Manitoba Law Journal*, vol. 3 (1992), 626 (hereinafter "Individual v. Collective"). "As outlined earlier, Hood J. decided in favour of the individual's right to security of the person over the group right to practice spirit dancing. This raises the issue of whether group rights should succumb to individual rights for Aboriginal peoples."

57. Robert Matas, "Native Rite Ruled Subject to Law," *The Globe and Mail*, 8 February 1992, A6.

58. Isaac, "Individual v. Collective," *supra*, 630.

59. Ibid., 618. "The facts and reasons for judgment of the decision provide a superb opportunity to examine the issue of individual rights of Aboriginal people versus group Aboriginal rights."

60. Ibid.

61. Ibid., 621.

62. Ibid., 622, quoting *Thomas*, *supra*, 159.

63. *Thomas*, *supra*, 160.

64. Isaac, "Individual v. Collective," *supra*, 623. "Thus, section 35 rights are to be exercised in accordance with the criminal law (which prohibits certain kinds of conduct) and the civil law which protects persons who may be injured by the exercise, in this instance, of Aboriginal rights."

65. Ibid., 625. "An 1803 Act, and an 1821 Act, extended the jurisdiction of the colonial governments to include crimes and offenses within 'Indian territories.' Thus, the criminal law was clearly applicable to Aboriginal people long before Confederation. Bruce Clark notes that this restricts any Aboriginal claims of an inherent right to self-government to 'civil matters.'" The author's references included: *An Act for Extending the Jurisdiction of the Courts of Justice in the Provinces of Lower and Upper Canada, to the Trial and Punishment of Persons Guilty of Crimes and Offenses within Certain Parts of North America Adjoining to the Said Provinces* (U.K.) (1803), 43 Geo. 3, c. 138; *An Act for Regulating the Fur Trade, and Establishing a Criminal and Civil Jurisdiction within Certain Parts of North America* (U.K.) (1821), 1 and 2, Geo. 4, c. 66; Bruce Clark, *Native Liberty, Crown Sovereignty: The Existing Right of Aboriginal Self-Government in Canada* (Montreal: McGill-Queen's University Press, 1990), 125.

66. *Thomas*, *supra*, 232. "He lives in a free society and his rights are inviolable. He is free to believe in, and to practise, any religion or tradition, if he chooses to do so. He cannot be coerced or forced to participate in one of any group purporting to exercise their collective rights in doing so. His freedoms and rights are not 'subject to the collective rights of the aboriginal nation to which he belongs.'"

67. Michael Hartney, "Some Confusions Concerning Collective Rights," *Canadian Journal of Law and Jurisprudence*, vol. 4, no. 2 (1991): 239.

68. Philip P. Frickey, "Marshalling Past and Present: Colonialism, Constitutionalism and Interpretation in Federal Indian Law," *Harvard Law Review*, vol. 107, no. 2 (1993), 395. The author found that the existence of congressional plenary power has been established by the courts, but the exercise of the power is open to scrutiny. Similarly, the exercise of powers under sections 91 and 92 are open to the *Charter* tests. In other words, parliamentary supremacy is not an issue. The question is whether legislatures under section 32 exercised their legislative powers in keeping with the *Charter of Rights and Freedoms*.

69. Isaac, "Individual v. Collective," *supra*, 627.

70. McDonald, "Communities," *supra*, 225. "In a liberal state, right-holders must be more than merely passive beneficiaries of rights; right-holders must be active exercisers of their rights."

71. Ibid., 227.

72. Ibid.

73. Ibid., 226–7. McDonald quotes Justice Deschenes in *Quebec Protestant School Board* v. *Quebec A.-G.*, 140 D.L.R. (3d) 33, 64–5:

    The court is amazed, to use a euphemism, to hear this argument from a government which prides itself in maintaining in America the flame of French civilization with its promotion of spiritual values and its traditional respect for liberty.

In fact, Quebec's argument is based on a totalitarian conception of society to which this court does not subscribe. Human beings are, to us, of paramount importance and nothing should be allowed to diminish the respect due to them. Other societies place the collectivity above the individual. They use the Kolkhoze steamroller and see merit only in the collective result even if some individuals are left by the wayside in the process.

This concept of society has never taken root here— even if certain political initiatives seem at times to come dangerously close to it—and this court will not honour it with its approval. Every individual in Canada should enjoy his rights to the full when in Quebec, whether alone or as a member of a group; and if the group numbers 100 persons, the one hundredth has as much to benefit from all privileges of citizens as the other ninety-nine. The alleged restriction of a collective right which would deprive the one hundredth member of the group of the right guaranteed by the *Charter* constitutes, for this one hundredth member, a real denial of his rights. He cannot simply be counted as an accidental loss in a collective operation; our concept of human beings does not accommodate such a theory.

74. Wendy Moss, "Indigenous Self-Government in Canada and Sexual Equality Under the Indian Act: Resolving Conflicts Between Collective and Individual Rights," *Queen's Law Journal*, vol. 15 (1990), 279.

75. *Santa Clara Pueblo* v. *Martinez*, 436 U.S. 49 (1978).

76. Moss, *supra*, 289.

77. *Indian Civil Rights Act of 1978*, Public Law No. 90-284, 88 Stat. 77 cited in Carla Christofferson, "Tribal Courts' Failure to Protect Native American Women: A Reevaluation of the Indian Civil Rights Act of 1978," *The Yale Law Journal*, vol. 101 (1991), 170.

78. Carla Christofferson, "Tribal Courts' Failure to Protect Native American Women: A Reevaluation of the Indian Civil Rights Act," *The Yale Law Journal*, vol. 101 (1991), 170.

79. Ibid.

80. Ibid., 175.

81. McDonald, "Communities," *supra*, 228: "from a liberal perspective group rights, like individual rights, appear to be non-justiciable because they are inherently political. Thus, Dworkin assigns to the judiciary the task of adjudicating claims on the basis of rights. The role of judges is to postulate foundational rights, which Dworkin contends will centre on individual autonomy. This leaves the care of groups to the legislature, which has the task of advancing the general good in a totalitarian way."

82. Darlene Johnson, "Native Rights as Collective Rights: A Question of Group Self-Preservation," *Canadian Journal of Law and Jurisprudence*, vol. 2, no. 1 (1989), 28.

83. Moss, *supra*, 301.

84. McDonald, "Communities," *supra*, 219.

85. Storrow and Morellato, "Aboriginal Law," *supra*, 1.1.09 citing *Pasco* v. *C.N.R.* (1989), 34 B.C.L.R. (2d) 344; *Joe* v. *Findlay* (1981), 26 B.C.L.R. 376 (B.C.C.A.). In *Pasco*, the court noted: "It is a mistake ... to ignore the historical fact that the rights Aboriginal are communal, and that they are possessed today by the descendants of persons who originally held them. They are not personal rights in the sense that they exist independently of the community, but are personal in the sense that a violation of the communal rights affects the individual members' enjoyment of those rights."

86. Jamieson, *supra*, 91–2: "At the time of the *Lavell* case there were no women on the National Indian Brotherhood NIB executive council and the Iroquois and Allied Indian group, who first enlisted the help of the Solicitor-General and turned the tide against Lavell, represented 20,000 Indian men. At present (February 1978) the Indian Brotherhood executive council has eleven members none of whom are women. At the September 1977 annual NIB conference, out of 68 delegates, only one was a woman (from B.C.)."

References

Articles

Asch, Michael, and Patrick Macklem. "Aboriginal Rights and Canadian Sovereignty: An Essay on *R. v. Sparrow*." *Alberta Law Review*, vol. 29, no. 2 (1991).

Binnie, W. Ian C. "The Sparrow Doctrine: Beginning of the End or End of the Beginning?" *Queen's Law Journal*, vol. 15 (1992).

Blaustein, Albert P., and Carol Tenney. "Understanding 'Rights' and Bills of Rights." *University of Richmond Law Review*, vol. 25, no. 3 (1991).

Christofferson, Carla. "Tribal Courts' Failure to Protect Native American Women: A Reevaluation of the Indian Civil Rights Act." *The Yale Law Journal*, vol. 101 (1991).

Frickey, Philip P. "Marshalling Past and Present: Colonialism, Constitutionalism, and Interpretation in Federal Indian Law." *Harvard Law Review*, vol. 107, no. 2 (1993).

Hartney, Michael. "Some Confusions Concerning Collective Rights." *Canadian Journal of Law and Jurisprudence*, vol. 4, no. 2 (1991).

Isaac, Thomas. "Individual Versus Collective Rights: Aboriginal People and the Significance of *Thomas v. Norris*." *Manitoba Law Journal*, vol. 3 (1992).

Isaac, Thomas, and Mary Sue Maloughney. "Dually Disadvantaged and Historically Forgotten? Aboriginal Women and the Inherent Right to Self-Government." *Manitoba Law Journal* (1992).

Johnson, Darlene M. "Native Rights as Collective Rights: A Question of Group Self-Preservation." *Canadian Journal of Law and Jurisprudence*, vol. 2, no. 1 (1989).

Kirkness, Verna. "Emerging Native Women." *Canadian Journal of Women and the Law*, vol. 2 (1987–88).

Matas, Robert. "Native Rite Ruled Subject to Law." *The Globe and Mail*, 8 February 1992, A6.

McDonald, Michael. "Should Communities Have Rights? Reflections on Liberal Individualism." *Canadian Journal of Law and Jurisprudence*, vol. 4, no. 2 (1991).

Moss, Wendy. "Indigenous Self-Government in Canada and Sexual Equality Under the Indian Act: Resolving Conflicts Between Collective and Individual Rights." *Queen's Law Journal*, vol. 15 (1990).

Pentney, William. "The Rights of the Aboriginal Peoples of Canada in the Constitution Act, 1982, Part II, Section 35: The Substantive Guarantee." *University of British Columbia Law Review*, vol. 22 (1987).

Slattery, Brian. "Understanding Aboriginal Rights." *Canadian Bar Review*, vol. 66 (1987).

Weaver, Sally M. "Indian Women, Marriage and Legal Status." In *Marriage and Divorce in Canada*, ed. K. Kriswaren. Toronto: McGraw-Hill Ryerson, 1978.

Books

Canada. Department of Justice. *Federal Issues Document on Violence Against Women*. Ottawa: Department of Justice, May 1994.

Canada. Department of Justice. *Draft Report on the Role of Aboriginal Women in Justice Reform*. Ottawa: Department of Justice, May 24, 1994.

Canada. Parliament. House of Commons. *Report of the Sub-Committee on Indian Women and the Indian Act*. Ottawa: Queen's Printer, 1982.

Canada. *The Elimination of Sex Discrimination from the Indian Act*. Ottawa: Minister of Indian Affairs and Northern Development, 1982.

Hobsbawn, Eric, and Terence Banger. *The Invention of Tradition*. Cambridge: Cambridge University Press, 1983.

Jamieson, Kathleen. *Indian Women and the Law in Canada: Citizens Minus*. Ottawa: Department of Indian Affairs and Northern Development, 1978.

Krosenbrink-Gelissen, Lillianne Ernestine. *Sexual Equality As an Aboriginal Right: The Native Women's Association of Canada and the Constitutional Process on Aboriginal Matters, 1982–1987*. Saarbrucken, Germany: Verlag Breitenback Publishers, 1991.

Leslie, John, and Ron Macguire. *The Historical Development of the Indian Act*. Ottawa: Department of Indian and Northern Affairs Canada, 1979.

Lowes, Warren. *Indian Giver: A Legacy of North American Native People*. Toronto: Canadian Alliance in Solidarity with Native Peoples, 1985.

Storrow, R.V., and Maria A. Morellato. *Aboriginal Law: Fishing Rights and the Sparrow Case*. Vancouver: Continuing Legal Education, 1990.

Trigger, Bruce G. *Natives and Newcomers: Canada's "Heroic Age" Reconsidered*. Montreal: McGill-Queen's Press, 1986.

Unpublished Works

Christos Sirross, Minister of Natural Resources and Minister Responsible for Native Affairs. "Notes for a Speech to the Federal-Provincial-Territorial Meeting of Ministers Responsible for Native Affairs and Leaders of the National Aboriginal Organizations." Quebec City, 17 May 1994.

Cases

A.-G. B.C. v. *MacDonald* (1961), 131 C.C.C. 126.

A.-G. Canada v. *Lavell* (1973), 38 D.L.R. (3d) 481 (S.C.C.).

A.-G. Canada v. *Lavell, Isaac* v. *Bedard* (1973), 1974 S.C.R. 1349.

Calder v. *A.-G. B.C.* (1973), 34 D.L.R (3d) 145 (S.C.C.).

Cunningham v. *Tomey Homma* 1903 A.C. 151.

Derrickson v. *Derrickson* (1986), 26 D.L.R. (4th) 175 (S.C.C.C.).

Edwards v. *A.-G. Canada* 1930 A.C. 124.

In the Matter of a Reference as to the Meaning of the Word "Persons" in section 24 of the British North America Act, 1867 1928 S.C.R. 276.

Joe v. *Findlay* (1981), 26 B.C.L.R. 376 (B.C.C.A.).

Lovelace v. *Canada* 1982 1 C.N.L.R. 1.

Native Women's Association of Canada v. *Canada* (1992), 95 D.L.R. (4th) 106 (F.C.A.).

Pasco v. *C.N.R.* (1989), 34 B.C.L.R. (2d) 344.

Paul v. *Paul* (1986), 26 D.L.R. (4th) 196 (S.C.C.).

Quebec Protestant School Boards v. *Quebec A.-G.*, 140 D.L.R. (3d) 33.

R. v. *Flett* (1989), 6 W.W.R. 166.

R. v. *Sparrow* (1990), 70 D.L.R. (4th) 385 (S.C.C.).

Re Lavell and A.-G. of Canada (1971), 22 D.L.R. (3d) 182 (Co. Ct.); rev'd (1971), 22 D.L.R. (3d) 188 (F.C.A.).

Santa Clara Pueblo v. *Martinez*, 436 U.S. 49 (1978).

Simon v. *The Queen* (1985), 24 D.L.R (4th) 390, 410–12 (S.C.C.)

Thomas v. *Norris* 1992 2 C.N.L.R. 139 (B.C.S.C.).

Union Colliery v. *Bryden* 1899 A.C. 580.

Statutes

An Act for the Better Protection of the Lands and Property of the Indians in Lower Canada, 1850.

An Act to Encourage the Gradual Civilization of the Indian Tribes, 1857.

An Act for the Gradual Enfranchisement of Indians, the Better Management of Indian Affairs, and to Extend the Provisions of the Act 31st Victoria, Chapter 42, S.C. 1869, c. 6.

Bill C-31, *An Act to Amend the Indian Act*. R.S.C. 1985, c. 32 (1st Supp. 1985).

Electoral Franchise Act. S.C. 1885, c. 40, s. 2.

Family Relations Act. R.S.B.C. 1979, c. 121, s. 77.

Fisheries Act. R.S.C. 1985, c. F-14.

Indian Act. R.S.C. 1970, s. 12(1)(b).

International Instruments

Declaration on Elimination of All Forms of Discrimination Against Women. Art. 5, 1967 U.N.Y.B. 518, U.N. Doc. A/6716/1967.

Declaration on Human Rights. 1948 3 Y.B. Int'l Comm'n 15, U.N. Doc. AK/811/1948.

Indian Civil Rights Act of 1978. Public Law No. 90-284, 82 Stat. 77.

Women's Movements and State Feminism: Integrating Diversity into Public Policy

L. Pauline Rankin and Jill Vickers

In Canada, the existence of a formal, institutionalized relationship between women's organizations and bureaucratic structures began in 1954 with the establishment of the Women's Bureau within the federal Department of Labour. Like many later developments, this initiative was part of an international effort to focus attention on the position of women in the paid work force. Canadian labour activists and other women involved in the Congress of Canadian Women (formed in 1950) saw the Bureau primarily as a source of research data of the sort that the International Labor Organization was compiling about women in the paid work force. The Bureau was also necessary to inform government on the issues raised by the data. This structure, the first example of status-of-women machinery in Canada, was based on a similar structure within the U.S. Department of Labor that dated back to 1920.

The Women's Bureau developed within a government department that had a culture of advocacy and reflected the government's need to understand the greater participation by Canadian women in the paid labour force.[1] This model was replicated at the sub-national level. The successful campaign for equal pay for equal work legislation achieved in Ontario in 1954 further mobilized support for this kind of mechanism and women's bureaus spread across the country. These agencies began as advocacy-based organizations, but advocacy became more difficult as labour laws in Canada developed and established governments as neutral in labour–management relationships.

In the 1960s, women's groups in Francophone and Anglophone Canada joined forces to demand a royal commission on the status of women. The federal Liberal Government, sensitive to national unity issues, was eager to support movements it believed cut across linguistic cleavages and, therefore, fostered its relationship with the women's movement by agreeing to strike a royal commission to investigate women's equality needs.

When the Commission reported in 1970, it recommended the creation of an implementation committee to monitor the adoption of the report's 167 recommendations. Initially located within the Privy Council Office, the Implementation Committee was designated as a separate agency in 1976 and renamed Status of Women Canada (SWC).

Another recommendation was the establishment of an arm's length, non-partisan status of women council that would be pan-Canadian in scope and directly responsible to Parliament for evaluating programs that affected women. Although Canadian women were granted an advisory council, the organizational practices chosen by the Trudeau Government produced long-term representational weaknesses. For example, the Canadian Advisory Council on the Status of Women (CACSW), created in 1973, was established through an order-in-council and not by the passage of legislation. This meant it continued at the "pleasure" of the government of the day. Instead of reporting to Parliament directly, it reported through the Minister Responsible for the Status of Women. If the Council had continued to be led by presidents of major women's organizations, as was the practice in the early years, the representational capacity of this state feminist institution would have been enhanced, and the relationship between women's movements and the bureaucracy might have developed a quite different history. Instead, governments began to use the Council to make patronage appointments, some of whom were very knowledgeable about women's concerns, while others were less so. Vacancies on the Council were not advertised nor were members nominated by women's organizations. Gradually, the structure lost legitimacy except for its research in some periods and was replaced by the National Action Committee on the Status of Women (NAC) as the main focus of the movement/federal government interface. In fact, there has never been an effective consultative structure within Canadian state feminism that enjoyed the sustained confidence of women's movement organizations. Instead, from the mid-1970s, NAC served effectively as a peak organization representing many women's groups in English Canada. Arguably, the existence of NAC permitted the neglect of consultative mechanisms within the federal government.

The network of state feminist institutions in place from the 1970s to the 1990s included:

- Status of Women Canada: A policy agency, reporting to the Minister Responsible for the Status of Women. Status of Women Canada also emerged as a focus for government policy development within the state and became the central vehicle for representing Canada's international position on gender issues.

- Minister Responsible for the Status of Women: Created in 1971. Throughout the 1970s, the post was often assigned to a very senior (male) minister. Since the 1980s it is generally assigned to junior (female) ministers.

- Women's Program, Citizenship Branch, Secretary of State: This agency provided funding for women's organizations and movement activities.

- Canadian Advisory Council on the Status of Women:[2] Reported to Parliament via the Minister Responsible for the Status of Women.

- Women's Labour Bureau: Produced materials on women's labour force participation.

- Expertise-Based Agencies: Within Health and Welfare/Health Canada and the Department of Justice, these structures involved government-driven consultations on an irregular basis.

Concurrent to the development of state feminism at the federal level, provinces and territories also created women's machinery that generally included a policy directorate and an advisory council. Some jurisdictions developed more effective models than others. Some adopted the federal model with all its structural confusion. Others developed their own, often more coherent, structural basis for state feminism. In Newfoundland, for example, the Women's Policy Unit was integrated into the decision-making structure through the government's Executive Council. Similarly, the Newfoundland and Labrador Provincial Advisory Council was created with a guarantee that women's movements would participate in nominating Council members from their activist communities. There were assurances that the Advisory Council would have a public role and autonomy as an independent agency (Rankin 1996). As women's movements grew across Canada in the 1970s and 1980s, the orientation of these movements to the state differed. As we illustrate, in some contexts, such as Quebec, the relationship was relatively positive. In others, such as Alberta, the relationship was frequently acrimonious because governments were hostile to feminist demands. In most jurisdictions, the relationship changed over time.

The structures of state feminism at the federal level have been compressed significantly since the election of the Liberals in 1993. To reduce duplication of services and provide a more comprehensive approach to women's equality in Canada, the Liberal Government dismantled the Advisory Council and transferred its research and public inquiries function, along with the Women's Program to Status of Women Canada (Wilcox 1997). As a consequence, SWC now exists as the central mechanism for the advancement of women's equality. This amalgamation was set within an economic rationalist discourse and the argued need to enhance the efficiency and effectiveness of the bureaucracy as a whole. Under the leadership of Status of Women Canada, however, this restructuring has not strengthened the consultative process between women's movements and the state for a number of reasons.

Our focus groups revealed that, although there was not widespread respect for the now defunct Advisory Council mainly because of the partisan/patronage composition of its membership, women activists believe there is now a vacuum in the federal machinery for gaining women's input. Some women's organizations describe recent efforts at consultations with governments as "disastrous." Others note an increased distancing between bureaucrats and feminists, and express frustration that access, previously enjoyed, has disappeared. Clearly, at least at the level of the federal structures of state feminism, there are serious problems of unmet expectations and a disruption in effective communication for many long-term activists.

Three issues merit exposure. First, the women's bureaucratic machinery, which developed more or less topsy-turvy in Canada at the federal level, differed significantly from the original femocrat model of state feminism. Many argue that this was a negative, not a positive, innovation. Second, the women's state machinery that developed in Canada was based on the idea that women's organizations were best able to convey women's ideas for change, and their needs, to government directly. Particularly in the 1970s, when very few women were members of Parliament, or bureaucrats who understood the issues, this founding principle was accepted. Moreover, the arm's-length research activities of the Advisory Council and the role of NAC brought together the views of many women's groups, resolved some of their conflicts, and presented them to government as "women's views." This served the interests of government actions and majority women. Third, models of state feminism have emerged in other countries that form the basis of the paradigm being promoted by international agencies. This model relies on feminist "experts" and gender-based or gender-sensitive analysis undertaken by academics and bureaucrats. They are now increasingly the focus of state feminism replacing the role of women's organizations in conveying their views to femocrats within the state. Although women's movements in Canada were generally willing to engage with state institutions for the two decades after 1970, the negative experiences many report in recent years are leading some to refocus their attention away from official politics. Ironically, this is occurring at just the time when state feminist agencies are promoting the brave new world of governments ready to subject all policies to gender-based analysis. A subnational comparison of state feminism reveals that many models of women's policy machinery have emerged. Some provide important opportunities for successful collaboration between women's movements and their provincial governments. Quebec is one such example.

State Feminism in Quebec

Although all ministries within Quebec share responsibility for improving the social conditions and the overall status of women, the Ministère responsable de la condition de la femme, created in 1979, has the lead role in ensuring the co-ordination, coherence, and development of government actions around women's equality. The Secrétariat à la condition féminine answers directly to the minister, providing administrative support for the Ministry and supplying the minister with analysis and recommendations on matters of policy development. The Secrétariat is also responsible for co-ordinating the network of status of women co-ordinators which exist in over 30 ministries. Beyond these functions, the Secrétariat is also the driving force behind the implementation of gender analysis in the province.

The Conseil du statut de la femme (CSF) works at arm's length from the government. It is an agency for consultation and research founded in 1973. It promotes and defends the rights of women in Quebec through a two-pronged mandate of advising the government on all issues that are linked to the status of women as well as communicating information to women's organizations and the general public about the conditions and rights of Quebec women. The Conseil responds to government requests for advice linked to the status of women, but also raises issues when it deems that government intervention may be necessary and offers recommendations to the government on a range of policy matters. The Conseil mandate includes monitoring government activities through analysis of bills and policies that affect the status of women. The Conseil also initiates research projects on issues linked to the status of women. Additionally, the Conseil publishes *La Gazette des Femmes*, which informs the public on various issues pertinent to women and updates Conseil activities.

As Marie Lavigne (1997), a former president of the Conseil explains, the relationship between the Conseil and the women's movement is complex: the Conseil supports the agenda of the women's movement, but does not act as a direct representative for the movement. The members of the Conseil are appointed by the Quebec government, but the vital links to the women's movement are reflected in the appointment process. For example, another former president, Diane Lemieux, previously held the position of co-ordinator of the Regroupement Québeçois des centres d'aide et de lutte contre les agressions à caractère sexuel, which suggests that action on violence against women has a strong advocate within the Conseil. The other members of the Conseil are also government appointees, but these appointments are based on the recommendations of various groups. Four members are recommended by feminist organizations, two by universities, two by socio-economic groups and two by unions. This model is not the norm for advisory council appointments elsewhere in Canada and reflects a substantial commitment on the part of the Quebec government to representing its women citizens appropriately through state feminist institutions. The Conseil also has a permanent staff, approximately one third of which is deployed in regional offices.

What is unique about the Conseil is its presence throughout Quebec as a result of its decentralization. Consequently, it is accessible to women's groups and able to initiate studies that correspond to the realities of the different regions. The task of the regional offices includes regional research projects and support to the tables de concertations des groupes de femmes, which were set up in 1982. The regionalization of the Conseil was part of the mandate between 1978 and 1984. Currently, the Conseil boasts a complement of 12 regional offices that allows the Conseil to maintain a visible profile among Quebec women.[3]

What is most interesting in a period marked both domestically and internationally by budgetary restraint and retrenchment, is that although the staff has been reduced from 73 to 64 employees, the budget of the Conseil has remained relatively stable. While there has been fluctuation in the budget throughout the 1990s, the current level is slightly higher than at the beginning of the decade.[4]

Why Bother with State Feminism?

Our analysis thus far isolates some serious weaknesses in the model of state feminism that unfolded at the federal level in Canada. Nevertheless, we contend there are models of state feminism which work well and demonstrate that women's involvement in official politics in various ways has paid off, especially, but not exclusively, for majority women. Later in this document, we profile some successful relationships between women's movements and state feminism that operate in Quebec. We also argue that the political opportunity structure women activists face is rapidly changing in Canada, and to realize substantive improvements in women's lives, women's movements must reconsider their strategic choices vis-à-vis the state. Any assessment of the political opportunities now available for feminists must include careful consideration of how the state has been restructured, the characteristics of electoral systems, party systems and bureaucratic systems, as well as analysis of the ideological climate in which activism now occurs.

How women can act politically in the realm of official politics is partly a matter of choice. How they can act *effectively* is shaped by the structure of the political opportunities they face. Through their interaction with governments in the last three decades, women activists have played some role in shaping the "women's machinery" now in place. The large-scale restructuring governments are involved in is radically altering the kind of state women activists will face in the future. Despite the challenges and constraints characterizing state feminism in Canada, feminists still have much to gain by working with femocrats to pursue equality goals. Below we discuss seven reasons to consider.

Pragmatic Reasons

State feminism is working effectively in some countries and provinces with positive results for many women. We analyze a positive case to identify why state feminism has worked. If state feminism can be an effective vehicle in other contexts, we believe it can function similarly in Canada.

Rights-Based Reasons

Having women's concerns and needs taken seriously by governments is a right of citizenship. As members of a national community, women have civil, political, and social rights that must be protected by their states. As citizens, the right to participate in decision-making processes is fundamental to a healthy democracy. Special "women's machinery" was developed in recognition of women's historic marginalization in institutions dominated by men, as all state institutions in Canada still are. Therefore, engagement with these decision-making processes can be argued for from a rights-based perspective.

Responsibility-Based Reasons

To date, women have tended to view themselves largely as consumers of state policies and programs. Women also have an obligation as citizens to contribute ideas about the issues facing women in order to improve society for the population as a whole. Because political parties continue to be male-dominated, women must access alternative institutions in order to integrate women-centred perspectives in decision-making processes.

Representation-Based Reasons

There have been improvements in women's presence in the elected and appointed institutions of official politics, but these women remain a small minority and have found it difficult to achieve change in isolation. Significant structural barriers to women's participation in official politics, on the same basis as men, remain. Special structures to channel women's ideas and views, such as those offered in state feminist institutions, will be needed for some time to afford women substantive representation.

Diversity Reasons

At the nation-state level, it is difficult to move beyond consideration of "women's issues," which treat women as an undifferentiated category. Strong local decision-making should enhance women's participation; good consultative structures at all levels of state feminism can also make it easier for differently located women's views to be heard.

Changing Bureaucratic Cultures

The character of the bureaucracy within a jurisdiction profoundly affects the potential success of state feminism. For example, the bureaucratic cultures of some regional and federal governments encouraged advocacy, making the femocrat project acceptable. Such a pattern is evident in Quebec, Newfoundland, and British Columbia. In other jurisdictions, however, especially in the Canadian federal case, the norms of bureaucratic neutrality have invalidated the adoption of state feminism by ordinary public sector structures. The development of an expertise-based, gender-based analysis approach provides a focus for examining this problem. The impact of gender-based analysis on advocacy-based analysis obtained via consultation will require women involved with state feminism to monitor these developments.

Multi-Level Governance

Multi-level governance is the new reality even in non-federal states as decision-making devolves to more local authorities but is still shaped by transnational levels of governance. For women, the nation-state level will continue to be important and, therefore, regularizing access to governments through both federal and provincial/territorial channels of state feminism may prove critical to achieving meaningful policy results.

The Changing Political Opportunity Structure and State Feminism

Sidney Tarrow developed the concept of a "political opportunity structure in his work on the relationship between social movements and the state" (Phillips 1992). The term refers to the institutional arrangements and ideological climate of political systems at any one time and is useful in identifying the limitations and opportunities that confront movements which attempt change through state-directed action. Throughout the last decade, a number of developments strained the relationships between structures of state feminism and women's movements as feminists experienced radical alterations in the nature of the political opportunity structure. For example, far more women became active in electoral politics as members of Parliament and cabinet ministers, and in senior bureaucratic positions. This resulted in conflicts among femocrats, women politicians, and women's organizations about who best represents women. Undoubtedly, the neo-liberal "turn" in domestic and international politics precipitated a dramatic contraction of the welfare state and the downloading of responsibilities. This shift in the political opportunity structure radicalized some women's organizations and led to more confrontational stances. Not surprisingly, when there are fewer opportunities for women to get what they need and want from governments, women's groups often become more oppositional. This trend also had an impact on solidarity within the women's movement. Many majority women had made significant personal gains in their equality struggles and the most vocal women's groups, such as NAC, were seen, increasingly, as vehicles for less affluent, more marginalized women. Important efforts to deal with critical, complex issues such as racism, ableism, and homophobia within feminist institutions, such as NAC, unfortunately, resulted in diminished solidarity.

As we have argued, the restructuring of women's machinery federally reduced its legitimacy with many women's organizations. The trend toward the realignment of state feminist institutions throughout Canada reflects international developments. A recent report of the United Nations Experts Advisory Group on National Machineries stated that one of the most significant obstacles that women's equality machinery faces today, throughout the world, is the frequent restructuring of governments, in both developing and developed countries (as quoted in Wilcox 1997). These frequent changes disrupt the continuity of national machineries, leading to significant constraints in the ability of these mechanisms to advance women's equality. In Canada, a similar realignment both of state feminist institutions, and government structures more broadly, is precipitating a profound recasting of the linkages between women's movements and their government. As one focus group participant lamented:

> Overall, what we find difficult is that the structures of government are constantly changing. We are constantly having to make new contacts, learn the new policies, the changes in philosophies and requirements, and how these people function. It is difficult to make advances in such contexts.

Another participant echoed similar sentiments.

> [B]y the time we've figured out where we fit and how it all works, which almost requires one to have an M.A. or Ph.D., they [the government] change the structure again. We are stuck in a

wave of change which leads to a demobilization of the various groups.

More generally, globalization is reducing women's belief that governments can provide them with what they need and want, even if the political will to do so is present. The increased complexity of federalism in Canada has made it harder and harder for women to relate effectively to state feminism because of confusion over which level of government is responsible for policy areas. That does not mean this route to change should be abandoned. Instead, the women's movement must explore how state feminism can be "retooled" to meet the needs of feminism in the new millennium. A crucial step in shaping those decisions involves a careful evaluation of the overall governmental structures in which state feminism is located in order to understand the realities of the current political opportunity structure.

Recommendations

Our vision for state feminism in Canada is of a system in which co-operation, co-ordination, and regular exchanges of information on strategies, alliances, what works, and what does not occur regularly using new technology. To realize this vision, however, also requires the rebuilding of trust among increasingly fragmented women's movements. Rebuilding trust between femocrats and activists is crucial, but so too is rebuilding trust between majority and minority women on a new basis of mutual respect and equality. We believe that some new structures and practices are needed for this rebuilding to occur. As one activist argued:

> The institutional changes important to us are at the level of consultation. What is difficult about this is that there are several actors who all have differing interests …. However, the government needs to be increasingly aware of the way citizens empower themselves to have a voice and ask

for change. They need to listen to us …. This is a recognition that we are a democratic society and the work that we are doing contributes to upholding democratic principles.

In keeping with these comments and based on our analysis of the changing nature of feminist activism and women's relationship to the state in a globalizing and decentralizing era, we recommend the following.

A new permanent consultative body should be established. Given the restructuring of state feminist institutions, we call for the creation of a new council that could include the presidents of 50 women's organizations, 10 of which would change each year. A steering committee would be selected from among the council members. The council would serve as a body to convey the positions of their organizations and members to government in areas of mutual concern. The council would meet annually with femocrats and ministers.

The steering committee could be convened more frequently. It is crucial that such a council not be subject to patronage appointments as was the CACSW. Its function should be to represent to government the views of women's organizations in areas of pressing policy concerns. *It will be especially important that minority and marginalized women's groups are well represented in such a forum.* The model of Quebec's Conseil du statut de la femme should be explored for insights in how to achieve ongoing legitimacy.

Formal policy networks need to be established working primarily through information technology in areas such as the anti-violence portfolio. These networks should include activists, women's groups, service providers, academics, femocrats, and interested politicians. As a minimum, such on-line policy networks can keep the major actors in policy and program development informed of one another's thinking. Ideally, the sort of

synergy and creativity we see emerging in the area of women's health policy will develop.

An annual conference should be developed at which women from different contexts and localities can meet, exchange ideas and experiences, and come to understand one another better. These should not take the form of a lobby. Rather, women activists, front-line workers, politicians, and femocrats should meet as women with different roles to play and learn about one another's situation and constraints. The core of such a conference could well be an annual meeting of federal and provincial ministers and femocrats *in conjunction with* a meeting of their movement counterparts. It would be especially useful if such a conference could move to different parts of the country so participants can learn about the diversity of women's lives and experiences as activists. This sort of initiative should be supported by a full range of communication technologies, including Web sites, a list-server, and teleconferencing.

Given the opportunities and constraints at play between women's movements and the state, these suggestions represent a tentative step toward retooling state feminism for the new millennium. In an era marked by the pressures of globalization and decentralization, we argue these and other similar initiatives are vital to reposition women's groups in relation to their governments and ensure that gender and diversity are integrated substantively into public policy. The new realities challenging feminist activists also require researching models used elsewhere to probe how best to restructure our relationships with the state. We believe that "bothering with government" can still provide women with opportunities to achieve feminist goals. Indeed, our collective ability to rethink interactions with governments in creative and innovative ways may well be the critical test for the achievement of equality and justice for all women.

Notes

1. The early history of women's policy machinery is documented in Linda Geller-Schwartz, "An Array of Agencies" in Stetson and Mazur (1995).
2. For a more complete treatment of the CACSW, consult Burt (1998).
3. These regional offices are located in Bas-Saint-Laurent, Gaspésie, Îles-de-la-Madeleine; Saguenay, Lac-St-Jean; Québec, Chaudière, Apalaches; Mauricie, Centre du Québec; Lanaudière, Laurentides; Abitibi-Témiscamingue; Estrie; Montréal; Laval; Montérégie; Outaouais and Côte-Nord.
4. The Conseil's budget in 1990–91 was $3,898,468 compared to $3,947,069 in 1997–98. The Conseil's budget peaked in 1992–93 at $4,231,500 (CSF annual reports).

References

Lavigne, Marie. 1997. "Structures institutionnelles en condition féminine—le cas de Conseil du statut de la femme du Québec." In *Women and the Canadian State*. Edited by Caroline Andrew and Sanda Rodgers. Montréal-Kingston: McGill-Queen's University Press.

Phillips, Susan D. 1992. "New Social Movements and Unequal Representation: The Challenge of Influencing Public Policy." In *Democracy with Justice*. Edited by Alain-G. Gagnon and Brian Tanguay. Ottawa: Carleton University Press.

Rankin, L. Pauline. 1996. "Experience, Opportunity and the Politics of Place: A Comparative Analysis of Provincial and Territorial Women's Movements in Canada." Unpublished doctoral thesis. Carleton University: Department of Political Science.

Wilcox, Krista. 1997. "Getting Government Right? Government Reform and the Impact on the Federal Women's Equality Machinery." Unpublished master's research essay. Ottawa: Carleton University, Department of Political Science.

Marriage and Love[*]

Emma Goldman

The popular notion about marriage and love is that they are synonymous, that they spring from the same motives, and cover the same human needs. Like most popular notions this also rests not on actual facts, but on superstition.

Marriage and love have nothing in common; they are as far apart as the poles; are, in fact, antagonistic to each other. No doubt some marriages have been the result of love. Not, however, because love could assert itself only in marriage; much rather it is because few people can completely outgrow a convention. There are today large numbers of men and women to whom marriage is naught but a farce, but who submit to it for the sake of public opinion. At any rate, while it is true that some marriages are based on love, and while it is equally true that in some cases love continues in married life, I maintain that it does so regardless of marriage, and not because of it.

On the other hand, it is utterly false that love results from marriage. On rare occasions one does hear of a miraculous case of a married couple falling in love after marriage, but on close examination it will be found that it is a mere adjustment to the inevitable. Certainly the growing-used to each other is far away from the spontaneity, the intensity, and beauty of love, without which the intimacy of marriage must prove degrading to both the woman and the man.

Marriage is primarily an economic arrangement, an insurance pact. It differs from the ordinary life insurance agreement only in that it is more binding, more exacting. Its returns are insignificantly small compared with the investments. In taking out an insurance policy one pays for it in dollars and cents, always at liberty to discontinue payments. If, however, woman's premium is her husband, she pays for it with her name, her privacy, her self-respect, her very life, "until death doth part." Moreover, the marriage insurance condemns her to life-long dependency, to parasitism, to complete uselessness, individual as well as social. Man, too, pays his toll, but as his sphere is wider, marriage does not limit him as much as woman. He feels his chains more in an economic sense.

Thus Dante's motto over Inferno applies with equal force to marriage. "Ye who enter here leave all hope behind."

---

[*]   First published in 1917.

That marriage is a failure none but the very stupid will deny. One has but to glance over the statistics of divorce to realize how bitter a failure marriage really is. Nor will the stereotyped Philistine argument that the laxity of divorce laws and the growing looseness of woman account for the fact that: first, every twelfth marriage ends in divorce; second, that since 1870 divorces have increased from 28 to 73 for every hundred thousand population; third, that adultery, since 1867, as ground for divorce, has increased 270.8 per cent.; fourth, that desertion increased 369.8 per cent.

Added to these startling figures is a vast amount of material, dramatic and literary, further elucidating this subject. Robert Herrick, in *Together*; Pinero, in *Mid-Channel*; Eugene Walter, in *Paid in Full*, and scores of other writers are discussing the barrenness, the monotony, the sordidness, the inadequacy of marriage as a factor for harmony and understanding.

The thoughtful social student will not content himself with the popular superficial excuse for this phenomenon. He will have to dig deeper into the very life of the sexes to know why marriage proves so disastrous.

Edward Carpenter says that behind every marriage stands the life-long environment of the two sexes; an environment so different from each other that man and woman must remain strangers. Separated by an insurmountable wall of superstition, custom, and habit, marriage has not the potentiality of developing knowledge of, and respect for, each other, without which every union is doomed to failure.

Henrik Ibsen, the hater of all social shams, was probably the first to realize this great truth. Nora leaves her husband, not—as the stupid critic would have it—because she is tired of her responsibilities or feels the need of woman's rights, but because she has come to know that for eight years she had lived with a stranger and borne him children. Can there be anything more humiliating, more degrading than a life-long proximity between two strangers? No need for the woman to know

anything of the man, save his income. As to the knowledge of the woman—what is there to know except that she has a pleasing appearance? We have not yet outgrown the theologic myth that woman has no soul, that she is a mere appendix to man, made out of his rib just for the convenience of the gentleman who was so strong that he was afraid of his own shadow.

Perchance the poor quality of the material whence woman comes is responsible for her inferiority. At any rate, woman has no soul—what is there to know about her? Besides, the less soul a woman has the greater her asset as a wife, the more readily will she absorb herself in her husband. It is this slavish acquiescence to man's superiority that has kept the marriage institution seemingly intact for so long a period. Now that woman is coming into her own, now that she is actually growing aware of herself as being outside of the master's grace, the sacred institution of marriage is gradually being undermined, and no amount of sentimental lamentation can stay it.

From infancy, almost, the average girl is told that marriage is her ultimate goal; therefore her training and education must be directed towards that end. Like the mute beast fattened for slaughter, she is prepared for that. Yet, strange to say, she is allowed to know much less about her function as wife and mother than the ordinary artisan of his trade. It is indecent and filthy for a respectable girl to know anything of the marital relation. Oh, for the inconsistency of respectability, that needs the marriage vow to turn something which is filthy into the purest and most sacred arrangement that none dare question or criticize. Yet that is exactly the attitude of the average upholder of marriage. The prospective wife and mother is kept in complete ignorance of her only asset in the competitive field—sex. Thus she enters into life-long relations with a man only to find herself shocked, repelled, outraged beyond measure by the most natural and healthy instinct, sex. It is safe to say that a large percentage of the unhappiness, misery, distress, and physical suffering of matrimony is due to the criminal ignorance in sex matters that is being extolled as a great virtue. Nor is it at all an exaggeration when I say that more than one home has been broken up because of this deplorable fact.

If, however, woman is free and big enough to learn the mystery of sex without the sanction of State or Church, she will stand condemned as utterly unfit to become the wife of a "good" man, his goodness consisting of an empty brain and plenty of money. Can there be anything more outrageous than the idea that a healthy, grown woman, full of life and passion, must deny nature's demand, must subdue her most intense craving, undermine her health and break her spirit, must stunt her vision, abstain from the depth and glory of sex experience until a "good" man comes along to take her unto himself as a wife? That is precisely what marriage means. How can such an arrangement end except in failure? This is one, though not the least important, factor of marriage, which differentiates it from love.

Ours is a practical age. The time when Romeo and Juliet risked the wrath of their fathers for love, when Gretchen exposed herself to the gossip of her neighbors for love, is no more. If, on rare occasions, young people allow themselves the luxury of romance, they are taken in care by the elders, drilled and pounded until they become "sensible."

The moral lesson instilled in the girl is not whether the man has aroused her love, but rather it is, "How much?" The important and only God of practical American life: Can the man make a living? Can he support a wife? That is the only thing that justifies marriage. Gradually this saturates every thought of the girl; her dreams are not of moonlight and kisses, of laughter and tears; she dreams of shopping tours and bargain counters. This soul poverty and sordidness are the elements inherent in the marriage institution. The State and Church approve of no other ideal, simply because it is the one that necessitates the State and Church control of men and women.

Doubtless there are people who continue to consider love above dollars and cents. Particularly this is true of that class whom economic necessity has forced to become self-supporting. The tremendous change in woman's position, wrought by that mighty factor, is indeed phenomenal when we reflect that it is but a short time since she has entered the industrial arena. Six million women wage workers; six million women, who have equal right with men to be exploited, to be robbed, to go on strike; aye, to starve even. Anything more, my lord? Yes, six million wage workers in every walk of life, from the highest brain work to the mines and railroad tracks; yes, even detectives and policemen. Surely the emancipation is complete.

Yet with all that, but a very small number of the vast army of women wage workers look upon work as a permanent issue, in the same light as does man. No matter how decrepit the latter, he has been taught to be independent, self-supporting. Oh, I know that no one is really independent in our economic treadmill; still, the poorest specimen of a man hates to be a parasite; to be known as such, at any rate.

The woman considers her position as worker transitory, to be thrown aside for the first bidder. That is why it is infinitely harder to organize women than men. "Why should I join a union? I am going to get married, to have a home." Has she not been taught from infancy to look upon that as her ultimate calling? She learns soon enough that the home, though not so large a prison as the factory, has more solid doors and bars. It has a keeper so faithful that naught can escape him. The most tragic part, however, is that the home no longer frees her from wage slavery; it only increases her task.

According to the latest statistics submitted before a Committee "on labor and wages, and congestion of population," ten per cent. of the wage workers in New York City alone are married, yet they must continue to work at the most poorly paid labor in the world. Add to this horrible aspect the drudgery of housework, and what remains of the protection and glory of the home? As a matter of fact, even the middle-class girl in marriage cannot speak of her home, since it is the man who creates her sphere. It is not important whether the husband is a brute or a darling. What I wish to prove is that marriage guarantees woman a home only by the grace of her husband. There she moves about in HIS home, year after year, until her aspect of life and human affairs becomes as flat, narrow, and drab as her surroundings. Small wonder if she becomes a nag, petty, quarrelsome, gossipy, unbearable, thus driving the man from the house. She could not go, if she wanted to; there is no place to go. Besides, a short period of married life, of complete surrender of all faculties, absolutely incapacitates the average woman for the outside world. She becomes reckless in appearance, clumsy in her movements, dependent in her decisions, cowardly in her judgment, a weight and a bore, which most men grow to hate and despise. Wonderfully inspiring atmosphere for the bearing of life, is it not?

But the child, how is it to be protected, if not for marriage? After all, is not that the most important consideration? The sham, the hypocrisy of it! Marriage protecting the child, yet thousands of children destitute and homeless. Marriage protecting the child, yet orphan asylums and reformatories overcrowded, the Society for the Prevention of Cruelty to Children keeping busy in rescuing the little victims from "loving" parents, to place them under more loving care, the Gerry Society. Oh, the mockery of it!

Marriage may have the power to bring the horse to water, but has it ever made him drink? The law will place the father under arrest, and put him in convict's clothes; but has that ever stilled the hunger of the child? If the parent has no work, or if he hides his identity, what does marriage do then? It invokes the law to bring the man to "justice," to put him safely behind closed doors; his labor, however, goes not to the child, but to the State. The child receives but a blighted memory of his father's stripes.

As to the protection of the woman—therein lies the curse of marriage. Not that it really protects her, but the very idea is so revolting, such an outrage and insult on life, so degrading to human dignity, as to forever condemn this parasitic institution.

It is like that other paternal arrangement—capitalism. It robs man of his birthright, stunts his growth, poisons his body, keeps him in ignorance, in poverty, and dependence, and then institutes charities that thrive on the last vestige of man's self-respect.

The institution of marriage makes a parasite of woman, an absolute dependant. It incapacitates her for life's struggle, annihilates her social consciousness, paralyzes her imagination, and then imposes its gracious protection, which is in reality a snare, a travesty on human character.

If motherhood is the highest fulfillment of woman's nature, what other protection does it need, save love and freedom? Marriage but defiles, outrages, and corrupts her fulfillment. Does it not say to woman, Only when you follow me shall you bring forth life? Does it not condemn her to the block, does it not degrade and shame her if she refuses to buy her right to motherhood by selling herself? Does not marriage only sanction motherhood, even though conceived in hatred, in compulsion? Yet, if motherhood be of free choice, of love, of ecstasy, of defiant passion, does it not place a crown of thorns upon an innocent head and carve in letters of blood the hideous epithet, Bastard? Were marriage to contain all the virtues claimed for it, its crimes against motherhood would exclude it forever from the realm of love.

Love, the strongest and deepest element in all life, the harbinger of hope, of joy, of ecstasy; love, the defier of all laws, of all conventions; love, the freest, the most powerful moulder of human destiny; how can such an all-compelling force be synonymous with that poor little State and Church-begotten weed, marriage?

Free love? As if love is anything but free! Man has bought brains, but all the millions in the world have failed to buy love. Man has subdued bodies, but all the power on earth has been unable to subdue love. Man has conquered whole nations, but all his armies could not conquer love. Man has chained and fettered the spirit, but he has been utterly helpless before love. High on a throne, with all the splendor and pomp his gold can command, man is yet poor and desolate, if love passes him by. And if it stays, the poorest hovel is radiant with warmth, with life and color. Thus love has the magic power to make of a beggar a king. Yes, love is free; it can dwell in no other atmosphere. In freedom it gives itself unreservedly, abundantly, completely. All the laws on the statutes, all the courts in the universe, cannot tear it from the soil, once love has taken root. If, however, the soil is sterile, how can marriage make it bear fruit? It is like the last desperate struggle of fleeting life against death.

Love needs no protection; it is its own protection. So long as love begets life no child is deserted, or hungry, or famished for the want of affection. I know this to be true. I know women who became mothers in freedom by the men they loved. Few children in wedlock enjoy the care, the protection, the devotion free motherhood is capable of bestowing.

The defenders of authority dread the advent of a free motherhood, lest it will rob them of their prey. Who would fight wars? Who would create wealth? Who would make the policeman, the jailer, if woman were to refuse the indiscriminate breeding of children? The race, the race! shouts the king, the president, the capitalist, the priest. The race must be preserved, though woman be degraded to a mere machine—and the marriage institution is our only safety valve against the pernicious sex awakening of woman. But in vain these frantic efforts to maintain a state of bondage. In vain, too, the edicts of the Church, the mad attacks of rulers, in vain even the arm of the law. Woman no longer wants to be a party to the production of a race of sickly, feeble, decrepit, wretched human beings, who have neither the strength nor moral courage to throw off the yoke of poverty and slavery. Instead she desires fewer and better children, begotten and reared in love and through free choice; not by compulsion, as marriage imposes. Our pseudo-moralists have yet to learn the deep sense of responsibility toward the child, that love in freedom has awakened in the breast of woman. Rather would she forego forever the glory of motherhood than bring forth life in an atmosphere that breathes only destruction and death. And if she does become a mother, it is to give to the child the deepest and best her being can yield. To grow with the child is her motto; she knows that in that manner alone can she help build true manhood and womanhood.

Ibsen must have had a vision of a free mother, when, with a master stroke, he portrayed Mrs. Alving. She was the ideal mother because she had outgrown marriage and all its horrors, because she had broken her chains, and set her spirit free to soar until it returned a personality, regenerated and strong. Alas, it was too late to rescue her life's joy, her Oswald; but not too late to realize that love in freedom is the only condition of a beautiful life. Those who, like Mrs. Alving, have paid with blood and tears for their spiritual awakening, repudiate marriage as an imposition, a shallow, empty mockery. They know, whether love last but one brief span of time or for eternity, it is the only creative, inspiring, elevating basis for a new race, a new world.

In our present pygmy state love is indeed a stranger to most people. Misunderstood and shunned, it rarely takes root; or if it does, it soon withers and dies. Its delicate fiber can not endure the stress and strain of the daily grind. Its soul is too complex to adjust itself to the slimy woof of our social fabric. It weeps and moans and suffers with those who have need of it, yet lack the capacity to rise to love's summit.

Some day, some day men and women will rise, they will reach the mountain peak, they will meet big and strong and free, ready to receive, to partake, and to bask in the golden rays of love. What fancy, what imagination, what poetic genius can foresee even approximately the potentialities of such a force in the life of men and women. If the world is ever to give birth to true companionship and oneness, not marriage, but love will be the parent.

Myth and Reality

Simone de Beauvoir

The myth of woman plays a considerable part in literature; but what is its importance in daily life? To what extent does it affect the customs and conduct of individuals? In replying to this question it will be necessary to state precisely the relations this myth bears to reality.

There are different kinds of myths. This one, the myth of woman, sublimating an immutable aspect of the human condition—namely, the division of humanity into two classes of individuals—is a static myth. It projects into the realm of Platonic ideas a reality that is directly experienced or is conceptualized on a basis of experience; in place of fact, value, significance, knowledge, empirical law, it substitutes a transcendental Idea, timeless, unchangeable, necessary. This idea is indisputable because it is beyond the given: it is endowed with absolute truth. Thus, as against the dispersed, contingent, and multiple existences of actual women, mythical thought opposes the Eternal Feminine, unique and changeless. If the definition provided for this concept is contradicted by the behaviour of flesh-and-blood women, it is the latter who are wrong: we are told not that Femininity is a false entity, but that the women concerned are not feminine. The contrary facts of experience are impotent against the myth. In a way, however, its source is in experience.

Thus it is quite true that woman is other than man, and this alterity is directly felt in desire, the embrace, love; but the real relation is one of reciprocity; as such it gives rise to authentic drama. Through eroticism, love, friendship, and their alternatives, deception, hate, rivalry, the relation is a struggle between conscious beings each of whom wishes to be essential, it is the mutual recognition of free beings who confirm one another's freedom, it is the vague transition from aversion to participation. To pose Woman is to pose the absolute Other, without reciprocity, denying against all experience that she is a subject, a fellow human being.

In actuality, of course, women appear under various aspects; but each of the myths built up around the subject of woman is intended to sum her up *in toto*; each aspires to be unique. In consequence, a number of incompatible myths exist, and men tarry musing before the strange incoherencies manifested by the idea of Femininity. As every woman has a share in a majority of these archetypes—each of which lays claim to containing the sole Truth of woman—men of today also are moved again in the presence of their female companions to an astonishment like that of the old sophists who failed to understand how man could be blond and dark at the same time! Transition towards the absolute was indicated long ago in social phenomena: relations are easily congealed in classes, functions in types, just as relations, to the childish mentality, are fixed in things. Patriarchal society, for example, being centred upon the conservation of the patrimony, implies necessarily, along with those who own and transmit wealth, the existence of men and women who take property away from its owners and put it into circulation. The men—adventurers, swindlers, thieves, speculators—are generally repudiated by the group; the women, employing their erotic attraction, can induce young men and even fathers of families to scatter their patrimonies, without ceasing to be within the law. Some of these women appropriate their victims' fortunes or obtain legacies by using undue influence; this role being regarded as evil, those who play it are called "bad women." But the fact is that quite to the contrary they are able to appear in some other setting—at home with their fathers, brothers, husbands, or lovers—as guardian angels; and the courtesan who "plucks" rich financiers is, for painters and writers, a generous patroness. It is easy to understand in actual experience the ambiguous personality of Aspasia or Mme de Pompadour. But if woman is depicted as the Praying Mantis, the Mandrake, the Demon, then it is most confusing to find in woman also the Muse, the Goddess Mother, Beatrice.

As group symbols and social types are generally defined by means of antonyms in pairs, ambivalence will seem to be an intrinsic quality of the Eternal Feminine. The saintly mother has for correlative the cruel stepmother, the angelic young girl has the perverse virgin: thus it will be said sometimes that Mother equals Life, sometimes that Mother equals Death, that every virgin is pure spirit or flesh dedicated to the devil.

Evidently it is not reality that dictates to society or to individuals their choice between the two opposed basic categories; in every period, in each case, society and the individual decide in accordance with their needs. Very often they project into the myth adopted the institutions and values to which they adhere. Thus the paternalism that claims woman for hearth and home defines her as sentiment, inwardness, immanence. In fact every existent is at once immanence and transcendence; when one offers the existent no aim, or prevents him from attaining any, or robs him of his victory, then his transcendence falls vainly into the past—that is to say, falls back into immanence. This is the lot assigned to woman in the patriarchate; but it is in no way a vocation, any more than slavery is the vocation of the slave. The development of this mythology is to be clearly seen in Auguste Comte. To identify Woman with Altruism is to guarantee to man absolute rights in her devotion, it is to impose on women a categorical imperative.

The myth must not be confused with the recognition of significance; significance is immanent in the object; it is revealed to the mind through a living experience; whereas the myth is a transcendent Idea that escapes the mental grasp entirely. When in *L'Age d'homme* Michel Leiris describes his vision of the feminine organs, he tells us things of significance and elaborates no myth. Wonder at the feminine body, dislike for menstrual blood, come from perceptions of a concrete reality. There is nothing mythical in the experience that reveals the voluptuous qualities of feminine flesh, and it is not an excursion into myth if one attempts to describe them through comparisons with flowers or pebbles. But to say that Woman is Flesh, to say that the Flesh is Night and Death, or that it is the splendour of the Cosmos, is to abandon terrestrial truth and soar into an empty sky. For man also is flesh for woman; and woman is not merely a carnal object; and the flesh is clothed in special significance for each person and in each experience. And likewise it is quite true that woman—like man—is a being rooted in nature; she is more enslaved to the species than is the male, her animality is more manifest; but in her as in him the given traits are taken on through the fact of existence, she belongs also to the human realm. To assimilate her to Nature is simply to act from prejudice.

Few myths have been more advantageous to the ruling caste than the myth of woman: it justifies all privileges and even authorizes their abuse. Men need not bother themselves with alleviating the pains and the burdens that physiologically are women's lot, since these are "intended by Nature"; men use them as a pretext for increasing the misery of the feminine lot still further, for instance by refusing to grant to woman any right to sexual pleasure, by making her work like a beast of burden.[1]

Of all these myths, none is more firmly anchored in masculine hearts than that of the feminine "mystery." It has numerous advantages. And first of all it permits an easy explanation of all that appears inexplicable; the man who "does not understand" a woman is happy to substitute an objective resistance for a subjective deficiency of mind; instead of admitting his ignorance, he perceives the presence of a "mystery" outside himself: an alibi, indeed, that flatters laziness and vanity at once. A heart smitten with love thus avoids many disappointments: if the loved one's behaviour is capricious, her remarks stupid, then the mystery serves to excuse it all. And finally, thanks again to the mystery, that negative relation is perpetuated which seemed to Kierkegaard infinitely preferable to positive possession; in the company of a living enigma man remains alone—alone with his dreams, his hopes, his fears, his love, his vanity. This subjective game, which can go all the way from vice to mystical ecstasy, is for many a more attractive experience than an authentic relationship with a human being. What foundations exist for such a profitable illusion?

Surely woman is, in a sense, mysterious, "mysterious as is all the world," according to Maeterlinck. Each is *subject* only for himself; each can grasp in immanence only himself, alone: from this point of view the *other* is always a mystery. To men's eyes the opacity of the self-knowing self, of the *pour-soi*, is denser in the *other* who is feminine; men are unable to penetrate her special experience through any working of sympathy: they are condemned to ignorance of the quality of woman's erotic pleasure, the discomfort of menstruation, and the pains of childbirth. The truth is that there is mystery on both sides: as the *other* who is of masculine sex, every man, also, has within him a presence, an inner self impenetrable to woman; she in turn is in ignorance of the male's erotic feeling. But in accordance with the universal rule I have stated, the categories in which men think of the world are established *from their point of view, as absolute*: they misconceive reciprocity, here as everywhere. A mystery for man, woman is considered to be mysterious in essence.

Her situation makes woman very liable to such a view. Her physiological nature is very complex: she herself submits to it as to some rigmarole from outside; her body does not seem to her to be a clear expression of herself; within it she feels herself a stranger. Indeed, the bond that in every individual connects the physiological life and the psychic life—or better the relation existing between the contingence of an individual and the free spirit that assumes it—is the deepest enigma implied in the condition of being human, and this enigma is presented in its most disturbing form in woman.

But what is commonly referred to as the mystery is not the subjective solitude of the conscious self, nor the secret organic life. It is on the level of communication that the word has its true meaning: it is not a reduction to pure silence, to darkness, to absence; it implies a stammering presence that fails to make itself manifest and clear. To say that woman is mystery is to say, not that she is silent, but that her language is not understood; she is there, but hidden behind veils; she exists beyond these uncertain appearances. What is she? Angel, demon, one inspired, an actress? It may be supposed either that there are answers to these questions which are impossible to discover, or, rather, that no answer is adequate because a fundamental ambiguity marks the feminine being: and perhaps in her heart she is even for herself quite indefinable: a sphinx.

The fact is that she would be embarrassed to decide *what* she *is*; but this is not because the hidden truth is too vague to be discerned: it is because in this domain there is no truth. An existent *is* nothing other than what he does; the possible does not extend beyond the real, essence does not precede existence: in pure subjectivity, the human being *is not anything*. He is to be measured by his acts. Of a peasant woman one can say that she is a good or a bad worker, of an actress that she has or does not have talent; but if one considers a woman in her immanent presence, her inward self, one can say absolutely nothing about her, she falls short of having any qualifications. Now, in amorous or conjugal relations, in all relations where the woman is the vassal, the other, she is being dealt with in her immanence. It is noteworthy that the feminine comrade, colleague, and associate are without mystery; on the other hand, if the vassal is male, if, in the eyes of a man or a woman who is older, or richer, a young man, for example, plays the role of the inessential object, then he too becomes shrouded in mystery. And this uncovers for us a substructure under the feminine mystery which is economic in nature.

A sentiment cannot be supposed to *be* anything. "In the domain of sentiments," writes Gide, "the real is not distinguished from the imaginary. And if to imagine one loves is enough to be in love, then also to tell oneself that one imagines oneself to be in love when one is in love is enough to make one forthwith love a little less." Discrimination between the imaginary and the real can be made only through behaviour. Since man occupies a privileged position in this world, he is able to show his love actively; very often he supports the woman or at least helps her financially; in marrying her he gives her social standing; he makes her presents; his economic and social independence allows him to take the initiative: it was M. de Norpois who, when separated from Mme de Villeparisis, made twenty-four-hour journeys to visit her. Very often the man is busy, the woman idle: he *gives* her the time he passes with her; she takes it: is it with pleasure, passionately, or only for amusement? Does she accept these benefits through love or through self-

interest? Does she love her husband or her marriage? Of course, even the man's evidence is ambiguous: is such and such a gift granted through love or out of pity? But while normally a woman finds numerous advantages in her relations with a man, his relations with a woman are profitable to a man only in so far as he loves her. And so one can almost judge the degree of his affection by the total picture of his attitude.

But a woman hardly has means for sounding her own heart; according to her moods she will view her own sentiments in different lights, and as she submits to them passively, one interpretation will be no truer than another. In those rare instances in which she holds the position of economic and social privilege, the mystery is reversed, showing that it does not pertain to *one sex* rather than the other, but to the situation. For a great many women the roads to transcendence are blocked: because they *do* nothing, they fail to *make themselves* anything. They wonder indefinitely what they *could have* become, which sets them to asking about what they *are*. It is a vain question. If man fails to discover that secret essence of femininity, it is simply because it does not exist. Kept on the fringe of the world, woman cannot be objectively defined through this world, and her mystery conceals nothing but emptiness.

Furthermore, like all the oppressed, woman deliberately dissembles her objective actuality; the slave, the servant, the indigent, all who depend upon the caprices of a master, have learned to turn towards him a changeless smile or an enigmatic impassivity; their real sentiments, their actual behaviour, are carefully hidden. And moreover woman is taught from adolescence to lie to men, to scheme, to be wily. In speaking to them she wears an artificial expression on her face; she is cautious, hypocritical, play-acting.

But the Feminine Mystery as recognized in mythical thought is a more profound matter. In fact, it is immediately implied in the mythology of the absolute Other. If it be admitted that the inessential conscious being, too, is a clear subjectivity, capable of performing the *Cogito*, then it is also admitted that this being is in truth sovereign and returns to being essential; in order that all reciprocity may appear quite impossible, it is necessary for the Other to be for itself an other, for its very subjectivity to be affected by its otherness; this consciousness which would be alienated as a consciousness, in its pure immanent presence, would evidently be Mystery. It would be Mystery in itself from the fact that it would be Mystery for itself; it would be absolute Mystery.

In the same way it is true that, beyond the secrecy created by their dissembling, there is mystery in the Black, the Yellow, in so far as they are considered absolutely as the inessential Other. It should be noted that the American citizen, who profoundly baffles the average European, is not, however, considered as being "mysterious": one states more modestly that one does not understand him. And similarly woman does not always "understand" man; but there is no such thing as a masculine mystery. The point is that rich America, and the male, are on the Master side and that Mystery belongs to the slave.

To be sure, we can only muse in the twilight byways of bad faith upon the positive reality of the Mystery; like certain marginal hallucinations, it dissolves under the attempt to view it fixedly. Literature always fails in attempting to portray "mysterious" women; they can appear only at the beginning of a novel as strange, enigmatic figures; but unless the story remains unfinished they give up their secret in the end and they are then simply consistent and transparent persons. The heroes in Peter Cheyney's books, for example, never cease to be astonished at the unpredictable caprices of women: no one can ever guess how they will act, they upset all calculations. The fact is that once the springs of their action are revealed to the reader, they are seen to be very simple mechanisms: this woman was a spy, that one a thief; however clever the plot, there is always a key; and it could not be otherwise, had the author all the talent and imagination in the world. Mystery is never more than a mirage that vanishes as we draw near to look at it.

We can see now that the myth is in large part explained by its usefulness to man. The myth of woman is a luxury. It can appear only if man escapes from the urgent demands of his needs; the more relationships are concretely lived, the less they are idealized. The fellah of ancient Egypt, the Bedouin peasant, the artisan of the Middle Ages, the worker of today has in the requirements of work and poverty relations with his particular woman companion which are too definite for her to be embellished with an aura either auspicious or inauspicious. The epochs and the social classes that have been marked by the leisure to dream have been the ones to set up the images, black and white, of femininity. But along with luxury there was utility; these dreams were irresistibly guided by interests. Surely most of the myths had roots in the spontaneous attitude of man towards his own existence and towards the world around him. But going beyond experience towards the transcendent Idea was deliberately used by patriarchal society for purposes of self-justification; through the myths this society imposed its laws and customs upon individuals in a picturesque, effective manner; it is under a mythical form that the group-imperative is indoctrinated into each conscience. Through such intermediaries as religions, traditions, language, tales, songs, movies, the myths penetrate even into such existences as are most harshly enslaved to material realities. Here everyone can find sublimation of his drab experiences: deceived by the woman he loves, one declares that she is a Crazy Womb; another, obsessed by his impotence, calls her a Praying Mantis; still another enjoys his wife's company: behold, she is Harmony, Rest, the Good Earth! The taste for eternity at a bargain, for a pocket-sized absolute, which is shared by a majority of men, is satisfied by myths. The smallest emotion, a slight annoyance, becomes the

64

Feminisms and Womanisms

reflection of a timeless Idea—an Illusion agreeably flattering to the vanity.

The myth is one of those snares of false objectivity into which the man who depends on ready-made valuations rushes headlong. Here again we have to do with the substitution of a set idol for actual experience and the free judgements it requires. For an authentic relation with an autonomous existent, the myth of Woman substitutes the fixed contemplation of a mirage. "Mirage! Mirage!" cries Laforgue. "We should kill them since we cannot comprehend them; or better tranquillize them, instruct them, make them give up their taste for jewels, make them our genuinely equal comrades, our intimate friends, real associates here below, dress them differently, cut their hair short, say anything and everything to them." Man would have nothing to lose, quite the contrary, if he gave up disguising woman as a symbol. When dreams are official community affairs, clichés, they are poor and monotonous indeed beside the living reality; for the true dreamer, for the poet, woman is a more generous fount than is any down-at-heel marvel. The times that have most sincerely treasured women are not the period of feudal chivalry nor yet the gallant nineteenth century. They are the times—like the eighteenth century—when men have regarded women as fellow creatures; then it is that women seem truly romantic, as the reading of *Liaisons dangereuses*, *Le Rouge et le noir*, *Farewell to Arms*, is sufficient to show. The heroines of Laclos, Stendhal, Hemingway are without mystery, and they are not the less engaging for that. To recognize in woman a human being is not to impoverish man's experience: this would lose none of its diversity, its richness, or its intensity if it were to occur between two subjectivities. To discard the myths is not to destroy all dramatic relation between the sexes, it is not to deny the significance authentically revealed to man through feminine reality; it is not to do away with poetry, love, adventure, happiness, dreaming. It is simply to ask that behaviour, sentiment, passion be founded upon the truth.[2]

"Woman is lost. Where are the women? The women of today are not women at all!" We have seen what these mysterious phrases mean. In men's eyes—and for the legion of women who see through men's eyes—it is not enough to have a woman's body nor to assume the female function as mistress or mother in order to be a "true woman." In sexuality and maternity woman as subject can claim autonomy; but to be a "true woman" she must accept herself as the Other. The men of today show a certain duplicity of attitude which is painfully lacerating to women; they are willing on the whole to accept woman as a fellow being, an equal; but they still require her to remain the inessential. For her these two destinies are incompatible; she hesitates between one and the other without being exactly adapted to either, and from this comes her lack of equilibrium. With man there is no break between public and private life: the more he confirms his grasp on the world in action and in work, the more virile he seems to be; human and vital values are combined in him. Whereas woman's independent successes are in contradiction with her femininity, since the "true woman" is required to make herself object, to be the Other.

It is quite possible that in this matter man's sensibility and sexuality are being modified. A new aesthetics has already been born. If the fashion of flat chests and narrow hips—the boyish form—has had its brief season, at least the over-opulent ideal of past centuries has not returned. The feminine body is asked to be flesh, but with discretion; it is to be slender and not loaded with fat; muscular, supple, strong, it is bound to suggest transcendence; it must not be pale like a too shaded hothouse plant, but preferably tanned like a workman's torso from being bared to the sun. Woman's dress in becoming practical need not make her appear sexless: on the contrary, short skirts made the most of legs and thighs as never before. There is no reason why working should take away woman's sex appeal. It may be disturbing to contemplate woman as at once a social personage and carnal prey.

For a woman to hold some "man's position" and be desirable at the same time has long been a subject for more or less ribald joking; but gradually the impropriety and the irony have become blunted, and it would seem that a new form of eroticism is coming into being—perhaps it will give rise to new myths.

What is certain is that today it is very difficult for women to accept at the same time their status as autonomous individuals and their womanly destiny; this is the source of the blundering and restlessness which sometimes cause them to be considered a "lost sex." And no doubt it is more comfortable to submit to a blind enslavement than to work for liberation: the dead, for that matter, are better adapted to the earth than are the living. In all respects a return to the past is no more possible than it is desirable. What must be hoped for is that the men for their part will unreservedly accept the situation that is coming into existence; only then will women be able to live in that situation without anguish. Then Laforgue's prayer will be answered: "Ah, young women, when will you be our brothers, our brothers in intimacy without ulterior thought of exploitation? When shall we clasp hands truly?" Then Breton's "Mélusine, no longer under the weight of the calamity let loose upon her by man alone. Mélusine set free ... " will regain "her place in humanity." Then she will be a full human being, "when," to quote a letter of Rimbaud, "the infinite bondage of woman is broken, when she will live in and for herself, man—hitherto detestable—having let her go free."

Notes

1. cf. Balzac: *Physiology of Marriage:* "Pay no attention to her murmurs, her cries, her pains; *nature has made her for our use* and for bearing everything: children, sorrows, blows and pains inflicted by man. Do not accuse yourself of hardness. In all the codes of so-called civilized nations, man has written the laws that ranged woman's destiny under this bloody epigraph: '*Vae victis!* Woe to the weak!'"

2. Laforgue goes on to say regarding woman:

> "Since she has been left in slavery, idleness, without occupation or weapon other than her sex, she has over-developed this aspect and has become the Feminine ... We have permitted this hypertrophy; she is her in the world for our benefit .... Well! that is all wrong .... Up to now we have played with woman as if she were a doll. This has lasted altogether too long! ... "

The Crisis in Woman's Identity

Betty Friedan

I discovered a strange thing, interviewing women of my own generation over the past ten years. When we were growing up, many of us could not see ourselves beyond the age of twenty-one. We had no image of our own future, of ourselves as women.

I remember the stillness of a spring afternoon on the Smith campus in 1942, when I came to a frightening dead end in my own vision of the future. A few days earlier, I had received a notice that I had won a graduate fellowship. During the congratulations, underneath my excitement, I felt a strange uneasiness; there was a question that I did not want to think about.

"Is this really what I want to be?" The question shut me off, cold and alone, from the girls talking and studying on the sunny hillside behind the college house. I thought I was going to be a psychologist. But if I wasn't sure, what did I want to be? I felt the future closing in—and I could not see myself in it at all. I had no image of myself, stretching beyond college. I had come at seventeen from a Midwestern town, an unsure girl; the wide horizons of the world and the life of the mind had been opened to me. I had begun to know who I was and what I wanted to do. I could not go back now. I could not go home again, to the life of my mother and the women of our town, bound to home, bridge, shopping, children,

husband, charity, clothes. But now that the time had come to make my own future, to take the deciding step, I suddenly did not know what I wanted to be.

I took the fellowship, but the next spring, under the alien California sun of another campus, the question came again, and I could not put it out of my mind. I had won another fellowship that would have committed me to research for my doctorate, to a career as professional psychologist. "Is this really what I want to be?" The decision now truly terrified me. I lived in a terror of indecision for days, unable to think of anything else.

The question was not important, I told myself. No question was important to me that year but love. We walked in the Berkeley hills and a boy said: "Nothing can come of this, between us I'll never win a fellowship like yours." Did I think I would be choosing, irrevocably, the cold loneliness of that afternoon if I went on? I gave up the fellowship, in relief. But for years afterward, I could not read a word of the science that once I had thought of as my future life's work; the reminder of its loss was too painful.

I never could explain, hardly knew myself, why I gave up this career. I lived in the present, working on newspapers with no particular plan. I married, had children, lived according to the feminine mystique as a suburban housewife. But still the question haunted me. I could sense no purpose in my life, I could find no peace, until I finally faced it and worked out my own answer.

I discovered, talking to Smith seniors in 1959, that the question is no less terrifying to girls today. Only they answer it now in a way that my generation found, after half a lifetime, not to be an answer at all. These girls, mostly seniors, were sitting in the living room of the college house, having coffee. It was not too different from such an evening when I was a senior, except that many more of the girls wore rings on their left hands. I asked the ones around me what they planned to be. The engaged ones spoke of weddings, apartments, getting a job as a secretary while husband finished school. The others, after a hostile silence, gave vague answers about this job or that, graduate study, but no one had any real plans. A blonde with a ponytail asked me the next day if I had believed the things they had said. "None of it was true," she told me. "We don't like to be asked what we want to do. None of us know. None of us even like to think about it. The ones who are going to be married right away are the lucky ones. They don't have to think about it."

But I noticed that night that many of the engaged girls, sitting silently around the fire while I asked the others about jobs, had also seemed angry about something. "They don't want to think about not going on," my ponytailed informant said. "They know they're not going to use their education. They'll be wives and mothers. You can say you're going to keep on reading and be interested in the community. But that's not the same. You won't really go on. It's a disappointment to know you're going to stop now, and not go on and use it."

In counterpoint, I heard the words of a woman, fifteen years after she left college, a doctor's wife, mother of three, who said over coffee in her New England kitchen:

The tragedy was, nobody ever looked us in the eye and said you have to decide what you want to do with your life, besides being your husband's wife and children's mother. I never thought it through until I was thirty-six, and my husband was so busy with his practice that he couldn't entertain me every night. The three boys were in school all day. I kept on trying to have babies despite an Rh discrepancy. After two miscarriages, they said I must stop. I thought that my own growth and evolution were over. I always knew as a child that I was going to grow up and go to college, and then get married, and that's as far as a girl has to think. After that, your husband determines and fills your life. It wasn't until I got so lonely as the doctor's wife and kept screaming at the kids because they didn't fill my life that I realized I had to make my own life. I still had to decide what I wanted to be. I hadn't finished evolving at all. But it took me ten years to think it through.

The feminine mystique permits, even encourages, women to ignore the question of their identity. The mystique says they can answer the question "Who am I?" by saying "Tom's wife ... Mary's mother." But I don't think the mystique would have such power over American women if they did not fear to face this terrifying blank which makes them unable to see themselves after twenty-one. The truth is—and how long it has been true, I'm not sure, but it was true in my generation and it is true of girls growing up today—an American woman no longer has a private image to tell her who she is, or can be, or wants to be.

The public image, in the magazines and television commercials, is designed to sell washing machines, cake mixes, deodorants, detergents, rejuvenating face creams, hair tints. But the power of that image, on which companies spend millions of dollars for television time and ad space, comes from this: American women no longer know who they are. They are sorely in need of a new image to help them find their identity. As the motivational researchers keep telling the advertisers, American women are so unsure of who they should be that they look to this glossy public image to decide every detail of their lives. They look for the image they will no longer take from their mothers.

In my generation, many of us knew that we did not want to be like our mothers, even when we loved them. We could not help but see their disappointment. Did we understand, or only resent, the sadness, the emptiness, that made them hold too fast to us, try to live our lives, run our fathers' lives, spend their days shopping or yearning for things that never seemed to satisfy them, no matter how much money they cost? Strangely, many mothers who loved their daughters—and mine was one—did not want their daughters to grow up like them either. They knew we needed something more.

But even if they urged, insisted, fought to help us educate ourselves, even if they talked with yearning of careers that were not open to them, they could not give us an image of what we could be. They could only tell us that their lives were too empty, tied to home; that children, cooking, clothes, bridge, and charities were not enough. A mother might tell her daughter, spell it out, "Don't be just a housewife like me." But that daughter, sensing that her mother was too frustrated to savor the love of her husband and children, might feel: "I will succeed where my mother failed, I will fulfill myself as a woman," and never read the lesson of her mother's life.

Recently, interviewing high-school girls who had started out full of promise and talent, but suddenly stopped their education, I began to see new dimensions to the problem of feminine conformity. These girls, it seemed at first, were merely following the typical curve of feminine adjustment. Earlier interested in geology or poetry, they now were interested only in being popular; to get boys to like them, they had concluded, it was better to be like all the other girls. On closer examination, I found that these girls were so terrified of becoming like their mothers that they could not see themselves at all. They were afraid to grow up. They had to copy in identical detail the composite image of the popular girl—denying what was best in themselves out of fear of femininity as they saw it in their mothers. One of these girls, seventeen years old, told me:

I want so badly to feel like the other girls. I never get over this feeling of being a neophyte, not initiated. When I get up and have to cross a room, it's like I'm a beginner, or have some terrible affliction, and I'll never learn. I go to the local hangout after school and sit there for hours talking about clothes and hairdos and the twist, and I'm not that interested, so it's an effort. But I found out I could make them like me—just do what they do, dress like them, talk like them, not do things that are different. I guess I even started to make myself not different inside.

I used to write poetry. The guidance office says I have this creative ability and I should be at the top of the class and have a great future. But things like that aren't what you need to be popular. The important thing for a girl is to be popular.

Now I go out with boy after boy, and it's such an effort because I'm not myself with them. It makes you feel even more alone. And besides, I'm afraid of where it's going to lead. Pretty soon, all my differences will be smoothed out, and I'll be the kind of girl that could be a housewife.

I don't want to think of growing up. If I had children, I'd want them to stay the same age. If I had to watch them grow up, I'd see myself growing older, and I wouldn't want to. My mother says she can't sleep at night, she's sick with worry over what I might do. When I was little, she wouldn't let me cross the street alone, long after the other kids did.

I can't see myself as being married and having children. It's as if I wouldn't have any personality myself. My mother's like a rock that's been smoothed by the waves, like a void. She's put so much into her family that there's nothing left, and she resents us because she doesn't get enough in return. But sometimes it seems like there's nothing there. My mother doesn't serve any purpose except cleaning the house. She isn't happy, and she doesn't make my father happy. If she didn't care about us children at all, it would have the same effect as caring too much. It makes you want to do the opposite. I don't think it's really love. When I was little and I ran in all excited to tell her I'd learned how to stand on my head, she was never listening.

Lately, I look into the mirror, and I'm so afraid I'm going to look like my mother. It frightens me, to catch myself being like her in gestures or speech or anything. I'm not like her in so many ways, but if I'm like her in this one way, perhaps I'll turn out like my mother after all. And that terrifies me.

And so the seventeen-year-old was so afraid of being a woman like her mother that she turned her back on all the things in herself and all the opportunities that would have made her a different woman, to copy from the outside the "popular" girls. And finally, in panic at losing herself, she turned her back on her own popularity and defied the conventional good behavior that would have won her a college scholarship. For lack of an image that would help her grow up as a woman true to herself, she retreated into the beatnik vacuum.

Another girl, a college junior from South Carolina told me:

I don't want to be interested in a career I'll have to give up.

My mother wanted to be a newspaper reporter from the time she was twelve, and I've seen her frustration for twenty years. I don't want to be interested in world affairs. I don't want to be interested in anything beside my home and being a wonderful wife and mother. Maybe education is a liability. Even the brightest boys at home want just a sweet, pretty girl. Only sometimes I wonder how it would feel to be able to stretch and stretch and stretch, and learn all you want, and not have to hold yourself back.

Her mother, almost all our mothers, were housewives, though many had started or yearned for or regretted giving up careers. Whatever they told us, we, having eyes and ears and mind and heart, knew that their lives were somehow empty. We did not want to be like them, and yet what other model did we have?

The only other kind of women I knew, growing up, were the old-maid high-school teachers; the librarian; the one woman doctor in our town, who cut her hair like a man; and a few of my college professors. None of these women lived in the warm center of life as I had known it at home. Many had not married or had children. I dreaded being like them, even the ones who taught me truly to respect my own mind and use it, to feel that I had a part in the world. I never knew a woman, when I was growing up, who used her mind, played her own part in the world, and also loved, and had children.

I think that this has been the unknown heart of woman's problem in America for a long time, this lack of a private image. Public images that defy reason and have very little to do with women themselves have had the power to shape too much of their lives. These images would not have such power, if women were not suffering a crisis of identity.

The strange, terrifying jumping-off point that American women reach—at eighteen, twenty-one, twenty-five, forty-one—has been noticed for many years by sociologists, psychologists, analysts, educators. But I think it has not been understood for what it is. It has been called a "discontinuity" in cultural conditioning; it has been called woman's "role crisis." It has been blamed on the education which made American girls grow up feeling free and equal to boys—playing baseball, riding bicycles, conquering geometry and college boards, going away to college, going out in the world to get a job, living alone in an apartment in New York or Chicago or San Francisco, testing and discovering their own powers in the world. All this gave girls the feeling they could be and do whatever they wanted to, with the same freedom as boys, the critics said. It did not prepare them for their role as women. The crisis comes when they are forced to adjust to this role. Today's high rate of emotional distress and breakdown among women in their twenties and thirties is usually attributed to this "role crisis." If girls were educated for their role as women, they would not suffer this crisis, the adjusters say.

But I think they have seen only half the truth.

What if the terror a girl faces at twenty-one, when she must decide who she will be, is simply the terror of growing up—growing up, as women were not permitted to grow before? What if the terror a girl faces at twenty-one is the terror of freedom to decide her own life, with no one to order which path she will take, the freedom and the necessity to take paths women before were not able to take? What if those who choose the path of "feminine adjustment"—evading this terror by marrying at eighteen, losing themselves in having babies and the details of housekeeping—are simply refusing to grow up, to face the question of their own identity?

Mine was the first college generation to run head-on into the new mystique of feminine fulfillment. Before then, while most women did indeed end up as housewives and mothers, the point of education was to discover the life of the mind, to pursue truth and to take a place in the world. There was a sense, already dulling when I went to college, that we would be New Women. Our world would be much larger than home. Forty percent of my college class at Smith had career plans. But I remember how, even then, some of the seniors, suffering the pangs of that bleak fear of the future, envied the few who escaped it by getting married right away.

The ones we envied then are suffering that terror now at forty. "Never have decided what kind of woman I am. Too much personal life in college. Wish I'd studied more science, history, government, gone deeper into philosophy," one wrote on an alumnae questionnaire, fifteen years later. "Still trying to find the rock to build on. Wish I had finished college. I got married instead." "Wish I'd developed a deeper and more creative life of my own and that I hadn't become engaged and married at nineteen. Having expected the ideal in marriage, including a hundred-per-cent devoted husband, it was a shock to find this isn't the way it is," wrote a mother of six.

Many of the younger generation of wives who marry early have never suffered this lonely terror. They thought they did not have to choose, to look into the future and plan what they wanted to do with their lives. They had only to wait to be chosen, marking time passively until the husband, the babies, the new house decided what the rest of their lives would be. They slid easily into their sexual role as women before they knew who they were themselves. It is these women who suffer most the problem that has no name.

It is my thesis that the core of the problem for women today is not sexual but a problem of identity—a stunting or evasion of—growth that is perpetuated by the feminine mystique. It is my thesis that as the Victorian culture did not permit women to accept or gratify their basic sexual needs, our culture does not permit women to accept or gratify their basic need to grow and fulfill their potentialities as human beings, a need which is not solely defined by their sexual role.

Biologists have recently discovered a "youth serum" which, if fed to young caterpillars in the larva state, will keep them from ever maturing into moths; they will live out their lives as caterpillars. The expectations of feminine fulfillment that are fed to women by magazines, television, movies, and books that popularize psychological half-truths, and by parents, teachers and counselors who accept the feminine mystique, operate as a kind of youth serum, keeping most women in the state of sexual larvae, preventing them from achieving the maturity of which they are capable. And there is increasing evidence that woman's failure to grow to complete identity has hampered rather than enriched her sexual fulfillment, virtually doomed her to be castrative to her husband and sons, and caused neuroses, or problems as yet unnamed as neuroses, equal to those caused by sexual repression.

There have been identity crises for man at all the crucial turning points in human history, though those who lived through them did not give them that name. It is only in recent years that the theorists of psychology, sociology, and theology have isolated this problem, and given it a name. But it is considered a man's problem. It is defined, for man, as the crisis of growing up, of choosing his identity, "the decision as to what one is and is going to be," in the words of the brilliant psychoanalyst Erik H. Erikson:

I have called the major crisis of adolescence the identity crisis; it occurs in that period of the life cycle when each youth must forge for himself some central perspective and direction, some working unity, out of the effective remnants of his childhood and the hopes of his anticipated adulthood; he must detect some meaningful resemblance between what he has come to see in himself and what his sharpened awareness tells him others judge and expect him to be ....
In some people, in some classes, at some periods in history, the crisis will be minimal; in other people, classes and periods, the crisis will be clearly marked off as a critical period, a kind of "second birth," apt to be aggravated either by widespread neuroticisms or by pervasive ideological unrest.[1]

In this sense, the identity crisis of one man's life may reflect, or set off, a rebirth, or new stage, in the growing up of mankind. "In some periods of his history, and in some phases of his life cycle, man needs a new ideological orientation as surely and sorely as he must have air and food," said Erikson, focusing new light on the crisis of the young Martin Luther, who left a Catholic monastery at the end of the Middle Ages to forge a new identity for himself and Western man.

The search for identity is not new, however, in American thought—though in every generation, each man who writes about it discovers it anew. In America, from the beginning, it has somehow been understood that men must thrust into the future; the pace has always been too rapid for man's identity to stand still. In every generation, many men have suffered misery, unhappiness, and uncertainty because they could not take the image of the man they wanted to be from their fathers. The search for identity of the young man who can't go home again has always been a major theme of American writers. And it has always been considered right in America, good, for men to suffer these agonies of growth, to search for and find their own identities. The farm boy went to the city, the garment-maker's son became a doctor, Abraham Lincoln taught himself to read—these were more than rags-to-riches stories. They were an integral part of the American dream. The problem for many was money, race, color, class, which barred them from choice—not what they would be if they were free to choose.

Even today a young man learns soon enough that he must decide who he wants to be. If he does not decide in junior high, in high school, in college, he must somehow come to terms with it by twenty-five or thirty, or he is lost. But this search for identity is seen as a greater problem now because more and more boys cannot find images in our culture—from their fathers or other men—to help them in their search. The old frontiers have been conquered, and the boundaries of the new are not so clearly marked. More and more young men in America today suffer an identity crisis for want of any image of man worth pursuing, for want of a purpose that truly realizes their human abilities.

But why have theorists not recognized this same identity crisis in women? In terms of the old conventions and the new feminine mystique women are not expected to grow up to find out who they are, to choose their human identity. Anatomy is Woman's destiny, say the theorists of femininity; the identity of woman is determined by her biology.

But is it? More and more women are asking themselves this question. As if they were waking from a coma, they ask, "Where am I ... what am I doing here?"

For the first time in their history, women are becoming aware of an identity crisis in their own lives, a crisis which began many generations ago, has grown worse with each succeeding generation, and will not end until they, or their daughters, turn an unknown corner and make of themselves and their lives the new image that so many women now so desperately need.

In a sense that goes beyond any one woman's life, I think this is the crisis of women growing up—a turning point from an immaturity that has been called femininity to full human identity. I think women had to suffer this crisis of identity, which began a hundred years ago, and have to suffer it still today, simply to become fully human.

Note

1. Erik H. Erikson, *Young Man Luther, A Study in Psychoanalysis and History*, New York, 1958, pp. 15 ff. See also Erikson, *Childhood and Society*, New York, 1950, and Erikson, "The Problem of Ego Identity," *Journal of the American Psychoanalytical Association*, Vol. 4, 1956, pp. 56–121.

The Middle-Class Myth of Love and Marriage

Germaine Greer

Loveless marriage is anathema to our culture, and a life without love is unthinkable. The woman who remains unmarried must have missed her chance, lost her boy in the war, or hesitated and was lost; the man somehow never found the right girl. It is axiomatic that all married couples are in love with each other. Sympathy is often expressed for those people, like kings and queens, who cannot be solely directed by Cupid's arrow, although at the same time it is tacitly assumed that even royal couples are in love. In the common imagination nuns are all women disappointed in love, and career women are compensating for their failure to find the deepest happiness afforded mankind in this vale of tears. But it was not always believed even if the normality of the idea persuades us that it must have been. The mere mention of Cupid's arrow ought to remind us that there was a far different concept of love which prevailed not so long ago, a concept not only separate from pre-nuptial courtship, but quite inimical to marriage. Even in the brief lifetime of the concept of nuptial love it has not always been the same idea: many of the defenders of marriage for love in the sixteenth century would be horrified if they could know the degree of romantic and sexual passion with which their ideal is now invested. Gradual changes in basic assumptions have obscured the traces of the development of the myth of falling-in-love-and-getting-married; demographic information about its early stages is hard to come by. Acknowledging all these uncertainties with due humility we may embark upon a speculative exploration.

> The art of managing men has to be learned from birth. It is easier as you acquire experience. Some women have an instinctive flair, but most have to learn the hard way by trial and error. Some die disappointed. It depends to some extent on one's distribution of curves, a developed instinct, and a large degree of sheer feline cunning.
> —Mary Hyde, *How to Manage Men*, 1955, p. 6

I am 39 and have been submitting to corporal punishment from my husband ever since we married 15 years ago. We have both treated this matter of punishment as a normal sort of proceeding. It was not until recently, when we saw some letters in *Forum* that we realized there were people who had guilt complexes about spanking their mates.

Our ideas are quite simple. My husband happens to believe that in marriage the husband should be the boss. I agree with him and I recognize that wrong-doing should be punished. We both think that the simplest, most convenient, most effective and most natural way for a man to punish the faults of his woman is to spank or whip her; but not too severely, certainly not brutally.

—Letter in *Forum*, Vol. II, No. 3

It is by now commonplace to point out that in feudal literature romantic love was essentially antisocial and adulterous. The discussions of de Rougemont and his ilk are well-known, at least in their gist.[1] The term "courtly love" has become a cliché of historical criticism. The tales of Guinevere and Iseult were the product of the minority culture of the ruling class, at which the serfs and yeomen must have marveled when they heard them recounted in song and folk-tale. They were the product of the feudal situation in which a noble wife was a wife only when her warrior husband was at home (which with any luck was seldom); otherwise she ruled a community of men, many of them young and lusty, with the result that they entertained fantasies about the unobtainable to whom they could not even address their advances. She exploited their servility, which was the original of chivalry, and may or may not have served her own lusts by them. To her husband she was submissive and offered him her body as his fief. Victorian scholars exclaimed in horror at the description of marital love given in tracts like *Hali Maidenhead*,[2] and joyously acclaimed the Protestant reformers for bringing the first breath of "fresh air into the cattle shed" of marital theory.[3] The monkish author of the fourteenth-century tract *Hali Maidenhead* put it to the virgins he was addressing that if they really liked reading in Latin, illuminating manuscripts, embroidering (not antimacassars and guest towels but precious vestments and magical tapestries which are now among the finest art treasures of European museums), and writing poetry and music, then they were better off in the all-female society of a convent, where they were not surrounded by the bustle and brutality of a barracks, condemned to dangerous childbirth and the rough caresses of a husband too used to grappling with infidel captives and military whores to be aware of their emotional and sexual needs. He did not say but we might infer that the loves of clerks and nuns were more likely to be satisfying than the infatuation of young squires and the endless exacerbation of unfulfilled desire which is the whole motive behind Provençal minstrelsy. Rabelais combined the elements of medieval humanist fantasy of sexual and intellectual adjustment in his jolly secular monastery of Theleme.[4] Rattray Taylor has listed the period as a matrist one, and however dubious his classification may ultimately be, it is true that the influence of women upon the character of medieval civilization was great,[5] and appears greater when we consider that all culture which was not utterly ephemeral was the culture of a tiny minority. It is perhaps significant that most of the women who made a valuable contribution to medieval culture were either religious or women living in celibacy within or after marriage, like Hilda, Queen Edith, the sainted Margaret, her daughters Matilda and Mary, and Lady Margaret Beaufort.

The amorous character in the feudal castle was the young squire, not eligible for knight-service until he was twenty-one. His beardless youth and beauty were most often described as effeminate for he was long-haired, dressed in embroideries, skilled at musical performance with voice and instrument, and at dancing, and penning poetry. It was inevitable that a lad torn from his mother's breast to serve first as page and then as squire should yearn for the affection of his liege-lord's wife. The exigencies of adolescent flesh insured that he would suffer sexual aches and pains and naturally he attached them to his beloved lady-image. It was a submissive, tearful, servile posture; once he attained his majority and came to know the permissive society of the battle-field, this compulsive feeling became more intellectual and less immediate as he became more manly, less effeminate, and perforce less sexually obsessed. The situation was full of hazards: the lord's wife was often closer to her fellow vassal in age and temperament; he was certainly more attractive to her physically than her gruff stranger husband. If she should fall from grace and compromise the legitimacy of her heirs, the only outcome was disaster. Divorce was impossible, adultery was punishable by death be it the husband's *crime passionel* or the sentence of the law. The community attempted to exorcize this deep fear by externalizing it. Stories of ill-fated passion were cautionary tales. Love was a blight, a curse, a wound, death, the plague. Sex itself was outlawed, except in desire of issue. The chastity belt and its attendant horrors are reminders of the intense pressure built up in such a situation. The body-soul dichotomy which characterizes medieval thought operated to protect the status quo. Servant girls and country bumpkins were debauched without mercy, while the passion for the lady of the manor became exalted into a quasi-religious fervor. The literature of adulterous passion was, like the modern stories of obsession, fetishism, and perversion, a series of vicarious peeps into a region so fraught with dangers that only a lunatic would venture there. Every young clerk learnt from his dominies what *love* was:

> Set before thyne eyen howe ungoodly it is, how altogether a mad thing, to love, to waxe pale, to be made leane, to wepe, to flatter and shamefully to submyte thyselfe onto a stynkyng harlot most filthy and rotten, to gape and synge all nyght at her chambre wyndowe, to be made to the lure & to be obedyent at a becke, nor dare to do anything except she nod or wagge her head, to suffre a folyshe woman to reigne over the, to chyde the, to lay unkyndnesse one against ye other to fall out, to be made at one agayne, to gyve thyselfe wyllynge unto a Queene that she

might mocke, knocke, mangle and spoyle the. Where I beseche amonge all these thinges the name of a man? Where is thy berde? Where is that noble mynde created unto most beautyfull and noble thynges?[6]

But the more he strove to heed their teachings and disdain love, the more likely he was to be struck down unsuspecting by the bright glance of another man's chaste wife, which is what happened one fateful day to Francesco Petrarca. The effect on European letters was to last five hundred years. Petrarch was, besides a genius, very astute and he understood pretty clearly the nature of his passion. He managed to integrate it into his whole philosophical system, sublimating it by a thoroughly conscious and meticulous process. Laura became the mediatrix of all love and all knowledge of which God himself is the only Begetter. Her death made the process easier. Love of Laura, the lady of the laurel, the topaz and the ermine, the white deer, the madonna, was his greatest cross and his greatest blessing. By bearing it conscientiously all his life he made it his salvation. In almost every sonnet Petrarch achieves a reconciliation between his joy and his pain, his body and his soul, but his myriad followers were neither so intelligent nor so fortunate. In fact only Dante had ever achieved the same sort of dynamic equilibrium with his Beatrice, consciously demonstrating it in the *Purgatorio* and the *Paradiso* when she takes over from Virgil and leads him to the beatific vision. For lesser men Petrarchism became a refinement of adulterous sensuality. One of the factors in the survival of Petrarchism was that Petrarch was not living in a feudal situation. Laura was not the wife of his lord but of a peer, the citizen of a city-state which was bureaucratic and not hierarchic in structure. He managed singlehanded the transfer of courtly love from the castle to the urban community in a form which enables it to survive the development of the mercantile community and centralized government.

With the breakdown of the feudal system came the corrosion of hierarchic, dogmatic religion. Medieval Catholicism had based its authority upon the filial station of the celibate clergy. Celibacy was incessantly promoted by edicts of the Church in favor of sexual abstemiousness not only in the clergy but even in the married. It would be tiresome, if shocking, to relate the prohibitions which the Church laid upon intercourse within the marriage, before communion, during Advent and Lent and on rogation days and fast days, or the prurient interrogatories which priests were instructed to conduct in the confessional. Marriage was a station in life inferior to vowed celibacy and infantile virginity and the abstention of widows. Second marriage was not allowed a blessing in the Catholic rituals. It was considered better for a priest to have a hundred whores than one wife. Mystics and saints compelled to be married by their station in life, like Edward the Confessor, made vows of celibacy within marriage. The second-class status of marriage became one of the principal issues in the Reformation. Martin Luther, the Augustinian friar, had barely posted his thirty-nine articles on the door of the church in Württemberg when he took himself a wife.

Perhaps the best way of understanding the Reformation is to connect it with the decline of the feudal system in those northern countries where it took place. In England its course seems to reflect pretty clearly the impact of lower-class values on upper-class culture. The poor do not marry for dynastic reasons, and they do not marry out of their community in alliances with their peers. Goings-on in the castle have never been based upon practice in the cottage, except when a lord decided to take unto himself a supermenial as he does in the story of Patient Griselda, told by Boccaccio in the fourteenth century and taken up by the Renaissance in a big way;[7] possibly the fascination that this story of the lord who married a peasant girl had for the Renaissance throughout Europe was an indication of the rethinking about marriage that is insensibly and unofficially going

on. Griselda, taken from her hovel, is installed as her lord's humble and uncomplaining wife. Even when he takes a new, young, and noble wife, she does not abate her servility, for she welcomes her and dresses her for the wedding, and as a result wins her lord back. He of course claims he was testing her. The story reflects the general effect of the impact of lower-class *mores* on the attenuated and neurotic sexuality of the ruling class, albeit in a distorting mirror. When Adam delved and Eve span there was little point in lady-worship. Nostalgic and probably mythical accounts of marriage and giving in marriage in Merrie England are unanimous in their praise of the young folk who grow up working side by side in the tight-knit agricultural community. A boy made his choice from the eligible girls of his own village, lovingly steered by his parents and hers, indulgently watched during the permitted revels at Maying and nutting, pursuing a long courting process of token-giving and kiss-stealing, until there was space in his home for his bride, and need of a new hand in the butter- and cheese-making, the milking, the brewing, the care of lambs and chickens, at the spinning wheel and the loom. Books of husbandry listed the qualities he should look for in a wife—health, strength, fertility, good-will, and good-humor as well as her proper complement of household skills.[8] He respected her as a comrade and provided they were both healthy and strong they desired each other. The obsession of romantic love was simply irrelevant. Provided they agreed in age and social standing (a condition guaranteed by dowry and jointure) there was no obstacle except the tiresome caprice of the Church laws against affinity, which had to be bought off by dispensations seeing as by the sixteenth century they disqualified nearly all the members of a village from marriage through either blood relationship or the imaginary ties of gossipry, the spiritual relationships incurred by baptismal sponsors.

By the sixteenth century this placid picture, which resembles the courting situation which still pertains in the extended kinship system of feudal Calabria and Sicily, was broken up by the effects of enclosures, the increased exactions of the Church, and the rise of urban centers. Increased mobility, especially of the young men, increased the likelihood of marriage outside the known community. Changes in land tenure came to mean that a young man could not marry until his parents died and left him master of his own small property. By the seventeenth century a new pattern was established in England; late marrying was combined with betrothal followed by cohabitation. Peter Laslett found that parish registers showed christenings following hard on weddings, while marriage at thirty must be construed, in terms of the average life-span, as senile marriage.[9] The Church had long since lost control of the parish and her own courts were inadequate to deal with the results of her unrealistic laws about affinity and kinship. Too many parishes were left without competent clergy, and common-law marriage was on the increase. The religious reformers began to forge a new ideology of marriage, as public and holy, so holy that it had first been celebrated by God in heaven. It was extolled as the highest state of life and the condition of attainment of the status of citizenship and manhood. The increase in literacy and the advent of printing gave new scope to theory and literary example. The first tales of courtship and marriage found their way into written forms, now printed for the new, semiliterate readership. Much of this was didactic and set out ways and whys of marrying; some of it was cautionary, some escapist, and some direct polemic. Ballads appeared, containing the exempla of the marriageable girl, possibly based on old songs of wooing like *Jone can call by name her cowes*.

Any girl who was personable, healthy, and good-natured[10] was likely to be heartily wooed, but love was always subject to firm considerations of suitability and advantageousness. Her husband must not be old or disfigured or cruel or a whoremaster. She was not married away vilely for money, for the heroes of ballads and their admirers strongly condemned the practice of the nobility in disposing of their children like stud cattle; on the other hand a girl could not be married out of her father's house until a suitable groom presented himself in a proper manner. She agreed to treat him well, respect him, and joyfully to do his will in bed, but there is no indication that she expected her life to be transfigured by love. She considered herself to be as others thought her, a sexual creature ready for mating, and her husband was chosen as *likely* in this fashion too. On her marriage day she would be awakened by her bride knights and maidens, dressed in her best gown, stuck over with rosemary and crowned perhaps with ears of wheat, and taken in procession to the village church, where she would be assured of her husband's protection and a share in his fortunes. The blessing would promise children and freedom from nameless fear and jealousy. Feasting would last all day while the young couple chafed to be alone, for weddings were held in midsummer when the sun does not set until eleven; then they would be escorted to bed and left alone.

This is what happened according to the folklorists of the sixteenth century. Too often it did not, but it supplies the justification for the boast of the country to the court, that it alone knew the secrets of "true love," based on familiarity and parental control.[11] But the legacy of Petrarchan passion, with the invention of printing, became more and more accessible as an idea and reacted on the sensibilities of young folk whose brains were already inflamed by the sexual abstinence imposed by a system of late marrying. Schoolmasters, preachers, and reformers raged and wept over the prevalence of lecherous books and plays; prose works spun out long tales of chivalry debased into adventure; poems sang of adultery and the delights of sexual titillation; plays set forth images of juvenile infatuation and clandestine marriage. Young men in search of uncontaminated women, for the arrival of venereal disease at the beginning of the sixteenth century had complicated many things, rode up and down the country wooing country girls of substance with snatches of Serafino, Marino, and Anacreon, justified in the name of the great Petrarch whom few Englishmen had ever read.[12] The Elizabethan press thundered with denunciations of the lewd seducers of silly country girls. Elizabeth and Mary both brought out the severest edicts against young men who charmed country wenches, lured them into marriage, wasted their dowries, and then cast them off.[13] The Church authorities insisted on the reading of the banns in the parishes of both parties, but often they were read in quite the wrong places and more often not read at all. Religious turmoil added to the confusion. Parishes left without incumbents depended upon hedgepriests to legitimize children; the preposterously ramified laws which could nullify marriage were unknown until invoked by an interested and better-informed party. We will probably never know how many people suffered from the confusion about ecclesiastical law, which dealt with all questions of marriage and inheritance, and the changes of official religion in the sixteenth century. Perhaps it was only the reforming clergy persecuted by Mary, and disappointed by Elizabeth's refusal to recognize clerical marriage, who created the myth of perfect marriage, but minorities change the culture of majorities and certainly a change was occurring.

By the end of the sixteenth century love and marriage was already established as an important theme in literature. The nuclear household was certainly typical of urban households, and a greater proportion of the total population now lived in cities, but even the agricultural majority was also following the trend to triadic families. But it was still a developing argument, and not yet an escapist theme. The town took its cue from the country, where marriage was tolerance and mutual survival in a couple of rooms, where winter was longer than summer, and dearth more likely than plenty. The disastrous step to marriage as the *end* of the story, and the assumption of "living happily ever after" had not yet been taken. One of the most significant apologists of marriage as a

way of life and a road to salvation was Shakespeare. It is still to be proved how much we owe of what is good in the ideal of exclusive love and cohabitation to Shakespeare, but one thing is clear—he was as much concerned in his newfangled comedies to clear away the detritus of romance, ritual, perversity, and obsession as he was to achieve happy endings, and many of the difficulties in his plays are resolved when we can discern this principle at work. Transvestism is a frequently discussed Shakespearean motif, but it is rarely considered as a mode of revelation as well as a convention productive of the occasional frisson. Julia (in *Two Gentlemen of Verona*) and Viola (in *Twelfth Night*) are both transvestite heroines on close terms with the audience, who are explicitly contrasted with Petrarchan idols living on another plane of ceremony and imagery, Silvia and Olivia. These goddesses are debased in the course of the play by their own too human tactics, and even in the case of Silvia by an attempted rape. The girls in men's clothing win the men they love by a more laborious means, for they cannot use veils and coquetry; they must offer and not exact service, and as valets they must see their loved ones at their least heroic. In *As You Like it* Rosalind finds the means to wean Orlando off his futile Italianate posturing, disfiguring the trees with bad poetry; love at first sight for a stranger lady who addressed kind words to him on a day of victory becomes the love of familiarity for a sexless boy who teaches him about women and time, discovering her own role as she teaches him his, thereby leaping the bounds of femininity and tutelage. In *Romeo and Juliet* the same effect is got by Romeo's overhearing Juliet's confession of love, so that she cannot dwell on form, however fain. Because their love is not sanctioned by their diseased society they are destroyed, for Shakespearean love is always social and never romantic in the sense that it does not seek to isolate itself from society, family, and constituted authority. In *Midsummer Night's Dream* obsession is shown as hallucination and a madness, exorcized by the communal rite. Portia in *The Merchant of Venice* only manages to show Bassanio the worth of what he really found in his leaden casket when she dons an advocate's gown to plead for Antonio, her husband's friend and benefactor, so that her love is seen to knit male society together, not to tear it apart.

When the choice lies between the ultrafeminine and the virago, Shakespeare's sympathy lies with the virago. The women of the tragedies are all feminine—even Lady Macbeth (who is so often misinterpreted as a termagant), especially Gertrude, morally unconscious, helpless, voluptuous, and her younger version, infantile Ophelia, the lustful sisters, Goneril and Regan, opposed by the warrior princess Cordelia who refuses to simper and pander to her father's irrational desire. Desdemona is fatally feminine, but realizes it and dies understanding how she has failed Othello. Only Cleopatra has enough initiative and desire to qualify for the status of female hero.

The opposition between women who are people and women who are something less does not only rest in the vague contrast between the women of the comedies and the women of the tragedies. There are more explicit examples of women who may earn love, like Helena, who pursued her husband through military brothels to marriage and honor in *All's Well*, and women who must lose it through inertia and gormlessness, like Cressida. In *The Taming of the Shrew* Shakespeare contrasted two types in order to present a theory of marriage which is demonstrated by the explicit valuation of both kinds of wooing in the last scene. Kate is a woman striving for her own existence in a world where she is a *stale*, a decoy to be bid for against her sister's higher market value, so she opts out by becoming unmanageable, a scold. Bianca has found the women's way of guile and feigned gentleness to pay better dividends: she woos for herself under false colors, manipulating her father and her suitors in a perilous game which could end in her ruin. Kate courts ruin in a different

way, but she has the uncommon good fortune to find Petruchio, who is man enough to know what he wants and how to get it. He wants her spirit and her energy because he wants a wife worth keeping. He tames her as he might a hawk or a high-mettled horse, and she rewards him with strong sexual love and fierce loyalty. Lucentio finds himself saddled with a cold, disloyal woman, who has no objection to humiliating him in public. The submission of a woman like Kate is genuine and exciting because she has something to lay down, her virgin pride and individuality: Bianca is the soul of duplicity, married without earnestness or good-will. Kate's speech at the close of the play is the greatest defense of Christian monogamy ever written. It rests upon the role of a husband as protector and friend, and it is valid because Kate has a man who is capable of being both, for Petruchio is both gentle and strong (it is a vile distortion of the play to have him strike her ever). The message is probably twofold: only Kates make good wives, and then only to Petruchios; for the rest, their cake is dough.

There is no romanticism in Shakespeare's view of marriage. He recognized it as a difficult state of life, requiring discipline, sexual energy, mutual respect, and great forbearance; he knew there were no easy answers to marital problems, and that infatuation was no basis for continued cohabitation. His lifetime straddled the decay of the ancient state and the development of the new, the collapse of Catholicism and the solidification of English Protestantism, and the changes in the concept of the created universe, of ethics and science and art, which we call the English Renaissance. Much of his writing deals expressly with these changes and their meaning, balancing notions of legitimacy and law with co-operation, spontaneity, and moral obligation, nature, and mercy against authority and vengeance.

The new ideology of marriage needed its mythology and Shakespeare supplied it. Protestant moralists sought to redeem marriage from the status of a remedy against fornication by underplaying the sexual component and addressing the husband as the wife's friend.[14] It was unthinkable to them that children should marry without consent of their parents, but unthinkable also that parents should oppose a match which was suitable in the sense that the parties were of the same social standing and wealth, of an age and not disqualified by illness or criminality. Now that the property to be parceled and transferred in marriage was more divisible and portable, girls may have had more freedom of choice, but by the same token the old safeguards had ceased to apply. Parents demanded the right to know something of a bridegroom's background, and feared marriage with a stranger who might prove to be bigamous or a pauper. The country still taunted the city with the differences between their marryings but now the urban community was growing at the expense of the agrarian, and the rural community was losing its cohesiveness.

Where the wife was actively employed in production, helping with planting out and harvesting as well as minding the women's work, she was naturally not the family's chief consumer in circumstances of vicarious leisure. She was not primarily chosen for her obvious charms, not used to manipulating them for her own ends, had no opportunity to gad about, wear fine clothes, and make mischief. The subjects of popular farces about marrying and cuckoldry were the town-wives who were not employed in running their husband's business with them, who sat about with their gossips all day, flirting, drinking, flaunting new fashions, and making mischief by carrying assignations and rumors, or entertaining the priest. Antoine de la Sale's very circumstantial account, *Les Quinze Joies de Mariage*, enjoyed several centuries of popularity and was even translated and adapted by Dekker at the end of the sixteenth century.[15] This was no mere misogynist's account, but the heart-felt cry of a man who felt that he had been exploited by women all his life. In the larger community of the town there was more sexual competition and girls learnt early to enhance

their chances by the use of cosmetics and other forms of sexual display, laying forth their breasts and padding their buttocks. Their mothers superintended the process and instructed their daughters in the arts of sexual bargaining; if the worst came to the worst, and dalliance with a lusty young buck menaced an advantageous match with untimely progeny, mother arranged for an abortion or for the patching up of a hasty wedding with a more or less wealthy gull. The tensions in the situation were exaggerated by the laws which prevented apprentices from marrying until their long articles were over: many a master craftsman, free at last to wive, picked out a juicy young thing only to find that he had some soldier's or apprentice's leavings. Many of the city wives were idle, but, unlike women in other countries where urban dwelling had developed at an earlier epoch, they were not chaperoned and supervised and kept indoors, but allowed to walk forth freely and salute their acquaintances. The staple of French and English farce was the unwitting cuckoldom of the hardworked and henpecked husband whose wife will not keep house or cook for him.[16] The miserable husband reflected that her lust seemed to fire at the sight of every man but him, that she nagged, wheedled for fine clothes to attract strangers, that the first pregnancy meant the decline of her health and the assumption of permanent valetudinarianism. Obviously, such a dismal picture is an exaggeration, but the characteristics of middle-class marriage are already present: the wife is chief consumer and showcase for her husband's wealth: idle, unproductive, narcissistic, and conniving. She had been chosen as sexual object, in preference to others, and the imagery of obsession became more appropriate to her case. This is the class who were most exposed to the popular literature of escapist wedding which grew out of the collision of upper-class, adulterous romance and the simple stories of peasant weddings. As long as literature kept the essential character of marriage in sight, stories of love and marriage remained vibrant, ambiguous, and intelligent, but true love was quick to become a catch-phrase: the country had used it to mean their innocent couplings leading to a life of shared hardship and endeavor; the religious reformers added the notion which they culled from the scripture, "Rejoice in the wife of thy youth, may her breasts delight thee always." Sexual pleasure within marriage was holy; nevertheless marriage was also meant to be a remedy for lechery in that a good wife restrained her husband's passion and practiced modesty and continence within marriage, especially when breeding. Unrestrained indulgence was thought to lead to illness, barrenness, disgust, and deformity of issue. For this, reason it was considered particularly horrible when a woman married against her better judgment.[17] It was originally considered to be a mistake to marry a woman with whom you had been "in amors," at whose feet you had groveled and wept, to whom you had made flattering poems and songs. Shakespeare made his comment on the disparity between what is promised to the courted woman and what the wife can realistically expect in his picture of Luciana and Adriana in *The Comedy of Errors*. The divine mistress was to dwindle into a wife within hours of her wedding: the goddess was to find herself employed as supermenial.

> These London Wenches are so stout,
>   They are not what they do;
> They will not let you have a Bout,
>   Without a Crown or two.
>
> They double their Chops, and Curl their Locks,
>   Their Breaths perfume they do;
> Their tails are pepper'd with the Pox,
>   And that you're welcome to.
>
> But give me the Buxom Country Lass,
>   Hot piping from the Cow;
> That will take a touch upon the Grass,
>   Ay, marry, and thank you too.

> Her Colour's as fresh as a Rose in June
>   Her temper as kind as a Dove;
> She'll please the Swain with a wholesome Tune,
>   And freely give her Love.
>   —English Ballad, c. 1719

Despite all pressures to the contrary from religious reformers, intelligent poets, and playwrights, and the desperate interest of propertied parents in retaining control of marriage behavior, love and marriage took over, ending in that triumph of kitsch, the white wedding. Part of the explanation can be found in the story of what happened to Petrarchism in Protestant England. The English sonnet sequences of the 1590s were either frankly adulterous like Sir Philip Sidney's or totally honorific like Daniel's artificial passion for the Countess of Pembroke. Wyatt had been unable to keep a note of genuine physical tension out of his dramatic and colloquial translations of Petrarch, but he never ceased to battle with this irrelevant sensuality. Sidney makes no such effort. His sexual successes with Penelope Rich are chronicled in the poetry.[18] Reaction to this license in a society crusading for marriage as a sacred condition and deeply conscious of the differences in the practice of the nobility after a half-century of scandals was not slow in making an appearance on the same literary level. The Puritans were agitating for severer punishments for fornication as standing at the church door in a white sheet was treated by some blades as a sign of prowess and prestige. The reaction to the adulterous element in the courtly literature of the nineties can be found in the epithalamia, which were written as public relations work for marriage. Spenser's, the best of them, was also virtually the first, for its precedents were mainly fescennine and Latinate. In it he combined reminiscences of the rural modes of celebrating bridals with imagery from the Song of Songs and a platonic injection of veneration for intellectual beauty. The result is a poetical triumph, although the sonnet sequence of which it is the climax is a failure. The adoption of the Petrarchan mode to describe the methodical steps of Spenser's very proper wooing is simply a mistake, but it is a mistake which continues to be made. The anguish and obsession of the Petrarchan lover is artificially stimulated by his lawful betrothed in fits of pique or capriciousness: the lawful wooer lashes himself into factitious frenzies at her father's frown.[19] William Habington followed the new pattern of Petrarchan wedding in a dreary sequence called *Castara*,[20] which ought to have proved beyond further dispute that adultery provided greater inspiration than marriage. Playwrights succeeded better than poets at establishing marriage as the *non plus ultra* of romantic love, but the real source of the marrying-and-living-happily-ever-after myth is that art form invented to while away the vacant hours of idle wives, the love-novel.

Richardson's *Pamela* is the source of all, but it had various founts to draw upon for its own being. The invention of printing had meant that literature was no longer the prerogative of the nobility, and developments in education under the Tudors, buttressed by the Protestant anxiety that all should be able to read the Bible, led to the development of a market for all forms of escapist literature, many of which treated marriage as an adventure. The daughters of up-and-coming burghers learnt romance from the same sources that they learnt to use knives and forks and how to avoid farting in public. The notion of marriage as exploit first appears in stories like those told to the gentle craft of shoemakers, stories of the abduction of princesses by humble cobblers.[21] Bit by bit the archetypal story of the winning of the nobleman by the virtuous commoner like the Fair Maid of Fressingfield was developed.[22] The novels of Nashe, Defoe, and other writers of the picaresque were not proper reading for ladies. Moll Flanders and Fanny Hill were not fit heroines for the gentle sex. The pattern of the trials of *Pamela* is the pattern of the *Golden Legend*, in which virgin saints fought off all the machinations of the devil and his earthly agents to present themselves as unsullied spouses to Christ himself in heaven.[23] Pamela's divine spouse is the squire, and heaven is several thousand pounds a year. Richardson continued the story, but its proper ending, if the story is to correspond to the structure of sexual fantasy, is entry upon married life and unimaginable bliss. Richardson's followers did not attempt to describe the indescribable. The great bulk of the novel industry has been maintained until our own age by the lending libraries, which depend largely upon the category called *romance*, escapist literature of love and marriage voraciously consumed by housewives. Now the market is contested by the cheap paperback and the cinema, women's magazines, and love comics and photoromance. Gillian Freeman was offered work by one women's magazine which set out her staple plot in these terms.

> The girl in the story should be a secretary ... the boyfriend must be elevated above her socially— he could be the son of the boss, an advertising executive, a student or a serviceman ... or a young doctor. The story had to have a happy ending, there was to be no mention of religion or race, and lovemaking must be restricted to a kiss.[24]

The myth is still as widely dispersed as it ever was, although permissiveness is loudly argued to have made great inroads upon it. It has no demonstrable relation to what actually happens in the majority of cases, but this fact itself reflects nothing upon its sway as a myth. The myth has always depended upon the riches, the handsomeness, the loverliness, the considerateness of a man in a million. There are enough women prepared to boast of having got a man in a million to persuade other women that their failure to find a man rich enough, handsome enough, skilled enough as a lover, considerate enough, is a reflection of their inferior deserts or powers of attraction. More than half the housewives in this country work outside the home as well as inside it because their husbands do not earn enough money to support them and their children at a decent living standard. Still more know that their husbands are paunchy, short, unathletic, and snore or smell or leave their clothes lying around. A very high proportion do not find bliss in the conjugal embrace and most complain that their husbands forget the little things that count. And yet the myth is not invalidated as a myth. There is always an extenuating circumstance, the government, high taxation, or sedentary work, or illness, or perhaps a simple mistake or a failure in the individual case, which can be invoked to explain its divergence from the mythical norm. Most women who have followed in the direction indicated by the myth make an act of faith that despite day-to-day difficulties they are happy, and keep on asserting it in the face of blatant contradiction by the facts, because to confess disappointment is to admit failure and abandon the effort. It never occurs to them to seek the cause of their unhappiness in the myth itself.

> Chances are, when a fellow asks you out for dinner, you're someone pretty special in his life. A dinner-date means he doesn't mind spending a wallet-full of wampum on you—and more important, a great deal of time just sitting across at table from you with nothing to do but eat and talk. And it also means he expects to be proud of you as he follows you and the head-waiter to the table.
> —*Datebook's Complete Guide to Dating*,
> 1960, p. 115

The women of the lower classes have always labored, whether as servants, factory hands or seamstresses, or the servants of their own households, and we might expect that the middle-class myth did not prevail as strongly in their minds. But it is a sad fact that most working-class families are following a pattern of "progress" and "self-improvement" into the ranks of the middle class. In too many cases the wife's work is treated as a stop-gap, a contribution to buying or furnishing a house, and the omnipotent husband looks forward to the day when she will be able to stay at home and have babies. They too consider even if they cannot exactly manage it that mum *ought* to be at home keeping it nice for dad and the kids. In extreme cases a husband may even object to the sight of his wife scrubbing the floor as an affront to his male romanticism. Too often his wife's work merely supplies him with the property or the mortgage necessary to admit him once and for all to the middle class; behind it the myth lurks secure and unthreatened.

The wedding is the chief ceremony of the middle-class mythology, and it functions as the official entrée of the spouses to their middle-class status. This is the real meaning of saving up to get married. The young couple struggles to set up an image of comfortable life which they will be forced to live up to in the years that follow. The decisions about the cost of the celebration are possibly less important than the choice of a shop whereat to place the *list*. The more class the families can pretend to, the more they can exact in the way of presents at showers, kitchen teas, and the like. A list placed at the most expensive store in town embeds the couple and their interlacing families in the high-consumption bracket. The result is big business and mutual satisfaction. Harrods assures the bride that all she needs to do is "find the groom, we'll do the rest." Some stores bombard girls whose engagements are announced in the newspapers with invitations to place their lists with them. One store in London turns over five to eight million dollars a year in this business, mainly by manipulating the bride's mother. The more expensive stores expect a list to fetch about $1250 turnover, although the most expensive finds to its chagrin that only half the guests buy the wedding present from them.[25] The true pattern is already set in that it is the bride who initiates and controls all this spectacular consumption, just as the bride's gown and jewelry and the female guests' attire will establish the modishness of the whole clan, just as her girlfriend estimated her success in the marriage stakes by the size of the rock she sported when her engagement was first announced. The high consumption factor is maintained throughout by the imagery of films and plays and books about marriage, in which every household is warm and light, every wife is slim and elegant, and every husband successful.

> ... when through man's social and economic organization she became dependent, and when in consequence he began to pick and choose ... women had to charm for her life; and she not only employed the passive arts innate with her sex, but flashed forth in all the glitter that had been one of man's accessories in courtship, but which he had dispensed with when the superiority acquired through occupational pursuits enabled him to do so. Under new stimulation to be attractive, and with the addition of ornament to the repertory of her charms, woman has assumed an almost aggressive attitude towards courtship ....
> —W. I. Thomas, *Sex and Society*, 1907, p. 235

> It is not really surprising to hear of the number of men whose wives do not reach a satisfactory climax. As vibrators have been mentioned, may I add that it need not be the penis-shaped battery model which is difficult to "disguise" if found by your children. We have a standard Pifco and this is really fantastic. I would defy anyone to claim that his wife would not reach a magnificent climax if her clitoris were teased with one of these.
> —R. W. (Cheshire) *Forum*, Vol. II, No. 8

The myth is effortlessly pervasive like the forlorn hope of winning the pools. Any shabby, overworked female reading of a millionaire's wife in the *Sunday Times* can dream that she had "three children, one cook/ housekeeper, one nanny, two cleaners, two gardeners, one Rolls-Royce, one Fiat, one staff car, one helicopter, country home in Cheshire, London flat in Belgravia" and "my husband bought me a lovely little crocodile bag on chains from Gucci which goes with most things. Of course, I don't know how much it cost. He also gave me a mink, dark brown, by Maxwell Croft, which one can practically live in .... I buy my negligées and nightgowns from Fortnum's, of course. I've no idea how much they cost. Sometimes my husband gives me them, which pleases me greatly .... My husband's awfully good at present of jewelry."[26] It would all be spoilt if the envious little woman reading her *Sunday Times* had a vision of the industrialist's secretary reminding him that it was his anniversary, and slipping out at lunchtime with a check to pick up a piece selected by the jeweler's sales manager. Love seems to perish in hardship or to go underground, so that the valiant wife says "I know he loves me. He doesn't say much and we're past all that petting and stuff. But he'd never do anything to hurt me or the kids." It is easy to imagine that love survives in a cottage with roses round the door, or in a house in Cheshire with a cook/housekeeper, a nanny, two gardeners, and two cleaners, where the lady of the house is always scented and beautiful, draped in fine stuffs from Fortnum's, rested and happy in her triumphant husband's loving arms.

> We all know that the male instinctively looks to the woman for chastizement. It is a natural emotion born of the mother and child relationship. I am a willing partner in my husband's recurring urge to be disciplined, not simply for the eroticism of the event but also because my endeavours in this field are amply rewarded in other ways.

I have found that my husband has an almost insatiable desire to please me, not only in sexual affairs but also in general household matters. He has assumed responsibility for the housework, shopping, washing and ironing. I have only to mention that I need a new shelf, that the oven needs cleaning or a room decorating to find it done in no time at all. I am now encouraging him to take an interest in the culinary arts.

I am convinced not only by my own experience but also from other marriages that my husband is not abnormal. I'm sure that nine husbands out of 10, if asked by their wives if they would like to be caned, would answer yes. (Mrs.) L.B., Essex.

—*Forum*, Vol. II, No. 3

But it isn't true and it never was, and now for sure it never will be.

NOTES

1. Denis de Rougemont, *Love in the Western World, cf.* C.S. Lewis, *The Allegory of Love.*
2. *Hail Maidenhad*, ed. O. Cockayne, Early English Text Society Publications No. 19 (1866), pp. 28–39.
3. C.L. Powell, *English Domestic Relations 1487–1653* (Columbia, 1927), p. 126.
4. Rabelais, *Five Books of the Lives, Heroick Deeds and Sayings of Gargantua and His Sonne Pantagruel* (London, 1653), Caps LII–LVIII.
5. Gordon Rattray Taylor, *Sex in History* (London, 1965), p. 138.
6. Erasmus, *Two dyaloges wrytten in Laten ... one called Polythemus or the Gospeller, the other dysposing of thynges and names* translated into Englyshe by Edmonde Becke, Sig. M5 verso.
7. The story appeared in the *Decamerone*, not for the first time, and was instantly taken up as a theme by Petrarch, who wrote a Latin treatment of it, and then several French versions appeared to proliferate in the sixteenth century in a rash of ballads and poems and plays e.g., *The Ancient True and Admirable History of Patient Grissel* (1619), *The Pleasant and Sweet History of Patient Grissel* (1630), *The Pleasant Comodie of Patient Grissel* (H. Chettle, T. Deloney, and T. Haughton, 1603), *The Most Pleasant Ballad of Patient Grissel ... To the Tune of the Brides Goodmorrow.* (T. Deloney? 1600 and 1640).
8. E.g., *The Boke of Husbandry ... Made First by the Author Fitzherbert, ...* Anno Domini 1568, fol. xxxvi verso.

The ten properties of a woman: The .i. is to be mery of chere, ye. ii. to be well placed, the .iii. to haue a broad forhed, the .iiii. to haue brod buttocks, the .v. to be hard of ward, ye .vi. to be easy to leap upon, ye .vii. to be good at long iourney, ye .viii. to be wel sturring under a man, the .ix. to be always busy wt ye mouth, ye .x. euer to be chewing on ye bridle.

9. Peter Laslett, *The World We Have Lost* (London, 1965).
10. John Campion, *Two Books of Airs*; "Jack and Joan they think no ill, But loving live and merry still ..."
11. Nicholas Breton, *The Court and Country* (1618), *The Works in Verse and Prose of Nicholas Breton*, ed. A.B. Grosart (London, 1879), Vol. II.
12. E.g., Barclay in *The Ship of Fools*, Ascham in *The Scholemaster*, Lodge in *Wits Miserie*, among many others.
13. 4 & 5 Philip and Mary c. 8, and 39 Elizabeth c. 9.
14. E.g., the popular Elizabethan ballad, *The Brides Goodmorrow*. (The version in the B.M. dates from 1625.)
15. Antoine de la Sale, *Les Quinze Joies de Mariage* rendered by Thomas Dekker as *The Batchelar's Banquet* (1603).

16. One farce which exists in both French and English and demonstrates the archetypal pattern is *Johan Johan and Tyb His Wife*.

17. When Lady Mary Gray, a tiny woman bred too close to royalty for her own comfort, married Keys, a sergeant porter of no breeding and a huge man, for her own safety, the scandal was very great (Strype, *Annals of the Reformation* [1735–31], Vol. II, p. 208.)

18. Sir Philip Sidney, *Astrophel and Stella*, especially Sonnets XXIX, XXXVI, XLI, LXXII, LXXVI, LXXXI, LXXXII, *cf.* Samuel Daniel, *Delia* and Sir Thomas Wyatt, Poems from the Egerton MS.

19. Edmund Spenser, *Amoretti* and *Epithalamion*, published in 1595.

20. William Habington, *Castara* published anonymously in 1634. The first part deals with courtship and the second, which deals with marriage, has the epigraph *Vatumque lascivos triumphos, calcat Amor, pede coniugali*.

21. E.g., Thomas Deloney, *The Gentle Craft, a Discourse Containing Many Matters of Delight* (London, 1637). Chapter 5 relates "How the Emperours Fair Daughter Ursula, fell in love with young Crispine coming with shooes to the Court; and how in the end they were secretly married by a blind Frier."

22. The Fair Maid of Fressingfield is the subject of the subplot of *Friar Bacon and Friar Bungay* (1592) by Robert Greene.

23. *The Golden Legend* was a compilation of saints stories made according to the calendar of feasts by Jacobus de Voragine, Bishop of Genoa in the thirteenth century. It was one of the first books to be printed, and went through edition after edition in all places where there were printing presses, the first international best-seller.

24. Gillian Freeman, *The Undergrowth of Literature* (London, 1969), pp. 50–1.

25. *Sunday Times*, 3.8.1969, "Making Money Out of Marriage."

26. *Sunday Times*, 15.6.1969, "First Catch Your Millionaire."

Life between the Lines

Gloria Steinem

There have been days in the last ten or twelve years when I thought my collected works would consist entirely of fund-raising letters, scribbled outlines of speeches, statements hammered out at the birth of some new coalition, and introductions to other people's books.

I'm not regretful of the time I've devoted to those projects. Writing that leads to action, puts some common feeling into words, or introduces people to one another may be just as important in the long run as much of the fact and fiction published in conventional ways. If I were to name an emotional highpoint of my twenty or so years as a writer, it might be the two sleepless days I spent as an invited outside scribe for diverse caucuses at the 1977 National Women's Conference (an event also described here in "Houston and History"). Women representing every group of "minority" Americans, from Indian nations to new Vietnamese refugees, had decided to forge a shared resolution. As words were found to describe the common experiences of women of color while preserving the special issues of each group, and as that unprecedented shared resolution passed by acclamation of two thousand delegates representing every part of the country, I felt pride in being a writer that was at least as pleasurable as the pride that comes from seeing one's own more personal words in print.

In the same way, and supposing there is such a thing as posterity, I might be just as pleased if my part in it were much shorter than a book or an essay: perhaps the invention of something as brief and pithy as the phrase *reproductive freedom*, a democratic substitute for such old paternalisms as *population control*, and a Fifth Freedom of special importance to the female half of the world. Finding language that will allow people to act together while cherishing each other's individuality is probably the most feminist and therefore truly revolutionary function of writers. Just as there can be no big social change without music (as Emma Goldman said, "If I can't dance, it's not my revolution"), there can be none without words and phrases that first create a dream of change in our heads.

But it's one of the ironies of trying to be a writer and an activist at the same time that just when you feel you have the most to say, you have the least time to say it.

I regret very much, after more than a dozen years of traveling at least a couple of days a week as an itinerant speaker and feminist organizer, that I never kept a diary. Though most of the ideas and observations in this essay were born during those travels [....] I could have written a book-length, blow-by-blow account of just one early year. For instance, one year that included being the first woman speaker for the powerful few at the National Press Club in Washington (they gave me a tie) and a Harvard Law Review banquet (where, being supplied with research from the few women students at this school that began admitting females only in the 1950s, I committed the sin of talking specifically about Harvard instead of generally about The World). Or finding three thousand people gathered for a speech in a basketball stadium in Wichita, Kansas, while the media was still reporting feminism as the invention of a few far-out women on either coast, and New York colleagues were predicting either indifference or the strong possibility of my being stoned to death. Or meeting women who were protesting everything from sex-segregated help-wanted ads in Pittsburgh to Nevada's practice of pressuring welfare mothers into prostitution in order to save money and increase tourist attractions.

Several more years like that one at the start of the 1970s taught me, despite deprecations the media were then reporting about "Women's Lib" or "bra burners," that daily rebellions and dreams of equality—inside families and in public life—were sprouting up everywhere. And these new ideas were not confined to any predictable demographics of age, race, education, or geography. If anything, rebellion was less rhetorical and more real in parts of the country where women's alternatives were more restricted than in the big cities of New York or California, and at economic levels where women's salaries were even more crucial than among the middle-class rebels who were the focus of the press.

Those regular travels also gave me good news to bring back to New York women writers and editors who were growing impatient with the old "feminine" and "masculine" stereotypes in the media, and who had just held historic sit-ins at The Ladies' Home Journal and RAT, a so-called radical paper that actually prospered on pornography. The good news was that there were more than enough readers for a new kind of women's magazine for, by, and about women. Though feminism

was (and sometimes still is) a misunderstood word, many women readers wanted a magazine that supported its real definition: the equality and full humanity of women and men. After all, even those magazines directed to women were totally male-owned and controlled, and mostly edited by men. In order to right the balance, women needed a national forum—indeed, many such forums.

Meetings with other women in the publishing world uncovered war stories that either made you laugh or cry. Look magazine told Patricia Carbine, who had been essentially running that magazine for years as executive editor, that a woman could never have the editor's title. At The Ladies' Home Journal where I was an occasional consultant and writer, one of its two top editors (both men, of course) was so convinced that I was nothing like its readers (whom he described as "mental defectives with curlers in their hair") that he used to hand me a manuscript and say, "Pretend you're a woman and read this." Even at that, he was more flexible than the owner of Seventeen, who ordered an end to my editorial consulting there when he discovered I was raising money for the legal-defense fund of Angela Davis. An editor at New York magazine, where the women's movement was at least understood as an important news event, still insisted the whole thing was a minor upper-class discontent that could be solved by importing more maids from Jamaica. The New York Times Magazine seemed to be continuing its usual practice of allowing women, minorities, and homosexuals to write first-person confessional pieces, but, in the name of objectivity, assigning white male "authorities" to write definitive articles on these groups. A memo smuggled out by a woman office worker at Playboy magazine in Chicago was a three-page diatribe by Hugh Hefner against publishing an article on the women's movement that one of his editors had assigned to a professional male journalist, and thus had come out too "objective" and "well-balanced" for Hefner's purposes. As he wrote, "Doing a piece on the pros and cons of feminism strikes me as rather pointless for *Playboy*. What I'm interested in is the highly irrational, emotional, kookie trend .... These chicks are our natural enemies .... It is time to do battle with them .... What I want is a devastating piece ... a really expert, personal demolition job on the subject." (I remember assuming that her release of that memo to the press would have a chilling effect on anyone who cared about journalism, if not women's equality, but it was treated with chuckles and smiles. Objectivity was for serious concerns, not for anything relating to women.)

There was an even bigger problem for women of color. Black women reported, for instance, that the senior editorial jobs of major national magazines included not one of their number. Even a brand-new magazine for black women was partly owned by *Playboy*, and, in the pattern of other women's magazines, was published by two men. As one woman put it, "At least you're getting hostility. We're still The Invisible Woman."

It was stories and meetings like those that rounded up the energy and professionalism for a national, inclusive, female-controlled magazine for women. With little capital and no intention of duplicating the traditional departments designed around "feminine" advertising categories—recipes to reinforce food ads, beauty features to mention beauty advertisers, and the like—we knew it would be economically tough. (Fortunately, we didn't know *how* tough. Attracting ads for cars, sound equipment, beer, and other things not traditionally directed to women still turns out to be easier than convincing advertisers that women look at ads for shampoo without accompanying articles on how to wash their hair, just as men look at ads for shaving products without articles on how to shave.) Given all these obstacles, we never would have continued if readers hadn't encouraged us. We produced one sample issue of this new editorial content—a magazine designed to stay on newsstands for three months—and it sold out in eight days.

There was a lot more hard work and uncertainty before we could begin publishing every month. Trying to start a magazine controlled by its female staff in a world accustomed to the authority of men and investment money should be the subject of a musical comedy.

Nonetheless, *Ms.* magazine was born [....]

At the same time, however, my life was less a magazine than a novel. For the four or five years surrounding the birth of *Ms.*, I was traveling and speaking as a team with a black feminist partner: first Dorothy Pitman Hughes, a child-care pioneer, then lawyer Florynce Kennedy, and finally activist Margaret Sloan. By speaking together at hundreds of public meetings, we hoped to widen a public image of the women's movement created largely by its first homegrown media event, *The Feminine Mystique*. (The English translation of Simone de Beauvoir's *The Second Sex* had caused a stir even earlier, but its message had been diminished by the idea that the rebellious women came from some other country, not our own.) Despite the many early reformist virtues of *The Feminine Mystique*, it had managed to appear at the height of the civil rights movement with almost no reference to black women or other women of color. It was most relevant to the problems of the white well-educated suburban homemakers who were standing by their kitchen sinks justifiably wondering if there weren't "more to life than this." As a result, *white-middle-class movement* had become the catch phrase of journalists describing feminism in the United States (unlike Europe, where early writings and actions were much more populist), and divisions among women were still deep.

There was little public understanding that feminism, by its very definition, has to include females as a caste across economic and racial boundaries, just as a movement against racial caste includes each individual marked by it, regardless of sex or class. There was even less understanding that sex and race discrimination are so pragmatically linked and anthropologically interdependent that one cannot be successfully uprooted without taking on the other.

So, to be feminist in both form and content, we went out in what Flo Kennedy used to describe cheerfully as "Little Eva teams—something for everyone." Or, as Margaret Sloan put it, "We travel in pairs—like nuns." After Dorothy Pitman Hughes and her husband Clarence had a baby who was nursing and so traveled with us, we were a trio for a while. Dorothy was convinced that some people might suspect us of renting this baby to demonstrate the integration of children into daily life; an important part of our message. In fact, one or two people behaved as if we had somehow given birth to a baby daughter by ourselves. It was a time when even one feminist speaker was a novelty, and interracial teams of feminists seemed to be unheard of since the days of Sojourner Truth.

That rarity brought us stares and opposition, but also great support. Our presence on the stage together made a point that women seemed hungry for, especially in the South. We attracted bigger and more diverse audiences than each of us would have had on our own, and we were complementary in other ways. As a journalist, my name was publicized, so I was more likely to attract the one paid speech around which we could build other meetings and benefits. On the other hand, Dorothy could talk personally about equality in marriage and parenthood, and both Flo and Margaret were far more experienced speakers. I always spoke first to lay a groundwork (as anyone in those audiences would tell you, speaking second also would have made me an anticlimax after the energy and style of Margaret or Flo), but the most important part of any lecture came after both of us—a long audience discussion and organizing meeting.

It was then that people began to answer one another's questions ("How can I stop feeling guilty about asking my husband to do housework?") with their own tried-and-true solutions ("Divide the housework as you would if you were living with another woman, and then don't lower your standards"). They informed one another of problems we never could have known about (a local factory that refused to hire women, a college hushing up a campus rape to protect its reputation, a high school counselor who advised girls to be nurses and minority boys to be veterinarians). They passed around literature from current feminist groups, sign-up sheets for new ones, and the addresses of politicians who deserved to be lobbied or demonstrated against. They picked up ideas or actions from the lengthening list we recited from our travels in other parts of the country, or they decided to do something entirely new.

Small all-women discussion groups that followed the lectures were even more honest, just as consciousness-raising or networking groups were (and still are, as reported here in an essay on "Networking") the basic cells of long-term change. But we discovered that the ideal proportion for a big public audience was about two-thirds women and one-third men. When matched by men in even numbers, women still restrained their response and looked to see how the men were reacting; but in clear majorities, they eventually forgot about any male presence at all and responded as women do when we are on our own. That gave many women a rare chance to speak honestly, and some men an even more rare chance to hear them.

Most of all, women in those audiences discovered they were not alone. And so did we.

Though we tried to focus on parts of the country that were most removed from the little feminist activity that then existed, there were so few feminist speakers that we ended by going to almost every kind of community and, I think, every state but Alaska. There were times when we felt like some combination of Susan B. Anthony and a lost company of *Blossom Time*.

[…] other scenes come flooding back:

• Reporters at press conferences who routinely assumed I could answer questions about all women but Dorothy could answer only about black women, or perhaps only about the few black male leaders whose names they knew. Just as *male* was universal but *female* was limited, *white* was universal but *black* was limited. (We tried to turn this into a learning experience by letting the questions go on for a while—and then pointing the problems out.)

- White train conductors in the North who let me pass into the parlor car, then explained to Dorothy that the cheaper seats were in the rear.
- A black minister in Dorothy's tiny southern hometown who wouldn't let women in his church do anything but cook and sing—not even be deacons or pass the collection baskets that women's hard-earned coins did the most to fill.
- A white stewardess who pronounced Dorothy's nursing her baby onboard "obscene."
- An irate man in one audience who screamed at Dorothy to "go home to Russia where you belong," causing both her and the audience to break up with laughter at the idea of her Russian roots.
- A snobbish boys' prep school that gave us our toughest audience and a lifetime friend, the mother of one of the boys, who announced that she had an executive husband who liked to hunt, and two obnoxious sons who thought girls were inferior. She became a full-time volunteer for Dorothy's child-care center—where she worked for years thereafter.
- Margaret standing bravely with her arms crossed to block a man storming the stage against our "blasphemous" talk of equality.
- Late-night discussions in endless motel rooms where black women suggested we radicalize white women so they would stop offering themselves as doormats to black men, thus allowing some black men to accuse black women of being "too strong"; and where we listened to many women's stories of outrages to become

known later as "sexual harassment," "battered women," or "displaced homemakers."

- A woman in Chicago who capsulized our long explanation of why welfare was a woman's issue (it was then considered an entirely racial one) by explaining that, with young children to care for, "most women in this country are only one man away from welfare."
- Gyms, auditoriums, church basements, and union halls filled to overflowing with women (and men) who applauded and laughed with relief at hearing the sexual politics of their lives described out loud.
- Stirring up rebellion at a women's university in Texas where campus guards were suspected of raping the women they were paid to protect, or among factory workers whose insurance covered men who had hair transplants but not women who had babies.
- Talking with Flo about her first book, *Abortion Rap*, in a Boston taxi and hearing its elderly Irish woman driver say the much-to-be-quoted words: "Honey, if men could get pregnant, abortion would be a sacrament."
- Trying to keep up with Flo's generosity and energy, from helping prostitutes organize against pimps and for decriminalization to encouraging rich wives to break the trusts that passed their family money from one generation of men to the next.
- Learning from Flo's experience as a lawyer how much more common were domestic violence and incest than I had ever dreamed. (She said, "Talk to any group of five or six women. One of them was probably sexually abused as a child by a man in her own family circle." I asked—and it was true.)
- Watching Flo transform lives by any available magic, from bullying an unconfident woman

reporter into trying her own radio show, to convincing a shy clerk in a small-town dry-goods store that it was okay for Flo to buy her the purple pantsuit she'd been coveting for months.

- Most of all, learning from Flo's example that you didn't have to accept the opposition's terms. For instance, when a hostile man asked if we were lesbians (as frequently happened; why else would a white and black woman be colleagues?), Flo would just look him in the eye and ask, "Are you my alternative?"

It was Flo especially who taught me that a revolution without humor is as hopeless as one without music. Her own outrageousness allowed me to say things I might otherwise have confined to my former job as a writer of satire for the television show, "That Was the Week That Was," and feminism itself encouraged me to go beyond conventional subjects for humor (as you will see from a fantasy called "If Men Could Menstruate," an improvisation from later lectures). Flo also rescued me from a habit that might be okay in articles but is death in speeches: citing a lot of facts and statistics. After one such lapse before an audience that seemed especially skeptical about the existence of any discrimination at all, she took me aside. "Look," she said kindly. "If you're lying in the ditch with a truck on your ankle, you don't send somebody to the library to find out how much the truck weighs. You get it *off*."

The friendship and company of all three of my lecture partners helped me get over something else—an almost pathological fear of speaking in public. In the past, when magazines had booked me on a radio or television show, as writers routinely are asked to do, I had canceled out at the last minute so often that a few shows banned me as a guest. Though I wasn't shy about bearding lions on a den-by-den basis, as journalists must do, the very idea of speaking to a group, much less before a big audience, was enough to make my heart pound and my mouth go

dry. The few times I tried it, I became obsessed with getting to the end of each sentence without swallowing, and then obsessed for days afterward with what I should have said.

It was self-conscious. It was wasteful. I berated myself for this idiotic inability to talk on my own. When I once did show up on television to talk about the organizing efforts of migrant workers, host Bill Cosby tried to still my chattering teeth by explaining during a break that I had no *right* to be so nervous when I was speaking for a man as important as Cesar Chavez. That didn't help at all. After experiencing police riots at the 1968 Chicago Democratic Convention, I got angry enough to try again, but only as a team with Jimmy Breslin, my colleague at *New York* magazine. That time, I got out about three sentences—and didn't even have the confidence to resist false eyelashes that television makeup men then glued on female guests, thus making the medium contradict the message.

On the theory that I knew no one in Canada and so failure wouldn't be as humiliating there, I did a Canadian television series in the late sixties that included long interviews with James Earl Jones, Congressman Adam Clayton Powell, and Prime Minister Pierre Trudeau. (I also didn't have the confidence to suggest women.) But that series offered the comfort of a very professional cohost and tapes that could be edited later. It was still a long way from standing in front of an audience with the sole responsibility for an hour of dead air.

I even consulted a speech teacher. She told me that writers and dancers had the most difficulty learning to talk in public, because each had chosen a profession in which they could communicate without speech. I had been both. Long before becoming a writer, I had been a semiprofessional dancer dreaming of tap dancing my way out of Toledo. I decided to give up on trying to say anything in public.

And I would have remained silent, like so many women who were giving up on various aspects of their human abilities, if I hadn't been lucky enough to live through a time when a few women were beginning to figure out that the gigantic lack of confidence in females wasn't all our individual faults. A profound system of sexual politics was at work here.

I say all this about speaking not only because it has been a major hurdle in my life, but also because it's a problem that seems to be common to many people who feel overly dependent on the approval of others. (Layers of political cause and effect peeled away more for me when I researched [my essay] "Men and Women Talking." […]) One of the most helpful things ever said to me came from poet Sandra Hochman: "Don't think about it. Just pretend you're Eleanor Roosevelt and you have to do this idiotic television show before you can go on to do something *really* important." Perhaps this is the Art of Zen Speaking.

Years of actually getting up in front of audiences have taught me only three lessons: 1) you don't die; 2) there's no right way to speak, only *your* way; and 3) it's worth it. A mutual understanding can come from being in a room together, and a sense of character and intention can come through the television screen that could never happen on a printed page.

Now, I continue to travel and organize almost every week, sometimes alone, sometimes with other women, depending on the issue and audience at hand. If we were to do another road show like that earlier one (and perhaps we should), we would need a repertory company of a dozen or so women even to begin to symbolize who American feminists really are; from Chicana to Alaskan Native, from Puerto Rican to Pacific Islander. We would still need women who have made different choices, from a traditional homemaker who wants honor for her work to a lesbian who wants honor for her life-style. Indeed, we would now need some men, too. There are many more who can call themselves feminists with pride and justification. But the goal would still be the same: to give people a chance to hear feelings confirmed, know they

are not alone, and thus discover they didn't need "outside agitators" after all. In any one audience, there is enough energy, skill, anger, and humor for a revolution.

As an itinerant organizer, my own two biggest rewards are still a sense of making a difference and the birth of ideas. The first would be enough in itself, for that is how we know we are alive, but the second is magic. On a good night, a roomful of people can set off a chain of thought that leads us all to a new place—a sudden explosion of understanding, a spontaneous invention. We hear ourselves saying things we had felt but never named. It will take a lifetime to write them all down.

Nonetheless, I wouldn't be honest if I blamed only activism for the fact that, after more than twenty years of making a living as a writer, [*Outrageous Acts and Everyday Rebellions*] is the first book I can call my own.[1]

Writers are notorious for using any reason to keep from working: over-researching, retyping, going to meetings, waxing the floors—anything. Organizing, fund-raising, and working for *Ms.* magazine have given me much better excuses than those, and I've used them. As Jimmy Breslin said when he ran a symbolic campaign for a political office he didn't want, "Anything that isn't writing is easy." Looking back at an article I published in 1965, even when I was writing full-time and in love with my profession, I see, "I don't like to write. I like to have written."

That thought comes from "What's in It for Me," the subject on which *Harper's* had invited a group of writers to contribute. In fact, most of my reasons in that essay still hold.

- There is freedom, or the illusion of it. Working in spurts to meet deadlines may be just as restricting as having to show up at the same place every day, but I don't think so …. Writing about a disliked person or theory or institution usually turns out to be worthwhile, because pride of authorship finally takes over from prejudice.

Words in print assume such power and importance that it is impossible not to feel acutely responsible for them.

- Writing, on the other hand, keeps me from believing everything I read.
- Women whose identity depends more on their outsides than their insides are dangerous when they begin to age. Because I have work I care about, it's possible that I may be less difficult to get along with when the double chins start to form.
- I don't have to specialize. If one year can include articles on suburban integration, electronic music, Saul Bellow, college morals, John Lennon, three Kennedys, the space program, hiring policies in television, hard-edge painting, pop culture, draftees for Vietnam, and James Baldwin, nonfiction writing may be the last bastion of the generalist.
- For me, writing is the only thing that passes the three tests of metier: (1) when I'm doing it, I don't feel that I should be doing something else instead; (2) it produces a sense of accomplishment and, once in a while, pride; and (3) it's frightening.[2]

Nevertheless, I'm surprised by the quantity of writing I was doing then; not just in that single year of 1965 but for most of the sixties. I hadn't reread these pieces until I dug them out for this collection and rejected almost all of them as outdated or off-the-point. (Only two of the most personal ones survive, "I Was a Playboy Bunny" and the earlier parts of "Campaigning.") If I had realized at the time that trying to write like other reporters and essayists is precisely what makes the results more interchangeable and perishable, I would have been less hesitant about writing in the first person. (You were supposed to say nothing more personal than "this reporter.") I was trying to be a professional writer-on-assignment; a worthy calling but not one that makes for

much original thinking. Nonetheless, some themes of those articles emerge.

I was clearly trying to learn from other writers by choosing them as subjects for profiles. James Baldwin was high on the list because I identified with his sense of outrage and vulnerability (though at the time, I had no idea why I, a middle-class white person, should share these feelings). Saul Bellow's *The Adventures of Augie March* was the only novel that captured a certain crazy American class mobility I also had experienced while growing up in the Midwest with many books and show-business pretensions, but in either a housetrailer, or a house with rats and no heat. So I spent a memorable day following Bellow around as he revisited his childhood haunts in Chicago. I wrote about Truman Capote twice because I was so moved by his early fiction and its bittersweet evocation of an outsider's childhood, as well as by his ability to write seriously and empathetically about women (including the rape of a black woman trapped by white men in a roadside ditch—a scene I shall never forget). John Lennon was a subject I wrote about so long ago that I was more attracted by his pun-filled, Liverpudlian poetry than his music, but the only article I could sell was a pretty conventional account of following the Beatles during their first visit to New York. Interviewing Dorothy Parker, one of the few female writers about whom women's magazines cared enough to publish a profile, was like meeting an acerbic old friend. My mother had quoted her verses and I knew many by heart. In fact, we did become friends. Long after the article was published, I kept visiting her in the apartment where she was trapped by illness, and once got her out to a ballet. "My dear, that Round Table thing was *greatly* over-rated, you know," she said, with her delightful habit of debunking past glories. "It was full of people looking for a free lunch and asking, 'Did you hear the funny thing I said yesterday?'"

Most of my assignments reflected the media's interest in celebrities: Mary Lindsay, wife of the newly elected New York mayor, and actor Michael Caine for *The New York Times Magazine*; Margot Fonteyn and Lee Radziwill for *McCall's*; Paul Newman and a newer star named Barbra Streisand for *The Ladies' Home Journal*; and many more. (The Newman assignment, typical of the hazards of working for certain women's magazines, was to find out "how that plain little girl hangs on to the world's handsomest movie star." When I reported back that Joanne Woodward was at least as interesting as her husband—and that, if anything, the balance seemed to be the other way around—my male editor said I couldn't write it that way. *Journal* readers would be threatened by interesting wives. When I finally did Newman on his own, it was a hard-won compromise.) I sneaked in a few less-well-known women whose work I admired: Marisol as an iconoclastic sculptor; Renata Adler as a very smart young writer and movie critic for *The New York Times*; Pauline Frederick as an older and excellent television reporter who might have been Walter Cronkite had she been a man and thus allowed to age on camera; Barbara Walters as the first woman on the "Today" show who wasn't a coffee-serving beauty-contest winner and who actually did her own reporting. But there weren't many of those. I didn't fight hard enough. I was grateful for celebrity profiles as a step up from the traditional "girl writer" assignments I was inevitably given and to which I sometimes succumbed.

They included things like: reporting on a hotel sale whose chief attraction was ZsaZsa Gabor's bed; going to London to interview a new hairdresser named Vidal Sassoon (who turned out to be a serious person, but *Glamour* wasn't interested in his life on a kibbutz); writing about designer Rudy Gernreich (who also turned out to be an innovator of comfortable clothes, but only a long fight with *The New York Times Magazine* got anything but his topless bathing suits included in the article); and, probably the low point in my writing life, a long, endlessly researched article on textured stockings. That last one was for *The New York Times Magazine*, the source of my most frivolous and seductive assignments. After turning down three or four on such subjects as a profile of Park Avenue (with instructions to stop where it entered Spanish Harlem and *Times* readers diminished), I would think, *Well, it is* The New York Times, and find myself writing on something I didn't care about. The good gray *Times* also had a high incidence of editors who asked you to go to a hotel with them in the afternoon, or, failing that, to mail their letters for them on the way out.

For *Life* magazine, I did write a long semi-sociological report on pop culture, but only after being sent home by the first editor I saw there. ("We don't want a pretty girl," he explained. "We want a writer.") There were also many proto-feminist, philosophical essays for *Glamour*: a little saccharine but not without a germ of personal experience or real feeling. I still meet an occasional woman who tells me that she did or didn't have an affair, leave home, or otherwise do what she wanted to do anyway because one of those essays said it was okay. There were cultural columns for *Look* magazine; show business and college features for *Show* magazine and *Esquire*; such odd one-time projects as a concert booklet for Peter, Paul, and Mary; and book reviews for almost everybody.

In other words, I was making a living as a writer.

But most of this work was a long way from the writing I had hoped to do when I lived in India just after college, discovered that its standard of living, not ours, was the norm for most of the world, and kept a diary of walking through village caste riots with nothing but a cup, a sari, and a comb. After I first came home in 1958, I had naïvely tried to sell some of that writing, as well as a guidebook designed to lure Westerners into traveling beyond the Taj Mahal, but I was unknown and the time was much too early. Even the Beatles hadn't yet discovered India.

In fact, a lot of the work I published pre-feminism was schizophrenic, even when compared to the life I was leading in New York.

I was volunteering for political campaigns, but writing *fumetti* and satirical photo captions for a successor to

Mad magazine called *Help!*; sneaking endless pizzas and cigarettes to a group of Puerto Rican radicals, including some early feminists, while they occupied a church in Spanish Harlem, but writing about ancient Christmas traditional foods for *Glamour*; traveling in 110 degree heat with Cesar Chavez and his Poor People's March to the Mexican border in order to organize press coverage, but reporting on tropical vacations; raising bail and collecting clothes for migrant workers organizing on Long Island, but interviewing James Coburn about some James Bond-type movie.

As one of the few "girl reporters," I also was traveling among the Beautiful People I was writing about, and was sometimes photographed as one of their lesser members, yet at the same time, I was paying $62.50 a month for an apartment and having my American Express card—on which I had charged all the expenses of that march to the Mexican border that the farmworkers couldn't afford—repossessed.

Much of this disparity was my fault. I didn't take myself very seriously either. Besides, there had been the early mistake of accepting an assignment from *Show* magazine to work as a Playboy Bunny in order to write the exposé included in [*Outrageous Acts and Everyday Rebellions*]. Though I returned an advance payment for its expansion into a book, thus avoiding drugstore racks full of paperbacks emblazoned with my name, "I Was a Playboy Bunny," and god-knows-what illustration, that article quickly became the only way I was publicly identified. It swallowed up my first major signed article: an *Esquire* report on the contraceptive revolution that had been published a year earlier and was attracting assignments from other editors. (I see that this twenty-one-year-old article ended with: "The only trouble with sexually liberating women is that there aren't enough sexually liberated men to go around." It's interesting that I could understand that much and still be blind to all the rest.) I lost a hard-won assignment to do an investigative article on the United States Information Agency, whose

accurate reflection of this country I had come to doubt after seeing its operations in India. Instead, I got a leering suggestion that I pose as a call girl and do an exposé of high-level prostitution.

Eventually, dawning feminism made me understand that reporting about the phony glamour and exploitative employment policies of the Playboy Club was a useful and symbolic thing to do. Posing as a call girl (which I didn't do because I found the idea both insulting and frightening) would have been an assignment worthy of Nellie Bly. But at the time, I had no protection against the sex jokes and changed attitudes that the Bunny article brought with it; and my heart sank whenever I was introduced as a former Playboy Bunny or found my employee photograph published with little explanation in *Playboy*. (Even twenty years later, both these events continue. The latter is *Playboy*'s long-running revenge.) Though I always identified emotionally with other women, including the Bunnies I worked with, I had been educated to believe that my only chance for seriousness lay in proving my difference from them.

It wasn't until *New York* magazine was founded in 1968 and I became one of its contributing editors and political columnists that my work as a writer and my own interests began to combine. For *New York*'s inaugural issue, I wrote a short article called "Ho Chi Minh in New York"—a probable American experience in the life of that mysterious anticolonial leader whose affection for this country and respected status as "the George Washington of South Asia" I knew from living in India after college. It was only now, a decade later, that I was able to use any experience from those two crucial years in my life. They also had taught me that a white woman was less threatening than a white man, and had an easier time traveling in other cultures. That helped when, after Martin Luther King was murdered and I sat staring mutely at my TV set, I got a call from *New York* editor Clay Felker to "get the hell up to Harlem, and just talk to people." I knew that, as in India, safety lay in staying close to other women for protection. I felt like a reporter for the first time. When a newly elected President Nixon sent Nelson Rockefeller on a tour of Latin America, I was assigned by *New York* to go along on the press plane. The result was an account of his very unpopular trip called "The Sound of One Hand Clapping." I reported on John Lindsay as mayor and Ed Koch as a congressman; on wounded Vietnam vets who returned to a hospital in Queens direct from the battlefield, only to find themselves victims of the peace movement as well as the war; on the discovery in the Bronx of kwashiorkor, a protein-deficiency disease once thought to be confined to the famines of Africa; neighborhood battles over child-care centers; anti-Vietnam demonstrations and peace mobilizations; and the attitudes of journalists on presidential campaign planes. (Samples of these travels are part of "Campaigning.") For the first time, I wasn't writing about one thing, while caring about something else.

Nonetheless, it wasn't until I went to cover a local abortion hearing for *New York* that the politics of my own life began to explain my interests.

In protest of an official hearing that had invited fourteen men and one nun to testify on the liberalization of New York State's anti-abortion laws, a local feminist group had asked women to testify about their real life experiences with illegal abortion. I sat in a church basement listening to women stand before an audience and talk about desperately trying to find someone who would help them, enduring pre-abortion rapes from doctors, being asked to accept sterilization as the price of an abortion, and endangering their lives in an illegal, unsafe medical underground. It was like the "testifying" I had heard in southern churches and civil rights meetings of the earlier sixties: emotional, rock-bottom, personal truths.

Suddenly, I was no longer learning intellectually what was wrong. I knew. I had had an abortion when I was newly out of college, and had told no one. If one in three

or four adult women shares this experience, why should each of us be made to feel criminal and alone? How much power would we ever have if we had no power over the fate of our own bodies?

I researched as much as I could about reproductive issues and other wellsprings of a new feminism and wrote a respectable, objective article (not one *I* in the whole thing) called "After Black Power, Women's Liberation." It contained none of the emotions I had felt in that church basement, and certainly not the fact that I, too, once had an abortion. (Though hearing those women had made me free to say it for the first time, I still thought that writers were more credible when they concealed their personal experience. I had a lot to learn.) But I did predict that if these younger, more radical women from the peace and civil rights movements could affect what were then the middle-class reformists of the National Organization for Women, and join with poor women already organizing around welfare and child care, a long-lasting and important mass movement would result.

That article would now seem about as new as the air we breathe, but in 1970, a year after its publication, it won a Penney-Missouri Journalism Award as one of the first above-ground reports on this wave of feminism. From my male friends and colleagues, however, it won immediate alarm. Several took me aside kindly: Why was I writing about these crazy women instead of something serious, political, and important? How could I risk identifying myself with women's stuff when I'd worked so hard to get "real" assignments? Interestingly, the same men who had thought working as a Bunny and writing a well-publicized article was just fine for my career were now cautionary about one brief article on a political movement among women.

For the first time, I began to question the honor of being the only "girl reporter" among men, however talented and benevolent they might be. And all the suppressed anger of past experiences I had denied or tried to ignore came flooding back: the apartments I couldn't get because landlords assumed a single woman couldn't pay the rent (or if she could, she must be a hooker); the political assignments lost to younger and less-experienced male writers; the assumption that any work I did get was the result of being a "pretty girl" (even at a time, I suddenly realized, when all of my editors had been women); the lowered payments because women didn't really need the money; the innuendos that came along with any recognition ("easier than you think," was how *Newsweek* had captioned my photograph as a young writer—a quotation that turned out to be from my own statement that freelance writing was "easier than you think"); the well-meaning friends who kept encouraging me to marry any man I was going out with who had talent or money; a lifetime of journalists' jokes about frigid wives, dumb blonds, and farmers' daughters that I had smiled at in order to be "one of the boys."

That was the worst of it, of course—my own capitulation to all the small humiliations, and my own refusal to trust an emotional understanding of what was going on, or even to trust my own experience. For instance, I had believed that women couldn't get along with one another, even while my own most trusted friends were women. I had agreed that women were more "conservative" even while I identified emotionally with every discriminated-against group. I had assumed that women were sexually "masochistic" even though I knew that trust and kindness were indispensable parts of my sexual attraction to any man. It is truly amazing how long we can go on accepting myths that oppose our own lives, assuming instead that we are the odd exceptions. But once the light began to dawn, I couldn't understand why I hadn't figured out any of this before.

I began to read every piece of feminist writing I could lay my hands on, and talk to every active feminist I could find. For the few magazines then interested, I wrote articles that reflected this growing movement: the possibility of a woman president in the White House for *Look*, more columns that commented on sexual politics for *New York*, an essay on "What It Would Be Like If Women Win" that ran with *Time* magazine's sensationalized cover story on Kate Millett, and others. (Though, as I discovered later, I was paid less than male journalists who had written similar *Time* essays—so much for women winning.)

But most magazines said, "Sorry, we published our feminist article last year." Or, "If we publish one article saying women are equal, then we'll have to be objective by publishing one right next to it saying they're not." Editors who had assumed I had some valuable biological insight into food, male movie stars, and textured stockings now questioned whether I or other women writers were biologically capable of writing objectively about feminism.

Responses like those drove me to try speaking instead of writing in order to report the deeper realities that I had first glimpsed the night of that abortion hearing. I began to learn from other women, to figure out the politics of my own life, and to experiment with telling the truth in public. That was the beginning.

But not the end. The first flash of consciousness reveals so much that it seems like the sun coming up. In fact, it's more like a first candle in the dark.

For instance, I could have collected those early profiles and articles long before they were out of date. I also could have attempted a single piece of work that would have been a book in itself. Why did I never do the former? And why, even now, do I continue to resist the latter?

Before feminism, I told myself that my work couldn't possibly be good enough. That excuse concealed the fact that I was still assuming my real identity would come from the man I married, not the work I did. It also kept me from admitting that I was too insecure to attempt a long and lonely piece of work. I needed the reinforcement that comes from short articles frequently published.

Immediately post-consciousness, I noticed that many of my male contemporaries who were felling forests and filling bookstores with their hard-cover works were not better writers than I. Some were much worse. Others had imitative ideas that hardly seemed worth the death of one tree. In the first light of early consciousness, I also noticed that most of them had wives, secretaries, and girlfriends who researched, typed, edited, and said reverential things like, "Shhh, Norman is working." Meanwhile, I felt so "unfeminine" about admitting that I, too, loved and was obsessed with my work that, unlike those male colleagues, I never asked friends and lovers for help with research or other support, and rarely put writing ahead of their social schedules. I never even said firmly, "I want to work." Instead, I shuffled and apologized and said, "I'm terribly sorry, but I have this awful deadline."

Only later did I understand that a need for external emergencies to justify "unfeminine" work is common to many women (a phenomenon also explored in the essay on "The Importance of Work"). In fact, one measure of women's ingenuity may be the wide variety of ways we have found male authority, economic circumstance, or other good reasons to justify doing what we wanted to do anyway. This subterfuge allows us to maintain a passive, "feminine" stance while secretly rebelling. Like most deceptions, it is a gigantic waste of inventiveness and time.

Only much later did I realize that my resistance to undertaking a long piece of work—or to planning far into the future for any goal—was another common symptom of powerlessness. Even after I had stopped assuming that my life would be decided by whatever man I happened to marry (a pretty big "after"), I still had (and have) a hard time saying, "This is where I want to be in five years—or even next year." Class brings to poor men the same feeling of being out of control and subject to the whims of others, though rarely in the same degree as women who are trained to feel subject to the needs of a real or potential husband and children as well as to any lack of money. Writing "The Time Factor," [...], made me understand that planning ahead is a function of caste and class in general, and that I as an individual am just learning.

As old assumptions fall away, each layer of new observation has truth to it. Growing consciousness expands but doesn't negate the vision that went before. For instance, lately I've been wondering, *What is so sacred about a long and continuous piece of writing?* Life isn't always experienced in book-length themes. Shorter forms or a series of insights that surround a subject may be just as useful and give prose more of the economy and depth that poetry has always had. The idea of episodic techniques might release a lot of male writers who now struggle to create lineal and unrealistically neat connections, not to mention all the women writers who must work episodically at their kitchen tables with only a few hours to concentrate until the children come home. After all, spontaneity, flexibility, and a talent for living in the present are the other side of an inability to control our time and to plan. While women are discovering what we need to learn, we shouldn't jettison or undervalue what we already know.

For example, when I'm asked about the rewards and punishments of my life now, I always feel the need to come up with continuous themes and neat conclusions. In fact, I can only think of intense scenes and sense memories. Furthermore, the categories of reward or punishment aren't always clear. Some of the worst punishments turned out to be so instructive that they eventually were rewarding, and some of the supposed rewards are not only punishments but very difficult to complain about. (For instance, sympathies for the problems of becoming well known are about as limited as sympathies for the rich.) Taking an intention to punish at face value, however, here are some scenes from the down side.

- Waking up to the "Today" show and an ad for an exploitation novel that features a scantily clad woman with my hair and glasses slinking toward a table on which there is a necklace with a large feminist symbol, while a male announcer's voice says something like: "The Symbol. She used men ... but preferred women." In fact, this example of "any rebellious woman is a lesbian" turned out to be a useful lesson. Women who hadn't seen lesbianism as a feminist issue before wrote to say they now understood that all women could be stopped or divided by this accusation until we all succeeded in taking the sting out of it by making lesbianism an honorable choice.

- Opening a mass-mailed Christmas letter from a cousin and his wife with the misfortune of having the same last name as mine and, between the news of their fishing trip and other retirement activities, discovering an announcement that they had formally disowned me. As a feminist, I was "disloyal" to God, Man, and Country. Their announcement hurt my mother, but after I discovered they were still segregationists and had been at odds with my suffragist grandmother years before I was born, it began to seem like an honor and a family tradition.

- Watching Al Capp denounce me on television as both the "Shirley Temple of the New Left" and someone comparable to Richard Speck, the sadistic murderer of eight nurses—indeed, he went on to compare all "women's liberation leaders" with "mass murderers"—I guess on the theory that feminism kills women. Later, I discovered that Al Capp's public career was marred by allegations and a lawsuit about his own sexual approaches to young women while he was a frequent speaker on campus. But his words hurt nonetheless.

- Watching Richard Speck explain on television that not *all* the women he had murdered were "like Gloria Steinem." Though he was being interviewed in prison, his women hatred and gynocide are far from unique to him. His words were frightening.

- Being told by the elevator man that another tenant in my office building had said, "I hear Gertrude Stein works in this building. So how come I never see her in the elevator?" At first I thought this was only funny, until I realized that the image of one rebellious woman was being used to include all of us. We all look alike.

- Going to give a speech in Texas and seeing dozens of people outside the amphitheater with signs: GLORIA STEINEM IS A HUMANIST. I thought, *How nice, they must be friends*. But as I got closer and saw the hatred in their faces, I realized they were right-wing pickets to whom *humanist*—or any other word that means a belief in people instead of their authoritarian god—is the worst thing you can be.

- Being consistently opposed by the right (because feminism is "a leftwing plot to destroy the family") and occasionally by the left (because feminism is "a rightwing plot to divide the left"). From this I learned that Feminists Will Be Accused of Everything.

- Being accused both of communist agentry (because I went to two Soviet-sponsored Youth Festivals twenty-four and twenty-one years ago) and government agentry (because Americans who went to them were partly subsidized by foundations that wrongly took funds from the U.S. government). Or being accused of both things as a result of supporting lesbian rights (which have been called the inevitable "anti-family communist plot," and even "an FBI plot to discredit the Women's Movement"). I find such accusations unreasonably painful. They all imply that your mind and your acts are not your own.

- Being said to "use men" to get published, get ahead, even to succeed as a feminist—whatever. Since this accusation is generally leveled at women who succeed in anything, it may be the root cause of all of those above. As long as women who do well in the world are rare, even other women will wrongly assume that they must be following men's orders. The only question then is, *Which* men?

- Seeing displayed on news-stands all over New York a *Screw* magazine centerfold of a woman with my face and glasses, a nude body drawn in labial detail, a collection of carefully drawn penises bordering the page, and a headline instruction to PIN THE COCK ON THE FEMINIST. Feeling helpless and humiliated, I sent a lawyer's letter to *Screw*'s editor Al Goldstein—and got back a box of candy with a note that said "Eat It." Only Bella Abzug's humor rescued me from my depression. When I explained to her about this nude centerfold in full labial detail with my face and head, she deadpanned, "and my labia."

There are, of course, the occasional bomb threats designed to clear the hall (generally phoned in by a self-described "Right-to-Lifer"), the hurtful articles you learn not to read because you can do nothing about them, the frustration at not being able to retain the legal rights to your own life, and the anger at seeing survival issues ridiculed or misunderstood. There is also the great reward of working full time at something I care about so much that I would do it for no money at all, plus the problems of making far less money than would be possible outside a social movement. The last would be okay if "rich and famous" weren't one phrase. Being resented for money that doesn't *exist* is not a great combination. Still, all of the punishments are somehow easier to describe than the rewards that mean much more. Perhaps women are more accustomed to singing the blues—even to using humor as a palliative for rage—than to victories and celebrations. In fact, there are many scenes and sense memories of emotional and factual rewards.

- Listening to five women say they have jobs they love that wouldn't have been open to them without feminism—a pregnant flight attendant, a fire-fighter, the highest woman official in New York State, a union carpenter, and the first female astronaut—and hearing all of these in one day.

- Being stopped in the street by a truck driver who tells me that the woman he loves and has been living with for three years wouldn't marry him or have children because he didn't want her to go on working; then he heard some interview in which I asked men to consider how they would feel if they were exactly the same people but had been born female. He tried this exercise for a while, and changed so much that he and his friend were now happily married. He is thanking me—but the miracle is his own empathy.

- Seeing every day on my way to work a middle-aged black woman traffic cop who is the Toscanini of Manhattan's busiest intersection, who smiles at me and says "Give 'em hell," and leaves me with an unreasonable feeling of womanpride and well-being.

- Discovering that my excellent dentist has retired and left his practice to a calm, equally excellent young woman.

- Going on a speaking tour of Minnesota, from the Iron Range to farming villages, and finding that each church basement and school gym is full of women and men who matter-of-factly refer to themselves as feminists.

- Speaking at campuses that students warn me are "conservative" or "apathetic," and finding Women's Studies, clerical workers organizing, demonstrations against local porn theaters, a rape hot line, the beginning of child care for students and faculty, a partnership between women students and professors—all things that probably weren't there ten or even five years ago.

- Meeting a midwestern Catholic priest who prays to "God the Mother" as some reparation for five thousand years of patriarchy and who invites me to preach the homily from the pulpit; reading public statements by nuns who oppose their bishops' position against abortion; hearing a woman rabbi and a woman cantor who conduct a beautiful and inclusive memorial service for the death of a friend's mother in New York; meeting a woman Episcopalian priest in Washington who broke the barriers for herself and others with an ecclesiastical lawsuit; finding schools and Bible classes that honor as martyrs the millions of women burned as witches for resisting a cruel and patriarchal god.
- Getting on planes whose flight attendants tell me about their latest lawsuit, seat me in first class though I have a tourist ticket, come to lectures in strange cities, volunteer for lobbying, and send me home with slips of paper to remind me that they need news of this or that issue or the address of the nearest feminist group.
- Hearing over and over again "Feminism saved my life," or "Thank you for my mother," or "I understand my wife better now," or "My daughter will be what I never could have been," and being constantly entrusted with the personal gratitude and triumphs of strangers.
- Sitting in an ethnic hall in Detroit, at a local celebration of *Ms.* magazine's tenth birthday,

and being tapped on the shoulder by a small, gray-haired woman with gnarled, hardworking hands and a starched cotton housedress that is clearly her best. "I just want you to know," she says softly, "that you are the inside of me." All reward came together in one moment. Remembering now that woman's touch and words, I still feel the tears behind my eyes.

I used to have a recurring dream. I was fighting with one person or many people, struggling and kicking and hitting as hard as I could because they were trying to kill me or to hurt someone I loved. I fought with all my strength, as fiercely as I could, harder and harder; but no matter what I did, I couldn't hurt any of them. No matter how hard I fought, they just smiled.

In the 1970s, I told this dream to some other women and discovered that they shared similar emotions. My dream was a classic scenario of anger, humiliation, and powerlessness.

Sometime in the 1980s, I stopped having the dream. Thinking of that woman in Detroit, I realize now that I associate its disappearance with her words. They crystallized in one moment what women can do and are doing. We are offering each other a new and compassionate kind of power.

In fact, women and men have begun to rescue one another in many ways, large and small. [I hope that you will find a rescuing moment or fact or idea within the pages of this book.]

—New York City, 1983

Notes

1. There were two semibooks: *The Thousand Indias*, a guidebook I wrote for the Indian government while on a fellowship there in 1957 and 1958, but never published here; and *The Beach Book* (Viking, 1963), which was my anthology but mostly other people's writing.

2. "What's in It for Me," *Harper's*, November 1965, 169.

Womanist: A Letter to the Editor of *MS*

Alice Walker

I realized at the National Black Feminist Organization conference that it had been much too long since I sat in a room full of black women and, unafraid of being made to feel peculiar, spoke about things that matter to me. We sat together and talked and knew no one would think, or say, "Your thoughts are dangerous to black unity and a threat to black men." Instead, all the women understood that we gathered together to assure understanding among black women, and that understanding among women is not a threat to anyone who intends to treat women fairly. So the air was clear and rang with earnest voices freed at last to speak to ears that would not automatically begin to close. And then to hear Shirley Chisholm speak: to feel all of history compressed into a few minutes and to sing "We love Shirley!"—a rousing indication of our caring that we could not give to Sojourner Truth or Harriet Tubman or Mary McLeod Bethune. To see her so small, so impeccable in dress, in speech, and in logic, and so very black, and to think of her running for President of this country, which has, in every single age, tried to destroy her. It was as if, truly, the faces of those other women were just beneath the skin of Shirley Chisholm's face. And later, at the same general meeting, being one among and with all those black women, I thought of all the questions about us I have been asking myself.

For four or five years I have been watching the faces of young black men and women as they emerge from the movie houses of this city, their faces straight from Southern black homes and families, which means *upright, Christian, striving* homes with mothers and fathers who are shown respect. I've watched them, innocence and determination to grow mingling in their bodies, respond to images of black women and men they never have seen before. Watched them stagger, slink, or strut away from the Sweetback flicks ... a doomed look on the faces of the young women, a cruelty or a look of disgust beginning behind the innocence on the faces of the young men. And I have asked myself: Who will stop this slinging of mud on the character of the black woman? Who will encourage the tenderness that seeks to blossom in young black men? Who will stand up and say, "Black women, at least, have had enough!" And I began to feel, at the conference, that, yes, there are black women who will do that.

And I looked again at Shirley Chisholm's face (which I had never seen before except on television) and was glad she has kept a record of her political and social struggles, because our great women die, often in poverty and under the weight of slander, and are soon forgotten. And I thought of how little we have studied any of our ancestors, but how close to zero has been our study of those who were female ... and I have asked myself: Who will secure from neglect and slander those women who have kept our image as black women clean and strong for us? And at the conference, I met women who are eager to do this job.

And of course I thought of Frederick Douglass. And knew that *his* newspaper would have been pleased to cover our conference, because we are black and we are women and because we intend to be as free as anyone. He understood that it is not incumbent upon the slave to make sure her or his uprising is appropriate or "correct." It is the nature of the oppressed to rise against oppression. Period. Women who wanted their rights did not frighten him, politically or socially, because he knew his own rights were not diminished by theirs. I'm sure he would have sent someone from his newspaper to see what things—abortion, sterilization, welfare rights, women in the black movement, black women in the arts, and so forth—we were talking about. I don't think he would have understood—any more than I do—why no representatives from black magazines and newspapers came. Are not black women black news?

And then, when I came home, I stood looking at a picture of Frederick Douglass I have on my wall. And I asked myself: Where is your picture of Harriet Tubman, the General? Where is your drawing of Sojourner Truth? And I thought that if black women would only start asking questions like that, they'd soon—all of them—have to begin reclaiming their mothers and grandmothers—and what an enrichment that would be!

When we look back over our history it is clear that we have neglected to save just those people who could help us most. Because no matter what anyone says, it is the black woman's words that have the most meaning for us, her daughters, because she, like us, has experienced life not only as a black person, but as a woman; and it was *different* being Frederick Douglass than being Harriet Tubman—or Sojourner Truth, who

only "looked like a man," but bore children and saw them sold into slavery.

I thought of the black women writers and poets whose books—even today—go out of print while other works about all of us, less valuable if more "profitable," survive to insult us with their half-perceived, half-rendered "truths." How simple a thing it seems to me that to know ourselves as we are, we must know our mothers' names. Yet, we do not know them. Or if we do, it is only the names we know and not the lives.

And I thought of the mountain of work black women must do. We must work as if we are the last generation capable of work—for it is true that the view we have of the significance of the past will undoubtedly die with us, and future generations will have to stumble in the dark, over ground we should have covered.

Someone claimed, rhetorically, that we are the only "true queens of the universe." I do not want to be a queen, because queens are oppressive, but even so the thought came to me that any true queen knows the names, words, and actions of the other queens of her lineage and is very sharp about her herstory. I think we might waive the wearing of a crown until we have at least seriously begun our work.

I thought about friends of mine whose views do not differ very much from mine, but who decided not to come to the conference because of fear. Fear of criticism from other black people (who, I assume, consider silence a sign of solidarity), and fear of the presence of lesbians. The criticism will no doubt be forthcoming, but what can one do about that? Nothing, but continue to work. As for the lesbians—a black lesbian would undoubtedly be a black woman. That seems simple enough. In any case, I only met other black women, my sisters, and valuable beyond measuring, every one of them.

And we talked and we discussed and we sang for Shirley Chisholm and clapped for Eleanor Holmes Norton and tried to follow Margaret Sloan's lyrics and cheered Flo Kennedy's anecdotes. And we laughed a lot and argued some. *And had a very good time.*

1974

Note

Womanist

1. From *womanish*. (Opp. of "girlish," i.e., frivolous, irresponsible, not serious.) A black feminist or feminist of color. From the black folk expression of mothers to female children, "You acting womanish," i.e., like a woman. Usually referring to outrageous, audacious, courageous, or *willful* behavior. Wanting to know more and in greater depth than is considered "good" for one. Interested in grown-up doings. Acting grown up. Being grown up. Interchangeable with another black folk expression: "You trying to be grown." Responsible. In charge. *Serious.*

2. *Also:* A woman who loves other women, sexually and/or nonsexually. Appreciates and prefers women's culture, women's emotional flexibility (values tears as natural counterbalance of laughter), and women's strength. Sometimes loves individual men, sexually and/or nonsexually. Committed to survival and wholeness of entire people, male *and* female. Not a separatist, except periodically, for health. Traditionally universalist, as in: "Mama, why are we brown, pink, and yellow, and our cousins are white, beige, and black?" Ans.: "Well, you know the colored race is just like a flower garden, with *every* color flower represented." Traditionally capable, as in: "Mama, I'm walking to Canada and I'm taking you and a bunch of other slaves with me." Reply: "It wouldn't be the first time."

3. Loves music. Loves dance. Loves the moon. *Loves* the Spirit. Loves love and food and roundness. Loves struggle. *Loves* the Folk. Loves herself. *Regardless.*

4. Womanist is to feminist as purple to lavender.

Feminism: A Transformational Politic

bell hooks

We live in a world in crisis—a world governed by politics of domination, one in which the belief in a notion of superior and inferior, and its concomitant ideology—that the superior should rule over the inferior—affects the lives of all people everywhere, whether poor or privileged, literate or illiterate. Systematic dehumanization, worldwide famine, ecological devastation, industrial contamination, and the possibility of nuclear destruction are realities which remind us daily that we are in crisis. Contemporary feminist thinkers often cite sexual politics as the origin of this crisis. They point to the insistence on difference as that factor which becomes the occasion for separation and domination and suggest that differentiation of status between females and males globally is an indication that patriarchal domination of the planet is the root of the problem. Such an assumption has fostered the notion that elimination of sexist oppression would necessarily lead to the eradication of all forms of domination. It is an argument that has led influential Western white women to feel that feminist movement should be *the* central political agenda for females globally. Ideologically, thinking in this direction enables Western women, especially privileged white women, to suggest that racism and class exploitation are merely the offspring of the parent system: patriarchy. Within feminist movement in the West, this has led to the assumption that resisting patriarchal domination is a more legitimate feminist action than resisting racism and other forms of domination. Such thinking prevails despite radical critiques made by black women and other women of color who question this proposition. To speculate that an oppositional division between men and women existed in early human communities is to impose on the past, on these non-white groups, a world view that fits all too neatly within contemporary feminist paradigms that name man as the enemy and woman as the victim.

Clearly, differentiation between strong and weak, powerful and powerless, has been a central defining aspect of gender globally, carrying with it the assumption that men should have greater authority than women, and should rule over them. As significant and important as this fact is, it should not obscure the reality that women can and do participate in politics of domination, as perpetrators as well as victims—that we dominate, that we are dominated. If focus on patriarchal domination masks this reality or becomes the means by which women deflect attention from the real conditions and circumstances of our lives, then women cooperate in suppressing and promoting false consciousness, inhibiting our capacity to assume responsibility for transforming ourselves and society.

Thinking speculatively about early human social arrangement, about women and men struggling to survive in small communities, it is likely that the parent-child relationship with its very real imposed survival structure of dependency, of strong and weak, of powerful and powerless, was a site for the construction of a paradigm of domination. While this circumstance of dependency is not necessarily one that leads to domination, it lends itself to the enactment of a social drama wherein domination could easily occur as a means of exercising and maintaining control. This speculation does not place women outside the practice of domination, in the exclusive role of victim. It centrally names women as agents of domination, as potential theoreticians, and creators of a paradigm for social relationships wherein those groups of individuals designated as "strong" exercise power both benevolently and coercively over those designated as "weak."

Emphasizing paradigms of domination that call attention to woman's capacity to dominate is one way to deconstruct and challenge the simplistic notion that man is the enemy, woman the victim; the notion that men have always been the oppressors. Such thinking enables us to examine our role as women in the perpetuation and maintenance of systems of domination. To understand domination, we must understand that our capacity as women and men to be either dominated or dominating is a point of connection, of commonality. Even though I speak from the particular experience of living as a black woman in the United States, a white-supremacist, capitalist, patriarchal society, where small numbers of white men (and honorary "white men") constitute ruling groups, I understand that in many places in the world oppressed and oppressor share the same color. I understand that right here in this room, oppressed and oppressor share the same gender. Right now as I speak, a man who is himself victimized, wounded, hurt by racism and class exploitation is actively dominating a woman in his life—that even as I speak, women who are ourselves exploited, victimized, are dominating children. It is necessary for us to remember, as we think critically about domination, that we all have the capacity to act in ways that oppress, dominate, wound (whether or not that power is institutionalized). It is necessary to remember that it is first the potential oppressor within that we must resist—the potential victim within that we must rescue—otherwise we cannot hope for an end to domination, for liberation.

This knowledge seems especially important at this historical moment when black women and other women of color have worked to create awareness of the ways in which racism empowers white women to act as exploiters and oppressors. Increasingly this fact is considered a reason we should not support feminist struggle even though sexism and sexist oppression is a real issue in our lives as black women (see, for example, Vivian Gordon's *Black Women, Feminism, Black Liberation: Which Way?*). It becomes necessary for us to speak continually about the convictions that inform our continued advocacy of feminist struggle. By calling attention to interlocking systems of domination—sex, race, and class—black women and many other groups of women acknowledge the diversity and complexity of female experience, of our relationship to power and domination. The intent is not to dissuade people of color from becoming engaged in feminist movement. Feminist struggle to end patriarchal domination should be of primary importance to women and men globally not because it is the foundation of all other oppressive structures but because it is that form of domination we are most likely to encounter in an ongoing way in everyday life.

Unlike other forms of domination, sexism directly shapes and determines relations of power in our private lives, in familiar social spaces, in that most intimate context—home—and in that most intimate sphere of relations—family. Usually, it is within the family that we witness coercive domination and learn to accept it, whether it be domination of parent over child, or male over female. Even though family relations may be, and most often are, informed by acceptance of a politic of domination, they are simultaneously relations of care and connection. It is this convergence of two contradictory impulses—the urge to promote growth and the urge to inhibit growth—that provides a practical setting for feminist critique, resistance, and transformation.

Growing up in a black, working-class, father-dominated household, I experienced coercive adult male authority as more immediately threatening, as more likely to cause immediate pain than racist oppression or class exploitation. It was equally clear that experiencing exploitation and oppression in the home made one feel all the more powerless when encountering dominating forces outside the home. This is true for many people. If we are unable to resist and end domination in relations where there is care, it seems totally unimaginable that we can resist and end it in other institutionalized relations of power. If we cannot convince the mothers and/or fathers who care not to humiliate and degrade us, how can we imagine convincing or resisting an employer, a lover, a stranger who systematically humiliates and degrades?

Feminist effort to end patriarchal domination should be of primary concern precisely because it insists on the eradication of exploitation and oppression in the family context and in all other intimate relationships. It is that political movement which most radically addresses the person—the personal—citing the need for transformation of self, of relationships, so that we might be better able to act in a revolutionary manner, challenging and resisting domination, transforming the world outside the self. Strategically, feminist movement should be a central component of all other liberation struggles because it challenges each of us to alter our person, our personal engagement (either as victims or perpetrators or both) in a system of domination.

Feminism, as liberation struggle, must exist apart from and as a part of the larger struggle to eradicate domination in all its forms. We must understand that patriarchal domination shares an ideological foundation with racism and other forms of group oppression, that there is no hope that it can be eradicated while these systems remain intact. This knowledge should consistently inform the direction of feminist theory and practice. Unfortunately, racism and class elitism among women has frequently led to the suppression and distortion of this connection so that it is now necessary for feminist thinkers to critique and revise much feminist theory and the direction of feminist movement. This effort at revision is perhaps most evident in the current widespread acknowledgement that sexism, racism, and class exploitation constitute interlocking systems of domination—that sex, race, and class, and not sex alone, determine the nature of any female's identity, status, and circumstance, the degree to which she will or will not be dominated, the extent to which she will have the power to dominate.

While acknowledgement of the complex nature of woman's status (which has been most impressed upon everyone's consciousness by radical women of color) is a significant corrective, it is only a starting point. It provides a frame of reference which must serve as the basis for thoroughly altering and revising feminist theory and practice. It challenges and calls us to re-think popular assumptions about the nature of feminism that have had the deepest impact on a large majority of women, on mass consciousness. It radically calls into question the notion of a fundamentally common female experience which has been seen as the prerequisite for our coming together, for political unity. Recognition of the inter-connectedness of sex, race, and class highlights the diversity of experience, compelling redefinition of the terms for unity. If women do not share "common oppression," what then can serve as a basis for our coming together?

Unlike many feminist comrades, I believe women and men must share a common understanding—a basic knowledge of what feminism is—if it is ever to be a powerful mass-based political movement. In *Feminist Theory: From Margin to Center*, I suggest that defining feminism broadly as "a movement to end sexism and sexist oppression" would enable us to have a common political goal. We would then have a basis on which to build solidarity. Multiple and contradictory definitions of feminism create confusion and undermine the effort to construct feminist movement so that it addresses everyone. Sharing a common goal does not imply that women and men will not have radically divergent perspectives on how that goal might be reached. Because each individual starts the process of engagement in feminist struggle at a unique level of awareness, very real differences in experience, perspective, and knowledge make developing varied strategies for participation and transformation a necessary agenda.

Feminist thinkers engaged in radically revisioning central tenets of feminist thought must continually emphasize the importance of sex, race, and class as factors which *together* determine the social construction of femaleness, as it has been so deeply ingrained in the consciousness of many women active in feminist movement that gender is the sole factor determining destiny. However, the work of education for critical consciousness (usually called consciousness-raising) cannot end there. Much feminist consciousness-raising has in the past focussed on identifying the particular ways men oppress and exploit women. Using the paradigm of sex, race, and class means that the focus does not begin with men and what they do to women, but rather with women working to identify both individually and collectively the specific character of our social identity.

Imagine a group of women from diverse backgrounds coming together to talk about feminism. First they concentrate on working out their status in terms of sex, race, and class using this as the standpoint from which they begin discussing patriarchy or their particular relations with individual men. Within the old frame of reference, a discussion might consist solely of talk about their experiences as victims in relationship to male oppressors. Two women—one poor, the other quite wealthy—might describe the process by which they have suffered physical abuse by male partners and find certain commonalities which might serve as a basis for bonding. Yet if these same two women engaged in a discussion of class, not only would the social construction and expression of femaleness differ, so too would their ideas about how to confront and change their circumstances. Broadening the discussion to include an analysis of race and class would expose many additional differences even as commonalities emerged.

Clearly the process of bonding would be more complex, yet this broader discussion might enable the sharing of perspectives and strategies for change that would enrich rather than diminish our understanding of gender. While feminists have increasingly given "lip service" to the idea of diversity, we have not developed strategies of communication and inclusion that allow for the successful enactment of this feminist vision.

Small groups are no longer the central place for feminist consciousness-raising. Much feminist education for critical consciousness takes place in Women's Studies classes or at conferences which focus on gender. Books are a primary source of education, which means that already masses of people who do not read have no access. The separation of grassroots ways of sharing feminist thinking across kitchen tables from the spheres where much of that thinking is generated, the academy, undermines feminist movement. It would further feminist movement if new feminist thinking could be once again shared in small group contexts, integrating critical analysis with discussion of personal experience. It would be useful to promote anew the small group setting as an arena for education for critical consciousness, so that women and men might come together in neighborhoods and communities to discuss feminist concerns.

Small groups remain an important place for education for critical consciousness for several reasons. An especially important aspect of the small group setting is the emphasis on communicating feminist thinking, feminist theory, in a manner that can be easily understood. In small groups, individuals do not need to be equally literate or literate at all because the information is primarily shared through conversation, in dialogue which is necessarily a liberatory expression. (Literacy should be a goal for feminists even as we ensure that it not become a requirement for participation in feminist education.) Reforming small groups would subvert the appropriation of feminist thinking by a select group of academic women and men, usually white, usually from privileged class backgrounds.

Small groups of people coming together to engage in feminist discussion, in dialectical struggle make a space where the "personal is political" as a starting point for education for critical consciousness can be extended to include politicization of the self that focuses on creating understanding of the ways sex, race, and class together determine our individual lot and our collective experience. It would further feminist movement if many well-known feminist thinkers would participate in small groups, critically re-examining ways their works might be changed by incorporating broader perspectives. All efforts at self-transformation challenge us to engage in ongoing, critical self-examination and reflection about feminist practice, about how we live in the world. This individual commitment, when coupled with engagement in collective discussion, provides a space for critical feedback which strengthens our efforts to change and make ourselves new. It is in this commitment to feminist principles in our words and deeds that the hope of feminist revolution lies.

Working collectively to confront difference, to expand our awareness of sex, race, and class as interlocking systems of domination, of the ways we reinforce and perpetuate these structures, is the context in which we learn the true meaning of solidarity. It is this work that must be the foundation of feminist movement. Without it, we cannot effectively resist patriarchal domination; without it, we remain estranged and alienated from one another. Fear of painful confrontation often leads women and men active in feminist movement to avoid rigorous critical encounter, yet if we cannot engage dialectically in a committed, rigorous, humanizing manner, we cannot hope to change the world. True politicization—coming to critical consciousness—is a difficult, "trying" process, one that demands that we give up set ways of thinking and being, that we shift our paradigms, that we open ourselves to the unknown, the unfamiliar. Undergoing this process, we learn what it means to struggle and in this effort we experience the dignity and integrity of being that comes with revolutionary change. If we do not change our consciousness, we cannot change our actions or demand change from others.

Our renewed commitment to a rigorous process of education for critical consciousness will determine the shape and direction of future feminist movement. Until new perspectives are created, we cannot be living symbols of the power of feminist thinking. Given the privileged lot of many leading feminist thinkers, both in terms of status, class, and race, it is harder these days to convince women of the primacy of this process of politicization. More and more, we seem to form select interest groups composed of individuals who share similar perspectives. This limits our capacity to engage in critical discussion. It is difficult to involve women in new processes of feminist politicization because so many of us think that identifying men as the enemy, resisting male domination, gaining equal access to power and privilege is the end of feminist movement. Not only is it not the end, it is not even the place we want revitalized feminist movement to begin. We want to begin as women seriously addressing ourselves, not solely in relation to men, but in relation to an entire structure of domination of which patriarchy is one part. While the struggle to eradicate sexism and sexist oppression is and should be the primary thrust of feminist movement, to prepare ourselves politically for this effort we must first learn how to be in solidarity, how to struggle with one another.

Only when we confront the realities of sex, race, and class, the ways they divide us, make us different, stand us in opposition, and work to reconcile and resolve these issues will we be able to participate in the making of feminist revolution, in the transformation of the world. Feminism, as Charlotte Bunch emphasizes again and again in *Passionate Politics*, is a transformational politics, a struggle against domination wherein the effort is to change ourselves as well as structures. Speaking about the struggle to confront difference, Bunch asserts:

> A crucial point of the process is understanding that reality does not look the same from different people's perspective. It is not surprising that one way feminists have come to understand about differences has been through the love of a person from another culture or race. It takes persistence and motivation—which love often engenders—to get beyond one's ethnocentric assumptions and really learn about other perspectives. In this process and while seeking to eliminate oppression, we also discover new possibilities and insights that come from the experience and survival of other peoples.

Embedded in the commitment to feminist revolution is the challenge to love. Love can be and is an important source of empowerment when we struggle to confront issues of sex, race, and class. Working together to identify and face our differences—to face the ways we dominate and are dominated—to change our actions, we need a mediating force that can sustain us so that we are not broken in this process, so that we do not despair.

Not enough feminist work has focused on documenting and sharing ways individuals confront differences constructively and successfully. Women and men need to know what is on the other side of the pain experienced in politicization. We need detailed accounts of the ways our lives are fuller and richer as we change and grow politically, as we learn to live each moment as committed feminists, as comrades working to end domination. In reconceptualizing and reformulating strategies for future feminist movement, we need to concentrate on the politicization of love, not just in the context of talking about victimization in intimate relationships, but in a critical discussion where love can be understood as a powerful force that challenges and resists domination. As we work to be loving, to create a culture that celebrates life, that makes love possible, we move against dehumanization, against domination. In *Pedagogy of the Oppressed*, Paulo Freire evokes this power of love, declaring:

> I am more and more convinced that true revolutionaries must perceive the revolution, because of its creative and liberating nature, as an act of love. For me, the revolution, which is not possible without a theory of revolution—and therefore science—is not irreconcilable with love .... The distortion imposed on the word "love" by the capitalist world cannot prevent the revolution from being essentially loving in character, nor can it prevent the revolutionaries from affirming their love of life.

That aspect of feminist revolution that calls women to love womanness, that calls men to resist dehumanizing concepts of masculinity, is an essential part of our struggle. It is the process by which we move from seeing ourselves as objects to acting as subjects. When women and men understand that working to eradicate patriarchal domination is a struggle rooted in the longing to make a world where everyone can live fully and freely, then we know our work to be a gesture of love. Let us draw upon that love to heighten our awareness, deepen our compassion, intensify our courage, and strengthen our commitment.

Why Are You a Feminist?[*]

Samantha Sacks

"Oh, so you're in university ...."
The eyes of those professing interest in my occupation light up; the prospect of an interesting area of study, maybe something they know. Hey, perhaps they think they can teach me a little, tell me what it was like in the good old days.

"What's your major?" asks my new-found friend.

And while the potential for sparkling conversation still lingers sweetly in the air (I can almost hear the clinking of good cutlery and wine glasses), I alone have the seasoned prescience of a thousand encounters of an identical nature to know that momentarily I will squash out any titillating *tête-à-tête* with the oppressive weight of my major ....

"Women's Studies."

And of course, a glassy-eyed stare settles over my partner's face. Sometimes it conveys condescending humour, sometimes hate, sometimes astonishment, sometimes indifference spliced with ignorance. The combinations are endless. If I were to mix the ingredients of these myriad gawks and gapes and leers, I could make a vicious cocktail, as the one thing these ogles have in common is their absence of genuine interest.

Regardless, I will still be asked to testify on my own behalf ....

"WHY ARE YOU A FEMINIST?"

And this is what I will say ....

Because at the dawn of a new century we have so much death in our lives. Nature struggles to catch its breath. The earth heaves gently as the last drops of juice are sucked from its bowels. Sanitized lives hang leaden in the hot, rotting air. Intolerance seeps into our kitchens through radioactive TV screens. Breastless women, their faces lit with the gaunt glow of chemotherapy, cruise florescent supermarket aisles, where delicacies from the four corners of the earth meet in prepared meals, elegantly displayed on styrofoam trays—microwave-ready cultural diversity. The first oxygen bar opens in Toronto and with AIDS comes the death of love.

Because the only security I feel leaving my home at night comes from countless self-defense courses. Because my body is qualified, quantified, valued, and valueless; bought and sold on every street corner and television advertisement that invades my solitude—on purpose. Because where would we be without hysteria? Without anxiety we may be able to get a grip, our claws in,

* First published in CWS/cf's Spring 1997 issue, "Bridging North and South: Patterns of Transformation" (Volume 17, Number 2).

perhaps, to reality, or the power structures that comprise it.

Because our lives are histories. The culmination of a thousand stories, myths, and oracles; recorded over many thousands of years by the most prestigious members of the most powerful societies, throughout time—as they see it. A myopic vision, a false prophecy. Where am I in your history? I look in the mirror, craning my neck to see past a distorted body image, a castrated, manipulated sexual identity, to see myself. But you built the chrome and glass and you can't see me. In this world I don't count unless I raise my fucking voice.

"WHY ARE YOU A FEMINIST?"

Recently I was asked this question in a very different context. I was in Honduras and had the opportunity to interview a group of women called "*Las Amas de Casa*," or "The Mistresses of the Home" or "The Housewives." It is a community group comprised of women whose husbands immigrated illegally to the United States to find work. For the most part their husbands found work, new wives, and new families. *Las Amas de Casa* is a group of single mothers. They secure latrines for their homes, build schools, and organize technical training programs.

After a thousand different questions from me regarding the role of feminism in Honduras, the relevancy of academics, and who they would or would not accept money from, and under which circumstances, the group's leader, Gloria Reina Santos Montes, asked me with a cold stare why I am a feminist.

And this is what I said ….

Feminism is about change, about a redistribution of power. It is about challenging the status quo. It is call for the redefinition of the family, the mosque, the temple, the church, the synagogue, and of love. Change is threatening to those of us who wield power and those who do not. And because it is threatening, it is electric and alive and powerful and I want to touch it.

And Gloria Reina Santos Montes stared at me, from her world that looked like Eden fixed between a garbage dump and a Coca-Cola billboard, and said (and I paraphrase) ….

"I don't care what you call it, I just want to feed my babies and maybe someday shit in a toilet."

Then the world stands still. The earth stops spinning, the sun shines in one single long ray and except for my pulse throbbing gently in my ears, silence is everywhere. For a wrinkle in time I'm breathless and speechless and I want to puke because no matter how many post-colonial, post-modern binary pedagogies I suck from the lily white asshole of some underexposed academic, YOU CAN'T THEORIZE BREAKFAST.

Hungry children are not concerned with political nuances.

Where is the value of my course in Strategic Adjustment Policy in this land where the American-owned Standard Fruit Company is mother's milk, the juice of life, fueling the Honduran economy while matricide pulses through the blood of the people? Who do I think I am in this wild west armed only with a university degree?

And Gloria Reina Santos Montes and I lock eyes and I recognize what it is I have seen in her stare from the moment we met. She knows me. She was expecting my armament of questions, my textbook sensitivity. She has merely been watching to see if I will recognize myself. If I will catch a glimpse of my reflection in the mirrors that are her eyes.

And now that I have, what will I do? Will I escape from this parallel universe, slinking away, tail between my legs in search of a more comfortable reality? Will I return to fill my head with someone else's words? Until I forget the hot green stink of the earth and those omniscient eyes, my thoughts sterilized and sanitized, my brain rocked into an academic stupor by the embryonic lull of saniflush? Or perhaps I will go home to twist and bend and shape my words until, like bulimic consumption and eruption of meaning, I can purge my mixed-up self. And pass it on to you.

So as I stand before you, my bones racked with the ache of expulsion, perhaps we can build a bridge, or do something lyrical and metaphorical and uplifting. That will make us all feel better. Conflict resolution. Or closure, or some such thing.

Or maybe, for a brief moment, we will take a breath between the spewing forth of academic bile. Because if somebody says the word "problematic" one more time, I'm going to scream. A silent beat between syllables. In our ugly language, our long vowels that reek of imperialism. We will stop and shiver as a gust of reality makes this comfortably heated room seem cold. And know ourselves.

And now the shimmering edges between questions and answers become blurred, wavering in the stifling heat of revelation. And I'm still wondering ....

WHY AM I A FEMINIST?

Women Who Run from the Wolves: Feminist Critique As Post-Feminism

Anne-Marie Kinahan

For some time now I have been intrigued by the discourses on post-feminism consistently articulated within popular media. In an attempt to interrogate and understand the rise of this post-feminist movement, this essay discusses three of the most popular treatments of the topic: René Denfeld's *The New Victorians* (1995), Katie Roiphe's *The Morning After* (1993), and Christina Hoff Sommers's *Who Stole Feminism?* (1994). Specifically concerned with how these works define feminism, how they articulate the "crisis" of the movement, and what solutions they propose, I am interested in uncovering what is at stake in these debates. The similarities between these books (all published in the early 1990s, all discussing campus feminism, all written by feminist-identified, university-educated women) allow for an assessment of how these young, white, well-educated women position themselves against a movement once thought to be theirs alone. While each author claims to offer insight into the current crisis facing feminism, it is my contention that, collectively, these works signal a fear of the perceived radicalism of feminism on university campuses, a radicalism which these authors attribute to the increasing influence of queer theory, "radical" lesbians, and feminists of colour. These fears over the potential radicalization of young women

belie a concern over the loss of literary and canonical traditions, as well as an attendant concern over the legacy of the university as a cultural, intellectual, and social institution.

In *The New Victorians*, René Denfeld (1995) argues that contemporary feminism has fallen victim to a repressive ideology reminiscent of Victorian feminism. Essentially concerned with explaining the reasons why so many young women feel alienated from contemporary feminism, Denfeld launches an analysis that discusses victimology, date rape, pornography, women's studies courses, and feminist activism on university campuses. Articulating the current crisis facing feminism, Denfeld defines herself and others of her generation as feminist: "That my generation has taken the women's movement to heart is illustrated by the numbers. We don't believe in sexual inequality, and we don't believe in confining ourselves—or one another—to traditional sex roles. Simply put, we are feminist—in action, if not in name" (5). Denfeld asserts that feminism has undergone a radical change. It is no longer about equality, rights, and justice but has "become bogged down in an extremist moral and spiritual crusade that has little to do with women's lives. It has climbed out on a limb of academic theory that is all but inaccessible to the uninitiated" (5).

Arguing that there are two different types of women's movements today, Denfeld articulates the crisis with which feminist academics have struggled over the past few years: the discrepancy between women's lives and feminist inquiry and critique. As expressed by Denfeld, one women's movement is cultural, characterized by magazines such as *Glamour* and populated by young, independent women who shirk the feminist label. The reasons for this reticence in embracing feminism, according to Denfeld, is the existence of the "other" women's movement characterized by the National Organization of Women (NOW), feminist leaders, and women's studies courses. This "other" feminism is ideological, organized, radical, and distanced from the everyday lives of American women (5–6).

While feminist academics have addressed these concerns seriously and with great commitment in the hope of overcoming divisions with feminism (see Hennessy; hooks; Modelski; Moraga and Anzaldúa), Denfeld characterizes the discrepancy as a fundamental flaw within contemporary feminism. Her critique focuses on issues of sexuality, arguing that contemporary feminism has lost devotees because it is repressive, puritanical, and moralistic. The emphasis on issues such as sexual harassment, sexual violence, date rape, and pornography by feminists like Andrea Dworkin and Catharine MacKinnon has created a climate of fear and victimization. Denfeld asserts that this is further reinforced in women's studies courses that discuss lesbianism as a political choice and offer critiques of the social construction of patriarchy and heterosexuality.

Katie Roiphe's *The Morning After: Sex, Fear and Feminism on Campus* (1993) has been the subject of much discussion among feminist academics, journalists, and scholars. Decrying the loss of sexual freedom and the increasing co-mingling of fear and sexuality, Roiphe analyzes the ways that feminism on campus has contributed to this climate of fear and victimization. Controversial for her questioning of date rape statistics,

Roiphe's analysis is really quite polemical, personal, and not particularly scholarly. She argues that feminism has become the domain of extremist radicals and, like Denfeld, asserts that it has little or no connection to the lives of contemporary women. Ostensibly a lament for the lost days of sexual freedom, *The Morning After* attributes the climate of fear and danger around sexuality to feminist activism on issues such as date rape, sexual violence, pornography, and sexual harassment. Like Denfeld, she also asserts that feminism on campus is closely connected to Victorian feminism, promulgating the perception of women as victimized, powerless, and in need of protection. Also defining herself as feminist, Roiphe argues that feminism should be helping women to become sexually assertive, self-possessed, and responsible; instead, it is fostering a climate in which women learn to be afraid.

Christina Hoff Sommers's *Who Stole Feminism? How Women Have Betrayed Women* (1994), like *The New Victorians* and *The Morning After*, argues that feminism has become too radical and extreme for many American women. The most comprehensive and scholarly of the books under consideration, *Who Stole Feminism?* critiques the climate of repression and political correctness on campuses and argues that women's studies courses, "Take Back the Night" marches, and feminist activism have alienated scores of women from the traditional feminist movement. Like Denfeld and, to a lesser extent, Roiphe, Hoff Sommers postulates the existence of two types of feminism, which she terms "equity" feminism and "gender" feminism:

Most American women subscribe philosophically to that older "First Wave" kind of feminism whose main goal is equity, especially in politics and education. A First Wave, "mainstream," or "equity" feminist wants for women what she wants for everyone: fair treatment, without discrimination. The equity agenda may not yet be fully achieved, but by any reasonable measure, equity feminism has turned out to be a great American success story (22).

Against this liberal, egalitarian, and democratic perception of feminism, Hoff Sommers constructs a second type of feminism, subscribed to by feminist leaders like Gloria Steinem, as the belief that women, even modern American women, are in thrall to "a system of male dominance" variously referred to as "'heteropatriarchy' or the sex/gender system .... Sex/gender feminism ('gender feminism' for short) is the prevailing ideology among contemporary feminist philosophers and leaders. But it lacks a grass roots constituency" (22).

Similar to the work of Denfeld and Roiphe, Hoff Sommers's book accuses the contemporary feminist movement of being too radical and too distanced from the lives of ordinary women. Taken together, these three books launch an analysis of the crisis in feminism—why contemporary women feel alienated from a movement meant to represent them—and attempt to postulate the future of such a movement.

Aside from the stated topic of examination, these books also share several similarities: each accuses the modern women's movement of repression, puritanism, and anti-male bias. From the title of Denfeld's book to the content and analyses of Roiphe and Hoff Sommers, each of these women draws parallels between contemporary and Victorian feminism. All three discuss feminism as their own personal birthright: each identifies as feminist and does so in language that suggests its taken-for-grantedness. Hence, the women offer a critique of contemporary feminism as both women and feminists. Cleverly inverting the oft-recited qualifier "I'm not a feminist, but ..." to "I am a feminist, but ...," these authors attempt to reclaim feminism for their generation. In doing so, each constructs a specific type of feminism. Alternatively referred to as cultural feminism, liberal feminism, or equity feminism, this is a feminism devoid of history, politics, and systemic critique. Furthermore, in "wresting" feminism away from its more radical proponents, these treatises marginalize the critiques of feminists of varying races, ethnicities, and sexual orientations. Each author does attempt to reclaim feminism, and the feminism she so desperately wants to preserve is white, middle-class, and predominantly heterosexual. That none of these authors seriously investigates the work of feminists of colour or lesbians is indicative of a blindness to the sustained critiques of "mainstream" feminism that have emerged from these quarters. That such critiques inform the work of these women is beyond doubt. That they do not devote space, time, or consideration to this work is emblematic of their desire to reclaim feminism as a white, middle-class, straight woman's movement.

The Lesbian Menace

Denfeld argues that the increasing prominence of lesbian issues and theory is at least partially responsible for the alienation of heterosexual women from the contemporary feminist movement. She argues that contemporary feminism has offered lesbianism as the only appropriate sexual choice for enlightened feminists and quotes the San Francisco *NOW Times* to demonstrate her point:

> Embracing lesbianism, or lesbian-feminist theory, is pivotal to the feminist movement, which works to change society through the elimination of gender-defined roles ... heterosexism and male supremacy reinforce one another in maintaining our oppression. Both must be eliminated for any woman to be free (12).

Arguing that this is demonstrative of anti-male bias, Denfeld asserts that any attempt to challenge such a perception is shrouded in silence, since to raise objections would be perceived as homophobic. What is significant about Denfeld's inclusion of these comments is not that they demonstrate the male bias of which she speaks but that they clearly articulate the importance of lesbian-feminist critique. Misinterpreting the statements to argue that lesbianism should be mandatory, Denfeld is unable to contextualize these comments as reflective of a particular viewpoint. Far from advocating lesbianism as the only appropriate sexual choice, these comments illustrate the challenge that lesbian theory poses to heterosexual norms. What Denfeld fails to articulate is the distinction between heterosexism and heterosexuality. Interpreting these comments to mean that all feminists must be lesbian, Denfeld conflates the critique of heterosexism with the practice of heterosexuality. Her concern over the increasing radicalism of feminism is belied by her unstated and unwritten fear that the feminism with which she grew up—the feminism she has taken for granted—is in danger of being appropriated by lesbians. She argues that the work of Adrienne Rich, listed with others who advocate a retreat from heterosexual relations, is indicative of the attempt to enforce a single sexual standard:

> "I am suggesting that heterosexuality, like motherhood, needs to be studied as a political institution ...." writes feminist author Adrienne Rich in her immensely influential essay "Compulsory Heterosexuality and Lesbian Existence." One of the most common assignments in women's studies classes—taught from the University of California at San Diego to Rutgers University in New Jersey—this essay stresses that heterosexuality is the "model for every form of exploitation." Destroy this institution and you will destroy all oppression (31).

While there is a large amount of feminist work that is characterized as lesbian separatist, Denfeld, I think, misinterprets Rich's arguments. What Rich is stressing is not that all women should cease being heterosexual but that heterosexuality must be analyzed as a historical, political, and cultural construction. The importance of Rich's work (the reason why it is included on several women's studies syllabi) is not that she articulates a lesbian takeover but that she questions the taken-for-grantedness of heterosexuality and seeks to uncover the power relations that are buttressed by institutions such as motherhood, marriage, and heterosexuality.

As these passages indicate, what is characteristic of Denfeld's discussion of the influence of lesbian theory on the feminist movement is her complete inability to seriously address and understand its critical power. She employs these passages in the attempt to present such arguments as, at best, ludicrous and, at worst, dangerous. In Denfeld's narrative, lesbian theory is cast as responsible for what she sees as the radicalism and intolerance of academic feminism.

While Roiphe does not specifically blame lesbian theory for the radicalism and intolerance of academic feminism, she nonetheless argues that the climate of sexual fear has its roots in the panic over AIDS, which she characterizes as a marginal issue for the majority of university students.

> Most straight college students don't actually think they're going to get AIDS. Most of us probably think of it as a disease out there for somebody else .... I remember a friend telling me that our chances of actually getting AIDS were about the same as the chance a piano would fall on your head .... AIDS may not brush directly against our lives [but] it affects the way we think about our actions (24).

While Roiphe is trying to make a point about how the threat of AIDS has been internalized, she is also making a distinction between those who should be concerned over AIDS and those who are not "directly" affected by it. Through the conflation between safe sex seminars and an attendant panic around sex, Roiphe suggests that the hard-won sexual freedom that characterized liberal democracy has been co-opted by marginalized groups with specific agendas. Hence, she reinforces the perception that AIDS is a problem only for "high-risk groups" while also acknowledging that these concerns have affected the attitudes and behaviour of everyone (an argument which is most certainly belied by the number of heterosexual women and men who have tested HIV-positive).

In her discussion of the climate of intolerance and political correctness on university campuses, Hoff Sommers also betrays the perception of increasing homosexual influence. She argues that "feminized" universities (those that teach "re-conceptualized" courses) should print a disclaimer warning parents of the potential effects of this type of education on their daughters (sons, apparently, are beyond the pale of concern):

> We will help your daughter discover the extent to which she has been in complicity with the patriarchy. We will encourage her to reconstruct herself through dialogue with us. She may become enraged and chronically offended. She will very likely reject the religious and moral codes you raised her with. She may well distance herself from family and friends. She may change her appearance, and even her sexual orientation. She may end up hating you (her father) and pitying you (her mother). After she has completed her reeducation with us, you will certainly be out tens of thousands of dollars and very possibly be out one daughter as well (91).

All facetiousness aside, the warning issued by Hoff Sommers is demonstrative of a fairly traditional response to the seeming radicalism of universities. The assumptions inherent in her comments indicate how feminism, queer theory, and revisionist history are perceived as threats to traditional value systems. Hoff Sommers's comments belie the inherent assumption that the typical female university student is white, heterosexual, and from a middle- to upper-class family with enough money to fund her post-secondary education. The threat posed by feminism and other radical disciplines that Hoff Sommers excoriates is the threat to traditional hierarchies of morality, religion, and the nuclear family, not to mention the traditional pedagogical structures of universities.

Like Denfeld and Roiphe, Hoff Sommers characterizes the radicalism of campus feminism as a lesbian takeover, symbolized by the young, impressionable heterosexual woman who returns from university politicized, angry, and, horror of all horrors: a lesbian!! Part and parcel of this concern is the belief that feminist and queer theory function only as a means of converting women into accepting, practising, and celebrating the lesbian lifestyle. Beyond consideration for Hoff Sommers is the suggestion that such texts may function to encourage critical thought and engagement. Clearly, what is also at issue for Hoff Sommers is the proper role of a university education for young women. In discussing the effects of such radical instruction on the nation's daughters, Hoff Sommers employs a paternalistic attitude, characterizing universities as present-day finishing schools. Within the context of these comments, her concern rests with assuring that the parents of these students get their money's worth.

The Classroom as Indoctrination: Teaching Women's Studies

All three authors express concern over the state of post-secondary education, and each expresses this concern with respect to the effects on female students. What is perhaps most disturbing about their arguments is the extent to which they assume that young women need strict, well-organized, canonized courses in order to learn effectively. Their concerns over the radicalism of feminism or queer theory also belie the assumption that young women are easily confused, alienated, distracted, or overwhelmed by course content.

All three women devote some discussion to official, academic feminism, characterized by women's studies courses. René Denfeld, in order to back up her claim that feminism is interested only in promoting lesbianism, discusses the syllabi of several women's studies courses taught throughout the United States. Stating that works such as Andrea Dworkin's *Pornography: Men Possessing Women*, Adrienne Rich's *Compulsory Heterosexuality and Lesbian Existence*, and Cheryl Clarke's "Lesbianism: An Act of Resistance" appear on several syllabi, Denfeld asserts that these courses are either indoctrinating women or making them feel ashamed of their heterosexuality. She cites a passage from Andrea Dworkin in an attempt to demonstrate the type of radicalism that young women are exposed to in these courses: "The epidemic of cesarean sections in this country ... is a sexual, not medical phenomenon. The doctors save the vagina—the birth canal of old—for the husband; they fuck the uterus directly, with a knife" (Dworkin qtd. in Denfeld 33).

Denfeld's accompanying comments trivialize the work of Dworkin and women's studies courses generally: "Yes, the students are taught this in all seriousness: Dworkin's work is assigned under the section 'Violence Against Women'" (33). Denfeld's assumption here is that students will be unable to critique this work, that the professors will not enable such critiques, and that these classrooms are merely sites of indoctrination. The polemical bite of her critique of women's studies courses once again trades on her assumption that young women are unwilling or unable to engage critically with such work.

All of this talk about masculine ideals, hierarchies, androcentric this and phallocentric that can be very confusing to women encountering feminist theory—

especially in women's studies classes and feminist literature, where such lingo is used with wild abandon but seldom backed up by any coherent reasoning. A woman trying to unravel just how feminist theory applies to her out of this snarled mess of vague terms is easily daunted (158–59).

In attempting to demonstrate that young women are easily daunted by such material, Denfeld decontextualizes these courses and readings and assumes that students passively absorb such information, if they manage to understand it at all. That Andrea Dworkin's work is polemical, extreme, and essentialist has been duly noted by feminist critics. That Denfeld invokes Dworkin as an example of how women are taught to think about heterosexuality is a polemical tactic that does not consider the possibility that women, feminists even, are resistant to her work. Furthermore, she unquestioningly assumes that women's studies courses do not foster critical thought. It does not enter Denfeld's mind that Dworkin's work is representative of a radical feminist approach to violence against women and that it may in fact be presented as such within the context of the class. Intent on making her own polemical argument about the totalitarian feminist classroom, Denfeld refuses to consider the very real possibility that students are able and encouraged to challenge and critically assess such material.

Roiphe devotes less time to an actual discussion of the content of women's studies courses and instead provides characterizations of classmates who considered themselves feminist. These characters range from the earth-mother Sarah to the glamour feminist Lauren to the careerist feminist critic Amanda. What is striking about Roiphe's arguments is the extent to which she personalizes the feminist politics of these women, attempting to render such critiques disingenuous or futile. Sarah, for example, dresses in baggy clothes that disguise her figure and cares for depressed friends and abandoned animals but is actually the well-bred daughter of an affluent family (120). Lauren, the glamour feminist with her "green eyes, her pale skin, and her long red hair," is embracing of and conflicted over her sexuality (121). And Amanda, the careerist, latches onto feminist criticism because it will likely lead to a job: "Her conversation is peppered with words like inscription, appropriation, hegemonic and transgress. In her world, things don't just exist, they are 'constructed.' People don't just write, they 'position themselves within the dominant discourse'" (127).

Not familiar with these women personally, I have no intention of disputing Roiphe's characterizations. However, I do think it is important to illustrate how her characterization of her classmates serves to reinforce the perception that feminist criticism, pedagogy, and politics are not to be taken seriously. Her examples reinforce the perception that feminists are either social misfits, sexually conflicted, or merely opportunistic. While Roiphe does not argue that these women are emblematic of all feminists, she does invoke them as examples of feminism on university campuses.

Her description of Amanda is perhaps the most telling example of the perceived threat of academic feminism. She states that her friend

> does not waste too much time with the books themselves but instead devotes herself to the books written about the books themselves. She has not read Clarissa, for instance—who could plow through more than a thousand pages— but she has read at least ten books written about Clarissa. With her shining analytical mechanisms, her gears turning toward the job market, she reminds me of a well-oiled machine. She has mapped out popular theory, churned out the requisite papers, and calculated her way into the profession (129–30).

While it is not my intent to launch a spirited defence of Amanda's interests, I do think it is telling that Roiphe's problem with Amanda, and others like her, is her

perceived lack of respect for the literary canon. Clearly, the challenge posed by literary critics and cultural theorists may be articulated as an attack upon the cherished traditions that have defined and justified the study of English literature.

This concern over the apparent threat to pedagogical traditions also characterizes the concerns of Hoff Sommers, who devoted a large portion of her research for *Who Stole Feminism?* to attending women's studies classes and conferences. Concerned with the state of contemporary education and determined to discover the path to improvement, Hoff Sommers launches an analysis of women's studies courses and concludes that they are tantamount to indoctrination. Characterizing them as determined to convince students they are oppressed, Hoff Sommers contends that these courses are indicative of feminism's distance from women's lives: "But it is fair to say that most students are not 'buying into' gender feminism. Many resent the attempt to recruit them. Even more resent the shift away from a traditional pedagogy whose primary objective is teaching students a subject matter that will be useful to them" (92).

Inherent within her comment is the assumption that feminist theory, history, and criticism is useless. Following the arguments of Denfeld and Roiphe, Hoff Sommers also challenges the legitimacy of traditionally marginalized discourses. Part and parcel of her analysis here is that post-secondary education is not providing an adequate return on student's and parent's investments. Following on the heels of her mission statement for "feminized" colleges, this statement further reinforces her perception that universities must fulfil specific tasks, although what those specific tasks are, she does not say.

An underlying concern throughout Hoff Sommers's writing is the belief that something has gone terribly wrong in our universities. No longer the space for open discussion, critique, and learning, universities have become indoctrination camps where powerless, naïve, and unthinking students unquestioningly endorse all radical views to which they are exposed. Her argument is contradictory, however, in that while she is claiming that radicals have too much influence on the curriculum and are intent on radicalizing our youth, she also asserts that many students are resistant to such recruitment. Charges of feminist "recruitment" aside for a moment, if students are resistant to this radicalism, it cannot possibly pose the drastic danger that Hoff Sommers articulates.

Feminism as the New McCarthyism

In attempting to demonstrate the irrelevance of organized feminism in contemporary women's lives, Denfeld, Roiphe, and Hoff Sommers devote some discussion to the problems of pornography, rape, and sexual harassment. Arguing that the feminist focus upon issues of sexual violence has reinforced the perception of women as victims, these women attempt to draw parallels between contemporary and Victorian feminism. Each of the books under consideration charges contemporary feminism with embodying a repressive, anti-sex, anti-male viewpoint that hearkens back to the Victorian era. The feminist activism embodied by critics such as Andrea Dworkin, Susan Brownmiller, and Catharine MacKinnon is discussed by all three authors, who maintain that it promulgates the perception that women are powerless and victimized. Most prominent in the work of Denfeld, the spectre of the spinster haunts these women, and their books may be seen as an attempt to assert women's sexual identity.

Horrified at having received an excerpt from Sheila Jeffreys's *The Spinster and Her Enemies* in an information package on pornography from NOW, Denfeld declares that contemporary feminism is actively embracing the figure of the spinster:

> According to Jeffreys, the early feminist campaigns against non-reproductive sexuality, sexual material, and prostitutes were wonderfully

feminist, truly revolutionary. The fact that current feminist crusades against porn and "compulsory heterosexuality" mirror these repressive Victorian crusades does not escape Jeffreys; she applauds this similarity as a sign that feminists are on the right track (241).

Denfeld's critique of Jeffreys is instructive, and this is one of the central problems facing feminists who oppose pornography. That Jeffreys reclaims the spinster as the vanguard of nineteenth-century feminism without an interrogation into the race and class imperatives at work in social purity campaigns is a serious problem within her analysis. However, what Denfeld fails to acknowledge is that while nineteenth-century feminists campaigned against prostitution, they did so to draw attention to the sexual double standard that "forced 'virtuous' middle and upper class women into a straightjacket of chastity while men were encouraged to expend excess sexual energy upon a class of 'fallen' women" (Backhouse 387).

Several critics have drawn rhetorical comparisons between the Victorian perceptions of ideal womanhood and contemporary feminist critiques of pornography, rape, and sexual harassment. Roiphe discusses the characterization of male sexuality postulated by Catharine MacKinnon and argues that it also recapitulates Victorian feminism in its assumption that women are weak, powerless, and victimized. She draws a comparison between MacKinnon's views on male sexuality and pornography (see "Not a Moral Issue") and the nineteenth-century feminist concern over prostitution and social purity:

> Like MacKinnon, the nineteenth century proto-feminists worried about something called social purity. Instead of pornography, for them prostitution was the metonymy of evil. They spoke of female prostitutes in terms similar to

those in which MacKinnon speaks of the women employed in the pornography industry—as if they had no will, as if they had been captured and exploited and forced like slaves to serve the base desires of men. As many historians have noted, this was simply not an accurate portrait of all nineteenth century prostitutes, and it is not an accurate portrait of all twentieth century workers in the sex industry. As MacKinnon talks, the ideal of social purity burning in her inflamed rhetoric, you can hear the legacy of the nineteenth century in her voice (148–49).

Roiphe's analysis of MacKinnon's rhetoric comprises the most thoughtful and interesting aspect of her book. However, that MacKinnon has faced these criticisms from within the feminist movement for years now is not mentioned by Roiphe. An analysis of the polemical rhetoric employed by MacKinnon and Dworkin, as well as other anti-pornography feminists, has been the subject of a large amount of feminist work over the past several years (Segal and McIntosh; Williams; Vance). What is significant about these critiques is the extent to which they have been articulated within feminist circles and yet have not spelled the end of feminism as we know it.

Politics and Pedagogy: From False Reports to Political Correctness

As a graphic demonstration of feminist extremism, Denfeld and Roiphe both recite the example of a Princeton student who falsely accused another student of rape (Denfeld 261; Roiphe 39–41). Roiphe's account is the more personal of the two, recounting how "Mindy" told the story of the attack at a "Take Back the Night" rally; reported the incident to administration, who told her not to pursue the matter; later published her account in the *Daily Princetonian*; and revealed the name of the attacker to several students. It was subsequently revealed that Mindy had not reported any attack, did not speak to administration about it, and, furthermore, had never met the student she named as the attacker. Roiphe argues that this event was politically motivated and characteristic of the new militant feminism that condones false reports in the name of political and public awareness. Denfeld discusses this example briefly to illustrate the extreme measures that some campus feminists undertake in the name of political awareness. She argues that such extremism further demonstrates the extent to which campus feminism does not represent the opinions of most young women. What is significant about this example is that both women cite it as demonstrative of repression, extremism, and moral fervour, asserting that Mindy's story is exemplary of the new radicalism of contemporary feminism. The unwritten assumption from Denfeld's and Roiphe's narratives is the not-too-subtle suggestion that if one false report was exposed, then how many other women actually "get away with" making such claims?

In addition to the false allegation story, Roiphe and Hoff Sommers cite the case of a University of Michigan student who was almost charged with sexual harassment by his female teaching assistant. Writing a paper about public opinion polls, the student provided an example using the character of Dave Stud, entertaining ladies in his apartment, interrupted by a telephone call from a pollster. The teaching assistant, offended by what she perceived as sexism, approached the male course instructor, who urged her to view the example as sexual harassment. She did not press charges but warned the student not to use such examples in scholarly work. Roiphe contends that assuming a male student can harass a female teaching assistant is naïve and assumes that women are inherently powerless (89). Hoff Sommers contends that it is an example of the increasingly censorious climate on college campuses (94). While the teaching assistant may have overreacted, telling the student she had decided not to press charges but that if he used such examples again, she would proceed with her claim, it is telling that there has been so much attention devoted to this one instance. That Denfeld, Roiphe, and Hoff Sommers each offer the same examples of such extremism is also quite telling. While it may be explained as providing interpretations of what were newsworthy stories, it also suggests the extent to which Denfeld, Roiphe, and Hoff Sommers have focused upon isolated instances of extremism as indicative of the movement as a whole.

Post-Feminism as Conservative Critique

In her attempt to demonstrate how feminism has become increasingly extreme, Denfeld offers a criticism of women's studies courses that are too radical and off-putting to young women:

> they read two poems by black feminist radicals and Audre Lorde's classic essay "The Master's Tools Will Never Dismantle the Master's House" … that wraps up the week dedicated to feminist visions of the future. Far from being a brief foray into delirium, this extremism simply mirrors the rest of the course … and almost lost among dozens of radical works by the likes of Cheryl Clarke, bell hooks, Susan Griffin, Shulasmith Firestone (a diatribe claiming "men can't love"), and Adrienne Rich are only a handful of more moderate works, such as the NOW Bill of Rights. A young woman who takes this class will likely walk away believing that being a feminist means being a fanatical kook (162–63).

So the problem with feminism, identified by Denfeld, is the voice of lesbians and feminists of colour (Audre Lorde, Shulasmith Firestone, bell hooks, Adrienne Rich). The preferred "moderate" approach is found in NOW, a largely white, middle-class collection of women. In dismissing the work of feminists of color and lesbians, Denfeld asserts that the feminism that speaks for her, and presumably for the majority of women, is that which is articulated by middle-class, heterosexual, white women.

That the work of Denfeld, Roiphe, and Hoff Sommers demonstrates some painful truths about the state of contemporary feminism cannot be denied. Many of their criticisms regarding the feminist opposition to pornography and the problems with censorship are well informed and will continue to be addressed by feminists. But the problem with their work is that they refuse to acknowledge such critiques within feminism. Collectively, these books represent a concerted attempt to reclaim feminism from its radical proponents and reassert its coherence as a middle-class, white women's movement.

Each of the books under consideration counsels a retreat from organized, ideological feminism. Denfeld argues that contemporary feminism must concern itself with political parity, economic equality, and safe, reliable birth control and must dispense with the academic feminism preached in women's studies courses. Roiphe argues that feminism must counsel individual responsibility and move away from repressive, anti-sex tactics. Hoff Sommers's project is to abandon ideological feminism in favour of an equity feminism that hearkens back to the turn of the century. As she states, "feminism itself is as American as apple pie and it will stay" (275). While some of their critiques are valid, these books are also concerned inherently with a reclamation of feminism. Fundamental to the vision of feminism postulated here is its liberalism. Denfeld, Roiphe, and Hoff Sommers all write of equity feminism as something they grew up with, something their mothers fought for, and something to which they are entitled. As a result, their treatises are motivated by a profound sense of alienation from a social movement that they thought was rightfully theirs. The projects undertaken by Denfeld, Roiphe, and Hoff Sommers are not necessarily misdirected—the past shortcomings and mistakes of feminist scholars and activists should be interrogated. The problem is that, while they critique feminism from a middle-class, white perspective, they do not include the work of feminists who have also articulated such critiques. While they make mention of Adrienne Rich, bell hooks, and Audre Lorde, they are cited only as decontextualized examples of extremism.

In the narratives of Denfeld, Roiphe, and Hoff Sommers, the feminism that is their birthright has been subverted and perverted by the radicalism of lesbians and feminists of colour. These post-feminist works, then, function collectively as extended laments for the feminism of the 1960s and 1970s, a movement that politicized their mothers and secured their sexual, political, and educational freedom. While the post-feminists articulate problems that have been the subject of extended discussion within feminist circles, they characterize the contributions of lesbians and feminists of colour as potentially destructive to the movement as a whole. Hence, these discussions of the current crisis in feminism serve to reassert the logic of feminism as a predominantly white, middle-class women's movement through derisive treatment of its more radical proponents.

This essay has been concerned with the deconstruction of the arguments by Denfeld, Roiphe, and Hoff Sommers and their popularity as exemplars of post-feminism. What is interesting about the works under consideration is the extent to which they have enjoyed mainstream media attention. Anxious to proclaim the crisis in feminism, these works explore the reasons why women feel alienated from the movement. That each of these women identifies as feminist lends credibility to their claims. What is striking about these books is the extent to which they are really quite benign in their criticisms of contemporary feminism. Collectively cautioning against extremism, false reports, and unsubstantiated accusations, the arguments articulated by these women strike the reader as mere "common sense." The feminism that they reclaim—a liberal, egalitarian approach to full equality—is a project that most people would have difficulty criticizing. Certainly, no right-minded individual would argue that falsely accusing someone of rape is a necessary component of feminist activism.

What remains a compelling feature of the arguments presented by Denfeld, Roiphe, and Hoff Sommers is their conservatism. While they have all been described as the leaders of a new post-feminism, their views of feminism, education, and equality are hardly the vanguard of social criticism. What is significant about these works is that the stated concern over the crisis in feminism is in fact belied by a larger concern over the status of a university education. That each of these women defends traditional literary and academic canons against the threat of radicalism is indicative of the attempt to preserve "liberal education." That these critiques deliberately and unapologetically marginalize, discount, and disqualify the work of feminists of varying races, classes, creeds, and sexual orientations further establishes the extent to which such "challenging criticism" may actually serve to reinforce traditional structures of knowledge and pedagogy.

References

Backhouse, Constance. "Nineteenth Century Prostitution Law: Reflection of a Discriminatory Society." *Social History/ Histoire Sociale* 8.35 (1985): 387–423.

Denfeld, René. *The New Victorians: A Young Woman's Challenge to the Old Feminist Order*. New York: Warner, 1995.

Hennessy, Rosemary. *Materialist Feminism and the Politics of Discourse*. New York: Routledge, 1993.

Hoff Sommers, Christine. *Who Stole Feminism? How Women Have Betrayed Women*. New York: Simon, 1994.

hooks, bell. *Talking Back: Thinking Feminist, Thinking Black*. Toronto: Between the Lines, 1988.

Jeffreys, Sheila. *The Spinster and Her Enemies: Feminism and Sexuality, 1880–1930*. London: Pandora, 1985.

MacKinnon, Catharine A. *"Not a Moral Issue." Feminism Unmodified: Discourses on Life and Law*. Cambridge, MA: Harvard University Press, 1987. 146–61.

Modelski, Tania. *Feminism without Women: Culture and Criticism in a "Postfeminist" Age*. New York: Routledge, 1991.

Moraga, Cherrié, and Gloria Anzaldúa. *This Bridge Called My Back: Writings by Radical Women of Color*. New York: Kitchen Table, Women of Color Press, 1981.

Roiphe, Katie. *The Morning After: Sex, Fear and Feminism on Campus*. Boston: Little, Brown, 1993.

Segal, Lynne, and Mary McIntosh. *Sex Exposed: Sexuality and the Pornography Debates*. New Brunswick, NJ: Rutgers University Press, 1992.

Vance, Carol S., ed. *Pleasure and Danger: Exploring Female Sexuality*. London: Routledge and Kegan Paul, 1984.

Williams, Linda. *Hard Core: Power, Pleasure and the "Frenzy of the Visible."* Berkeley: University of California Press, 1989.

Section Two

DIVERSITY

The Five Sexes, Revisited[*]

Anne Fausto-Sterling

As Cheryl Chase stepped to the front of the packed meeting room in the Sheraton Boston Hotel, nervous coughs made the tension audible. Chase, an activist for intersexual rights, had been invited to address the May 2000 meeting of the Lawson Wilkins Pediatric Endocrine Society (LWPES), the largest organization in the United States for specialists in children's hormones. Her talk would be the grand finale to a four-hour symposium on the treatment of genital ambiguity in newborns, infants born with a mixture of both male and female anatomy, or genitals that appear to differ from their chromosomal sex. The topic was hardly a novel one to the assembled physicians.

Yet Chase's appearance before the group was remarkable. Three and a half years earlier, the American Academy of Pediatrics had refused her request for a chance to present the patients' viewpoint on the treatment of genital ambiguity, dismissing Chase and her supporters as "zealots." About two dozen intersex people had responded by throwing up a picket line. The Intersex Society of North America (ISNA) even issued a press release: "Hermaphrodites Target Kiddie Docs."

It had done my 1960s street-activist heart good. In the short run, I said to Chase at the time, the picketing would make people angry. But eventually, I assured her, the doors then closed would open. Now, as Chase began to address the physicians at their own convention, that prediction was coming true. Her talk, titled "Sexual Ambiguity: The Patient-Centered Approach," was a measured critique of the near-universal practice of performing immediate, "corrective" surgery on thousands of infants born each year with ambiguous genitalia. Chase herself lives with the consequences of such surgery. Yet her audience, the very endocrinologists and surgeons Chase was accusing of reacting with "surgery and shame," received her with respect. Even more remarkably, many of the speakers who preceded her at the session had already spoken of the need to scrap current practices in favor of treatments more centered on psychological counseling.

What led to such a dramatic reversal of fortune? Certainly, Chase's talk at the LWPES symposium was a vindication of her persistence in seeking attention for her cause. But her invitation to speak was also a

---

[*]   Portions of this essay were adapted from Anne Fausto-Sterling's book *Sexing the Body: Gender Politics and the Construction of Sexuality* (2000).

watershed in the evolving discussion about how to treat children with ambiguous genitalia. And that discussion, in turn, is the tip of a biocultural iceberg—the gender iceberg—that continues to rock both medicine and our culture at large.

Chase made her first national appearance in 1993, in these very pages, announcing the formation of ISNA in a letter responding to an essay I had written for *The Sciences*, titled "The Five Sexes" [March/April 1993]. In that article I argued that the two-sex system embedded in our society is not adequate to encompass the full spectrum of human sexuality. In its place, I suggested a five-sex system. In addition to males and females, I included "herms" (named after true hermaphrodites, people born with both a testis and an ovary); "merms" (male pseudohermaphrodites, who are born with testes and some aspect of female genitalia); and "ferms" (female pseudohermaphrodites, who have ovaries combined with some aspect of male genitalia).

I had intended to be provocative, but I had also written with tongue firmly in cheek. So I was surprised by the extent of the controversy the article unleashed. Right-wing Christians were outraged, and connected my idea of five sexes with the United Nations-sponsored Fourth World Conference on Women, held in Beijing in September 1995. At the same time, the article delighted others who felt constrained by the current sex and gender system.

Clearly, I had struck a nerve. The fact that so many people could get riled up by my proposal to revamp our sex and gender system suggested that change—as well as resistance to it—might be in the offing. Indeed, a lot has changed since 1993, and I like to think that my article was an important stimulus. As if from nowhere, intersexuals are materializing before our very eyes. Like Chase, many have become political organizers, who lobby physicians and politicians to change current treatment practices. But more generally, though perhaps no less provocatively, the boundaries separating masculine and feminine seem harder than ever to define.

Some find the changes under way deeply disturbing.

Others find them liberating.

How many Intersexuals Are There?

Who is an intersexual—and how many intersexuals are there? The concept of intersexuality is rooted in the very ideas of male and female. In the idealized, Platonic, biological world, human beings are divided into two kinds: a perfectly dimorphic species. Males have an X and a Y chromosome, testes, a penis, and all of the appropriate internal plumbing for delivering urine and semen to the outside world. They also have well-known secondary sexual characteristics, including a muscular build and facial hair. Women have two X chromosomes, ovaries, all of the internal plumbing to transport urine and ova to the outside world, a system to support pregnancy and fetal development, as well as a variety of recognizable secondary sexual characteristics.

That idealized story papers over many obvious caveats: some women have facial hair, some men have none; some women speak with deep voices, some men veritably squeak. Less well known is the fact that, on close inspection, absolute dimorphism disintegrates even at the level of basic biology. Chromosomes, hormones, the internal sex structures, the gonads, and the external genitalia all vary more than most people realize. Those born outside of the Platonic dimorphic mold are called intersexuals.

In "The Five Sexes" I reported an estimate by a psychologist expert in the treatment of intersexuals, suggesting that some 4 percent of all live births are intersexual. Then, together with a group of Brown University undergraduates, I set out to conduct the first systematic assessment of the available data on intersexual birthrates. We scoured the medical literature for estimates of the frequency of various categories of intersexuality, from additional chromosomes to mixed gonads, hormones, and genitalia. For some conditions we could find only anecdotal evidence; for most, however, numbers exist. On the basis of that evidence, we calculated that for every 1,000 children born, seventeen are intersexual in some form. That number—1.7 percent—is a ballpark estimate, not a precise count, though we believe it is more accurate than the 4 percent I reported.

Our figure represents all chromosomal, anatomical, and hormonal exceptions to the dimorphic ideal; the number of intersexuals who might, potentially, be subject to surgery as infants is smaller—probably between one in 1,000 and one in 2,000 live births. Furthermore, because some populations possess the relevant genes at high frequency, the intersexual birthrate is not uniform throughout the world.

Consider, for instance, the gene for congenital adrenal hyperplasia (CAH). When the CAH gene is inherited from both parents, it leads to a baby with masculinized external genitalia who possesses two X chromosomes and the internal reproductive organs of a potentially fertile woman. The frequency of the gene varies widely around the world: in New Zealand it occurs in only forty-three children per million; among the Yupik Eskimo of southwestern Alaska, its frequency is 3,500 per million.

Defining Intersexuality

Intersexuality has always been to some extent a matter of definition. And in the past century physicians have been the ones who defined children as intersexual—and provided the remedies. When only the chromosomes are unusual, but the external genitalia and gonads clearly indicate either a male or a female, physicians do not advocate intervention. Indeed, it is not clear what kind of intervention could be advocated in such cases. But the story is quite different when infants are born with mixed genitalia, or with external genitals that seem at odds with the baby's gonads.

Most clinics now specializing in the treatment of intersex babies rely on case-management principles developed in the 1950s by the psychologist John Money and the psychiatrists Joan G. Hampson and John L. Hampson, all of Johns Hopkins University in Baltimore, Maryland. Money believed that gender identity is completely malleable for about eighteen months after birth. Thus, he argued, when a treatment team is presented with an infant who has ambiguous genitalia, the team could make a gender assignment solely on the basis of what made the best surgical sense. The physicians could then simply encourage the parents to raise the child according to the surgically assigned gender. Following that course, most physicians maintained, would eliminate psychological distress for both the patient and the parents. Indeed, treatment teams were never to use such words as "intersex" or "hermaphrodite"; instead, they were to tell parents that nature intended the baby to be the boy or the girl that the physicians had determined it was. Through surgery, the physicians were merely completing nature's intention.

Although Money and the Hampsons published detailed case studies of intersex children who they said had adjusted well to their gender assignments, Money thought one case in particular proved his theory. It was a dramatic example, inasmuch as it did not involve intersexuality at all: one of a pair of identical twin boys lost his penis as a result of a circumcision accident. Money recommended that "John" (as he came to be known in a later case study) be surgically turned into "Joan" and raised as a girl. In time, Joan grew to love wearing dresses and having her hair done. Money proudly proclaimed the sex reassignment a success.

But as recently chronicled by John Colapinto, in his book *As Nature Made Him*, Joan—now known to be an adult male named David Reimer—eventually rejected his female assignment. Even without a functioning penis and testes (which had been removed as part of the reassignment) John/Joan sought masculinizing medication, and married a woman with children (whom he adopted).

Since the full conclusion to the John/Joan story came to light, other individuals who were reassigned as males or females shortly after birth but who later rejected their early assignments have come forward. So, too, have cases in which the reassignment has worked—at least into the subject's mid-twenties. But even then the aftermath of the surgery can be problematic. Genital surgery often leaves scars that reduce sexual sensitivity. Chase herself had a complete clitoridectomy, a procedure that is less frequently performed on intersexuals today. But the newer surgeries, which reduce the size of the clitoral shaft, still greatly reduce sensitivity.

Failed Cases

The revelation of cases of failed reassignments and the emergence of intersex activism have led an increasing number of pediatric endocrinologists, urologists, and psychologists to re-examine the wisdom of early genital surgery. For example, in a talk that preceded Chase's at the LWPES meeting, the medical ethicist Laurence B. McCullough of the Center for Medical Ethics and Health Policy at Baylor College of Medicine in Houston, Texas, introduced an ethical framework for the treatment of children with ambiguous genitalia. Because sex phenotype (the manifestation of genetically and embryologically determined sexual characteristics) and gender presentation (the sex role projected by the individual in society) are highly variable, McCullough argues, the various forms of intersexuality should be defined as normal. All of them fall within the statistically expected variability of sex and gender. Furthermore, though certain disease states may accompany some forms of intersexuality, and may require medical intervention, intersexual conditions are not themselves diseases.

McCullough also contends that in the process of assigning gender, physicians should minimize what he calls irreversible assignments: taking steps such as the surgical removal or modification of gonads or genitalia that the patient may one day want to have reversed.

Finally, McCullough urges physicians to abandon their practice of treating the birth of a child with genital ambiguity as a medical or social emergency. Instead, they should take the time to perform a thorough medical workup and should disclose everything to the parents, including the uncertainties about the final outcome. The treatment mantra, in other words, should be therapy, not surgery.

I believe a new treatment protocol for intersex infants, similar to the one outlined by McCullough, is close at hand. Treatment should combine some basic medical and ethical principles with a practical but less drastic approach to the birth of a mixed-sex child. As a first step, surgery on infants should be performed only to save the child's life or to substantially improve the child's physical well-being. Physicians may assign a sex— male or female—to an intersex infant on the basis of the probability that the child's particular condition will lead to the formation of a particular gender identity. At the same time, though, practitioners ought to be humble enough to recognize that as the child grows, he or she may reject the assignment—and they should be wise enough to listen to what the child has to say. Most important, parents should have access to the full range of information and options available to them.

Sex assignments made shortly after birth are only the beginning of a long journey. Consider, for instance, the life of Max Beck: Born intersexual, Max was surgically assigned as a female and consistently raised as such. Had her medical team followed her into her early twenties, they would have deemed her assignment a success because she was married to a man. (It should be noted that success in gender assignment has traditionally been defined as living in that gender as a heterosexual.) Within a few years, however, Beck had come out as a butch lesbian; now in her mid-thirties, Beck has become a man and married his lesbian partner, who (through the miracles of modern reproductive technology) recently gave birth to a girl.

Transsexuals, people who have an emotional gender at odds with their physical sex, once described themselves in terms of dimorphic absolutes—males trapped in female bodies, or vice versa. As such, they sought psychological relief through surgery. Although many still do, some so-called transgendered people today are content to inhabit a more ambiguous zone. A male-to-female transsexual, for instance, may come out as a lesbian. Jane, born a physiological male, is now in her late thirties and living with her wife, whom she married when her name was still John. Jane takes hormones to feminize herself, but they have not yet interfered with her ability to engage in intercourse as a man. In her mind Jane has a lesbian relationship with her wife, though she views their intimate moments as a cross between lesbian and heterosexual sex.

It might seem natural to regard intersexuals and transgendered people as living midway between the poles of male and female. But male and female, masculine and feminine, cannot be parsed as some kind of continuum. Rather, sex and gender are best conceptualized as points in a multidimensional space. For some time, experts on gender development have distinguished between sex at the genetic level and at the cellular level (sex-specific gene expression, X and Y chromosomes); at the hormonal level (in the fetus, during childhood and after puberty); and at the anatomical level (genitals and secondary sexual characteristics). Gender identity presumably emerges from all of those corporeal aspects via some poorly understood interaction with environment and experience. What has become increasingly clear is that one can find levels of masculinity and femininity in almost every possible permutation. A chromosomal, hormonal, and genital male (or female) may emerge with a female (or male) gender identity. Or a chromosomal female with male fetal hormones and masculinized genitalia—but with female pubertal hormones—may develop a female gender identity.

The medical and scientific communities have yet to adopt a language that is capable of describing such diversity. In her book *Hermaphrodites and the Medical Invention of Sex*, the historian and medical ethicist Alice Domurat Dreger of Michigan State University in East Lansing documents the emergence of current medical systems for classifying gender ambiguity. The current usage remains rooted in the Victorian approach to sex. The logical structure of the commonly used terms "true hermaphrodite," "male pseudohermaphrodite," and "female pseudohermaphrodite" indicates that only the so-called true hermaphrodite is a genuine mix of male and female. The others, no matter how confusing their body parts, are really hidden males or females. Because true hermaphrodites are rare—possibly only one in 100,000—such a classification system supports the idea that human beings are an absolutely dimorphic species.

At the dawn of the twenty-first century, when the variability of gender seems so visible, such a position is hard to maintain. And here, too, the old medical consensus has begun to crumble. Last fall the pediatric urologist Ian A. Aaronson of the Medical University of South Carolina in Charleston organized the North American Task Force on Intersexuality (NATFI) to review the clinical responses to genital ambiguity in infants. Key medical associations, such as the American Academy of Pediatrics, have endorsed NATFI. Specialists in surgery, endocrinology, psychology, ethics, psychiatry, genetics, and public health, as well as intersex patient-advocate groups, have joined its ranks.

One of the goals of NATFI is to establish a new sex nomenclature. One proposal under consideration replaces the current system with emotionally neutral terminology that emphasizes developmental processes rather than preconceived gender categories. For example, Type I intersexes develop out of anomalous virilizing influences; Type II result from some interruption of virilization; and in Type III intersexes the gonads themselves may not have developed in the expected fashion.

Moving beyond the Five Sexes

What is clear is that since 1993, modern society has moved beyond five sexes to a recognition that gender variation is normal and, for some people, an arena for playful exploration. Discussing my "five sexes" proposal in her book *Lessons from the Intersexed*, the psychologist Suzanne J. Kessler of the State University of New York at Purchase drives this point home with great effect:

> The limitation with Fausto-Sterling's proposal is that … [it] still gives genitals … primary signifying status and ignores the fact that in the everyday world gender attributions are made without access to genital inspection…. What has primacy in everyday life is the gender that is performed, regardless of the flesh's configuration under the clothes.

I now agree with Kessler's assessment. It would be better for intersexuals and their supporters to turn everyone's focus away from genitals. Instead, as she suggests, one should acknowledge that people come in an even wider assortment of sexual identities and characteristics than mere genitals can distinguish. Some women may have "large clitorises or fused labia," whereas some men may have "small penises or misshapen scrota," as Kessler puts it, "phenotypes with no particular clinical or identity meaning."

As clearheaded as Kessler's program is—and despite the progress made in the 1990s—our society is still far from that ideal. The intersexual or transgendered person who projects a social gender—what Kessler calls "cultural genitals"—that conflicts with his or her physical genitals still may die for the transgression. Hence legal protection for people whose cultural and physical genitals do not match is needed during the current transition to a more gender-diverse world. One easy step would be to eliminate the category of "gender" from official documents, such as driver's licenses and passports. Surely attributes both more visible (such as height, build, and eye color) and less visible (fingerprints and genetic profiles) would be more expedient.

A more far-ranging agenda is presented in the International Bill of Gender Rights, adopted in 1995 at the fourth annual International Conference on Transgender Law and Employment Policy in Houston, Texas. It lists ten "gender rights," including the right to define one's own gender, the right to change one's physical gender if one so chooses, and the right to marry whomever one wishes. The legal bases for such rights are being hammered out in the courts as I write and, most recently, through the establishment, in the state of Vermont, of legal same-sex domestic partnerships.

No one could have foreseen such changes in 1993. And the idea that I played some role, however small, in reducing the pressure—from the medical community as well as from society at large—to flatten the diversity of human sexes into two diametrically opposed camps gives me pleasure.

Sometimes people suggest to me, with not a little horror, that I am arguing for a pastel world in which androgyny reigns and men and women are boringly the same. In my vision, however, strong colors coexist with pastels. There are and will continue to be highly masculine people out there; it's just that some of them are women. And some of the most feminine people I know happen to be men.

Growing up White: Feminism, Racism, and the Social Geography of Childhood

Ruth Frankenberg

Whiteness: a privilege enjoyed but not acknowledged, a reality lived in but unknown.[2]

Introduction: Personal and Contextual Notes

This essay is about the ways racism shapes white women's lives, the impact of race privilege on white women's experience and consciousness. Just as both men's and women's lives are shaped by their gender, and both heterosexual and lesbian women's experiences in the world are marked by their sexuality, white people and people of colour live racially structured lives. In other words, any system of differentiation shapes those upon whom it bestows privilege as well as those it oppresses. At a time in the histories of both the US and UK when we are encouraged, as white people, to view ourselves as racially and culturally "neutral" rather than as members of racially and culturally *privileged* or *dominant* groups, it is doubly important to look at the "racialness" of white experience.[3] This essay traces the early lives of five white US women to help concretize these ideas and contextualize some of my questions about feminist theory and anti-racist feminist politics.

For the last two decades and more, women of colour have worked to transform feminism, challenging white feminists' inattention to race and other differences between women, and the falsely universalizing claims of much "second wave" feminist analysis (for the 1970s see, among others: Cade, 1970; Garcia, 1990; for the 1980s and 1990s, key works include Moraga and Anzaldua, 1981; hooks, 1981, 1984; Sandoval, 1982, 1991). Women of colour in North America and Black women in Britain have mapped the ways racism and ethnocentrism limit feminist theory and strategy over issues such as family structures (Carby, 1981; Bhavnani and Coulson, 1986) and reproductive rights (A.Y. Davis, 1981; see also S.E. Davis, 1988, for a more recent analysis that takes seriously the intersections of gender and sexuality with race and class) as well as making feminist institutions exclusive, be they workplaces, journals, or conferences (Zinn et al., 1986; Sandoval, 1982).[4] Alongside this critique feminist women of colour and, more recently, white feminists also, have analyzed women's lives as marked by the simultaneous impact of gender, sexuality, race, and class (the founding text here is, I believe, Combahee River Collective, 1979; Zavella, 1987; Alarcon, 1990; Haraway, 1991; Sandoval, 1982) and generated visions and concepts of multi-racial coalition work (notably Moraga and Anzaldùa, 1981: 195–6; Reagon, 1983). In this context, white feminists like myself have learned a great deal about the meaning of race privilege. The interviews presented here, and my analysis of them, represent one approach to understanding the meaning of being white in a racist society such as the USA, one piece of the broad task of doing anti-racist work, within feminism and beyond.

White Privilege

Today I got permission to do it in graduate
    school,
That which you have been lynched for,
That which you have been shot for,
That which you have been jailed for,
Sterilized for,
Raped for,
Told you were mad for—
By which I mean
Challenging racism—
Can you believe
The enormity
Of that?

(Frankenberg, 1985)

I came to the United States from Britain in 1979, a Marxist Feminist. My anti-racist activism had involved participating in the Anti-Nazi League, Rock against Racism, and the All-Cambridge Campaign against Racism and Fascism—organizations that emerged in the mid-1970s in reaction to a resurgence of far-right, organized racism in the UK. I marched in London, picketed in Cambridge, and declared myself ready to join in physically defending the boundaries of Black neighbourhoods from the incursions of racist gangs.[5] In that context, I saw racism as entirely external to me, a characteristic of extremists or of the British State, but not a part of what made *me*, or shaped my activism. Ironically, however,

and exemplifying the extent to which racism constructed my outlook, I barely noticed, much less questioned, the reality that the All-Cambridge Campaign was almost entirely white in its membership. My "externalizing" of racisms changed in the United States, where, initially through university, I met, learned from, and later wrote, co-taught, and lived with lesbian women of colour and white working-class women, who pushed the limits of my perceptions of racism beyond the purely external, so that I increasingly saw its ever-present impact on daily lives—mine and theirs. In the context of a group called the Women's Work and the Capitalist State Collective, we struggled to teach, write, and analyze in new ways— to develop modes of working that might join, but not falsely unify all of our divergent, yet linked, experiences as women.[6]

Through the early 1980s I and my white feminist sisters groped for a language with which to talk about racism and feminism, racism, and ourselves. By the mid-1980s as white feminists continued acting out elements of racism and ethnocentrism, I felt the need for a more systematic analysis of the situation. I wanted to ask *why* white feminist thought and practice replicated the racism of the dominant culture, about the social processes through which white women take our places in a racially hierarchical society like the US, and what we might do to challenge racism from within those places. My presumption here was one I'd held to since I first came to political activism in the early 1970s—that knowledge about a situation is a critical tool in dismantling it.

Between 1984 and 1986, I undertook in-depth life history interviews with thirty white women, ranging in age from twenty-one to ninety, diverse in class, family and household situation, sexuality, political orientation, and geographical region of origin, but all living in northern California. While interviewing women and analyzing their narratives, I looked not only for the stories white women told, but also thought critically about the languages available to us in the 1980s and 1990s, for talking about race, culture, selfhood, otherness, whiteness. I wanted to think about what those languages made visible and what they concealed, as well as the historical moments in which they had come into being (I have written about this work in Frankenberg, 1993).

Racial identity is complex and in no way reducible to biological terms. In fact, as the history of the USA amply shows, race, race difference, and racial identity are politically determined categories, intimately tied to racial inequality and racism, and constantly transformed through political struggles. Thus the names that groups of people give themselves, and the names ruling groups give to others, change over time.[7] My study worked with an avowedly political, provisional, historically, and geographically specific understanding of race difference. As such, I viewed groups in US society who are targets of racism—including Native, Latino, African, and Asian Americans and other immigrants of colour—as racially different from white people and from each other.

As is the case for people of colour in the US (itself a chosen name with the specific purpose of coalition-building in the United States), "white" is neither a fixed nor a homogeneous label. My study set out to explore some of its meanings for white women and to understand the political and social shifts which have given whiteness its present shape. I came to view whiteness as having at least three dimensions. Firstly, it is a position of structural advantage, associated with "privileges" of the most basic kind, including, for example, higher wages, reduced chances of being impoverished, longer life, better access to health care, better treatment by the legal system, and so on. (Of course, access is influenced by class, sexuality, gender, age, and in fact "privilege" is a misnomer here since this list addresses basic social rights.) Secondly, whiteness is a "standpoint" or place from which to look at oneself, others, and society. Thirdly, it carries with it a set of ways of being in the world, a set of cultural practices, often not named as "white" by white folks, but looked on instead as "American" or "normal." For reasons of space, this essay for the most part examines the first two dimensions of whiteness, rather than the third (see

Frankenberg, 1993, Chapter 7, whiteness and cultural practice).

My analysis of white women's childhoods is organized around what I call "social geographies of race," exploring the ways racism as a system helps shape our daily environments, trying to identify the historical, social, and political processes that brought these environments into being. *Geography* refers to the physical landscape—the home, the street, the neighbourhood, school, parts of town visited or driven through on rare or regular occasions, places visited on vacation. My interest is in how physical space was divided, who inhabited it, and of course for my purposes that "who" is a racially or ethnically identified being. *Social* geography suggests that the physical landscape is peopled—by whom? How did the women I interviewed conceptualize and relate to the people around them? What were they encouraged, forced, or taught by example to do with the variously racially identified people in their environments? And how is the white sense of self constructed with reference to notions of race or ethnicity? *Racial* social geography, then, refers to the racial and ethnic mapping of a landscape in physical terms, and enables also a beginning sense of the conceptual mapping of self and other with respect to race operating in white women's lives.

Ultimately, the concept of social geography came to represent for me a complex mix of material and conceptual ingredients for I saw increasingly that, as much as white women are located in racially marked *physical* environments, we also inhabit "conceptual environments" or environments of ideas, which frame and limit what we see, what we remember, and how we interpret the physical world. They tell us, for example, what race is, what culture is, and even what racism means. Just as material environments have histories which are political and the product of social change or of oppression, so too do the conceptual frameworks through which we view them. For example, women I interviewed at times saw people of colour through the filter of racist ideas generated in the context of West European colonial expansion, or were raised to live by the rules of segregation associated with an explicit white supremacism. Other white women did not "see" racism, and failed to recognize cultural difference, in part because of the "melting pot" and "colourblind society" myths which have dominated thinking on race in the US for much of the post-war era. Or more positively, some women had begun valuing cultural diversity and recognizing structural racism, here drawing on the anti-imperialist, anti-racist, and feminist struggles of recent decades. All of these ways of being and seeing with respect to race were, in short, the product of historical and political process—not surprisingly, for racism is as unnatural as the concept of race itself.

The landscapes of childhood are important because, from the standpoint of children, they are received rather than chosen (although of course from an adult standpoint they are chosen and crafted in complex, conscious, and unconscious ways). As the narratives discussed below will show, none of the women I interviewed was passive in relation to her childhood environment. However, beyond a point, children do not define the terms in which the world greets them; they can only respond. And while throughout their lives people can and do make profound changes in the ways they see themselves and the world, it seems to me that the landscapes of childhood are crucially important in creating the backdrop against which later transformations must take place. Looking at the social geography of race in white women's childhoods may then provide information and tools useful to us in the project of comprehending and changing our places in the relations of racism.

As I compared narratives with one another, common threads and lines of differentiation emerged. Narratives typified certain experiences, separable into four modes, of social geography of race. Of these, one seemed at first to be characterized by an absence of people of colour from the narrator's life, but turns out, as I will explore below, to be only *apparently* all-white. Secondly, there

were contexts organized in terms of *explicit* race conflict, hierarchy, and boundary-marking. Thirdly, there were contexts in which race difference was present, but unremarked, that is, in which race difference organized white women's perceptions, feelings, and behaviour, but was not, for the most part, consciously perceived. Finally, white women described experiences I have interpreted as "quasi-integrated," that is, as integrated, but not fully so, for reasons that should become clear below.

Growing up White

This section explores in detail the childhood and teenage years of five women, with one drawn from each of the four modes just named, and one extra from the "quasi-integrated" group. All five of the women in this group were between twenty-five and thirty-six years old at the time of the interviews, their childhoods and teenage years spanning the mid-1950s, 1960s, and early 1970s. One woman, Beth Ellison, grew up middle class, the other four—Pat Bowen, Sandy Alvarez, Clare Traverso, and Louise Glebocki—in working-class homes. Pat grew up in Maryland, Beth in a Southern family in Alabama and Virginia, Sandy and Louise are from the Los Angeles area, and Clare from a small town outside San Diego, California. The women are referred to by pseudonyms, with an effort to give them surnames reflecting their own or their spouses' ethnicities. Thus Beth's and Pat's "real" surnames suggested Anglo, or Scottish heritage, and Louise's her Polish ancestry. Clare's married name reflected her husband's Italian-American identity, and Sandy's the fact that her husband is Chicano.

These women's stories all bear the marks of an era of challenges and transformations in terms of race, racism, and anti-racism. Sandy's mother, for example, was a political activist involved in struggles for integration. By contrast, as will be seen, Beth's mother was ambivalent in the face of challenges to the racial status quo in her all-white, middle-class neighbourhood. All five women spent at least part of their childhoods in racially desegregated schools, indicative of the effects of the Civil Rights movement on the patterning of children's daily lives. However, as will be abundantly clear, the women's material and conceptual environments were shaped in complex ways by long histories of racism. Regional histories also differentiated the racial and ethnic landscapes of these women's childhoods. Thus for Southerners Pat Bowen and Beth Ellison, the people of colour with whom they had contact were mainly African American (or in the language of the time, Black). By contrast, Clare Traverso grew up on the US–Mexican border, in the same town as Native Americans and Mexican Americans. And both Sandy Alvarez and Louise Glebocki grew up in racially heterogeneous (Latino, Asian, Black) working-class, Los Angeles neighbourhoods.

As adults, these five women were also distinctive in the extent to which they had thought about, or acted on, anti-racism. Two of them, Sandy Alvarez and Clare Traverso, taught in high schools whose students were predominantly Asian and Latino and, for each of them, teaching was to some extent tied to social change. Thus, for example, Sandy had tried (with limited success) to raise faculty consciousness about racism, and Clare had worked to make student literacy a vehicle for empowerment. Louise was active in a left party. And while neither Pat Bowen nor Beth Ellison described themselves as activists, both had thought a great deal about the interracial dynamics with which they had grown up. In addition, Louise and Sandy were both in long-term primary relationships with Chicano men. One of the five, Beth, was lesbian, the others heterosexual.

These women, were, then, unusual in certain ways, politically and in their life choices. However, their accounts of childhood resonated with those of more conservative interviewees and, like the others, their experience ran the gamut from explicitly articulated or *de facto* segregation, to what I will refer to below as "quasi-integration." There was, then, no predictive relationship between ways of growing up and adult perspectives. (Indeed, even Sandy, whose mother, as noted above, was an active integrationist, described her sister as having become "racist" in her attitudes, as an adult.)[8]

Beth Ellison: An "Apparently All-White" Childhood

Many of the women whose childhoods were apparently all-white shared suburban middle-class childhoods. Beth, born in 1956, grew up in a white, middle-class, professional suburb in a town in Virginia. Today, she describes herself as a feminist. She is an artist who makes a living as a retail worker. Beth said of her childhood:

> I was born in Alabama, and spent my real early years in New Orleans. I was five when we moved to Virginia. I remember living in a professional subdivision, our neighbours were all doctors and lawyers [...]. It was a white neighbourhood [...] The only specifically racist thing I remember from growing up in Virginia was when a Black doctor and his family moved into the neighbourhood [...] At that time I guess maybe I was fourteen and I still didn't think about racism [...] I wasn't interested in politics [...] but I vaguely remember neighbours banding together to see if they could keep this family from moving in and I remember thinking that was disgusting but I was more concerned with my life and being a young teenager.

In the telling of this incident, Beth categorizes racism as "politics," and as separate from her daily life as a teenager. Her description highlights a key difference between many white people's experience of racism and that of most people of colour: for the latter, racism is very frequently pushed to the forefront of consciousness, as a construct that organizes hardship and discrimination (see, for example, many contributions to Moraga and Anzaldùa, 1981). The statement that the only *specifically* racist incident was the attempted exclusion of a Black family from the neighbourhood implies a limited definition of racism, including only individual, conscious acts of "discrimination" or "prejudice." Yet, the very existence of a neighbourhood whose residents are all white itself bespeaks a history of the racist structuring of that community. Elements of that history include both the "redlining" of neighbourhoods by realtors to prevent Black people from buying property in them, and also the economic dimensions of racism which would place affluent neighbourhoods beyond the reach of most Black families. The incident that drew Beth's attention to racism was, then, only the tip of the iceberg.

There *were*, in fact, Black people not too far away. For Beth says,

> I saw a lot of Black people around [...] on the street and [...] in class and downtown, but [...] I don't remember there being many Black and white people hanging out together, I just don't remember seeing that. And also I didn't pay real close attention to it, either.

She continues:

> [...] now that we're talking about this, I remember seeing a lot of Black people around, and I remember not really hanging out with them [...] it wasn't any kind of conscious decision but it was just not what I did.

Thus, with or without conscious decision on Beth's part, her experience of friendship and community was racially structured in multiple ways.

Unlike some of the other women with apparently all-white childhoods, who described obeying their parents'

explicit instructions to stay away from particular neighbourhoods or subway stops, Beth said that there had been no sections of town that she avoided. In fact, in the town where she spent her teenage years, the poorest—and Black—part of town was *en route* to the downtown record and bookstores, so Beth crossed it regularly.

However, if Beth felt no anxiety, her mother seemed to oscillate between what Beth called a "humanist" belief in at least a limited integration and the sense of a need to keep her children apart (and in her perception, *safe*) from Black children and adults. This is illustrated in Beth's description of school integration, which for her began in fifth grade.

> I would have been about ten when schools desegregated [in 1965]. I don't remember anyone in my family being upset about it, or my mother trying to withdraw me from school or anything. [...] I was [...] a little bit excited about it because it was something new. [...] My mother tried really hard to be—she's kind of a humanist, so I don't remember her saying anything like, "don't hang out with the Black kids."

But, later, in high school, Beth was involved in an incident in which she was pushed up against the wall of the gym changing room by a Black girl. This, Beth felt, was directly connected with her parents' decision to move Beth to a segregated private school:

> [W]e didn't talk about it at the time, but as I look back on it now [...] it seems evident to me that they did this because it was a school where there wouldn't be, uh, what they might consider rowdy Black girls for me to have to contend with.

Beth's mother seemed similarly ambivalent or conflicted on the question of residential integration. On the one hand, Beth did not think her mother had taken part in the effort to keep the Black family out of her neighbourhood. However, her response was very different when Beth, at twenty, moved to a poor, racially mixed part of the same town:

> I do remember my mother being really concerned and I don't know if that's because there were a lot of Black people living there or because it was an extremely poor part of town where you'd be more inclined to be ripped off [...] [but she] wouldn't let my younger brother come visit me.

So Beth grew up in a context in which Black people were the "significant others" of colour, and where race and income were intertwined. Being white and middle class meant living somewhere different from Black people. The social distance between white and Black people—which was significant—was produced and reproduced both through the conscious efforts of white people, including Beth's mother, and the neighbours, and through the more diffuse but still intentional effects of the interplay of the class structure with racism. White people like Beth's mother deliberated over the permissibility and safety of living in the same terrain as Black people, seemingly projecting their fear of Black people when they made such decisions.[9] What is not seemingly visible, however, are the forms of personal and structural violence directed towards African Americans by white people, which marked both residential and school desegregation, and the period of Civil Rights struggle in general.

In any event, Beth, received mixed messages. Her environment was shaped by at least three factors. First, there was a pre-existing arrangement of racial segregation and inequality, reproduced, for example, by the all-white private school. Second, Beth's mother's verbal messages about segregation espoused ideas about equality or what Beth called "humanism." Thirdly, and contrasting with her humanism, there were Beth's mother's actions in response to Beth's experiences and choices, which as Beth tells it, frequently leaned in the direction of segregationism and hostility towards Black people. The result was that, without trying, Beth could continue to live a mostly racially segregated life.

Thus, the ways racial inequality shaped Beth's own life was for the most part, "a reality lived in but unknown," or at least a reality known in rather limited terms. However, if the impact of racism on *herself* was not always obvious to Beth, the effects of race and class hierarchy on others were at times very clear: she says of the two communities she knew well, growing up:

> Beth: In [one] it seems like it was mostly poor neighbourhoods where Black people lived, but there were also a lot of poor white people that lived there too. But in [the other], there was a Black part of town and a white part of town. There was the rich part of the white town, the middle-class and then the poor white section. And then there was shanty town and it was literally shacks.
>
> RF: So the shanty town was really the Black part of town?
>
> Beth: Yeah [...] these tiny little shacks that looked like they'd been thrown together out of plywood and two-by-fours. The difference was incredible, because you could drive for one minute in your car and go through rich, beautiful neighbourhoods to [...] what looked squalid to me.

Comparing Beth's words here with her memories of her own neighbourhood, it is striking that Beth is much more sharply aware of racial *oppression* shaping Black experience than of race *privilege* in her own life. Thus,

Beth can be alert to the realities of economic discrimination against Black communities, while still conceptualizing her own life as "racially neutral"—non-racialized, non-political.

It is, in fact, conceptually rather than physically that people of colour (here, Black people) are distant: for Beth and the other women in this "apparently all-white" category, there are in fact at least one or two people of colour not too far away. In this regard, one feature of several accounts of apparently all-white childhoods is the sudden appearance in the narratives of people of colour as employees, mainly Black, mainly female, and mainly domestic workers. As always there is an embedded history here, since up until the 1960s as many as half of all Black women in paid employment worked as domestic workers (Malveaux, 1988). Thus, what is striking here is not the presence of domestic workers as such, so much as the way in which they are talked about. For most often these Black women are *not* summoned into white women's accounts of their lives by means of questions like, "Were there any people of colour in your neighbourhood?" or "Who lived in your household, growing up?" Rather, they arrive previously unheralded, in context of a discussion about another topic.

In Beth's narrative, the mention of black women domestic workers came when I asked her if she remembered the first time she became conscious of race difference, or that there were Black and white people in the world. Beth responded that her first consciousness of race as a difference was at about four years old, when her mother chastised her for referring to a Black woman as a "lady." Here, of course, we are not just seeing race as difference but as hierarchy. We are also seeing the limits of Beth's mother's discourse of humanism. However, Beth said:

> [...] ever since I was a baby, Black people have been around, the person who taught me to walk was a Black woman, that was a maid for our

family [...] pretty much all throughout my childhood, there was a maid around [...]

She added that, although she had not really noticed at the time, she realized now that when her mother remarried, the family stopped employing anyone to do housework. Thus Black domestic workers, despite involvement in Beth's life on the very intimate level of teaching her to walk, seemed on another level to have been so insignificant as not to have merited mention earlier in conversation. Nor were they noticeable enough for their departure from the household after a certain point in her life to have been called to attention.

The image of the forgotten and suddenly remembered domestic worker recurs across several of these white, middle-class childhoods. In another instance, Tamara Green, raised in her words "solidly middle class" in suburban Los Angeles, said:

> I totally forgot until I just started thinking about it—we had housekeepers who, all but one from the time we lived in California, were Latin American, Mexican, Columbian, Honduran, Salvadoran. There was one British Honduran who was Black. And I had a close relationship with one of them.

Why is the story told in this particular way? It may be the status of domestic workers from the standpoint of white middle-class women, or the status of people of colour from the purview of a white and middle-class childhood, that makes these women invisible and seems to strip them of subjectivity in the landscapes of childhood (Rollins, 1985: 207ff describes at length the "invisibility" of Black women domestic workers in the households in which they worked). But whether or not it is race *per se* that creates the form in which the domestic worker of colour appears in the interviews, it is primarily through employer-employee, class-imbalanced relationships that women from "apparently all-white" homes encounter women of colour. If not themselves in positions of clear authority, these white middle-class women must have seen their parents in such positions, able to summon and dismiss the "racially different other" at will. It is perhaps in this sense of control and authority that the home was indeed all-white, and the neighbourhood similarly so.

Patricia Bowen: Race Conflict and "Segregation"

Patricia Bowen grew up in Maryland in the 1960s:

> I grew up in a town that was semi-Southern [...] a fairly small town and pretty much in a working-class family. The town was very racist, it was very segregated. Everyone was aware of race all the time and the races involved were pretty much white and Black people.

Pat describes her town as "segregated": yet as will be seen, she and her family had more interaction with people of colour (specifically, Black people) than either Beth (above) or Clare (whose narrative follows). Segregation, in Pat's experience, meant a complex system of interactions and demarcations of boundary, rather than complete separation. In fact, Black and white people lived near together:

> [We] lived on a street that was all-white, and there were no Black people on that street. But the back of our house—our front door faced an all-white street, the back door faced an all-Black street and that was all-Black. It was completely separate.

The boundary between white and Black was thus very clear. And differences between the streets were also obvious to Pat: the houses on the "Black street" were poorer, more "shacky" (her term), and there were more children playing outside. Added to these sharp distinctions was a feeling of fear on the part of Pat:

> We were kind of told that it wasn't safe to walk down the Black street. [...] [Black children would] yell at you [...] I never got hurt but [they] threatened you a little bit. [...] So I grew up learning that Black people were dangerous.

Pat never actually came to any harm on the "Black street": the idea of danger was introduced by adults and by the taunts or threats of the Black children (apparently never carried out) but, in fact, Pat went in *fear* rather than in danger. As an explanation for the threats she experienced, Pat suggested that the Black children "weren't used to whites walking through"—yet Pat explained that she and other white children routinely used the "Black street" as a shortcut. One is tempted to interpret the situation as another aspect of boundary demarcation, or gesture of turf maintenance on the part of African-American children frustrated at their treatment by their white neighbours. In any event, in Pat's experience, difference, opposition, and threat lived right on the back doorstep.

However, as Pat describes others in her family, it seems for them the issue was not fear so much as maintaining a complex balance of association with and differentiation from Black people. African American and white people used the same stores. As the person in charge of the household, Pat's grandmother took care of shopping. As a result, Pat explained, her grandmother knew many of the Black women in the other street. She would chat and even visit their homes but:

> Pat: she'd tell me proudly or just very self-righteous, "Well, you know, I would never sit down when I go in their house. I would go over and talk to them, but I wouldn't sit down." You

know, because to sit down would imply some equal relationship and she wouldn't do that. They would come up to the back door.

RF: Instead of the front door?

Pat: Yes.

This kind of elaborate and contradictory process of boundary maintenance was undertaken by other relatives too:

My uncle was pretty young [...], a teenager when I lived there. He and his friends would play with the boys who were Black, but again they didn't really consider them friends in the same way [...] Black culture was really cool, they would imitate them all the time, and the funny thing was they spoke exactly like them [...] it was pretty much the accent something like they had anyway. The way they danced was really cool and everyone listened to Black music all the time [...], but at the same time there was this "niggers, niggers, niggers," it was this weird contradiction.

The direct teaching Pat received from family members about racism was equally mixed. On the one hand:

[M]y mother was more liberal [...] so she would always tell me not to say "nigger," that Black people weren't any worse than white people.

On the other:

I remember this one incident [...] When I was about eight or nine and walking with my uncle down the street and kind of mutually bumping into a Black woman. I just said "Excuse me," and he said, "Don't ever say excuse me to a nigger. If you bump into them or they bump into you, it's always their fault." And I said, "How is it their fault if I bumped into them?"

It is important to notice here Pat's memories of resistance or at least puzzlement, in the face of explicitly racist socialization. Like Beth, Pat was not, perhaps, always an unquestioning recipient of her environment.

Pat's descriptions of two relationships she had with young Black teenagers, in junior high school years, dramatize the room for manoeuvre that young people managed to find in relation to racism, even in the very constrained context of segregationism:

There are some things about friendships that I developed with Blacks at that time that are kind of interesting. There were two in particular that I really remember. One was a guy in my junior high [...] who was kind of a leader, very charismatic person, and he started hassling me a lot, he wanted to pick on me and he would tease me and kind of threaten me, pull my hair or whatever and I was terrified of him. This went on for a while and then one Halloween my friends and I were out trick-or-treating—we were teenagers and were tagging along with the little kids. [...] We saw him with a friend also trick-or-treating and we laughed, it was a kind of bonding because we were both these obnoxious teenagers out trick-or-treating, trying to get candy with the kids. So I had a feeling he kind of really liked me after that [...] The relationship kind of switched from him threatening me to being a real friendly relationship, I wasn't afraid of him anymore.

But the way that got played out [was by means of] a lot of jokes about racism acted out, like he would pretend to threaten me or tease me in front of people, like Black and white people who were there, and I would play with him back, and everyone would be nervous and thought a fight was going to break out. [...] It was something where we would never really talk or become friends, but it was a neat little thing.

Similarly, with a girlfriend:

She was a very, very large woman and she would pretend to threaten me sometimes and I remember some Black girls going "Ooh" because I was much smaller than she was. We'd play around with that.

In playing with the segregation system like this, Pat and friends are taking at least a small step towards subverting it. By acting out their roles as enemies but not really fighting, they at least signal that they know what it is that they are caught in; the dramatization is a kind of stepping aside from the assigned role, although not necessarily changing it. For Pat, one could say that this involves *acting* being white, simultaneously with *being* white.

However, alongside the subversion there is also another, less self-conscious inversion of social reality here. For if Pat's Black friends were playing with the racial order by pretending to threaten her, that threat itself inverts the institutionalized relations of the dominant culture where, in fact, Black people have much more to fear from whites than vice versa. Commonplace as is white people's fear of people of colour, and especially of Black people, it is important to step back from it and realize that it is a socially constructed fear and thus in need of analysis. I will return to this issue below.

In any event, most of the time Pat and others around her lived out the rules of segregation without subverting them. The same girlfriend with whom Pat "played" racial tension also experienced it directly in an incident that Pat describes:

There were three of us that hung around together, [...] Janet, who was Black, and my friend Sandra and me. Sandra—again, like I had this whole liberal interpretation I got from my mother about Black people and race. Sandra was just more—"nigger"—she would whisper that word and things like that—yet we were both friends with Janet. [...] I remember one night— this is really an awful, painful thing—we were at Janet's house just hanging around, she was drinking coke out of a can and she passed it to my friend Sandra, and Sandra [...] said "No," and we all knew it was because she wouldn't drink out of a can after a Black person, but yet this was our friend that we hung around with. I remember Janet just looking really sad, but also accepting, like it hurt her. [...] I guess it never occurred to me not to drink the coke.

Pat, Sandra, and Janet were all around twelve years old at the time that they were friends. It is worth noting that Pat does not state the colour of her white friend, Sandra: as is often the case, white stands for the position of racial neutrality, or racially unmarked category. Pat commented further on this incident:

We never really talked about race, it was just too taboo a subject.

In the context of Pat's childhood, race difference and racism seem never to be far from the forefront of consciousness and experience. Pat lives a life visibly defined by race hierarchy. Here, segregation as a practice is linked to the presence rather than absence of people of colour. This may be partly a result of class. Pat points out that middle-class whites in the town would probably have had less contact with African Americans than she did, and in fact one can speculate that, had Pat been middle class the racial social geography of her childhood might have resembled Beth's.

The process of boundary demarcation of physical space—being in the same street or house, sitting or standing, making physical contact, sharing a drink, seemed to be a major concern for the white people Pat describes, probably precisely because of the proximity of white and Black people in the context of an ideology and practice of white superiority and segregation. However, boundary maintenance was an issue in other women's stories too, evidenced, for example, in Beth's all-white neighbourhood.

Clare Traverso: Race Difference As a Filter for Perception

Clare was born in 1954 and grew up in a small, rural town, not far from San Diego. The town, said Clare, was

> kind of like a redneck town, actually. [...] Very conservative, politically. People off to themselves, don't want to be bothered with government or politics or other people, love to drink beer and drive around and stuff like that.

The situation described in Clare Traverso's narrative is a complex mix of noticing and not noticing "difference" and people of colour. The question of whether Clare saw that people of colour were seen as "different" or "the same as herself" was similarly complex. Clare's parents were, in her words, "fundamentalist Christian, but not moral majority" people who had moved to California from South Dakota with their children. Clare, fifth child out of six, was born in California. Describing how her time was spent as a child, Clare said:

> We lived sort of off into the hills. We didn't really go into town much [...] the amount of times I went out to eat before I went to college was maybe five times [...] See, my parents had more

traditional values from the Midwest—always saving money and [...] we never went on vacations. I went on two, but they were back to South Dakota to visit my relatives.

Consequently, aside from school, and later, church-related activities, Clare spent much of her early years playing on the land around her family's house.

None the less, Clare was able to describe the racial composition of the town. Aside from the white people, said Clare:

> The town itself is located right next to an Indian reservation. [...] There was also a small Mexican-American population, that went to our high school, but I would say probably, no Blacks. Maybe one or two.

Clare's standpoint here is clearly different from that of the African-American townspeople themselves, for whom it would be impossible to confuse existence with non-existence. Rather than measuring their physical presence, what Clare's cloudy memory indicates, I think, is the lack of importance accorded to Black people in her community. Clare's first conscious contact with people of colour was when she began travelling on the school bus. At that point, like Pat, her response was one of fear:

> The bus I rode, there were these [...] Mexican-American families, lived on the hill across from us, so they rode our bus, and they always had the reputation for being really tough. And I was really scared of this one girl, I remember, because she used to get in fights with this other girl.

Clare speculated that her fear was probably bolstered by her brother who was also in class with one of the "tougher" Mexican-American boys.[10] Again like Pat,

Clare's fear did not come from experience of personal attack so much as from a sense of different behaviour perceived as louder or rowdier than her own:

> They used to yell, flip people off—I came from a more sheltered environment. My parents never did things like that.

In a sense the comment, "my *parents* never did things like that," suggests that, unconsciously, a cultural explanation is being advanced for the difference in behaviour: it is placed in the realm of things taught. However, although the fact that this group is Mexican American is clearly a part of the anecdote, once off the bus and in school, Mexicanness becomes less important as a feature of conscious differentiation:

> RE: So your [kindergarten] class was all white?
>
> Clare: I'm pretty sure it was—probably—oh, wait, I had one little friend, Ralph Vasquez. Their whole family was Mexican American, my sister went through school with one girl in that family. [...] But, I never really thought of them as, like, different from me. I don't think I was aware of them being culturally different.

A similar pattern is repeated in Clare's description of her sense of Native-American schoolmates, later on in school. On the one hand:

> I was so unaware of cultural difference that I probably wouldn't have noticed they were different from me.

On the other hand, she remembers Native Americans in school as a distinct group, noting that they were in the remedial classes. Differences were thus both seen and not seen, or perhaps seen but only partially. Race difference entered into Clare's conscious perception of her environment only on those rare occasions when it carried a feeling, real or imagined, of potential threat to herself (as when she was afraid on the school bus). The ways in which racism did seem to cause hardship for students of colour, by contrast, were perceived only dimly, accessible to memory but not remembered as having made a strong impact on Clare at the time. For, presumably, racism accounted for the location of the Native-American students in remedial classes and, more indirectly, perhaps for their intra-group fights too.

Clare's friendship group in high school further supports this picture of a daily life that was in effect patterned by race. Structured around the student council and a church youth group, it was all-white. What shapes Clare's descriptions of all three groups, whites, Mexican Americans, and Native Americans, is, on the one hand, the absence of a conscious conceptualization of cultural and racial difference *per se* but, on the other, the *experience* of a racially structured environment, not understood as such at the time. In sum, Clare saw individuals in her immediate community through a racial lens, but did not consciously see race, cultural difference or racism.

Clare came to awareness of all three concepts as she grew older, but in relation to communities other than her own. She says:

> Clare: In sixth grade I started learning Spanish and learning a bit about Latin culture, Latin America. My awareness of race came through that rather than Mexican-American people. [...]
>
> RF: So what did you learn about Latin America?
>
> Clare: Pyramids, music, sometimes we'd listen to the radio. I was fascinated by the Aztecs and the Incas.

Latin America thus appears to Clare as a site of more real or authentic cultural difference, and as the proper adjunct to learning Spanish. In the education process, cultural difference was located at a distance and in the past, rather than nearer to home. At the same time, in a contradictory vein, Clare commented that Spanish seemed like the appropriate language to study in school, rather than German or French, "because we were living around and across the border from people who spoke it."

If Latin culture was conceived as being far away, then, it was clear that the Spanish language was closer at hand. In this nearer context though, difference referred to social inequality more directly than to cultural difference. The Mexican border was less than two hours drive from Clare's home and for some, although not for Clare's family, border towns like Tijuana were places to visit, on day trips. However, Clare *did* visit across the border in rather different circumstances, described in the following story:

> Clare: [...] even though I had Spanish in high school, I didn't really speak it—once when we went down to Tecate at Christmas to give away clothes and we spoke a little bit of Spanish to real people who spoke it. [...]

One may note here the implication that Mexican Americans or Chicanos somehow do not really count as members of a Latino, Spanish-speaking culture. Again the issue is one of the perceived inauthenticity of Latinos on the US side of the border. Clare's story continues:

> Clare: This Spanish teacher I had [...] every year they used to collect all these clothes and bring it down and give it away to people in Tecate. I think we did that twice. And you'd give away the clothes to people, the poor people there.

RF: So how do you do that?

Clare: You just walk up to people and say, "Hey, do you need something?"

RF: Just like that?

Clare: Yeah, It was kind of weird, really. [...] We would walk around—and, yeah, we had trucks or cars or something. [...] Our teacher knew someone there. I think he knew the mayor. [...] I felt really odd about giving away things like that, even though they didn't have anything and I know they needed things. They needed food and clothes. You could tell by the way their houses were, just like little shacks, really—dirt floors [...] I remember feeling a real contrast between myself and them. [...]

RF: Do you remember any comments, from your parents, or from school?

Clare: I'm sure they thought it was good [...] We all felt happy that we'd helped poor people out.

In this incident Clare is unwittingly inscribed into the power relations involved in any act of charity. While the sharing of wealth in almost any form is of course useful, here the process is controlled entirely by the giver. In a process that dramatizes power imbalance between Mexico and the US, the adult Mexican receiver is dependent on the mercy of the North American schoolchildren who, at their teacher's behest, walk the streets asking, "Do you need anything?" One wonders if this power imbalance may in part have accounted for Clare's feelings that something was not quite right about the situation. In going to Tecate, Clare becomes starkly aware of the imbalance of resources on either side of the border. However, it was not clear from our conversation how, if at all, this imbalance was explained. Rather than seeing ways in which the US is partially responsible for Mexico's poverty, it is most likely in this context that the US would become identified with the giver and the side of "good."

This expedition took place in the context of learning a language. As adjuncts to the language, Clare was taught about ancient and distance *culture* exemplified by her fascination with Aztec and Inca culture, along with present-day, physically nearer *poverty*. This pattern replicates the classic colonialist view of the conquered society: a view of past glories and present degradations, from which, within a colonialist ideology, it is the conqueror's duty to save the poor native.

Further, authentic difference of any kind was placed firmly outside Clare's home community. Asked about the possibility of practising Spanish with Mexican-American fellow-students, Clare was unsure whether any of them spoke Spanish. Clare sums up this contradictory situation thus:

I think I was so—like I say, we never went to Mexico, we never had contact with other races, really, and if they were there I wasn't aware that they were from another race, I mean vaguely, only looking back on it.

Towards the end of high school, social studies classes analyzing global inequality, as well as her sister's involvement in the movement against the Vietnam War gave a political outlook and set of values which, she felt, were more "liberal" than those of most people in her family and home town. However, again the focus was largely outside her immediate community. The same was true in terms of the process whereby Clare began to *see herself* as a culturally specific being:

I went away to college [in Minnesota] and I met [...] all these people who had a real sense of "I

am Swedish," "I am Norwegian." And then when I went to [stay in] Mexico. That was the two strongest things, I think.

The social geography of race for Clare differed from Beth's "apparently all-white" context described above, in the greater number of people of colour she encountered and the absence of the racially divided employer-employee relationships in the family. Her story also differed from Pat's, such that racial difference was not to the forefront of consciousness, nor was the situation one of such visible ongoing conflict.

However, aside from their differences, one feature common to all three stories is the description of white women's fear of people of colour. As I have suggested, this fear needs careful analysis, both because of its prevalence and because of its status as an inversion of reality. In general, people of colour have far more to fear from white people than vice versa, given, for example, the ongoing incidence of white supremacist terrorism around the United States, which targets African, Asian, Native, Latino, and Jewish Americans (in addition to gay men and lesbians); the problematic relationship between the police and many communities of colour, which leaves men and women of colour with, at the very least, a sense that they lack legal and physical protection.

White people's fear of people of colour is, I think, an inversion that can be contextualized in multiple ways. Most importantly, it must be understood as an element of racist discourse crucially linked to "essentialist racism," or the idea that people of colour are fundamentally "Other" than white people: different, inferior, less civilized, less human, more animal, than whites. Further, US history is marked by multiple moments when the power of racist imagery constructing men of colour as violent, dangerous, or sexually threatening has been renewed, as rationale or pretext for white hostility, in the context of political and economic conflicts between particular communities of colour and white Americans.

Thus for example, a key aspect of white women's fear of Black men has to do with the persistent, racist image of the Black man as rapist. As Angela Davis has clarified, the production of this myth took place alongside the abolition of slavery and efforts, by Black and white people, towards reconstruction of the Southern economy and polity along more racially egalitarian lines. The lynching of Black people was a means of social and political repression, with accusations of rape used as an alibi for what were in effect politically motivated death squads. Here, a discourse ostensibly about threat or danger was in fact a rationale for repression or control (Davis, 1981: 172–201). Similarly, it was in tandem with white, Nativist movements for immigration control and economic protectionism that, from the late nineteenth century into the first decades of the twentieth, first Chinese, then Japanese, then Filipino male immigrants were represented in the white-owned press as sexually lascivious and physically violent (Osumi, 1982). Most recently in the United States, in context of the Los Angeles Rebellion of May 1992, once again newspaper and television reports described African-American protesters as "savage," "roving bands," engaged in a "feeding frenzy" of looting. More generally in the present, I would further speculate that white people's fear of men and women of colour may have to do with the projection or awareness of the anger of individual people of colour over white accountability for racism.

Beyond these few examples of contextualization, white people's fear of people of colour, and the distinctively gendered dimensions of it, require far more extensive discussion than is possible here (a discussion of the imperialist context for the social construction of white women's fear of men of colour is a key theme in Ware, 1992). And it is also crucial to ask what "interrupts" or changes white people's fear of people of colour: for those who are not afraid, what made, or makes, the difference? I do not know how to answer these questions,

but register them here as important ones for us as white women to address.

Quasi-integration: Sandy and Louise

The final pair of narratives to be examined here are those of Sandy Alvarez and Louise Glebocki, both of whom grew up in contexts that I choose to call "quasi-integrated," which is to say seemingly or apparently integrated. I qualify "integration" in this way because it seems to me that true integration would require a broader antiracist social context than existed in the US while Sandy and Louise were growing up. It might involve, for example, that no area of physical space be marked by racial hierarchy and that racist ideas be entirely absent: a situation that is impossible in the context of the United States as presently constituted. As Sandy and Louise's narratives show, neither woman's life circumstances in any sense placed her outside the system of racism. However, their experience of close, peer relationships with men and women of colour none the less marks them off from the other women whose narratives have been discussed so far.

Both women grew up working class in Los Angeles. Sandy was born in 1948. She teaches English as a second language, in a high school. Her husband is Chicano and she has two small children. Louise was born in 1958. She cleans houses, not a job she enjoys but which she feels is "OK for now." She describes herself as always learning, growing, and active. She and her partner of seven years were about to get married at the time of the interview. Like Sandy's husband, he is Chicano.

Sandy Alvarez
Sandy said of the neighbourhood where she lived before she was five years old:

The main things I remember [...] are some friends [...] the Vernons were two sisters and they had a little brother too, just like our family, and they were Black. And the Frenches [...] they were white.

I'm only mentioning race because of this interview [...] as a kid it wasn't until I went to elementary school that I really became aware that these people were different races. Before that you just played with everybody.

From the beginning Sandy had friends from ethnic and racial groups different from her own. At five, she moved to a community, still in Los Angeles, that was, in her words, "equal thirds Japanese, Mexican and white, with two Black families," and her friends reflected this mix. Sandy says that she played with Japanese boys and with the only girl in the neighbourhood, who was in Sandy's terminology "Anglo." Her school friends were Mexican and white. Her "crushes" (again to use her word) and boyfriends were Anglo, Mexican, Guamanian. Also, a Black woman who was Sandy's neighbour when she was growing up is to this day "like a second mother" to Sandy:

[She] is one of my dearest friends. She always thought of me as her daughter. She never had a daughter, and couldn't have any more kids She really loves me and I really love her, and it's a real close relationship.

Looking at the differences in Sandy's experience and Beth's, the first and obvious precondition for Sandy's more racially mixed childhood is that people of colour and whites were living nearer to each other. But in addition, physical proximity was responded to in a particular way and need not have led to the mixed friendship groups Sandy describes. This point is underlined by comparison with the largely tense, conflictual, and unequal relationships, and the elaborate

boundary maintenance between Black and white people in Pat Bowen's neighbourhood (above). By contrast, there was much visiting back and forth between the Vernons and Sandy's household. The Vernon children would often stay overnight at her house.

The other major difference between Sandy as a child who grew up "integrated" and most of the other women I interviewed, was her parents' explicit anti-racism and activism. I asked Sandy what her mother thought of her having friends who were Black. She responded,

Well my mother is really—she's a radical, politically [...] the church we went to [...] the community had turned primarily Black and it was an all-white church and [my parents] were really into helping to integrate the church.

Manifestly, Sandy's mother was a woman unlikely to object to her children having Black friends—and for preschoolers, parental co-operation is key to social interaction. Less obvious is Sandy's awareness that her childhood was unusual and requires explanation, such that she cites her mother's activism to account for it. Sandy's parents may well have been different from other whites in the neighbourhood: otherwise, integrating the church would not have required work. Later in the interview, Sandy made explicit her sense of being unusual, saying:

I don't know that a lot of people have had the integrated experience that we've had growing up, where it wasn't just our acquaintances but our real good friends and all our peers were of different races.

How are race and cultural difference conceptualized in this context? As suggested earlier, Sandy felt that before the age of five she was not aware of race difference between herself and her peers. She explained:

In second grade [...] there are just two pictures in my mind, and I just remember a Black boy, about my age. I don't remember if he was just one of the things that made me aware [...] I just remember becoming aware different kids were different races. And this one girl that I'll never forget. I was really aware she was culturally different, because—she may not have been Mexican, she could have been Filipina, I don't know which culture—somehow I think she was Mexican because the neighbourhood was about a third Mexican—But she'd wear her hair up in a bun, and um, she must have been Asian, because she had those big chopsticks in her hair and in the playground she fell down once and one went right inside her skull and they had to take her to emergency hospital. And, uh, I was just aware that was a big cultural difference, that I would never wear those in my hair.

Here, specifics of cultural difference are perhaps more imaginary than real in any substantive sense. Sandy, drawing on the memories and perceptions of herself at six, did not know which ethnic group the little girl belonged to—she may have been Mexican, Filipina, or East Asian. However, the key here is not whether Sandy could or can answer this question correctly, so much as that we can witness the process of her struggle as a child to make some sense of cultural difference. At six, Sandy remembers herself as registering cultural and race differences as things that shape appearance and what might happen to one; moreover, unlike Clare and Pat, an awareness that her schoolmates and friends were culturally and racially different did *not* evoke in Sandy any sense of fear for herself.

It was not until adulthood, Sandy claims, that she was conscious of people of colour seeing her as white and therefore belonging to a dominant, even oppositionally situated, group. When I asked Sandy whether her sense of race changed as she grew older, she said:

> As you grow older you see how others perceive you, look at yourself. Before that you just act, you are who you are. In that sense [...] that's the only change.

I continued, "So in junior college and at university you were still 'acting,' rather than thinking about how you were acting?" Sandy said, "Yes." So I asked, "At any point in your life did you think of yourself as white?" Sandy replied, "From elementary school on up I guess I was aware of that."

Here, strikingly, Sandy describes herself as having noted her whiteness without any negative or positive charge, in contrast with most contexts in today's US where, I suggest, white either connotes superiority or is "neutralized" and ignored. Often—and this may be the most common experience for white feminists of the 1980s and 1990s—"white" is a concept learned simultaneously with a negative connotation, in terms of its attachment to privilege and exclusionism. However, for Sandy in this early period, "white" or "Anglo" apparently merely described another ethnic group. One cannot help but see this as connected to the multi-racial context within which she experienced her ethnicity: one in which, at least within the local conditions of home, elementary school, and the neighbourhood, racial and ethnic identities were not hierarchically ordered.

However, it is important not to present a falsely utopian picture of Sandy's experience. For one thing, although her friendship groups were racially mixed from preschool to college, she points out that there was racial tension and division elsewhere in the schools she attended. Secondly, it is of course quite possible that Sandy's friends of colour were more conscious of racial hierarchy than was Sandy herself. Thirdly, Sandy was not immune to the impact of racist ideology. For example, she told me that a Black, male schoolfriend had asked her out on a date. She explained that she did not accept, because she could not bring herself to face the stares that she knew they would receive as an inter-racial, especially as a Black and white, couple. Sandy is not convinced by the element of racist discourse which says that only "bad" white women date Black men. However, she is still afraid to challenge it in public.

In other words, growing up in a racially mixed context did not mean that racism was absent from the environment, nor that the environment was not racially structured. Rather, Sandy's childhood, while clearly characterized by an anti-racist intent on the part of her parents and a sense of interpersonal racial equality between Sandy and those in her immediate world, was equally clearly surrounded and ultimately challenged and disrupted by, the broader, racially hierarchical social order. In fact, Sandy's was an integrating family, rather than a family living in an integrated environment. This was also true for two of the other women, whose childhoods were marked by what I call a "quasi-integration." Their parents were also radicals, and both of them felt it necessary to offer this fact to explain a state of affairs they know to be abnormal (although desirable) in a racist society.

Louise Glebocki

The final narrative in this article is that of Louise Glebocki, who was born in 1958. While not coming from a family that spoke of integration or anti-racism, Louise's own experience growing up was one of more thorough-going connection with a community of colour than the rest of the women I interviewed. Like Sandy, Louise had grown up in Los Angeles. Having spent her first six years on the East Coast, Louise, with her mother and two older sisters, came west, moving "into a barrio, basically around all Spanish-speaking people." Louise added:

Besides Mexicanos, the others that lived there were poor whites. [...] It was just a poor, small community.

Right from the start, Louise and her sisters began having boyfriends. And more of Louise's boyfriends and female friends were Mexicano, or Chicano, than white.

Louise: I remember I had a white boyfriend and then a Chicano one. But I started hanging around more with the Chicanos. But both—always.

RF: How come you hung out more with the Chicanos?

Louise: To me they were more—at that point I did have white friends too. I don't know, there was just something real honest about them, and real friendly, and real close relationships formed, I remember, around a couple of girlfriends I had. Just visiting their families was a really nice atmosphere—kind of like ours. Because for a white family, while we were poor, we grew up [around] a lot of people. We had a lot of relatives in the LA area. It was always a lot of activity, and hustle and bustle. And a lot of times I guess, among the whites, even if they were poor, it was kind of like more snobby, more uppity.

In short, Louise viewed Chicano families as similar to her own, rather than different from it. Louise is also commenting here on class and people's perceptions of themselves. She suggests, in effect, that there was a link between class position and cultural style, linking her own working-class position with a liveliness shared with Chicano families. However, the suggestion is, other poor whites acted differently, aspiring to a style of life associated with a higher-class position. Louise preferred the Chicanos' mode of being, viewing it as more "down to earth," more honest, and more like her own. Of course, Louise's words are adult ones: it is hard to know exactly what form these thoughts would have taken in the consciousness of a younger person.

In fact, Louise's extended family was not only similar to the Chicanos, part of it actually *was* Chicano. For as Louise explained, a good number of her mother's sisters and brothers had Mexican-American partners.

RF: Did it feel to you like you were in a bi-cultural family, or a family with two cultures? [...]

Louise: I never looked at it like it was two separate cultures. I just kind of looked at it like, our family and our friends, they're Mexican and Chicanos, and that was just a part of our life.

More than any of the other women described here, Louise's childhood was one in which a community of colour played a consciously central role for the interviewee. The following description from Louise's narrative underlines three things: firstly, the closeness of Louise's connection to Chicano or Mexican culture; secondly, the fact that at the same time, Louise and her relatives were clear that she was white; and thirdly, the extent to which white culture remained, at least linguistically, Louise's point of reference:

RF: If you would go to your aunt's house or your uncle's house, would there be things about how their house was and how they raised their kids, things that they would have on the walls or would do, that came from the fact that it was a partly Mexican and partly white household?

Louise: Yeah. Like I remember my aunt, she was married to this Mexican dude. And his background was really, *strongly* into the whole Mexican scene. [...] He was real strong in terms of what he was. I mean, he would never want to be anything else but Mexican. And he had a real strong "machismo." He had something like thirteen kids in his previous marriage. [...] And she really took all that in. In fact she's still constantly like that [...] her attitude is, well, a woman should be a woman, and in her place—the whole mentality was, I don't know, really a trip.

But I remember like, with these relatives, the Chicanos, they would always joke around, you know, around us being Polish, and white. There would be a lot of joking and stuff, oh you know, "You honkys gotta learn more ..." and stuff.

And in terms of their house? They'd play a lot of Mexican music, and a lot of regular music, and have stuff on the Indians up on the walls, and from Mexico.

There are contradictions and complexities here. On the one hand, Louise said that she did not conceptualize the two cultures as separate, yet it is clearly possible for her to do so descriptively. The sense of Chicano culture as more sexist (assuming that "machismo" connotes sexism in Louise's usage of it) is jarring, given Louise's view elsewhere that Chicano culture was better, more "in tune with reality." The distinction between "Mexican" and "regular" music suggests that the dominant culture remains in her description the reference point, the cultural practice that requires no name or explanation.

However, Louise is also conscious of her whiteness in this description as, it seems were her Chicano relatives. The use of the, usually negative, "honky" to describe Louise and her white family members suggests that no one has lost sight of the wider context of race conflict. At the same time, taking on board and using the word honky in a playful way suggests, I think, a context in which it has been possible to situationally subvert racial hierarchy, to bracket it while simultaneously not evading consciousness of racial inequality.

Curiously, despite this mix of relatives on her mother's side of the family, Louise's father had very different ideas, including, as Louise put it, "racist tendencies." For example:

> My parents had been saving money, and they wanted to buy a house. [...] I'm pretty sure one of the things my dad really emphasized was [...] a nice, white community.

However, although the family moved to a white section of a small town in the Los Angeles area, their situation ended up little different from the previous community,

> because our school just ended up being pretty poor, and the majority was Chicanos, and a lot of them were people who had just come over from Mexico, so there was a lot of Spanish-speaking people. And there was a whole section of whites too, but it wasn't this pure, middle-class, white area, it was once again a real mixture.

Through school and into adulthood, Louise continued to be close friends with Chicanos, as much or more than with whites. But like Sandy, she may well have been unusual in this, for she described increasing racial and cultural conflict amongst students, throughout her school career:

> When we were in elementary school, everybody was together, playing. By junior high, things started really dividing up, into groups of people. Hey! By high school—to me, the school system really helped set it down. You had your sections. By that time, you had a whole section of these white racists that were into surfing—very outspoken on being racist. I just started seeing a whole lot of divisions—a whole lot of different

lifestyles coming together and just crashing. [...] low riders, [...] gangs. Things started becoming more segregated, more separate.

Louise described the "surfers" attempts to recruit her to their side, and her refusal to move over: "I saw myself with pride as an anti-racist white." In addition, Louise saw herself as Polish, identified as such by her surname:

> We had to put up with [...] a lot of racist, Polish jokes, but I looked at it—I just laughed, you know, I just looked at it like, "It doesn't bother me! I feel great!"

In Louise's life, then, despite her own connections to Chicano culture, a level of explicit racial conflict was as visible in her environment as that which Pat Bowen experienced in Maryland. Louise responded to it, though, by means of a much more explicit anti-racism, self-consciously rejecting the attentions of racist white students. Like Sandy, class and, in fact, poverty were preconditions for greater racial equality between Louise and those around her: only because Louise's family was almost as poor as those of her neighbours of colour was it possible for her to approach them as peers. Louise's narrative also challenges the assumption that all families are racially homogeneous, and in doing so, indicates from Louise's point of view some of the complexities of negotiating membership in multi-racial family and community, in a racially hierarchical society.

As noted earlier, despite the extent to which Sandy and Louise grew up with close ties with Chicano (and in Sandy's case, also Black and Asian) people, there are reasons to argue that experiences like Sandy's and Louise's represent only a partial or qualified integration. Nor can they be anything else in a racist society, if racial integration is taken to mean the absence of race hierarchy and racist ideas.

Conclusion: White Women's Lives As Sites for the Reproduction of Racism—and for Challenges to It

In all five narratives discussed in this essay, landscape and the experience of it were racially structured. This was true whether those narratives were marked predominantly by the seeming presence or absence of people of colour. This is of course not to say that race was the only principle by which the social context was organized. For example, class intersected with race in differentiating Pat's and Beth's relationships with Black communities, and in making possible the "quasi-integrated" experiences of Louise and Sandy. Again, controls on sexuality link up with racism in creating frequent hostility towards relationships between African-American men and white women.

In addition, once in a landscape structured by racism, a conceptual mapping of race, of self and others, takes shape, which follows from and feeds the physical context. Thus, for example, Sandy experiences the term "Anglo" initially without any negative or positive connotation; Clare both sees through the lens of racial stratification in her own environment, *and* does not perceive racial stratification as such. Even the presence and absence of people of colour seem to be as much social-mental as they are social-physical constructs. Here one can cite the positioning and invisibility of African-American and Latina domestic workers in some apparently all-white homes.

These narratives have some implications for a white feminist analysis of racism. To begin with, they clarify some of the forms, obvious and subtle, that racism and race privilege may take in the lives of white women: including educational and economic privilege, verbally expressed assertions of white superiority, the maintenance of all-white neighbourhoods, the "invisibility" of Black and Latina domestic workers, white people's fear of people of colour, and the "colonial" notion that the cultures of peoples of colour were great only in the past. Racism thus appears not only as an ideology or political orientation chosen or rejected at will; it is also a system and set of ideas embedded in social relations.

My analysis underscores the idea that there is no place for us to stand "outside" racism any more than we can stand "outside" sexism. In this context, it seems foolish to imagine that as individuals we can escape complicity with racism as a social system. We cannot, for example, simply "give up" race privilege. I suggest that as white feminists we need to take cognizance both of the embeddedness of racism in all aspects of society and the ways this has shaped our own lives, theories, and actions. Concretely, this means work in at least three linked areas: work on re-examining personal history and changing consciousness; thorough-going theoretical transformation within feminism; and participation in practical political work towards structural change.

Re-examining personal history is necessary in part because it is possible that white feminists continue relating to people of colour, as well as doing feminist work, on the basis of patterns and assumptions learned early on. For example, there could be a connection between white women's "not noticing" people of colour in their childhood environments, and white feminists' capacity to continue "forgetting" to include women of colour in the planning of conferences and events. This forgetting may, in other words, be a socially constructed one.

Reconceptualization of past experience in fact marked each of the narratives discussed here. Although this was not the case for all the women I interviewed, this group indicated as they told their stories that, with hindsight, they had become more aware of how race differences and racism had been a feature of their childhoods. Phrases like, "Now that we're talking about this I remember ..." and "I was so unaware of cultural differences that ..." signal both lack of awareness of racism *and* moments of recognition or realization of it.

In addition, each woman's experience is complex and contradictory. Thus the two women most explicitly raised to "be racist," Beth and Pat, found contexts and moments, however fleeting, to question the racist status quo. Conversely, Sandy and Louise, raised to find spaces *not* to be racist, were none the less in no sense outside the reach of racism: racism as well as anti-racism shaped their environments, and both women at times drew on white-centred logics in describing and living their lives.

It is from these places of contradiction that the work of revisioning begins. For white women in "mostly racist" contexts, the moments of questioning are perhaps moments when the door opens on to other realms of possibility, other ways of being. Those moments should give us hope. For white women who grew up in situations of "quasi-integration," the racism that still pervades reminds us that this is not a simple struggle, that it is all too easy for us, as white women, to be ethnocentric or patronizing, at the same time as being consciously and purposively anti-racist.

For these five white women (as for most white feminists) access to information about the impact of racism on people of colour, and/or direct or indirect access to the intellectual and political work of people of colour, seem to be crucial to the process of rethinking racism. Thus, for example, Louise's awareness of racism first came about as she saw her friends of colour "tracked" into vocational and remedial classes in high school. And, as an adult, Beth Ellison described how reading African-American women authors such as Toni Morrison and Alice Walker, as well as meeting African Americans, had pushed her to question many of the assumptions about racism and about African Americans with which she had been raised. Pat Bowen described participating in discussions about racism in university Women's Studies classes. And although her cohort was mainly white, the impetus for these discussions had come from the challenges posed by activist women of colour. Pat Bowen's experience raises a further point: the call to accountability raised by women of colour must be met in part by white women learning from one another, teaching each other, and thinking together, for example, about race privilege and its effects on feminism, rather than expecting women of colour to do all of this work for us. This kind of work is going on in the published writings of white anti-racist women (Bulkin, Pratt, and Smith, 1988; Segrest, 1985 among others) as well as through (usually multi-racial) "unlearning racism" workshops and racism consciousness-raising groups (sometimes multi-racial, sometimes not) developed in feminist communities around the country. None the less, the painful truth is that white feminists continue to "forget," to "not think," and this means that the bulk of anti-racist work is being done by people of colour.

There is another link between the reconceptualization of experience and the making of feminism, given that white feminists have often relied on notions of "women's experience" in order to develop theory and strategy for feminism. As mentioned earlier, the experience referred to by white feminists has almost always been white women's experience over generalized. Rarely and only recently have white feminists begun to examine the intersection of their gender and class positions with race privilege. Much white feminist theory generated "from experience" has thus been flawed on two counts, very often assessing *neither* differences between white women and women of colour *nor* adequately describing the race-privileged positions of white women ourselves. (The same points may in fact be made in relation to other groups marginalized within feminism, such as women with disabilities.)

The relationship between experience and the process of interpreting or describing it is by no means simple: as the narratives showed, there were multiple ways in which women named, forgot, remembered, and reinterpreted their experience through the lenses of racism and anti-racism. Accounts of experience are partial, and we must review them as always being open to change. It is also critical, as white women examine and re-examine our complicity with racism, that we go beyond our immediate daily environments to learn more about the history of racist ideas. We need to do this in order to understand the contexts for the production of our "racist lenses," including, for example, the ways white women "fear" people of colour, or the ways we view whiteness as "neutral." Reaching cognitive understandings of the history of white racist consciousness may be a valuable step towards loosening its grip on our daily lives and practice.

As we formulate anti-racist practices, focusing on issues of consciousness is, while necessary, not sufficient. As should be clear from what has been said here, challenging racism is not a project that can take place only on the level of ideas, but one which calls for major changes in the social, economic, and legislative orders. These hold in place the unequal life chances of white people and people of colour, and indeed create what I have called the "social geographies of race" in white women's experience. By itself, reformulating ideas will change none of this. For example, I work in the arena of higher education. I am active in developing multi-racial Women's Studies curricula. However, it is clear to me that we cannot progress very far towards multi-racial curricula unless we make strides towards more multi-racial composition of faculty and student bodies. This in turn implies that we must work to strengthen affirmative action, challenge cutbacks in student financial aid, demand daycare facilities on campus for women with children, improve funding for public high schools, and so on.

In short, there is a delicate balance to be maintained in white feminist practice, for it is precisely racist ideas and lack of awareness that have often prevented white women from challenging racism structurally. Unlearning racism, however, is not the same thing as ending it. Nor can we wait for a moment when we feel we have finished changing our "race consciousness" before becoming active in working against racism in the world at large. Examining whiteness is as urgent now as it ever was, because of the persistence of systemic racism. In the last decade, at the urging of women of colour, white feminists like myself have learnt a lot about the meaning of race privilege. I believe that we can turn the corner into the next century knowing more about what "being white" means than we did two decades ago. Moreover, we will know it from a standpoint that is specifically anti-racist, one that will at the very least challenge the apparent invisibility or neutrality of whiteness,[11] and at best will also see whiteness as a place from which to participate actively in struggles for racial equality. The story of what we will, in practical terms, do with that consciousness in our politics and daily lives continues to unfold, as we transform feminist demands and agendas, and build feminist organizations and institutions. For as always in feminist thinking, new ideas are not merely ends in themselves, but tools to assist in the larger project of social change.

Notes

1. This essay is offered with love to the memory of Rosa Maria Villafañe Sisolak. The essay is adapted from a chapter of *White Women, Race Matters: The Social Construction of Whiteness*, Minneapolis: University of Minnesota Press, 1993, and was originally a doctoral thesis, History of Consciousness, University of California, Santa Cruz, 1988. Warm thanks are due to the thirty white women interviewed for the book. Advisers, friends, family, comrades, and colleagues, including among others, Susan Alexander, Terry Berman, Nancy Chodorow, Jim Clifford, Reyna Cowan, Donna Haraway, Carol Lopes, Chela Sandoval, David Wellman, and, above all, Lata Mani, have given me continued and unstinting support and advice on the project. Jacqui Alexander, Kum-Kum Bhavnani, Mab Segrest, and

several anonymous readers have commented on this essay in particular. Finally, Rosamaria Zayas and Gloria Watkins/ bell hooks initiated a sea-change in my outlook on life when they taught me how urgently I needed to look at the world, and feminism, through the prism of anti-racism.

2. These are the words of Cathy Thomas, one of the white women I interviewed in the research described here. Cathy Thomas is a pseudonym—unfortunately, given the confidentiality of the research, I cannot give Cathy credit by name for this acute observation about the meaning of whiteness for many white people socialized in contexts where the ideology of a "colourblind" society overlays systemic racial inequality.

3. Here and throughout this essay, I assume neither that white women occupy equal positions of advantage in US society, nor that whites' cultures are equally powerful, equally formative of dominant cultural practices.

4. Racism and ethnocentrism are key terms in this essay, so that their meanings unfold throughout the piece. However, a preliminary note on how I would distinguish between these two terms may be in order. I use racism very broadly to denote the structures, institutions, practices, and patterns of thought implicit in a system of domination, of unequal relations of power, constructed around the notion of "race." I do not view racism as an unchanging, timeless, or inevitable system, but rather as one that is changing and historically specific, reproduced in conjunction with other social relations. In parallel, I view the term "race" itself as referring to a socially constructed and historically specific categorization system, rather than to a set of essentially real, unchanging differences. I use ethnocentrism more narrowly than racism to refer to the holding of presumptions about the universality, normalcy, superiority, or "generic" status of attitudes, practices, and forms of social organization that are in reality culturally and historically specific. Ethnocentrism can then refer simply to attitudes, or to patterns of thought embedded in particular instances of theorization and analysis, as well as in actions, practices, and institutions.

5. I am using "Black" here in the "British" sense, to refer to people of Asian and African-Caribbean descent. However,

it should be noted that elsewhere in this essay, when I and the women I interviewed spoke of "Black people," we used the term in the "American" sense, to refer to Americans of African descent.

6. None of that writing was ever published, although we did present our perspective in workshops, both at the University of California, Santa Cruz, and at the University of Oregon, Eugene, in the early 1980s. Our collectively taught class, "Women and Work," University of California, Santa Cruz, January to March 1983, also exemplified our method. Finally, I have written about the collective and its method in "Different Perspectives: Interweaving Theory and Practice in Women's Work," History of Consciousness, University of California at Santa Cruz, June 1988.

7. For example, Gould (1985) describes the history of the reduction of race to biological differences; Omi and Winant (1986: 3–4 and elsewhere) indicate the historical mutability of racial naming and the strong ties between naming and political struggle; Baldwin (1984) analyzes the consolidation of white racial identity in the United States, again in context of political struggle, and the consolidation of power and privilege.

8. Given the constraints of a short essay, many kinds of experience explored in the research are left out of this article: for example, those of older and younger women, women with a stronger sense of cultural or ethnic identity, including Jewish women, women who have *not* critically rethought childhood experience.

9. Discussion of the decisions Beth's mother made are beyond the scope of this essay since I did not interview her, but her daughter. However, it is possible to speculate that, in relation to the Black doctor and his family, a sense of class similarity overrode or mitigated race difference in making Beth's mother feel it was acceptable for the family to move in. In contrast, she did not accept Beth's move to a racially mixed, low-income neighbourhood (in other words a neighbourhood different from Beth's family's in both race and class terms). It is also possible that for Beth's mother, the presence of one or two Black people did not for her disrupt the "whiteness" of the environment, whereas a

greater number of Black people, in school or in a neighbourhood, were more disturbing.

10. I have chosen to stay with Clare's term, "Mexican American" here, for it is impossible to know what name or names the Mexican-descended community in that town might have chosen for themselves and, in fact, "Mexican" and "Mexican American" are good guesses, given the region and timeframe in question.

11. Conscious articulations of whiteness are, however, not necessarily anti-racist. For most of US history, use of the term "white" has been deployed in the context of biology-based racist discourses and hierarchical constructions of "difference." Moreover, in the present, the US white supremacist movement continues to use the term "white" to articulate its sense of white superiority. A good source of information about white supremacist activity is the Center for Democratic Renewal's newsletter, *The Monitor*, PO Box 50469, Atlanta, GA 30302.

References

Alarcon, Norma. (1990) "The Theoretical Subjects of *This Bridge Called My Back* and Anglo-American Feminism" in Anzaldùa, G. editor (1990) *Haciendo Caras: Making Face, Making Soul*. San Francisco: Aunt Lute, 356–69.

Anzaldùa, Gloria, editor. (1990) *Haciendo Caras: Making Face, Making Soul*. San Francisco: Aunt Lute.

Baldwin, James. (1984) "On Being White and Other Lies." *Essence* April, 80–1.

Bhavnani, Kum-Kum, and Coulson, Margaret. (1986) "Transforming Socialist Feminism: The Challenge of Racism." *Feminist Review* 23.

Bulkin, Elly, Pratt, Minnie Bruce, and Smith, Barbara. (1988) *Yours in Struggle: Three Feminist Perspectives on Racism and Antisemitism*. Ithaca: Firebrand Books (original publisher, Long Haul Press, 1984).

Cade, Toni. (1970) *The Black Woman: An Anthology*. New York: Mentor.

Carby, Hazel. (1981) "White Woman Listen! Black Feminism and the Boundaries of Sisterhood" in Center for Contemporary Cultural Studies (1981), *The Empire Strikes Back: Race and Racism in '70s Britain*. London: Hutchinson, 212–35.

Center for Democratic Renewal. *The Monitor,* PO Box 50469, Atlanta, GA 30302.

Combahee River Collective. (1979) "A Black Feminist Statement," in Eisenstein, Zillah R., editor (1979) *Capitalist Patriarchy and the Case for Socialist Feminism*. New York and London: Monthly Review Press.

Davis, Angela Y. (1981) *Women, Race and Class*. New York: Random House.

Davis, Susan E., editor. (1988) *Women under Attack: Victories, Backlash and the Fight for Reproductive Freedom*. Boston: South End Press.

Frankenberg, Ruth. (1985) "White Privilege," unpublished.

_____. (1993) *White Women, Race Matters: The Social Construction of Whiteness*. Minneapolis: University of Minnesota Press. London: Routledge.

Garcia, Alma. (1990) "The Development of Chicana Feminist Discourse, 1970–1980" in DuBois, Ellen Carol, and Ruiz, Vicki L., editors (1990) *Unequal Sisters: A Multicultural Reader in US Women's History*. New York: Routledge, 418–31.

Gould, Stephen Jay. (1985) "Human Equality Is a Contingent Fact of History." *The Flamingo's Smile*. New York: W.W. Norton, 185–97.

Haraway, Donna J. (1991) "Situated Knowledges: The Science Question and the Privilege of Partial Perspective." *Simians, Cyborgs and Women: The Reinvention of Nature*. New York: Routledge, 183–202.

hooks, bell. (1981) *Ain't I a Woman? Black Women and Feminism*. Boston: South End Press.

_____. (1984) *Feminist Theory: From Margin to Center*. Boston: South End Press.

Malveaux, Julianne. (1988) "Ain't I a Woman: Differences in the Labor Market Status of Black and White Women," in Paula S. Rothenberg, editor (1988) *Racism and Sexism: An Integrated Study*. New York: St. Martin's Press, 76–9.

Moraga, Cherrie, and Anzaldùa, Gloria, editors. (1981) *This Bridge Called My Back: Writings by Radical Women of Color*. Watertown: Persephone Press (reprinted by Kitchen Table/Women of Color Press, 1983).

Omi, Michael, and Winant, Howard. (1986) *Racial Formation in the United States: From the 1960s to the 1980s*. New York and London: Routledge & Kegan Paul, 3–4.

Osumi, Megumi Dick. (1982) "Asians and California's Antimiscegenation Laws," in Tsuchida, Nobuya, editor (1982) *Asian/Pacific American Experiences: Women's Perspectives*. Minneapolis: Asian/Pacific American Learning Resource Center and General College, University of Minnesota, cited in Amott, Teresa L., and Matthaei, Julie A. (1991) *Race, Gender and Work: A Multicultural Economic History of Women in the United States*. Boston: South End Press, 195.

Reagon, Bernice Johnson. (1983) "Coalition Politics: Turning the Century," in Smith, Barbara, editor (1983) *Home Girls: A Black Feminist Anthology*. New York: Kitchen Table/Women of Color Press, 356–69.

Rollins, Judith. (1985) *Between Women: Domestics and Their Employers*. Philadelphia: Temple University Press.

Sandoval, Chela. (1982) "The Struggle Within: Women Respond to Racism—Report on the National Women's Studies Conference, Storrs, Connecticut." Oakland, California: Occasional Paper, Center for Third World Organizing (revised version in Anzaldùa 1990) 55–71.

_____. (1991) "US Third World Feminism: The Theory and Method of Oppositional Consciousness in the Postmodern World." *Genders* 10, 1–24.

Segrest, Mab. (1985) *My Mama's Dead Squirrel: Lesbian Essays on Southern Culture*. Ithaca, NY: Firebrand Books.

Ware, Vron. (1992) *Beyond the Pale: White Women, Racism and History*. London: Verso.

Zavella, Patricia. (1987) "The Problematic Relationship of Feminism and Chicana Studies"; paper delivered to conference on "Women: Culture, Conflict and Consensus," University of California, Los Angeles.

Zinn, Maxine Baca et al. (1986) "The Cost of Exclusionary Practices in Women's Studies." *Signs* Winter.

Caribbean Feminism
versus Canadian Feminism

Yvonne Bobb-Smith

One day, one day, congotay[1]

Caribbean-Canadian women [in my study] proved they belong to those ancestors of the Caribbean region who charted a legacy of resistance: Aboriginal, African, Asian, and, least in numbers of all, European. These women belong to a people whose histories are interconnected, and whose experiences under the evil forces of imperialism are interrelated. Because they have "come from the nigger yard," the "coolie yard," the "bound yard,"[2] and often they remain "strangers in a hostile landscape."[3] To this new landscape of Canada, Caribbean women brought their resilience to sexism within Black communities and to racism within the White feminist organizations. The rejection experienced in these two sites of struggle, during the eighties, precipitated a strongly aggressive thrust by many Caribbean-Canadian women to find space for their voices to explore issues of identity in race, gender, and sexuality. As a consequence, a Caribbean brand of feminism was adopted to examine comprehensively the oppressions that subordinated them and affected not only their rights, but those of their communities as well. Their efforts crystallized in a formation of a women's movement which was an alternative to White and mainstream feminist organizing.

These Caribbean-Canadian women practiced a Caribbean feminism which, as Rhoda Reddock (1990) argues, identifies Caribbean women with a historic struggle in opposition and resistance to a dual system of capitalism and patriarchy. Their fight for liberation has produced a counter ideology to many ideas of women's roles in Western society. This ideology includes Caribbean women fundamentally, as workers, who seek female emancipation through proficiency in skills to achieve social and economic independence. As well, it includes their sense of humanity to join Caribbean men in leadership of anti-colonial and labour struggles.

Thus, Caribbean feminism had some major ideological differences with Canadian feminism. One, those who described themselves as feminists at that time in Canada were White, middle-class women who were often well-educated. Caribbean-Canadian women who were active in the struggle against racism were cross-class, and had not yet, in numbers, achieved levels of education nor career-based opportunities as White Canadian feminists had, though they were intellectually active. Two, the Canadian feminists saw "home" significantly as one of the sites of oppression. Caribbean-Canadian women were opposed to centralizing home negatively because their experiences of home meant nurturing and connection with "family" to support their strategies of resistance against issues of race and gender. Three, Canadian feminists opted for a hegemonic approach to identity; that is, they did not attempt to define or recognize diversity and difference among women. Caribbean-Canadian women comprised a group of diverse heritages, though, collectively they, at that time, identified as Black. There were others who chose a single identity—Indo-Caribbean or Chinese-Caribbean—who were also engaging at disparate sites in the struggle. Four, Canadian feminists failed to see racism as an issue for White women within their primary politics. For Caribbean-Canadian women, their true lives were submerged under a loss of identity occasioned by ongoing discriminatory practices of State and public, which constituted racism.

Therefore, on these four counts, Caribbean-Canadian women "felt silenced and robbed" (Ruth Pierson 1993:207) Experiences of these differing ideologies amounted to condescension, patronage, and defensiveness in the movement, as Rowena says:

My initial foray into politics here was in feminist politics, the Women's Movement, in the late seventies and early eighties, which was extremely white. I dropped out because I was not taken seriously. I was tired of women who weren't getting it. And there were no women of colour. Me was tired of dey tekkin me fuh a nice likkle brown girl.[4] (Interview no. 37, 31 August 1995)

First of all, Caribbean-Canadian women, in particular those who worked in the domestic service of the majority of White homes, could not see the negativity in "home" espoused by White feminists. As domestic service workers, the experience of long separations from their families made their home their haven whenever they got there, and the employers' home a site of oppression. As well, these workers' identities were afflicted with White feminists' insensitivity to race issues, because, in the "historical and contemporary treatment of domestic workers from the Caribbean," White women employers always seem to pathologize a Caribbean woman's identity (Daiva Stasiulis 1987:6). There is also an argument that failure to see racism as a burning issue for migrant women, coupled with many White feminists' denial to apprehend its ill effects, might have been due to their inability to recognize how their social power "revictimized" Black women (Ruth Pierson 1993:189) Therefore, for many Caribbean-Canadian women, socially conscious and active in the movement towards social change, feminism, under White jurisdiction, was another marginalizing process towards their settlement in Canada.[5]

Caribbean-Canadian women's experience of everyday racism focuses mainly on incidents in their workplaces, in housing, in school, and in social and health service institutions.[6] These women applied an ethic of independence and created oppositional activities, within community organizing, to dissolve some of these experiences. They chose sites of involvement such as: immigration and refugee issues, social service practices, cultural production, and eventually the politics of women-centred issues. Their repetitive strategic efforts in response to issues of discrimination and victimization, which formulated sites of pro-action and reaction, I interpret as a development of a social movement in its particularity. I label this process comprehensively, the *1980s Alternative Women's Movement in Canada (AWMC)*. This movement encouraged individual initiatives to anti-racism efforts in the Black community; also, it enabled reform of racist biases in institutions to which these women were directly related. Added to that, it fostered the collaboration, inclusiveness, and solidarity among migrant women from Africa, Asia, Caribbean, the Philippines, as well as with women of the First Nations of Canada. Like the mainstream movement it was dependent on State recognition and its funding, as well as financial contributions from corporate and community sources.

However, the differences in gender ideologies between Canadian and Caribbean feminism cause segregation of the AWMC. Caribbean-Canadian women, who were involved in this movement, claim a social reality existed which was the face of a Caribbean legacy of resistance embracing community, men, and children in the struggle for liberation.[7] Their responsibility for Caribbean men conflicted with degrees of radical feminism, which could have forced them to preclude Caribbean male issues around race and gender. These differences in gender ideologies, for Caribbean-Canadian women, raised some doubts about the rectitude of adapting fully to White thought on gender and leaving Caribbean men out of their concerns. As Maya comments:

I could see the oppression, and yes, the sexism as the source of violence. Yet it never made me want to do away with men in my community. I recognized they are oppressed on the basis of race, as well. So, for me, it became a struggle. I had to think much about an argument from lesbians, in particular, that we can't be supportive of men because we are feminists. It is something I never agreed with. (Interview no. 26, 27 June 1995)

Aita further clarifies how that brand of Caribbean feminism became operable to produce this alternative women's movement, as she says:

I call myself a feminist; I do! Because I believe in the liberation of women. Believe you me, I don't believe in the liberation of women outside the liberation of the family and the community. (Interview no. 20, 14 June 1995)

Notes

1. Standard English translation: *Some day it is obliged to happen*.
2. Meaning: Estate tenement house or logies.
3. I borrow meanings from Martin Carter's (1969) recognition of dehumanization in slavery, Walter Rodney's (1981) references to disparate locations of working people of Guyana, and Meiling Jin's (1990) notion of marginality among indentured workers to emphasize the depth of oppression among the diversity of Caribbean peoples.
4. Standard English translation: *I was tired of the assumption that I was a naïve and good girl that would not oppose any ideas*.
5. Black Canadian women, born in North America, had developed, before this period, different sites of organizing. For example, in 1951, the Canadian Negro Women's Club was founded in Toronto. The purpose was to raise consciousness and to bring public awareness to the merits of Black life in Canada. In order to exert influence at a national level, many of its members were represented in organizations like the Young Women's Christian Association, the Medical Association of Canada, and the National Council of Churches.
6. "Everyday racism," as theorized by Philomena Essed (1991), is a body of prevalent "systematic, recurrent and familiar practices," which distinguishes it from racism at the macro level—the political charting of lack of access to resources (3–4). Experiences of everyday racism are located in the stories that people relate about life in their social contexts.
7. The film production of *Children Are Not the Problem* was among the social action objectives of the Congress of

Black Women (Toronto Chapter) in 1988, as well as advocacy work with the Black Action Defense Committee, a male-dominated organization against police racial profiling and targeting of Black men in the Toronto community.

References

Carter, Martin. (1969). "I Come from the Nigger Yard." In *Selected Poems* (61–63). Georgetown, Guyana: Demerara Publishers Ltd.

Essed, Philomena. (1991). *Understanding Racism: An Interdisciplinary Theory.* Newbury Park, NJ: Sage Publications.

Jin, Meiling. (1990). "Strangers on a Hostile Landscape." In Ramabai Espinet (Ed.), *Creation Fire: A CAFRA Anthology of Caribbean Women's Poetry* (129–132). Toronto: Sister Vision Press.

Pierson, Ruth Roach. (1993). *Canadian Women's Issues: Twenty-Five Years of Women's Activism in English Canada.* Toronto: James Lorimer.

Reddock, Rhoda E. (1990). The Caribbean Feminist Tradition. *Womanspeak* 26/27: 12–14.

Rodney, Walter. (1981). *A History of the Guyanese Working People, 1881–1905.* Baltimore: The Johns Hopkins University Press.

Stasiulis, Daiva K. (1987). Rainbow Feminism: Perspectives on Minority Women in Canada. *RFR/DFR.* 16(1): 5–9.

Modest and Modern: Women As Markers of the Indian Nation State

Amita Handa

In my interviews with young South Asian women, conflicts with parents emerged as the most salient and persistent issue. All of the women spoke about the restrictions on their lives and tied this into the expectations around being a girl. While some were able to escape these confines, others, because of limiting family circumstances and lack of networks, were unable to risk committing any significant acts of disobedience.[1] Although I experienced my adolescent years fifteen years prior to them, I was struck by the degree to which I could relate to the issues and concerns they were raising. There was almost an immediate understanding over how parents and community work to regulate young women's lives. For instance, parents used a particular brand of disciplining with their daughters, and during the interviews we often laughed at the identical phrases of chastisement, which usually focused on an unstated effort to protect women's sexuality.

For South Asian women, negotiating their femininities doesn't just affect their sexual reputations; it also reflects their degree of allegiance to an ethnic collectivity. Rupinder, for example, spoke extensively about how her recent backtalk to her parents in reference to the "unreasonable" restrictions they were placing on her raised concerns not only about her rebelliousness but also about the extent to which she was South Asian.

Rupinder: You say, "Well, you don't let me do what I want to do, so why should I do what you want me to do?" They're like, "Well, we're Indian, we're not white."

Amita: What do you think they mean by that? What do they see as Indian and what do they see as white?

Rupinder: I guess Indian means being wholesome and not being able to talk back to your parents, do whatever they say, and just go to school and home and home to school and work and have no social life. And being white, I guess they see people being as like sluts and rebels and just a lot of rebellionism, I guess.

"Rebellionism" here is challenging parental authority. This concept of authority, however, draws on understandings of "Indian" and "white," as well as on generational differences. The dictates around appropriate femininity are maintained through labelling transgressions as "Western" or "white": challenging parental restrictions makes Rupinder "white." Crossing the boundaries of appropriate behaviour not only signifies a gender transgression but also a cultural one. A real Indian girl would not talk back to her parents and would not want to go out, and so Rupinder's desire for self-determination puts into question her cultural allegiance.

Looking back to history as a way of understanding this dynamic has shown me how women, in the context of larger political struggles, become positioned as representative of cultural, ethnic, and national identities, and how ethnic boundaries depend on notions of gender. Notions of women's sexuality are used to mark the boundaries of cultural and ethnic identity, preservation, and authenticity.

During the nationalist struggle for independence from British rule, for example, certain notions of womanhood, tradition, and culture were used by both British colonialists and Indian nationalists to forge a distinction between East and West. [2] The female body became the site for testing out the modern way of life, and this is still the case: the modern is often presented as a sexual threat for women, and women continue to be the site of an East-West cultural battle.[3] As a result, current questions of cultural authenticity and cultural preservation are inextricably tied to the history of regulation of women's sexualities.

Lata Mani defines colonial discourse as "a mode of understanding Indian society that emerged alongside colonial rule and over time was shared to a greater or lesser extent by officials, missionaries and the indigenous elite, although deployed by these various groups to different, often ideologically opposite ends."[4]

Colonial understandings of women, tradition, and culture persist in the Canadian context in situating young South Asian women. The positioning of South Asians vis-à-vis a dominant white/anglo population continues to be accomplished by drawing boundaries around notions of tradition, culture, and women related to those that operated in colonial India. In fact, "South Asian" is a meaningful category because it is continually marked and distinguishable from the dominant norm.

While youth can be understood as symbolic of both fear and anticipation of modern change, women have come to represent the flip side of modern civilization and the possibility of being outside the effects of modernization. Women are associated with the memory of all that is seen to be good from premodern times. In this sense, they could provide the antidote to the anxieties associated with modern social progress—namely the possibility that limitless freedom might bring about moral and social disintegration.[5]

The question becomes how to preserve women's innocence without sacrificing modern social progress. Indian nationalists fashioned a feminine identity representative of the nation that was modern and Eastern. In colonial India, notions of spirituality, innocence, and purity were enmeshed in a debate about culture and cultural difference. Women became synonymous with these characteristics and were also positioned as the moral guardians and keepers of a particular brand of Indian culture.

Protecting the Khan Dhan:[6] It's All Relative

Much of what is considered fixed, natural, and objective ethnic and national identity is actually based on changing political, economic, and social goals. Certainly, what it is means to be an American today is markedly different from what it meant before September 11, 2001. The boundaries around America have literally and figuratively changed, as have the passion and sentiment behind protecting what is perceived to be the American way of life. At this moment of history it is clear that the American sense of identity is very much in reference to the external world. Joseph Levenson argues that there has been a shift from culturalism to nationalism. The former, which he locates in premodern history, based its notion of community in a natural belief of cultural superiority; it did not seek approval or justification outside of the collectivity itself. Only when cultural values had to seek legitimation in relation to an outside threat in the late nineteenth century, according to Levenson, do we begin to see a disintegration of culturalism and a swift transition to nationalism.[7] Similarly, the Asian historian Duara Prasenjit argues that the notion of ethnicity and its association with the nation-state are modern phenomena. Nationalism, here, is understood as culture being protected by the state or as the politicization of culture.[8] Prasenjit explains how notions of community and nation are mobilized:

> Nationality is formed when the perception of the boundaries of community are transformed, namely, when soft boundaries are transformed into hard ones. This happens when a group succeeds in imposing a historical narrative of descent and/or dissent on both heterogeneous and related cultural practices .... The narrative of discent is used to define and mobilize a community, often by privileging a particular cultural practice (or set of practices) as the constitutive principle of the community—such as language, religion or common historical experience—thereby heightening the self-consciousness of this community in relation to those around it.[9]

Both Levenson and Prasenjit perceive power struggles between communities as having an important impact on community consciousness. Awareness of identity is seen to be heightened in relation to an outside threat.

The power struggle between East and West, and the construction of their respective identities, is based on their relationship to one another; the meaning of each is constructed through the marking out of symbolic boundaries. Women are central to this boundary. This East/West relationship is, of course, not an equal one. In constructing its own oppositional narrative as a marginal community, both currently in the West and previously during the colonial era, South Asian Canadian and Indian nationalist discourses use (or used) certain symbols of community identity as a strategy to assert their own right to cultural (self) determination from a marginal location. Nations can be understood as imagined communities that are built on certain cultural and historical symbols.[10] South Asian community identity in Canada is accomplished by mobilizing certain discourses around ethnicity and cultural preservation. The community imagines itself by using certain historical (colonial) notions of tradition, culture, and gender.

Historians have sought to uncover how gender has been used as a political and ethnic marker in times of change, resistance, and revolution, both in liberal and conservative discourses. Floya Anthias and Nira Yuval-Davis argue that the boundary of ethnicity is inseparable from notions of gender. They contend that women are responsible for upholding the norms and consequent identity of an ethnic collective:

> The boundary of the ethnic is often dependent on gender and there is a reliance on gender attributes for specifying ethnic identity: much of ethnic culture is organized around rules relating to sexuality, marriage and the family, and a true member will perform these roles properly. Communal boundaries often use differences in the way that women are socially constructed as markers. Such markers (for example, expectations about honour, purity, the mothering of patriots, reproducers of the nation, transmitters of ethnic culture) often symbolize the use of women as an ethnic resource.[11]

In the early 1990s, my partner in crime Vinita Srivastava and I put in a proposal at a community radio station (CKLN 88.1 FM) for a bhangra show.[12] We were inspired by the female British Asian DJ Ritu, who hosted the BBC's "Bhangra in Bed." The bhangra explosion in the

UK was unprecedented. While the explosion included groups such as Alaap and Apna Sangeet who maintained a traditional Punjabi folk style but exchanged "back-home" content for a longing for "back home," it also included the likes of Bally Sagoo and Apache Indian who mixed or blended old classical songs with a ragga backbeat rap and reggae-style vocals. What emerged as a central question about music fusion was also the question that underlies the kind of conflict that Rupinder and her parents had: the issue of authenticity and what is truly Indian. The feeling was that this fusion would offend cultural authenticity. Whether the music was played eight years ago in Toronto or for the first time in the new millennium in Trinidad and Tobago, the response was the same: what will the parents think? Won't heads of the community be upset and/or offended? The battle here was between viewing culture as fixed and unchanging and seeing it as always forming, in flux and in fusion. The idea of tradition as fixed, static, and synonymous with certain notions of Hindu Indian femininity can be dated back to colonial understandings of Indian culture and tradition [....]

The genesis of the Indian nation-state provides a good example of how gender and ethnicity worked together to carve out notions of national identity. British colonialists used women as a yardstick to measure the extent of modernization in India: the low status of Indian women indicated to the British the backward condition of the entire country [....]

*****

Women became the focus of a struggle for national independence that was integrally linked to a politics of cultural authenticity: for Indian nationalists, the category "woman," and more accurately, certain notions of the Hindu woman, became emblematic of an Indian national identity.[13]

Indian Femininity As Virtuous and Chaste

For young South Asian women in Canada, nose piercing is a way of calling attention to their ethnic/racial identity. While it has also been associated with the (white) punk rock movement, the nose ring in a Western context indicates a link to South Asian heritage. It is also a gendered performance of ethnicity in a predominantly white context. In Punjabi it is referred to as *koka*, *nath*, or *long*, and the symbolic meaning of this fashion accessory has changed with each generation depending on the cultural and political context. I have witnessed these changes in my own lifetime. I first remember the nose ring on the face of my grandmother. For my mother's generation of middle-class, educated Punjabi women, the nose ring represented a backward (unmodern) practice. Some modern women growing up at the dawn of modern India did not wear one. The absence of this accessory helped to distinguish a (middle-class, educated) modern femininity from a traditional one. When I began to wear a nose ring, my mother saw it as an act of rebellion. For me it was an act of (cultural) assertion, a way of marking difference in the Canadian context that acknowledged and reclaimed to myself and others the idea that being different from white was not necessarily negative.

In interviews with young South Asian women, I found that there was a definite understanding of how certain feminine behaviours were linked to and defined being Indian, while others were associated with being un-Indian. Nina, like all the other girls, spoke to me at length about conflicts with her parents that she saw as having to do with both her gender and culture: "Like if you want to drink, Indian girls can't drink, Indian girls can't smoke, Indian girls can't do this, you can't date."

These concepts of Indian femininity can be found in Indian nationalist visions of Indian identity. During the late nineteenth and early twentieth centuries, Indian nationalists sought to differentiate themselves from both the idea of past tradition and from the West. During "the entire phase of national struggle, the crucial need was to protect, preserve, and strengthen the inner core of national culture, its spiritual essence."[14] Women, substantially, became the sign of this inner identity that was in need of protection and preservation. Indian nationalists attempted to preserve the innocence of women while simultaneously meeting the needs of modernization. They proposed a new kind of woman, one who could enjoy the freedoms of the modern world, such as education and paid employment, while at the same time attending to the responsibilities of the home and upholding cultural norms and the virtues associated with spirituality. Keeping up with modern progress would keep India on par with the British. This nationalist project promoted a notion of civilization which, while rooted in post-Enlightenment understandings of progress and modernity, sought to set itself apart both from a disgraceful past that the British pointed to as a mark of inferiority, and from the West.

What developed, Patha Chatterjee argues, was

> a dominant characteristic of femininity in the new construct of "woman" standing as a sign for "nation," namely spiritual qualities of self-sacrifice, benevolence, devotion, religiosity, and so on. This spirituality did not, as we have seen, impede the chances of woman moving out of the physical confines of the home; on the contrary, it facilitated it, making it possible for her to go into the world under conditions that would not threaten her femininity. In fact the image of woman as goddess or mother served to erase her sexuality in the world outside her home.[15]

Chatterjee maintains that Indian nationalist discourse can only be understood in relation to the dichotomy between the private and the public, or what he calls "the home" and "the world." Indian nationalists asserted that the essential identity of the East "lay in its distinctive, and superior, spiritual culture" (the home) which had not been and did not have to be colonized, yet they also saw keeping abreast with the modern material world as imperative.[16]

The nationalist agenda based its vision of woman on certain assumptions about femininity, about woman as closer to nature, nurturing, and spirituality. Mahatma Gandhi, the influential national leader most strongly associated with his nonviolent strategy to overthrow British rule, also espoused prevailing notions of masculinity and femininity. He wrote in the 1920s: "The female sex is not the weaker sex; it is the nobler of the two: for it is even today the embodiment of sacrifice, silent suffering, humility, faith and knowledge."[17] Women were seen to be inherently sacrificing and to possess the virtues of innocence, purity, and suffering. They were best suited to symbolize civil disobedience, because according to Gandhi, "women optimally embodied ... a dual impulse for 'obedience and rebellion against authority' primarily within the family" that he felt he could mobilize for a revolution against colonial rule. These qualities were glorified as the standard that women should uphold in the nationalist struggle.[18]

This vision of spirituality affects significant aspects of female sexuality. For women, when spirit and body meet, the female body—bearing the mark of the sexual and in this sense overdetermined by it—contains the threat of sexuality. As the active agent of her sexuality, woman is powerful. The only way to make the body-spirit union unthreatening for men is to completely subsume woman's sexuality into the spiritual realm, leaving behind "the realms of the psychic, of desire, of pleasure."[19]

Women therefore became desexualized in the process of nation-building. The idea of the new woman was advanced in the interests of the nation. Her sexuality became the marker of virtue and a symbol of what differentiated her from the Western woman. Modesty, as a code of dress, behaviour, and the proper use of the body (refraining from smoking or drinking), became the symbolic marker of this cultural difference. Chatterjee explains: "A woman identified as westernized, for instance, would invite the ascription of all that the 'normal' woman (mother/sister/wife/daughter) is not— brazen, avaricious, irreligious, sexually promiscuous."[20] The new Indian woman was forged on the grounds of her difference from her Western counterpart. This narrative represented the white woman as everything the Indian woman was not. There are also ethnic and class dimensions of the nationalist project that promised "superiority over the western woman for whom, it was believed, education meant only the acquisition of material skills to compete with men in the outside world and hence a loss of feminine (spiritual) virtues; superiority over the preceding generation of women in their own homes who had been denied the opportunity of freedom by an oppressive and degenerate social tradition; and superiority over women of the lower classes who were actually incapable of appreciating the virtues of freedom."[21]

The Indian identity also became inseparable from a notion of Hindu femininity. The Hindu woman, her fasts and prayers, became the object of aspiration, the symbol of morality and national identity.[22] "Woman" in this process is commissioned as carrier of the nation, the marker of national distinctness symbolized in the specificity of certain cultural practices. I am suggesting that by extension, women are also seen as the carriers of culture. British colonialists contributed to establishing links among woman, tradition, and national identity by refuting the interpretative nature of religious texts and advancing their own civilized notions of practices involving women. This intervention was a show of superiority in order to justify the rightful place of British colonial rule in India.

*****

Conclusion

Identified with nature and the act of procreation, women have been relegated to the task of upholding the virtues associated with all that modern change is said to reject. They, like youth, are associated with purity and innocence, which, if left untouched and protected from the ills of the modern world, could help to preserve some vestiges of a past golden age and thereby alleviate the downfalls of rapid change. However, in nationalist Indian discourses women were placed in a position of having to preserve premodernity in a way that was not at odds with modern change, but distinguished itself from Westernism.

Women are markers of ethnic difference and nationhood. Both Indian nationalists and British colonialists were concerned about the authenticity and boundaries of their respective cultural collectives in the struggle over political rule. Indian nationalists resolved the contradiction between modernization and westernization by allowing women to modernize without forsaking what was perceived to be a true Indian identity. Notions of womanhood were used not only to resolve the ambivalence between premodernity and modernity but also to assert the claim to Indian self-rule. Concepts of femininity in the context of colonial India became inseparable from a politics of cultural authenticity, preservation, and Indian identity itself.

*****

Notes

1. For example, some women had older siblings whom they could go out with or who would "cover" for them, and some had friends or relatives they could rely on as a network of support or as a means of access to public spaces, such as a dance or club.

2. Lata Mani, "Contentious Traditions: The Debate on *Sati* in Colonial India," in *Recasting Women: Essays in Indian Colonial History*, ed. Kumkum Sangari and Sudesh Vaid (New Brunswick: Rutgers University Press, 1990), pp. 88–126; Lata Mani, *Contentious Traditions*, University of California Press, 1999; Partha Chatterjee, *The Nation and Its Fragments: Colonial and Post-Colonial Histories* (New Jersey: Princeton University Press, 1993); Partha Chatterjee, *Wages of Freedom: Fifty Years of the Indian Nation State* (Delhi: Oxford University Press, 1998); Jasodhara Bagchi, "Colonialism and Socialization: The Girl Child in Colonial Bengal," *Resources for Feminist Research* 22, no. 3/4 (Fall/Winter 1993): 23–30.

3. Nalini Natarajan argues, in the context of India, that women have become the terrain of a nationalistic message of "containment of the threat to national culture from diasporic Indian populations" living outside of the Indian subcontinent (Natarajan, "Women, Nation and Narration in *Midnight's Children*," in *Scattered Hegemonies: Postmodernity and Transitional Feminist Practice*, ed. Inderpal Grewal and Caren Kaplan [Minneapolis: University of Minneapolis Press, 1994], p. 87).

4. Mani, "Contentious Traditions," p. 90.

5. The contradiction for women within modernity is that the notion of womanhood has to incorporate the freedoms supposedly opened up by modern progress while simultaneously attending to the responsibility attributed to women, of preserving the morality of the individual and the social order, especially through the family. See Joan Landes, "Women and the Public Sphere: A Modern Perspective," *Social Analysis* 15 (1984): 20–31. To refer to Franco Moretti's argument. the notion of modern self-government includes both the individual's capacity to govern the self through the ability to reason, and the social capacity to self-govern through democratic participation. Within this construction, the only way that traditional notions of responsibility can be maintained is if the individual perceives the norms of social order as her/his own. As Moretti argues: "The ideal of the self-determining or self-legislating individual meant that social order could no longer be maintained by the force of tradition, and consent to that order could not longer be gained through the exercise of the authority of a sovereign form of power .... The problem was posed in terms of how the 'free individual' could be required to be, at the same time, the 'convinced citizen'— not as a fearful subject, but as one who perceives 'the social norms as one's own'" (as paraphrased in Leslie Johnson, *The Modern Girl: Girlhood and Growing Up*, [Philadelphia: Open University Press, 1993] p. 37).

6. *Khan dhan* means "kinship/extended family."

7. Joseph Levenson, *Confuscian China and Its Modern Fate: A Trilogy* (Berkeley: University of California Press, 1965).

8. Duara Prasenjit, "Bifurcating Linear Histories in China and India," in *Rescuing History from the Nation: Questioning Narratives of Modern China*, by Duara Prasenjit (Chicago: University of Chicago Press, 1995), p. 56.

9. Ibid., p. 66. Prasenjit invents the term *discent* to indicate both "dissent" and "descent."

10. See Benedict Anderson, *Imagined Communities: Reflections on the Origin and Spread of Nationalism*, rev. ed. (London: Verso Press, 1991) for more information on nations as imagined communities.

11. Floya Anthias and Nira Yuval-Davis, introduction to *Woman-Nation-State*, ed. Floya Anthias and Nira Yuval-Davis (London: Macmillan, 1989), pp. 113–14.

12. Vinita Srivastava, currently a freelance journalist in New York, is the co-founder of "Masala Mixx" and founder of the on-line magazine (e-zine) *Brownsugar* (www.brownsugaronline.com)—a culture and arts magazine for South Asian women.

13. See Natarajan, "Women, Nation and Narration"; Bagchi, "Colonialism and Socialization," pp. 22–30; Kumkum

Sangari and Sudesh Vaid, eds., *Recasting Women: Essays in Indian Colonial History* (New Brunswick: Rutgers University Press, 1990); Mani, "Multiple Mediations," pp. 24–41; Mani, "Contentious Traditions"; Mani, *Contentious Traditions*.

14. Chatterjee, *Nation and Its Fragments*, p. 121; also see pp. 116–34.

15. Ibid., p. 131.

16. Ibid., p. 121.

17. As quoted in Kumari Jayawardena, *Feminism and Nationalism in the Third World* (New Delhi: Kali for Women, 1986), p. 95.

18. Ketu Ketrak, "Indian Nationalism, Gandhian Satyagraha and the Representations of Female Sexuality," in *Nationalism and Sexualities*, ed. Andre Parker et al. (New York: Routledge, 199), p. 396.

    Ketrak argues that Gandhi deliberately chose certain mythological heroines over others because they best embodied these virtues. For example, Gandhi praised the virtues of figures like Sita and Draupadi who, according to Hindu mythology, embodied notions of strength that lay in self-sacrifice and passivity. He chose these symbols over such heroines as the Rani of Jhansi who cloaked herself in male attire and in 1857 led troops into battle against the British Raj (p. 398).

19. Ibid., p. 391.

20. Chatterjee, *Nation and Its Fragments*, p. 131. The West was aligned with the kind of modernity nationalists wanted to distinguish themselves from; they saw Western modernism as contradictory to the Indian identity that needed preserving. According to nationalist discourses, the inner core of this identity was contained within the private sphere, and could be preserved by women. A multitude of claims were made by Indian nationalists about the superior moral character of women that justified their suitability for this role. Women and the true essence of Indian identity became synonymous, and both were seen as in need of protection from the threat of Western modernity.

21. Ibid., p. 391.

22. For more on Hindu womanhood and Indian national identity, see Bagchi, "Colonialism and Socialization."

Man Royals and Sodomites: Some Thoughts on the Invisibility of Afro-Caribbean Lesbians

Makeda Silvera

I will begin with some personal images and voices about woman-loving. These have provided a ground for my search for cultural reflections of my identity as a Black woman artist within the Afro-Caribbean community of Toronto. Although I focus here on my own experience (specifically, Jamaican), I am aware of similarities with the experience of other Third World women of colour whose history and culture has been subjected to colonisation and imperialism.

I spent the first thirteen years of my life in Jamaica among strong women. My great-grandmother, my grandmother, and grand-aunts were major influences in my life. There are also men whom I remember with fondness—my grandmother's "man friend" G., my Uncle Bertie, his friend Paul, Mr. Minott, Uncle B., and Uncle Freddy. And there were men like Mr. Eden who terrified me because of stories about his "walking" fingers and his liking for girls under age fourteen.

I lived in a four-bedroom house with my grandmother, Uncle Bertie, and two female tenants. On the same piece of land, my grandmother had other tenants, mostly women and lots of children. The big verandah of our house played a vital role in the social life of this community. It was on the verandah that I received my first education on "Black women's strength"—not only from their strength, but also from the daily humiliations they bore at work and in relationships. European experience coined the term "feminism," but the term "Black women's strength" reaches beyond Eurocentric definitions to describe what is the cultural continuity of my own struggles.

The verandah. My grandmother sat on the verandah in the evenings after all the chores were done to read the newspaper. People—mostly women—gathered there to discuss "life." Life covered every conceivable topic— economic, local, political, social, and sexual: the high price of salt-fish, the scarcity of flour, the nice piece of yellow yam bought at Coronation market, Mr. Lam, the shopkeeper who was taking "liberty" with Miss Inez, the fights women had with their menfolk, work, suspicions of Miss Iris and Punsie carrying on something between them, the cost of school books ....

My grandmother usually had lots of advice to pass on to the women on the verandah, all grounded in the Bible. Granny believed in Jesus, in good and evil, and in repentance. She was also a practical and sociable woman. Her faith didn't interfere with her perception of what it meant to be a poor Black woman; neither did it interfere with our Friday night visits to my Aunt Marie's bar. I remember sitting outside on the piazza with my grandmother, two grand-aunts, and three or four of their women friends. I liked their flashy smiles and I was fascinated by their independence, ease, and their laughter. I loved their names—Cherry Rose, Blossom, Jonesie, Poinsietta, Ivory, Pearl, Iris, Bloom, Dahlia, Babes. Whenever the conversation came around to some "big 'oman talk"—who was sleeping with whom or whose daughter just got "fallen," I was sent off to get a glass of water for an adult, or a bottle of Kola champagne. Every Friday night I drank as much as half a dozen bottles of Kola champagne, but I still managed to hear snippets of words, tail ends of conversations about women together.

In Jamaica, the words used to describe many of these women would be "Man Royal" and/or "Sodomite." Dread words. So dread that women dare not use these words to name themselves. They were names given to women by men to describe aspects of our lives that men neither understood nor approved.

I heard "sodomite" whispered a lot during my primary school years, and tales of women secretly having sex, joining at the genitals, and being taken to the hospital to be "cut" apart were told in the school yard. Invariably, one of the women would die. Every five to ten years the same story would surface. At times, it would even be published in the newspapers. Such stories always generated much talking and speculation from "Bwoy dem kinda gal naasti sah!" to some wise old woman saying, "But dis caan happen, after two shutpan caan join"— meaning identical objects cannot go into the other. The act of loving someone of the same sex was sinful, abnormal—something to hide. Even today, it isn't unusual or uncommon to be asked, "So how do two 'omen do it? ... what unnu use for a penis? ... who is the man and who is the 'oman?" It's inconceivable that women can have intimate relationships that are whole, that are not lacking because of the absence of a man. It's assumed that women in such relationships must be imitating men.

The word "sodomite" derives from the Old Testament. Its common use to describe lesbians (or any

strong independent woman) is peculiar to Jamaica—a culture historically and strongly grounded in the Bible. Although Christian values have dominated the world, their effect in slave colonies is particular. Our foreparents gained access to literacy through the Bible when they were being indoctrinated by missionaries. It provided powerful and ancient stories of strength, endurance, and hope which reflected their own fight against oppression. This book has been so powerful that it continues to bind our lives with its racism and misogyny. Thus, the importance the Bible plays in Afro-Caribbean culture must be recognised in order to understand the historical and political context for the invisibility of lesbians. The wrath of God "rained down burning sulphur on Sodom and Gomorrah" (*Genesis* 19:23). How could a Caribbean woman claim the name?

When, thousand of miles away and fifteen years after my school days, my grandmother was confronted with my love for a woman, her reaction was determined by her Christian faith and by this dread word sodomite—its meaning, its implication, its history.

And when, Bible in hand, my grandmother responded to my love by sitting me down, at the age of twenty-seven, to quote Genesis, it was within the context of this tradition, this politic. When she pointed out that "this was a white people ting," or "a ting only people with mixed blood was involved in" (to explain or include my love with a woman of mixed race), it was strong denial of many ordinary Black working-class women she knew.

It was finally through my conversations with my grandmother, my mother, and my mother's friend five years later that I began to realise the scope of this denial which was intended to dissuade and protect me. She knew too well that any woman who took a woman lover was attempting to walk on fire—entering a "no man's land." I began to see how commonplace the act of loving women really was, particularly in working-class communities. I realised, too, just how heavily shame and silence weighed down this act.

A conversation with a friend of my mother:

Well, when I growing up we didn't hear much 'bout woman and woman. They weren't "suspect." There was much more talk about "batty man business" when I was a teenager in the 1950s.

I remember one story about a man who was "suspect" and that every night when he was coming home, a group of guys use to lay wait him and stone him so viciously that he had to run for his life. Dem time, he was safe only in the day.

Now with women, nobody really suspected. I grew up in the country and I grew up seeing women holding hands, hugging up, sleeping together in one bed and there was no question. Some of this was based purely on emotional friendship, but I also knew of cases where the women were dealing but no one really suspected. Close people around knew, but not everyone. It wasn't a thing that you would go out and broadcast. It would be something just between the two people.

Also one important thing is that the women who were involved carried on with life just the same, no big political statements were made. These women still went to church, still got baptised, still went on pilgrimage, and I am thinking about one particular woman name Aunt Vie, a very strong woman, strong-willed and everything, they use to call her "man-royal" behind her back, but no one ever dare to meddle with her.

Things are different now in Jamaica. Now all you have to do is not respond to a man's call to you and dem call you sodomite or lesbian. I guess it was different back then forty years ago because it was harder for anybody to really conceive of two woman sleeping and being sexual. But I do remember when you were "suspect," people would talk about you. You were definitely classed as "different," "not normal," a bit "crazy." But women never really got stoned like the men.

What I remember is that if you were a single woman alone or two single women living together and a few people suspected this ... and when I say a few people I mean like a few guys, sometimes other crimes were committed against the women. Some very violent, some very subtle. Battery was common, especially in Kingston. A group of men would suspect a woman or have it out for her because she was a "sodomite" or because she act "man-royal" and so the men would organise and gang rape whichever woman was "suspect." Sometimes it was reported in the newspapers, other times it wasn't—but when you live in a little community, you don't need a newspaper to tell you what's going on. You know by word of mouth and those stories were frequent. Sometimes you also knew the men who did the battery.

Other subtle forms of this was "scorning" the women. Meaning that you didn't eat anything from them, especially a cooked meal. It was almost as if those accused of being "man-royal" or "sodomite" could contaminate.

A conversation with my grandmother:

I am only telling you this so that you can understand that this is not a profession to be proud of and to get involved in. Everybody should be curious and I know you born with that, ever since you growing up as a child and I can't fight against that, because that is how everybody get to know what's in the world. I am only telling you this because when you were a teenager, you always say you want to experience everything and make up your mind on your own. You didn't like people telling you what was wrong and right. That always use to scare me.

Experience is good, yes. But it have to be balanced, you have to know when you have too much experience in one area. I am telling you this because I think you have enough experience in this to decide now to go back to the normal way. You have two children. Do you want them to grow up knowing this is the life you have taken? But this is for you to decide ....

Yes, there was a lot of women involved with women in Jamaica. I knew a lot of them when I was growing up in the country in the 1920s. I didn't really associate with them. Mind you, I was not rude to them. My mother wouldn't stand for any rudeness from any of her children to adults.

I remember a woman we use to call Miss Bibi. She live next to us—her husband was a fisherman, I think he drowned before I was born. She had a little wooden house that back onto the sea, the same as our house. She was quiet, always reading. That I remember about her because she use to go to the little public library at least four days out of the week. And she could talk. Anything you want to know, just ask Miss Bibi and she could tell you. She was a mulatto woman, but poor. Anytime I had any school work that I didn't understand, I use to ask her. The one thing I remember, though, we wasn't allowed in her house by my mother, so I use to talk to her outside, but she didn't seem to mind that. Some people use to think she was mad because she spent so much time alone. But I didn't think that because anything she help me with, I got a good mark on it in school.

She was colourful in her own way, but quiet, always alone, except when her friend come and visit her once a year for two weeks. Them times I didn't see Miss Bibi much because my mother told me I couldn't go and visit her. Sometimes I would see her in the market exchanging and bartering fresh fish for vegetables and fruits. I use to see her friend too. She was a jet Black woman, always had her hair tied in bright coloured cloth and she always had on big gold earrings. People use to say she live on the other side of the island with her husband and children and she came to Port Maria once a year to visit Miss Bibi.

My mother and father were great storytellers and I learnt that from them, but is from Miss Bibi that I think I learnt to love reading so much as a child. It wasn't until I move to Kingston that I notice other women like Miss Bibi ....

Let me tell you about Jones. Do you remember her? Well she was the woman who live the next yard over from us. She is the one who really turn me against people like that, why I fear so much for you to be involved in this ting. She was very loud. Very show-off. Always dressed in pants and man-shirt that she borrowed from her husband. Sometimes she use to invite me over to her house, but I didn't go. She always had her hair in a bob hair cut, always barefoot and tending to her garden and her fruit trees. She tried to get me involved in that kind of life, but I said no. At the time I remember I needed some money to borrow and she lent me, later she told me I didn't have to pay her back, but to come over to her house and see the thing she had that was sweeter than what any man could offer me. I told her no and eventually paid her back the money.

We still continued to talk. It was hard not to like Jonesie—that's what everybody called her. She was open and easy to talk to. But still there was a fear in me about her. To me it seem like she was in a dead end with nowhere to go. I don't want that for you.

I left my grandmother's house that day feeling anger and sadness for Miss Jones—maybe for myself, who knows. I was feeling boxed in. I had said nothing. I'd only listened quietly.

In bed that night, I thought about Miss Jones. I cried for her (for me) silently. I remember her, a mannish looking Indian woman, with flashy gold teeth, a Craven A cigarette always between them. She was always nice to me as a child. She had the sweetest, juiciest Julie, Bombay, and East Indian mangoes on the street. She always gave me mangoes over the fence. I remember the dogs in her yard and the sign on her gate. "Beware of bad dogs." I never went into her house, though I was always curious.

I vaguely remember her pants and shirts, though I never thought anything of them until my grandmother pointed them out. Neither did I recall that dreaded word being used to describe her, although everyone on the street knew about her.

A conversation with my mother:

Yes, I remember Miss Jones. She smoke a lot, drank a lot. In fact, she was an alcoholic. When I was in my teens she use to come over to our house—always on the verandah. I can't remember her sitting down—seems she was always standing up, smoking, drinking, and reminiscing. She constantly talked about the past, about her life, and it was always on the verandah. And it was always women: young women she knew when she was a young woman, the fun they had together, and how good she would make love to a woman. She would say to whoever was listening on the verandah, "Dem girls I use to have sex with was shapely. You shoulda know me when I was younger, pretty, and shapely just like the 'oman dem I use to have as my 'oman."

People use to tease her on the street, but not about being a lesbian or calling her sodomite. People use to tease her when she was drunk, because she would leave the rumshop and stagger down the avenue to her house.

I remember the women she use to carry home, usually in the daytime. A lot of women from downtown, higglers and fishwomen. She use to boast about knowing all kinds of women from Coronation market and her familiarity with them. She had a husband who lived with her and that served as her greatest protection against other men taking steps with her. Not that anybody could easily take advantage of Miss Jones, she could stand up for herself. But having a husband did help. He was a very quiet, insular man. He didn't talk to anyone on the street. He had no friends so it wasn't easy for anyone to come up to him and gossip about his wife.

No one could go to her house without being invited, but I wouldn't say she was a private person. She was a loner. She went to the rumshops alone, she drank alone, she staggered home alone. The only time I ever saw her with somebody were the times when she went off to the Coronation market or some other place downtown to find a woman and bring her home. The only times I

remember her engaging in conversation with anybody was when she came over on the verandah to talk about her women and what they did in bed. That was all she let out about herself. There was nothing about how she was feeling, whether she was sad or depressed, lonely, happy. Nothing. She seemed to cover up all that with her loudness and her vulgarness and her constant threat—which was all it was—to beat up anybody who troubled her or teased her when she was coming home from the rumshop.

Now Cherry Rose—do you remember her? She was a good friend of Aunt Marie and of Mama's. She was also a sodomite. She was loud too, but different from Miss Jones. She was much more outgoing. She was a barmaid and had lots of friends—both men and women. She also had the kind of personality that attracted people—very vivacious, always laughing, talking, and touching. She didn't have any children, but Gem did.

Do you remember Miss Gem? Well she had children and she was also a barmaid. She also had lots of friends. She also had a man friend name Mickey, but that didn't matter because some women had their men and still had women they carried on with. The men usually didn't know what was going on, and seeing as these men just come and go and usually on their own time, they weren't around every day and night.

Miss Pearl was another one that was in that kind of thing. She was a dressmaker, she use to sew really good. Where Gem was light complexion, she was a very black Black woman with deep dimples. Where Gem was a bit plump, Pearl was slim, but with big breast and a big bottom. They were both pretty women.

I don't remember hearing that word sodomite a lot about them. It was whispered sometimes behind their backs, but never in front of them. And they were so alive and talkative that people were always around them.

The one woman I almost forgot was Miss Opal, a very quiet woman. She use to be friends with Miss Olive and was always out at her bar sitting down. I can't remember much about her except she didn't drink like Miss Jones and she wasn't vulgar. She was soft spoken, a half-Chinese woman. Her mother was born in Hong Kong and her father was a Black man. She could really bake. She use to supply shops with cakes and other pastries.

So there were many of those kind of women around. But it wasn't broadcast.

I remembered them. Not as lesbians or sodomites or man royals, but as women that I liked. Women who I admired. Strong women, some colourful, some quiet.

I loved Cherry Rose's style. I loved her loudness, the way she challenged men in arguments, the bold way she laughed in their faces, the jingle of her gold bracelets. Her colourful and stylish way of dressing. She was full of wit; words came alive in her mouth.

Miss Gem: I remember her big double iron bed. That was where Paula and Lorraine (her daughters, my own age) and I spent a whole week together when we had chicken pox. My grandmother took me there to stay for the company. It was fun. Miss Gem lived right above her bar and so at any time we could look through the window and onto the piazza and street, which was bursting with energy and life. She was a very warm woman, patient and caring. Every day she would make soup for us and tell us stories. Later on in the evening she would bring us Kola champagne.

Miss Pearl sewed dresses for me. She hardly ever used her tape measure—she could just take one look at you and make you a dress fit for a queen. What is she doing now, I asked myself? And Miss Opal, with her calm and quiet, where is she—still baking?

What stories could these lesbians have told us? I, an Afro-Caribbean woman living in Canada, come with this baggage—their silenced stories. My grandmother and mother know the truth, but silence still surrounds us. The truth remains a secret to the rest of the family and friends, and I must decide whether to continue to sew this cloth of denial or break free, creating and becoming the artist that I am, bring alive the voices and images of Cherry Rose, Miss Gem, Miss Jones, Opal, Pearl, and others ....

There is more at risk for us than for white women. Through three hundred years of history we have carried memories and the scars of racism and violence with us. We are the sister, daughter, mothers of a people enslaved by colonialists and imperialists. Under slavery, production and reproduction were inextricably linked. Reproduction served not only to increase the labour force of slave owners but also, by "domesticating" the enslaved, facilitated the process of social conditions by focusing on those aspects of life in which they could express their own desires. Sex was an area in which to articulate one's humanity, but, because it was tied to attempts "to define oneself as human," gender roles, as well as the act of sex, became badges of status. To be male was to be the stud, the procreator; to be female was to be fecund, and one's femininity was measured by the ability to attract and hold a man, and to bear children. In this way, slavery and the post-emancipated colonial order defined the structures of patriarchy and heterosexuality as necessary for social mobility and acceptance.

Socio-economic conditions and the quest for a better life has seen steady migration from Jamaica and the rest of the Caribbean to the US, Britain, and Canada. Upon my arrival, I became part of the so-called "visible minorities" encompassing Blacks, Asians, and Native North Americans in Canada. I live with a legacy of continued racism and prejudice. We confront this daily, both as individuals and as organised political groups. Yet for those of us who are lesbians, there is another struggle: the struggle for acceptance and positive self-definition within our own communities. Too often, we have had to sacrifice our love for women in political meetings that have been dominated by the "we are the world" attitude of heterosexual ideology. We have had to hide too often that part of our identity which contributes profoundly to make up the whole.

Many lesbians have worked, like me, in the struggles of Black people since the 1960s. We have been on marches every time one of us gets murdered by the police. We have been at sit-ins and vigils. We have flyered, postered, we have cooked and baked for the struggle. We have tended to the youths. And we have all at one time or another given support to men in our community, all the time painfully holding onto, obscuring, our secret lives. When we do walk out of the closet (or are thrown out), the "ideologues" of the Black communities say "Yes, she was a radical sistren but, I don't know what happen, she just went the wrong way." What is implicit in this is that one cannot be a lesbian and continue to do political work, and not surprisingly, it follows that a Black lesbian/artist cannot create using the art forms of our culture. For example, when a heterosexual male friend came to my house, I put on a dub poetry tape. He asked, "Are you sure that sistren is a lesbian?"

"Why?" I ask.

"Because this poem sound wicked; it have lots of rhythm; it sounds cultural."

Another time, another man commented on my work, "That book you wrote on domestic workers is really a fine piece of work. I didn't know you were that informed about the economic politics of the Caribbean and Canada." What are we to assume from this? That Afro-Caribbean lesbians have no Caribbean culture? That they lose their community politics when they sleep with women? Or that Afro-Caribbean culture is a heterosexual commodity?

The presence of an "out" Afro-Caribbean lesbian in our community is dealt with by suspicion and fear from both men and our heterosexual Black sisters. It brings into question the assumption of heterosexuality as the only "normal" way. It forces them to acknowledge something that has always been covered up. It forces them to look at women differently and brings into question the traditional Black female role. Negative response from our heterosexual Black sister, though

more painful, is, to a certain extent, understandable because we have no race privilege and very, very few of us have class privilege. The one privilege within our group is heterosexual. We have all suffered at the hands of this racist system at one time or another and to many heterosexual Black women it is inconceivable, almost frightening, that one could turn her back on credibility in our community and the society at large by being lesbian. These women are also afraid that they will be labelled "lesbian" by association. It is that fear, that homophobia, which keeps Black women isolated.

The Toronto Black community has not dealt with sexism. It has not been pushed to do so. Neither has it given a thought to its heterosexism. In 1988, my grandmother's fear is very real, very alive. One takes a chance when one writes about being an Afro-Caribbean lesbian. There is the fear that one might not live to write more. There is the danger of being physically "disciplined" for speaking as a woman-identified woman.

And what of our white lesbian sisters and their community? They have learnt well from the civil rights movement about organising, and with race and some class privilege, they have built a predominantly white lesbian (and gay) movement—a pre-condition for a significant body of work by a writer or artist. They have demanded and received recognition from politicians (no matter how little). But this recognition has not been extended to Third World lesbians of colour—neither from politicians nor from white lesbian (and gay) organisations. The white lesbian organisations/groups have barely (some not at all) begun to deal with or acknowledge their own racism, prejudice, and biases—all learned from a system which feeds on their ignorance and grows stronger from its institutionalised racism. Too often white women focus only on their oppression as lesbians, ignoring the more complex oppression of non-white women who are also lesbians. We remain outsiders in these groups, without images or political voices that echo our own. We know too clearly that, as non-white lesbians in this country, we are politically and socially at the very bottom of the heap. Denial of such differences robs us of true visibility. We must identify and define these differences, and challenge the movements and groups that are not accessible to non-whites—challenge groups that are not accountable.

But where does this leave us as Afro-Caribbean lesbians, as part of this "visible minority" community? As Afro-Caribbean women we are still at the stage where we have to imagine and discover our existence, past and present. As lesbians, we are even more marginalised, less visible. The absence of a national Black lesbian and gay movement through which to begin to name ourselves is disheartening. We have no political organisation to support us and through which we could demand respect from our communities. We need such an organisation to represent our interests, both in coalition-building with other lesbian/gay organisations, and in the struggles which shape our future—through which we hope to transform the social, political, and economic systems of oppression as they affect all peoples.

Though not yet on a large scale, lesbians and gays of Caribbean descent are beginning to seek each other out—are slowly organising. Younger lesbians and gays of colour are beginning to challenge and force their parents and the Black community to deal with their sexuality. They have formed groups, "Zami for Black and Caribbean gays and lesbians" and "Lesbians of Colour," to name two.

The need to make connections with other Caribbean and Third World people of colour who are lesbian and gay is urgent. This is where we can begin to build that other half of our community, to create wholeness through our art. This is where we will find the support and strength to struggle, to share our histories, and to record these histories in books, documentaries, film, sound, and art. We will create a rhythm that is uniquely ours—proud, powerful, and gay, naming ourselves, and taking our space within the larger history of Afro-Caribbean peoples.

SECTION THREE

SOCIALIZATION AND GENDER ROLES

X—A Fabulous Child's Story

Lois Gould

Once upon a time, a baby named X was born. This baby was named X so that nobody could tell whether it was a boy or a girl. Its parents could tell, of course, but they couldn't tell anybody else. They couldn't even tell Baby X, at first.

You see, it was all part of a very important Secret Scientific Xperiment, known officially as Project Baby X. The smartest scientists had set up this Xperiment at a cost of Xactly 23 billion dollars and 72 cents, which might seem like a lot for just one baby, even a very important Xperimental baby. But when you remember the prices of things like strained carrots and stuffed bunnies, and popcorn for the movies and booster shots for camp, let alone twenty-eight shiny quarters from the tooth fairy, you begin to see how it adds up.

Also, long before Baby X was born, all those scientists had to be paid to work out the details of the Xperiment, and to write the *Official Instruction Manual* for Baby X's parents and, most important of all, to find the right set of parents to bring up Baby X. These parents had to be selected very carefully. Thousands of volunteers had to take thousands of tests and answer thousands of tricky questions. Almost everybody failed because, it turned out, almost everybody really wanted either a baby boy or a baby girl, and not Baby X at all. Also, almost

everybody was afraid that a Baby X would be a lot more trouble than a boy or a girl. (They were probably right, the scientists admitted, but Baby X needed parents who wouldn't *mind* the Xtra trouble.)

There were families with grandparents named Milton and Agatha, who didn't see why the baby couldn't be named Milton or Agatha instead of X, even if it *was* an X. There were families with aunts who insisted on knitting tiny dresses and uncles who insisted on sending tiny baseball mitts. Worst of all, there were families that already had other children who couldn't be trusted to keep the secret. Certainly not if they knew the secret was worth 23 billion dollars and 72 cents—and all you had to do was take one little peek at Baby X in the bathtub to know if it was a boy or a girl.

But, finally, the scientists found the Joneses, who really wanted to raise an X more than any other kind of baby—no matter how much trouble it would be. Ms. and Mr. Jones had to promise they would take equal turns caring for X, and feeding it, and singing it lullabies. And they had to promise never to hire any baby-sitters. The government scientists knew perfectly well that a baby-sitter would probably peek at X in the bathtub, too.

The day the Joneses brought their baby home, lots of friends and relatives came over to see it. None of them knew about the secret Xperiment, though. So the first thing they asked was what kind of a baby X was. When the Joneses smiled and said, "It's an X!" nobody knew what to say. They couldn't say, "Look at her cute little dimples!" And they couldn't say, "Look at his husky little biceps!" And they couldn't even say just plain "kitchy-coo." In fact, they all thought the Joneses were playing some kind of rude joke.

But, of course, the Joneses were not joking. "It's an X" was absolutely all they would say. And that made the friends and relatives very angry. The relatives all felt embarrassed about having an X in the family. "People will think there's something wrong with it!" some of them whispered. "There *is* something wrong with it!" others whispered back.

"Nonsense!" the Joneses told them all cheerfully. "What could possibly be wrong with this perfectly adorable X?"

Nobody could answer that, except Baby X, who had just finished its bottle. Baby X's answer was a loud, satisfied burp.

Clearly, nothing at all was wrong. Nevertheless, none of the relatives felt comfortable about buying a present for a Baby X. The cousins who sent the baby a tiny football helmet would not come and visit any more. And the neighbors who sent a pink-flowered romper suit pulled their shades down when the Joneses passed their house.

The *Official Instruction Manual* had warned the new parents that this would happen, so they didn't fret about it. Besides, they were too busy with baby X and the hundreds of different Xercises for treating it properly.

Ms. and Mr. Jones had to be Xtra careful about how they played with little X. They knew that if they kept bouncing it up in the air and saying how *strong* and *active* it was, they'd be treating it more like a boy than an X. But if all they did was cuddle it and kiss it and tell it how *sweet* and *dainty* it was, they'd be treating it more like a girl than an X.

On page 1,654 of the *Official Instruction Manual*, the scientists prescribed: "plenty of bouncing and plenty of cuddling, *both*. X ought to be strong and sweet and active. Forget about *dainty* altogether."

Meanwhile, the Joneses were worrying about other problems. Toys, for instance. And clothes. On his first shopping trip, Mr. Jones told the store clerk, "I need some clothes and toys for my new baby." The clerk smiled and said, "Well, now, is it a boy or a girl?" "It's an X," Mr. Jones said, smiling back. But the clerk got all red in the face and said huffily, "In that case, I'm afraid I can't help you, sir." So Mr. Jones wandered helplessly up and down the aisles trying to find what X needed. But everything in the store was piled up in sections marked "Boys" or "Girls." There were "Boys' Pajamas" and "Girls' Underwear" and "Boys' Fire Engines" and "Girls' Housekeeping Sets." Mr. Jones went home without buying anything for X. That night he and Ms. Jones consulted page 2,326 of the *Official Instruction Manual*. "Buy plenty of everything!" it said firmly.

So they bought plenty of sturdy blue pajamas in the Boys' Department and cheerful flowered underwear in the Girls' Department. And they bought all kinds of toys. A boy doll that made pee-pee and cried, "Pa-pa." And a girl doll that talked in three languages and said, "I am the Pres-i-dent of Gen-er-al Mo-tors." They also bought a storybook about a brave princess who rescued a handsome prince from his ivory tower, and another one about a sister and brother who grew up to be a baseball star and a ballet star, and you had to guess which was which.

The head scientists of Project Baby X checked all their purchases and told them to keep up the good work. They also reminded the Joneses to see page 4,629 of the *Manual*, where it said, "Never make Baby X feel *embarrassed* or *ashamed* about what it wants to play with. And if X gets dirty climbing rocks, never say 'Nice little Xes don't get dirty climbing rocks.'"

Likewise, it said, "If X falls down and cries, never say 'Brave little Xes don't cry.' Because, of course, nice little Xes *do* get dirty, and brave little Xes *do* cry. No matter how dirty X gets, or how hard it cries, don't worry. It's all part of the Xperiment."

Whenever the Joneses pushed Baby X's stroller in the park, smiling strangers would come over and coo: "Is that a boy or a girl?" The Joneses would smile back and say, "It's an X." The strangers would stop smiling then, and often snarl something nasty—as if the Joneses had snarled at *them*.

By the time X grew big enough to play with other children, the Joneses' troubles had grown bigger, too. Once a little girl grabbed X's shovel in the sandbox, and zonked X on the head with it. "Now, now, Tracy," the little girl's mother began to scold, "little girls mustn't hit little—" and she turned to ask X, "Are you a little boy or a little girl, dear?"

Mr. Jones, who was sitting near the sandbox, held his breath and crossed his fingers.

X smiled politely at the lady, even though X's head had never been zonked so hard in its life. "I'm a little X," X replied.

"You're a *what?*" the lady exclaimed angrily. "You're a little b-r-a-t, you mean!"

"But little girls mustn't hit little Xes, either!" said X, retrieving the shovel with another polite smile. "What good does hitting do, anyway?"

X's father, who was still holding his breath, finally let it out, uncrossed his fingers, and grinned back at X.

And at their next secret Project Baby X meeting, the scientists grinned, too. Baby X was doing fine.

But then it was time for X to start school. The Joneses were really worried about this, because school was even more full of rules for boys and girls, and there were no rules for Xes. The teacher would tell boys to form one line, and girls to form another line. There would be boys' games and girls' games, and boys' secrets and girls' secrets. The school library would have a list of recommended books for girls, and a different list of recommended books for boys. There would even he a bathroom marked BOYS and another one marked GIRLS. Pretty soon boys and girls would hardly talk to each other. What would happen to poor little X?

The Joneses spent weeks consulting their *Instruction Manual* (there were 249½ pages of advice under "First Day of School"), and attending urgent special conferences with the smart scientists of Project Baby X.

The scientists had to make sure that X's mother had taught X how to throw and catch a ball properly, and that X's father had been sure to teach X what to serve at a doll's tea party. X had to know how to shoot marbles and how to jump rope and, most of all, what to say when the Other Children asked whether X was a Boy or a Girl.

Finally, X was ready. The Joneses helped X button on a nice new pair of red-and-white checked overalls, and sharpened six pencils for X's nice new pencilbox, and marked X's name clearly on all the books in its nice new bookbag. X brushed its teeth and combed its hair, which just about covered its ears, and remembered to put a napkin in its lunchbox.

The Joneses had asked X's teacher if the class could line up alphabetically, instead of forming separate lines for boys and girls. And they had asked if X could use the principal's bathroom, because it wasn't marked anything except BATHROOM. X's teacher promised to take care of all those problems. But nobody could help X with the biggest problem of all—Other Children.

Nobody in X's class had ever known an X before. What would they think? How would X make friends?

You couldn't tell what X was by studying its clothes— overalls don't even button right-to-left, like girls' clothes, or left-to-right, like boys' clothes. And you couldn't guess whether X had a girl's short haircut or a boy's long haircut. And it was very hard to tell by the games X liked to play. Either X played ball very well for a girl, or else X played house very well for a boy.

Some of the children tried to find out by asking X tricky questions, like "Who's your favorite sports star?" That was easy. X had two favorite sports stars: a girl jockey named Robyn Smith and a boy archery champion named Robin Hood. Then they asked, "What's your favorite TV program?" And that was even easier. X's favorite TV program was "Lassie," which stars a girl dog played by a boy dog.

When X said that its favorite toy was a doll, everyone decided that X must be a girl. But then X said that the doll was really a robot, and that X had computerized it, and that it was programmed to bake fudge brownies and then clean up the kitchen. After X told them that, the other children gave up guessing what X was. All they knew was they'd sure like to see X's doll.

After school, X wanted to play with the other children. "How about shooting some baskets in the gym?" X asked the girls. But all they did was make faces and giggle behind X's back.

"How about weaving some baskets in the arts and crafts room?" X asked the boys. But they all made faces and giggled behind X's back, too.

That night, Ms. and Mr. Jones asked X how things had gone at school. X told them sadly that the lessons were okay, but otherwise school was a terrible place for an X. It seemed as if Other Children would never want an X for a friend.

Once more, the Joneses reached for their *Instruction Manual.* Under "Other Children," they found the following message: "What did you Xpect? *Other Children* have to obey all the silly boy-girl rules, because their parents taught them to. Lucky X—you don't have to stick to the rules at all! All you have to do is be yourself. P.S. We're not saying it'll be easy."

X liked being itself. But X cried a lot that night, partly because it felt afraid. So X's father held X tight, and cuddled it, and couldn't help crying a little, too. And X's mother cheered them both up by reading an Xciting story about an enchanted prince called Sleeping Handsome, who woke up when Princess Charming kissed him.

The next morning, they all felt much better, and little X went back to school with a brave smile and a clean pair of red-and-white checked overalls.

There was a seven-letter-word spelling bee in class that day. And a seven-lap boys' relay race in the gym. And a seven-layer-cake baking contest in the girls' kitchen corner. X won the spelling bee. X also won the relay race. And X almost won the baking contest, except it forgot to light the oven. Which only proves that nobody's perfect.

One of the Other Children noticed something else, too. He said: "Winning or losing doesn't seem to count to X. X seems to have fun being good at boys' skills *and* girls' skills."

"Come to think of it," said another one of the Other Children, "maybe X is having twice as much fun as we are!"

So after school that day, the girl who beat X at the baking contest gave X a big slice of her prizewinning cake. And the boy X beat in the relay race asked X to race him home.

From then on, some really funny things began to happen. Susie, who sat next to X in class, suddenly refused to wear pink dresses to school any more. She insisted on wearing red-and-white checked overalls—just like X's. Overalls, she told her parents, were much better for climbing monkey bars.

Then Jim, the class football nut, started wheeling his little sister's doll carriage around the football field. He'd put on his entire football uniform, except for the helmet. Then he'd put the helmet *in* the carriage, lovingly tucked under an old set of shoulder pads. Then he'd start jogging around the field, pushing the carriage and singing "Rockabye Baby" to his football helmet. He told his family that X did the same thing, so it must be okay. After all, X was now the team's star quarterback.

Susie's parents were horrified by her behavior, and Jim's parents were worried sick about his. But the worst came when the twins, Joe and Peggy, decided to share everything with each other. Peggy used Joe's hockey skates, and his microscope, and took half his newspaper route. Joe used Peggy's needlepoint kit, and her cookbooks, and took two of her three baby-sitting jobs. Peggy started running the lawn mower, and Joe started running the vacuum cleaner.

Their parents weren't one bit pleased with Peggy's wonderful biology experiments, or with Joe's terrific needlepoint pillows. They didn't care that Peggy mowed the lawn better, and that Joe vacuumed the carpet better. In fact, they were furious. It's all that little X's fault, they agreed. Just because X doesn't know what it is, or what it's supposed to be, it wants to get everybody *else* mixed up, too!

Peggy and Joe were forbidden to play with X any more. So was Susie, and then Jim, and then *all* the Other Children. But it was too late; the Other Children stayed mixed up and happy and free, and refused to go back to the way they'd been before X.

Finally, Joe and Peggy's parents decided to call an emergency meeting of the school's Parents' Association, to discuss "The X Problem." They sent a report to the principal stating that X was a "disruptive influence." They demanded immediate action. The Joneses, they said, should be *forced* to tell whether X was a boy or a girl. And then X should be *forced* to behave like whichever it was. If the Joneses refused to tell, the Parents' Association said, then X must take an Xamination. The school psychiatrist must Xamine it physically and mentally, and issue a full report. If X's test showed it was a boy, it would have to obey all the boys' rules. If it proved to be a girl, X would have to obey all the girls' rules.

And if X turned out to be some kind of mixed-up misfit, then X should be Xpelled from the school. Immediately!

The principal was very upset. Disruptive influence? Mixed-up misfit? But X was an Xcellent student. All the teachers said it was a delight to have X in their classes. X was president of the student council. X had won first prize in the talent show, and second prize in the art show, and honorable mention in the science fair, and six athletic events on field day, including the potato race.

Nevertheless, insisted the Parents' Association, X is a Problem Child. X is the Biggest Problem Child we have *ever* seen!

So the principal reluctantly notified X's parents that numerous complaints about X's behavior had come to the school's attention. And that after the psychiatrist's Xamination, the school would decide what to do about X.

The Joneses reported this at once to the scientists, who referred them to page 85,759 of the *Instruction Manual*. "Sooner or later," it said, "X will have to be Xamined by a psychiatrist. This may be the only way any of us will know for sure whether X is mixed up—or whether everyone else is."

The night before X was to be Xamined, the Joneses tried not to let X see how worried they were. "What if—?" Mr. Jones would say. And Ms. Jones would reply, "No use worrying." Then a few minutes later, Ms. Jones would say, "What if—?" and Mr. Jones would reply, "No use worrying."

X just smiled at them both, and hugged them hard and didn't say much of anything. X was thinking, What if—? And then X thought: No use worrying.

At Xactly nine o'clock the next day, X reported to the school psychiatrist's office. The principal, along with a committee from the Parents' Association, X's teacher, X's classmates, and Ms. and Mr. Jones, waited in the hall outside. Nobody knew the details of the tests X was to be given, but everybody knew they'd be *very* hard, and that they'd reveal Xactly what *everyone* wanted to know about X, but were afraid to ask.

It was terribly quiet in the hall. Almost spooky. Once in a while, they would hear a strange noise inside the room. There were buzzes. And a beep or two. And several bells. An occasional light would flash under the door. The Joneses thought it was a white light, but the principal thought it was blue. Two or three children swore it was either yellow or green. And the Parents' Committee missed it completely.

Through it all, you could hear the psychiatrist's low voice, asking hundreds of questions, and X's higher voice, answering hundreds of answers.

The whole thing took so long that everyone knew it must be the most complete Xamination anyone had ever had to take. Poor X, the Joneses thought. Serves X right, the Parents' Committee thought. I wouldn't like to be in X's overalls right now, the children thought.

At last, the door opened. Everyone crowded around to hear the results. X didn't look any different; in fact, X was smiling. But the psychiatrist looked terrible. He looked as if he was crying! "What happened?" everyone began shouting. Had X done something disgraceful? "I wouldn't be a bit surprised!" muttered Peggy and Joe's parents. "Did X flunk the *whole* test?" cried Susie's parents. "Or just the most important part?" yelled Jim's parents.

"Oh, dear," sighed Mr. Jones.

"Oh, dear," sighed Ms. Jones.

"*Sssh*," ssshed the principal. "The psychiatrist is trying to speak."

Wiping his *eyes* and clearing his throat, the psychiatrist began, in a hoarse whisper. "In my opinion," he whispered—you could tell he must be very upset— "in my opinion, young X here—"

"Yes? Yes?" shouted a parent impatiently.

"*Sssh!*" ssshed the principal.

"Young *Sssh* here, I mean young X," said the doctor, frowning, "is just about—"

"Just about *what?* Let's have it!" shouted another parent.

"… just about the *least* mixed-up child I've ever Xamined!" said the psychiatrist.

"Yay for X!" yelled one of the children. And then the others began yelling, too. Clapping and cheering and jumping up and down.

"*SSSH!*" SSShed the principal, but nobody did.

The Parents' Committee was angry and bewildered. How *could* X have passed the whole Xamination? Didn't X have an *identity* problem? Wasn't X mixed up at *all?* Wasn't X *any* kind of a misfit? How could it *not* be, when it didn't *even* *know* what it was? And why was the psychiatrist crying?

Actually, he had stopped crying and was smiling politely through his tears. "Don't *you* see?" he said. "I'm crying because it's wonderful! X has absolutely no identity problem! X isn't one bit mixed up! As for being a misfit— ridiculous! X knows perfectly well what it is! Don't you, X?" The doctor winked. X winked back.

"But what *is* X?" shrieked Peggy and Joe's parents. "*We* still want to know what it is!"

"Ah, yes," said the doctor, winking again. "Well, don't worry. You'll all know one of these days. And you won't need me to tell you."

"What? What does he mean?" some of the parents grumbled suspiciously.

Susie and Peggy and Joe all answered at once. "He means that by the time X's sex matters, it won't be a secret any more!"

With that, the doctor began to push through the crowd toward X's parents. "How do you do," he said, somewhat stiffly. And then he reached out to hug them both. "If I ever have an X of my own," he whispered, "I sure hope you'll lend me your instruction manual."

Needless to say, the Joneses were very happy. The Project Baby X scientists were rather pleased, too. So were Susie, Jim, Peggy, Joe, and all the Other Children. The Parents' Association wasn't, but they had promised to accept the psychiatrist's report, and not make any more trouble. They even invited Ms. and Mr. Jones to become honorary members, which they did.

Later that day, all X's friends put on their red-and-white checked overalls and went over to see X. They found X in the back yard, playing with a very tiny baby that none of them had ever seen before. The baby was wearing very tiny red-and-white checked overalls.

"How do you like our new baby?" X asked the Other Children proudly.

"It's got cute dimples," said Jim.

"It's got husky biceps, too," said Susie.

"What kind of baby is it?" asked Joe and Peggy.

X frowned at them. "Can't you tell?" Then X broke into a big, mischievous grin. "*It's a Y!*"

Nakedness: Pride and Shame

Naomi Wolf

So you see that to be a girl is very special ....
Your body begins to mature beautifully ... you'll
begin to develop the pretty curves that make
older girls so proud of themselves. Suddenly a
waistline will show. Your legs and arms will
become rounder and your hips curvier. Breasts
will begin to form on what was previously a flat
chest .... Each year from now on, that very special
feminine quality that has been yours from the
moment you were born will become ... more
noticeable.
>   —Kimberly-Clark, "The Miracle of You,"
>   1968, 1973

The very consciousness of their nature must
evoke [in women] feelings of shame.
>   —Clement of Alexandria, *Pædagogus*

Girls' normal anxieties about nakedness were
intensified for us by the growth of the sex
industry. Something new was happening, for
what had been hidden from middle-class children since
the Victorians had invented childhood's privileged space
was now being exposed to them. During our childhoods,
the sex industry moved from being confined to the world
of adults—specifically adult men—to being an ever-
growing part of the visible universe of children. During
the 1970s, in many parts of California, "distribution
locations" for the sex industry proliferated twentyfold.
Our demographic counterparts in 1869 would have been
exposed to almost no graphic images of female sexuality.
In 1942, Anne Frank's ignorance of the adult world of
sexual images may have left her better able to characterize
with little ambivalence the sweet feeling she had for a
boy whom she had a crush on. Her vague fantasies of
being kissed are appropriate to her age. After 1969, my
friends and I were exposed, just by walking to our schools
and playgrounds, to fantasies that were in no way
appropriate to our psychic ages, that belonged to the
daily-more-expressive imaginations of adults.

The images we had of what it would mean to grow
up and grow sexual were more complicated year by year.
At eleven, my friend Cath and I would go on long bus
journeys through the city. On our trips we saw scene
after scene that we needed to think about. We understood
that they bore intimately on the changes our bodies would
soon undergo.

On Broadway, there was a line of huge neon signs
demarcating what became the sex-club district. On that
block was the famous club the Condor. As everyone

knew, the stripper Carol Doda worked there. Even the breakfast-table columnists in the city newspaper wrote about her. I had the impression that she actually lived in the Condor. I understood that she was a joke and that what had happened to her breasts was a joke. They had always been huge, and they had become even huger because of silicone. It was funny that now she was a famous pair of breasts. There were lots of punch lines involving the local landmark, Twin Peaks.

A sign that stood about twelve feet high advertised her. It was made in the shape of her body. Perched on the sign's immense neon breasts were two red lights that blinked comically on and off. The whole atmosphere around her was absurd, and the absurdity was about what happened to women when they have breasts. I understood that someday my own breasts would grow and might make me a laughingstock as well. I wondered why some women's breasts were funny and other women got away with just having them, without being a joke, and I wanted to know how I could be sure to be in the second category.

Another sign on the block read: SEE AND TALK TO A NAKED GIRL FOR ONE DOLLAR. A naked girl? For a dollar? Cath and I discussed this but could come to no certain conclusions. "See and talk to": what was the importance to men, I wondered, of that—would women not talk to them otherwise or let men see them? And what about this clearly valuable, desirable commodity: "a naked girl"? I did not yet understand where the special value lay in that. Underneath my raveling sweaters and the bellbottoms with the patched knees, even *I* was a naked girl; so were all my friends, and our older sisters.

"We used to drive to the Bay Bridge," Sandy recalled when I spoke to her as an adult. "And I was so shocked— there were these signs *everywhere* saying 'naked girls.' And my mind was blown away. What *is this?* There were signs saying things like 'topless,' 'bottomless,' 'totally nude.' And I pictured these torsos ... half a woman."

"Did you ever talk to your parents about this?" I asked her.

"I knew I was not supposed to ask them. I understood that I was supposed not to see it, that it didn't matter and it wasn't there. But I thought it was exciting. I would cross my fingers and hope my parents would drive down that street so I could look at these signs.

"The one that really got me was a sign that showed a naked lady kneeling, wearing a mortarboard. It said: 'totally nude college coeds.' That was the first time I had ever heard the word 'coed.' And I thought, whatever a coed is, it must be really special because they've got a sign about them naked.

"That was the most prominent image of a college-educated woman that I had in my life. It affected my idea of schooling. It was not like you saw images of women in college attire anywhere else when you were a little girl."

We knew the women in those images were exciting but also silly. Was this imagery only a form of comedy? I wondered about that, too. I could tell that a sense of awe and almost of fear drove the comedy. Though Carol Doda was a joke, she was also a sort of deity. The sign of her body was bigger than anything else on that street. Behind her massive curving hips and the blinking of her nipples, the hill dropped off precipitously and you could see the sweep of the Bay Bridge and the white-steel shine of the surface of the bay, but none of it could dwarf the great figure of the woman mounted high over the street.

Farther down the block was the Garden of Eden; that sign showed Adam and Eve, and Eve was represented, again in neon, as a slim nude girl, seen from the back, standing, with a serpent coiled around her body. On the sign for the World of Eros, a sixteen-foot half-draped woman was painted on half a block of wall space, lying recumbent across from a parking lot. Another sign proclaimed: LIVE GIRLS. LIVE LIVE LIVE. I wondered at this too: What else would they be?

I wanted to understand how it worked, for this was Sexland. I wanted to explore Sexland the way I wanted to visit Disneyland. And though nothing was keeping me out, I had a sense that there would be a price to pay if I drew closer. There was always a man standing by a stack of magazines, yelling something as if guarding the gate. His hands were in his front pockets, making fists. I was afraid of him.

The "naked girl" seemed to have little value to the dispensers of sex newspapers that had begun to appear at child's-eye height on street corners. These were much more graphic and raw than the old-fashioned "burlesque" listings in the newspaper. Passing these dispensers on my way home from school, I would stop outside Cala Foods where we shopped; the cranky old crossing guard would gesture to me to stay where I was. I would look and not look at these newsprint representations of "sex"—of the fate of all big girls. These naked women were young—as young as our favorite, least authoritative substitute teachers—smiling their strained smiles. Their slender but quite ordinary bodies were contorted this way and that in hapless calisthenics. And I wondered: Are they there because they are having fun? How can they be having fun if there are no boys with them? What is fun about this for them—for big girls? I knew this imagery was "sexy," though it did not look to me like "sex." But I could not see what was in it for women. I still recall those bodies in all their postures, like a human alphabet, presented week by week on cheap newsprint on the street corners of my hometown. Like Sandy, I remember how odd it seemed that they were everywhere, but neither the crossing guard nor the ladies behind the counter at Cala nor my mother who took me by the hand seemed to see them at all. They seemed actively to avoid them.

There were more congenial images of female sexuality, too. My favorite was the scene in the bronze fountain at Ghirardelli Square, where two young mermaids played. They were surrounded by pond lilies, and on each lily pad was a welter of jolly toads. The scene was lewd: toads were kissing, small toads jumped on the backs of big toads, and water spouted over it all.

One mermaid held out her arms, and toads leapt from her outstretched fingers. The mermaid bodies, though cast in metal, looked at once soft and strong. Each was a little pouchy in the belly and a little slack in the full breast. One mermaid cradled a merbaby in her arms. The baby was laughing. The grown mermaids were naked in the most public of spaces—yet merry, confident, young, and maternal. This also seemed to me to be part of Sexland but of a different kind. The fountain was reassuring to me. These mermaids were happy and playful as well as "sexy." The bronze mermaids were imaginary, of course, and Carol Doda was real, but to me they seemed more real than she did. As I grew older, the Carol Doda images proliferated and became active and three-dimensional and the glimpses of what the mermaids represented grew rarer and quainter.

Wending our way among these divergent images, my friends and I had to follow complex and contradictory rules about girls' nakedness. By the time my Bay Area friends and I were twelve, we had developed, as a way of creating order out of chaos, a byzantine sense of what was just naked enough and what was too naked. We were not sluts. The way we negotiated being "not-sluts" had to do with paying close attention to excruciatingly subtle rules. Midriff-baring shirts were fashionable that year. If you showed an inch of belly too much, the look was "slutty." But if too little belly showed, you risked being a "doggie," a loser in the sexual hierarchy.

That year I went away to overnight camp for the first time. In our barracklike dormitories, we practiced preparing and evaluating our nakedness. Bras and shaving were the mediums for this activity, which took place in communal dressing-up sessions for the Friday-night dance. Bras were important. Wearing no bra at all was considered to be too naked; a bra made of what must have been some newly invented polymer blend, an early forerunner of spandex, that shimmered over the skin, hooked brazenly in front, and showed the shape of the breast was just naked enough; a training bra that showed nothing was not sufficiently naked. Bras—their outlines, their straps—were the badge. Panties were less important. No one, we reckoned, was going to see our panties for a good long time.

Shaving was important, too. Big girls shaved their legs. We would lather our shins up to the kneecap—beyond, up to the thigh, for the most daring—and then take turns shaving, using steady, unchildlike upward strokes and being careful not to nick. The shaving was full of implications: we were signaling that these particular expanses of tanned skin were to be transformed in anticipation of the touch of a boy. Beyond kissing, we knew that it was here—with these smooth calves—that it would all begin.

The first time I shaved my legs, that summer, it was in defiance of my mother's warning: "Once you start, you can never stop, it only grows back coarser." To me, this caution was exciting: "Once you start, you can never stop …" I recognized these words, on a subliminal level, as the eternal caution of mothers to virgin daughters. Her words echoed in my ears as I made the first swipe. There, Mom! My skin was denuded in my first irrevocable act.

Then each girl would put on her underclothing. The more developmentally advanced of the girls would wear real bras. These fastened with intriguing hook-and-eye devices and had underwiring. The wiring distinguished those who had arrived from those who were still aspiring. The most daring girls had obtained the new spandex brassieres that were so excitingly translucent. (They also discovered the bras pilled, and fell apart in the wash.) The less-advanced girls—including, predictably, me—did not subject themselves to the ridicule that pretensions to such garments would inspire. Facing the fact of our untransformed and unwished-for selves, we pulled on the simple white cotton brassieres that were sold folded up in utilitarian cardboard containers. Little corn-fed blond girls smiled on the boxes, just as they did on the white plastic Wonder Bread packaging. There was no mystery

in that part of the girls' department of the store: AAA, AA, A ran the sizes, from smallest to "largest," and if you merited only the triple A, everyone understood that "bra" was a courtesy term for the seamless elastic garment with the babyish bow.

Through the bras, our nakedness was already graded. We understood that its quality corresponded to the quality of the prizes that went with it, and the bras were the prizes. Somehow, I would have to make the transition from the training bra to the Juniors' or Misses' section of the store, which smelled of perfume instead of starch, where the pearl- and rose-colored, even pure black, real brassieres hung on metal trees, shifting in the air-conditioning. It was entirely outside my control. There was no guarantee that I would ever make it over the threshold. In the meantime, I would try to follow the rules.

The problem was that the designation of "too naked" was not entirely within our control. The state of being too naked, we found, could inhere in the very structure of our physiognomy, no matter what clothes we wore.

Yet what were we to do? In San Francisco at that time, just about everyone, it seemed, was divesting him- or herself of clothing. Topless women, fur visible under proudly upraised arms, were marching in women's liberation parades; we saw their pictures in our moms' *Ms.* magazines. Gay men hung out on the sunny sidewalks in the Castro wearing nothing but leather chaps and jockstraps. Our moms and dads went to Esalen on weekends, or Big Sur, and sat around naked in hot tubs with other kids' moms and dads and other kids. "Take it off," purred an ad for shaving cream; "Take it *all* off." That was what cool people did—but it seemed that everyone was taking his or her clothes off in public except the only people most of us girls really wanted to take a look at—the boys we liked. The straight boys kept their baggy army-surplus shorts on and smugly surveyed the scene.

In the autumn of my twelfth year, I was in Israel with my family. In some ways, that visit, which took me out of a culture increasingly influenced by the sex industry, gave me a perspective on my peers' new femininity that was both more innocent and more authentic. My girlfriends in the modern neighborhood in Jerusalem where we lived were less affected by sexual expectations than my San Francisco friends had been—the Orthodox-dominated city had little sexual imagery on display—but they were much more curious on their own terms. When the Israeli girls and I played together we'd go to the house of whoever's mother was out, turn up the fans, take off our shirts, and inspect one another. Our interest was almost clinical. We would turn upon one girl or another and dare her to take off her shirt. She had to. The peer pressure against refusing was intense. We would ignore the girl if she declined. When she did our bidding, we would gather like medical students and scrutinize the buds of her breasts. We were both fascinated and repelled by the inflamed aureoli on the still-boyish chest, the first stage of breast development that characterized almost all of us. We knew these weren't real breasts yet. Another girl might share the information that if you pinch these buds, they would get harder from a rush of blood. A third might dispute this. Then we would pressure the first girl into demonstrating. She would blush and protest, but the pressure from the alternating taunts and cajoling would only grow more insistent.

"All right. I'll show you. But," she would bargain, "only if you will all come out with me on the balcony and flash the traffic."

A deal. This sort of bargain had an inner logic in the dreamtime of the room. We were fixated on dares and were always on the lookout for a good one. This was the kind of dare we longed to be goaded into, just as we goaded our day's designated specimen into taking off her shirt.

In a close, awkward group, we would edge out to the balcony. Then, huddling at the threshold, with little shrieks, our hearts pounding, we would push one another out into the sun. "You go!" "You!" "Now!" In one desperate moment, by unspoken agreement, all of us would rush out, flip up our T-shirts, and then duck, howling, back into the living room.

Afterward, our chests tingled. We were being girls together, flaunting what was happening to us and proud of it. We would tuck our shirts back in, thrilled with ourselves. And the traffic would flow on, ignorant of the little girls too high up anyway to be seen, who for an instant had felt electric with arrogance and power.

This "compare-and-contrast" ritual seems widespread. Sandy's took place at summer camp, a "hippie camp." "At camp," she recalls, "we spent a lot of time swimming around naked. At that age you've got girls at all stages of development. By eleven I had friends with fully developed breasts, friends who were menstruating, and everything in between."

The girls, she said, had different names for the different stages of breast development. "'Nuzzies,'" she recounted as if doing an inventory. "They were the little mosquito bites. 'Squeeners' were where they get kind of pointy, starting to stick out. 'Dudleys' were when they got kind of round. 'Bonkers' were normal adult women's breasts. And 'bongaydie ladies'—I don't know how you'd spell that—were the women with breasts that hung down to the navels. My campmates and I just made these up. 'Cause we were all in these different stages. This was the vocabulary we had to talk about what was going on in our bodies. I remember singing this song about 'We are bosom buddies—some are big, some are small. But what the hell, we've got 'em all.' It had nothing to do with sexually interacting with boys," she explained. "This was just about being girls together.

"There was a part of it," she went on, "that made developing okay. That was the word: 'developing.' I got to see that it was normal. I think all girls had these questions about themselves and other girls, whether they were lying around together naked or not. But it was also a hazing ritual: you had to be comfortable being naked to be part of this group. We would tease other campers who didn't want to take off their bathing suits. We'd make them cry.

"I was a late bloomer," she said. "I felt very inadequate because boys were interested in the girls with larger breasts and they weren't interested in me. Girls with bigger breasts seem to have taken part in more sexual activities with boys—this is by thirteen. The friends I had who weren't virgins any more at thirteen were larger breasted. Because their bodies developed at a younger age, they got hit on younger. I had a few years' grace."

I knew what she was talking about. When I returned to California, that innocent sense of pride and pleasure I had had on the balcony became elusive again. Dangers loomed larger. It seemed that no matter how hard we tried to make and stick to rules about nakedness, we were confounded. You could wear a training bra and a work shirt and jeans, and a grown man would say "Mama!" to you, a little girl, on the street: you had been too naked. A judge in California ruled, at around that time, that a high school boy who had raped a girl in a school stairwell was not culpable because of the girl's revealing clothing: jeans. The other women remember the same ruling; a homeroom teacher told their class about it to scare them. The ruling did scare us. We all wore jeans.

A young woman named Daria, from a Baptist background, also told me a story about her own early experiment with nakedness. In this case, the moral of the story, in her eyes, is the shame her nakedness had first caused her.

"I must have been twelve or thirteen," she said. "I was just becoming an adolescent and had been changing, but there was no acknowledgment of my 'becoming a woman' whatsoever at home. I always wore baggy clothes, little girls' loose clothing. I didn't want to draw attention to the change: it was too frightening to do so; I was afraid that my grandfather would say that I looked like a harlot. And that my mother would disapprove: I would no longer be someone she liked, no longer deserve to be 'her girl.'"

One night in Albuquerque, where she, her three younger half brothers, and her grandparents, who were raising her, were living, the whole family went out to an old-fashioned restaurant.

The evening was a romantic prospect for Daria. The restaurant was grown-up: it had banquettes and a maître d'. The newness of the setting, the fact that she would probably never see any of the grown-ups eating there that night again, the southwestern springtime, the teenage coat-check boy who had been chivalrous as he took her jacket—all these made Daria take a risk.

She excused herself and went to the ladies' room. She washed her hands, using up all the pink soap. The restaurant had provided hand lotion: she spread it all over her face and throat. It was called "Cashmere Bouquet," a name that to her was suggestive of being adult and exotic. She then reached into her bag, took out the lipstick and mascara she had bought at Woolworth's and had kept hidden like a talisman in her sock drawer, and painted her face for the first time. She took off the detachable collar of her little-girl velvet dress and undid the top two buttons. The black velvet suddenly looked sophisticated. It was almost, she thought, as if she was dressed in "evening wear." Her skinny child's arms metamorphosed before her eyes into the arms of a young woman waiting to be caressed. Daria looked in the mirror and saw herself beautifully changed into her next and more powerful self.

Downstairs, in the restaurant, she joined her family. Everyone started to whisper urgently at her. "Go wash that off!" hissed her perfectly groomed grandmother.

"What is this nonsense?" muttered her grandfather.

"There's stuff running all down your face." Her little half brother giggled, picking up the cue. "You don't even know how to put it on."

What Daria heard was: You're no woman; just the thought is ludicrous. Your nakedness is a failure. She fled back to the bathroom. It felt to her as if the whole restaurant was laughing at her.

When she looked at her face and body, it was those that she blamed, and her desires that had led her to make such a humiliating mistake. There was no soap left in the dispenser, so Daria rubbed her face red with scratchy paper towels and hot water.

Later, her grandmother apologized. Nonetheless, Daria says that she got the message that her grandmother would not love her as much if she were sexual and that her "becoming a woman" in any visible way would embarrass her grandfather. She spent her teenage years hiding her body and denying her own growing up. "Well," Daria ended her story, "as you can imagine, I didn't try that again soon."

Daria's story is common. What feels like sexual pride one moment can turn into shame the next.

When I went home to talk to the girls, now women, with whom I grew up, we talked at a restaurant about how we learned to associate our emerging grown-up nakedness with shame. Pattie looked out the window, swirled the ice in her glass, and recalled: "No one has shamed my body like women have. The shaming experiences I have had, when I was just beginning to develop, were from other girls first. My best friend, Melinda, and me—we'd get dressed up together, at about eleven. And I'd like to look at my reflection. I really started developing early, and at that age you really love looking at your reflection. And she'd say: 'You really *love* looking at yourself.' And I'd think: So *what*? It wasn't okay to like yourself. And then, a little later, I remember my same friend telling me my breasts looked like 'blups.'"

"Blups?" I asked. It was a word that was distressing and funny at once.

"Big blups," Pattie said. "It was just cruel. Now, I can say, What was going on with you that you had to put me down? But then, it was awful. By then I was twelve or so. By 'blups' she meant big and no shape or something. I didn't respond angrily to that. I just absorbed it. There was no one to help me. No one I could go to and say, Why are people making fun of my breasts? Is something wrong with me, or is it them?"

Pattie leaned her head against a hand. "Yes," she reiterated, "it was the girls. Right when I was discovering my curves, I had this bikini. It was so great. And I'd put it on, and just *love* the way it looked. I liked my body at first. 'Well, what do you think of my bathing suit?' I'd ask my sister. And she'd say, 'Well, if you want to flaunt your body I guess it looks okay.' It made me feel ... *bad*. Like, So: I'm not supposed to enjoy my body? What I absorbed was: there's something wrong with showing my body."

I asked her, "Any woman's body? Or yours in particular?"

Pattie answered: "Any woman's, because I remember, at about that time, becoming judgmental of other girls, the way they were being judgmental of me."

Sandy smiled dryly. "When my friends were getting breasts, but eons before I was, they would say I was on the Itty-bitty Titty Committee. They would also tease: 'You're a sailor's dream: a sunken chest.' Boys would never say that. Just girls. And—remember this?" Sandy began singing, making fists and flapping her elbows, somewhat startling the nearby diners:

We must, we must, we must increase our bust.
For fear, for fear, the boys will disappear.
The bigger the better, the tighter the sweater,
the boys depend on us.

Trina said, "I used to tease girls myself. I remember as a group of girls—seventh grade—we would tease one another about our breasts or being fat."

I asked, "Would you tease the big-breasted girls or the small-breasted ones?"

"The big ones, of course," said Trina. "We did it to each other. It wasn't meant to be a competition, trying to cut each other down. At least, it didn't start out that way. It was more about our changing bodies and not being able to handle it or deal with it. And making fun of it as a result."

I asked the women, "Do you think the fact that there were not a lot of messages saying 'Don't laugh at the girls'' sexuality intensified this inclination to mock one another or tease?"

Pattie said, "If only there had been some sorts of events for us, where girls were there to support one another about their changing bodies—*something*, saying that we were all of like gender, and this is what to expect, and that there's—" she paused, and thought "—a *goodness* for us in it."

"You didn't see messages that there was a goodness in it?" I asked. Trina said gently, her confident voice now almost a whisper, "It was *so … scary*."

Like Pattie's bikini, a single article of clothing, which we remember forever, can symbolize a stage of the passage from childhood to nubility. At thirteen, I saw a dress in the window of a boutique on San Francisco's Judah Street. It looked like the hippest outfits that Millie the Model wore in the comic-book series. Made of blue-and-cream-striped Egyptian cotton that was a little nubby to the touch, it had the "midriff top," very fashionable at the time, that tied above the belly, and a wraparound skirt. It was definitely sexy. In my culture at home it said "Sexy hippie earth mama." I saved up babysitting money for a long time. It really mattered to me. It was the first outfit I ever wore in which I felt I could pass for a woman.

I went back to Israel that summer, and this time there would be no frolicking on balconies. We had all grown real, if tentative, breasts. I made friends with another American girl, Ofra, who was visiting her Orthodox relatives. When I went to get her one afternoon to hang out, I wore my dress. Her uncle intercepted me. He looked to me like Mr. Brocklehurst in *Jane Eyre*: a terrifying pillar of black. "You can't visit Ofra," he said in Hebrew. "Don't try to see her again. We don't approve of you. You are dressed like a whore." I was stricken mute, partly by the shock of being reflected in his disapprobation—no one had thought of me as a bad influence until then—but also by something in his cold

eyes and voice that I had never heard before. He feared me; me, a little girl. He was shaming me because he was afraid of me. What I had considered something to be proud of—my emerging sexuality—was something to be ashamed of. In the Haight, I had absorbed the idea that God liked sexuality; through Ofra's uncle I saw the possibility, which I had never considered up to that point, that God hated it—and, in particular, that God localized it in women; in my belly, which I had passed up so many desserts to reveal; and in my nice blue-striped cotton dress with the ruffle along the skirt that had cost me all that money. What I offered was an affront.

In the West, it is rare for a woman to encounter this sexual shaming as late in life as I did. In Western culture's debate, images of female sexualized nakedness are assumed, by progressives and conservatives and apolitical concerned mothers alike, to be innately degrading to women. The trouble with this is that it locates the degradation of the women *within* the sex or the nakedness itself, rather than in the distorted value *assigned* to that sex and that nakedness.

In our culture, women's nudity is typically seen as exposing women—in the sense of making them vulnerable—for the sake of more powerful, less vulnerable men. But, as Havelock Ellis argued in his *Studies in the Psychology of Sex*, other cultures have organized female nakedness very differently. At the turn of the twentieth century, according to Ellis, among the Uapas of the Amazon rain forest, for instance, men always covered their genitals while women were free to roam about naked; the women of Tierra del Fuego, off the coast of South America, were comfortable in public wearing nothing but a tiny patch of animal skin between their legs, consenting to raise it only when they made love; and Moru women carefully covered their buttocks with aprons made of leaves at all times, but their genitals remained in full view.

Various attitudes to nudity have prevailed in the West as well. Fifth-century Alexandrian women aristocrats lent themselves to the pleasures of being washed and massaged by their slaves, including males, and were comfortable, according to a critic, stripping before spectators. In Germany until the sixteenth century, "the sight of complete nakedness was the daily rule" in crowded households, mixed-sex nude bathing in both water and steam was commonplace, women were often naked under their petticoats, and it was considered great sport by men and women of both the town and the country to play a game during dances in which the man hoisted his dance partner so high in the air that her dress flew upward.

In the early Middle Ages, some women in Ireland undressed as a sign of welcome; it is reported in G. Rattray Taylor's *Sex in History* that the Queen of Ulster and the ladies of her court greeted the hero Cuchulainn thus. One traveler in Ireland reported that, as late as 1617, naked young girls were to be seen grinding corn in public. At about the same time in Venice and Padua,

in the summer, observers wrote that "wives, widows and maids all walked with naked breasts." Even at the end of the eighteenth century, in sophisticated circles in Paris that were responsive to the Greek revival, a fashion arose for dresses made of sheer gauze that outlined and even displayed women's nakedness. This style so charmed these aristocratic women that some were happy "even to walk abroad in the Champs-Elysées without any clothing; that, however, was too much for the public."

Could nakedness have many meanings? We knew of only two, and neither was of our choosing. For friends of mine like Sandy, female nakedness was not shameful, but it also signified total availability. For Daria, as for so many of the women who have told me their stories, the new revelation of female sexuality seemed to be partially constituted of shame. Was there yet a third way to think about what was going on with us, in us? If there was, we had no notion of it.

Mothers, Daughters, and Feminism Today: Empowerment, Agency, Narrative, and Motherline[*]

Andrea O'Reilly

I have a good mother.
Her voice is what keeps me here.
Feet on ground, heart in hand, facing forward.
Be yourself.

—Jann Arden, "Good Mother"

This essay examines contemporary feminist writing on the mother-daughter relationship; in particular it looks at the various ways this scholarship theorizes feminist mothering of girls. My intent is *not* to draft a blueprint of feminist mothering: what mothers *don't* need is yet another normative discourse of the good mother. My aim is to describe, rather than prescribe, the themes of feminist mothering of girls as found in the literature—empowerment, agency, narrative, and motherline—with particular attention to how the mother-daughter bond has been constructed as a site of empowerment for mother and daughter alike.

At the age of 37 I am a mother, a feminist, and a feminist mother. My two daughters, Erin, age eleven, and Casey, age nine, identify themselves as feminist.[1] I also have spent most of my adult life researching and

teaching the subjects of motherhood and mothers and daughters, first as a graduate student and later as a professor.[2] Adrienne Rich opened *Of Woman Born: Motherhood as Experience and Institution*, recognized as the first and arguably still the best feminist study of motherhood, with the observation that "we know more about the air we breathe, the seas we travel than about the nature and the meaning of motherhood" (11). In the close-to-a-quarter century since the publication of *Of Woman Born* the topic of motherhood has emerged as a salient issue in feminist scholarship. In her recent book, *Motherhood Reconceived: Feminism and the Legacies of the Sixties*, Laura Umansky details the increasing centrality of motherhood to feminist activism and scholarship and challenges the frequently-made claim that motherhood, in the words of one critic, "is the problem that modern feminists cannot face" (Hewlett quoted in Umansky 1). Feminist attention to motherhood emerged from and gave rise to a parallel interest in the mother-daughter relationship; specifically feminists seek to imagine and implement a truly feminist mode of mothering daughters. Today there is more written on

[*] First published in CWS/cf's Summer/Fall 1998 issue, "Looking Back, Looking Forward: Mothers, Daughters, and Feminism" (Volume 18, Numbers 2 and 3).

mothers and daughters than on motherhood itself; from the highly theoretical psychoanalytic discourse of New French Feminism taught in universities to the pop-psychology of self-help manuals found at local bookstores, feminists celebrate the mother-daughter relation as a site of female renewal and feminist resistance.

The scholarship on mothers, daughters, and feminism falls into four interconnected themes: empowerment, agency, narrative, and the motherline. All four centre upon and call for reciprocal mother-daughter identification to achieve a lasting politics of empowerment. The most popular of the four, particularly among lay feminists, is the first concern. Particularly big in the '70s and early '80s, this approach committed itself to non-sexist childrearing practices; its goal was to circumvent traditional gender socialization by destabilizing the assumed gender behaviour and assigned gender roles of girls and boys by way of an androgynous mode of childrearing. Girls handed over their dolls for trucks; boys traded in their hockey sticks for ballet slippers in the hopes that the masculine would be made more available to girls and likewise the feminine for boys. Many parents, aware of the damage inflicted by traditional gender socialization, have engaged in some form of non-sexist childrearing. I dressed my infant son in pink sleepers and at bedtime I revised traditional fairytales—Sleeping Beauty agreed to marry the prince only upon the completion of her Ph.D. In recent years the aim of feminist mothering has shifted and now focuses almost exclusively on the empowerment of adolescent girls.

Groundbreaking books, such as *In a Different Voice* by Carol Gilligan, *Meeting at the Crossroads* by Lyn Mikel Brown and Carol Gilligan, and *Reviving Ophelia: Saving the Selves of Adolescent Girls* by Mary Pipher, document the loss of the female self in adolescence, investigate the various reasons for this self-effacement, and consider strategies on ways this loss may be resisted. Mary Pipher in *Reviving Ophelia*, for example, argues that "with puberty girls crash into junk culture .... This culture is just too hard for most girls to understand and

master at this point in their development" (13). The solution for Pipher "is to strengthen girls, guide and protect them, and most importantly to create a culture that is less complicated and more nurturing, less violent and sexualized and more growth-producing" (13). In Virginia Beanne Rutter's *Celebrating Girls: Nurturing and Empowering Our Daughters* self-esteem is emphasized; mothers, through affirmation and celebration of the feminine in everyday practice and ritual, allow girls to claim power and gain self-worth in and through their female identity. She writes:

> We are all aware of the severe pressures and dangers that diminish girls' self-esteem as they approach adolescence. As concerned mothers, we read all this depressing news and wonder if there is anything we can do about it. I believe the answer is a decided yes: Mothers and other adult women in girls' lives can raise girls with a vital, intact feminine spirit. [...] [T]he mother-daughter relationship is the ground for teaching, taking, and sharing the feminine experience and the more we empower that experience, the healthier our girls will be. We need to secure our daughters' sense of self-worth, in their minds and their bodies, so that they will not turn away from us and from themselves. (2, 9–10)

Rutter, along with Pipher, maintains that the daughter's empowerment through either cultural critique/change and/or the valuation of the feminine depends upon a close and vital mother-daughter relationship: a strong mother-daughter connection, for these writers, is what makes possible a strong female self. However, western culture in general, and normative psychological theory in particular, mandates separation from parents in adolescence to enable the emerging adult to achieve an autonomous sense of self. Recent feminist writers on adolescent girls' empowerment, most notably Elizabeth deBold, Marie Wilson, and Idelisse Malave in *Mother-*

Daughter Revolution, call into question this "sacred cow" of developmental theory—the equivalency of separation and autonomy—and argue that it constitutes a betrayal of both mothers and daughters. They explain:

> Separation and autonomy are not equivalent: [daughters] need not separate from mothers emotionally to be autonomous. Under the domain of experts, mothers are urged to create a separation and disconnection from daughters that their daughters do not want. Early childhood and adolescence are the two stages of life where separation has been decreed as imperative to the independence and autonomy of children. To mother "right," women disconnect from their daughters and begin to see them as society will. Rather than strengthen girls, this breach of trust leaves girls weakened and adrift. (36)

What is most disturbing about this pattern of separation and betrayal is its timing. "In childhood," they write, "girls have confidence in what they know, think, and feel" (11). With the onset of adolescence girls between the ages of nine and 12 come up against what they call the wall. "The wall is our patriarchal culture that values women less than men .... To get through the wall girls have to give up parts of themselves to be safe and accepted within society" (12). Daughters are thus abandoned by their mothers when they need them the most. Central to *Mother-Daughter Revolution* is the belief that mothers can aid daughters in their resistance to the wall. The key to the mother's resistance is the reclamation of her own girl self:

> If mothers decide to join with daughters who are coming of age as women, mothers first must reclaim what they themselves have lost. Reclaiming is the first step in women's joining girls' resistance to their own dis-integration. Reclaiming is simply a process of discovering, describing, and reappropriating the memories and feelings of our preadolescent selves. (101)

This reclamation empowers the mother and enables her to aid the daughter in her resistance.

Feminist writers on daughters all agree that the mother-daughter connection is vital for young women's empowerment. However, the perspective of this literature is quite often daughter-centric; the mother's identity, particularly as it is lived outside of motherhood, is rarely, if at all, examined. Earlier feminist writers on the mother-daughter relationship, most notably Judith Arcana and Adrienne Rich, recognized the importance of the mother's empowerment for her own life and that of the daughter. Mother-daughter connection empowers the daughter if, and only if, the mothers with whom the daughters are identifying are themselves living lives of agency, authority, and autonomy. "We must live as if our dreams have been realized," Arcana writes:

> we cannot simply prepare other, younger daughters for strength, pride, courage, and beauty. It is worse than useless to tell young women and girls that we have done and been wrong, that we have chosen ill, that we hope they'll be more "lucky." (33)

Adrienne Rich goes on to ask:

> What do we mean by the nurture of daughters? What is it we wish we had, or could have, as daughters; could give, as mothers? Deeply and primarily we need trust and tenderness, surely this will always be true of every human being. But women growing into a world so hostile to us need a very profound kind of loving in order to learn to love ourselves. But this loving is not simply the old institutionalized, sacrificial, "mother-love" which men have demanded; we want courageous mothering. The most notable

fact that culture imprints on women is the sense of our limits. The most important thing one woman can do for another is to illuminate and expand her sense of actual possibilities. For a mother, this means more than contending with the reductive images of females in children's books. It means that the mother herself is trying to expand the limits of her life. To refuse to be a victim; and then to go on from there. (246)

Kate, a daughter who contributed to Karen Payne's *Between Ourselves: Letters between Mothers and Daughters*, attributed her empowerment to that of her mother:

When Mum finally left Dad she was giving up female martyrdom; she was waving farewell to that womanly virtue of self sacrifice. And if she could escape that bondage than so could I .... In setting herself free, [my mother] set me free. (244)

Another daughter in Payne's collection eloquently described the inspiration and joy she felt as she came upon her mother dancing alone in the living room:

[A]s I watched you I suddenly saw a different Eunice. I saw you before you met Dad, before you had two children. I saw you dancing before the onset of responsibilities .... For once I didn't see you as the parent or the wife, but as the woman yourself, unfettered by any lack of confidence or distrust. You were yourself that night dancing in the living room, joyous, spontaneous, full of life, smiling (306).

In the same collection renowned sociologist Jesse Bernard wrote to her daughter: "For your sake, as well as mine, I must not allow you to absorb me completely.

I must learn to live my own life independently in order to be a better mother to you" (272).

What daughters need, therefore, in the words of Rich,

[are] mothers who want their own freedom and ours .... The quality of the mother's life— however embattled and unprotected—is her primary bequest to her daughter, because a woman who can believe in herself, who is a fighter, and who continues to struggle to create livable space around her, is demonstrating to her daughter that these possibilities exist. (247)

Writing of lesbian mothering in *Politics of the Heart*, Baba Cooper describes "radical mothers [as] involving children in disloyalty to the culture the mother is expected to transmit at the expense of woman-bonding and female empowerment" (238). Reciprocal mother-daughter empowerment depends upon mothers claiming, in the words of Mary Kay Blakely, an identity as "[an] outlaw from the institution of motherhood" to engage in gynocentric mothering that nurtures the power of her female self and that of her daughter. Whether it be termed courageous mothering as Rich describes it, or radical mothering as defined by Cooper, this practice of mothering calls for the empowerment of daughters *and* mothers and recognizes that the former is only possible with the latter. As Judith Arcana concludes: "If we want girls to grow into free women, brave and strong, we must be those women ourselves" (33).

The transformation of mothering to effect change both inside and outside the home underpins most feminist thinking on the empowerment of daughters. Advocates of reciprocal mother-daughter empowerment however, recognize that knowledge of mothers' lives, and of female history generally, necessary for this connection is often difficult to come by. As girls need to experience firsthand their mothers' struggles against patriarchy, they also need to be told female narratives of resistance. In *Writing a Woman's Life* Carolyn Heilbrun observes:

Lives do not serve as models, only stories do that. And it is a hard thing to make up stories to live by. We can only retell and live by stories we have heard .... Stories have formed us all: they are what we must use to make new fictions and new stories. (32)

In 1976 Adrienne Rich lamented the dearth of maternal stories; in 1992 journalist Marni Jackson called maternal space "the mother zone; [the] hole in culture where mothers [go]" (13). Motherhood, Jackson writes, "is an unexplored frontier of thought and emotion that we've tried to tame with rules, myths, and knowledge. But the geography remains unmapped" (9). Feminist scholarship on motherhood in the '80s and '90s sought to give voice to maternal subjectivity. While recognizing how difficult it is to speak that which has been silenced, disguised, and marginalized, feminist maternal theory, since the publication of *Of Woman Born*, has been concerned with making the maternal story narratable.

Feminist interest in maternal narrative may be attributed to the realization among writers on girls' empowerment that girls need to hear their mothers' stories in order to forge a strong mother-daughter bond and to construct a female-defined identity. The authors of *Mother-Daughter Revolution* maintain that the compromise of female selfhood in adolescence may be resisted or, at the very least, negotiated, when the mother connects with the daughter through story. The mother, in recalling and sharing with her daughters her own narrative of adolescence, gives her daughter strategies of resistance, and hence constructs an alternative script of coming into womanhood. As my girls mature, I am made more and more aware of the importance of female narrative in strengthening our relationship and in aiding their own growth into womanhood. These stories unite mothers and daughters as girls realize that their mothers were once girls and young women; additionally they provide, by lived examples, road maps of the journey into womanhood. What I have also discovered is that as

I tell my narrative, my daughters construct their own. When my eldest daughter turned ten I gave her the journal I kept as a teenager; she now is writing her own journal that someday may be passed on to her daughter. My daughters are both avid storytellers; in either a fictional or autobiographical voice they narrate their own dreams and struggles as girls at the end of the millennium. When I asked my nine-year-old daughter Casey, as I was writing this piece, to describe what it means to be the daughter of a feminist mother she, not surprisingly, put it in narrative form:

She teaches me a lot of things. Like what sexism means. So I know a lot of things. I try to tell my friends. One time we were studying fishing and my teacher kept saying "He caught the fish or fisherman"!! So I raised my hand and asked if women could be fishers. She said "I can't think of why not, can anybody tell me otherwise?" and a boy in my class said they can't because they look in the mirror too much and they are scared of fish and water. That is what sexism means.

"Mothers and daughters," Rich writes,

have always exchanged with each other—beyond the verbally transmitted lore of female survival—a knowledge that is subliminal, subversive, pre-verbal: the knowledge flowing between two alike bodies, one of which has spent nine months inside the other (220).

Told and retold, stories between mothers and daughters allow us to define female experience outside the phallocentric narrative of patriarchy.

Maternal narrative, the third theme in current feminist writing on the mother-daughter relationship, brings us to the final theme, namely the importance of herstory or more specifically the motherline in the empowerment of daughters. In *Stories from the Motherline: Reclaiming the Mother-Daughter Bond, Finding Our Souls* Naomi Lowinsky describes her book as being "about a worldview that is as old as humankind, a wisdom we have forgotten that we know: the ancient lore of women—the Motherline" (1). She goes on to say:

> Whenever women gather in circles or in pairs, in olden times around the village well, or at the quilting bee, in modern times in support groups, over lunch, or at the children's party, they tell one another stories from the Motherline. These are stories of female experience: physical, psychological, and historical. They are stories about the dramatic changes of woman's body: developing breasts and pubic hair, bleeding, being sexual, giving birth, suckling, menopause, and of growing old. They are stories of the life cycles that link generations of women: mothers who are also daughters, daughters who have become mothers; grandmothers who also remain granddaughters (1–2).

Daughters today, at least among the middle class, are living lives radically different from those of their mothers. These daughters, Lowinsky argues, "[have] paid a terrible price for cutting [themselves] off from [their] feminine roots" (31). Severing their motherline, these daughters have lost the authenticity and authority of their womanhood; to reclaim that authority and authenticity they must reconnect to the motherline. She writes:

> When a woman today comes to understand her life story as a story from the Motherline, she gains female authority in a number of ways. First, her Motherline grounds her in her feminine nature as she struggles with the many options now open to women. Second, she reclaims carnal knowledge of her own body, its blood mysteries and their power. Third, as she makes the journey back to her female roots, she will encounter ancestors who struggled with similar difficulties in different historical times. This provides her with a life cycle perspective that softens her immediate situation .... Fourth, she uncovers her connection to the archetypal mother and to the wisdom of the ancient world view, which holds that body and soul are open and all life is interconnected. And, finally she reclaims her female perspective from which to consider how women are similar and how they are different (13).

Writing about Lowinsky's motherline in her book *Motherless Daughters: The Legacy of Loss*, Hope Edelman emphasizes that

> motherline stories ground a ... daughter in a gender, a family, and a feminine history. They transform the experience of her female ancestors into maps she can refer to for warning or encouragement (61).

They enable daughters to derive strength from their identities as women. These stories, made available to daughters through the female oral tradition or what we disparagingly call today gossip and old wives' tales, reunite mothers and daughters and reconnect the daughter to her motherline, thus making possible the gynocentric mother-daughter bond needed to effect change in the home and in the larger patriarchal culture.

My eleven-year-old daughter Erin, when asked her thoughts on feminism, quickly corrected me and explained that she was not a feminist, she was an equalist. "I believe that all creatures (not just people) on this planet are as good as each other. There is no better species." My daughter is a vegetarian and is deeply engaged with environmental issues. Her words inspired and humbled me: the feminism I have taught her and lived by has indeed been accepted, but on different terms. It is as if she returned the dress I selected for her and chose one of the same design but in a style more befitting her self and world. But this is ultimately the success of feminism; chameleon-like, it changes its hues as each generation recasts it in its own image. Commenting further, Erin remarked:

> My friends at school often make fun of me because of my belief in equalism and feminism .... I don't have many friends but I know that it is important to be yourself. That is what is important! This is what my parents have taught me.

Her words again comfort and sadden me. I am pleased and proud that her sense of self is so strongly grounded. But the aloneness of her feminist awareness concerns me. I can only hope that the empowerment, agency, voice, and motherline that is affirmed in the feminist literature is enough to sustain her and other girls as they grow into womanhood. I believe it is. To return to the quotation by Jann Arden that opens this essay: it is the voice of the mother in agency and narrative that empowers the daughter by returning her to the motherline so that she may claim the authority and authenticity of womanhood to face forward, with feet on ground, and be herself.

Notes

1. I am also the mother of a fourteen-year-old son, Jesse. He, along with his sisters, has been raised in a feminist household. This essay addresses only feminist mothering of daughters. Please refer to my edited book, *Mothers and Sons and Feminist Theory* (Routledge 2000). While this essay refers to feminist mothering the themes discussed may be applicable to fathers: men can practice feminist mothering. In our household my spouse and I both practice feminist mothering in the raising of our daughters and our son.

2. I designed and taught a first course on "Mothers and Daughters" 1993 to 1997; my third-year "Mothering–Motherhood" has been taught at York since 1992. In 1996 and 1997 the course was redesigned and taught in the Distance Education program; over two hundred took the course each year, studying the material through audio and video lectures.

References

Arcana, Judith Pilders. *Our Mothers' Daughters*. Berkeley, CA: Shameless Hussy Press, 1979.

Blakey, Mary Kay. *American Mom: Motherhood, Politics, and Humble Pie*. Chapel Hill, NC: Alonquin Books, 1994.

Brown, Lyn Mikel and Carol Gilligan. *Meeting at the Crossroads: Women's Psychology and Girls' Development*. Cambridge, MA: Harvard University Press, 1992.

Cooper, Baba. "The Radical Potential in Lesbian Mothering of Daughters." *Politics of the Heart: A Lesbian Parenting Anthology*. Eds. Sandara Pollack and Jeanne Vaughn. Ithaca, NY: Firebrand Books, 1987.

Debold, Elizabeth, Marie Wilson, and Idelisse Malavé. *Mother–Daughter Revolution: From Good Girls to Great Women*. New York: Bantam Books, 1994.

Edelman, Hope. *Motherless Daughters: The Legacy of Loss*. New York: Delta, 1994.

Gilligan, Carol. *In a Different Voice: Psychological Theory and Women's Development*. Cambridge, MA: Harvard University Press, 1982.

Heilbrun, Carolyn. *Writing a Woman's Life*. New York: Ballantine Books, 1988.

Jackson, Marni. *The Mother Zones: Love, Sex, and Laundry in the Modern Family*. Toronto: Macfarlane Walter and Ross, 1992.

Lowinsky, Naomi. *Stories from the Motherline: Reclaiming the Mother-Daughter Bond, Finding Our Female Souls*. Los Angeles: Jeremy P. Tarcher, 1992.

Payne, Karen, ed. *Between Ourselves: Letters between Mothers and Daughters*. Boston: Houghton Mifflin, 1983.

Pipher, Mary. *Reviving Ophelia: Saving the Selves of Adolescent Girls*. New York: Grosset/Putman, 1994.

Rich, Adrienne. *Of Woman Born: Motherhood as Experience and Institution*. New York: W.W. Norton, 1986.

Rutter, Virginia Beane. *Celebrating Girls: Nurturing and Empowering Our Daughters*. Berkeley, CA: Conari Press, 1996.

Umansky, Laura. *Motherhood Reconceived: Feminism and the Legacies of the Sixties*. New York: New York University Press, 1996.

How I almost Killed My Mother in Childbirth

Michelle Hammer

J'avais sept ans lorsque je suis tombée de bicyclette et que j'ai couru à la maison en saignant. Ma mère s'est exclamée: « Oh, mon Dieu! oh, mon Dieu » et ses yeux se sont exorbités à la vue de mon sang. Ma mère avait du mal avec les accidents, à cause de son expérience dans le camp de concentration d'Auschwitz. Me raconter des histoires était une façon de m'apaiser. C'est pour ça qu'elle me raconta comment je l'avais presque tuée à ma naissance. « Tu étais en retard de deux semaines, dit-elle, et le médecin dit à ton père qu'il ne pouvait en sauver qu'une seule de nous deux. Ton père décida de sauver sa jeune femme et la vie de l'enfant à venir. Le médecin, un sacré athée, déclara que c'était un miracle de Dieu que nous ayons survécu toutes les deux. » Ma mère me répéta souvent cette histoire, dessinant pour moi le cercle infernal du sang et de la féminité.

The summer I turned seven I rode the bike my father bought for me on a pebbled path in the playground of our apartment building. When I fell off my bike the pebbles dug deep into my face and knees and soon the blood dripped on the sharp white and grey pebbles. I abandoned my new bike on the side of the gravel road, not checking for damage, but rushed home, leaving a bloody trail behind, like Hansel and Gretl's breadcrumbs in the wild forest. The sight of my unfortunate accident drew the attention of the children in the playground and they followed me, pointing at my bloodied body, their voices filling the air in a cacophony of questions.

"What happened to you?"

"Who pushed you?"

I sobbed, but kept walking, ignoring their questions.

"She fell off her new bike," one girl shouted. "I saw it all."

In front of our building the children stopped and turned to find a new item of interest, while I climbed to the fourth floor.

I opened the door, looking around the apartment. Noise rose from the kitchen, a chopping knife banging on a wooden board, a familiar sound of my mother dicing onions or slicing peppers for the Sabbath meal. I closed the door behind me and sneaked into the bathroom. I didn't want to be noticed. Not just yet. Not until I cleaned the blood off my face and knees.

"You are home?" my mother called out from the shrine of pots and pans. "Why don't you answer me?"

My mother did not cope well with emergencies. The sight of blood, or an open wound, drove her into a state of panic. I imagined this was the result of her time in Auschwitz, something we didn't discuss often.

I started to wash the blood off my face with a hand towel, but fresh rivulets of blood dripped slowly over my face and I had to start over again. My mother appeared at the door, her eyes wide as she stood frozen, like Lot's wife. Oh, my god, oh, my god, and her eyes almost popped out, mouth open, like the fish that swam in our bathtub every week. Suddenly she took two wide steps toward me, grabbing the towel out of my hands. I almost fell backwards into the bathtub, where two carp swam back and forth before their makeover into gefilte fish.

"I knew I shouldn't have let you ride THAT BIKE," my mother hissed while trying to stop the bleeding, pressing on the bloodied gashes with the wet towel.

"Ouch, it hurts," I moaned.

"Be still," she warned, "or you'll lose all your blood, like I did when I gave birth to you."

I looked in the mirror and saw a clown's face with a red nose and red blotches, and started to cry.

"Why are you crying?"

"I look like a monster! I'll never be able to go outside again."

Mother started to laugh. I didn't appreciate her making light of my situation.

"You need to take a bath," she said.

"What! With the fish?"

"No, silly, without the fish."

When Mother attempted to catch the slippery carp, its tail shook in a furious frenzy. When she finally caught the squirming fish, she held it tightly inside her apron, hugging it like a baby. She had to place both fish in the small kitchen sink, and I imagined the carp flying in the air, like dolphins in a movie I had once seen. What if they landed in the pot of chicken soup, I worried, playing the scene in my mind, but not telling my mother any of this as she cleaned the bathtub for my bath.

Mother knelt on the hard floor and rubbed the tub with a scouring pad and a cleanser smelling of sharp Ammonia, moaning about the delay in cooking for the Friday night meal, and why did you ride your bike today of all days?

"It's going to smell of fish," I groaned when Mother finally got up and motioned for me to undress.

"Don't be silly, we do this every week," she said.

When I didn't budge, she relented and gave the tub one more scrubbing with an extra sprinkling of Ammonia cleanser and let the water wash over the tub's surface a long time before filling it up for my bath.

My mother had her cooking schedule planned and she managed to feed the four of us without help and work six days a week. The cooking was done from scratch, without the occasional relief from a delicatessen or a fast food counter. On Wednesdays she started cooking the chicken soup and meat dishes for Friday night. She also bought the two carp on Shenkin Street and left them in the tub overnight. On Thursday night she made gefilte fish. She baked that night too, two loaves of Hungarian cakes, one filled with crushed walnuts, the other with cinnamon and raisins.

The aroma of cinnamon and yeast rose from the kitchen, warm and enticing, filling the apartment with a reminder of the sweetness of the Sabbath. I slumped in the weightlessness of my warm bath. Mother scrubbed my legs with a yellow sponge, trying to erase my injuries. She washed the blood off my face, and I squirmed as she applied stinging alcohol with a cotton ball.

"Ima, stop," I shouted, splashing water over the rim of the bathtub.

"It's for your own good," she said with a firm hand. At times like this Mother resorted to story-telling, her favorite educational tool. She had a story for every occasion and I loved listening to her stories because it was the only time I had my mother's attention all to myself.

"Did I ever tell you about the blood transfusion?" she asked, trying to divert my mind from my smarting bruises on my skin that felt as though I fell into a field of broken glass.

I didn't answer right away. She never waited for an answer.

"The day I gave birth to you I lost a lot of blood and almost died. You were two weeks overdue," my mother continued to scrub my wounded knees, her voice fluctuating with the demands of the story line. "The doctor in Sziget told your father—'I can save only one. Which one will it be?'"

My miraculous beginning was cloaked in my mother's blood and my father's love for his unborn child. Every family has a story, like a legend that shapes the lives of its people, and the story that shaped my life was the way I almost killed my mother at birth.

"Your father said, 'I want both.' When asked, 'How will you do that?' your father moved me to a large hospital in Kluj and after finding the best doctor he presented him with large bills of money. It was after the war, don't forget, people didn't have a lot of money, but your father's business flourished and he made a lot of money when most Jews were still in D.P. camps and without a penny to their name."

"What happened next?" I asked, while my mother got up to fetch a towel. I knew the story well, but my favorite part was coming up. I dried my aching body. The towel, stiff from hanging outside on the line, felt like sandpaper scraping my bruises. Mother continued her story in the kitchen, while attending to her pots and pans. She cooked

chicken soup and chicken paprikash for the Friday night meal, but continued telling the blood transfusion story in a voice that rose above the bubbling pots.

"You were stuck to the walls of my uterus," Mother laughed, "almost as if you didn't want to leave my belly."

I didn't laugh, just wondered how I could be so mischievous and naughty before my birth.

"Your father was praying in the hallway and the nurse came to tell me how worried he looked."

Mother decided to sit down, as though the story was too heavy to tell while standing up. She stopped to catch her breath before rising to a crescendo: "I could hear the doctor shouting for a blood transfusion. The nurses panicked when they could not find the proper needles. The doctor yelled at the nurses, how could they not prepare the right needles and the blood. Oh, my god, can you imagine how frightened I had been when I heard his loud voice shouting, 'blood transfusion, blood transfusion.'"

Every time my mother told this part of the story of my birth, her voice got loud and excited, throwing me into a state of fear and confusion. I had no idea how a child is born, but the word 'blood' created an image of red pools gushing out of my mother's belly, and my tiny body swimming out, like a fish, sucking air, trying to float above the red sea of blood.

"What happened then?" I asked my mother, who got up to taste the chicken soup.

"First, I closed my eyes and prayed to the souls of my mother and father who perished in Auschwitz."

"And then?"

"Well, that's when they asked your father to give blood. In those days you had to ask relatives to give blood when you went in for an operation. When you came out of my womb, the doctor said to the nurses, 'God gave birth to this baby, not I.'"

"Why?"

Mother added the punch line:

"This was a miracle," she said. "The doctor was a sworn atheist before your birth, but when it was over, he realized how close to death I had been, and while witnessing this miracle he became a believer in God's power."

In the days following my birth my mother never held me, except for the obligatory breast feedings, but my father cradled me in his arms, rocking me to sleep with the lullaby from "IL TROVATORE," which he sang to me in lieu of my mother's arms. On the fourth day after giving birth to me, my mother woke up in the middle of the night, and since no one was around, she scratched the tiny brown mole off the tip of my nose and accepted me into her life.

Later that evening, when Father returned from work, he saw my swollen face and red bruises, he turned pale, and asked my mother in a hushed voice what had happened to me.

"It's the bike you bought for her," Mother answered in a loud and accusatory voice. "I told you she doesn't need a bike."

"All children ride bikes."

"Not in this house," she said.

"You can't keep her from living a normal life," he said. "We're not living in the ghetto."

"How do you know about those days," she exclaimed, "when you haven't been to Auschwitz."

I wished my father had spoken up to defend himself, but he always retreated. His silence, like negative space in a painting, created uncertainty about the way I would perceive him as a man.

Father, what did you do during the war?—I'll tell you when you are all grown up.

How will I know I'm all grown-up?—Don't worry, I'll remind you.

My father never revealed his survival story. My mother depicted my birth on many occasions, with the same passion as that first time, drawing me into the circle of womanhood and blood.

Crush Crash

Margaret Cho

I fell for one of the writers of the show. It was rather unexpected, but I was in a state of serious distress. The show had been on for two months, starting very strong, but with ratings that dropped week after week. The headaches and nausea from diet pills were slowly killing me. The bad reviews and backlash from the Asian community left me heartbroken and enraged at the same time. Having no friends anymore outside of work made me question what was real and what wasn't. Finally, with the situation in North Korea continuing downhill and with no word yet on the future of the show, I needed something or someone to take my mind off it all. I found Jon.

I decided that I was going to have a crush on him. Crushes allow us to step outside ourselves and view ourselves as the crush might.

Very often, a crush is not about the other person, but about us and how we think we are in the world. By looking at this reflection of ourselves through another person, we find a way to achieve self-love without actual self-esteem, a way to admire oneself without admitting that is what you are really doing.

Crushes are about fantasy colliding with reality, the fantasy of who we think we are matched with the reality of who we are. Other people have little to do with it.

When I set off on a crush I spend a lot of time on my appearance: buying clothes, working out, immersing myself in the crush's perceived culture. I imagine that I can be closer to the crush if I surround myself with the things he likes. I feel that it will rub off on me, making me more attractive in the glow of the familiar. It also serves as a way to get to know him without actually having to speak to him and risk rejection, or having him say something that might not coincide with the imagined life I have given him. I take a spare collection of facts and trivia, mix it with things he has said, fortify it with my own personal research about him, throw in a bit of profiling for good measure and there we have it—crush! *Here's one I made earlier…*

I needed that escape more than anything. Maybe Jon did, too, although I have trouble distinguishing what really happened with what happened in my imagination. This was not only the craziest I ever got with a guy, it was the most insanity I have displayed ever. That is saying a lot.

Jon was not handsome or sexy or particularly attractive in any way. He was having a hard time in his personal life. His mother and his uncle were both dead of cancer in the space of a week. Jon traveled on weekends back and forth from the East Coast, and he looked sad and tired on Mondays when he returned to the set.

He wanted to talk to me about things. He was leaving his job. He needed the time. His family wouldn't stop crying, he said. Maybe we could get together and talk. Maybe.

He came over to my newly rented Hollywood Hills house and sat on my red couch and didn't have much to say about anything. He felt sorry that things were going so wrong for me, too. He had the most understanding expression on his face. I don't know what he was trying to do. I hoped he had come to save me.

I was alternating between depression and denial. *All-American Girl* was on the verge of being cancelled. I hated the show, and so did the rest of the world, it seemed. I had to stand behind it, because to abandon it would mean I'd have to leave myself behind in the wreckage.

It was a dark time for both of us, and the last nail in my coffin was Jon and my obsession with him. I see now that it wasn't him at all — I just needed to be rescued and he was the frog I kept kissing. I was drowning in quicksand and he was the dry twisted branch that I held onto, even as it broke off and splintered in my hand.

He was subtly persuasive in his way. There was something about him that obsessed women. It had to do with the way he withheld. He was like a geisha, or a Victorian ingénue, offering a tantalizing glimpse of his inner being. This frustrated me and many like me to total madness. I think he was proud of it.

He told me that he once volunteered on a suicide hotline. A disturbed woman became fixated on him and he tried to break away. He had the hotline transfer all her calls. She got angry and threatened to do something bad. He did not believe her.

When she finally got him on the phone, she told him she had pulled out her eyes. The Bible said that if her eye offended God, to pluck it out, so she was calling him to tell him she had done it. She was stunned and

creepily calm and not yet feeling the pain. Then suddenly, she felt it. She screamed at him fearful, primal screams, and the whole time he was trying to get her to tell him where she lived so that he could send her an ambulance. He had to talk her through it all, stand in the darkness with her. He said it was the scariest thing he had ever done.

Later they would meet. She, of course, was now blind, and had become a nun. I thought about them meeting and how maybe she would be curious about how he looked. I thought she would ask to put her hands on his face, and he would let her, reluctantly, as he did everything.

When he told me that story, it made me feel strangely inadequate, as if my obsession with him would always pale in comparison. I wanted to kiss him when he was in my house, but he wouldn't let me. He was already cheating on his fiancée with another woman who worked on my show and he didn't want to three-time her.

What was so seductive about him was that I thought he cared about me when nobody else did. That bound me to him. I wanted him to kiss me so bad and he did and then he didn't. He pushed me onto the floor and left. That place in my house is haunted by the electricity that went through me. Later, when I missed him I would lie in that space and remember his hands on me.

Right after he left, he called from the car and said he didn't want things to be strained between us. He was sorry, but he wasn't sure for what.

He'd call every couple of months, to vaguely make plans that would never happen, or to put me off, or to be friendly, or to leave a message to call him, which he'd never be around to receive, pushing me further and further into my obsession. Days went by with me dressing and waiting by the phone and it never, ever rang. Not once.

I would keep putting on makeup and the sun would move across the sky. Finally, it would be too late for anyone to be calling or making plans, even though I thought he still might, and I would just get high and wait longer, phone by the bed. I'd fall asleep on top of the covers, completely dressed and made-up. It would be morning and the birds would be singing and I would wake with a sharp intake of breath and a realization that I had wasted an entire day waiting. The lights from the night before would still be on, throughout the house, and ashamed and desperate that I had lost another twenty-four hours of my life, waiting for a man that did not care if I existed, I would get up and do it again.

After thirteen episodes had been shot, *All-American Girl* was on hiatus, so I had nothing to do but spend my life in preparation to meet him. I went to a silversmith and ordered a beautiful flask engraved with, "Astronauts, Movie Stars, Politicians. I know you would if you could …"—a sort of attempted private joke that was so private that I am sure only I got it. It was a cryptic reference to the fact that I had been loved by all these illustrious men and that he would love me if he could be as accomplished as they were or something ridiculous like that. I realized somewhere along the way that it was insane, and I never gave it to him. Now, I display it prominently in my house as a reminder to never let myself go insane again.

I was so fucking crazy and I did so many drugs just to keep this fantasy of him alive. He did take me to dinner once at Off Vine. I tried too hard to seduce him during dinner, and unconvincingly licked red wine off my fingers. He said that I would have to do a lot more than lick red wine off my fingers.

He took me home in his stupid Acura Vigor with the ugly sheepskin seat covers and drove me up Vine. Later in my obsession, depression, I would drive myself up Vine and feel special. What kind of life is that?

It was just like being dead, and this waiting and wanting was with me for two years. I never got over it. I heard through the grapevine that he had broken off with his fiancée. I saw her ad in the *Recycler*: "Wedding Dress For Sale $800, Never Worn, Call Reese S_____."

That set me off trying on bridal gowns like *Muriel's Wedding*. I found out that I don't look good in them

anyway. What I loved about it was that everyone at the bridal boutique was so *nice*. It was the happiest place on earth: the women trying on gowns, and the women with them on the verge of tears anytime anybody came out of the dressing room. It was the joy that was so seductive. When I left those shops, I couldn't help thinking that I really *was* getting married to Jon, and it would be only a matter of time until he would realize it.

"The Wedding Fantasy" has been one of my most lasting and persistent daydreams. They go back as far as T. Sean, my blue-eyed Texan beau, from when I was just twenty. I saw marrying him in quickie Vegas fashion. Smoking a cigarette in a pink shantung silk suit, '60s style, tapping my foot impatiently, holding a tiny bouquet of baby roses in a trembling gloved hand.

Curiously, I also saw our make-believe marriage fall apart, and me drunkenly stalking him into his next relationship. I fantasized about being found by his young son from his next marriage, passed out on their porch early in the morning wearing a fur coat and pearls and nothing else, and clutching a broken champagne glass— *That's Dad's first wife before Mommy. She's having some trouble letting go. Can I call the ambulance? Please? Please?*

I saw getting married to Jude, a country-western crooner I had a brief affair with, just as clearly. That particular ceremony was held in a stone church in wine country, C&W all the way down to the white cowboy boots. The justice o' the peace would be Col. Sanders, and he, of course, would also cater the event. Jude would sing to me, and all the girls would cry at the romance of it all and the fact that he was taken for good.

My fantasy wedding to Marcel, my last most horrible boyfriend, seemed far more real. We'd go to the South of France, to Provence, where he had attended a wedding years before. The theme would be turn-of-the-century peasant, and we would serve stone soup. There would be fiddles and tiny flowers weaved into my unruly mass of *Manon of the Spring* hair. All the men with their black vests and pocket watches like old-time bankers would lift the heavy oak table and set it outside in the field, where we would dance and drink the night away.

I never pictured my parents at these functions because they represented the awful truth, the bad shit, not that they were awful, bad, or shitty—they were just *real*, and I could not live without lying. They were the black watermelon seeds of my existence. I wanted to just have what I thought were the good parts of my life, seedless and sweet.

I got deeply into this fantasy, thinking I could go to 1900, that expensive boutique on Main that is open by appointment only, just to price antique cotton, to see what a dress would be like should this fantasy come true. I didn't want to lose my head about my wedding dress as many a young bride is known to do. There were so many new magazines to buy—*Bride's* and *Modern Bride* and such, just like *Vogue* but with a sense of purpose and direction. The gowns in there were ugly and puffy. I always realized I'd have to go the vintage route, or perhaps design it myself.

I thought about the bridesmaid dresses. Lemon yellow granny dresses, sort of '70s Gibson girls with big bubbly bun hairdos, which of course they'd never wear again, but who cares? Who wears anything again? I saw myself in Victoriana, white gauze and delicate white lace and daisies in my bouquet, and the bridesmaids, my friends Siobhan, Ebby, and Marcel's sister Louise, in yellow to match the yolk of the daisy.

And suddenly, it wasn't a fantasy anymore, it was outright planning. Later, when the relationship went sour and I could barely stand the sight of Marcel, I still didn't want to break up because I had spent so much time on my fantasy. In fact, I was being held hostage by my fantasy. I was willing to let myself be miserable in this relationship, to stay with someone I hated, someone who tortured me every time he looked at me, talked to me, or touched me. I was going to endure a lifetime of hell for the pleasure of ONE IMAGINED DAY!!!!!!!

No matter how hard it is, I am not going to fashion a wedding fantasy for my next crush. I will stop living life for a future of happiness that does not and may never exist. I will live for now and stop wasting my time. Every moment I live can be as beautiful as a fantasy. Every second of life is precious. I vow to stop wasting my time on these dreams that turn my life into a nightmare. I vow to live, to be mindful, to pay attention to life, and hold it hard to my heart. Every beat another second going by.

It was so hard then to not want to lose myself in the lacy, white emotions, the soft, womanly caresses of the bridal salon. I was insane, I was being a lunatic. Trying on wedding dresses, preparing for a wedding to someone who would never even call me back. But the ladies at the boutique didn't know that. They just wanted to help me be ready for my Special Day, the one which I would remember for my entire life.

I tried on a dress, which didn't look good on me anyway. I went to wait outside for Sledge to pick me up. Curiously, he didn't think anything I was doing was strange.

I was standing on a corner of Ventura Boulevard and this guy drove up and looked at me and then went and parked his car and walked back. He started talking to me and saying that I was attractive and asked what I was doing. It took me a long time to realize that he thought I was a prostitute! Sledge came roaring up in his Acura and I got into his car and he drove my crazy ass home.

The Feminist Wife?
Notes from a Political "Engagement"

Patricia Payette

Can one be within the framework of a marriage?
—May Sarton, *Journal of a Solitude*

The summer after I graduated from college, my high school friend Heather married her college sweetheart, Jeff. When it came time for the single women to circle together to compete for the bride's bouquet, my friend Vonda and I obediently joined the small cluster of women. As Heather's bouquet flew toward us, I discreetly ducked out of its path. I don't remember who caught the bouquet but I do remember my distinct feeling at that moment: I was twenty-one years old, a newly minted college graduate contemplating my career choices and a whole new life. The last thing I had on my mind was becoming the next bride.

Ten years later, in 1998, I am the bride-to-be, living with my fiancé, struggling with a new set of feelings about getting married. There would be no bouquet tossing at my reception. In recent years, I became embarrassed when single women herded together at a reception to compete for the bouquet, as if getting "lucky" enough to be the next bride was all they had on their minds. I began to hide out in the bathroom during the event and felt relieved whenever a bride decided to forgo this tradition.

During the nine months I spent as a fiancée, I documented my emotional journey to the altar in a computer journal I simply named "engaged." Reading over the journal a year after my engagement, I see now that while I was writing, I was actively "engaged" in a process of sorting through the meaning of marriage and the significance of wedding traditions. I experienced waves of varying emotions—excitement, astonishment, chagrin, ambivalence, confidence—as a self-proclaimed feminist about to engage in one of the most traditional feminine rites of all.

My story as an independent, feminist woman who also desired to be married, and struggled with that desire, is not an uncommon one. Stacey D'Erasmo, writing in the *New York Times Magazine*, observes the abundance of contemporary tales tracing the single woman's search for a husband, as evidenced by the television shows *Sex and the City* and *Ally McBeal* and the fiction bestsellers *Bridget Jones's Diary* and *The Girls' Guide to Hunting and Fishing*. D'Erasmo writes: "In nearly every medium, the marital quest of the fashionable, sexually well-traveled, thirty-something woman has become so popular as to seem like the dominant narrative of life on earth right now." Noting the "melodrama" and "misadventure" that follow these single heroines as they pursue a husband, D'Erasmo believes these narratives prove that feminism is "over" and has "failed."[1] Her reasoning suggests that yearning for marriage is not only incompatible with feminist beliefs, the fact that the desire exists proves feminism is dead. My experience proves feminism isn't dead; it's merely undergoing a transformation at the hands of young women like myself who are refusing to submit to outmoded paradigms that tell us what we should and shouldn't desire for ourselves. The abundance of contemporary narratives about outspoken single women questing for satisfying personal and professional lives is a testament to our determination to speak truthfully about our generation's unique needs and desires. Hundreds of women like myself are struggling with age-old prejudices in order to reinvent the meaning of single life and the matrimonial urge.

The second wave adage "A woman without a man is like a fish without a bicycle" doesn't serve women or men in coming to terms with the thorny issues surrounding equality, mutuality, and marriage in this national and historical moment. Portraying women as either domesticated victims of male patriarchy or angry, man-hating feminists doesn't permit the nuances of real women's lives to come into clear view, just as the assumption that single women who long to be married must be "unfeminist" obscures a more complete picture of contemporary women's psyches. I endorse a new approach to the marriage bond that undermines the power dynamics of male-female relationships in which we must choose between being master or slave, as Jessica Benjamin describes relationships in *The Bonds of Love: Psychoanalysis, Feminism and the Problems of Domination*. Benjamin concludes that the only way to avoid becoming trapped in a dualism of our relationships is to embrace the paradox "posed by our simultaneous need for recognition and independence," to sit comfortably with the desire to be both autonomous and to be connected.[2]

I grew into feminism as I grew up. Like many third wave feminists who grew up in the 1970s and 1980s, I was raised in a familial atmosphere of feminist ideals nurtured by my mother and my aunts. I learned a great deal from my female relatives through the example they set in their lives. My mother worked part-time during part of my growing up years, first as a dental hygienist when my brother and sister and I were very young, and then later, when we reached school age, she earned an M.A. in education and was a lab instructor in anatomy and physiology at the college in the small town where we lived. She was the first woman elected to the water board in that town and later was active in the League of Women Voters. My mother's scope of activities and interests has always ranged outside the home.

Even my mother's mother has been a dynamic role model for me, for she was, and is, a lively, active, and witty grandmother who treated me and my siblings to solo vacations with her to special places. While growing up, I learned as well that men could be feminists when my father, an auto dealer, supported women's equality in his traditionally male-dominated field by hiring women managers and even promoting a woman to general manager of his dealership. For the past twenty years, his dealership has sponsored a free workshop called "Women's Day" to help women become more comfortable buying and maintaining their cars.

My mother's eldest sister, Pat, is a nun whose extensive travels, business savvy, and spirited sense of humor forever nullified in my mind the stereotype of a nun as passively church bound. My Aunt Maddie also became a nun and garnered much attention by speaking out on behalf of feminism. Maddie eventually left the convent, got married, and retained her last name, had a baby, and started a successful career as a social worker and therapist, all the while remaining active in feminist causes. One summer my Aunt Molly, an activist and lawyer, arrived at our home during a trip cross-country by way of motorcycle. Throughout my childhood, Molly encouraged my interest in books and writing, and when she carved out special time for us to spend together, she talked to me as her peer and was comfortable and open about her sexual orientation, bringing her female partners to family events. My youngest aunt, Terry, also talked to me honestly and openly about sexuality, and lived for several years with her boyfriend before marrying him. She, too, kept her own last name.

In fifth grade, I questioned the gym teacher, Mr. Lando, about why he chose only boys to serve as team captains. Although I don't remember his response, I do remember that after I challenged him, he sent me to the office to fetch his coffee. Later, in high school, I got better results when I gently corrected my civics teacher— "congressperson"—aloud in class. He thanked me and corrected himself. Shortly after that, he and his wife began hiring me to babysit for their daughter.

As a preteen, I spent a great deal of time reading and writing stories and plays. My younger sister Maggie, interested in horses and talented in art, also picked up some sewing and cooking skills from my mother, but I was not interested in acquiring those skills and my parents never pushed me to learn them. These events did not seem unusually significant to me at the time, but I now understand Maggie and I were granted "permission" to be the kind of girls we wanted to be.

Nevertheless, I became self-conscious of those moments in life when the values of feminism appeared to be at odds with my own desires and impulses. During my undergraduate years at the University of Michigan, I was thrilled to find like-minded feminists among my peers, both men and women. Although we sometimes dressed and acted the part of "feminine" women and "masculine" men, we were acutely aware of our social conditioning as gendered subjects and often mocked our conformist impulses with sarcastic humor. If I broke a nail, I expressed displeasure and made fun of my reaction at the same time. We acted upon our sexual freedoms, but sometimes felt bound by ancient dating rituals and found prefeminist sexual assumptions hard to shake. Even though we knew we could make our own rules, my girlfriends and I wondered what it *meant* if we slept with a man on the first or second date.

In *Third Wave Agenda: Being Feminist, Doing Feminism*, Leslie Heywood and Jennifer Drake describe the third wave movement as "feminisms" that grew out of the social context of the late 1970s through the late 1980s: "Because our lives have been shaped by struggles between various feminisms as well as by cultural backlash against feminism and activism, we argue that contradiction—or what looks like contradiction, if one doesn't shift one's point of view—marks the desires and strategies of third wave feminists."[3] The second wave generation of the 1960s frequently constructed the freedoms of feminism in opposition to the social strictures of femininity, but I have consistently sought balance between what I saw as the feminine and feminist sides of myself, precisely because I do not see them as contradictory.

Although "third wavers" hold strong to the belief that men are not the enemy, we take a cautious stance toward the twenty-something wedding mania as witnessed in pop culture portrayals of young women like Monica on the popular sitcom *Friends*. During my college years, and throughout my twenties, I savored a sense of emotional and financial independence that grew over the years. Time enough later for marriage, I told myself as I became absorbed by getting my M.A. and cultivated a strong connection to friends, family, and various community activities. I never eliminated the possibility of meeting Mr. Right during those dating years, but the search for a marriageable man didn't dominate my life. My single friends and I discovered that a happy and successful life didn't require a husband, or even a boyfriend.

This attitude toward marriage is commonplace among the third wave generation. Journalists and sociologists are sitting up and taking notice of the growing number of women staying single longer, and the abundance of "never married" women and their stereotype-shattering lives. In a 1996 issue of *Psychology Today*,[4] Anatasia Toufexis dispels the popular assumptions about "never-married" women as "unloved, unwanted, unhealthy" by citing the numerous healthy, happy, successful single women buying houses, running companies, and having children on their own. I read Toufexis's article the year I turned thirty, and I identified with her "single woman as heroine of her own life" thesis, yet I also found myself more and more longing to be in a committed relationship.

Gradually, the freedoms that I had cherished in my twenties began to lose their charm, not because I felt incomplete without a man, but because I finally felt ready to take on a serious, loving, committed relationship with a man. I witnessed the settled homes and shared happiness that many of my peers, including my younger sister, had found with a mate, and I felt increasingly impatient with my charmingly noncommittal boyfriends, yet I still resented the frequent, worrisome questioning from my parents and others regarding my persistent single status. Why did they find that topic so much more pressing than the promising academic career in English literature I recently embarked upon? What happened to my feminist parents who raised me to cherish

independence, but now pestered me about settling down with one of my male friends? Although I didn't perceive myself as one of the "never marrieds" for whom Toufexis advocates, I strongly related to her assertion that single women "have been staging a quiet revolution, battling social prejudice, family expectations, and their own apprehensions to set a new standard for what it means to be successful, fulfilled, and content women."[5] The essay helped me realize, for the first time, that a lot of my worries stemmed from internalizing the "social prejudice" and "family expectations" Toufexis names. Regardless of their intellectual commitment to women's independence, my parents had no personal experience to help them imagine what it was like to be a "never-married" thirtysomething adult with a fulfilling life. Marrying in their early twenties and then turning their attention immediately to raising children, they had no idea what life was like for a woman in my situation. I mailed them a copy of Toufexis's article. They seemed relieved.

*****

Notes

1. Stacey D'Erasmo, "Single File: Why do the Sexy, Savvy New Heroines Want Nothing So Much as Rings on Their Fingers?" in New York Times Magazine, 28 August 1999, 13–14.

2. Jessica Benjamin, The Bonds of Love: Psychoanalysis, Feminism and the Problems of Domination (New York: Norton), 221.

3. Leslie Haywood and Jennifer Drake, Eds., Third Wave Agenda: Being Feminist, Doing Feminism (Minneapolis: University of Minneapolis Press, 1997).

4. Anatasia Toufexis, "When the Ring Doesn't Fit …," in Psychology Today, November/December 1996.

5. Ibid., 52.

SECTION FOUR

IDENTITY, BODY, AND HEALTH

The Construction of a Negative Identity

Kim Anderson

Drunken squaw.
Dirty Indian.
Easy.
Lazy.

Every Canadian knows these words to commonly describe and identify Aboriginal women. Many Canadians are fooled by this construction of Native womanhood. This imagery is so ingrained in the North American consciousness that even Native people have, in dark times, internalized these beliefs about their grandmothers, their aunties, their daughters, and themselves.

Perhaps people begin to see alcohol abuse, sexual dysfunction, and poverty through the lens of these stereotypes. There are many people in our communities who are still using alcohol to drown the shame and confusion that festers within such negative definitions of their ancestry. We have a lot of family and sexual dysfunction because of the imposition of Christianity, western morality, and abuses endured in the residential school system. Yet, when we consider our lived experience, the drunken, easy squaw is not a character that Aboriginal people know. I would not describe my

Native female relations as lazy and dirty. I don't know any squaws. So where did these images come from? How did they become so widespread, and how do they affect the day-to-day living of contemporary Native women?

As I began to explore these questions, I discovered how this negative understanding of Native womanhood was constructed. The dirty, easy squaw was invented long before poverty, abuse, and oppression beset our peoples. She was invented and then reinforced because she proved useful to the colonizer. The "uncivilized" squaw justified taking over Indian land. She eased the conscience of those who wished to sexually abuse without consequence. She was handy to greedy consumers. Dirty and lazy, she excused those who removed her children and paved the way for assimilation into mainstream culture. She allowed for the righteous position of those who participated in the eradication of Native culture, language, and tradition.

To me, these images are like a disease that has spread through both the Native and the non-Native mindset. In tracing this development, I hope to highlight a renewed understanding of Native womanhood that will help us to recover our strength, self-esteem, and dignity.

Roots of a Negative Female Image

In both western and Indigenous frameworks, Native women have historically been equated with the land. The Euro-constructed image of Native women, therefore, mirrors western attitudes towards the earth. Sadly, this relationship has typically developed within the context of control, conquest, possession, and exploitation. The Euro-Canadian image of Native women has been constructed within this context and has evolved along with the evolving relationship of European people to this continent.

When they first arrived on Turtle Island in the sixteenth century, Europeans produced images of Native womanhood to symbolize the magnificent richness and beauty they encountered. This was the phase of the great mother, the Indian Queen. Cherokee scholar Rayna Green describes the personification of "America" typical to this period (1575–1765):

> Draped in leaves, feathers, and animal skins, as well as in heavy jewelry, she appeared aggressive, militant, and armed with spears and arrows. Often she rode on an armadillo, and stood with her foot on the slain body of an animal or human enemy. She was the familiar mother-goddess figure—full bodied, powerful, nurturing but dangerous—embodying the wealth and danger of the New World.[1]

"Exotic, powerful, dangerous and beautiful," this Native female symbol represented both "American liberty and European virtue,"[2] but as the European settler became more familiar with the land, the queen was demoted. Colonial claims to the land would only work if the queen became more accessible, less powerful, and within the grasp of the white man. Out of this need, the "Indian princess" was born. The queen was transformed from a mother-goddess figure to a girlish-sexual figure, for who can own mother or dominate the gods?

"Indian princess" imagery constructed Indigenous women as the virgin frontier, the pure border waiting to be crossed.[3] The enormous popularity of the princess lay within her erotic appeal to the covetous European male wishing to lay claim to the "new" territory. This equation of the Indigenous woman with virgin land, open for consumption, created a Native female archetype which, as Elizabeth Cook-Lynn has pointed out, could then be "used for the colonizer's pleasure and profit."[4]

The erotic image of Native female as "new" territory in the American narrative persists to this day. You need only to glance at posters of Walt Disney's *Pocahontas* to be confronted with a contemporary example of this archetype. We see a voluptuous yet innocent looking Native (but not too Native) "girl," who will soon become involved with an adventurous young white male. As Emma LaRocque points out, Disney's *Pocahontas* combines a lot of the overarching stereotypes about Native people. LaRocque sees a Pocahontas who is "so oversexualized, kind of crouching around, slithering around on the rocks," part noble savage, part princess, part loose squaw. This archetype has been perpetrated again and again throughout North American his-story. It has been promoted through other popular his-storical characters like Sacajewea, the Shoshone woman who led "explorers" Lewis and Clarke into the interior of the North American continent. In Spanish colonial history, there is la Malinche, the Aztec woman who birthed the mestizo children of Cortez and interpreted for Spanish troops.

It is possible to interpret characters like Pocahontas, Sacajewea, and la Malinche as strong Indigenous leaders,[5] but the mainstream interpretation of these mythic characters is quite the opposite: Native women (and, by association, the land) are "easy, available and willing" for the white man.[6] This mythology ensures that the "good" Native woman who willingly works with white men is rewarded with folk hero or "princess status."[7] Racism dictates that the women of these celebrated liaisons are elevated above the ordinary Indigenous female status; they must be some kind of royalty. The ultimate "reward" for the Indian princess is marriage to a white man, providing her the ability to transcend into his world.

What, then, of the Native woman who does not comply with the colonizer?

As with other colonial his-stories, once Indigenous peoples began to resist colonization, the archetypes changed. Indigenous women worldwide became symbols of the troublesome colonies, and in the Americas the squaw emerged. Carol Douglas Sparks has traced the princess-to-squaw devolution in colonizer accounts of the Navajo.[8] The virgin-princess, so commonly found in white male adventurer records of the nineteenth century, is soon transformed. While the princess held erotic appeal for the covetous imperial male wishing to claim the "new" territory, the squaw drudge justified the conquest of an uncivilized terrain:

> ... Americans found squaw drudges far more comfortable than these outspoken and powerful women, whose presence defied colonial rationalizations. Not only could the squaw be pitied, but her very existence justified American intrusion into her land and society.[9]

In her book, *Capturing Women: The Manipulation of Cultural Imagery in Canada's Prairie West*, Sarah Carter demonstrates how both the Canadian state and the national press deliberately promoted "dirty squaw" imagery in the late 1800s.[10] At the time of settler invasion in western Canada, "dirty squaw" fiction was useful for a number of reasons. The uncivilized squaw provided a backdrop for the repressive measures against the Native population of the time. Like the men who were depicted as savage warriors, the women were reported to be "violent instigators of atrocities" (against whites),[11] thereby justifying colonial violence against Indigenous peoples. The image of the Native woman as the beast of burden

in her society was drawn up to demonstrate the superiority of European womanhood and femininity (after all, women did not "labour"), and the necessity for replacing Native womanhood with European womanhood. This distortion of Native women's physical labour and contribution to their community is at the root of the longstanding "squaw-drudge" image. Rather than being seen as significant players in the economic structure of society, Native women were framed as drudges and beasts of burden.

As Native people moved off the land, and women lost their status and role as producers within the economic structure of their societies, they were cast as lazy and slovenly. Women were no longer able to provide for their families because they had lost the means to produce primary goods, such as clothing and food. They became dependent upon purchased goods and an economy in which they held no power. The dirty squaw emerged, conveniently taking the blame for the increasing poverty on reserve and deflecting attention from government and public complicity in the devastation of Indigenous peoples. If Native women were constructed as "squaws," dirty, lazy, and slovenly, it was easier to cover up the reality of Native women who were merely struggling with the increasingly inhuman conditions on reserve:

> In the unofficial and unpublished reports of reserve life ... it was widely recognized that problems with reserve housing and health had little to do with the preferences, temperament, or poor housekeeping abilities of the women. Because of their poverty, the people were confined in one-room shacks, which were poorly ventilated and were impossible to keep clean because they had dirt floors and were plastered with mud and hay. One inspector of the agencies noted in 1891 that the women did not have soap, towels, wash basins, or wash pails, nor did they have any means of acquiring them. Similarly, it

was frequently noted that the women were short of basic clothing and had no textiles or yarn to work with. Yet in official public statements, the tendency was to ascribe blame to the women rather than drawing attention to conditions that would injure the reputation of government administration.[12]

Similarly, if Native women were portrayed as poor parents, it was then excusable for the state to remove Native children and place them in residential schools and foster homes.

Native female sexuality was also transformed into the "squaw" who was "lewd and licentious" and morally reprehensible. This representation was projected onto Native women to excuse the mistreatment they endured from white settler males. Within the context of late-nineteenth-century morality, it was easier to blame Native women than to challenge the behaviour of the heroes on the frontier. The narrative espousing how "easy" Native women were was developed to cover up the fact that white males were involved in unmarried sexual activity and that state officials were perpetrators of sexual assault. This tactic is common in rape cases and is well entrenched in the western consciousness: blame women for the sexual deviance of certain men. As part of the Native woman-blaming campaign, the *Toronto Daily Mail* of February 2, 1886, railed, "The character of the men of this country has been assailed."[13]

The squalor of the media-driven, uncivilized, easy squaw was further intended to guard against interracial marriages, thus protecting racial "purity" in the new country: "There were fears that the Anglo-Celts might be overrun by more fertile, darker and lower people, who were believed to be unable to control their sexual desires."[14] The moral reform movement of the late 1880s in the West embraced images of the dirty squaw in an effort to keep the races segregated and to keep the white race pure.

The dirty, dark squaw not only justified the deplorable treatment of Aboriginal peoples, she also created a gauge against which white femininity could be measured and defined. Where Native women were powerful physical workers, white women were encouraged to be weak and frail. The Native woman thus was re-invented as a drudge. Where Native women had sexual liberty, white women were restricted from pleasure. The Native woman had then to be perceived as easy. Where Native women resisted the increasing restrictions and poverty of reserves, white women were expected to be models of domesticity, industriousness and obedience. The Native woman had to be reconstructed as deficient in order to prop up the image of the white woman:

> The particular identity of white women depended for its articulation on a sense of difference from Indigenous women. What it meant to be a white woman was rooted in a series of negative assumptions about the malign influence of Aboriginal women. The meanings of and different ways of being female were constantly referred to each other, with Aboriginal women always appearing deficient.[15]

Since contact with the European, Native women have been trapped within a western dichotomous worldview, where everything is either good or bad; dark or light; pure or corrupt. The Euro-constructed Indigenous woman with her dark ways, her squalor, and corruption makes the construction of whiteness all the more attractive. In the absence of white women, Native women can represent both characters: the "Indian princess," bathed in a sublime light (and well on her way to becoming white), or the "easy squaw," hunched and wallowing in her darkness. In terms of female identity, the Native woman must endure the western framework of virgin-whore, which was translated to princess-squaw and slapped on top of the complex understanding of Native womanhood that had existed for tens of thousands of years. This his-story continues to interfere with the lives of contemporary Native women.

Ghosts of the Squaw and the Princess

The majority of Native women will tell you that, at some point in their experience they have been called a "squaw." Depending on the degree of overt racism in their environment, this will happen to a greater or lesser extent. Sometimes it is applied in the context of "friendly" joking; often in the form of a violent assault. Whatever the context, the "squaw" label has been applied to Native women right across North America; there are accounts from women of nations as widespread as the Mi'kmaq (Rita Joe) and the Pawnee/Otoe (Anna Lee Walters).[16]

Native girls begin to hear racial/sexual slurs from an early age, often before they even understand the terms themselves. Ojibway Professor Shirley Williams says she remembers hearing white boys singing, "Squaws along the Yukon aren't good enough for me." The boys would follow up with, "Would two dollars be enough?" playing on the myth that Native women are "easy." Williams states that she thought "squaw" must be an English word "because it sounded like something dirty." Laverne Gervais-Contois, a woman of Ojibway, Cree, and Sioux heritage recalls the slurs she heard while growing up in Winnipeg. Typically, the images were (and are) steeped with degrading sexual innuendo. She recalls hearing Native women referred to as "dark coffee," which was implicitly sexual, as the boys would say, "Dark coffee is good if you like it good and strong."

When negative images of Native women are so ingrained in the Canadian consciousness that even children participate in using them, it is easy to see how Native women might begin to think of themselves as "easy squaws." Janice Acoose describes how these negative images affected her consciousness:

I learned to passively accept and internalize the easy squaw, Indian-whore, dirty Indian, and drunken Indian stereotypes that subsequently imprisoned me, and all Indigenous peoples, regardless of our historic, economic, cultural, spiritual, political, and geographical differences … I shamefully turned away from my history and cultural roots, becoming, to a certain extent, what was encouraged by the ideological collusiveness of textbooks, and the ignorant comments and peer pressure from non-Indigenous students.[17]

Many Native female writers—including Joanne Arnott, Beth Brant, Maria Campbell, Janet Campbell Hale, Beatrice Culleton, Paula Gunn Allen, Lee Maracle, and Anna Lee Walters[18]—have provided accounts of how they or other Native women have fostered destructive and hateful attitudes towards themselves. This self-hatred is rooted in internalized racism that comes from the negative self-concepts of racist stereotypes. Internalized racism spreads like a disease through Native communities.[19] It makes us doubt the validity of the existence of our people, and thus ourselves. This results in self-destructive behaviours, including addictions and involvement in violent relationships.

Less destructive and overt but equally as false is the princess. This is a stereotype that I am more familiar with in my personal experience. My class, age, and stature likely play into this interpretation of my being. The fact that I am half-white also helps. Remember, the Indian princess is well on her way to becoming white, so it follows that those of us who are more assimilated qualify for this racist nobility. Mixed-bloods have "exotic" appeal because we look "different," yet we are accessible to white people.

No one would ever call you a princess, but you can see it in their approach. Sometimes people glow all over you about your heritage; others want to use you as some kind of showpiece. It is a sexualized identity, which, in my case, has, for example, resulted in the humiliating experience of being called "my little Indian" as a measure of affection. I have felt stalked by Canadian and European men because of my Indianness, which, to them, was a "bonus" to whatever interest they had in me as a female.

When I read bell hooks for the first time, I felt a wash of relief to discover that I hadn't been imagining this syndrome; that, in fact, several people have written about it. As I discussed earlier, hooks provided me a name for it: "eating the Other." In an essay so named, she explains how it has become fashionable to "enjoy racial difference." She demonstrates, for instance, how advertising has picked up on this desire, and has used people of colour to sell products.[20]

People with a desire for "eating the Other" do not see themselves operating within a racist framework; rather, they think they are progressive in their desire to make contact. Hooks suggests that relations of this nature may further be used to assuage guilt and "take the form of a defiant gesture where one denies accountability and historical connection."[21] People need to believe that their desire to befriend an Indian or to sleep with a woman of colour is proof that we have all transcended the racism that plagues the Americas, and that in so doing we are tucking our racism safely in the past. But what is implied in this type of contact? What narratives are we replaying?

I see Pocahontas looming in the background. There is a desire to cross some kind of frontier, to be transformed by the experience and, finally, to take possession. Hooks relates her experience of hearing some white college boys talk about how many Black, Aboriginal, and Asian women they could "fuck" before graduation. To these boys, sex with the Other represents a rite of passage into a more "worldly" state. Whether overtly stated or covertly desired, transformation through contact with the "exotic" is played out in the forum of certain white-dark sexual relations. These attitudes

reinforce colonial power relations, where the dark, earthly, and sensual paradise is there for the enjoyment of the white newcomer.

Whether princess or squaw, Native femininity is sexualized. This understanding finds its way into our lives and our communities. Sometimes, it means constantly having to fend off the advances of people with an appetite for the "Other." It may involve a continual struggle to resist crass, sexualized interpretations of one's being, as in the experience of these (anonymous) women:

> I can't stand at night in any place by myself because all the men think that I am trying to pick them up. I am telling you, it doesn't matter where I am .... They think that all the Native women in the world, we are there just to [have sex with them]. All the time—it doesn't matter where—poor area, rich area, it doesn't matter.[22]

> I found that I was constantly, throughout my life, pestered by men who were drunk, alcoholics, feeling like they had a chance with me. I found this really insulting. I mean, I may not be rich, but I'm well educated, I'm hard-working, I'm not an alcoholic—you know, to me I've got a lot of positive things going for me, and I feel that I should have men who are at least my equal coming after me. And I've found throughout my life that I have not had that. I have them coming up for one-night stands. They don't want a relationship with me, they just want sex. And this is quite upsetting.[23]

This sexualized understanding of Native women can be seen in our communities, where, as Lee Maracle has observed, "it is nearly impossible for Native men to cherish the femininity of Native women. They have grown up in a world in which there is no such thing as dark-skinned femininity. There is only dark-skinned sensuality."[24]

In terms of overt violence, Plains Cree/Métis professor Emma LaRocque asserts that "the dehumanizing portrayal of the squaw and the over-sexualization of Native females such as Disney's Pocahontas surely render all Native female persons vulnerable."[25] After telling me, "Since childhood, I have had to walk through a maze of racist and sexist assaults on me," she told me a story that offered a striking image of the perceived worthlessness of Native female existence as it has too often been understood by the dominant society:

> My first experience of when I was conscious of this kind of assault happened when I was about ten years old. I was sitting in a café in my home town, reading a comic book, as I was wont to do. Minding my own business. I don't know where my parents were, but I just remember a big, fat, red-faced white guy coming in. Leering at me. I don't even think I could identify what that look was, because I had been so safe at home and in my community. I had never been attacked, and I didn't know what on earth that was. This guy, he throws a quarter. I still remember, and I still see that quarter rolling right past my coke bottle. He threw a quarter and he said, "Want to go for a ride, little squaw?"

LaRocque acknowledges the danger she was in at that moment, and how racist stereotypes endanger Native girls and women: "To this day, I am profoundly grateful he did nothing else. He could have just picked me up and taken me away. Nobody would have known the difference." She asks, "Where do these men get off on attacking little children, teenagers, regular aged women, and grandmothers? It has to come from some conditioning, some horrendous sociological, racist and sexist conditioning, to be so inhumane to your co-human beings. It is really stunning."

Negative images of Native women, whether in historical accounts, anecdotes, jokes, movies, or Canadian literature,[26] are at the root of stories like that of Helen Betty Osbourne, a sixteen-year-old Native woman who was picked up by four white men and brutally raped and murdered in The Pas, Manitoba, in 1972. This story remains fixed in the consciousness of many Native women, as it demonstrates how mainstream society interprets violence against Native women, especially when it is committed by whites. In my conversation with Gertie Beaucage (Ojibway), she pointed out that Osbourne was killed because she was expected to be "easy," and yet she resisted the sexual assault of the white men who attacked her. As Emma LaRocque has further pointed out, "In the minds of 'good boys who did bad things,' it is not the place of 'squaws' to resist white power, especially power snakily connected to the male ego."[27]

The Osbourne case eventually received a moderate amount of publicity because of the injustices it represented. There are, however, many more Native women's tales that would reveal the minimal worth placed on Native female lives. In our conversations, Lee Maracle (Sto:lo) and Catherine Martin (Mi'kmaw) have demonstrated to me that the notion that Native women are there for the sexual taking has been acted out from one side of the continent to the other. Maracle recalls her childhood on the West Coast:

> In my village, every single weekend ... men came into the village, picked up little children, took them to the gravel pit, raped them—sometimes killed them—and were never prosecuted. I personally was chased in automobiles by white men. And when I went to swear out a complaint, they said it was in my imagination. I had charged a white man with assault, and I was called not a credible witness. Those things happen in our personal lives.

Maracle attributes this to the "permission that white society gave to white men to enter our communities, murder, pillage, rape and plunder us at will, right up until 1963."

A Mi'kmaw from Nova Scotia, Catherine Martin recalls, "In my grandmother's time, during the war, during the time when the Indian Agent had total rule, atrocities happened to our women. I know that." This was a time when, in the absence of Indian men, women were even more subject to attack. But Martin knows that racist ideology was at work:

> Our women were raped. They weren't just raped back in cowboy and Indian days, they are still raped. But that myth or misperception about our women [being easy] is in the minds of the mainstream society, which is why our women end up being attacked and raped. The fact that we have been raped tends to make them think that we are easy. It is a way to excuse the rapist, or to ignore the race issue.

Hereditary Wit'suwet'en Chief Theresa Tait lives in central British Columbia. When I spoke with her about this issue, she told me that in the last decade there have been at least five Aboriginal women who have been killed in her local area. There is little investigation and next to no media coverage about these incidents. Tait contrasts the lack of attention to violence against Aboriginal females with cases involving white women who go missing in Vancouver: "There, you have the media, you have everybody on side."

Native women seeking justice against the violence in their lives are overshadowed by the image of the squaw. In her study of how race figures into sexual abuse trials, Sherene Razack notes that Aboriginal women are treated as "inherently rapeable" because of assumptions made about Native female promiscuity and the insistence that a rape victim who has passed out because of alcohol is considered to have suffered less of a violation.[28] A Native

woman who is drunk is deemed particularly unworthy of human treatment, and Native women who are involved in abusive relationships may not feel comfortable calling police in the case of domestic violence because they may be seen "at fault," or deserving of the abuse.[29]

The construction of a negative identity can rule a Native woman's experience, as these women have described. The triangle of oppression, developed by the Doris Marshall Institute,[30] is a useful tool for analysing how the oppression functions:

Each point of the triangle supports the others to maintain the oppression of Native women. If Native women are constructed as "easy squaws" and are locked into this imagery through the behaviour of individuals, they will continue to be rendered worthless in public institutions such as courtrooms or hospitals. If we treat Native women as easy or drunken squaws in the court system, we feed negative stereotypes that will further enable individuals to abuse Native females, and so on. Negative Native female images are part of a vicious cycle that deeply influences the lives of contemporary Native women. We need to get rid of the images, the systems that support them, and the abusive practices carried out by individuals.

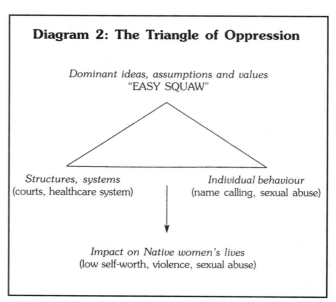

Diagram 2: The Triangle of Oppression

Dominant ideas, assumptions and values
"EASY SQUAW"

Structures, systems
(courts, healthcare system)

Individual behaviour
(name calling, sexual abuse)

Impact on Native women's lives
(low self-worth, violence, sexual abuse)

Notes

1. Rayna Green, "The Pocahontas Perplex: The Image of the Indian Woman in American Culture," *Sweetgrass* (July–August 1984), 19.

2. Ibid.

3. This was a typical application of Indigenous women in other colonial contexts, as explained in Ann McClintock, *Imperial Leather: Race, Gender and Sexuality in the Colonial Context* (New York: Routledge, 1995).

4. Elizabeth Cook-Lynn, *Why I Can't Read Wallace Stegner and Other Essays* (Madison: University of Wisconsin Press, 1996), 97–107.

5. Beth Brant, *Writing as Witness: Essay and Talk* (Toronto: Women's Press, 1984), 83–103; Clara Sue Kidwell, "Indian Women as Cultural Mediatators," *Ethnohistory* 39, no. 2 (Spring 1992), 97–107.

6. Cook-Lynn, *Why I Can't Read Wallace Stegner and Other Essays*, 106.

7. Green, "The Pocahontas Perplex," 20.

8. Carol Douglas Sparks, "The Land Incarnate: Navajo Women and the Dialogue of Colonialism," in Nancy Shoemaker, ed., *Negotiators of Change: Historical Perspectives on Native American Women* (New York: Routledge, 1995), 135–156.

9. Ibid., 147.

10. Sarah Carter, *Capturing Women: The Manipulation of Cultural Imagery in Canada's Prairie West* (Montreal: McGill-Queen's University Press, 1997), 158–193.

11. Ibid., 160.

12. Ibid., 162.

13. Ibid., 183.

14. Ibid., 191.

15. Ibid., 205.

16. Rita Joe, *Song of Rita Joe: Autobiography of a Mi'kmaq Poet* (Charlottetown, PEI: Ragweed Press, 1996), 62; Anna Lee Walters, *Talking Indian: Reflections on Survival and Writing* (Ithaca, NY: Firebrand Books, 1992), 211.

17. Janice Acoose, *Iskwewak: Kah'Ki yaw NiWakhomakanak: Neither Indian Princesses nor Easy Squaws* (Toronto: Women's Press, 1995), 29.

18. Joanne Arnott, *Breasting the Waves: On Writing and Healing* (Vancouver: Press Gang, 1995), 76; Brant, *Writing as Witness*, 13, 119–120; Maria Campbell, *Halfbreed* (Toronto: McClelland and Stewart Limited, 1973), 47, 90; Janet Campbell Hale, *Bloodlines: Odyssey of a Native Daughter* (New York: Harper-Perennial, 1993), 139–140; Beatrice Culleton, *In Search of April Raintree* (Winnipeg: Pemmican Publications, 1983); Paula Gunn Allen, *The Sacred Hoop: Recovering the Feminine in American Indian Tradition* (Boston: Beacon Press, 1986), 48–49; Lee Maracle, *I am Woman* (Vancouver: Press Gang, 1996), 14–19; Anna Lee Walters, *Talking Indian: Reflections on Survival and Writing* (Ithaca, NY: Firebrand Books, 1992), 52.

19. Barbara Helen-Hill, *Shaking the Rattle: Healing the Trauma of Colonization* (Penticton, BC: Theytus Books, 1995).

20. bell hooks, *Black Looks: Race and Representation* (Toronto: Between the Lines Press, 1992), 21–39.

21. Ibid., 25.

22. Quoted in Bonita Lawrence, "'Real' Indians and Others: Mized-Race Urban Native People, *The Indian Act*, and the Rebuilding of Indigenous Nations" (PhD thesis, Ontario Institute for Studies in Education of the University of Toronto, 1999), 261–262.

23. Ibid.

24. Maracle, *I Am Woman*, 56.

25. Emma LaRocque, "The Colonization of a Native Woman Scholar," in Patricia Chuchryk and Christine Miller, eds., *Women of the First Nations: Power, Wisdom, and Strength* (Winnipeg: The University of Manitoba Press, 1996), 12.

26. See Acoose, *Iskwewak*.

27. Emma LaRocque, "Tides, Towns and Trains," in Joan Turner, ed., *Living the Changes* (Winnipeg: University of Manitoba Press, 1990), 87.

28. Sherene Razack, *Looking White People in the Eye: Gender, Race and Culture in Courtrooms and Classrooms* (Toronto: University of Toronto Press, 1998), 68–72.

29. Anne McGillivary and Brenda Comaskey, *Black Eyes All of the Time: Intimate Violence, Aboriginal Women, and the Justice System* (Toronto: University of Toronto Press, 1999), 100.

30. Rick Arnold, Bev Burke, Carl James, D'Arcy Martin, and Barb Thomas, *Educating for a Change* (Toronto: Between the Lines and the Doris Marshall Institute for Education and Action, 1991), 91–92.

Eat and Disorder

Julie Glaser

Part One: Eat

They link her to my rejection of meat.
Days of plates of cabbage rolls, fried moose steak, the thanksgiving bird,
rabbit I was told was chicken, deer meat, steak tartar, goose, the christmas
bird, breaded veal, glazed ham, stewed beef, the easter bird, head cheese
which is not really cheese at all
and once,
bear.
Not ones to waste, make haste and make room for the organs and innards:
kidney and liver and tongue and tripe, stuffing up arteries like bursting,
bar-b-qued bratwurst, dripping slow deaths of ambiguous hunger. My
brain cells waded through the pools of fat in a last ditch effort to digest
reality.

Years ago, while still in school, I felt the need to cleanse my system of pigs
and deer and bear and cow and moose and rabbit and turkey and goose
and chicken. Flush my soul of creatures consumed against their will.
    That year I learned how to cook and eat without grimace, tofu and
chickpeas. It was the same year I first read Foucault and stopped
shaving my legs. At christmastime, I received four angora sweaters from various
family members, and an Epilady. They saw me off at the train station with
a case of sardines weighing down my suitcase. I couldn't explain to their
satisfaction that I was feeding myself with a steady diet of fresh herbs, gin-
ger root, and Virginia Woolf. I bartered the sardines for marijuana and tick-
ets to see experimental theatre.

On weekends, I paraded an array of boyfriends by them. Mostly skinny, much to their disappointment. The melodrama and sensitivity and situational poverty of the young, budding actor or artist were under-appreciated in my family. Once or twice, I brought home a couple of bigger ones, athletic types, good feeders, and polite, always accepting seconds and occasionally thirds. Watching them eat was the highlight of our relationships: they filled me to no other capacity beyond entertaining my family with their voracious appetites. My Oma would ask: what is their last name again? and what nationality is that? are they Jewish?

God forbid I bring home to their table a Jew, or a black, or an Indian, or a dirty gypsy.

Eye-talians were pretty much suspect too for that matter. And later, as I pushed the meat around on my plate and eventually passed it by altogether, they added to the list socialists, environmentalists, and academics. Artists continued to invoke laughter much like the gag reflex. It just never occurred to them at all that I might bring home

a girl.

Flesh not of my own brought to my lips makes me a carnivore. Hands and lips and breasts and tongue and thighs and sighs from flesh of my flesh make me a lesbian. Dirty, sick, shameless. Condemned to death by my own blood, thrown onto the heap of bodies akin   to me in our difference: gypsies, Jews, homosexuals, crazies. Warming me in our criss-crossing faggot of fire roasted to perfection. They'd rather have me eat another than love my own. Pile my plate with nazi propaganda. Learn by rote the family recipe for normalcy, the ingredients needed to make a good girl who'll grow up to (1) work at A Job, (2) buy a house in Suburbia close enough to all relations to make them neighbours, and (3) consume goods from The Mall. Lick the plate clean after each serving.

I starve there: skin breaks out and hair falls out and teeth rot.

We made pudding our first greedy night together. Not enough eggs to double the recipe, we multiplied the fractions and added the remainders to form a thick, chocolate brew. Laugh and argue over the calculations, counting on fingers. Numbers making us dizzy, banter making us breathless. Turning up the heat to a slow boil. Her hand brushed against my back and the world
stopped.

Tastebuds explode on the exotic fruit. I have fallen far from the family tree,
plump and tart, juice dripping between my sapling limbs at just the
thought of another like me.

I am nine.
Sensing the badness of something I know nothing about, innocent lips curl
around a hiss as I ask the Grand Mother: Was Opa a nazi?
Twenty years later the Grand Mother hisses back at me: Are you a lesbian?
Evil wearings on my back, I bade the beasts before you. I know what lies
behind those eyes. Locking me up, charged with your indignities.
Membership lost at sea, salty like my earthly endeavors, dissolved in tears
that followed. Outside to your inside, peeping Pam I am.

When I arrived home it was to her. Two women, she and I, makin' a go of
it, eh? Hopeless-chest-china and newspaper all over the floor. Dog hair
and little pebbles of kitty litter woven into the carpet. Save it for later.
Vacuuming's the last thing on my mind.

In his backyard, accordion and lederhosen hung out to dry. Guilt, crusty
mud cracking in the seams.

It seems that I was out of order, out of line to suggest such a thing.
A nazi?
A nazi?
A trisket a trasket, a green and yellow basket.
I went to bed with a lump on my head,
and didn't wake up in the morning.

Don't mention it.
Don't ever   mention it   again.
I didn't.
Until I could sleep no longer.
And so ...

Once upon a time, years later in a place not too far, far away, I rose from
my bed of thorns and imported duvets (german ducks produced the best
feathers, they said) and tasted the fruit before me. She was sweet, and she
offered me cups and bowls and spoonfuls of her. A geyser of seductive
truth poured forth from her and I wept with acceptance. Lustily, I led her

to the kitchen, where I could eat my fill of her. We set our bed up where
the table should be, and began the feast.

Part Two: Disorder

Prepared for the questions they do not ask, I carry on as usual. Usually I
just carry on.
And what I expect is what is to be expected.
The phone doesn't ring. Just the proverbial pregnant pause while they
await my change of mind.

As if I would change my mind.

And then
a voice croaks through the dusty receiver, full of warning and shaming
and saving my soul.
As she did her own, I suppose, half a century ago.

Her eyes grey steel. Were they blue once? She tells me they are blue, but
she maintains that she is taller than me too, which she has not been since
I have been a
fraction of her age.

There are pictures I have seen: first years in Canada mostly, a few of herself as a girl in Germany. Taller, rounder, hair falling loosely from her head
in curls. Bosom soft, eyes laughing at something outside the camera. She
was a girl once; I have seen the evidence.

    There was a boy too, who I have not seen, but heard about. Once. And I
have seen the evidence of this too: a silver band, melted-down and shaped
to fit her finger, gently hammered by his own hands. He joined up with the
German army, she said, and died shortly thereafter. She told me this only
once. And at that moment she transformed before my eyes into a woman
I had not known but had been waiting to meet my whole life. Her beauty
and passion cleared the kitchen of its antiseptic and sauerkraut smells. The
room awhirl with her hopes. I hoped for her too.

And then the ring is snatched from my hand and she dashes up the stairs,
to hide it away in her piles of things hiding other things. I try when we are
alone together to get more scoop out of her. I try other family members for
details, but no one seems to know what I'm talking about, including her

now too, who looks at me like I'm crazy when I bring it up. Apparently I don't know what I am talking about. Apparently I am crazy. I am always the crazy one. Of course I am. How quickly I forget.

There are the things we remember and the things we forget. And then there are the other things that exist to prompt the remembering or secure the forgetting.

My shape mirrors hers: hearty Russian peasant bones, big hands for the size of us, nose and chin that will meet in time. My bosom, however, pales in comparison. My skin is darker too. Popped out like some brown and hairy little foreigner. The gypsy, they called me. Defects attributed to my mother's gene pool. Imperfections abound in the British; years of scandalous trading with the colonies.

Sugar & spice, all things nice, I add garlic to everything.

I am nine.
Summer of 1976. We—my parents, a cousin, and his wife—are packed into some sort of hot rod car, travelling west to Vancouver. We eat Niagra cherries out of a paper bag and spit the seeds out of the window. It's so damn hot we strip down to what is legally permissible. I am conscious of growing out my bangs, which is probably more conscious than my parents believe me capable of. I marvel at the way my father rockets determinedly across a country, never consulting a map, never losing us. I marvel too at his silky armpit hair, catching some breeze through his crooked arm out the window, hand beating rhythm on the door to a seventies soundtrack. Freddie Mercury, a blazing streak of groin lust turning up the heat in our hot rod. The women fall asleep, sticking their thighs to mine. In their purses I dig out tampons, fluff them out and marker wee mice faces on them. Line them up on the back dash. I keep my eyes peeled for prairie dogs, imagining them trainable rodents.
We stay over at the farm of our cousin's cousin, somewhere in dry and dusty Saskatchewan. The cousin's cousin has produced a herd of children, none of whom appear to ever brush hair or teeth. They are strangely quiet and screamingly hysterical at the same time. They sleep everywhere. I sleep on a couch next to a kitchen table. It smells like beer and wet dog. I wake up early and the girl nearest my age takes me out behind the barns, through a field, into scrub bush sprouting rusted appliances. The doors should be off, I think, all panicky. Hasn't anyone told them that the doors

should be off? Else children crawl into dryers and freezers and ovens and get locked inside. They suffocate there on their own exhale, in darkness and the echo of quiet. The girl beckons me behind a line-up of refrigerators, only a couple with doors hanging open on their on hinges. I lurch past them, eyes spinning to the back of my head on the lookout for small, withered hands emerging from a Westinghouse. The girl is behind the wheel of a burnt out vehicle. I crawl in next to her, perch on a crate where a seat should be. There is a sleeping bag in the back. She pulls out a pack of cigarettes from underneath what remains of the driver's seat. *This is where we do it*, she tells me. *Sometimes they give me nickels.*

I stay on the porch awhile gathering air in my lungs. The girl has gone inside to get a plate of bacon and toast. I think I should tell my parents before we leave about the children who might be trapped in the appliances. But then I think that our cousin's cousin might not let us go if they know that we know. And no one would know where we were, in the middle of nowhere, in the middle of Saskatchewan, severed and roasting in prairie-sun-powered ovens. I feel a fever coming on and lay out on the porch, one eye peeled on a sorrowful black dog eyeballing me, and one ear tuned and alert to the footsteps of a mangy teenage boy.

When we say our thank-you's and goodbye's to our cousin's cousin's family, I can barely wait to get in the car. I am so unsteady on my feet that my father insists that I use the outhouse one last time before we go, otherwise he's leaving me here. The girl catches me on the way out of the hut that up until now I had been peeing behind. She pulls me close to her and my lungs catch on bacon grease and cigarette smoke and wet dog. *I could come visit you. We could be pen pals, and I could visit you in Ontario.* I give her my hair barrette that is holding back my bangs and tell her, ok.

Our cousin's cousin gives my father directions back to the main roads. He tells us to roll up our windows going through the Indian reservation, just like the man at the ticket booth of the African Lion Safari told us to. We emerged from the African Lion Safari with our soft-top roof torn to shreds from the monkeys. I sat horrified mute throughout the entire experience, holding back sympathetic tears for captured beasts on display. *I'm sorry I'm sorry I'm sorry.* I telepathically plead to them. I anticipate the worst going through the reservation, and for the remainder of the trip keep a close eye on our cousin. I discover a feathered roach clip in his wife's purse and add an Indian tampon mouse to my brood.

Twenty years pass and my cousin and his wife are travelling the Yukon in an RV equipped with an oxygen tank. They have routed their journey

according to oxygen refill stations, and my cousin waits for a lung trans-
plant. Twenty years pass and the Grand Mother's cellar is lined with an
armour of cans: cherries and ham and tomatoes and corn and beans steeling themselves against some unprovoked, anticipated attack multiplying
in the dark. How long before their insides poison with ancient aluminum?
How long before decaying ham and corroding metal bubble a life of their
own?

Twenty years pass and I know no more about family secrets than I ever
did, other than that I have become one. My sexual orientation is about as
well tolerated as my preference for not eating meat. It is never acknowledged nor taken seriously. Apparently if they ignore these things long
enough, I might revert. I might just conveniently forget that I don't eat
hormone-injected beef or by-products, that I sleep with girls, that I need to
know where I come from. Discontent with silence I create my own noise.
I make my own dinner and my own bed. I piece together my family history like a raggedy old quilt, a thing of purpose, not of beauty. It doesn't keep
me particularly warm at night, but I feel better knowing that it's there.

Twenty years pass and my CV is filled with acts of disobedience, challenges to social structures, mindsets and political whimsy. Twenty years
pass and around my Thanksgiving table assemble my friends: socialists,
academics, poets, deviants. We thank the good farmers of Ontario and eat:

Curried Squash Soup
Fennel & Pomegranate Salad
Marinated Portobello Mushrooms
Roasted New Potatoes with Garlic & Fresh Herbs
Kale (from my garden) with Chevre & Balsamic Vinegar
&
Berries & Custard, for Dessert

It's a party,   afterall.

Fat and Fabulous: Resisting Constructions of Female Body Ideals

Kathleen LeBesco

"You can never be too rich or too thin." The linking of economic status and body size in this popular adage is far from coincidental. In fact, the unprecedented abundance of food resources in much of the Western world and the accompanying shift from the manual labor of the industrial age to the more sedentary bodies of the flourishing service and information economies have made it easier than ever before to be fat.

However, cultural ideals of beauty tend to follow from that which is difficult to attain in a given context. In a world where our jobs require little physical exertion, where media are best enjoyed while immobile, and where overprocessed fast food is increasingly convenient and ubiquitous, it is then unsurprising that the aesthetic ideal for women—a lean, gym-toned physique—signifies a clear departure from the logic of the culture itself. While there is certainly much profit to be made in the fattening process, there are even greater returns when fat and average-sized women are made to feel anxious and ashamed about their bodies. Diet and fitness industries prey upon the very insecurities that they help to create, reaping billions of dollars in annual revenue as a result.

It is vital to remember, in the face of professionally cultivated body shame, that spending one's money on diet products and more generally, buying into diet rhetoric, means allowing that shame to thrive unchecked. For many fat women, the only way to avoid derision by peers is to submit to the notion that there is something wrong with them and to confess a drive for change. Women who claim "fat pride" and inhabit their culturally scorned bodies comfortably get little refuge from the critical, discriminatory glare of those around them. On the other hand, those who internalize the perception that they would be incomparably improved if they could only lose weight—whether or not they actually *do* diet—are granted a bit of breathing space. Those women who fail to take up their own body as a project, who instead direct their attention to more pressing social and political projects, are given more than a slap on the wrist. They are pushed to the margins of society, *abjected*, making the objectification faced by their slimmer sisters look like a dream state.

Electronic and print media are some of the most notorious carriers of punishing messages about women's bodies. Fashion magazines aimed at young women showcase spreads featuring near-skeletal models and ads for diet products and flaw-masking cosmetics alongside articles about female empowerment—the bait and switch, indeed. Lad magazines aimed at young men so radically alter images of the actresses on their covers, thinning them down to peg-leg proportions, that the stars themselves (Kate Winslet, for example) complain.

Few genres of television programming feature women of average or even ample size, and when fat women do show up, they're often portrayed one-dimensionally as unhappy and lovelorn or zany comic figures (Mimi from *The Drew Carey Show*, for one). "Real" fat women appear on television in daytime talk shows, where they either capitulate to audience consensus that they're deeply flawed, or where they are roundly mocked for taking pleasure in their own bodies. Entertainment television reports also devote significant attention to the weight gain of actresses, real women whose bodily dimensions are the stuff of much public speculation. In recent years, numerous women inhabiting what many of us would consider conventionally beautiful bodies have been flayed in entertainment media for "betraying" the public by gaining a few pounds, including Alicia Silverstone, Kathleen Turner, Catherine Zeta-Jones, and others. Mainstream film treads similar ground, with few exceptions highlighting slender beauties as leading ladies and relegating their fatter counterparts to second-banana status. Even films that portend to take aim at fat-phobia and looks-ism like the Farrelly brothers' *Shallow Hal* end up reinscribing notions that beauty comes in a size six and that fat jokes pandering to the lowest common denominator are comedic gold.

One should not get carried away in pointing fingers at the media for promoting narrow body ideals, however, without examining how everyday talk about bodies—the kind that each one of us participate in—reinforces cultural prejudices against fat people. At a pool party, I recently overheard the following conversation about a middle-aged woman at the far end of the pool dressed in a fairly ample bikini and tank-top coverup whose large belly and fleshy hips made her an unusual wearer of a bikini-style swimsuit. The onlookers, both women, exchanged goofy smiles, and the first exclaimed, "Brave woman!" to which the

second muttered, "More like CRAZY! What makes her think the public wants to see her big gut?" Even in a private chat, such conversational censure functions to police bodies that fail to correspond to bigoted standards. Similarly, when women describe their experience of having an "off" day as "having a fat day," fat is irrevocably positioned negatively. For mainstream body ideals to change, we must not only create and support more complex, sophisticated media representations of fat characters, but we must take responsibility in our own speech for how *we* present fat bodies.

This issue of responsibility rears its head quite frequently in discussions of whether fat women deserve to be treated respectfully, despite their differences from currently idealized body types. A fat body, like a lesbian body, a Black body, or a disabled body, is marked as "different" from what our culture idealizes. Racism and able-ism remain discouragingly prevalent in the North American context, though most people recognize that one does not choose one's race or disability. In contrast, battles over whether sexuality is an inherent orientation or instead a "lifestyle" choice continue to inform the decisions of many as to how homosexuals should be treated. The jury still seems to be out on fat people, as well, with many hoping that the identification of a "fat gene" will let fat folk off the hook, show that they're not responsible for their culturally maligned position, and augur some respect. Still other fat activists argue that regardless of the extent to which one is culpable (through eating and exercise habits) in one's own fatness, respectful treatment is *always* warranted.

Rather than despairing over the apparently maligned position of fat women in mainstream Western culture, one could look to the work of fat acceptance activists and culture workers for a blueprint to the anti-diet revolution. Groups like the radical Fat Underground from the 1970s and the more assimilationist National Association to Advance Fat Acceptance have labored to change our understandings of and responses to fatness.

Less formal networks of fat women have collaborated on public actions like an ice cream eat-in in front of a Jenny Craig diet center and a scale-smashing in Seattle that seek in a highly visible manner to show their dissatisfaction with our culture's regard for them. Others use the Internet as a forum for hashing out more acceptable and sometimes celebratory meanings for fat women's bodies. Even corporate media have seen fit to show us complex fat female heroines; Emmy-winner Camryn Manheim of *The Practice* sets many hearts aflutter! Whatever the location, these forms of resistance demonstrate that female body ideals are being contested in profound ways.

In stepping up to the challenge of resisting mainstream notions of what a woman's body should be, we need to guard against the tendency to claim innocent intentions. To cave in to the rhetoric that "we can't help being fat, thus we shouldn't be treated poorly" is to allow our emotional safety to exist at the expense our dignity and subjectivity. Never have I heard a Jewish woman defend herself from anti-Semitism by claiming "I was born this way, and I can't do anything about it—so leave me alone." To do so would be to undermine her agency and her faith. I believe that we need to encourage women to inhabit their bodies comfortably, whatever their size and shape, and to understand that it doesn't really matter how a body got to be the way it is for it to be respected. In this way, women can begin to abandon their "body projects" and give up the fantasies of what their lives would be like if only they were thin, and live *today*.

Angry Naked Women

Mariko Tamaki

Did you ever have one of those days when you look like shit and you feel like shit and then someone gives you like a *minute* dosage of attitude and you think, "Well it should just be legal to kill this person?"

Okay, well that's what this is about.

To all the little-butted, skinny people in the audience, I apologize in advance. All I can say is that you should all just be grateful that I'm here today and beyond that, you should be thankful that I didn't come here nude. Because let me tell you, as of late I am getting closer and closer to angry nakedness. The next time you see me I'll just be a pissed off vagina. This past Wednesday at Toronto's Women's Bathhouse, when I looked around at all the naked bodies what I saw was not an erotic display, but a practical option in a world where finding anything above a size 12 is like finding a virgin at a university dormitory.

I spent 6 hours yesterday scouring Toronto for a decent outfit that would fit over my thighs and I came to 3 conclusions:

1. This city sucks—it's hot, it contains no changing rooms bigger than my cat's litter, and it's hot.
2. I hate all sales people and blame them for the part they play in pushing a line of clothing that only fits a small fraction of the population (even if they aren't the ones who make the clothes, I blame them anyway).
3. All well-dressed fat people should be fucking worshipped and hailed as the Gods they are.

Should I not choose to walk around for the rest of my days angry and nude, I'm going to opt instead to wear a t-shirt that says *I'm a well-dressed fat person and I deserve your respect for my efforts.*

And for those of you fed up with us fat chicks and our bitching about our big fat asses and the problems they cause us, let me assure you no one is more tired of listening to me bitch about my big fat ass than me.

The only person who is possibly more wary of my big fat ass than me might be the retailer who tried to help me find an outfit amongst the racks at a store that shall remain nameless. Okay, it was The Gap. This poor man whose skinny ass I chewed into tiny bits after an hour of searching for something that would squeeze over my thighs … I swear, this poor man with all his efforts never had a chance of becoming anything more than a pot-hole in the road of my rage.

"You know," he said, as we neared the finale of my fitting routine, "maybe you should try a plus-size store."

I gathered my things, my courage, and my dignity, and pushed my way out of the tiny pen that had served as my dressing room.

"What's your name?" I asked.

"Ben." He said.

"Ben." I said, "Here's the situation, Ben, I have to give this performance tomorrow and you know, Ben, I was going to do a poem about my VISA card, but you know what I'm going to do now, Ben? I'm going to do a piece about snot-nosed GAP boys with little asses who work at boutiques that sell clothes for anorexic picks who make up all of 7% of the population."

"Don't you think that's just a little bitter," asked Ben.

"Do I look BITTER to you Ben," I asked, edging my sweaty body further and further into his personal space, "or do I look dangerously agitated?"

I left a sticker on the door that said:

WHEN THE REVOLUTION COMES, YOU AND YOUR COHORTS WILL BE THE FIRST UP AGAINST THE WALL.

You think it's a joke, but I'm serious.

In the end, no thanks to Ben, I did find myself an outfit that day (a little polka dotted number that makes me look immature but well-dressed), but memories of that particular exchange (and others like it) remain.

I have a plan.

I'll take my naked body to the streets in protest.

I'll pummel the public with what it insists on denying and avoiding: tons of mountainous, sexy flesh. I'll bare my boobs and squish my sweaty bum at strangers. I'll squeak against every available surface and leave strange marks to embarrass the public. I'll gather an army of fat angry naked soldiers and we'll take to the streets. We'll go to The Gap and touch all their clothes and use up all their perfume samples 'til they agree to stock size 16 to 30 as standard practice.

We'll bring Toronto the Timid to its knees with the vengeance of our vaginas.

Look out, Ben, the revolution is coming.

Mark my words.

Blood and Cunts

Inga Muscio

One fine spring day, after the lunchtime recess in sixth grade, Miss Cothran announced that all the boys were to join Mr. Rogers out on the playground for a game of softball, while all us girls were mandatorially invited to accompany her to the cafeteria.

My friends 'n me knew what was up. We had heard about the infamous Period Movie around fourth grade. Most of the boys were no less familiar with this legendary film and teased us relentlessly as they filed out to the softball diamond.

In the cafeteria, the girls from Mrs. Wolff's class, Mr. Rogers's class, and mine assembled into tittering rows. The school nurse stood in the front of the room, between the pullout movie screen and a table displaying all of the various disposable bleeding paraphernalia we would one day come to know so well. She explained the ways to affix pads to our panties and dabbled a little into tampondom; then the Film Projector Monitor was called to do her duty, and the Period Movie started.

To date, it is the most intellectually impaired film I've ever seen, taking into account the *combined* fatuity of *Basic Instinct* and *Ace Ventura: Pet Detective.*

A cartoon of the female form demonstrated how this dot in your head travels down to your cunt and makes you bleed. The doctorly sounding male narrator insisted that we not take baths or exercise during this "special time," but be sure to keep *spotlessly clean* with lots and lots of soap and showers because menstruating girls tend to stink up the room if they're not completely at one with personal hygiene. He also informed us that any pain or discomfort we might feel resided "in our heads," and had been collectively imagined by womankind for thousands of years.

Were we told anything about how our uteruses are almost exactly like the moon, shedding their linings, growing new ones and shedding all over again? Did the Period Movie teach us *thing one* about how miraculously cool and sublime the human body's reproductive system is when you're a girl?

Fuck no.

All I truly gleaned from this experience was that my cunt was the yucksville reason I had to sit in that stupid cafeteria watching some hack nurse show me how to safety pin a three-mile-wide wad of cotton to a pair of brief underpanties even my grandma wouldn't be caught dead in, while the other half of the sixth grade population was out in the sunshine playing softball. This was the first formal instruction in estrangement from my cunt—within a lifetime's barrage—that I consciously recall.

With all the prepubescent hoopla surrounding periods, I was inclined towards totally vivid nightmarish visions of complete humiliation that would usher in my initiation to womanhood. A recurring one was related to the shower scene Carrie endured—where she was pelted with tampons—in the Hollywood/Stephen King rendition of menstruation commencement. I was *wholly unprepared* for the simplicity and intuition I encountered at the inauguration of my blood.

In seventh grade, I was walking home from school with Teresa Greco and Joyce McCullough. We were halfway down Tunnel Street and suddenly I *knew* I was bleeding. It was the first time I remember *knowing* something in this manner. I told Teresa and Joyce, "Hey, I just started my period," and that was that. I went home, grabbed a pad out of my mom's store, and bled on it.

Tampons didn't come along until my fourth period, when Amy Ajello instructed me in great detail over my teen talk phone line. It was tricky holding the phone to my ear and inserting a tampon for the first time but, thank god, I managed, 'cause pads creeped me out the door. Whenever I wore one, I imagined Jimmy Vallejo and Andrew Vasquez pointing at the gigantic bulge moshing up my ass as I walked down the hall. In my vision, they howled, à la Beavis and Butthead, and everyone else, of course, would hear about it and I'd be the laughingstock of the whole middle school.

Shame kept a close watch on me and all my girlfriends.

It was shameful to bleed, to be seen bleeding, for blood-soaking paraphernalia to be visible on or about one's person at any time whatsoever, to speak of bleeding, to look like we were bleeding, to be excused from P.E. because of the crippling cramps which sometimes accompany bleeding; to display frailty, vulnerability, or mood swings because we were going to be bleeding soon; and to express any emotion other than contempt and disdain in reference to our blood.

No one, least of all my peers—who, verily, whispered about this proscriptive subject in hushy undertones,

behind closed doors, in only the most trusted of boyless locales—thought bleeding a pleasant reality.

Girls are told bleeding is a *bad thing*, an *embarrassing thing*, a *secret thing* that we should hide and remain discreet about come hell or high water.

Boys are told to go outside and play sports while the girls learn about some creepy, cootie-laden mystery that makes blood ooze out from our you-know-whats.

Given my swimmingly fetching cultural milieu, getting used to this bleeding business took quite a while. In the meantime, I fervently asked people why the hell this happened to us girls. Various sources consistently informed me that it was (big sigh) "just part of being a woman" (big sigh), or the good ol' standby curse we inherited from Eve.

My period was not only a "curse," but for the first years of bleeding, I was completely incapacitated with mind-numbing spasms of pain. For at least one day out of every month, I didn't go to school or work. I lay in bed and cried, unable to do anything about the agony of my uterus. Frequently, because of this "imagined" pain, I fainted and puked.

I find it fascinating that men's description of the pain enkindled by a knee to the groin sounds awfully similar to what I have experienced for up to thirty-six unflagging hours. And yet, imagine the hue and cry if men were informed that the horrifying symptom of pain accompanying a swift kick in the nuts was purely psychosomatic.

A coupla years after my period started, the newspapers across our fair nation announced that women *weren't* imagining those intense pains. *Scientific studies* proved that the pain is *real!* As you might surmise, this was but a *load* off my mind.

After all those days I vomited because the mid-section of my body was clenched in a fist of throbbing excruciation; when I sat in the bathtub crying for five hours straight; when I couldn't get out of bed or leave the house for fear of fainting in public; suddenly, because a group of men took the time to study a group of women and found there was indeed a rational reason for these symptoms to wrack our bodies once a month, I was allotted the pale comfort of knowing this pain *actually* existed!

Oh, joy.

Cynic that I am in such arenas of contemplation, I wonder if perhaps this generous allotment wasn't bestowed upon womankind because pharmaceutical companies came to the magnanimous conclusion that sales for pain relievers would skyrocket if only they invested in a little "research" to counter the "in her mind" myth and re-condition the general public into believing there was a veritable malady at hand.

In the spring of 1995, I had the momentous honor of interviewing Barbara G. Walker at her home in New Jersey. Among many other things, she told me about menarche parties women in her community have for the newly menstruating. Ms. Walker described a menarche she attended a few months prior to our interview. The honoree wore a red dress. Her mother made a beautiful, red cake for her. A bunch of women, young and old, brought her red gifts wrapped in red paper. The older women talked about the symbolism of the moon and the miraculous joys of both bleeding and not bleeding anymore, while the younger women who hadn't yet started to bleed duly expressed reverence for the honoree, and enthusiasm about starting their periods.

I mean, wouldn't that be wonderful?

Wouldn't you feel like a total princess if your mom or whoever did that for you? Wouldn't that put a whole new slant on bleeding from the get go?

I was deeply moved by Ms. Walker's account, but in all honesty I must acknowledge my bittersweet envy. My mom's a dang smart lady, and I admire her above and beyond all women on the planet, but it was a bummer to realize that if she hadn't been so busy dealing with the social constraints of single motherhood during the early '80s, sans the aid of a supportive community of women, she might have had the inspiration to hostess a menarche for my sister and me. Whereupon, I sincerely doubt I would've spent almost a decade of my life teaching myself to love the blood that coursed out my stunning cunt *every month*.

Throwing menarche parties for our younger sisters, nieces, and daughters is a very simple and profound way of effecting positive change for the next generation.

Get off your ass and do it.

If Pippi Longstocking were the nation's covergirl, rest assured that women would have a superlative role model in the fine science of accepting ourselves. Ms. Longstocking is extremely outspoken in response to negative social beliefs:

> [T]he children came to a perfume shop. In the show window was a large jar of freckle salve, and beside the jar was a sign which read: DO YOU SUFFER FROM FRECKLES?
>
> "What does the sign say?" asked Pippi. She couldn't read very well because she didn't want to go to school as other children did.
>
> "It says, 'Do you suffer from freckles?'" said Annika.
>
> "Does it indeed?" said Pippi thoughtfully. "Well, a civil question deserves a civil answer. Let's go in."
>
> She opened the door and entered the shop, closely followed by Tommy and Annika. An elderly lady stood back of the counter. Pippi went right up to her.
>
> "No!" she said decidedly.
>
> "What is it you want?" asked the lady.
>
> "No," said Pippi once more.
>
> "I don't understand what you mean," said the lady.

"No, I don't suffer from freckles," said Pippi.

Then the lady understood but she took one look at Pippi and burst out, "But, my dear child, your whole face is covered with freckles!"

"I know it," said Pippi, "but I don't suffer from them. I love them. Good morning."

(Lindgren, 1970, 1849)

Unfortunately, Pippi Longstocking is *not* the nation's covergirl.

All the way through my teens and into my twenties, I loathed my period. "Menstruation" was synonymous with unmitigated physical pain on a monthly basis.

But then I got to thinkin'.

Maybe because I was in college, and what are you supposed to do in college if not think? Maybe because I noticed a marked difference in the way women reacted toward menstruation at this point in human development. Maybe because for the first time in my life, I found myself surrounded by women who were greatly intrigued by the workings of our bodies. Maybe because by the time I went to college I'd taken enough psychotropic plant forms to feel more or less At One with the Universe, instead of lost at sea in the swimmingly fetching cultural milieu I'd previously more or less accepted as reality.

During this period of thinking, I read books and watched the moon.

All women throughout time have had the *opportunity* to see the moon. From Africa and Asia to the Americas and Europe, plenty of these ladies started noticing that the moon grows, recedes, and grows again, over and over every twenty-eight days. Those not detached from their menstrual cycle couldn't help but trip out on how their own rhythm also occurred over the span of approximately twenty-eight days.

This is how the moon links one up with a form of history none of the textbooks can possibly touch upon:

a *psychic* history with all the women who've ever bled on this planet.

By reading some books, investing in a lunar calendar, and poking my head out the window every night or so, I figured out how to tell time by the moon. I learned her phases and moods. The springtime full moon has a much different luminescence than the autumntime full moon. When I went to a party on a dark moon, I generally had a shitty time. When I went to a party during the moon's waxing phase, or better, when it was full, I had a whopping good time.

And on and on.

Soon after me and the moon got to be buddies, the strangest thing happened. The simple act of *hanging* with the moon invoked beliefs my brain had never computed before. Suddenly, all the period propaganda shoved down my throat since that fateful day in sixth grade was far away and beyond ridiculous.

Lo and behold, my period stopped hurting!

I designated the first day of my blood a Special Time where I consciously guarded my quiet. I soaked in mineral salted baths, read Pippi Longstocking, mended clothes (before this, shortening a skirt involved the use of duct tape and an iron), and cooked Creole Tomato Soup.

I quit taking ibuprofen. My period mellowed out even more. For the first time in my life, I actually *enjoyed* bleeding. I gauged myself with the movements and rhythms of the moon. I still got cramps, but I didn't faint or puke at all.

Hip, hip! ...

*****

Our society creates a hospitable climate for cuntpower to be generated into profits amassed by large corporations. Pharmaceutical and feminine hygiene companies, plastic surgeons, and weight-loss centers are designated to care for our bodies in our stead. We learn to rely on various "experts" and authority figures who patronizingly inform us how we should respond to our bodies. We are not offered the opportunity to consider how we'd like to respond to bleeding, nor are we presented with how women menstruated in the past or in other cultures.

Becoming responsible is about quitting the "expert" addiction, feeling and listening to what is going on inside of us, and responding in ways that feel good and right to us. Learning to be responsible for your body *takes time*. It's taken you *all your life* to learn how to alienate yourself to the point of total irresponsibility.

*****

A more material aspect of this revolution is downsizing the percentage of our funding to corporations that exist for no other purpose than to constrain women in the throes of body-alienation and perpetuate our deleterious relationships with our cunts.

*****

Why are words like "hygiene" and "sanitary"—which imply that a woman's cunt is unclean—acceptable in our society? Why are these people trying to sell me feminine deodorant spray? That's like hawking floral air freshener to a lady who lives in a rose garden.

Also, excuse me, but what's so clean about dicks?

One never hears of sanitary jock straps, deodorant condoms, perfumed Hershey-Squirt protection pads, or hygienic ball wipes, whereas I've heard tell of need for such products.

*****

Mother Root: Constant Craving

Nancy Graham

Six months into sessions with Dr. Cove, it happened:

[November, 1996—journal entry] *Walking my dog C.C. through the ravine behind our house, the mirage appears dancing seductively before me. Tears of enlightenment crystallize on my windblown cheeks as I listen to what the apparition whispers as she flits in amongst the trees, swaying in time to their eerily creaking branches. I walk alongside myself, an adult who remains a prisoner of childhood longings and teenage addictions, in an attempt to satisfy an almost constant craving for a nurturing female spirit. In my quest for that nurturing, I am inundated by more Freudian connotations than I can bear. But this spirit who surrounds yet eludes me is not daunted. She dangles a fine silken thread just out of my grasp, tempting, as always, my need to connect. I reach out between the virgin snowflakes, and grab hold of temptation. In an instant I discover who she is, in all of her many guises. She is the muse of a poem, the seed of a crush, the fleeting eye contact, the embodiment of those certain women whose paths cross mine. She is the mother who gave me birth, only to vanish thereafter. Making my way through the stillness of the woods, I instinctively know where to begin looking for her ...*

Part of me doesn't know how I had the gall to uproot the seeds once the idea poked through the soil. Between the covers of my journals, there emerged common thoughts and feelings that haunted my psyche. Seemingly out of the blue, I threw caution to the wind and confronted those feelings by locating Helen Michaels, my former high school English teacher. In the late 1970s, she represented everything that I feared and desired, that I lacked and that I craved, that I still carried with me unresolved. On the pretense of soliciting her assistance as a reader for this book, I rekindled that past when I met with her in mid-December 1996. The days and hours between my initial phone call and our subsequent rendezvous were unnervingly restless for me.

I was afraid I would embrace my destructive drinking patterns in an effort to smother the feelings that were resurfacing with a vengeance. My new counsellor at ARF, Christine, cautioned against meeting with someone who triggered such intense emotion within me. "You don't need to go through the fire," she advised. "Could you not find someone else to be a reader for your book?"

While her concern was valid, my short answer to her was "no." The long answer was far too complex. I was determined to go through the fire. It was the only way for me to make it over the bridge and toward the door I was compelled to re-open—a door that was opened for me many years ago, and behind which rested the source of a significant and symbolic undercurrent in my life. There was no relinquishing my hold of the delicate thread now. I was prepared to trace it back to the time when a shy adolescent was drawn towards someone who represented more than grammar rules.

I suppose I could well have kept the nature of the attraction safely in the past, had it not proceeded to shape me as an adult, in the way that I repeatedly connect with certain women at a deeper and more meaningful level than I had the capacity or maturity to understand as a teenager. The need to embrace that significance began to take on a life of its own. Though some things are better left unsaid, what you cannot communicate will run your life. While I harboured enormous conflict about reopening this door of the past, it was almost as if I did not have a choice. It even occurred to me that perhaps the door had never even been closed, but rather left ajar. On a cold, damp December day, I followed the thread through the door and found myself in a place I had never left.

I arrived early at our arranged meeting place on the outskirts of Hamilton with plenty of time to gulp down two very strong cups of coffee. Admittedly, it was not the wisest beverage choice for taming the butterflies within, but at least I refrained from the beer I would have preferred. As the minutes ticked by, I tried to occupy myself by writing about how damn nervous I was, hoping like hell I was not making a blind and foolish mistake. After repeated glances out the window, I happened to look up just in time to catch sight of a woman hurrying through the parking lot. My stomach tightened. It was she. Moments later, she walked through the door. She seemed to recognize her former pupil immediately, and

moved toward me. I stood to greet her, the colour rising to my face as if on command.

As we began our re-acquaintance, it was easily apparent why I had been drawn to this woman nearly 20 years previous. My nervousness slipped away, replaced by a comforting familiarity. It was as if I was somehow picking up where I had left off so many years ago.

Meeting with Mrs. Michaels unleashed a tide of emotion. As each wave washed over me, I was pulled toward the bridge leading me back to a fork in the road, when the conflict of striving to be a good daughter was challenged by a burgeoning sense of self that went against the grain of all things I knew to be "normal." The need to please my parents at all cost had always been in direct conflict with whatever I may have needed for myself. I had instinctively learned as a young child that Mom's needs necessitated a silencing of my own. Nevertheless, beneath the surface, some very basic needs existed. The need to be noticed and liked, the need to be listened to and accepted, the need for encouragement and praise; all became sources of shameful, rather than normal, neediness in my mind. Especially the need for affection.

On that mid-December afternoon, in the space of a mere two hours and over several more cups of coffee, I allowed myself to look across the table and into the eyes of the mirage from the ravine. I choked back the tears, my whole body recognizing that I was finally coming to terms with what I have always needed, but have fought to deny. With the safety mechanism of Dr. Cove in place, confronting those needs in meeting with Mrs. Michaels was critical to guiding me back further, to places I had never permitted myself to go.

My many moods assault me—leaving me along the way. A lost soul searching. And if I find, or when I find, my self, I know not from whence I came, other than from within her ...

Freud frequently attributed depression to loss in childhood and irretractable guilt. Though not a loss in the physical sense as through death, the emotional loss of Mom had begun with her post-natal depression. Deprived of solid maternal nurturing, of someone to always be there, maybe even with a smile or a hug, a vast emptiness grew within me. The absence of such intangibles that most children take for granted a mother will provide had far-reaching repercussions into my adult life. For nearly 35 years, part of me sought to dismiss the weight of that loss. Certainly any time it was raised by Dr. Cove as a possible influence on my present, I squirmed uncomfortably in my seat, simultaneously blinking back tears and irritated by the subtext of it all.

In retrospect, I did not know how to handle the validation she was offering. Once I allowed myself to let go of the denial, it was crystal clear that the way I move through the world is largely governed by a severed mother-daughter connection. That early rupture gave way to my difficulty identifying acceptable emotional and physical boundaries with others, particularly older women.

In lieu of whatever Mom was unable to provide physically or emotionally, I subconsciously began searching elsewhere. It was in meeting Mrs. Michaels back in the tenth grade that I first became aware of my unsettling longing to establish female bonds. Even though I was accustomed to being the "seen-but-not-heard daughter" and the timid student cowering in the back of the classroom, this woman was not about to let me get away with feigning such invisibility. When I'd sensed that, I had craved her attention, in a way I had never wanted anything before. It was a powerful undertow that drove me to impress her. All the while, I'd flirted with danger, as losing weight became an obsession and drinking destructively was embraced as a desperate attempt to dilute the intensity of the emotions she kindled in me. The confusion was overwhelming, for I feared I was craving something beyond that which could safely be spoken. At times, the craving was all-consuming, and I could barely meet her eyes, for fear she would read my mind, and know immediately how needy I was. It was as if I'd been testing the waters with her, to see how far in I could wade before I'd be over my head. I have been treading water ever since.

Can a drunken fish swim through fire without singeing all scales?

In the two decades since high school, the unsettled waters still churn within me. How resilient the craving has been to the passage of time, as I remain so easily attracted to certain women. Even the fleeting eye-contact or the most casual of conversations will stir a familiar need deep inside. For it is those brief moments in time that acknowledge my existence, my worth, my need to be liked to a fault. How I still fear eye contact will betray my need for female affection. As it began in a classroom so very long ago, so it continues. By the shores of the Red Sea, on a morning commuter train, over drinks in a bar, in the office of a psychiatrist, merely walking my dog around the block, virtually everywhere, I am susceptible to the magnetism of the female aura.

The guilt and shame of my needs are no less painful at age 35 than they were at 16. Although I am still prone to smother my feelings with alcohol and/or food, at least I better understand them. In working with Dr. Cove, I have managed to process and even reconcile the normalcy of some of my needs. In so doing, I am more cognizant of how alcohol does not drown, but rather magnifies the intensity of unresolved shame and guilt. Drink after drink, emotional boundaries become fluid and the temptation to cross over uncharted physical borders is heightened, at times with near immoral abandon. Although my logical mind now concedes there is no map, no way of navigating my way back to my mother through other women, I keep trying. Perhaps to stop would be like giving up on my mother. And I could never give up on the woman who gave me birth. Nor will I ever be able to make amends for the way my birth became her sadness.

Racism, Women's Health, and Reproductive Freedom

Carolyn Egan and Linda Gardner

Of all the forms of inequality injustice in health is the most shocking and inhumane.

—Martin Luther King, Jr.

Unfortunately there has been very little written on racism and women's health in Canada. We hope that this essay will be a useful contribution to the body of knowledge available, and will lead to more work being done on the topic. In the essay we intend to firstly review the findings of the research that is available that deals with the experiences of women of colour in the healthcare system, and examine the intersection of race, class, and gender. We will then analyze how one organization, the Ontario Coalition for Abortion Clinics, tried to relate to the health care needs of women of colour in its organizing for reproductive rights.

Racism has long been present in health care in this country. In Alberta between 1928 and 1972, 2844 people were forcibly sterilized through the province's sexual sterilization act. Under this legislation a eugenics board approved the operation, if reproduction involved the risk of "hereditary taint." Sixty-four percent of those sterilized were women, 20 percent were less than sixteen years old. They were for the most part poor and working class. The racism of its application is obvious. First Nations and Metis people represented 2.5 percent of the population, but accounted for 25 percent of the sterilizations in the law's later years.[1] Both Alberta and British Columbia had such laws in effect, and it is believed that hundreds of such operations were carried out in Ontario as well.

We believe that racism still permeates every facet of Canadian society, and medical services are no exception. A recent study, "Immigrant, Refugee and Racial Minority Women and Health Care Needs," carried out by the Women's Bureau of the Ontario Ministry of Health documents the health care experiences of minority women in Ontario. Researchers interviewed both individuals and groups of women in six regions: Ottawa, Thunder Bay, London, Windsor, Sudbury, and Toronto. These women outlined the situations they faced and the racism they experienced. The document concludes, "The most critical finding of this community consultation process was that immigrant, racial minority, and refugee women are discriminated against by the Ontario health care system."[2]

There are well over one million women who could be defined as immigrant, refugee, or racial minority in Ontario, at least one quarter of the female population of the province. There is, of course, an enormous range of difference in class, language abilities, racial, and ethnic backgrounds among these women, and therefore care has to be taken when making generalizations. The document does not differentiate between women of colour, and other immigrant and refugee women, which is unfortunate for our purposes. We know that the majority of immigrants to Canada today are from non-European countries.

You will see from the comments of the women themselves that they perceive their health is being jeopardized because of the racism and discrimination they face. Racial barriers were clearly identified in the study. Many of the respondents observed that those who are racially different are seen as inferior by white, Canadian health care providers. Women spoke of how they were treated disrespectfully and in a discriminatory manner. Structural barriers were outlined by the women, including the lack of access to language training and ghettoization in low-paying jobs, which restricts the time to access health services. Racism, limited language and literacy levels, combined with a lack of economic opportunities, inhibited the ability of respondents to use medical services, which has a huge impact on women's health.

Through no fault of their own, there is a lack of knowledge among immigrant and refugee women of health care practices that are available such us pap tests or breast screening. Very little effort is made in Ontario to make this information accessible in a racially sensitive manner, or in languages other than English or French. There is a lack of adequate translation and interpreter services, which creates real barriers and can greatly increase a sense of anxiety, alienation, and isolation. This can prevent women from using available services, and ensures that their needs remain unaddressed.

In Thunder Bay participants talked directly about their experience with racial discrimination and stereotyping by health care providers. Public health units were seen to be having a difficult time relating to them. Little effort has been made to develop programs and outreach initiatives, which were appropriate and responsive to minority women's needs. They spoke of how childbirth education programs were not reaching women. Concerns were also raised about the high number of Cesarean births and the over-medication of women involved in the study.

In Ottawa, women described a "softer but more pervasive" form of discrimination. Women spoke of a lack of understanding about their reality and the situations they were describing, as they spoke to health care providers. They felt very reticent to express concerns or feelings about their health, which contributed to stress and mental health problems. Health professionals were often dismissive, treating women as though they were stupid. The women spoke of a lack of trust, and felt no confidentiality in their interactions with health care providers. They felt that their experiences were devalued by the health care system.

In Sudbury women identified a particular need for information on gynecological care, pre- and postnatal services. Women underutilized pap tests and breast exams, because of the lack of outreach to their communities. They were being denied basic health services because of who they are. Many physicians were not aware of conditions such as sickle cell anemia, which can have devastating effects on women of colour.

The authors of the study told us that women's reactions ranged from "polite disappointment to outright anger." The report documented that immigrant, refugee, and racial minority women have obvious health care needs, but they make use of health care services at a significantly lower rate than other women. This is clearly due to the barriers they encounter, which are not only the biases of individual providers, but systemic barriers integrated into the health care delivery system itself. As the study states, "This contradiction is due in large measure to ... racial, linguistic, gender and class barriers embedded within the system, their needs are not being met by existing programs and services ... many areas of the health care delivery system are simply inappropriate for or insensitive to the needs of minority women."[3] Unfortunately we were not provided with a breakdown on the racial backgrounds of the women interviewed, how long they have been in Canada, or differences among the cities targeted. But the interviews make it clear that immigrant women and refugees, the majority of whom today are women of colour, experience the health care system differently than white women, because of the racism embedded within it.

An earlier study by the Immigrant Women's Health Centre (IWHC) in Toronto showed similar findings. The centre was established in 1975 and provides medical and educational services to women from a variety of communities. It also organizes around the health needs of immigrant women and women of colour. It is a multilingual, multi-racial collective with a central focus on sexual health. The counsellors are members of the communities, which the centre serves. They deal with birth control, pregnancy, childbirth, abortion, sexually transmitted diseases, and other gynecological issues, as well as stress management, nutrition, and patient's rights. The centre was started because of the racism that women encounter in mainstream health services, and the need for health care geared to meet their needs. It established specific outreach services, such as the Black Youth Hotline, a mobile unit, and has responded to the needs of the Tamil community and other recent immigrants to Toronto.

The IWHC conducted a study with the women who were using its mobile health unit, which visited work sites between January 1984 and August 1985. The study focused on working women between the ages of twenty-five and forty-five including women from the West Indian, Vietnamese, Chinese, and Spanish communities. Many of the women spoke very little English, did not have previous Canadian job experience, and were forced to work in low-paying jobs, often with unhealthy working conditions. They were often not able to find medical services that they could access and that were sensitive to their needs.

In the study, a health care worker at the IWHC said, "They ... are often taken advantage of without knowing what recourse to take. The implications for reproductive health, let alone reproductive rights, are limited. Unattended gynecological ailments, such as STD's, vaginal infections, information on breast examination, pap tests, and stress-related infections are seen at the Centre. The women are prey to poor quality health services because of their economic, cultural, and political status in society."[4] Mainstream health care did not provide for these women, and this put their health at serious risk.

Although we don't have data on the numbers of women from each community that participated in the study, we do know that today the majority of the women who are seen at the IWHC clinics are women of colour. The study reached 1500 working women at twelve workplaces. Using information gathered in a 1983 community health survey, done by the city of Toronto health department, they compared the preventative health practices of women in the IWHC target group, to those of other women in the city. They were asked questions about pap tests, breast examination by physician, and breast self-examination. The findings showed that only 43 percent of women in the IWHC target group had a pap test in the year prior to the interview, compared to 65 percent of other women. It was also found that women were even less likely to have had a pap test if they worked in semi-skilled or unskilled occupations. "The overall pattern suggests that women in the communities served by the IWHC, who worked in semi-skilled and unskilled jobs are at more risk of having undetected cervical dysplasia than women in any other groups."[5] In terms of breast examination by a physician, a similar pattern emerged in both number and percentage of women who had this performed in the year prior to the interviews. This was the case, not because the women had no concern about their health care needs, but because they had difficulty accessing services because of racism and systemic barriers.

The women seen by the IWHC tend to be concentrated in jobs where they work in assembly or product fabrication, as dishwashers, cleaners, cafeteria workers, waitresses, or domestic workers. The work makes women unable to take time off for routine health care. Treatable health problems, such as cervical or breast cancer, go undetected, jeopardizing chances of survival. Other health problems also go undiagnosed. For example, a woman with untreated high blood pressure is four times more likely to develop kidney disease. Women of colour face discrimination in employment, which makes it more likely that they will work in low-paying jobs, which do not allow easy access to medical services. They are denied health care that white, middle-class women take for granted.

In terms of reproductive issues, the study states, "women face a lack of options on family planning due to their economic condition and this has a direct relation to the measure of control they have or they don't have over their bodies. All of these must be taken into account; how the issue of birth control, pregnancy, abortion, etc., really affect women who work two jobs, who lack a facility in English, or who encounter racism in the society .... Women often seek abortions ... because their material conditions, i.e., housing, employment, lack of daycare, low salary jobs, have dictated to them how many children they may have at any given time in their reproductive life."[6] The intersection of race, class, and gender is very clear in the lives of the women interviewed in this study, and strongly impacts on how they experience health care in this country.

The racism that women of colour confront in the health care system is not confined to Ontario. In a study that specifically deals with the Chinese community in Vancouver, British Columbia the rate of cervical cancer was also found to be much higher.[7] A significant number of Chinese women in their late forties through late sixties were being diagnosed with cervical cancer in a province that was said to be leading the world in pap test screening. This was significantly higher than the general population. We do not know the class background of the women, but it is likely that they are poor or working class. Again it was a question of systemic racism, and the lack of appropriate community programs. Many Chinese women also found it unacceptable to be examined by male doctors, and this was not being taken into account by health providers.

There were a number of structural barriers. Pap screening was a provincial responsibility, but there was a very real absence of creative thinking or support for changes in the program that would make it more accessible to specific communities. Also, the Ministry of Health lacked a funding mechanism to allow for more accessible programs.

Women from the Chinese community took up the issue themselves. A pap smear campaign was highlighted in the Chinese media, featured at community health fairs, and training was provided for volunteers and health professionals from the community. An evening program was launched providing women with information and services in their own language and women doctors from their own community. Chinese women developed their own solutions to a critical problem, which was being ignored by the medical community.

Interestingly Statistics Canada reported in 1996 that recent immigrants report less health problems of a chronic nature than people born in Canada, but the longer they are resident the greater the incidence of chronic health problems. "The difference is particularly marked for recent immigrants from non-European regions, who now account for most of the immigration flow .... The evidence suggests that health status of immigrants weakens the longer they stay in Canada," said Edward Ng, an analyst for Statistics Canada.[8] The health status of people of colour deteriorates at a greater rate than white immigrants the longer they are in the country.

It is clear that government cutbacks are having an impact on the health care of the most vulnerable in Canadian society. Insufficient nutrition, emotional stress, isolation, poverty, and job or family pressures are contributing factors to the situation. Women of colour, because of the systemic racism that exists in the delivery of health care, and the class position that many of them occupy, are even more at risk.

We want to mention one last study that gives a national overview. At the fourth conference and biennial general meeting of the National Organization of Immigrant and Visible Minority Women, a document entitled "Political Participation for Change: Immigrant and Visible Minority Women in Action" was produced which examined a number of important issues confronting minority women. Health care was one of the concerns addressed. The document states, "The biological makeup of women and their role in society as child-bearers, mothers, nurturers, wives and sexual partners is an important component of life and calls for unique health care needs ... immigrant women with linguistic and cultural barriers are often denied and deprived of information and access to various options on reproductive health care

services." This document identified sexually transmitted diseases, infertility, and unintended pregnancies as areas that had to be addressed. "With the advancement in reproductive technologies, women have options to control pregnancy with a variety of birth control measures or even to terminate their pregnancies. Even though these options are relatively accessible through mainstream health care services, immigrant and visible minority women's access to information on birth control options, information regarding their right to access these birth control options, and their awareness of making informed decisions in controlling pregnancy is severely limited because of language and cultural barriers. Other barriers also exist that prevent immigrant and visible minority women from accessing appropriate birth control options. These include cultural insensitivity, lack of cross cultural awareness or even racism."[9] This indicates that the conclusions of the Ontario study cited earlier in this essay, that women of colour face racial barriers in the health care system, appear to be applicable nationally.

*****

Notes

1. Janice Tibbets, *The Ottawa Citizen*, June 12, 1995.

2. *Immigrant, Refugee and Racial Minority Women and Health Care Needs: Report of Community Consultations*, Women's Health Bureau, Ontario Ministry of Health (August 1993), 17.

3. *Immigrant, Refugee and Racial Minority Women and Health Care Needs: Report of Community Consultations*, Women's Health Bureau, Ontario Ministry of Health (August 1993), iii.

4. *Immigrant Women's Health Centre, Annual Report* (1986), 8.

5. *Immigrant Women's Health Centre: Mobile Health Unit Project. Preventative Health Care for Immigrant Women* (September 1995), 6.

6. *Immigrant Women's Health Care: Mobile Health Unit Project. Preventative Health Care for Immigrant Women* (September 1995), 7.

7. *What Women Prescribe: Report and Recommendations*, from the National Symposium, Women in Partnership: Working Toward Inclusive, Gender-sensitive Health Policies, Canadian Advisory Council on the Status of Women (May 1995), 68–9.

8. Edward Ng, "Immigrants Healthier than People Born Here," *Toronto Star* (April 2, 1996).

9. *Political Participation for Change: Immigrant and Visible Minority Women in Action*, Fourth National Conference and Biennial General Meeting of the National Organization of Immigrant and Visible Minority Women of Canada (March 1995), 38.

The Double Standard of Aging

Susan Sontag

"How old are you?" The person asking the question is anybody. The respondent is a woman, a woman "of a certain age," as the French say discreetly. That age might be anywhere from her early twenties to her late fifties. If the question is impersonal—routine information requested when she applies for a driver's license, a credit card, a passport—she will probably force herself to answer truthfully. Filling out a marriage license application, if her future husband is even slightly her junior, she may long to subtract a few years; probably she won't. Competing for a job, her chances often partly depend on being the "right age," and if hers isn't right, she will lie if she think she can get away with it. Making her first visit to a new doctor, perhaps feeling particularly vulnerable at the moment she's asked, she will probably hurry through the correct answer. But if the question is only what people call personal—if she's asked by a new friend, a casual acquaintance, a neighbor's child, a co-worker in an office, store, factory—her response is harder to predict. She may side-step the question with a joke or refuse it with playful indignation. "Don't you know you're not supposed to ask a woman her age?" Or, hesitating a moment, embarrassed but defiant, she may tell the truth. Or she may lie. But neither truth, evasion, nor lie relieves the unpleasantness of that question. For a woman to be obliged to state her age, after a "certain age," is always a miniature ordeal.

If the question comes from a woman, she will feel less threatened than if it comes from a man. Other women are, after all, comrades in sharing the same potential for humiliation. She will be less arch, less coy. But she probably still dislikes answering and may not tell the truth. Bureaucratic formalities excepted, whoever asks a woman this question—after "a certain age"—is ignoring a taboo and possibly being impolite or downright hostile. Almost everyone acknowledges that once she passes an age that is, actually, quite young, a woman's exact age ceases to be a legitimate target of curiosity. After childhood, the year of a woman's birth becomes her secret, her private property. It is something of a dirty secret. To answer truthfully is always indiscreet.

The discomfort a woman feels each time she tells her age is quite independent of the anxious awareness of human mortality that everyone has, from time to time. There is a normal sense in which nobody, men and women alike, relishes growing older. After thirty-five any mention of one's age carries with it the reminder that one is probably closer to the end of one's life than to the beginning. There is nothing unreasonable in that anxiety. Nor is there any abnormality in the anguish and anger

– 269 –

that people who are really old, in their seventies and eighties, feel about the implacable waning of their powers, physical and mental. Advanced age is undeniably a trial, however stoically it may be endured. It is a shipwreck, no matter with what courage elderly people insist on continuing the voyage. But the objective, sacred pain of old age is of another order than the subjective, profane pain of aging. Old age is a genuine ordeal, one that men and women undergo in a similar way. Growing older is mainly an ordeal of the imagination—a moral disease, a social pathology—intrinsic to which is the fact that it afflicts women much more than men. It is particularly women who experience growing older (everything that comes *before* one is actually old) with such distaste and even shame.

The emotional privileges this society confers upon youth stir up some anxiety about getting older in everybody. All modern urbanized societies—unlike tribal, rural societies—condescend to the values of maturity and heap honors on the joys of youth. This revaluation of the life cycle in favor of the young brilliantly serves a secular society whose idols are ever-increasing industrial productivity and the unlimited cannibalization of nature. Such a society must create a new sense of the rhythms of life in order to incite people to buy more, to consume and throw away faster. People let the direct awareness they have of their needs, of what really gives them pleasure, be overruled by commercialized *images* of happiness and personal well-being; and, in this imagery designed to stimulate ever more avid levels of consumption, the most popular metaphor for happiness is "youth." (I would insist that it is a metaphor, not a literal description. Youth is a metaphor for energy, restless mobility, appetite: for the state of "wanting.") This equating of well-being with youth makes everyone naggingly aware of exact age—one's own and that of other people. In primitive and pre-modern societies people attach much less importance to dates. When lives are divided into long periods with stable responsibilities

and steady ideals (and hypocrisies), the exact number of years someone has lived becomes a trivial fact; there is hardly any reason to mention, even to know, the year in which one was born. Most people in non-industrial societies are not sure exactly how old they are. People in industrial societies are haunted by numbers. They take an almost obsessional interest in keeping the score card of aging, convinced that anything above a low total is some kind of bad news. In an era in which people actually live longer and longer, what now amounts to the latter *two-thirds* of everyone's life is shadowed by a poignant apprehension of unremitting loss.

The prestige of youth afflicts everyone in this society to some degree. Men, too, are prone to periodic bouts of depression about aging—for instance, when feeling insecure or unfulfilled or insufficiently rewarded in their jobs. But men rarely panic about aging in the way women often do. Getting older is less profoundly wounding for a man, for in addition to the propaganda for youth that puts both men and women on the defensive as they age, there is a double standard about aging that denounces women with special severity. Society is much more permissive about aging in men, as it is more tolerant of the sexual infidelities of husbands. Men are "allowed" to age, without penalty, in several ways that women are not.

This society offers even fewer rewards for aging to women than it does to men. Being physically attractive counts much more in a woman's life than in a man's, but beauty, identified, as it is for women, with youthfulness, does not stand up well to age. Exceptional mental powers can increase with age, but women are rarely encouraged to develop their minds above dilettante standards. Because the wisdom considered the special province of women is "eternal," an age-old, intuitive knowledge about the emotions to which a repertoire of facts, worldly experience, and the methods of rational analysis have nothing to contribute, living a long time does not promise women an increase in wisdom either. The private skills expected of women are exercised early and, with the exception of a talent for making love, are not the kind that enlarge with experience. "Masculinity" is identified with competence, autonomy, self-control—qualities which the disappearance of youth does not threaten. Competence in most of the activities expected from men, physical sports excepted, increases with age. "Femininity" is identified with incompetence, helplessness, passivity, non-competitiveness, being nice. Age does not improve these qualities.

Middle-class men feel diminished by aging, even while still young, if they have not yet shown distinction in their careers or made a lot of money. (And any tendencies they have toward hypochondria will get worse in middle age, focusing with particular nervousness on the specter of heart attacks and loss of virility.) Their aging crisis is linked to that terrible pressure on men to be "successful" that precisely defines their membership in the middle class. Women rarely feel anxious about their age because they haven't succeeded at something. The work that women do outside the home rarely counts as a form of achievement, only as a way of earning money; most employment available to women mainly exploits the training they have been achieving since early childhood to be servile, to be both supportive and parasitical, to be unadventurous. They can have menial, low-skilled jobs in light industries, which offer as feeble a criterion of success as housekeeping. They can be secretaries, clerks, sales personnel, maids, research assistants, waitresses, social workers, prostitutes, nurses, teachers, telephone operators—public transcriptions of the servicing and nurturing roles that women have in family life. Women fill very few executive posts, are rarely found suitable for large corporate or political responsibilities, and form only a tiny contingent in the liberal professions (apart from teaching). They are virtually barred from jobs that involve an expert, intimate relation with machines or an aggressive use of the body, or that carry any physical risk or sense of adventure.

The jobs this society deems appropriate to women are auxiliary, "calm" activities that do not compete with, but aid, what men do. Besides being less well paid, most work women do has a lower ceiling of advancement and gives meager outlet to normal wishes to be powerful. All outstanding work by women in this society is voluntary; most women are too inhibited by the social disapproval attached to their being ambitious and aggressive. Inevitably, women are exempted from the dreary panic of middle-aged men whose "achievements" seem paltry, who feel stuck on the job ladder, or fear being pushed off it by someone younger. But they are also denied most of the real satisfactions that men derive from work— satisfactions that often do increase with age.

The double standard about aging shows up most brutally in the conventions of sexual feeling, which presuppose a disparity between men and women that operates permanently to women's disadvantage. In the accepted course of events a woman anywhere from her late teens through her middle twenties can expect to attract a man more or less her own age. (Ideally, he should be at least slightly older.) They marry and raise a family. But if her husband starts an affair after some years of marriage, he customarily does so with a woman much younger than his wife. Suppose, when both husband and wife are already in their late forties or early fifties, they divorce. The husband has an excellent chance of getting married again, probably to a younger woman. His ex-wife finds it difficult to remarry. Attracting a second husband younger than herself is improbable; even to find someone her own age she has to be lucky, and she will probably have to settle for a man considerably older than herself, in his sixties or seventies. Women become sexually ineligible much earlier than men do. A man, even an ugly man, can remain eligible well into old age. He is an acceptable mate for a young, attractive woman. Women, even good-looking women, become ineligible (except as partners of very old men) at a much younger age.

Thus, for most women, aging means a humiliating process of gradual sexual disqualification. Since women are considered maximally eligible in early youth, after which their sexual value drops steadily, even young women feel themselves in a desperate race against the calendar. They are old as soon as they are no longer very young. In late adolescence some girls are already worrying about getting married. Boys and young men have little reason to anticipate trouble because of aging. What makes men desirable to women is by no means tied to youth. On the contrary, getting older tends (for several decades) to operate in men's favor, since their value as lovers and husbands is set more by what they do than how they look. Many men have more success romantically at forty than they did at twenty or twenty-five; fame, money, and, above all, power are sexually enhancing. (A woman who has won power in a competitive profession or business career is considered less, rather than more, desirable. Most men confess themselves intimidated or turned off sexually by such a woman, obviously because she is harder to treat as just a sexual "object.") As they age, men may start feeling anxious about actual sexual performance, worrying about a loss of sexual vigor or impotence, but their sexual eligibility is not abridged simply by getting older. Men stay sexually possible as long as they can make love. Women are at a disadvantage because their sexual candidacy depends on meeting certain much stricter "conditions" related to looks and age.

Since women are imagined to have much more limited sexual lives than men do, a woman who has never married is pitied. She was not found acceptable, and it is assumed that her life continues to confirm her unacceptability. Her presumed lack of sexual opportunity is embarrassing. A man who remains a bachelor is judged much less crudely. It is assumed that he, at any age, still has a sexual life—or the chance of one. For men there is no destiny equivalent to the humiliating condition of being an old maid, a spinster. "Mr.," a cover from infancy

to senility, precisely exempts men from the stigma that attaches to any woman, no longer young, who is still "Miss." (That women are divided into "Miss" and "Mrs.," which calls unrelenting attention to the situation of each woman with respect to marriage, reflects the belief that being single or married is much more decisive for a woman than it is for a man.)

For a woman who is no longer very young, there is certainly some relief when she has finally been able to marry. Marriage soothes the sharpest pain she feels about the passing years. But her anxiety never subsides completely, for she knows that should she re-enter the sexual market at a later date—because of divorce, or the death of her husband, or the need for erotic adventure— she must do so under a handicap far greater than any man of her age (*whatever* her age may be) and regardless of how good-looking she is. Her achievements, if she has a career, are no asset. The calendar is the final arbiter.

To be sure, the calendar is subject to some variations from country to country. In Spain, Portugal, and the Latin American countries, the age at which most women are ruled physically undesirable comes earlier than in the United States. In France it is somewhat later. French conventions of sexual feeling make a quasi-official place for the woman between thirty-five and forty-five. Her role is to initiate an inexperienced or timid young man, after which she is, of course, replaced by a young girl. (Colette's novella *Chéri* is the best-known account in fiction of such a love affair; biographies of Balzac relate a well-documented example from real life.) This sexual myth does make turning forty somewhat easier for French women. But there is no difference in any of these countries in the basic attitudes that disqualify women sexually much earlier than men.

Aging also varies according to social class. Poor people look old much earlier in their lives than do rich people. But anxiety about aging is certainly more common, and more acute, among middle-class and rich women than among working-class women. Economically disadvantaged women in this society are more fatalistic about aging; they can't afford to fight the cosmetic battle as long or as tenaciously. Indeed, nothing so clearly indicates the fictional nature of this crisis than the fact that women who keep their youthful appearance the longest—women who lead unstrenuous, physically sheltered lives, who eat balanced meals, who can afford good medical care, who have few or no children—are those who feel the defeat of age most keenly. Aging is much more a social judgment than a biological eventuality. Far more extensive than the hard sense of loss suffered during menopause (which, with increased longevity, tends to arrive later and later) is the depression about aging, which may not be set off by any real event in a woman's life, but is a recurrent state of "possession" of her imagination, ordained by society—that is, ordained by the way this society limits how women feel free to imagine themselves.

There is a model account of the aging crisis in Richard Strauss's sentimental-ironic opera *Der Rosenkavalier*, whose heroine is a wealthy and glamorous married woman who decides to renounce romance. After a night with her adoring young lover, the Marschallin has a sudden, unexpected confrontation with herself. It is toward the end of Act I; Octavian has just left. Alone in her bedroom she sits at her dressing tale, as she does every morning. It is the daily ritual of self-appraisal practiced by every woman. She looks at herself and, appalled, begins to weep. Her youth is over. Note that Marschallin does not discover, looking in the mirror, that she is ugly. She is as beautiful as ever. The Marschallin's discovery is moral—that is, it is a discovery of her imagination; it is nothing she actually *sees*. Nevertheless, her discovery is no less devastating. Bravely, she makes her painful, gallant decision. She will arrange for her beloved Octavian to fall in love with a girl his own age. She must be realistic. She is no longer eligible. She is now "the old Marschallin."

Strauss wrote the opera in 1910. Contemporary opera-goers are shocked when they discover that the libretto indicates that the Marschallin is all of thirty-four years old; today the role is generally sung by a soprano well into her forties or fifties. Acted by an attractive singer of thirty-four, the Marschallin's sorrow would seem merely neurotic, or even ridiculous. Few women today think of themselves as old, wholly disqualified from romance at thirty-four. The age of retirement has moved up, in line with the sharp rise in life expectancy for everybody in the last few generations. The *form* in which women experience their lives remains unchanged. A moment approaches inexorably when they must resign themselves to being "too old." And that moment is invariably—objectively—premature.

In earlier generations the renunciation came even sooner. Fifty years ago a woman of forty was not just aging but old, finished. No struggle was even possible. Today, the surrender to aging no longer has a fixed date. The aging crisis (I am speaking only of women in affluent countries) starts earlier but lasts longer; it is diffused over most of a woman's life. A woman hardly has to be anything like what would reasonably be considered old to worry about her age, to start lying (or being tempted to lie). The crisis can come at any time. Their schedule depends on a blend of personal ("neurotic") vulnerability and the swing of social mores. Some women don't have their first crisis until thirty. No one escapes a sickening shock upon turning forty. Each birthday, but especially those ushering in a new decade—for round numbers have a special authority—sounds a new defeat. There is almost as much pain in the anticipation as in the reality. Twenty-nine has become a queasy age ever since the official end of youth crept forward, about a generation ago, to forty. Being thirty-nine is also hard; a whole year in which to meditate in glum astonishment that one stands on the threshold of middle age. The frontiers are arbitrary, but not any less vivid for that. Although a woman on her fortieth birthday is hardly different from what she was when she was still thirty-nine, the day seems like a turning point. But long before actually becoming a woman of forty, she has been steeling herself against the depression she will feel. One of the greatest tragedies of each woman's life is simply getting older; it is certainly the *longest* tragedy.

Aging is a movable doom. It is a crisis that never exhausts itself, because the anxiety is never really used up. Being a crisis of the imagination rather than of "real life," it has the habit of repeating itself again and again. The territory of aging (as opposed to actual old age) has no fixed boundaries. Up to a point it can be defined as one wants. Entering each decade—after the initial shock is absorbed—an endearing, desperate impulse of survival helps many women to stretch the boundaries to the decade following. In late adolescence thirty seems the end of life. At thirty, one pushed the sentence forward to forty. At forty, one still gives oneself ten more years.

I remember my closest friend in college sobbing on the day she turned twenty-one. "The best part of my life is over. I'm not young anymore." She was a senior, nearing graduation. I was a precocious freshman, just sixteen. Mystified, I tried lamely to comfort her, saying that I didn't think twenty-one was *so* old. Actually, I didn't understand at all what could be demoralizing about twenty-one. To me, it meant only something good: being in charge of oneself, being free. At sixteen, I was too young to have noticed, and become confused by, the peculiarly loose, ambivalent way in which this society demands that one stop thinking of oneself as a woman. (In America that demand can now be put off to the age of thirty, even beyond.) But even if I thought her distress was absurd, I must have been aware that it would not simply be absurd but unthinkable to a *boy* turning twenty-one. Only women worry about age with that degree of inanity and pathos. And, of course, as with all crises that are inauthentic and therefore repeat themselves compulsively (because the danger is largely fictive, a poison in the imagination), this friend of mine went on having the same crisis over and over, each time as if for the first time.

I also came to her thirtieth birthday party. A veteran of many love affairs, she had spent most of her twenties living abroad and had just returned to the United States. She had been good-looking when I first met her; now she was beautiful. I teased her about the tears she had shed over being twenty-one. She laughed and claimed not to remember. But thirty, she said ruefully, that really is the end. Soon after, she married. My friend is now forty-four. While no longer what people call beautiful, she is striking-looking, charming, and vital. She teaches elementary school; her husband, who is twenty years older than she, is a part-time merchant seaman. They have one child, now nine years old. Sometimes, when her husband is away, she takes a lover. She told me recently that forty was the most upsetting birthday of all (I wasn't at that one), and although she has only a few years left, she means to enjoy them while they last. She has become one of those women who seize every excuse offered in any conversation for mentioning how old they really are, in a spirit of bravado compounded with self-pity that is not too different from the mood of women who regularly lie about their age. But she is actually fretting much less about aging than she was two decades ago. Having a child, and having one rather late, past the age of thirty, has certainly helped to reconcile her to her age. At fifty, I suspect, she will be ever more valiantly postponing the age of resignation.

My friend is one of the more fortunate, sturdier casualties of the aging crisis. Most women are not as spirited, nor as innocently comic in their suffering. But almost all women endure some version of this suffering. A recurrent seizure of the imagination that usually begins quite young, in which they project themselves into a calculation of loss. The rules of this society are cruel to women. Brought up to be never fully adult, women are deemed obsolete earlier than men. In fact, most women don't become relatively free and expressive sexually until their thirties. (Women mature sexually this late, certainly much later than men, not for innate biological reasons but because this culture retards women. Denied most outlets for sexual energy permitted to men, it takes many women *that* long to wear out some of their inhibitions.) The time at which they start being disqualified as sexually attractive persons is just when they have grown up sexually. The double standard about aging cheats women of those years, between thirty-five and fifty, likely to be the best of their sexual life.

That women expect to be flattered often by men, and the extent to which their self-confidence depends on this flattery, reflects how deeply women are psychologically weakened by this double standard. Added on to the pressure felt by everybody in this society to look young as long as possible are the values of "femininity," which specifically identify sexual attraction in women with youth. The desire to be the "right age" has a special urgency for a woman that it never has for a man. A much greater part of her self-esteem and pleasure in life is threatened when she ceases to be young. Most men experience getting older with regret, apprehension. But most women experience it even more painfully: with shame. Aging is a man's destiny, something that must happen because he is a human being. For a woman, aging is not only her destiny. Because she is that more *narrowly* defined kind of human being, a woman, it is also her vulnerability.

To be a woman is to be an actress. Being feminine is a kind of theater, with its appropriate costumes, *decor*, lighting, and stylized gestures. From early childhood on, girls are profoundly mutilated (to the extent of being unfitted for first-class adulthood) by the extent of the stress put on presenting themselves as physically attractive objects. Women look in the mirror more frequently than men do. It is, virtually, their duty to look at themselves— to look often. Indeed a woman who is not narcissistic is considered unfeminine. And a woman who spends literally *most* of her time caring for, and making purchases to flatter, her physical appearance is not regarded in this society as what she is: a kind of moral idiot. She is thought to be quite normal and is envied by other women whose time is mostly used up at jobs or caring for large families.

The display of narcissism goes on all the time. It is expected that women will disappear several times in an evening—at a restaurant, at a party, during a theater intermission, in the course of a social visit—simply to check their appearance, to see that nothing has gone wrong with their make-up and hair styling, to make sure that their clothes are not spotted or too wrinkled or not hanging properly. It is even acceptable to perform this activity in public. At the table in a restaurant, over coffee, a woman opens a compact mirror and touches up her make-up and hair without embarrassment in front of her husband or her friends.

All this behavior, which is written off as normal "vanity" in women, would seem ludicrous in a man. Women are more vain than men because of the relentless pressure on women to maintain their appearance at a certain high standard. What makes the pressure even more burdensome is that there are actually several standards. Men present themselves as a face-and-body, a physical whole. Women are split, as men are not, into a body and a face—each judged by somewhat different standards. What is important for a face is that it be beautiful. What is important for a body is two things, which may even be (depending on fashion and taste) somewhat incompatible: first, that it is desirable and second, that it be beautiful. Men usually feel sexually attracted to women much more because of their bodies than their faces. The traits that arouse desire—such as fleshiness—don't always match those that fashion decrees as beautiful. (For instance, the ideal woman's body promoted in advertising in recent years is extremely thin: the kind of body that looks more desirable clothed than naked). But women's concern with their appearance is not simply geared to arousing desire in men. It also aims at fabricating a certain image by which, as a more indirect way of arousing desire, women state their value. A woman's value lies in the way she *represents* herself, which is more by her face than her body. In defiance of the laws of simple sexual attraction, women do not devote most of their attention to their bodies. The well-known "normal" narcissism that women display—the amount of time they spend before the mirror—is used primarily in caring for the face and hair.

Women do not simply have faces, as men do; they are identified with their faces. Men have a naturalistic relation to their faces. Certainly they care whether they are good-looking or not. They suffer over acne, protruding ears, tiny eyes; they hate getting bald. But there is a much wider latitude in what is esthetically acceptable in a man's face than what is in a woman's. A man's face is defined as something he basically doesn't need to tamper with; all he has to do is keep it clean. He can avail himself of the options for ornament supplied by nature: a beard, a mustache, longer or shorted hair. But he is not supposed to disguise himself. What he is "really" like is supposed to show. A man lives through his face; it records the progressive stages of his life. And since he doesn't tamper with his face, it is not separate from but is completed by his body—which is judged attractive by the impression it gives of virility and energy. By contrast, a woman's face is potentially separate from her body. She does not treat it naturalistically. A woman's face is the canvas upon which she paints a revised, corrected portrait of herself. One of the rules of this creation is that the face *not* show what she doesn't want it to show. Her face is an emblem, an icon, a flag. How she arranges her hair, the type of make-up she uses, the quality of her complexion—all these are signs, not of what she is "really" like, but of how she asks to be treated by others, especially men. They establish her status as an "object."

For the normal changes that age inscribes on every human face, women are much more heavily penalized than men. Even in early adolescence, girls are cautioned to protect their faces against wear and tear. Mothers tell their daughters (but never their sons): You look ugly when you cry. Stop worrying. Don't read too much. Crying, frowning, squinting, even laughing—all these human activities make "lines." The same usage of the face in men is judged quite positively. In a man's face lines are taken to be signs of "character." They indicate emotional strength, maturity—qualities far more esteemed in men than in women. (They show he has "lived.") Even scars are often not felt to be unattractive: they too can add "character" to a man's face. But lines of aging, any scar, even a small birthmark on a woman's face, are always regarded as unfortunate blemishes. In effect, people take character in men to be different from what constitutes character in women. A woman's character is thought to be innate, static—not the product of her experience, her years, her actions. A woman's face is prized so far as it remains unchanged by (or conceals the traces of) her emotions, her physical risk-taking. Ideally, it is supposed to be a mask—immutable, unmarked. The model woman's face is Garbo's. Because women are identified with their faces much more than men are, and the ideal woman's face is one that is "perfect," it seems a calamity when a woman has a disfiguring accident. A broken nose or a scar or a burn mark, no more than regrettable for a man, is a terrible psychological wound to a woman; objectively, it diminishes her value. (As is well known, most clients for plastic surgery are women.)

Both sexes aspire to a physical ideal, but what is expected of boys and what is expected of girls involves a very different moral relation to the self. Boys are encouraged to *develop* their bodies, to regard the body as an instrument to be improved. They invent their masculine selves largely through exercise and sport, which harden the body and strengthen competitive feelings; clothes are of only secondary help in making their bodies attractive. Girls are not particularly encouraged to develop their bodies through any activity, strenuous or not; and physical strength and endurance are hardly valued at all. The invention of the feminine self proceeds mainly through clothes signs that testify to the very effort of girls to look attractive, to their commitment to please. When boys become men, they may go on (especially if they have sedentary jobs) practicing a sport or doing exercises for a while. Mostly they leave their appearance alone, having been trained to accept more or less, what nature has handed out to them. (Men may start doing exercises in their forties to lose weight, but for reasons of health—their is an epidemic fear of heart attacks among the middle-aged in rich countries—not for cosmetic reasons.) At one of the norms of "femininity" in this society is being preoccupied with one's physical appearance, so "masculinity" means *not* caring very much about one's looks.

This society allows men to have a much more affirmative relation to their bodies than women have. Men are more "at home" in their bodies whether they treat them casually or use them aggressively. A man's body is defined as a strong body. It contains no contradiction between what is felt to be attractive and what is practical. A woman's body, so far as it is considered attractive, is defined as a fragile, light body. (Thus women worry more than men do abut being overweight.) When they do exercises, women avoid the ones that develop the muscles, particularly those in the upper arms. Being "feminine" means looking physically weak, frail. Thus, the ideal woman's body is one that is not of much practical use in the hard work of this world, and one that must continually be "defended." Women do not develop their bodies, as men do. After a woman's body has reached a sexually acceptable form by late adolescence, most further development is viewed as negative. And it is thought irresponsible for women to do what is normal for men: simply leave their appearance alone. During early youth they are likely to come as close as they ever will to the ideal image—slim figure, smooth, firm skin, light musculature, graceful movements. Their task is to try to maintain that image, unchanged, as long as possible. Improvement as such is not the task. Women care for their bodies—against toughening, coarsening, getting fat. They *conserve* them. (Perhaps the fact that women in modern societies tend to have a more conservative political outlook than men originates in their profoundly conservative relation to their bodies.)

In the life of women in this society the period of pride, of natural honesty, and unself-conscious flourishing is brief. Once past youth women are condemned to inventing (and maintaining) themselves against the inroads of age. Most of the physical qualities regarded as attractive in women deteriorate much earlier in life than those defined as "male." Indeed, they perish fairly soon in the normal sequence of body transformation. The "feminine" is smooth, rounded, hairless, unlined, soft, unmuscled—the look of the very young; characteristics of the weak, of the vulnerable, eunuch traits, as Germaine Greer has pointed out. Actually, there are only a few years—late adolescence, early twenties—in which this look is physiologically natural, in which it can be had without touching-up and covering-up. After that, women enlist in a quixotic enterprise, trying to close the gap between the imagery put forth by society (concerning what is attractive in a woman) and the evolving facts of nature.

Women have a more intimate relation to aging than men do, simply because one of the accepted "women's" occupations is taking pains to keep one's face and body from showing the signs of growing older. Women's sexual validity depends, up to a certain point, on how well they stave off these natural changes. After late adolescence women become the caretakers of their bodies and faces, pursuing an essentially defensive strategy, a holding operation. A vast array of products in jars and tubes, a branch of surgery, and armies of hairdressers, masseuses, diet counselors, and other professionals exist to stave off, or mask, developments that are entirely normal biologically. Large amounts of women's energies are devoted into this passionate, corrupting effort to defeat nature: to maintain an ideal, static appearance, against the progress of age. The collapse of the project is only a matter of time. Inevitably, a woman's physical appearance develops beyond its youthful form. No matter how exotic the creams or how strict the diets, one cannot indefinitely keep the face unlined, the waist slim. Bearing children takes its toll: the torso becomes thicker; the skin is stretched. There is no way to keep certain lines from appearing, in one's mid-twenties, around the eyes and mouth. From about thirty on, the skin gradually loses its tone. In women, this perfectly natural process is regarded as a humiliating defeat, while nobody finds anything remarkably unattractive in the equivalent physical changes in men. Men are "allowed" to look older without sexual penalty.

Thus, the reason that women experience aging with more pain than men is not simply that they care more than men about how they look. Men also care about their looks and want to be attractive, but since the business of men is mainly being and doing, rather than appearing, the standards for appearance are much less exacting. The standards for what is attractive in a man are permissive; they conform to what is possible or "natural" to most men throughout their lives. The standards for women's appearance go against nature, and to come anywhere near approximating them takes considerable effort and time. Women must try to be beautiful. At the least, they are under heavy social pressure not to be ugly. A woman's fortunes depend, far more than a man's, on being at least "acceptable" looking. Men are not subject to this pressure. Good looks in a man is a bonus, not a psychological necessity for maintaining normal self-esteem.

Behind the fact that women are more severely penalized than men are for aging is the fact that people, in this culture at least, are simply less tolerant of ugliness in women than in men. An ugly woman is never merely repulsive. Ugliness in women is felt by everyone, men as well as women, to be faintly embarrassing. And many features that count as ugly in a woman's face would be quite tolerable on the face of a man. This is not, I would insist, just because the esthetic standards for men and women are different. It is rather because the esthetic standards for women are much higher, and narrower, than those proposed for men.

Beauty, women's business in this society, is the theater of their enslavement. Only one standard of female beauty is sanctioned: the *girl*. The great advantage men have is that our culture allows two standards of male beauty: the *boy* and the *man*. The beauty of a boy resembles the beauty of a girl. In both sexes it is a fragile kind of beauty and flourishes naturally only in the early part of the life-cycle. Happily, men are able to accept themselves under another standard of good looks— heavier, rougher, more thickly built. A man does not grieve when he loses the smooth, unlined, hairless skin of a boy. For he has only exchanged one form of attractiveness for another: the darker skin of a man's face, roughened by daily shaving, showing the marks of emotion and the normal lines of age. There is no equivalent of this second standard for women. The single standard of beauty for women dictates that they must go heaving clear skin. Every wrinkle, every line, every gray hair, is a defeat. No wonder that no boy minds becoming a man, while even the passage from girlhood to early womanhood is experienced by many women as their downfall, for all women are trained to continue wanting to look like girls.

This is not to say there are no beautiful older women. But the standard of beauty in a woman of any age is how far she retains, or how she manages to simulate the appearance of youth. The exceptional woman in her sixties who is beautiful certainly owes a large debt to her genes. Delayed aging, like good looks, tends to run in families. But nature rarely offers enough to meet this culture's standards. Most of the women who successfully delay the appearance of age are rich, with unlimited leisure to devote to nurturing along nature's gifts. Often they are actresses. (That is, highly paid professionals at doing what all women are taught to practice as amateurs.) Such women as Mae West, Marlene Dietrich, Stella Adler, Dolores Del Rio, do not challenge the rules about the relation between beauty and age in women. They are admired precisely because they *are* exceptions, because they have managed (at least so it seems in photographs) to outwit nature. Such miracles, exceptions made by nature (with the help of art and social privilege), only confirm the rule, because what makes these women seem beautiful to us is precisely that they do not look their real age. Society allows no place in our imagination for a beautiful old woman who does look like an old woman—a woman who might be like Picasso at the age of ninety, being photographed outdoors on his estate in the south of France, wearing only shorts and sandals. No one imagines such a woman exists. Even the special exceptions—Mae West & Co.—are always photographed indoors, cleverly lit, from the most flattering angle and fully, artfully, clothed. The implication is they would not stand a closer scrutiny. The idea of an old woman in a bathing suit being attractive, or even just acceptable looking, is inconceivable. An older woman is, by definition, sexually repulsive—unless, in fact, she doesn't look old at all. The body of an old woman, unlike that of an old man, is always understood as a body that can no longer be shown, offered, unveiled. At best, it may appear in costume. People still feel uneasy, thinking about what they might see if her mask dropped, if she took off her clothes.

Thus, the point for women of dressing up, applying make-up, dyeing their hair, going on crash diets, and getting face-lifts, is not just to be attractive. They are ways of defending themselves against a profound level of disapproval directed toward women, a disapproval that can take the form of aversion. The double standard about aging converts the life of women into an inexorable march toward a condition in which they are not just unattractive, but disgusting. The profoundest terror of a woman's life is the moment represented in a status by Robin called *Old Age*: a naked old woman, seated, pathetically contemplates her flat, pendulous, ruined body. Aging in women is a process of becoming obscene sexually, for the flabby bosom, wrinkled neck, spotted hands, thinning white hair, waistless torso, and veined legs of an old

woman are felt to be obscene. In our direst moments of the imagination, this transformation can take place with dismaying speed—as in the end of *Lost Horizon*, when the beautiful young girl is carried by her lover out of Shangri-La and, within minutes, turns into a withered, repulsive crone. There is no equivalent nightmare about men. This is why, however much a man may care about his appearance, that caring can never acquire the same desperateness it often does for women. When men dress according to fashion or now even use cosmetics, they do not expect from clothes and make-up what women do. A face-lotion or perfume or deodorant or hairspray, used by a man, is not part of a disguise. Men, as men, do not feel the need to disguise themselves to fend off morally disapproved signs of aging, to outwit premature sexual obsolescence, to cover up aging as obscenity. Men are not subject to the barely concealed revulsion expressed in this culture against the female body—except in its smooth, youthful, firm, odorless, blemish-free form.

One of the attitudes that punish women most severely is the visceral horror felt at aging female flesh. It reveals a radical fear of women installed deep in this culture, a demonology of women that has crystallized in such mythic caricatures as the vixen, the virago, the vamp, and the witch. Several centuries of witch-phobia, during which one of the cruelest extermination programs in Western history was carried out, suggest something of the extremity of this fear. That old women are repulsive is one of the most profound esthetic and erotic feelings in our culture. Women share it as much as men do. (Oppressors, as a rule, deny oppressed people their own "native" standards of beauty. And the oppressed end up being convinced that they *are* ugly.) How women are psychologically damaged by this misogynistic idea of what is beautiful parallels the way in which blacks have been deformed in a society that has up to now defined beautiful as white. Psychological tests made on young black children in the United States some years ago showed how early and how thoroughly they incorporate the white standard of good looks. Virtually all children expressed fantasies that indicated they considered black people to be ugly, funny looking, dirty, brutish. A similar kind of self-hatred infects most women. Like men, they find old age in women "uglier" than old age in men.

This esthetic taboo functions, in sexual attitudes, as a racial taboo. In this society most people feel an involuntary recoil of the flesh when imagining a middle-aged woman making love with a young man—exactly as many whites flinch viscerally at the thought of a white woman in bed with a black man. The banal drama of a man of fifty who leaves a wife of forty-five for a girlfriend of twenty-eight contains no strictly sexual outrage, whatever sympathy people may have for the abandoned wife. On the contrary. Everyone "understands." Everyone knows that men like girls, that young women often want middle-aged men. But no-one "understands" the reverse situation. A woman of forty-five who leaves a husband of fifty for a lover of twenty-eight is the makings of social and sexual scandal at a deep level of feeling. No one takes exception to a romantic couple in which the man is twenty years or more the woman's senior. The movies pair Joanne Dru and John Wayne, Marilyn Monroe and Joseph Cotten, Audrey Hepburn and Cary Grant, Jane Fonda and Yves Montan, Catherine Deneuve and Marcello Mastroiani; as in actual life, these are perfectly plausible, appealing couples. When the age difference runs the other way, people are puzzled and embarrassed and simply shocked. (Remember Joan Crawford and Cliff Robertson in *Autumn Leaves*? But so troubling is this kind of love story that it rarely figures in the movies, and then only as the melancholy history of failure.) The usual view of why a woman of forty and a boy of twenty, or a woman of fifty and a man of thirty, marry is that the man is seeking a mother, not a wife; no one believes the marriage will last. For a woman to respond erotically and romantically to a man who, in terms of his age, could be her father is considered normal. A man who falls in love with a woman who, however attractive she

may be, is old enough to be his mother is thought to be extremely neurotic (victim of an "Oedipal Fixation" is the fashionable tag), if not mildly contemptible.

The wider the gap in age between partners in a couple, the more obvious is the prejudice against women. When old men, such as Justice Douglas, Picasso, Strom Thurmond, Onassis, Chaplin, and Pablo Casals, take brides thirty, forty, fifty years younger than themselves, it strikes people as remarkable, perhaps an exaggeration—but still plausible. To explain such a match, people enviously attribute some special virility and charm to the man. Though he can't be handsome, he is famous; and his fame is understood as having boosted his attractiveness to women. People imagine that his young wife, respectful of her elderly husband's attainments, is happy to become his helper. For the man a late marriage is always good public relations. It adds to the impression that, despite his advanced age, he is still to be reckoned with; it is the sign of a continuing vitality presumed to be available as well to his art, business activity, or political career. But an elderly woman who married a young man would be greeted quite differently. She would have broken a fierce taboo, and she would get no credit for her courage. Far from being admired for her vitality, she would probably be condemned as predatory, willful, selfish, exhibitionistic. At the same time she would be pitied, since such a marriage would be taken as evidence that she was in her dotage. If she had a conventional career or were in business or held public office, she would quickly suffer from the current of disapproval. Her very credibility as a professional would decline, since people would suspect that her young husband might have an undue influence on her. Her "respectability" would certainly be compromised. Indeed, the well-known old women I can think of who dared such unions, if only at the end of their lives—George Eliot, Colette, Edith Piaf—have all belonged to that category of people, creative artists and entertainers, who have special license from society to behave scandalously. It is thought to be a scandal for a woman to ignore that she is old and therefore too ugly for a young man. Her looks and a certain physical condition determine a woman's desirability, not her talents or her needs. Women are not supposed to be "potent." A marriage between an old woman and a young man subverts the very ground rule of relations between the two sexes, that is: whatever the variety of appearances, men remain dominant. Their claims come first. Women are supposed to be the associates and companions of men, not their full equals—and never their superiors. Women are to remain in the state of a permanent "minority."

The convention that wives should be younger than their husbands powerfully enforces the "minority" status of women, since being senior in age always carries with it, in any relationship, a certain amount of power and authority. There are no laws on the matter, of course. The convention is obeyed because to do otherwise makes one feel as if one is doing something ugly or in bad taste. Everyone feels intuitively the esthetic rightness of a marriage in which the man is older than the woman, which means that any marriage in which the woman is older creates a dubious or less gratifying mental picture. Everyone is addicted to the visual pleasure that women give by meeting certain esthetic requirements from which men are exempted, which keeps women working at staying youthful-looking while men are left free to age. On a deeper level everyone finds the signs of old age in women esthetically offensive, which conditions one to feel automatically repelled by the prospect of an elderly woman marrying a much younger man. The situation in which women are kept minors for life is largely organized by such conformist, unreflective preferences. But taste is not free, and its judgments are never merely "natural." Rules of taste enforce structures of power. The revulsion against aging in women is the cutting edge of whole set of oppressive structures (often masked as gallantries) that keep women in their place.

The ideal state proposed for women is docility, which means not being fully grown up. Most of what is cherished as typically "feminine" is simply behavior that is childish, immature, weak. To offer so low and demeaning a standard of fulfillment in itself constitutes oppression in an acute form—a sort of moral neo-colonialism. But women are not simply condescended by the values that secure the dominance of men. They are repudiated. Perhaps because of having been their oppressors for so long, few men really *like* women (though they love individual women), and few men ever feel really comfortable or at ease in women's company. This malaise arises because relations between the two sexes are rife with hypocrisy, as men manage to love those they dominate and therefore don't respect. Oppressors always try to justify their privileges and brutalities by imagining that those they oppress belong to a lower order of civilization or are less than fully "human." Deprived of part of their ordinary human dignity, the oppressed take on certain "demonic" traits. The oppressions of large groups have to be anchored deep in the psyche, continually renewed by partly unconscious fears and taboos, by a sense of the obscene. Thus, women arouse not only desire and affection in men but aversion as well. Women are thoroughly domesticated familiars. But, at certain times and in certain situations, they become alien, untouchable. The aversion men feel, so much of what is covered over, is felt most frankly, with least inhibition, towards the type of woman who is most taboo "esthetically," a woman who has become—with the natural changes brought about by aging—obscene.

Nothing more clearly demonstrates the vulnerability of women than the special pain, confusion, and bad faith with which they experience getting older. And in the struggle that some women are waging on behalf of all women to be treated (and treat themselves) as full human beings—not "only" as women—one of the earliest results to be hoped for is that women become aware, indignantly aware, of the double standard about aging from which they suffer so harshly.

It is understandable that women often succumb to the temptation to lie about their age. Given society's double standard, to question a woman about her age is indeed often an aggressive act, a trap. Lying is an elementary means of self-defense, a way of scrambling out of the trap, at least temporarily. To expect a woman, after "a certain age," to tell exactly how she is—when she has a chance, either through the generosity of nature or the cleverness of art, to pass for being somewhat younger than she actually is—is like expecting a landowner to admit that the estate he has put up for sale is actually worth less than the buyer is prepared to pay. The double standard about aging sets women up as property, as objects whose value depreciates rapidly with the march of the calendar.

The prejudices that mount against women as they grow older are an important arm of male privilege. It is the present unequal distribution of adult roles between the two sexes that gives men a freedom to age denied to women. Men actively administer the double standard about aging because the "masculine" role awards them the initiative in courtship. Men choose; women are chosen. So men choose younger women. But although this system of inequality is operated by men, it could not work if women themselves did not acquiesce in it. Women reinforce it powerfully with their complacency, with their anguish, with their lies.

Not only do women lie more than men do about their age but men forgive them for it, thereby confirming their own superiority. A man who lies about his age is thought to be weak, "unmanly." A woman who lies about her age is behaving in a quite acceptable, "feminine" way. Petty lying is viewed by men with indulgence, one of a number of patronizing allowances made for women. It has the same moral unimportance as the fact that women are often late for appointments. Women are not expected to be truthful, or punctual, or expert in handling and repairing machines, or frugal, or physically brave. They are expected to be second-class adults, whose natural state is that of a graceful dependence on men. And so they often are, since that is what they are brought up to be. So far as women heed the stereotypes of "feminine" behavior, they *cannot* behave as fully responsible, independent adults.

Most women share the contempt for women expressed in the double standard about aging—to such a degree that they take their lack of self-respect for granted. Women have been accustomed so long to the protection of their masks, their smiles, their endearing lies. Without this protection, they know, they would be more vulnerable. But in protecting themselves as women, they betray themselves as adults. The model corruption in a woman's life is denying her age. She symbolically accedes to all those myths that furnish women with their imprisoning securities and privileges, that create their genuine oppression, that inspire their real discontent. Each time a woman lies about her age she becomes an accomplice in her own underdevelopment as a human being.

Women have another option. They can aspire to be wise, not merely nice; to be competent, not merely helpful; to be strong, not merely graceful; to be ambitious for themselves, not merely for themselves in relation to men and children. They cannot let themselves age naturally and without embarrassment, actively protesting and disobeying the convention that stem from this society's double standard about aging. Instead of being girls, girls as long as possible, who then age humiliatingly into middle-aged women, they can become women much earlier—and remain active adults, enjoying the long, erotic career of which women are capable, far longer. Women should allow their faces to show the lives they have lived. Women should tell the truth.

The Howl: Resurrection of the Wild Woman

Clarissa Pinkola Estés

La Loba

There is an old woman who lives in a hidden place that everyone knows but few have ever seen. As in the fairy tales of Eastern Europe, she seems to wait for lost or wandering people and seekers to come to her place.

She is circumspect, often hairy, always fat, and especially wishes to evade most company. She is both a crower and a cackler, generally having more animal sounds than human ones.

They say she lives among the rotten granite slopes in Tarahumara Indian territory. They say she is buried outside Phoenix near a well. She is said to have been traveling south to Monte Alban[1] in a burnt-out car with the back window shot out. She is said to stand by the highway near El Paso, or ride shotgun with truckers to Morelia, Mexico, or that she has been sighted walking to market above Oaxaca with strangely formed boughs of firewood on her back. She is called by many names: *La Huesara*, Bone Woman; *La Trapera*, The Gatherer; and *La Loba*, Wolf Woman.

The sole work of *La Loba* is the collecting of bones. She is known to collect and preserve especially that which is in danger of being lost to the world. Her cave is filled with the bones of all manner of desert creatures: the deer, the rattlesnake, the crow. But her specialty is said to be wolves.

She creeps and crawls and sifts through the *montañas*, mountains, and *arroyos*, dry riverbeds, looking for the wolf bones, and when she has assembled an entire skeleton, when the last bone is in place and the beautiful white sculpture of the creature is laid out before her, she sits by the fire and thinks about what song she will sing.

And when she is sure, she stands over the *criatura*, raises her arms over it, and sings out. That is when the rib bones and leg bones of the wolf begin to flesh out and the creature becomes furred. *La Loba* sings some more, and more of the creature comes into being; its tail curls upward, shaggy and strong.

And *La Loba* sings more and the wolf creature begins to breathe.

And still *La Loba* sings so deeply that the floor of the desert shakes, and as she sings, the wolf opens its eyes, leaps up, and runs away down the canyon.

Somewhere in its running, whether by the speed of its running, or by splashing its way into a river, or by way of a ray of sunlight or moonlight hitting it right in the side, the wolf is suddenly transformed into a laughing woman who runs free toward the horizon.

So it is said that if you wander the desert, and it is near sundown, and you are perhaps a little lost, and certainly tired, that you are lucky, for *La Loba* may take a liking to you and show you something—something of the soul.

We all begin as a bundle of bones lost in the desert, a dismantled skeleton that lies under the sand. It is our work to recover the parts. It is a painstaking process best done when the shadows are just right, for it takes much looking. *La Loba* indicates what we are to look for—the indestructible life force, the bones.

This *cuento milagro*, miracle story, *La Loba*, shows up what can go right for the soul. It is a resurrection story about the underworld connection to Wild Woman. It promises that if we will sing the song, we can call up the psychic remains of the Wild Woman soul and sing her into a vital shape again.

In the tale, *La Loba* sings over the bones she has gathered. To sing means to use the soul-voice. It means to say on the breath the truth of one's power and one's need, to breathe soul over the thing that is ailing or in need of restoration. This is done by descending into the deepest mood of great love and feeling, till one's desire for relationship with the wildish Self overflows, then to speak one's soul from that frame of mind. That is singing over the bones. We cannot make the mistake of attempting to elicit this great feeling of love from a lover, for this women's labor of finding and singing the creation hymn is a solitary work, a work carried out in the desert of the psyche.

Let us consider *La Loba* herself. The symbol of the Old Woman is one of the most widespread archetypal personifications in the world. Others are the Great Mother and Father, the Divine Child, the Trickster, the Sorceress(er), the Maiden and Youth, the Heroine-Warrior, and the Fool(ess). Yet, *La Loba* is vastly different in essence and effect, for she is the feeder root to an entire instinctual system.

In the Southwest she is also known as old *La Que Sabé*, The One Who Knows. I first heard of *La Que Sabé* when I lived in the Sangre de Cristo mountains of New Mexico, under the heart of Lobo Peak. An old witch from Ranchos told me that *La Que Sabé* knew everything about women, that *La Que Sabé* had created women from a wrinkle on the sole of her divine foot. That is why women are knowing creatures; they are made, in essence, of the skin of the sole, which feels everything. This idea that the skin of the foot is sentient had the ring of truth, for an acculturated Kiché tribeswoman once told me that she'd worn her first pair of shoes when she was twenty years old and was still not used to walking *con los ojos vendados*, with blindfolds on her feet.

This *La Loba* Wild Woman who lives in the desert has been called by many names and crisscrosses all nations down through the centuries. These are some of the old names for her: *The Mother of Days* is the Mother-Creator-God of all beings and doings, including the sky and earth; *Mother Nyx* has dominion over all things from the mud and dark; *Durga* controls the skies and winds and the thoughts of humans from which all reality spreads; *Coatlique* gives birth to the infant universe, which is rascally and hard to control, but like a wolf mother, she bites her child's ear to contain it; *Hecate*, the old seer who "knows her people" and has about her the smell of hummus and the breath of God. And there are many, many more. These are the images of what and who lives under the hill, far off in the desert out in the deep.

In mythos and by whatever name, *La Loba* knows the personal past and the ancient past for she has survived generation after generation, and is old beyond time. She is an archivist of feminine intention. She preserves female tradition. Her whiskers sense the future; she has the far-seeing milky eye of the old crone; she lives backward and forward in time simultaneously, correcting for one side by dancing with the other.

La Loba, the old one, The One who Knows, is within us. She thrives in the deepest soul-psyche of women, the ancient and vital Wild Woman. The *La Loba* story describes her home as that place in time where the spirit of women and the spirit of wolf meet—the place where her mind and her instincts mingle, where a woman's deep life funds her mundane life. It is the point where the I and the Thou kiss, the place where women run with the wolves.

This old woman stands between the worlds of rationality and mythos. She is the knuckle bone on which these two worlds turn. This land between the worlds is that inexplicable place we all recognize once we experience it, but its nuances slip away and shape-change if one tries to pin them down, except when we use poetry, music, dance … or story.

There is speculation that the immune system of the body is rooted in this mysterious psychic land, and also the mystical, as well as all archetypal images and urges including our God-hunger, our yearning for the mysteries, and all the sacred instincts as well as those which are mundane. Some would say the records of humankind, the root of light, the coil of dark are also here. It is not a void, but rather the place of the Mist Beings where things are and also are not yet, where shadows have substance and substance is sheer.

One thing about this land is certain, it is old … older than the oceans. It, like *La Loba*, has no age; it is ageless. The Wild Woman archetype funds this layer, emanates the instinctual psyche. Although she can take on many guises in our dreams and creative experiences, she is not from the layer of the mother, the maiden, the medial woman, and she is not the inner child. She is not the queen, the amazon, the lover, the seer. She is just what she is. Call her *La Que Sabé*, The One Who Knows, call her Wild Woman, call her *La Loba*, call her by her high names or by her low names, call her by her newer names or her ancient ones, she remains just what she is.

Wild Woman as an archetype is an inimicable and ineffable force which carries a bounty of ideas, images, and particularities for humankind. Archetype exists everywhere and yet is not seeable in the usual sense. What can be seen of it in the dark cannot be seen in daylight.

We find lingering evidence of archetype in the images and symbols found in stories, literature, poetry, painting, and religion. It would appear that its glow, its voice, and its fragrance are meant to cause us to be raised up from contemplating the shit on our tails to occasionally travelling in the company of the stars.

At *La Loba*'s place, the physical body is, as poet Tony Moffeit writes, "a luminous animal,"[2] and the body's immune seems to be strengthened or weakened by conscious thought. At *La Loba*'s place, the spirits manifest as personages and *La Voz Mitológica*, The Mythological Voice of the deep psyche, speaks as poet and oracle. Things of psychic value, once dead, can be revived. Also, the basic material of all stories existent in the world *ever*, began with someone's experience here in this inexplicable psychic land, and someone's attempt to relate what occurred to them here.

There are various names for this locus betwixt the worlds. Jung called it variously the collective unconscious, the objective psyche, and the psychoid unconcious—referring to a more ineffable layer of the former. He thought of the latter as a place where the biological and psychological worlds share headwaters, where biology and psychology might mingle with and influence one another. Throughout human memory this place—call it Nod, call it the home of the Mist Beings, the crack between worlds—is the place where visitations, miracles, imaginations, inspirations, and healings of all natures occur.

Though this site transmits great psychic wealth, it must be approached with preparation, for one may be tempted to joyously drown in the rapture-trap from which people return unsteady, with wobbly ideas and airy presentments. That is not how it is meant to be. How one is meant to return is wholly washed or dipped in a revivifying and informing water, something which impresses upon our flesh the odor of the sacred.

Each woman has potential access to *Río Abajo Río,* this river beneath the river. She arrives there through deep meditation, dance, writing, painting, prayermaking, singing, drumming, active imagination, or any activity which requires an intense altered consciousness. A woman arrives in this world-between-worlds through yearning and by seeking something she can see just out of the corner of her eye. She arrives there by deeply creative acts, through intentional crafted practices, much of what occurs in this ineffable world remains forever mysterious to us, for it breaks physical laws and rational laws as we know them.

*****

La Loba parallels world myths in which the dead are brought back to life. In Egyptian mythos, Isis accomplishes this service for her dead brother Osiris, who is dismembered by his evil brother, Set, every night. Isis works from dusk until dawn each night to piece her brother back together before morning, else the sun will not rise. The Christ raised Lazarus, who had been dead so long he "stinketh." Demeter calls forth her pale daughter Persephone from the land of the Dead once a year. And *La Loba* sings over the bones.

This is our meditation practice as women, calling back the dead and dismembered aspects of ourselves, calling back the dead and dismembered aspects of life itself. The one who re-creates from that which has died is always a double-sided archetype. The Creation Mother is always also the Death Mother, and vice versa. Because of this dual nature, or double tasking, the great work before us is to learn to understand what around and about us and what within us must live, and what must die. Our work is to apprehend the timing of both; to allow what must die to die, and what must live to live.

For women, *Río Abajo Río*, the river-beneath-the-river world, the Bone Woman home place, contains direct knowing about the seedlings, root stock, the seed corn of the world. In Mexico, women are said to carry the *luz de la via*, the light of life. This light is located, not in a woman's heart, not behind her eyes, but *en los ovarios*, in her ovaries, where all the seed stock is laid down before she is even born. (For men, exploring the deeper ideas of fertility and the nature of seed, the cross-gender image is the furry bag, the scrotum.)

This is the knowing to be gained in being close to Wild Woman. When *La Loba* sings, she sings from the knowing of *los ovarios,* a knowing from deep within the body, deep within the mind, deep within the soul. The symbols of seed and bone are very similar. If one has the root stock, the basis, the original part, if one has the seed corn, any havoc can be repaired, devastations can be resown, fields can be rested, hard seed can be soaked to soften it, to help it break open and thrive.

To have the seed means to have the key to life. To be with the cycle of the seed means to dance with life, dance with death, dance into life again. The Wild Woman nature of women is the Life and Death Mother in her most ancient form. Because she turns in these constant cycles, I call her the Life/Death/Life Mother.

If something is lost, it is she to whom one must appeal, speak with, and listen to. Her psychic advice is sometimes harsh or difficult to put into practice, but always transformative and restorative. So when something is lost, we must go to the old woman who always lives in the out-of-the-way-pelvis. She lives out there, half in and half out of the creative fire. This is a perfect place for women to live, right next to the fertile *huevos*, their eggs, their female seeds. There the tiniest ideas and the largest ones are waiting for our minds and actions to make them manifest.

This old woman *La Loba* is the quintessential two-million-year-old woman.[3] She is the original Wild Woman who lives beneath and yet on the topside of the earth. She lives in and through us and we are surrounded by her. The deserts, the woodlands, and the earth under our houses are two million years old, and then some.

I'm always taken by how deeply women like to dig in the earth. They plant bulbs for the spring. They poke blackened fingers into mucky soil, transplanting sharp-smelling tomato plants. I think they are digging down to the two-million-year-old woman. They are looking for her toes and her paws. They want her for a present to themselves, for with her they feel of a piece and at peace.

Without her, they feel restless. Many women I've worked with over the years began their first session with some variation of: "Well, I don't feel bad, but I don't feel good either." I think that condition is not a great mystery. We know it comes from not enough muck. The cure? *La Loba*. Find the two-million-year-old woman. She is caretaker of the dead and dying of woman-things. She is the road between the living and the dead. She sings the creation hymns over the bones.

The old woman, Wild Woman, is *La Voz Mitológica*. She is the mythical voice who knows the past and our ancient history and keeps it recorded for us in stories. Sometimes we dream her as a disembodied but beautiful voice.

As the hag-maiden, she shows us what it means to be, not withered, but wizened. Babies are born wizened with instinct. They know in their bones what is right and what to do about it. It is innate. If a woman holds on to this gift of being old while she is young and young when she is old, she will always know what comes next. If she has lost it, she can yet reclaim it with some purposeful psychic work.

In the *La Loba* story, the old one in the desert is a collector of bones. In archetypal symbology, bones represent the indestructible force. They do not lend themselves to easy reduction. They are by their structure hard to burn, nearly impossible to pulverize. In myth and story, they represent the indestructible soul-spirit. We know the soul-spirit can be injured, even maimed, but it is very nearly impossible to kill.

You can dent the soul and bend it. You can hurt it and scar it. You can leave the marks of illness upon it, and the scorch marks of fear. But it does not die, for it is protected by *La Loba* in the underworld. She is both the finger and the incubator of the bones.

Bones are heavy enough to hurt with, sharp enough to cut through flesh, and when old and if strung, tinkle like glass. The bones of the living are alive and creatural in themselves; they constantly renew themselves. A living bone has a curiously soft "skin" to it. It appears to have certain powers to regenerate itself. Even as a dry bone, it becomes home for small living creatures.

The wolf bones in this story represent the indestructible aspect of the wild Self, the instinctual nature, the *criatura* dedicated to freedom and the unspoiled, that which will never accept the rigors and requirements of a dead or overly civilizing culture.

The metaphors in this story typify the entire process for bringing a woman to her full instinctual wildish senses. Within us is the old one who collects bones. Within us there are the soul-bones of Wild Woman. Within us is the potential to be fleshed out again as the creature we once were. Within us are the bones to change ourselves and our world. Within us is the breath and our truths and our longing—together they are the song, the creation hymn we have been yearning to sing.

This does not mean we should walk about with our hair hanging in our eyes or with black-ringed claws for fingernails. Yes, we remain human, but also within the human woman is the animal instinctual Self. This is not some romantic cartoon character. It has real teeth, a true snarl, huge generosity, unequaled hearing, sharp claws, generous and furry breasts.

This wolf-woman Self must have complete freedom to move, to speak, to be angry, and to create. This Self is durable, resilient, and possesses high intuition. It is a Self which is knowledgeable in the spiritual dealings of death and birth.

Today the *La Loba* inside you is collecting bones. What is she remaking? She is the soul Self, the builder of the soul-home. *Ella lo hace a mano*, she makes and re-makes the soul by hand. What is she making for you?

Even in the best of worlds the soul needs refurbishing from time to time. Just like the adobes here in the Southwest, a little peels, a little falls down, a little washes away. There is always an old round woman with bedroom-slipper feet who is patting mud slurry on the adobe walls. She mixes straw and water and earth, and pats it back on the walls, making them fine again. Without her, the house will lose its shape. Without her, it will wash down into a lump after a hard rain.

La Loba is the keeper of the soul. Without her, we lose our shape. Without an open supply line to her, humans are said to be soulless or damned souls. She gives shape to the soul-house and makes more house by hand. She is the one in the old apron. She is the one whose dress is longer in the front than in the back. She is the one who patta-pat-pats. She is the soul-maker, the wolf-raiser, the keeper of things wild.

So imaginistically—be you a Black wolf, a Northern Gray, a Southern Red, or an Arctic White—you are the quintessential instinctual *criatura*. Although some might really prefer you behave yourself and not climb all over the furniture in joy or all over people in welcome, do it anyway. Some will draw back from you in fear or disgust. Your lover, however, will cherish this new aspect of you—if he or she be the right lover for you.

Some people will not like it if you take a sniff at everything to see what it is. And for heaven's sakes, no lying on your back with your feet up in the air. Bad girl. Bad wolf. Bad dog. Right? Wrong. Go ahead. Enjoy yourself.

People do meditation to find psychic alignment. That's why people do psychotherapy and analysis. That's why people analyze their dreams and make art. That is why many read Tarot cards, cast I Ching, dance, drum, make theater, pry out the poem, and fire up the prayer. That's why we do all the things we do. It is the work of gathering all the bones together. Then we must sit at the fire and think about which song we will use to sing over

the bones, which creation hymn, which re-creation hymn. And the truths we tell will make the song.

These are some good questions to ask till one decides on the song, one's true song: What has happened to my soul-voice? What are the buried bones of my life? In what condition is my relationship to the instinctual Self? When was the last time I ran free? How do I make life come alive again? Where has *La Loba* gone to?

In the story, the old woman sings over the bones, and as she sings, the bones flesh out. We too "become" as we pour soul over the bones we have found. As we pour our yearning and our heartbreaks over the bones of what we used to be when we were young, of what we used to know if the centuries past, and over the quickening we sense in the future, we stand on all fours, four-square. As we pour soul, we are revivified. We are no longer a thin solution, a dissolving frail thing. No, we are in the "becoming" stage of transformation.

Like *La Loba*, we so often start out in a desert. We feel disenfranchised, alienated, not connected to even a cactus clump. The ancients called the desert the place of divine revelation. But for women, there is much more to it than that.

A desert is a place where life is very condensed. The roots of living things hold on to that last tear of water and the flower hoards its moisture by only appearing in early morning and late afternoon. Life in the desert is small but brilliant and most of what occurs goes on underground. This is like the lives of many women.

The desert is not lush like a forest or a jungle. It is very intense and mysterious in its life forms. Many of us have lived desert lives: very small on the surface, and enormous under the ground. *La Loba* shows us the precious things that can come from that sort of psychic distribution.

A woman's psyche may have found its way to the desert out of resonance, or because of past cruelties or because she was not allowed a larger life above ground.

So often a woman feels then that she lives in an empty place where there is maybe just one cactus with one brilliant red flower on it, and then in *every* direction, 500 miles of nothing. But for the woman who will go 501 miles, there is something more. A small brave house. An old one. She has been waiting for you.

Some women don't want to be in the psychic desert. They hate the frailty, the spareness of it. They keep trying to crank a rusty jalopy and bump their way down the road to a fantasized shining city of the psyche. But they are disappointed, for the lush and the wild is not there. It is in the spirit world, that world between worlds, *Río Abajo Río*, that river beneath the river.

Don't be a fool. Go back and stand under that one red flower and walk straight ahead for that last hard mile. Go up and knock on the old weathered door. Climb up to the cave. Crawl through the window of a dream. Sift the desert and see what you find. It is the only work we *have* to do.

You wish psychoanalytic advice?

Go gather bones.

Notes

1. Old Mexico.
2. Poem "Luminous Animal" by blues poet Tony Moffeit from his book *Luminous Animal* (Cherry Valley, NY: Cherry Valley Editions, 1989).
3. This ancient being is also called by some, "woman outside time."

Gerastology: A Feminist's View of Gerontology and Women's Aging

Margaret Cruikshank

Gerastology

Besides identifying the flaws and shortcomings of mainstream gerontology's understanding of old women, feminists must propose other approaches. This is the harder task. A few feminist essays have been published in the *Gerontologist* and in the *Journal of Women and Aging*, suggesting receptivity to alternative viewpoints, but gerastology will require multiple voices because of the breadth of women's aging issues. In the following pages, I consider several topics that lend themselves to a feminist analysis: the strengths evident among many old women; longevity; life changes; housing; aging research; standpoint theory, and crones.

Strengths

These have been noted [...] amongst the danger and the problems of women's aging. Feminists stress "agency," the concept that women are not completely controlled by their circumstances. Even though women are "variously molded" by social location and by cohort, they "resist denigration and domination by whatever means available" (Markson, 1999, 501). Literary examples bear this out. In Alice Walker's story "The Welcome Table," for example, an old black woman who is expelled from a segregated church finds her own way to Jesus. In "Trifles," a play by Susan Glaspell (1916), farm women conceal evidence that would convict their neighbor, a woman who has killed her abusive husband, of murder. Forms of resistance to domination differ in a group as heterogeneous as old women. Those sustained by an ethic of sturdy individualism will make different choices than those who live collectively, for example. Class privilege will insulate some older women but at the same time it may also pressure them to alter their bodies to disguise signs of physical aging.

Cross-cultural research demonstrates that in many societies, women's power and status increase with age. Old women are not only energetic and capable, they are leaders (Cool and McCabe, 1986, 108). Thus obstacles to old women functioning as powerful figures in mainstream American society are cultural, not biological. Certainly many were and are powerful among American Indians, Onondaga women of the Iroquois nation, for example. In *Women: An Intimate Geography*, Natalie Angier (1999) summarizes anthropological research suggesting that "selection favors robustness after menopause" because the food gathering skill of a grandmother helps increase the survival chances of her grandchild (248). The inference is that robustness after menopause could be seen as usual, not anomalous.

Some old women give each other informal help, an important aspect of women's aging that may be invisible to social science researchers. A drawback to documenting this help might be appearing to show that old women's needs can be met privately, for example, that the gaps created by cutbacks in home health care can be filled by individual effort. The informal help older women give each other has been called "peer care," an alternative to institutional care or care by families. Reciprocal help characterizes a relationship between two individuals, but peer care envisions networks of old women developing ways to care that "they both construct and manage" (Fiore, 1999, 247).[1] If women's longevity increases, such networks will be invaluable.

Longevity

The dramatic twentieth-century extension of longevity was caused by changes such as better diet and health care, notes Alice Rossi (1986), but these "environmental changes" (as opposed to genetic) could be reversed by other environmental changes, so that

> all future generations in developed societies may not necessarily live as well or as long as have recent generations. It is therefore only an optimistic faith in the persistence of improved diet and health that underlies the prediction that future generations in Western societies will be healthy, large, long-lived creatures, and that the age composition of society will be increasingly tipped to an older population. (112)

A pessimist might note that AIDS has already lowered longevity rates in Africa. Neither the government nor scientists can predict the impact on longevity of global warming, bio-chemical terrorism, air and water pollution, genetically modified food, or the increasing use of antibiotics and hormones on farm animals. In thinking about women's greater longevity, feminists must ask not

only what benefits it confers but also how it is suppressed by social policies that deprive many old women of adequate incomes and health care. If indeed selection favors robustness after menopause, how does cultural aging get in the way?

Change

Old women's potential for change [...] is expressed metaphorically by Gloria Wade-Gayles (2000):

> I was always interruptible, always accessible and available .... I was like a plant from which to take cuttings. A piece for this one. A piece for that one .... Although there were times when I could feel the blade, I did not regret the cuttings. They strengthened my roots ....
>
> But there is a time when a plant should be left still, when the number of cuttings should be reduced, when it should be left undisturbed in the light of its own nourishing sun. Now is that time for me. (20)

A survey of work on women's aging concluded that processes are more important than events; women go through "transitions and transformations" (Seltzer, 1994, 103), such as the one Wade-Gayles describes. We need primary sources to illuminate these changes: hundreds of diaries, oral histories, reminiscences, letters, novels, poems, plays, interviews, speeches, essays, and dialogues between women of different ethnic and class backgrounds. Other useful sources include labor archives, legislative testimony, and court records (Herzog, 1989, 151–52). The Canadian Film Board's outstanding documentary *Strangers in Good Company* offers a glimpse of the past and present lives of diverse old women, one of whom, Mary Meigs, described the process of making the film in her book titled *In the Company of Strangers*.

The importance of primary sources is emphasized by Gloria Wade-Gayles (2000) when she points out that she cannot find books in which black women describe *their* aging. "The way that racism exacerbates ageism, which is further exacerbated by class, is our project and nobody else's" (14). Unfortunately, many black writers have died before they could become old, including Audre Lorde, Pat Barker, Barbara Christian, Toni Cade Bambara, Rhonda Williams, and June Jordan. In "Indian Summer," Paula Gunn Allen (1993) reports seeing "virtually nothing written by elder women for elder women that is connected to my own experience in this part of my life journey" (186).

How can we teach ourselves and each other to heed our aging bodies? What constitutes close and loving attention to them? The study of old bodies could encourage us to perform ordinary actions like sitting, walking, standing, and driving more comfortably. How can we breathe more easily and deeply? Imagine a massage club for old women. No body shame here, no apologies for wrinkles, sagging skin, or thickened middles. No self-denigrating humor. To understand aging bodies, we need more work like Mary Felsteiner's (2000) essay "Casing My Joints: A Private and Public Story of Arthritis," in which she explores the meanings of rheumatoid arthritis as a woman's disease.

In another important essay, "The Embodiment of Old Women: Silences," Barbara Hillyer (1998) asks why so little has been written about the physical changes women experience. To notice them and not comment make the aging female body "an unspeakable subject or at least beneath notice" (53). Discussing physical changes should be a normal part of self care for women as they age. Instead, menopause is considered the most physical event for older women, accounts of "successful" aging focus on activity or accomplishments as if old bodies don't matter, and gerontologists do not inquire about physical changes unless they point to diseases or social problems. If an old woman talks about stiff joints or an unsteady gait, she may be discounted as a whiner. An old woman who honestly describes her bodily experience rebels against the expectation that she be cheerful (48–55).

Housing

To refute the stereotype that the old are lonely or isolated, gerontologists cite statistics about frequency of contact with families, but quality of contact eludes measurement. Suppose that living alone, the pattern for more than half of women over seventy-five, is not conducive to optimal physical and psychological health. It is true that many old women report a preference for living alone. They like the freedom from obligation. Would daily contact with a circle of friends better satisfy companionship needs? Old women alone in their houses, apartments, or rooms may pay a high price for the extreme individualism of our culture. Living alone, considered a personal choice, is perhaps more significantly a conditioned response to social circumstance.

Communal or group living for older women is imagined only as a confinement in board and care houses or nursing homes. But if a group of middle-class women pool their resources, they could have individual dwellings and common areas—dining room, laundry room, recreation room, reading room—an arrangement that might better suit them than living with families or living alone, the only choices now available. Many women could not envision such an arrangement because their lives center on family rather than friends. But families are not organized to meet the needs of old women, while alternative living could be so arranged. Intergenerational housing of nonrelatives could be one form. Why does housing designed for older people assume that they will be a married couple or a single woman? Why not have units for two or more women living together? (Burwell, 1984, 202).

Aging Research

What would aging research look like if old women themselves conducted in-depth interviews with thousands of diverse old women? Research on this scale would be hard to fund and carry out, and if a large quantity of data could be gathered, it might reveal the limits of generalization. Aging research was simpler when samples were 17,000 male doctors who went to Harvard. They are easy to find. Locating participants in barrios, on reservations, in hospitals and nursing homes, in community college classes, in rural churches, would be harder. Frieda Kerner Furman (1997) found her subjects in a beauty parlor. A large body of data would give feminists a clearer sense of the implications for social policy and for individual lives of women's greater longevity, chronic illness, and likelihood of living alone and being poor.

Feminists must ask questions that other women do not ask. How does lesbians' aging differ from that of heterosexual women, for example? When minority women elders age in a new homeland away from their extended family, will their experience be more isolating than that of men (Arber and Ginn, 1995, 12). What about gender difference in treatment of terminally ill patients?[2] What is unique about the concerns of the oldest women? How much of late-life physical and psychological illness of women is caused by or exacerbated by long-repressed memories of childhood abuse? That question is unasked in mainstream gerontology and in critical gerontology. The loss of driving ability signals social, religious, recreational, and aesthetic losses for old women in this culture; it marks official obsolescence (Carp, 1997, 256). How does a woman withstand this private shame? How will globalization and the loss of union jobs affect older women? (McDaniel, 2001, 43). What do we lose individually and collectively by attempting to reduce old age "to the wide and widening expanse of middle age," asks Martha Holstein (1999). Does aging still have a special place in human life (329)?

Obstacles to the development of feminist gerontology noted by Ruth Ray (1999) are the small number of women doing the work, the lack of places to publish, and the suspicion of colleagues that feminist gerontology is not scholarly. It's time to "step out of bounds," she concludes

(182). Out there we will need to find ways to bring health care, social science, and the humanities into closer alignment when the subject is old women. That ambitious agenda will require resistance to academic specialization as it is currently practiced.

A method for studying sexual harassment has applications for research on old women. Canadian scholars asked teenaged girls to keep journals recording their feelings about harassment they experienced. Groups met monthly to discuss relevant issues. Only after these had been identified and discussed by students did researchers formulate their questionnaires on sexual harassment (Larkin, 1997, 17–18). In a similar collaborative spirit, Sharon Jacobson (1996) designed her dissertation on lesbians and leisure with the help of an advisory panel who gave her feedback at every stage of her work. Members of Old Lesbians Organizing for Change created a slogan expressing their attitude toward research: "Nothing about Us without Us."

In both women's studies and gerontology, advocacy has an awkward relationship with academic specialization. When careers are built on the study of disadvantaged people, what are the ethical obligations to advocate for those whom one studies? If the group known as "the old" dissolves, who will lose power? The facile use of the term "empowerment" by some feminist gerontologists (in the way "diversity" and "multiculturalism" are invoked as feel-good words) suggests a benevolent regard for those seen as less able than themselves. Who has asked old women what power means to them?

Postmodernism complicates the relationship between advocacy and academic specialization by questioning traditional categories such as "woman" and "old" and by challenging the validity of authoritative statements because women are oppressed and feminism aims to improve women's lives (Gagnier, 1990, 24). While it is probably inevitable that academic feminists reject a belief in "one single unseamed reality 'out there' composed of facts which researchers can establish as 'truth' about social life" (Stanley, 1992, 263), there is a danger in seeing all as relative and contingent, for from this perspective, suffering and the political action that aims to alleviate it seem remote or futile.

Standpoint Theory

A lively debate among feminists centers on standpoint theory, the idea that women have access to a special knowledge, leading to a "truer (or less false) image of social reality" than the image available to white men (Harding, 1987, 185). Standpoint theory presupposes that people will develop different knowledge frameworks depending on their experiences and their circumstances (Hirschmann, 1992, 167) and that knowledge is particular rather than universal (Hekman, 2000, 25). A black woman's standpoint has a "legacy of struggle" at its core (Collins, 1997, 581), for example. The relevance of this debate for women's aging is that some have claimed for old women a special knowledge of the aging process. Shevy Healey (1994) believes, for example, that gerontology credentials do not create aging experts; the old themselves are "the *only* experts available" (109). But aging is not only an individual process; it is also a social construction whose workings are often hidden from view. Healey gives too much weight to personal experience. Being old does not by itself produce an understanding of the biology of aging, the ways that other cultures conceive of old age, or the intricacies of the federal aging bureaucracy. Gerontological knowledge is admittedly limited, partial, and contested, but some familiarity with it can inoculate against social control. The idea that old women have a special knowledge of aging is too attractive to cast aside, however. But which old women? Feminist theory posits that "women" is not a universal category. If the same is true of "old women," who are the privileged knowers of aging? Those who have paid the closest attention might be one answer.

Crones

In response to ageism, some feminists have created crone ceremonies to celebrate empowerment and creative aging when a woman turns fifty.[3] Perhaps we remember our mothers' dread of reaching this age and reluctance to acknowledge it. The received meaning of crone, an ugly, withered old woman, is rejected in favor of the wise and powerful. Crones defy social messages to conceal their age in shame. They are "free to be who we are and speak out as we must" (Onyx, Leonard, and Reed, 1999, 176). The Biblical figure Naomi is viewed as a crone by Shoni Labowitz (1998), who notes that "crone" is related to "crown" and that in many societies, the crone was the "crown citizen." Naomi gave advice wisely and self-confidently. "A crone, like Naomi, doesn't ask, 'Am I doing right? What are they thinking of me?' Instead she asks, 'Do I want to do this? How can I do it most consciously and effectively?'" (228–29, 239).

Although these notions of crones are attractive, crones and croning exemplify the social construction of aging by replacing negative stereotypes with positive ones; they still assume that chronology confers fixed meanings. Declaring women over fifty wise and powerful simply by virtue of their age obscures their individuality. It is a way of not seeing them. When young and middle-aged feminists attribute wisdom to women older than themselves, their efforts to be positive about aging perhaps masks their anxieties. At the end of her illuminating essay on menopause, Jacqueline Zita (1997) writes, "To deconstruct the meaning of menopause in a male gerontocracy is to construct a social and cultural space for the empowerment of crones," whom she praises as "unruly ... old, wise, and furiously heretical" (110). This statement essentializes old women. It sees them as monolithic. The notion that they should be unruly or heretical says more about the needs of younger women than about women themselves. When we project onto an old woman our wish that she be rebellious, we romanticize her.

Furthermore, when old women are positively stereotyped as crones, white women mistake their experience for universal experience. The crone is a European figure taken over by white Americans to compensate for the hatred of old women in mainstream culture. Blacks, Latinas/os, Indians, and Asian Americans are not burdened by this tradition, although they may be influenced by it because of its cultural dominance. Figures analogous to the crone may be familiar to them, *curanderas* in Latina culture, for example, and many grew up with grandmothers and other female relatives who were powerful and revered.[4]

Whisper the Waves, the Wind, a beautiful film about a diverse group of old women, takes place on a beach in La Jolla.[5] All wearing white, the women sit at round tables discussing their lives. A few stroll on the beach. They obviously love being together; later they gather for a reunion. They speak profoundly about their aging. As the film opens, the women are on a bus listening to one of the filmmakers thank them for participating. "You are our goddesses," she tells them, "you are our oracles, voices of experience that we can turn to." In the conversations that follow, however, neither the goddess nor the oracle appears, and the women do not present themselves as guides for others. The roles imposed on them by the filmmaker apparently have no meaning for them. Calling an old woman an oracle treats her as if her life were over. She is seen as a finished project.[6]

If, on the other hand, we think that an old woman continues to develop, we may be less likely to put her on a pedestal. Invoking positive stereotypes shows an understandable wish to take the sting out of aging, but instead makes signs and emblems of old women. Assigning attributes such as wisdom and power to a class of people was perhaps justified when only a few reached old age and those who did stood out. The situation is very different now. The crone holds an honored place, but she is not a template.

Conclusion

Whatever students take away from [this piece], I hope that their fears will be eased. Specific concerns are realistic—poverty, loss of mobility, age discrimination—but the generalized fear of getting old is an insidious and debilitating fear that feminists must bring into the light. If my students' aging will mirror others' attitudes about how it should unfold and if these attitudes are socially constructed, how much freedom will they have to age in their own ways, and how can they determine what their ways are? Years from now, hyper-awareness of their age by others may construct images that they will have to notice in order to resist. They will then share with women of color, poor women, and disabled women the need to expend psychic energy deflecting distorted images of themselves.

Aging has been called the "ultimate challenge in a woman's life, testing the limits of her resources and capabilities" (Gaylord, 2001, 64–65). Because her resources and to a lesser extent her capabilities will largely be determined by the politics of aging, gerastology must be skeptical of "successful" aging, "productive" aging, or other prescriptions that disguise inequity and power difference. "One size fits all" aging models will not do for women. Pressures to keep busy, for example, can coerce old women into prolonging the service role that gerontologists, including feminist gerontologists, have uncritically accepted as appropriate for them. If feminist gerontology develops theory connecting individual aging with the structures that shape it (McDaniel, 2001, 44), a bridge between women's studies and critical gerontology can be created.

The most pressing question in gerastology is how can we—we old women, we service providers inside and outside the home, we researchers, students, and teachers—improve the health, well-being, and social standing of women in late life? This question does not deny the value of knowledge for its own sake or require that every study have practical application. But it assumes a double-focus: the lives of old women and the professional work made possible by those lives. Twenty years ago, Nancy Datan (1981) wrote that old women are doubly disadvantaged by the "narrowing horizons of old age" compounded by traditional discriminations they face, but at the same time, their late-life potential is greater than that of men (124). This paradox still defines women's aging.

The influence of postmodernism on feminism has shifted the focus from things to words, "from concern with 'real' things—the *everyday realities of women's oppression*—to critiquing representations" of them (Rendell, 2000, 20). This insight helps to explain women's studies of neglect of aging, but whatever our reservations about postmodernism, we feminists cannot return to an essentialized, sentimentalized, and ultimately patronizing view of old women as either uniformly wise or universally oppressed. By virtue of their experience and their placement in the social hierarchy, some old women may have a special knowledge of aging, and previous neglect of them gives this knowledge great importance. But the category of wise old woman can be relinquished. At this unique, historical moment of a burgeoning population of old women, meaning lies in particulars. Having no models, we improvise. Later, perhaps, we organize.

Notes

1. See also the other essays in the "Living Arrangements" section of *Mother Time*: Anita Silvers on reciprocity and interdependence, Martha Holstein on home acre, and Joan C. Tronto on age-segregated housing.

2. See, for example, N. Jane McCandless and Francis P. Connor, "Working with Terminally Ill Older Women: Can a Feminist Perspective Add New Insight and Direction?" *Journal of Women and Aging* 11, nos. 2–3 (1999): 101–114; and S. Miles and A. August, "Courts, Gender, and the 'Right to Die,'" *Law, Medicine, and Health* 18 (1990): 85–95.

3. For interpretations of crones, see Edna Ward, *Celebrating Ourselves: A Crone Ritual Book* (Portland: Astarte Shell Press, 1992); Barbara Walker, *The Crone* (San Francisco: Harper and Row, 1985); and Ursula LeGuin, "The Space Crone" in *The Other Within,* ed. Marilyn Pearsall (Boulder, CO: Westview Press, 1997).

4. I thank Mirtha Quintanales for this connection.

5. *Whisper the Waves, the Wind*, directed by Suzanne Lacy and Kathleen Laughlin, produced by Suzanne Lacy, Terra Nova Films, 1986.

6. Stephanie Ross pointed this out to me.

References

Allen, Paula Gunn. "Indian Summer." In *Long Time Passing: Lives of Older Lesbians*. Edited by Marcy Adelman. Boston: Alyson, 1986.

Angier, Nancy. *Women: An Intimate Geography*. Boston: Houghton Mifflin Co., 1999.

Arber, Sarah, and Jay Ginn, eds. *Connecting Gender and Aging: A Sociological Approach*. Buckingham: Open University Press, 1995.

Burwell, Elinor J. "Sexism in Social Science Research on Aging." In *Taking Sex into Account: The Policy Consequences of Sexist Research*. Edited by Jill McCalla Vickers. Ottawa: Carleton University, 1984.

Carp, Frances M. "Living Arrangements for Midlife and Older Women." In *Handbook on Women and Aging*. Edited by Jean M. Coyle. Westport: Greenwood, 1997.

Collins, Patricia Hill. "Defining Black Feminist Thought." In *The Woman That I Am*. Edited by D. Soyini Madison. New York: St. Martin's, 1997.

Cool, Linda E., and Justine McCabe. "'The Scheming Hag' and the 'Dear Old Thing': The Anthropology of Aging Women." In *Growing Old in America*, 3rd ed. Edited by Beth B. Hess and Elizabeth W. Markson. New Brunswick: Transaction, 1986.

Datan, Nancy. "The Lost Cause: Aging Women in American Feminism." In *Toward the Second Decade*. Edited by Betty Justice and Renate Pore. Westport: Greenwood, 1981.

Felsteiner, Mary Lowenthal. "Casing My Joints: A Private and Public Story of Arthritis." *Feminist Studies* 26, no. 2 (2000): 273–85.

Fiore, Robin N. "Caring for Ourselves: Peer Care in Autonomous Aging." In *Mother Time*. Edited by Margaret Urban Walker. Lanham, MD: Rowman and Littlefield, 1999.

Furman, Frieda Kerner. *Facing the Mirror: Older Women and Beauty Shop Culture*. New York: Routledge, 1997.

Gagnier, Regenia. "Feminist Postmodernism: The End of Feminism or the End of Theory?" In *Theoretical Perspectives on Sexual Difference*. Edited by Deborah L. Rhode. New Haven: Yale, 1990.

Gaylord, Susan. "Women and Aging: A Psychological Perspective." In *Women as They Age*, 2nd ed. Edited by J. Dianne Garner and Susan O. Mercer. New York: Haworth, 2001.

Harding, Sandra. "Conclusion: Epistomological Questions." In *Feminist Methodologies*. Edited by Sandra Harding. Bloomington: Indiana University Press, 1987.

Healey, Shevy. "Diversity with a Difference: On Being Old and Lesbian." *Journal of Gay and Lesbian Social Services* 1, no. 1 (1994): 109–17.

Hekman, Susan. "Truth and Method: Feminist Standpoint Theory Revisited." In *Provoking Feminisms*. Edited by Carolyn Allen and Judith A. Howard. Chicago: University of Chicago, 2000.

Herzog, A. Regula. "Methodology Issues in Research on Older Women." In *Health and Economic Status of Older Women*. Edited by A. Regula Herzog, Karen C. Holden, and Mildred M. Seltzer. Amityville: Baywood, 1989.

Hillyer, Barbara. "The Embodiment of Old Women: Silences." *Frontiers* 19, no. 1 (1998): 48–60.

Hirschmann, Nancy J. *Rethinking Obligation. A Feminist Method for Political Theory*. Ithaca: Cornell, 1992.

Holstein, Martha. "Home Care, Women, and Aging: A Case Study of Injustice." In *Mother Time*. Edited by Margaret Urban Walker. Lanham: Rowman and Littlefield, 1999.

Jacobson, Sharon. "An Examination of Leisure in the Lives of Old Lesbians from an Ecological Perspective." Doctoral dissertation, University of Georgia, 1996.

Labowitz, Shoni. *God, Sex, and Women of the Bible*. New York: Simon and Schuster, 1998.

Larkin, June. *Sexual Harassment: High School Girls Speak Out*. Toronto: Second Story Press, 1997.

McDaniel, Susan. "A Sociological Perspective on Women and Aging as the Millennium Turns." In *Women as They Age*, 2nd ed. Edited by J. Dianne Garner and Susan O. Mercer. New York: Haworth, 2001.

Markson, Elizabeth. "Communities of Resistance: Older Women in a Gendered World." *Gerontologist* 39, no. 4 (1999): 495–502.

Meigs, Mary. *In the Company of Strangers*. Vancouver: Talonbooks, 1991.

Onyx, Jenny, Rosemary Leonard, and Rosslyn Reed, eds. *Revisioning Aging: Empowerment of Older Women*. New York: Peter Lang, 1999.

Ray, Ruth. "Researching to Transgress: The Need for Critical Feminism in Gerontology." *Journal of Women and Aging* 11, nos. 2–3 (1999): 171–184.

Rendell, Jane, Barbara Penner, and Iain Borden, eds. *Gender, Space, Architecture*. London: Routledge, 2000.

Rossi, Alice. "Sex and Gender in the Aging Society." In *Our Aging Society*. Edited by Alan Pifer and Lydia Bronte. New York: Norton, 1986.

Seltzer, Mildred. Review of *Women Growing Older: Psychological Perspectives* by Barbara Turner and Lillian E. Troll. *Contemporary Gerontology* 1, no. 3 (1994): 101–03.

Stanley, Liz. "The Impact of Feminism on Sociology in the Last 20 Years." In *The Knowledge Explosion: Generations of Feminist Scholarship*. Edited by Cheris Kramarae and Dale Van Tassel. New York: Teachers College Press, 1992.

Wade-Gayles, Gloria. "Who Says an Older Woman Can't/ Shouldn't Dance?" In *Body Politics and the Fictional Double*. Edited by Debra Walker King. Bloomington: Indiana University Press, 2000.

Zita, Jacqueline. "Heresy in the Female Body: The Rhetoric of Menopause." In *The Other Within*. Edited by Marilyn Pearsall. Boulder: Westview, 1997.

SECTION FIVE

WORK

Are These Clothes Clean?
The Campaign for Fair Wages and
Working Conditions for Homeworkers

Jan Borowy, Shelly Gordon, and Gayle Lebans

This is a story about fighting back against forces thought to be too large and too powerful to be confronted. Canadian workers, especially women, face a changed world economy in the 1990s. It's faster, leaner, and meaner than ever before. This essay is a story about some of those changes; how they affect a large group of immigrant women workers in Toronto; and how non-unionized workers, feminists, community groups, and a union are fighting back. It is part of a larger story about how unions are reshaping themselves and their strategies to meet the challenges of the 1990s and beyond.

Twenty years ago feminists within and outside trade unions were just beginning the fight to bring women and women's issues to the fore in the labour movement. Today, instead of struggling to get trade unions to take up issues like child care, women's and community groups and trade unions are exploring new ways of working together to achieve common goals, especially the larger goals of social change outside the traditional scope of collective bargaining. The Campaign for Fair Wages and Working Conditions for Homeworkers in Toronto is one example of new forms of alliances between unions, social movements, and community groups. While such a story is still not common, there are others in English-speaking Canada, in Quebec, and internationally.

The drive to organize homeworkers is long-term and continuing. It requires enormous resources and patience. The objective is for homeworkers to be able to exercise the right to join a union and sign collective agreements. Until that time, however, the experience of organizing homeworkers in an association or in a pre-union formation that addresses both work and social issues offers an example of and a direction for feminists and unions as they work to protect and improve working conditions in a changing economy.

This essay was written during an ongoing campaign, by women centrally involved in it, in the hope that our experience can be used by others. It is also an opportunity to reflect on the choices and decisions made during a campaign, on the various strategies for political action, and on the complexities of how to assist women workers in precarious employment to organize.

The Garment Industry

Jewish women, Italian women, Chinese women, South Asian women, Greek, Caribbean, Portuguese and Polish women, Vietnamese and Eastern European women—tens of thousands of women arriving in Canada over the last century—found their first job in the immigrant job-ghetto of Canada's garment manufacturing industry, the "rag trade." The pay was low, often piece-rate. The best-paying jobs went to men. The work was hard and hazardous. Employment was often seasonal. But you didn't need "Canadian experience" or "fluency in English" to get a job and be able to house and feed your family.

The garment industry plays a unique role in Canada's economy and labour market. It is often the first and only source of employment for many women, particularly immigrant women. While women make up twenty-nine percent of the workforce in the goods-producing sector as a whole, they are eighty percent of the garment manufacturing industry.[1] In Canada, sixty percent of garment production is conducted in Quebec, thirty percent in Ontario, and the remaining ten percent is spread throughout the rest of the country.

In Metro Toronto[2] in 1986, ninety-four percent of sewing machine operators were born outside of Canada, as were eighty-three percent of pattern-makers and cutters, and eighty-three percent of the employees in various textile industry occupations.[3]

Global Economic Restructuring and the Garment Industry

For the past twenty years the garment industry in Canada has been called a "sunset" industry. In an era of trade liberalization, it is seen as having little chance of survival without hefty tariffs and trade protection. Both manufacturers' associations and industry unions have focused historically on limiting imports as a way of protecting the industry in Canada. More recently, these same manufacturers and retailers have attempted to adjust to global market and labour supply changes by becoming importers themselves. The unions' strategy throughout the 1970s and 1980s consisted mainly of fighting the ever-growing number of imports, attempting to organize the ever-increasing number of small factories

and providing adjustment programs for the laid-off workers.

While the policy-makers and economists argued that the garment industry was in its sunset, employment figures reveal a different story. Between 1971 and 1988 employment in the garment industry actually rose by 11,000—at a time the industry was supposedly in decline. It was not until the late 1980s and the signing of the Free Trade Agreement that the garment industry began to face massive job loss. Employment dropped a full third from 95,800 in 1988 to an estimated 62,800 in 1992.[4] In Metro Toronto alone there were 24,711 workers in 1988, but by 1991 that number had fallen to 14,328.[5]

The thirty percent decline in the workforce in the garment industry is comparable to that in the manufacturing or goods-producing sector in general. Other industries in Metro Toronto have declined even more dramatically. For example, between 1983 and 1990 employment in the furniture, chemicals, and machinery industries declined by over fifty percent. Most manufacturing in Canada, not just garment, is experiencing globalization of production and markets.

Membership in the International Ladies' Garment Workers' Union (ILGWU) Ontario District declined much faster than overall employment because of the changes in the structure of the industry. Between 1985 and 1992 union membership dropped sixty percent, almost twice the rate of the general industry decline. The overall unionization rate within the industry fell to less than twenty percent, from a high of eighty percent fifty years earlier. Faced with this picture, the union needed to evaluate what was happening in the industry. What type of restructuring was taking place? How could it so devastate union membership?

Historically, homeworking has been part of garment manufacturing. The ILGWU was founded on trying to drive illegal sweatshops out of the industry. While apparel factories have not been as large as those typical of other manufacturing industries, throughout the post-war period, most clothing production generally occurred in larger factories employing fifty or more workers. Production was contracted out to smaller firms or homeworkers only in the busiest times. A large manufacturer or "jobber" would negotiate sales with the retailer, order the fabric, then cut and sew it in the factory. When the factory was at full capacity the manufacturer would use a contractor who was sent fabric directly and who then would sew and press the pieces.

By the late 1980s there had been a significant shift in the number of homeworkers and contracting shops. In 1971 only twenty-two percent of the industry was made up of shops with less than twenty workers. By 1991 this picture had reversed so that seventy-six percent of clothing production was in shops with less than twenty workers. The number of contracting shops in Ontario grew from only four in 1971 to over 116 in 1991. There is no way of counting the number of jobs that have migrated from the factories to homeworkers.

This trend posed a direct threat to the wages and working conditions secured in unionized factories. Sporadically used, contracting shops had not competed directly with larger unionized factories. However, in the 1980s, manufacturers began to lay people off and close unionized factories completely. Quite commonly, the owner would reappear with a smaller shop under a different name and hire only a cutter.

A centrally controlled hierarchical chain or pyramid of production began to emerge in the industry as retailers and manufacturers attempted to lower costs to compete with international suppliers. At the top of the pyramid are the huge retailers and a handful of large manufacturers with high-recognition labels like Alfred Sung. Three large retailers in Canada—the Hudson's Bay Company, Eaton's and Dylex—control access to forty percent of the clothing market.

The emerging trend in manufacturing is towards a hollow corporation, one where no actual production is done by the firm. Work is sub-contracted to contractors who employ as few as two workers or as many as thirty. These contractors then send the sewing work out to homeworkers. Homeworkers are at the bottom of the industry "pyramid."

The pyramid of production in the garment industry and the hollow manufacturing firm are a part of and a response to global economic restructuring. To lower costs, companies use new technologies to create a just-in-time production system with a just-in-time workforce. An electronic communications network—an electronic data interchange (EDI)—provides electronic hook-ups between the retailer and the jobber. When a garment is sold an electronic message is sent directly to the manufacturer or jobber ordering a new garment. Retailers carry much smaller inventories and demand production and delivery of garments with a quick turn-around time. Retailers create tighter and more direct links with fewer suppliers. To supply Eaton's, for example, a manufacturer must be linked with EDI.

The garment industry is undergoing increased concentration, with control by fewer and bigger retailers. Eaton's controls manufacturers through new technologies like EDI. According to some suppliers, the Hudson's Bay Co. exerts control throughout the entire market by the ownership of major retail chains in each price range. In addition to the Hudson's Bay stores, it owns Zellers, Simpson's, Robinsons, and Fields. The Hudson's Bay Co. has recently demanded garments at the previous year's price and often on consignment. In 1991 Hudson's Bay Co. had annual sales of $4.6 billion, with profits over $158 million. Dylex dominates the shopping mall market through ownership of Fairweather, Big Steel, Tip Top Tailors, Braemar, Bi-Way, Club Monaco, Harry Rosen, Suzy Shier, Thriftys, and Drug World (with combined annual sales of $1.83 billion in 1991).[6]

Manufacturers have had to make strategic choices in the face of relentless competition and increasing control and pressure from a few huge retailers.

Manufacturers and jobbers could modernize production and introduce state-of-the-art technology such as laser cutters and overhead automated bundle systems, or they could try to compete against imports by lowering labour costs—a low-wage strategy.

In general, manufacturers choose the low-wage strategy and rely on a global production system. A manufacturer may have fifty percent of production done off-shore in countries where labour costs are significantly lower. Manufacturers design the garment in Canada, buy the fabric here or abroad, and (perhaps) cut the garment in their own shops. The pieces are sent to Taiwan, the Philippines, Mexico, or Malaysia to be assembled and then shipped back to Canada for sale. The other half of the manufacturer's line is completed by homeworkers close to the large retailers in Canada for just-in-time production.

The shift toward homework in the garment industry is part of a larger trend toward increasingly precarious employment throughout the global economy. Precarious employment is insecure employment, including part-time, temporary, contract work, or own-account self-employment. Once considered unusual or non-standard employment in Canada, it is the most rapidly expanding sector of Canada's labour market. By 1989 one-third of Canada's workers were employed in non-standard jobs. In Metro Toronto, between 1983 and 1989, part-time employment grew by ninety-nine percent. Statistics Canada reports that in July 1992, 120,000 full-time jobs were lost while 100,000 part-time jobs were created. Women are more than seventy percent of all part-time workers.[7]

Precarious employment rises due to capital's drive for a flexible workforce to reduce labour costs. The process is often called the "casualization" of work. Businesses pursue a flexible low-cost labour strategy by "reducing their fixed labour force, making payment systems more flexible and using more contract workers, temporary labour and out-sourcing through the use of homeworkers, or subcontracting to small informal enterprises that are not covered by labour or other regulations and that bear the risks and uncertainties of fluctuating business."[8]

Multinational corporations first used this strategy in developing nations, using women workers in free trade or export zones. It is now being used around the world.[9]

Often the "flexibility" strategy involves three tactics: redeploying workers in new ways within a firm (for example, by "multi-skilling"), altering the size of the permanent workforce, and pushing for wage concessions.[10] In the case of the garment industry, firms first altered the size of the workforce by closing down larger factories and sending work out to "flexible" contract shops, which would in turn hire immigrant women (often, the same women who had worked in the factories) as homeworkers. Homeworkers are the ultimate in "just-in-time" or "flexible" workers.

The impact of this strategy on the labour force is the creation of two polar groups. A group of core factory workers maintains access to traditional collective bargaining. This group faces constant pressure for wage concessions. Surrounding this group are the peripheral "flexible" workers who have few benefits, and little or no real protection under employment law. The flexibility strategy and the "casualization" of work leaves the labour market polarized between a group of workers with higher wages, albeit under attack, and another group of workers with extremely low wages, few benefits, and in a vulnerable, precarious position. This occurred in the garment industry in Ontario. It posed a tremendous challenge to the unions.

The Union Responds

The International Ladies' Garment Workers Union—Ontario District (ILGWU) had to respond to the rapid decline in membership caused by the fundamental restructuring of the industry. In 1990 two factors came together which would help set a new direction for the ILGWU Ontario District. First, the Ontario District Council (the rank-and-file representatives' council) elected as district manager a feminist who knew the fight to save the union was integrally related to the industry's restructuring and its impact on immigrant women. Second, the union successfully applied for a research grant from the Technology Adjustment Research Project, a research fund administered by the Ontario Federation of Labour for the Ministry of Labour. The researchers hired were feminists. The research project provided the resources needed to permit a closer examination of the restructuring of the industry and its impact on labour and the opportunity to work out an industrial strategy that would reverse the trends.

In 1991 the ILGWU Ontario District began to investigate the wages and working conditions of homeworkers. An Information hotline was set up. Educational pamphlets on homeworkers' rights were distributed in English and Chinese. Thirty Chinese-speaking sewers were interviewed. The results were staggering. Conditions that the union had fought to eradicate at the turn of the century had re-emerged in the late twentieth century.

- Twenty-one of thirty homeworkers were not being paid the 1991 minimum wage of $5.40 per hour. One was earning as little as $1 per hour. The average wage was $4.64. Only two highly skilled workers earned an average of $7 an hour.

- Only one homeworker was being paid the vacation pay to which she was entitled. None of their employers were making unemployment insurance or pension contributions. Only one employer had a permit to employ homeworkers as required by the Employment Standards Act in Ontario.

- Homeworkers had to buy their own equipment and cover the cost of operating expenses out of their meagre wages. Their industrial sewing machines often cost more than $3,500.

- The average work week was forty-six hours. In busy times, homeworkers worked an average of seventy hours a week. (Homeworkers are exempted from the overtime pay provisions of Ontario law.)

- Almost half of the homeworkers reported that other family members, including children, assisted them, providing unpaid labour to the contractor.

- Twenty-seven of the thirty homeworkers interviewed had health problems related to their work—often allergies to fabric dust, stress resulting from the time pressure, and repetitive strain injuries or other problems associated with badly designed equipment.

- The homeworkers had no control over the scheduling of their work or the rate of pay. Twelve reported problems in getting paid for the work they had done. Twenty-one worked for sub-contractors, nine for factories, and all but four worked for more than one employer.

- All but one woman reported that they had turned to homework because they could not afford child care. More than two-thirds said they would rather work outside the home. With few exceptions, their last jobs had been in garment factories and they had begun to take in homework while on maternity leave.

- Only one of the women interviewed reported that she could converse in English. All but two had less than high school education, completed in their country of origin.[11]

Faced with these results, the ILGWU came to two conclusions. The union had to respond directly to the problems experienced by the homeworkers. Homeworkers were a super-exploited, flexible workforce at the bottom of the industry pyramid. This meant taking an approach that did not blame the victim but instead acknowledged the factors that oblige so many women to turn to homework.

The union understood that factory workers were being pitted against homeworkers. If the homeworkers continued to be exploited and exploitable, the union's own membership and collective agreements would be undermined. More shops would shut down and more work would be contracted out to homeworkers. During a time of high unemployment, apparel manufacturers and retailers would continue to use homeworkers.

Historically, the ILGWU fought for a ban on homework as part of its struggle for decent wages and working conditions in the industry. Trade unions in both the United States and Britain, at the turn of the century, argued it was impossible to organize homeworkers and that homework could never be regulated. In the worst cases, trade unionists blamed homework on the characteristics of women.[12]

The ILGWU in the United States won a legislated ban on homework in the garment industry. It would be completely contradictory for it to turn around and attempt to organize homeworkers—a public acknowledgement that the ban is not enforceable. To discourage homework, the ILGWU in the US has in some cases levied fines against union members who performed it. In Ontario, however, homework was legal, flourishing and threatening the union's foundation.

Deciding to Organize Homeworkers—ILGWU Ontario District

The ILGWU Ontario District decided to adopt a dual strategy to organize homeworkers into their own association or "pre-union" formation; to work with community and women's groups in a coalition to pressure

for legislative changes and accessible child care; and to build a public campaign to resist the impact of economic restructuring on women's work.

Organizing homeworkers poses considerable challenges. They are not at one location, such as a factory, and often work for more than one employer. The definition of bargaining units under the Ontario Labour Relations Act creates other problems for unionizing. And even if these difficulties are surmounted, the isolation of members and their geographic dispersal (to mention only two factors contributing to the vulnerability of homeworkers) are barriers to winning and then effectively enforcing a collective agreement. A union must be willing to commit itself to an extremely long-term and patient approach. Trade unions have been reluctant to take on this mammoth task. The resources required for organizing would have a very long-term payback, if any. However, the increasing use of just-in-time workers in non-standard forms of employment like part-time or casual work is challenging unions in the 1990s to find new ways of organizing.[13]

The homeworkers campaign provides a useful example of tactics for reaching workers in precarious employment. One of the biggest challenges in organizing homeworkers is finding them in the underground network of sub-contracting and homework. Individual homeworkers must be reached at the site of employment—their homes. One method is to hang around traditional garment district factories where contracting shops are located and follow the cars that pick up the bundles of cut garments. The ILGWU[14] tried this, but found it to be very labour-intensive, time-consuming, and not particularly successful.

The union had to make stronger links with organizations and groups within the particular communities, geographic or ethnic, to which the majority of homeworkers belonged. In Toronto the ILGWU started by working with the Chinese and Vietnamese communities, increasing the profile of the union as a place to call if a worker had employment problems.

It is almost impossible for homeworkers to become union members in the traditional sense of becoming members of a bargaining unit. Labour law defines a bargaining unit as having at least two members and one employer. Yet homeworkers needed an organization in which they could break down their isolation, share experiences, work together to improve their wages and working conditions, and receive some services. The history of the labour movement offers examples of other forms of associations. Industrial workers organized into Workers' Benevolent Societies, offering mutual assistance to members from the 1850s to the 1930s. There were attempts to organize homeworkers in France, Britain, and (to a lesser extent) the United States in the last century. In 1894 the British Women's Industrial Council evolved from the Women's Trade Union Association and supported the Liverpool Association of Homeworkers and Outworkers. Often US social reformers organized groups of homeworkers through neighbourhood settlement houses.[15]

During the mid-1980s, several US unions developed "associate memberships" to maintain connections with members who had lost their jobs. The associate membership program also enabled unions to assist previously unorganized groups, which had no tradition of a union and which may not have legally had the right to sign collective agreements, to come together to form a group [....][16]

While the move to organize homeworkers gained support in New York, there remained tension within the Ontario ILGWU. Many union members viewed homeworkers as taking their jobs away. The historical animosity towards homeworkers was deeply rooted. Members were worried that organizing homeworkers would simply allow homework to flourish. There was a lengthy debate. The argument was won when members became convinced that organizing homeworkers would help reduce the wage differential between unionized factory workers and homeworkers. In the long term, it was in the best interest of the union. One union member summed it up: "I have heard about the wages and the conditions of homeworkers. I joined this union forty-seven years ago to clean up the industry and stop this exploitation. We have to organize the homeworkers if we are really going to clean it up."

Slowly, union members began to revise their stereotypes of homeworkers. They realized that as manufacturers were restructuring their businesses they were pitting factory workers against homeworkers. Bargaining committees were being pushed to accept wage concessions, lengthened work weeks, and work speed-ups at the negotiating table because employers were obliging union members to compete with the less-than-minimum wage that homeworkers could be forced to accept.

The ILGWU Ontario District attempted to introduce new collective agreement language so homeworkers would be part of the bargaining unit with a particular employer. This strategy has not yet been successful. Other ways of reaching out to homeworkers and building unity between them and factory workers had to be found.

The Homeworkers' Association

Once the ILGWU Ontario District and the Coalition for Fair Wages and Working Conditions for Homeworkers set out to create a Homeworkers' Association, they confronted the problem of actually locating potential members.

A co-ordinator experienced in community development and workers' rights was hired in February 1992. Importantly, the co-ordinator spoke Vietnamese, Mandarin, and Cantonese as well as English.

The first attempt to attract women to the new organization was by contacting homeworkers who had been interviewed in the initial study and inviting them to a meeting on information about their rights as homeworkers. Only two of the forty women contacted appeared. Obviously, simply calling a meeting wasn't going to attract members to the Association.

The union and the co-ordinator conceived a different kind of organizing drive. They advertised the Homeworkers' Association in the Chinese and Vietnamese media, spoke about the Association at various functions, and placed leaflets on Homeworkers' Rights at all community centres. The key to the drive was to convince homeworkers that there was a place they could turn to for help and counselling—the union office.

The most successful tool of the homework drive involved extending the traditional notion of organizing to include social activities, especially for families. The homeworkers had reported in the interviews that social isolation was one of their major problems. Homeworkers stay at home working all day—and often all night—long. Production schedules left no time for social activities.

This was a gap the Association could fill. The co-ordinator organized a series of trips for families: trips to a maple sugar bush, to Niagara Falls for the Blossom Festival, to parks outside the city, and so on. The trips were advertised by leafleting factories which employ homeworkers and through media familiar to the South-East Asian community.

The response was excellent. While the focus of the trips was social, very important discussions took place on homework, the Association, the ILGWU, and unionization in general. Some myths were dispelled and information on both the situation and the rights of workers exchanged. It was simply not feasible, at that stage, to limit the trips to homeworkers and their families. However, homeworkers who did attend joined the Association and the participation of other workers created opportunities for news about the Association and its activities to travel by word of mouth through the community.

Between trips, drop-in social teas and legal clinics were held on Saturday afternoons at the union office, enabling women to meet, discuss their experiences, and do something about problems. The trips and teas were the most useful organizing and outreach strategies linking a woman's issues as a worker to other aspects of her day-to-day life.

In March 1992 four women joined, then two more, and then another three. By the end of the first year, the Homeworkers' Association boasted over fifty members—an incredible feat in view of the obstacles faced.

In June 1992, accompanied by the co-ordinator, a member of the Association flew to Miami as a delegate to the first convention of the ILGWU Associate Member (AIM) locals. Mrs. Chu[17] spoke at the convention and in an organizing workshop attended by both AIM and ILGWU convention delegates about the situation of homeworkers here and the activities of the Homeworkers' Association.[18]

Another milestone was reached at an ILGWU "retreat" in August that year. The union organized an educational weekend for members of the ILGWU and the Homeworkers' Association and the Coalition at Port Elgin, a union-owned educational facility on the shores of Lake Huron.[19] People brought their families and socialized as well as engaging in some hard-hitting discussion of problems.

Each side gained a better understanding of the other's situation and of common concerns. One participant, reflecting on the retreat, says: "Two groups met at Port Elgin. But, by the end of the weekend, we were one—workers, struggling to make ends meet in an industry whose future in Toronto is uncertain. We know we have to stick together."

A few weeks later, the Homeworkers' Association and ILGWU contingents marched together in the Labour Day parade, with members of both organizations intermingled beneath the two banners [....]

An example of both the exploitation which homeworkers encounter and the transformations which the Association brings is illustrated by Yen's story. Yen worked for an employer for several months. The company folded abruptly, leaving Yen with one month's wages owing, not to mention termination and vacation pay. Yen then began to do homework for another employer. She dropped off bundles of completed work, receiving in exchange only the promise of future pay. Then Yen picked up a bundle of silk blouses to sew. She was to be paid seven dollars a blouse, for a total of seventy dollars. She delivered the completed garments and requested payment for her work to date. The employer informed her that the work had been faulty (a lie) and that he could not sell the blouses. He told Yen that the selling price of the blouses was ninety dollars a piece, and that Yen's "error" had cost him nine hundred dollars. But because he was a "compassionate" man, he offered to split the loss with Yen, charging her fifty dollars for each blouse, for a total of five hundred dollars! Oddly enough, this amount was roughly equivalent to the total in wages owing to Yen. She was pounding the pavements again.

Her next employer owned a factory and retail outlets. Yen performed homework for this company until it closed up shop overnight, leaving her once again with unpaid wages. By this time Yen was a member of the Association. With the help of a legal clinic that is part of the Coalition, the Association made sure that Yen and other homeworkers received the monies owing to them. Before, the workers had said of their employers, "These people are like monsters, and I am just an ant. They can step on me easily." Now, as members of the Association, the workers had a way of fighting back.

One of the needs which the Association members identified at the August retreat was to acquire or improve English language skills. Two months later, the Association had set up classes with assistance from the Toronto Board of Education. Classes are held on Sundays, using materials developed specifically from the experiences of garment homeworkers. The Association has co-sponsored a number of workshops on workers' rights with other groups in the community.

In the first year, all the organizing was done in the South-East Asian community, where the ILGWU already had important links. Great strides have been made. The Coalition, however, is well aware that the scope of work being performed in homes is much broader than the garment trade and the workers involved are of diverse backgrounds.

When the Coalition members met with organizers from other ethno-linguistic communities, the response was always, "We're pretty sure homeworking must be happening in our community, but these workers are probably too busy, too isolated, to make contact with groups and services." Excellent suggestions and contact possibilities were shared with the Association. It has not yet, however, solved the major problem—how to find or fund the staff and resources necessary for outreach and follow-up in other communities.

Trips, socials, help with employment and other problems, English-as-a-second-language classes, health and welfare benefits—members are attracted to the Association for different reasons. Their employment remains so precarious that joining the Association is an act of bravery. But diverse motivations coalesce into a common purpose: "If we work together, we can change our situation." [...]

Building a Coalition and Launching a Campaign: September–December 1991

The principle aims of the campaign would be to win legislative changes that would offer greater protection to homeworkers and to assist in building an organization of homeworkers. In order to achieve these goals, the campaign would have to:

- Build alliances, especially a working coalition, with representation from unions, women's groups, and community groups, particularly those advocating for immigrant populations;
- Educate the general public, particularly activists in the labour and women's movements, about the conditions of homeworkers, to build broad public support;
- Lay the basis for an organization of homeworkers by making contact with homeworkers, initially by re-establishing the "Homeworkers' Hotline";
- Raise the long-term global economic issues underlying the increase in homework in the garment industry.

The Coalition decided to keep its focus on garment homeworkers. Coalition members wanted to understand and to explain that what was happening to garment workers was part of broader economic and labour market trends. But they agreed that they were more likely to be effective in taking on just one sector for now.

The Coalition initially discussed whether its ultimate goal would be to make homework a reasonable alternative for women, or to see it banned. Homework, it was decided, could only be an "alternative" if women had other options. The ILGWU study had demonstrated, and subsequent experience confirmed, that women become homeworkers because they can't find decent employment outside the home. They may not have the skills required to compete successfully in the Canadian labour market and they face racial, ethnic, and gender discrimination. There isn't accessible, high-quality, affordable child care; there aren't social supports that facilitate women working outside the home. Women are still almost solely responsible for the domestic sphere.

Women with whom the ILGWU spoke clearly stated that they did not want to be homeworkers. Would banning homework help to create jobs outside the home? The answer suggested by the US experience was "No." Such an approach could make the lives of homeworkers even more difficult by driving the work further underground, thus making homeworkers even more vulnerable to exploitation. Politically, a banning strategy could result in making women guilty by association with the illegal practices of their employers.

For these reasons, the Coalition rejected both the "reasonable alternative" and "banning" positions. Major transformations in the conditions of women's work have to be achieved for women to have real choices about where they work. Rather than trying to make homework illegal, the Coalition decided to try, through better employment legislation, stronger enforcement, and through organizing, to reduce the viability of homework as an attractive low-wage alternative for labour-intensive industries.

In the fall and winter of 1991 the Coalition held a press conference and a lobby of the provincial government and opposition parties and began planning an educational conference. The Ontario Federation of Labour convention unanimously adopted a resolution in support of the campaign.

The Coalition invited the Public Service Alliance of Canada (PSAC), the union representing federal government workers, to join in sponsoring a conference on homework. The trend toward a "flexible" workforce isn't confined to the private sector. The Treasury Board was developing a pilot project that would "allow" certain federal government employees to work from home rather than in the office. PSAC had initiated a research project to prepare the union's response. It was a very exciting partnership between labour and women's movement activists and academics. It was the first time that women in Canada explored the similarities and commonalities between industrial and electronic homework—the sweat shop and the "electronic cottage."

The Campaigns for Legislative Change and "Clean Clothes"

In early 1992 political discussion and debate in Ontario centred on the provincial government's proposals for reform of the Ontario Labour Relations Act (later, the controversial Bill 40). The government's stated intent was to reform the Act to facilitate access to collective bargaining for sectors of the labour market which historically had not been unionized and were often considered unorganizable. These are sectors of the economy which are expanding—personal service, retail, finance, insurance, and real estate. Women of all colours, immigrant, and young workers of both sexes are concentrated in these very sectors. More heavily unionized sectors such as manufacturing are declining.

The Coalition was part of an ad-hoc group of women who organized to respond to the government's discussion paper on reform of the Labour Relations Act. Women from the trade union movement INTERCEDE (The Toronto Organization of Domestic Workers), the retail and service sectors, the women's movement, and the Coalition all agreed that the proposed reforms, while a step in the right direction, would do little to change the situation for most women. Women for Labour Law Reform met with the Minister of Labour. While generally supporting the modest amendments being proposed, the group pointed out the limited impact they would have in female-dominated sectors of the labour force. They called on the government to strengthen and enforce the Employment Standards Act and to establish a task force to examine the potential for sectoral or broader-based bargaining.

Homeworkers are one of the groups that cannot unionize using existing labour relations laws. The ILGWU and the Coalition had been trying to develop a model of labour relations to allow homeworkers to organize as a sector and to negotiate jointly with their employers. The issue of broader-based or sectoral bargaining became more central as the year went on.

After the launch of the Coalition late in 1991, the ILGWU focused on analysing the specific structure of the Canadian apparel industry, putting names, faces, and numbers to the industry pyramid. The Coalition began discussing a campaign to pressure the three big retail firms that control the industry pyramid to take, or be held to, some responsibility for wages and working conditions down the production line. Such a campaign should continue public education, gather more public support, bring pressure to bear on the corporations to improve wages and working conditions, and put pressure on the government to implement and enforce legislation to protect homeworkers.

The Coalition talked about a consumer boycott, using one of the three large retail firms that essentially control the apparel industry in Canada as a straw-dog—specifically the Hudson's Bay. The Hudson's Bay Co., Canada's "oldest corporation," presents itself as one of the founding pillars of this country. It is possibly the worst of the big retailers in terms of setting conditions for manufacturers that pressure them into using homeworkers and importing from countries where workers are paid even lower wages. But there was apprehension about the boycott strategy. How could support for the boycott be obtained from workers directly employed by the Hudson's Bay Co.? What would the concrete objectives be? How would success be defined? Most of the Coalition members had grown up with the Kraft, Nestles, and green grape boycotts. While these had had some success, they required colossal effort and coordination on the part of thousands or tens of thousands of people.

Throughout the development of the Coalition there had been periodic correspondence with women in England who had been organizing and working with homeworkers throughout the 1980s. In the summer of 1992 one of the ILGWU staff went to England and met with two groups, the Leicester Outworkers' Campaign and the West Yorkshire Homeworkers' Unit. She brought back information about their "Clean Clothes Campaign."[20]

Responding to the same issues and industry structure that the Coalition faced in Canada, the Leicester Outworkers' Campaign had adopted a consumer education and preferential buying campaign directed at one large retail chain. They had drawn up a "Clean Clothes Code." Retailers who adopted it pledged to buy garments from manufacturers who:

- Abide by minimum wage and employment laws ...
- Give all workers a legally enforceable contract of employment, including homeworkers when used
- Allow free association of workers and the formation of independent worker organisations
- Do not enforce overtime
- Pay properly and promptly for all hours worked ... [21]

The retailer also pledged to ensure that their suppliers met these same standards.

The Toronto Coalition for Fair Wages and Working Conditions decided to formulate their campaign in a similar way. Rather than a boycott, there would be a campaign which asked consumers and retailers to become aware, to communicate their awareness to retailers, and to make positive choices. The Coalition produced background material about the use of homeworkers, their working conditions in the garment industry, and told the stories of three homeworkers who made designer-label clothes for less than the minimum wage. They created a "Clean Clothes Score Card" that shoppers could use to question retailers about their suppliers and evaluate which manufacturers they would like to buy from. They ran off tens of thousands of postcards for people to send to the presidents of Eaton's, the Hudson's Bay Co., and Dylex, demanding that they "Stop the Exploitation of Homeworkers—Buy from Manufacturers who pay Fair Wages and Working Conditions."

CLEAN CLOTHES SCORE CARD
Test your clothes: Are they clean?

The next time you buy clothes, ask the Retailer these questions:

1. Does the retailer or any of her/his suppliers use homeworkers?
2. Are they paid at least minimum wage?
3. Are homeworkers paid on time?
4. Are they paid for all hours of work?
5. Are homeworkers given reasonable turn around time to complete each job?
6. Has the original supplier registered for a Homeworkers permit, as required under the Employment Standards Act?
7. Does the original supplier/employer make contributions to Unemployment Insurance and Canada Pension Plan?
8. Were the homeworkers intimidated from joining the Homeworkers' Association? A score of less than 8 YESes means the homeworker is not receiving fair wages and working conditions. [...]

What Next

There is no conclusion to this story. It is part of a living campaign, one that will spread and grow in the time following the activities described here. Union organizing and negotiating, building the Coalition, lobbying government, publicizing the Clean Clothes Campaign, pressuring retailers, contacting homeworkers, fingering unlawful contractors, building the Association, increasing public awareness, learning more about homework and women's employment have all continued since this essay was written.

As the Coalition headed into 1993, the campaign for legislative change was at the top of its agenda. The Ontario government had made a promise, but the Coalition was convinced that it would have to keep up the pressure to hold them to that promise.

The Clean Clothes Campaign was just beginning. More research had to be done. More education had to be done about the causes and effects of women working in isolation in their homes for abysmal wages, with no benefits, and without child care.

The Coalition for Fair Wages and Working Conditions for Homeworkers[22] brought together community workers, trade unionists, religious leaders, lawyers, academics, and, most importantly, homeworkers. The basis of solidarity uniting the diverse membership of the Coalition is the realization that homeworkers are on the front lines of a common struggle for decent wages and working conditions, in the face of massive economic restructuring. If we are to win, sisterhood had better be powerful.

Notes

1. Statistics Canada, 1992.

2. Census Metropolitan Area.

3. Statistics Canada as reported in *The Toronto Star*, September 21, 1992, p. A1. (Forty-three percent of the overall workforce was born outside Canada.)

4. Employment estimates from Statistics Canada's Cat. 72-002: *Employment, Earnings and Hours*.

5. Statistics Canada counts only workers employed in factories and shops. While employers are required to register homeworkers under permit, enforcement is lax. Therefore no way of knowing the number of homeworkers in the industry exists. Unless or until we know how many jobs have gone from factories and shops to homeworkers, we cannot know the actual job loss in the industry.

6. Hudson's Bay Co. Annual Report, 1991; Dylex. Annual Report, 1991; *The Financial Post*'s "Report Card on Dylex," 1991.

7. See the Economic Council of Canada, "Good Jobs, Bad Jobs: Employment in the Service Economy" (Ottawa: Ministry of Supply and Services, 1990); A. Yalnizyan in "Full Employment Still a Viable Goal" in *Getting on Track: Social Democratic Strategies for Ontario* (Montreal: McGill-Queen's, 1991); H. Krahn in "Non-Standard Work Arrangements" in *Perspectives on Labour and Income* in Statistics Canada's Cat. 75-001E, Winter 1991.

8. G. Standing in "Global Feminization through Flexible Labour" in *World Development* Vol. 17, No. 7 (1989). Montreal: Elsevier Journals, p. 1079.

9. S. Mitter, *Common Fate, Common Bond: Woman in the Global Economy* (London: Pluto Press, 1986).

10. For an overview of flexibility strategies, see M. Macdonald in "Post-Fordism and the Flexibility Debate" in *Studies in Political Economy* Autumn 1992, pp. 171–201; S. Wood, *The Transformation of Work* (London: Unwin Hyman, 1989).

11. Barbara Cameron, "Chinese-Speaking Homeworkers in Toronto: Summary of Results of a Survey." Conducted by the International Ladies' Garment Workers Union (Toronto: ILGWU, 1991).

12. S. Rowbotham and S. Mitter, *Dignity and Daily Bread* (London: Routledge, 1994).

13. For more information on the history of organizing homeworkers, see E. Boris and C. Daniels, *Homework: Historical and Contemporary Perspectives on Paid Labour at Home* (Chicago: University of Illinois Press, 1989); West Yorkshire Homeworking Group, *A Penny a Bag: Campaigning on Homework* (Batley: Yorkshire and Humberside Low Pay Unit, 1990); S. Rowbotham, *Homeworkers Worldwide* (London: Merlin Press, 1993).

14. Unless otherwise specified, references to the ILGWU in the Coalition and in the organizing of homeworkers mean the ILGWU Ontario District.

15. S. Rowbotham, op. cit.

16. One of the first examples was the Service Employees' International Union, which linked up with a feminist working women's group, "9 to 5," in the US in an attempt to organize clerical workers into an associate membership group through feminist processes such as consciousness-raising. See K. Moddy, *An Injury to All* (London: Verso, 1989), p. 279.

17. Homeworkers' real names are not used in this essay to protect them from retaliation by their employers.

18. The AIM convention ran concurrently with the ILGWU convention.

19. The Port Elgin Family Education Centre is a Canadian Auto Workers facility.

20. The first Clean Clothes Campaign was a campaign for public health standards and enforcement at the beginning of this century. See C. Daniels in "Between Home and Factory: Homeworkers and the State" in Boris and Daniels, op. cit., pp. 13–31.

21. Traidcraft, Kingsway, Gateshead, England.

22. The authors decided not to use individual names in telling the story of the Coalition as some people would get mentioned often because they were the public spokeswomen and others might not be named at all. This would not reflect the fact that everyone contributed a great deal to the work of the Coalition. Nonetheless, we think it is important to acknowledge that it takes committed individuals to work for social change, not just faceless committees. We wish to acknowledge the following individuals: Alex Dagg (Ontario district manager of the International Ladies' Garment Workers' Union); Dr. Barbara Cameron (who conducted the initial research for the ILGWU); Teresa Mak of the ILGWU; Jan Borowy (currently research coordinator of the ILGWU); Danny Sun (ILGWU organizer); Holly Du (organizer for the Homeworkers' Association); Deena Ladd (ILGWU conference organizer); Liz Fraser, Kathleen Doran, and Rachel Seed (placement students at the ILGWU who assisted the Coalition); Shelly Gordon and David Kidd (Worker's Information and Action Centre of Toronto); Judy Fudge (Osgoode Hall Law School, representing NAC); Gayle Lebans, Sheila Cuthbertson, Gail Sax, Joanne Seamon, Kim Armstrong, and Laryssa Holynsky (staff and students from Parkdale Community Legal Services); Barbara Paleczny (Sisters of Notre Dame and Ecumenical Coalition for Economic Justice); Linda Yanz (Mujer à Mujer); Jennifer Stephen (Metro Labour Education Centre); Carla Lipsig-Mummé (York University Centre for Research on Work and Society); Margaret Oldfield, Sue Jones, and Helen Jackson (Public Service Alliance of Canada); Belinda Leach (McMaster University); Sandra Awang, Salome Loucas (Women Working with Immigrant Women); Julie Davis (secretary-treasurer of the Ontario Federation of Labour); Carrol Anne Sceviour (Ontario Federation of Labour). Even that list leaves out others whose assistance and support have been critical and those who have begun to participate in the Coalition more recently.

Class Is a Feminist Issue

Pat Armstrong and Hugh Armstrong

*****

Few would deny that capitalist societies are class societies or that women as a group are oppressed. But the question of whether or not there is a material basis to that oppression and of whether or not that basis is shared bodies or shared work is still a matter of debate. Are the fundamental divisions those between owners of the means of production and owners of labour power, those between men and women, or those between women and their bodies? Is the main enemy, to use Christine Delphy's terminology, capitalism, men, or female anatomy?[1]

While it is essential for a class analysis to locate women in relation to class, the answer cannot be one of these alternatives alone. Women are simultaneously subject to capitalism, male dominance, and their bodies. To pose the question in the form of alternatives is like asking whether ideas or material conditions structure women's subordination. They are inseparable. They act together. Patriarchy and capitalism are not autonomous, nor even interconnected systems, but the same system. As integrated forms, they must be examined together.

This is not to argue that women constitute a class. Although it is clear that most of those who own and control the means of production are male, most men own only their ability to work. There are also class differences among women. Lady Astor is not oppressed by her chauffeur and it is questionable whether her cleaning woman is more oppressed by her husband than her employer. Theorists have concentrated on exposing what women have in common, but not all theorists have ignored or dismissed class differences among women. Early in the domestic labour debate, Peggy Morton maintained that there were class differences among women—differences based on the class position of their husbands, their families, or their own labour force work.[2] Roberta Hamilton explored the different work experiences and life situations of women in peasant, craft, "tradesman," and noble families in the transition to bourgeois and proletarian households.[3] Situating women within the family, and the family in turn within the dominant mode of production, Dorothy Smith argued that capitalism changed all women's work into a personal service, but that there is a crucial difference between working-class and middle-class families. "The household for the working class woman is a means to meeting the needs of its members, and that is her work. Middle class women are oriented by contrast to the values and standards of an externalized order."[4] Bonnie Fox also distinguished between working-class and middle-class women—in this case on the basis of household income and resources.[5] The oppression takes different forms for these women. The consequences, nature, and responses to male dominance vary from class to class.

To argue that there are class differences among women and that they do not form a class on the basis of their bodies or their work is not to solve the problem of fitting women into classes. Locating women through their domestic labour either puts most women into the same class or places them automatically in the same class as their husbands. For those women with direct involvement in the labour market, the alternatives are independent class membership with other women because of the domestic labour they also perform. Gardiner's alternative of expanding the definition of the working class to include all those not directly involved in but dependent on the sale of labour power does expose the broad class cleavages, but fails to take into account the fundamental divisions between men and women in the working class.[6] Surely having an indirect, rather than a direct, relationship to production has important consequences for women's class sympathies—sympathies that cannot easily be equated with those of the young and unemployed whose dependency is temporary and transient. Furthermore, such an approach ignores the double work of women, their position as a particular kind of reserve army, their segregation into separate labour force jobs, and the ideology that reinforces and is reinforced by these divisions.

The problem here is more than one of counting, of figuring out how to classify women. Both bourgeois and Marxist categories treat sex differences as irrelevant to stratification and class systems. As Delphy points out, both approaches imply that "wider inequalities have no influence on the (assumed) 'equality' of the couple, and on the other hand that relationships within the couple because they are seen as equal cannot be the cause of wider inequalities."[7] Theories that lump all women together as a class ignore class differences among women. Theories that attach women to their husbands

or families ignore women's subordination, their domestic labour, and their labour force work. Theories that locate women in terms of their own paid employment forget both the segregation of the labour force and the domestic labour that most women perform. Theories that are blind to sex differences obscure not only divisions fundamental to all classes, but also the structure of capitalism. The working class, as well as the ruling class, has two sexes. Without acknowledging these divisions—without integrating them into a class analysis—neither capitalism nor households can be understood. This is not a plea to add women back in, but a challenge to a theory that has not made the system transparent, has not developed an analysis of class that accounts for a bifurcation of classes—a division that is central to an understanding of how capitalism itself works.

The domestic labour debate does lay the basis for a revision of theory based on an expansion of the class concept. Without denying that the most basic divisions are between those who own and control the means of production and those who own only their labour power—a primacy implied by the dominance of the wage system in capitalist society—it is possible to comprehend the antagonisms between the sexes, and among those of the same sex, by including all labour in our analysis. Those dependent directly or indirectly on the wage are objectively and subjectively divided by their material conditions, by their lived experiences, and by the work they do. If work for a wage (or the absence of work for a wage) and work required to transform that wage into consumable form, as well as work necessary to provide the next generation of workers, are included in our approach to class, then divisions between men and women and among women may be better understood. Such an approach would permit the domestic and wage labour of both men and women to be taken into account. Domestic labour would thus form an integral part of the explanation for men's interests just as wage labour would be a basis component in comprehending women's class position and relations. Connecting domestic and wage labour within classes would also extend the analysis to the relationship between domestic and wage labour—to the sex segregation in both areas of work. In this way, it would be possible to develop a theory that exposes the material basis of the subjective and objective antagonisms between sexes. The domestic labour debate suggests a movement in this direction; Marxism provides the tools; political economy should continue the work.

*****

Notes

1. Christine Delphy, "L'ennemi principal," reprinted in *Libération des femmes année zero*, Partisans (ed.) (Paris 1972).

2. Peggy Morton, "Women's Work Is Never Done," reprinted in *Women Unite!* (Toronto: Canadian Women's Educational Press, 1972).

3. Roberta Hamilton, *The Liberation of Women* (London: Allen and Unwin, 1978).

4. Dorothy Smith, "Women, the Family and Corporate Capitalism," in Marylee Stephenson (ed.), *Women in Canada* (Toronto: New Press, 1973), 45.

5. Bonnie Fox, "Women's Double Work Day: Twentieth-Century Changes in the Reproduction of Daily Life," in Bonnie Fox (ed.), *Hidden in the Household: Women's Domestic Labour under Capitalism* (Toronto: Women's Press, 1980).

6. Jean Gardiner, "Women in the Labour Process and Class Structure," in Alan Hunt (ed.), *Class and Class Structure* (London: Lawrence and Wishart, 1977), 158.

7. Christine Delphy, "Women in Stratification Studies," in Helen Roberts (ed.), *Doing Feminist Research* (London: Routledge and Kegan Paul, 1981), 115.

The World of the Professional Stripper

Chris Bruckert

If you wandered into one of the over 200 strip clubs in Ontario, you might notice the dim lighting, the pool tables and video games, the continually running pornographic movies, and the smell of stale beer. You might notice that this is clearly a "male space" that is, somewhat ironically, defined by the presence of (some) women. Women in scant attire "hanging out," women sitting and listening with apparently rapt attention to men, women at some phase of undress dancing on stage, women in champagne rooms[1] dancing for, or talking with, (clothed) men who are sitting only inches away from their naked bodies. At first glance the scene appears so imbued with the markers of gendered oppression, objectification, and exploitation that analysis is hardly necessary. Nonetheless, things are not as straightforward as they seem. From the perspective of the women "deep" in conversation or dancing on the stage, strip clubs are not about entertainment, or immorality, or sex. They are about work.

In this essay we explore the work of strippers through the lens of feminist labour theory. Using an approach informed by Marxism, symbolic interactionism, and feminism allows us to shift between analytic levels and consider the intersection and tension between market economy, social and gender relations, regulatory frameworks, dominant discourses, labour processes, and work site practices. When we step outside of morally loaded assumptions and attend to the understanding of industry workers, it is quickly apparent that strippers' work is both similar to and markedly different from other working-class women's labour.[2]

From Entertainment to Service

The trajectory of labour of Ontario's strippers over the last three decades speaks to the unique position of strip clubs as both commercial enterprises embedded in the market economy and, at the same time, the product and focus of dynamic social processes including moral and legal regulation. It also illustrates how broader labour market trends and economic shifts not only position clubs to exploit strippers but also condition the nature of that exploitation. In the mid and late 1970s strippers were entertainers who, in exchange for wages,[3] performed five sets of four songs (three fast, one slow floor show) during their six-hour shift. During the 1980s and into the 1990s Canada experienced periods of recession, a general stagnation of fiscal growth, and high rates of unemployment (Phillips, 1997:64). During this period of economic restructuring, manufacturing jobs were displaced, the service sector expanded exponentially, and women's labour market position was destabilized (Luxton and Corman, 2001). For working-class women labour market reorganization resulted in a move into labour-intensive consumer service sector employment characterized by low pay, low capital–labour ratio, limited job security, poor working conditions, and non-standard labour arrangements such as part-time, casual, and seasonal work. In principle protected through labour legislation, in practice marginal, non-unionized workers in this sector have limited recourse to legal protection and are susceptible to a range of exploitive practices (Duffy and Pupo, 1997). In addition, the vanishing social safety net compounded the vulnerability, economic need, and domestic responsibilities of this social strata. As a result, workers were not only, by default, increasingly employed in the service sector but situated to embrace work in the growing non-standard labour market, including casual and flexible self-account work, as an income-generating strategy that allowed them to fulfill their many social and personal obligations.

It was in this context of economic decline and dwindling options for working-class women that the new industry innovation of table dancing[4] was introduced in the early 1980s and used to justify cutting dancers' pay to $30 or $40 a day. At the same time shifts were increased from six to eight hours, and bar fees[5] were implemented. By the early 1990s as the economy continued to spiral downward threatening even the "bad jobs" in the service sector, clubs went from exploiting workers to the full appropriation of their labour. Many dancers found their pay eliminated, as they were offered the option of working for "tips" or not at all. In short, in Ontario between 1980 and 2000 stripping was "deprofessionalized,"[6] dancers were redefined as service providers, wages were reduced, and the labour requirements were substantially increased.

Today, while some dancers continue to work "on-schedule" earning between $35 and $45 for an eight-hour shift, most work as "freelancers"[7] receiving no financial compensation from the club. Under either arrangement dancers are expected to pay the established bar fee of between $10 and $20, follow house rules, remain in the bar for a predetermined period of time—hanging out and "looking like a hooker" (Debbie)[8]—and perform between one and five three-song "sets" on stage. Similar to other subcontracting relations (i.e., electricians) exotic dancers are responsible for furnishing tools, in this case music, costumes, and transportation. In exchange for labour, fees, and compliance with the expectations of the club, the bar provides the labour site—the physical space (bar, chairs, champagne rooms) and other co-ordinated and necessary labour by disk jockeys, bartenders, servers, and doormen. This setting is, of course, crucial. Without it, a dancer cannot solicit the private dances that constitute her income.[9]

In spite of receiving no, or minimal, pay the workers' labour and general deportment remains under the control of management, who establish the house rules governing attire and behaviour, expectations of stage shows, interactions with customers, and services offered in the champagne rooms. Compliance is realized through economic sanctions in the form of fines and by the club's power to deny access to customers. A dancer who is defined as troublesome, who complains "too much," who doesn't follow the house rules, or who leaves with a customer may be suspended or barred permanently. "Troublesome" dancers also risk being blacklisted. This can have dire consequences, since the marked dancer will be unable to pursue her trade anywhere in the city. Put this way, today strippers are in a contradictory space— on the one hand they are managed like employees and subject to disciplinary regimes if they fail to comply, while on the other hand they are denied the pay and protection generally associated with employment.

The exploitative nature of managerial attempts to extract maximum labour power notwithstanding, there have also been positive implications for workers in the shift from entertainment to service. With de-professionalization and lower labour costs, a new industry standard of continuous stages and lots of "girls" emerged. These changes in turn meant new employment opportunities and an opening up of the labour market as the demand increased. They also conditioned the relationship between management and dancers in new ways. Their limited commitment to a particular labour site affords individual dancers greater levels of autonomy and allows them to determine, within particular confines, where, when, and how much they work. Since the club no longer pays workers but exchanges fees and labour site access for free labour, the ability of management to control labour has been somewhat eroded. This is exacerbated by the managerial need for a stable work force and their subsequent hesitancy to alienate the dancers on whom they rely. This is particularly true for women with considerable organizational assets (i.e., a "sexy" appearance, a client list).

Moreover, the new organization not only conditions labour relations but also interacts with class to shape the labour site itself. In the past, the nature of the entertainment-based industry compelled dancers to work full-time and travel "the circuit." These conditions effectively excluded many women workers who embraced other "respectable" social roles: children, partners, school commitments, other jobs. Today, dancers can opt to work full-time, part-time, or occasionally; and either never, or only periodically, go "on the road" in response to particular financial difficulties. In real terms this, coupled with the impoverishment of women workers in Canada generally, opened up the industry to reputable working-class women and women from middle-class families whose eroding economic position (coupled with ideological changes regarding the meaning of nudity) has rendered morally suspect labour increasingly tenable. Tina, a sole-support mother, started working as a stripper when after years of steady employment she found herself:

On welfare for seven months. And it was hard and … I saw those, ah, those ads [in the newspaper]. And one day I decided to, to go, to try it y'know. But it was scary. I was 29 years old and I didn't know what was going on there.

Like Tina, these new workers need to overcome their own stereotypical assumptions about strip clubs; however, those who effectively deconstruct the dominant discourses sometimes remain in the occupation for considerable periods of time. In turn as these new workers bring to the labour site their own class culture and investment in respectability, these values have become embedded in the industry structure itself. Today, the markers of rough working-class culture—practices (partying, drugs), appearance (cut-off jean shorts, tattoos), values (being "solid"), and language (talking tough)—are either absent from strip clubs or are limited to one token "rough bar."[10]

In 1973, amendments to the provincial liquor Control Act expanded the definition of "theatre" (Ontario, 1973) and made it possible in Ontario to combine alcohol and nudity in a legal commercial endeavour. Since then, the trajectory of strip clubs in the province reveals how the complex interplay between market economy and labour structure shapes the labour process in marginal spheres at the same time as the labour process shapes the class origin of the available employee base. Workers are then positioned in a contradictory class location: they are both independent entrepreneurs who manage their own business—thus, are the bourgeois—and employees who sell (or in this case exchange) their labour power and who rely on, and must comply with the expectations of, an individual capitalist—in this case, the proletariat.

The Job

When we shift our focus and apply the feminist labour lens to the question of labour practices another set of questions emerge. What does the work entail? What skills and competencies are workers expected to bring to the labour site? What strategies do dancers employ to negotiate the occupational hazards? What are the particular challenges of the job? In addition, by retaining the focus on class, we are also positioned to ask: How does strippers' labour compare to that of working-class women more generally?

The Stage

Though frequently ignored in labour theory, sexuality does not operate outside of the labour market. Rather "sexuality is a structuring process of gender" (Adkins, 1992:208), and gender and sexuality are central "to *all* workplace power relations" [emphasis in original] (Pringle, 1988:84). Certainly in the consumer service sector where working-class women are clustered, workers are expected to bring to the labour market not only the ability to assume an attractive "made-up" appearance so that "part of the job for women consists of looking good," but also must offer, explicitly or implicitly, a feminine and sexualized presentation-of-self (Adkins, 1992: 216, 218). In fact much of the publicly visible labour (waitressing, flight attendants) that women traditionally undertake has a sexual subtext. Framed in this way, strippers' erotic labour situates them on a continuum of visible sexuality that frequently characterizes working-class women's labour force engagement. What marks the strip club as unique, however, is the self-conscious reliance on women's bodies. While other service industries may use women's bodies to make a product or service more appealing (Adkins, 1992), here the service and the body are conflated so that sexuality appears to define the labour.

A woman working in a strip club as a stripper first and foremost has to *act* like a *stripper*; whether she is on the stage or not, she is always *performing*. This involves both the ceremony common to visible employees of "playing [her] condition to realize it" (Goffman,

1959:76) and the fact that the dancer is allowed some creativity, although, like actors generally, she is required to assume a role that is not her own, nor of her making (Henry and Sims, 1970). To entertain, she has to "do a stage." This public erotic labour involves the ability to perform for, but also interact with, the audience, whose very presence legitimates the work.[11] In addition, a stripper's act requires a degree of comfort with nudity, a willingness to expose herself physically, and a self-assured and confident presentation-of-self. Many strippers develop a strong stage presence and are often competent dancers, proficient not only in the standard stripper "moves" but able to incorporate, and execute (in very high heels) their own eclectic mix of ballet, jazz, acrobatics, aerobics, and posing. On stage a dancer must continue to smile or at least assume the appropriate sexually vacant expression—"I think about doing laundry or watch the TV" (Debbie)—in the face of apathy and, sometimes, taunts. These kinds of verbal comments touch not only on her performance but, in light of the gendered appearance imperative, on her value as a woman. In short, she needs to develop the capacity to distance herself from the negative evaluation of the audience.

Although obscured by the performance component and nudity, stage shows are physically demanding labour. And, like so much physical labour, it can be dangerous.[12] In addition to the risks inherent to dancing in stiletto heels, there is the threat of infectious disease. While many dancers take protective measures,[13] the dressing rooms, washrooms, stage, and pole are, at least in some clubs, not particularly well-maintained. The work is also exhausting and technically difficult: "Pole work is a lot of hanging upside down, it's a lot of balance, muscle technique. It's hard to look sexy when you're upside down and all the blood's rushing to your head!" (Diane). Put another way, the "moves" can only be erotic if they appear effortless and natural, a feat that necessitates practice, skill, and considerable muscle development.[14] In short, constructing sexuality is not natural or easy but hard *work*; however, the more effective the illusion, the more sexual the portrayal, the more the *work* is invisible.

The question becomes: How is erotic labour understood and negotiated by participants? Perhaps the most telling finding was how few comments were made by interviewees about sexuality. It appeared to be largely incidental. While dominating public consciousness, nudity, sexual presentations, and interactions are normalized within the cultural environment of the strip club, so that the erotic nature of the labour is essentially a non-issue for participants. Moreover, unlike other labour sites, in the club sexuality is explicit and monetarily compensated: "it [sexual harassment] was all over, in what I do, *no* that's the place" [emphasis hers] (Tina). In addition, out in the open, sexuality can be managed:

> Wouldn't you say in a restaurant, the owners, the cooks, they're gonna grab you for free at their convenience? But in a bar, first of all they *don't* grab you, they're gonna be thrown out, and whatever happens they're always forking out the bucks for it [emphasis hers]. (Kelly)

Perhaps more important still are the meanings scripted onto the labour. A dancer engages with the indicators of sexuality, and these links to the erotic appear to define her job as a *stripper*. However, this explicitly erotic labour operates at the level of the visible body. It is not about sex but nudity and the visual presentations of the erotic: "You manipulate your body in a certain way and you throw a sexual aspect to it" (Debbie). Put another way, dancers engage in surface acting where "the body not the soul is the main tool of the trade. The actor's body evokes passion in the *audience*, but the actor is only *acting* as if he has the feeling" [emphasis in original] (Hochschild, 1983:37). The eroticized setting, available props, and their own expectations may ensure that the audience defines the entertainers as sexual, but the experience of workers is markedly different:

At the Blue Lagoon it's a lot easier because there's TVs. So I can't see anyone from the stage, so I watch TV. I'll listen to music, and I'll watch TV, and I'll just dance. I've been doing it, you know when you do it so often you're looking straight at people's eyes but you're going, you're kinda looking over yonder type, looking at the TV there. You're doing your little crawl and you're like giggling inside cause there's some show on. I mean I've lost it completely because I was doing a show and I was trying to talk to someone and *The Simpsons* came on TV and I started pissing myself laughing. I couldn't do it anymore. I walked off the stage. (Debbie)

The Floor

As previously noted, today's dancers must continually negotiate two discrete, and sometimes conflicting, jobs during their work day. The quasi-contractual obligation is to perform strip-tease shows and "hanging out"—tasks for which she receives not a paycheck but attains access to customers. As self-account service workers, all or most of the worker's income is directly paid by customers in fee-for-service arrangements. In order to "make her money" dancers must first solicit and sell their private dances by convincing "a guy that he really wants a dance" (Debbie). Here labour practices are constrained not only by house rules but also by individual inclination. Some dancers flatly refuse to approach customers: "Some girls go around and ask, 'hi baby how you doing' and start shaking their things in front of him. No! I don't like that at all. I just wait for them. If they want me bad enough, they'll come and get me, they'll signal me or tell the waitress" (Rachel). Others "work the floor"—socializing and engaging promising-looking customers in conversation. The most aggressive hustlers greet all customers. At a minimum they "give them the eye, just like you would in a bar" (Debbie).

Having "sold" her service, the dancer accompanies the patron to the champagne room where she seeks to maximize her income by employing a variety of special skills. "Once they come and get me, they're screwed. They're stuck with me, and I'm gonna keep them and siphon out every last dime I can get" (Rachel). While this may entail dirty dancing, more frequently dancers employ "straight" strategies to maximize income:

> I don't stop [dancing] until they tell me to stop, and then I tell them how much. I don't do one dance and then sit ... I used to do that, one dance and that's it. Then you don't get another dance. So I just keep dancing. (Sally)

In the champagne room a dancer needs to encourage the customer, retain his attention and good will, and yet remain firmly in control of the situation. The challenges have increased with the media and public discourses throughout the lap-dancing debates. Apparently, customers frequently equate surface presentations of sexuality with actual sexuality, so that dancers are wrongly presumed to be, if not prostitutes, then highly promiscuous. Today "99% by the customers, oh yes, 'You must have a price.' ... the way society is, they're allowed to expect it" (Marie). This means that an individual dancer is required to cope with customers' anticipation of sexual fulfillment while she labours in an environment where she is presumed to be, but cannot be, sexually available.

Not surprisingly given the physical space and discursive parameters, making money also renders dancers vulnerable to physical or sexual aggression. As a result, they must remain vigilantly attentive to clues that identify potentially dangerous patrons (body language, conversation, approach, intoxication). Dancers also routinely rely on each other for protection—"In the champagne room we're all watching each other's back" (Debbie)—and most of the more experienced dancers have perfected strategies that maximize their control of the interaction. One research participant described her atypically candid approach:

> I stand [and] I make them open their legs like this. If they give me a problem, my knees are right here. Ya, I'm serious! Every guy has to sit with their legs open. I want full range. Some of them say "why"—"cause if you get out of line I'll kick you right there." Fucking right, you hurt me, I'll hurt you right back. These are the rules, you don't like them, you get the fuck out, don't ask me to dance. A lot of them [dancers] sit with their legs wide open—he's going to get his hands to your crotch before you get your feet to the floor, 'cause he's got a hold of your legs. (Sally)

Emotional Labour

While erotic labour, either on the public stage or in the relatively private champagne rooms, appears to define strippers' labour, in practice strippers are increasingly required not only to engage in the surface acting essential for the selling and providing of private entertainment services but also to provide an interpersonal social service that necessitates a unique set of skills and strategies. Here Arlie Hochschild's (1983) concept of emotional labour has resonance.[15] Many customers are only marginally interested in nude entertainment whether it is on the public stage or in a private champagne room. Instead these men come to strip clubs because they "want someone to talk to" (Rachel) and will "spend a couple of hundred bucks and they sit there and talk to a girl that's nice to them and makes them feel good for a few hours" (Diane).

For the dancer this parody of social relations necessitates "playing a game .... It depends on the guy, the drippier you are, the more money you'll make. The more you laugh at his jokes, the more money you'll make" (Sally). In essence the dancer presents a cynical performance (Goffman, 1959:18), instrumentally and consciously playing to the expectations of an audience of one:

> I mean obviously they're going to be nice. They're being paid to be there, so it's not like it's not a good idea to be a bitch or something. Guys aren't gonna spend money on you. And that's what you're there for. (Diane)

Essentially, a dancer's livelihood depends on her ability to recreate social relations and "treat them like they're people. You don't just treat them like they're a ten dollar bill" (Rachel). Interactions are routinized charades where dancers create the illusion of a novel interaction with a "special" person. In short, strippers' daily labour involves not only continual performance—playing the role of a stripper—but also adopting other personas, in effect playing a number of roles, within a particular spectrum of possibilities, consecutively and sometimes concurrently:

> I used to give every guy a different age depending on what they wanted. I also gave different stories, but that's complicated to keep track of. Sometimes I acted really young and walk[ed] around the club in a skirt being cutesie. You don't even have to look that young, just act young. It's really weird. Different guys want different things. (Sarah)

Like other direct service workers, a stripper has to be able to manage her emotions and anger in the face of ignorant and trying customers. However, there is something more—she participates in a financial interaction that masquerades as a social relationship with its sense of reciprocity: "I should probably have my PhD in psychology by now for all the problems I've listened to and all the advice I've given" (Rachel). Social relationships are normally defined by mutual concern. In the strip club, however, the appearance of concern becomes a commodity that is purchased: "I feel guilty when they tell me things. Because personally I don't give a shit. But I have to pretend I do" (Jamie). Notably, unlike the professionals to whom Rachel compares herself, a dancer has neither the language nor the professional training on which to rely to guide them through the interaction; instead, she has to improvise as she continually reinvents herself and adapts her performance.

Although talking to customers appears to be a rather innocuous activity, many dancers express exasperation: "You have to go sit down with the guy and blah blah blah blah blah blah blah blah. I hate that" (Tina). In fact, the most distress was voiced by research participants about this activity. On reflection, this is not surprising. As capitalism expands and the service industry swells to include the supply of emotional and interpersonal services (for men) in a commercial imitation of authentic social relationships,[16] the boundaries are being blurred and the product is not only the service but the server herself. For strip industry workers this means they are alienated not just from their bodies—through their physical capacity to work or their labour power—nor from their surface sexual self-presentation in a way that was normal in burlesque theatres. They are alienated from something more—their social selves:

> Temporarily you're someone you're not, just for this guy, just so you can get his money. If he wants to believe something then you just play right along with it. "Ya I'm from wherever" and make yourself up to be something you're not. (Sally)

The result is a disassociated sense of self, so that "I pretend I'm somebody else and I get all glamorous and I go into work. I'm a completely different person in the club, a completely different person" (Debbie). Workers are very explicit about the need to distance and separate their different selves: "I have a very distinct difference between my job and my life, and I find if I mix the two of them that I can't keep it straight" (Ann). This assumption of separate identity is in part facilitated by the use of stage names so that "on stage I'm Kim so that's not me either" (Alex). It would appear that, as new areas of social and interpersonal life are transformed into services to be bought, the alienation inherent to the labour process in modern capitalist societies is also extended into a new arena.

Stripping Is Women's Work

To summarize the discussion so far, when we abandon morally loaded assumptions, explore labour structure and practices, and "normalize" the labour of strippers by making links to the "reputable" work of working-class women, similarities start to emerge. Today strippers are contractual own-account workers who experience the same sorts of issues confronting other working-class women in Canada, including a non-supportive work environment, exploitation and oppression by owners and managers, non-standard labour arrangements, lack of security, and minimal protection by the state. As part of the burgeoning consumer service sector they, like many other direct service workers, do a job that requires erotic and emotional labour. The job itself is physically exhausting, emotionally challenging, and definitely stressful.[17] Success is contingent on the development of complex skills and competencies including performance, construction of sexuality, sales, and finely tuned interpersonal skills. The very existence of these skills belie the customary focus on deviance rather than work process in much of the literature. Of course that these skills are largely dismissed, or rendered invisible, is not unique to

the strip trade but characterizes many working-class women's jobs (Gaskell, 1986). It does, however, affirm once again the relative and subjective nature of what is defined as skills.

It is women's work in another way as well. Traditionally women were expected to provide men with nurturance, care, and support. Dancers provide this service for men who "want someone to listen to their problems" (Sarah) on the market on a fee-for-service basis. Suspending momentarily what it says about the state of alienation in advanced capitalist society that men are prepared to pay $10 for every four minutes[18] they spend in the company of a woman ($85 per hour if they take the flat rate[19]), we can appreciate that this is fully consistent with the move of capital into the types of services traditionally performed in the home. In the context of intimate relations this empathetic support is not experienced as particularly challenging; within the labour market it proves to be difficult, emotionally taxing labour that requires both surface and deep acting and the implementation of complex skills. Like so much of the labour women do, it is obscured, even to participants, by the context in which it occurs and the taken-for-granted nature of the competencies. That is to say not only is the labour structured so that work is interspersed with social interaction but emotions do not "fit" into the language of work, so that while the strippers are fully aware that "it's hard on your head after a while" (Diane), they are, nonetheless, sometimes not fully cognizant of this as *labour* activity.

But Not a Job Like Any Other!

Recognizing this work as labour, we must exercise caution. While we can legitimately make links to more reputable labour sites for almost every aspect of the dancer's work, few jobs require this combination of skills and necessitate that the worker operate in such a complex and emotionally taxing labour environment. In this last section we attend to specificity and consider stripping as a *marginal* labour activity and reflect on the implications for workers.

First, we need to consider that stripping is a stigmatized labour location.[20] While participation in the paid labour force is a taken-for-granted imperative for most Canadians, the nature of an individual's work is something they are presumed to choose. "Choosing" a labour market location that is on the margins of legality, morality, or propriety can have profound implications, as the stigma of labour location is transformed into a stigma of the worker (Polsky, 1969). For women working as strippers, this is compounded by the conflation of the skin and sex trades in the dominant discourse that further vilifies strippers and personalizes the whore stigma:

> It's the reputation that goes with it. People— when you tell them what you do, they go "oh—really!" Oh ya. Oh ya. There is, um, to the outside, to the outside world—there is no difference between a prostitute and an exotic dancer. (Debbie)

These workers must contend with moral righteousness and stereotypical assumptions in interpersonal relations and in a range of social and economic areas from housing—"some places don't rent to strippers" (Diane)—to finance—"it's hard to get credit in a bank" (Marie)—that are generally assumed to operate outside of moral consideration. Put another way, *working* as a stripper becomes *being* a stripper, an identity marker with very real implications in the lives of women in the industry and that shapes the worker's experience of the wider world.[21] While most dancers deconstruct the discourses and challenge the assumptions that underlie the stigma (prostitution, drug abuse, immorality) and effectively manage their personal and social identities, they must, nonetheless, continually engage in social and

personal exchanges where their labour location is understood to be definitive.

The implications of participating in "disreputable" labour extend beyond questions of identity and social interaction. Dancers must also negotiate a web of state regulatory practices unknown to employees in more "reputable" occupations. Throughout the 1980s and into the early 1990s, in response to claims made by community groups that linked strip clubs to increased crime and vice, municipalities throughout Ontario began to regulate the industry through severe zoning restrictions, banning clubs from residential areas, restricting the clubs to commercial zones, and stipulating no strip-club parameters around churches and schools. They also introduced licencing that required the newly designated "exotic entertainment parlour attendants" to purchase annual licences under threat of fines and even imprisonment.[22] The nature of the licencing is revealing and speaks to the moral subtext of these strategies. For example, in Toronto strippers are categorized along with massage-parlour attendants, while in Ottawa attaining a licence is contingent on dancers first demonstrating they have not been convicted of indecent acts, procuring, prostitution, or for any offence under the Narcotics Control Act.

In 1995, as part of broader zero-tolerance health initiatives engendered by the fear of HIV/AIDS and Hepatitis C, the Ontario Labour Minister ruled that lap-dancing could expose workers to fatal disease and, therefore, that it constituted a potential health hazard for workers, contrary to the Occupational Health and Safety Act (Ontario Ministry of Labour, 1995). This labour law provided municipalities with a new regulatory tactic. In 1995 and 1996, a number of municipalities implemented bylaws outlawing lap-dancing by citing the newly established health risks associated with the practice. Finally, of course, strippers are at risk of being charged under Criminal Code prohibitions against presenting an indecent stage performance (section 169), public nudity (section 170), and being an inmate of a bawdy house (section 210).[23] In principle, these controls are intended to regulate the industry in the interests of broader society; in practice, they not only stigmatize and marginalize workers but also further restrict the employment options of women workers: some clubs are "zoned" out of existence, while live entertainment ceases to be economically viable for smaller clubs in light of the hefty annual fees.

Conclusion

If I have done my job well, it should be clear to the reader that the work women perform in strip clubs is *hard* work. In order to be able to practice her trade, a dancer has to appear periodically on stage, dance, and remove her clothes for a roomful (or worse, *not* a roomful) of men "for free." In order to "make her money," she has to present herself as an attractive "sexy" woman, sell her service to an individual patron, and retain his attention by engaging in erotic and/or emotional labour while carefully maintaining physical and psychological boundaries. In the champagne room, her naked body may well be inches from her client, but she is continually being monitored by the manager, the doorman, other dancers, and the police. Like a rape victim, if she is inappropriately touched, she is held responsible and sanctioned. All the while she has to cope with the particular stress of working in a leisure site as well as deal with the chaotic environment and interpersonal conflicts that abound. When she leaves the labour site, she continues to engage with the stigmatized nature of her occupation, managing her social and personal identity as well as coping with the stereotypical assumptions of her friends, intimate partners, and the state agencies with whom she interacts. In other words, while we can legitimately make links to more reputable labour sites for almost every aspect of the dancer's work, there are few jobs that require this combination of skills and necessitate that the worker operate in such a complex and emotionally taxing labour environment. Furthermore, the implication of stigma means that the labour has far-reaching costs in the worker's personal life.

At the same time, the implications of having a "job like no other" are not all bad. Unlike most workers who provide traditional women's work on the open market, a stripper is well compensated for her labour. Furthermore, not only does the job offer her a flexibility and autonomy seldom available to working-class women, it allows her to develop competencies that are useful outside the labour site—assertiveness, boundary maintenance, and interpersonal skills. In addition, although her work may leave her frustrated and angry, it also affords her a broader vision, enhanced self-esteem, good body image, comfort with her sexuality, and confidence—all worthwhile attributes and ones that many women continue to struggle to realize.

Notes

1.   These cubicles, measuring perhaps three feet by five feet each, are equipped with two (most often vinyl) chairs facing each other, an ashtray, and a ledge to hold drinks. While the cubicles are usually hidden from the general view of the club, they are open to be monitored by anyone passing down the aisle between them.

2.   This essay is based on data gathered during a year of participant observation in a southern Ontario strip club, fifteen in-depth, semi-structured interviews with women working as strippers, and a series of interviews with other industry employees including managers, doormen, bartenders, waitresses, and disk jockeys. For a more detailed

description of the methodology or for a further development of the arguments see Bruckert (2002).

3. Wages ranged from $275 to $600 a week in the late 1970s.

4. Table dances are a one-song strip show performed at the patron's table. Today, in spite of the advertised availability of $5 table dances, these are rare. Most dancers simply refuse to remove their clothes in the middle of the bar. At any rate, most patrons are easily persuaded to enjoy the privacy afforded by the champagne rooms, where for $10, the stripper either dances on a stool or sits in close proximity to the customer and moves—a dance in name only.

5. Dancers are required to pay bar fees or "DJ fees" of between $10 and $20 per shift. In practice this means that the dancer must "pay to work there" (Jamie). Depending on the club these fees compensate the disk jockey and sometimes the bartender, who also receive no pay in the traditional sense.

6. This redefining of labour as semi-skilled is consistent with the trend towards deskilling that Braverman (1974) identified as characteristic of twentieth-century capitalism. That deskilling is ideologically and economically useful (for capitalists) is revealed when we realize that throughout the 1980s and 1990s, at the same time as skills were being denied, employers in mainstream sectors of the labour market were establishing inordinate educational requirements (Rinehart, 1996:78). It would appear that labour-dependent personal service industries capitalize on existing age, gender, and racial stratifications by hiring marginal workers and then justify their low wages through reference to their marginal status (Reiter, 1991:148).

7. DERA (Dancer's Equal Rights Association of Ottawa) estimates that one in four Ottawa dancers are "on-schedule" (DERA, 2001).

8. On-schedule dancers are booked for eight-hour shifts, while freelancers must remain for a minimum period—usually four or five hours—established by the bar.

9. To perceive these arrangements as anomalous risks reaffirming marginality by locating it outside of established labour practices. In fact, in the way it is organized, stripping is comparable with the non-stigmatized service occupation of realty. Like strippers, real estate agents are in such a paradoxical relation to their "employers" that the term is hardly appropriate. Realtors are actively recruited by brokers; they are hired, and they can be fired. But since they receive no direct financial remuneration for their labour from their employer, the relationship is nuanced. In exchange for legal protection and access to the necessary legitimizing context (including the use of the name, licence, and insurance), means of production (phone services, office space, and technical support), the realtor commits her/himself to a particular brokerage firm (including providing "free" labour staffing the office).

10. There was a particular irony here. While the dominant discourse increasingly defines stripping as immoral, the clubs and workers are becoming progressively more committed to respectability: "they think of it as a business now, y'know, the newer generation; it's more like a business instead of just the stereotyped thing that people used to do. The girls are keeping their money. A lot less drugs" (Rachel). Furthermore, young women from the rough working class, who wear the markers with pride, are being marginalized within the industry. It is precisely these women whose employment options are restricted and who are the most exploited population of workers.

11. Her agency is noteworthy. Far from being solely an object of the male gaze, it is the dancer who establishes the interaction with the audience and determines the pace, actions, and movement of the show. The audience's reading of her sexualized form does not erase her authorship. We see this clearly when a dancer enacts a fine parody as she plays with her own and her audience's sexuality, although she is usually quite careful, given the economic-power dynamic, not to let the audience in on the joke.

12. While not all working-class jobs are manual, physically challenging jobs are overwhelmingly working class. Consequently, the labour sold frequently has a socially unacknowledged (though recognized by the wage-labourers themselves) youth imperative and uncompensated costs in terms of health and well-being (Dunk, 1991; Houtman and Kompier, 1995:221).

13. These include bringing their own towels to sit on and sometimes their own cleaning materials.

14. In addition, creating an erotic persona necessitates countless hours of labour in appearance, clothes, make-up, and sometimes tanning salons or plastic surgeries.

15. Hochschild (1983) argues that rather than simply selling her mental and physical labour, the modern service workers must now engage in emotional labour. This requires the worker, in exchange for a wage, to "induce or suppress feeling in order to sustain the outward countenance that produces the proper state of mind in others" (1983:7) and engage in "deep acting" by re-creating personal experiences in a commercial setting. Such a worker must manage her feelings not just for private social relations (which we all do), but as a commodity to benefit the corporation that pays her wage. The process, which requires her to transform her smile into a sincere smile, cannot avoid creating a sense of alienation from feelings (Hochschild, 1983:21).

16. It is possible that capitalism is responding to the market and exploiting men's insecurity in the changing gender relations that characterize the latter half of the twentieth century. With the erosion of male power that "is based on the compliance of women and the economic and emotional services which women provided" (Giddens, 1992:132), men struggle with the new expectations and their own need for intimacy (Giddens, 1992:180).

17. For dancers "role overload," identified as a key contributor to workplace stress (Levi et al., 1986:55), is normal. Dancers have to constantly negotiate two separate, sometimes conflicting, jobs during their work day. The quasi-contractual obligation of the stripper is to perform strip-tease shows and "hang out"—"looking like a hooker" (Debbie)—tasks for which she receives not a paycheck but the opportunity to "make her money"; that is, to take the chance to utilize the profitable skills of soliciting and playing the game. Her job not only requires her to fulfill a number of roles at the same time but also to continually manage the emotional and sexual demands of patrons. She must try to maximize her income while simultaneously engaging in boundary maintenance to protect her emotional and physical space. In addition dancers are subject to the stress shared by other labourers engaged in emotional work (Adelmann, 1995:372) as well as the particular stressors shared by entertainers—performance anxiety and a fear of even minor physical injury that can effectively curtail their career (Sternbach, 1995): "I can't work with black eyes, I can't work with big scars across my face" (Jessie).

18. These prices were in effect in 1999.

19. These prices were in effect in 1999.

20. Of course other occupations are also stigmatized—morticians, custodians, and used car salespeople, to name a few.

21. It is also a "sticky" stigma infecting those around the dancer as well (Goffman, 1963:30), so that her family may be, or may perceive themselves to be, stigmatized. Certainly, those who share her labour site are. It is also sticky in the sense of enduring even after participation in the industry has ceased. The almost inevitable linguistic designation of ex-strippers in the media speaks to an understanding that participation in the trades legitimates continued assumptions of immorality.

22. In 2001 there is considerable provincial disparity. Some municipalities, such as London and Kitchener, require clubs, but not attendants, to purchase licences. In municipalities that continue to licence dancers, costs can be quite high. In Windsor, dancers must pay $225 plus administration and photo fees annually.

23. For a more detailed discussion of this regulation, see Bruckert and Dufresne (2002).

References

Adkins, L. (1992). "Sexual Work and the Employment of Women in the Service Industries." In M. Savage and A. Witz (Eds.), *Gender and bureaucracy*. Oxford: Blackwell.

Adelmann, P. (1995). "Emotional Labour as a Potential Source of Job Stress." In S. Sauter and L. Murphy (Eds.), *Organizational Risk Factors for Job Stress*. Washington: American Psychological Association.

Braverman, H. (1974). *Labour and Monopoly Capital: The Degradation of Work in the Twentieth Century*. New York: Monthly Review Press.

Bruckert, C. (2002). *Taking it off, Putting it on: Women in the Strip Trade*. Toronto: Women's Press.

Bruckert, C. and Dufresne, M. (2002). Re-configuring the Margins: Tracing the Regulatory Context of Ottawa Strip Clubs. *Canadian Journal of Law and Society* (forthcoming).

Canada. (1998). *Pocket Criminal Code*. Scarborough, ON: Carswell.

DERA. (2001). Mission statement. Ottawa: Dancers Equal Rights Association of Ottawa Carleton. (n.p.)

Duffy, A. and Pupo, N. (1997). *Part-Time Paradox*. Toronto: McClelland and Stewart.

Dunk, T. (1991). *It's a Working Man's Town: Male Working Class Culture in Northwestern Ontario*. Montreal: McGill-Queen's University Press.

Gaskell, J. (1986). "Conceptions of Skill and Work of Women: Some Historical and Political Issues." In R. Hamilton & M. Barrett (Eds.), *The Politics of Diversity: Feminism, Marxism and Nationalism*. London: Verso.

Giddens, A. (1992). *The Transformation of Intimacy*. Palo Alto, CA: Stanford University Press.

Goffman, E. (1959). *The Presentation of Self in Everyday Life*. New York: Doubleday.

———. (1963). *Stigma*. Upper Saddle River, NJ: Prentice Hall.

Henry, W. and Sims, J. (1970). "Actors' Search for a Self." *Trans-Action* 7, 11.

Hochschild, A. (1983). *The Managed Heart: Commercialization of Human Feeling*. Berkeley, CA: University of California Press.

Houtman, I. and Kompier, M. (1995). "Risk Factors and Occupational Risk Groups for Work Stress in the Netherlands." In S. Sauter and L. Murphy (Eds.), *Organizational Risk Factors for Job Stress*. Washington: American Psychological Association.

Levi, L., Frankenhauser, M. and Gardell, B. (1986). "The Characteristics of the Workplace and the Nature of its Social Demands." In S. Wolf and A. Finestone (Eds.), *Occupational Stress: Health and Performance at Work*. Littleton, MA: PSG Publishing.

Luxton, M. and Corman, J. (2001). *Getting by in Hard Times: Gendered Labour at Home and on the Job*. Toronto: University of Toronto Press.

Ontario Government. (1973). "An Act to Amend the Liquor Licence Act." (Chapter 68, 69). *Statutes of the Province of Ontario*. Toronto: Thatcher.

Ontario Ministry of Labour (1995). *Occupational Health and Safety Act*. Toronto: Ministry of Labour.

Phillips, P. (1997). "Labour in the New Canadian Political Economy." In W. Clement (Ed.), *Understanding Canada: Building the New Canadian Political Economy*. Montreal: McGill-Queen's University Press.

Polsky, N. (1969). *Hustlers, Beats and Others*. Garden City, NJ: Anchor Press.

Pringle, R. (1988). *Secretaries Talk*. London: Verso.

Reiter, E. (1991). *Making Fast Food*. Montreal: McGill-Queen's University Press.

Rinehart, J. (1996). *The Tyranny of Work: Alienation and the Labour Process*. 3rd ed. Toronto: Harcourt Brace.

Sternbach, D. (1995). "Musicians: A Neglected Working Population in Crisis." In S. Sauter and L. Murphy (Eds.), *Organizational Risk Factors for Job Stress*. Washington: American Psychological Association.

Sundahl, D. (1987). "Stripper." In F. Delacosta and P. Alexander (Eds.) *Sex Work*. Pittsburgh, PA: Cleis Press.

In the Matter of "X":
Building "Race" into Sexual Harassment

Himani Bannerji

In the summer of 1992, I received a call from a law firm to work as an expert witness for a complaint of sexual harassment of a woman. There was a problem, however, to consider and to accommodate. She was not just a "woman" undergoing the usual sexual harassment common in workplaces, but she was a "black woman." How could we build that fact of blackness into the case so that we could say that racism was an integral part of the sexual harassment which she underwent? We knew that there were three oppressions (among others) at work in Canadian society—namely, racism, sexism, and classism—and that X's experience included all; but how were we to think of these oppressions in such a way that we could show her harassment as a composite or a crystallized form of both?

I decided to work on the case because X's oppression enraged me, and also offered a political and an analytical challenge. How to think of gender, race, and class in terms of what is called "intersectionality," that is, in terms of their interactiveness, their ways of mutually constructing or reinforcing each other, is a project that is still in the process of being worked out. Somehow, we know almost instinctively that these oppressions, separately named as sexism, racism, and class exploitation, are intimately connected. But when it comes

to showing how, it is always difficult, and strains the capacity of our conventional ways of speaking on such matters. And, if abstract theorization is partially possible, the concrete uncovering of how they actually work continues to have an elusive quality to it. The case of X is one of innumerable experiences of its kind, in varying degrees of intensity and complexity, which mark lives of black women in the West. Here the West means the US and Canada, but it includes Britain and other European countries as well. For that reason also, it was a challenge to think through a problem which exists within such a wide scope.

A Brief Outline of the Case

(outline provided by the firm of Cornish and Roland)

It is useful at the outset to specify who X is, though very briefly and mainly in terms of her work trajectory. But this offers some of the particulars with regard to which I tried to understand how she was specifically sexually harassed as a black woman. The following are some of the facts put forward as a part of the submissions of the claimant X.

Job Progression:

1. X is a 45-year-old black woman and sole-support mother.
2. X began working for Y company in 1980 on the assembly lines, first as a packer for detergent, then shampoo, then toothpaste, and finally soap. These jobs were classified as "light" and were predominantly female.
3. The work force at Y was predominantly white; also, to the best of X's knowledge, she was one of only two black female employees in the production area of the factory.
4. Towards the end of 1983 or the beginning of 1984, X applied for and was promoted to the position of packer "heavy-duty" in the soap department. "Heavy" jobs were historically performed exclusively by men and were performed in an area that was physically separated from the area in which X had previously been working. X was the only woman employed in that area. She was also one of very few visible minority employees in the area.
5. In mid-1984, X was again promoted—this time to "utility," a job demanding greater skill. She was required to learn how to trouble-shoot on the line and to drive a forklift, to obtain supplies for the line, and replace the operator for breaks and lunch. This job was also within the "heavy" tasks area and had been exclusively performed by men; X was the only woman employed in this capacity.
6. X was next transferred to "mills" as a prerequisite for promotion to the "operator" position within the heavy tasks area. In this area she mainly worked alone mixing soap for the assembly lines.
7. As an operator, X was responsible for overseeing a packing line operation. This included the requirement to work in a "lead hand" type of relationship with the utility and packer. The position required her to follow written instructions, document mechanical problems, and master the new vocabulary specific to the job. In addition, X was required to have a more in-depth knowledge of the operation and equipment on the line in order to adjust and trouble shoot its operation. Her performance would essentially be judged by the rate at which her line could maintain production; to do so, X required a high level of cooperation from her male co-workers who filled the packer and utility positions on her line.

    (Submissions of the Claimant "X," nos. 1–7)

X's experience of harassment at the workplace was extensive and ranged from job sabotages to being subjected to various obscenities. They may be summed up as:

a. active sabotage of the work for which she was responsible,
b. discriminatory treatment with respect to training and work assistance by senior co-workers,
c. forced exposure to hostile material, which denigrated both her race and sex, placed at and near her work station,
d. social isolation and ostracism by co-workers,
e. public pejorative name-calling and sexually and racially derogatory remarks.

    (Submissions, p. 2)

Particular details of this conduct, randomly selected by me, include the following:

11. ... X was subjected to adverse treatment: the white female lead hands would run the line she was packing at an unusually high speed, would damage her locker and referred to her publicly as "a fucking bitch."
12. Although X complained to management, the behaviour was allowed to continue. Further, when

her co-workers threatened to have her fired and complained about her to the foreman, she was transferred out of the area to the soap department.

19. Co-workers created an environment that was hostile to her gender and race. Pictures of "Sunshine Girls" [barely clothed women consistently featured on the third page of *The Toronto Sun*] were displayed in her work area. When X complained, the co-workers were told to remove them, but they refused. Despite the workers' insubordination, no action was taken against them. Note, however, that when white women walked through the area, the posters were taken down and hidden. X also heard racially derogatory comments directed at a Filipino male worker: She herself was repeatedly referred to as a "bitch."

21. ... Obscene pictures were left at her work station and in her toolbox. One was a hand drawn sketch in which a black woman was giving a "blow job" to a white man. Another was a picture also hand drawn of a black woman giving a white man a "hand job" while a gang of white men stood in line for their turn. X was repeatedly referred to as "a fucking bitch" and "cunt." One worker went so far as to throw a bar of soap at her, which hit her on her head; though her foreman was nearby, he did nothing. On one occasion, she went out to lunch with a male co-worker, the co-worker was asked on his return whether X had "fucked" him in the parking lot.
(Submissions, nos. 11, 12, 19, 21)

Though X remains anonymous in terms of her personal identity, these details allow us to imagine her more concretely.

*****

Reading X's Case

When the packer and utility finally returned, X attempted, for the second time, to start up the line. When she moved around in position to see whether the packer and utility were at work, she saw a group of white male employees standing around the line looking toward her. At that point she noticed that someone had placed a twelve inch long, bright green, *Irish Spring* soap carving of a penis with white foam at its tip, on the assembly line where X would be forced to see it.

The carving remained on the line for 30–45 minutes in full view of X and the group of white male co-workers who hovered around jeering and staring at X .... X recognized the incident to be not only humiliating and isolating, but a threat.
(Submissions, nos. 29, 30)

My reading of the case of X begins with this incident of the carved penis. In a history of incidents all of which amounted to small or big acts of harassment, this marks the culmination point. This event and her reaction to it must be seen as both a personal experience and a social moment, neither of which can be understood without an examination of her workplace. Her workplace, similar to others, cannot be seen only as a place of economic production, but must also be understood as a coherent social and cultural environment which is organized through known and predictable social relations, practices, cultural norms, and expectations. What happens in this environment, which is daily and highly regulated, cannot just be treated as random or unpredictable behaviour. As we shall see from the general pattern of her harassment (as submitted in X's complaint) there was nothing random about the carved penis incident.

This incident marked the moment of X's ultimate humiliation, where not only was she forced to see this repugnant object, but also to provide a spectacle for others in doing so. As we see from the submissions, X felt this to be not a joke, but rather an act of violence against her and a threat. In a manner of speaking it is in its intensity and singularity an archetypal experience, and it highlights for the reader the real quality of her six-year work life in this company. The perspective which I have introduced in the beginning of this essay is the lens through which we can now view X's work life and her workplace.

Let us begin with the organization and "race" composition of her workplace. It is significant for our purpose that X worked in an almost all-white workplace. When she worked in the women's section there was, to the best of her knowledge, only one other non-white woman working on the same floor with her. There were approximately fifty white women working with her. When she moved into the men's section not only were there were no women there, but the one or two non-white men who existed, appeared, and disappeared among a male white work force of about a dozen. This workplace (as in other industrial concerns) was divided in men's and women's, "heavy" and "light" labour sections, respectively. As a whole, then, the "normal" atmosphere was white, where the absence or exclusion of non-white people was nothing out of the ordinary.

This recognition of the "normal" character of her workplace allows us to treat her experience there as a piece of everyday life, which then needs to be broken down, or deconstructed to reveal a whole range of socio-cultural forces which play themselves out through forms of behaviour which can be called "harassment" (sexual or not). This deconstructive analytical method, which takes daily incidents apart, at the same time helps to situate or locate an event within its social space, within a matrix of social relations. Feminist sociology has often taken recourse to it. The work of Dorothy E. Smith, for

example, may be especially looked into for a clear idea of how such a situating critique might be put together. In this framework, a worker's or any person's experience is not seen just as her own, but as a possible experience with particular variations of all similar workers or persons within that setting and context. Similarly, the social and cultural relations of any particular workplace can be assessed as ongoing and unfolding social and cultural processes, practices and values present in the society as a whole. This is to treat "power" as a "concrete" social form and relation with a specific history and locale—not as an abstract concept, and this is the only way to point out the systemic socio-structural and historical aspects of sexism or racism. This moves our understanding of oppression from intentionality (good/bad people story) to a more fundamental notion of social organization, where such experiences are routinely possible because they are intrinsic to the properties of certain organizations.

This helps us to take the next step, to locate the characteristics of the workplace within the broader Canadian society. We need to show that the workplace displays characteristics which exist in the everyday Canadian world. Therefore, *individual* behaviour, workplace relations, daily life within its precincts all come within the purview of *social behaviour* and greater social and economic forces. Thus, X's work life, for example, cannot be fully understood outside of the general pattern of Canadian labour importation, labour market, labour process, and workplace. We have to consider which community works where, how, at what, and the reasons for doing so. A comparative study of work and workplaces brings this out clearly, as do cases brought to the labour and management mediating bodies, of peer behaviour brought to the personnel offices or the unions.

The socialization and organization of behaviour and social pattern and organization of workplaces and so on in terms of "race," gender, and class require an understanding of Canadian history. Issues of colonialism, indentured labour, and ethnicized immigration history need to be brought into view. Numerous studies in state or class formation in Canada provide an understanding for who become the working class, who is allowed to work here, at what jobs and wages, and what are the general socio-economic expectations from non-white immigrants. This essay will refer to this historical dimension only in so far as it speaks to this particular case and the present time in Canadian labour organization and economy. This means a broad overview of non-white, especially non-white women's, labour in Canada, and a study of the role played by the Canadian State (immigration policies and so on), which has constructed and manipulated notions such as "race" and ethnicity through its policy making and administrative procedures. Sometimes, more than others, the state has been explicit about this.

Finally, we must address daily cultural practices and everyday common sense perceptions of groups of people living in Canada regarding each other. They are connected with a historical popular consciousness and the creation of social meanings regarding different types of people. This extends to both their physical and cultural characteristics, giving rise to normative conventions and stereotypes which have powerful and daily socio-economic and political consequences. These stereotypes indicate something about the expected physical presences and absences of certain groups of people within any given social space. Sexual division of labour or gender roles express precisely this meaningful location of bodies and their physical functions within assigned social spaces or boundaries. Thus, for example, the female body is stereotypically conceived within a so-called private space (home) and the male in a public one (workplace). The former (supposedly) belongs to the world of reproduction (social and biological), the latter to that of production (economic and intellectual). The factual and actual presences of women in the public sphere has always been undercut by this ideological construction of the "two spheres" and cultural and moral assumptions and behaviour appropriate to that division. This has had dire personal and economic consequences for all women and has been the centre of debates regarding women in "non-traditional" jobs, or the value of housework.

*****

References

Aggarwal, Arjun. "Characteristics of Sexual Harassment." In *Sexual Harassment in the Workplace*. Toronto: Butterworths, 1972.

Armstrong, Frederick. "Ethnicity and the Formation of the Ontario Establishment." In *Ethnic Canada: Identities and Inequalities*, edited by L. Driedger. Toronto: Copp Clark Pitman, 1987.

Armstrong, Pat, and Hugh Armstrong. *The Double Ghetto: Canadian Women and their Segregated Work*. Toronto: McClelland and Stewart, 1984.

Bannerji, Himani, ed. *Returning the Gaze: Essays on Racism, Feminism and Politics*. Toronto: Sister Vision Press, 1993.

Brand, Dionne, and Krisantha Sri Bhaggiyadatta. *Rivers Have Sources, Trees Have Roots: Speaking of Racism*. Toronto: Cross Cultural Communications Centre, 1986.

Brittan, Arthur, and Mary Maynard. *Sexism, Racism and Oppression*. Oxford: Blackwell, 1984.

Centre for Contemporary Cultural Studies at Birmingham University. *The Empire Strikes Back Race and Racism in 70's Britain*. London: Hutchinson, 1982.

Chan, Anthony. *The Gold Mountain: The Chinese in the New World*. Vancouver: New Star Books, 1983.

Connelly, Patricia. *Last Hired, First Fired: Women and the Canadian Work Force*. Toronto: Women's Press, 1978.

Coverdale-Sumrall, Amber, and Dena Taylor, eds. *Sexual Harassment: Women Speak Out*. Freedom, CA: The Crossing Press, 1992.

Crenshaw, Kimberle. "Demarginalizing the Intersection of Race and Sex: A Black Feminist Critique of Antidiscrimination Doctrine, Feminist Theory and Antiracist Politics." In *The University of Chicago Legal Forum*. Chicago: University of Chicago Law School, 1989.

Davis, Angela Y. *Women, Race and Class*. New York: Vintage, 1983.

Estable, Alma. "Immigrant Women in Canada, Current Issues." A background paper prepared for the Canadian Advisory Council on the Status of Women, March 1986.

Gaskell, Jane. "Conceptions of Skill and the Work of Women: Some Historical and Political Issues." In *The Politics of Diversity*, edited by Roberta Hamilton and Michèle Barrett. Montreal: Book Centre, 1986.

Gates, Henry Louis, Jr., ed. *"Race," Writing and Difference*. Chicago: University of Chicago Press, 1986.

Government of Canada. *From Awareness to Action: Strategies to Stop Sexual Harassment in the Workplace*. Compiled and edited by Linda Geller-Schwartz. Ottawa: Women's Bureau of Human Resources Development Canada, 1994.

hooks, bell. *Ain't I A Woman: Black Women and Feminism*. Boston: South End Press, 1981.

Hurtado, Aida. "Relating to Privilege: Seduction and Rejection in the Subordination of White Women and Women of Color." *SIGNS: Journal of Women in Culture and Society* vol. 14 (1989).

Juteau-Lee, Danielle, and Barbara Roberts. "Ethnicity and Femininity: (d')après nos experiences." *Canadian Ethnic Studies* vol. 13, no. 1 (1981).

Law Union of Ontario. *The Immigrant's Handbook: A Critical Guide*. Montreal: Black Rose Books, 1981.

Mitter, Swasti. *Common Fate, Common Bond: Women in the Global Economy*. London: Pluto Press, 1986.

Nain, Gemma Tang. "Black Women, Sexism and Racism: Black or Antiracist Feminism?" *Feminist Review* 37 (1991).

Ng, Roxana. "Immigrant Women and Institutionalized Racism." In *Changing Patterns: Women in Canada*, edited by Sandra Burt et al. Toronto: McClelland and Stewart, 1988.

_____. "The Social Construction of 'Immigrant Women' in Canada." In *The Politics of Diversity*, edited by Roberta Hamilton and Michèle Barrett. Montreal: Book Centre, 1986.

Ontario Human Rights Commission. "Racial Slurs, Jokes and Harassment—Policy Statement and Guidelines." Reprinted in *Currents: Readings in Race Relations* vol. 6, no. 1 (1990).

Silvera, Makeda. *Silenced*. Toronto: Williams-Wallace, 1983.

Singh, B., and Peter Li. *Racial Oppression in Canada*. Toronto: Garamond Press, 1985.

Smith, Althea, and Abigail Stewart. "Approaches to Studying Racism and Sexism in Black Women's Lives." *Journal of Social Issues* 39 (1983).

Smith, Dorothy E. "Feminist Reflections on Political Economy." Paper presented at the Annual Meeting of Political Science and Political Economy, Learned Societies Meetings, Hamilton, June 1987.

Submissions of the Claimant X, prepared by the office of Cornish and Associates, on behalf of the worker, to the Workers' Compensation Board, Claim # B15878672T.

Wallace, Michele. *Black Macho and the Myth of the Superwoman*. New York: Dial Press, 1979.

SECTION SIX

THE CLASSROOM

Privileging Agency and Organizing: A New Approach for Women's Studies

Linda Briskin[*]

W omen have a long and remarkable history of organizing to resist oppression, expand their rights as women and citizens, protect their families and communities, defend traditional values, and change their societies. They have organized in, through, and sometimes against revolutionary, nationalist, and transnational movements; unions, autonomous women's movements, and mainstream political institutions; states, schools, workplaces, communities, and religious institutions; public and private spaces; and issues and identities. Too often, however, women's studies programmes have not highlighted this organizing. Where once it might have been difficult to mount courses on women's organizing given the lack of documentation and scholarship, this is no longer the case. The last decade has seen an explosion of publication in this area.[2]

I now teach both a graduate and undergraduate course on Women Organizing in the School of Women's Studies at York University in Toronto.[3] Initially I was prompted to introduce the undergraduate course because of inadequate background on women's organizing among the students in my fourth-year Feminist Theory class.

Without this kind of preparation, students found it difficult to contextualize theoretical works, and to assess theory in relationship to its implications (often buried) for making change. Now I believe that such courses can revitalize our women's studies programmes. Not only do they inspire and challenge students, but they offer a unique and accessible entry into current debates in feminist theory.

In the first instance, the study of women's organizing challenges students' political pessimism. The enormous gains that have resulted from women's organizing help to clarify the dialectic between agency and structure (Wharton 1991). What women have been able to accomplish even within terrible constraints resonates with Marx's comment that humans make history but not in circumstances of their own choosing.[4] Students come to understand that some degree of agency is always possible, and that resistance re-configures constraints.

One remarkable example is the Self-Employed Women's Association (SEWA) in India. The great majority of working women in India—ninety-four per cent—are self-employed, eking out marginal livelihoods as small-

---

* Originally published as "Women's Organizing: A Gateway to a New Approach for Women's Studies" in *Atlantis* 26:2 (Spring/ Summer 2002). Online at www.msvu.ca/atlantis.

scale vendors selling food, household goods, garments; home-based producers such as weavers, milk producers, handicraft producers; and labourers selling their services or labour including agricultural and construction workers, cooks, and cleaners. For these workers, conventional forms of trade unionism are not possible. Yet SEWA began in 1972 as a trade union of self-employed women, drawing on Gandhi's notion that a union should cover all aspects of workers' lives, both in the factory and at home. Not only does SEWA endorse trade unionism, it also organizes co-operatives as a vehicle to develop alternative economic systems through which workers control what they produce. SEWA's membership has grown from 6000 in 1981 to 46,000 in 1994; and from one co-operative to 40 (Jhabvala 1994). SEWA's inspiring success demonstrates to students that even the most vulnerable of women workers can organize effectively, and reminds those of us from the North how much we can learn from women in the South.

The wealth and breadth of women's organizing, some feminist, some not, also re-positions activism from a marginal to a mainstream activity. For those students who have internalized negative stereotypes of feminists, activists, and organizing, this represents an important shift. Engagement with this material also helps students to redefine their perceptions of what constitutes politics, and to deconstruct those ideologies which confine the political to the electoral. They can then recognize that "not being political," a stance many of them claim with a certain vigour, does not represent neutrality; in fact, nothing is outside the political or innocent of it. This process encourages students to understand themselves as political actors.

Second, women's studies courses undoubtedly function as a vehicle for consciousness raising (CR). Liz Kelly, Jill Radford, and Joan Scanlon (2000) argue that, in the UK, as the numbers of women's groups and popular publications have decreased, "academic women's studies is becoming the primary route of access to knowledge about and potential involvement in the women's movement"(9). I suspect there is a lot of truth in this statement in the Canadian context, especially for young women.

Out of the second wave CR process came an important insight: the personal is political. Although there have been a variety of interpretations of this slogan, a consensus emerged then that the problems women faced were political and social, not individual. Undoubtedly, this insight helped to inspire action-oriented political groups (Adamson, Briskin, and McPhail 1988). Although we need to problematize a focus on personal experience, self disclosure and "opinions" in an academic context (see Briskin 1998), women's studies classes do function, to some extent, like the CR groups of the second wave. However, unlike CR groups, they are not usually designed to stimulate the transformation of personal insight into political activity. The study of women's organizing is one curricular response to encourage this trajectory.

Third, although the study of women's organizing does not focus solely on organizing for women's rights,[5] students are often shocked to discover how much they have taken for granted about their liberal citizenship rights: about access to abortion, the right to vote, to own property, to control their own wages, to go to medical school, to have custody of their children. These revelations open up a useful discussion about the citizenship rights currently under attack and serve to problematize ideas about "progress."

Students often internalize the naturalization of progress: the commonsense belief in a linear movement towards equality. An ideology that things will naturally get better makes social justice organizing seem less necessary and less acceptable. The history of women's organizing demonstrates a much more contradictory movement toward improvement for women and challenges students' assumptions that what has been won is protected. It also helps students understand the postmodern challenge to teleological views of history and grand narratives such as "progress." Deconstructing "progress" highlights its fragility and simultaneously the importance of women's agency. A more positive future is possible but not inevitable. Only through individual and collective struggle will it happen.

Once progress is interrogated it is also possible to take on the "ethics of progress" embedded in modernist assumptions, for example, "the implication that countries that are more economically developed (in the sense of capitalist markets) are, for that very reason, farther along the path to the rational human ideal of progress and equality than other countries. This suggests that a paternalistic relationship between Northern and Southern countries is ethically justified" (Ferguson 1998, 97). Such paternalism (or maternalism) prompts a missionary attitude among students expressed in the desire to rescue Third World women, and simultaneously in a refusal to problematize the role of the North in producing the economic conditions in the South (Hase 2001).

Fourth, the literature on women's organizing helps students to envision alternatives to the current economic and political configurations. Dominant ideologies encourage students to feel that what exists is natural and as a result, no alternatives are possible. At the same time, at least one thread of students' discomfort with feminism is a concern that feminisms criticize without positive and hopeful alternatives. I continue to have great success using Marge Piercy's novel *Woman on the Edge of Time*. Students have also been excited by the historical work of Dolores Hayden (1984), Barbara Taylor (1983), and Meredith Tax (1980), and contemporary accounts of women's success (see, for example, Krauss 1998; Kemp 1995; Rowbotham and Mitter 1994; and Swerdlow 1989). In particular, the material on international and transnational organizing (discussed in more detail below) furnishes encouraging examples of working across complex differences (see, for example, Moghadam 2000; Christiansen-Ruffman 1996; Day 1996).

The innovative results of women's organizing challenge student resignation and make visible the "naturalism," which implies inevitability about social organization. Indeed, students make the link to the naturalization of the marketplace and then dispute the arguments that interventions into the market (for example, minimum wage laws, pay equity, employment equity) will disturb its natural workings.

Fifth, such courses help to problematize students' concerns about the lack of "unity" in the women's movement. The study of women's participation in large-scale "homogenous" movements (the strategic expression of unity) such as male-dominated unions, socialist, nationalist, or revolutionary movements graphically illustrates the way that such structures often disadvantage marginal voices. Although there is an indisputable (although abstract) attraction to bringing everyone together in one large movement, examining the contexts in which women are most empowered helps students to see the importance of the local. Local organizing, what students might see as "fragmentation," may provide the basis for coalition work in which such groups come together from positions of strength, preserving their particular voices while undertaking joint initiatives. Such coalitions and alliances offer an alternative paradigm to large-scale homogenous movements.

Sixth, courses on women's organizing provide a small laboratory in which to examine some of the issues that are raised in course material: about organizational strategies, dealing with diversity, and enhancing inclusivity and democracy. Linking these debates directly to classroom practices provides important learning moments.

Finally, the study of women's organizing demonstrates the relevance of some often inaccessible debates in feminist theory, for example, about fluid identities, feminism as process, and contextual and historical analysis. Below I explore four ways of examining women's organizing that provide an entry point into theory: the disaggregation of women's organizing and feminist organizing; the emphasis on context and strategic relativism; the move from identity politics to strategic alliances, and the construction of identities through coalition and negotiation; and the differentiation of international, global, and transnational organizing.

Disaggregating Women's Organizing and Feminist Organizing

Focusing on women's organizing rather than feminist organizing opens up space to study the considerable range of women's organizing that is not identified with feminisms (such as nationalist, maternalist, revolutionary, and social justice organizing) or is explicitly anti-feminist. It problematizes relationships rather than making *a priori* assumptions.

Such an approach resists the reification of feminisms. It allows the relationship between women's organizing and feminisms as ideologies, strategies, analyses, organizing practices, visionary alternatives, and complex self-identifications and identities to be interrogated. Feminisms emerge, then, not as abstract criteria or boundary markers against which women's organizing is assessed but as a fluid, contextually located set of meanings and practices. Feminisms are sites of struggle, moments of resistance, organizing tools; they help produce communities of interest but also patterns of exclusion.

Investigating rather than assuming the relationship between women's organizing and feminism is essential for exploring third world contexts. Such interrogation engages critiques of "western feminism," and challenges Eurocentric and classist assumptions that the subject of study should be "women's" issues. Simultaneously, it helps resist tendencies to homogenize "western feminism," recognizing instead the multiplicity of feminisms struggling for voice in the west.

Ella Shohat suggests that

Eurocentric definitions of feminism have cast "third world" women into a fixed stereotypical role, in which they play the part of passive victims lacking any form of agency. Within standard feminist historiography, for example, "third world women's" involvement in anticolonialist struggles has not been perceived as relevant for feminism. Since the anticolonialist struggles of colonized women were not explicitly labelled "feminist," they have not been "read" as linked or as relevant to feminist studies .... Yet the participation of colonized women in anticolonialist and antiracist movements did often lead to a political engagement with feminism .... I have reread the activism of third-world women through the period of colonization and decolonization as a kind of subterranean, unrecognized form of feminism, and, therefore, as a legitimate part of feminist historiography (2001, 1269–70).

Like Shohat, I am concerned that, as part of the women's studies project, we engage with the struggles of colonized women and resist their re-victimization through ethnocentric scholarship. I, too, would argue that these struggles are "relevant to feminism." However, I would caution about labelling such organizing as "feminist" in order to legitimize it. In fact, such labelling may itself contribute to both the hegemony and reification of western feminism, and to the privileging of those forms of women's organizing which are named as feminist. Rather, Women's Studies needs to valorize the study of women's organizing in all its complex and variegated forms, and to problematize the relationship of such organizing to feminisms.

For students, this framework challenges essentialized views of feminisms. They often envision a programmatic feminism "out there" which they have to accept or reject. As feminisms are understood less as a program and more as a political process, students are more likely to define a feminism that makes sense to them and to write themselves into the project of developing feminisms.

Strategic Relativism

The study of women's organizing challenges abstract programmatic commitments to particular strategies and highlights the significance of strategic relativism. It emphasizes contextual analysis of particular strategies and introduces students to the difference between historical materialist and transhistorical approaches. One cogent example which helps to historicize their sense of strategy has to do with separate organizing. This example is worth exploring since women's studies students tend to have strong feelings that separate organizing for women is either the quintessentially correct or incorrect strategy, their views often dependent on their understanding of the category of "woman" and their analyses of women's oppression.

The example of struggles around separate schooling shifts their thinking considerably. In the nineteenth century, many progressive women argued fiercely against separate schooling for girls because, in that context, separate schooling was a way of limiting access; it was a discriminatory practice. Similarly during the civil rights movement in the USA, blacks argued for school integration and school busing. However, in the current context, there have been progressive initiatives around separate schooling for girls and for black-focused schools. Concomitant with such progressive innovations are calls for separate religious schools, and class-based schools. Undoubtedly, the meaning of separate schooling is subject to constant re-negotiation and is re-constituted through struggle and resistance.

An historical perspective, then, illuminates the difference between separate structures which arise in the context of imposed or forced segregation, and those which are chosen by women to articulate their concerns and strengthen their voices. Rather than producing

discrimination, the latter represent a strategy to address discrimination (Briskin 1999a).

Another vivid illustration of how separate organizing must be situated within economic and ideological contexts can be found in recent work comparing women's organizing in Swedish and Canadian unions. In Canada, separate organizing has been a central and effective strategy of union women. In Sweden, women have been reluctant to organize separately, especially through formal structures, inside or outside the unions. These different approaches reflect dominant ideologies about equality and gender. In Sweden, an emphasis on common interests between women and men (a gender-neutral approach), which has supported innovative family and labour market policies, also translates into a discomfort with difference and with separate organizing. In Canada, a focus on power imbalances and on diversity of region, language, gender, race, and ethnicity provides support for it (Briskin 1999).

Although organizing separately appears grounded in the abstract sameness/difference debate, students come to reject this essentialist reading in favour of a more strategic and historical one. Separate organizing is neither accepted nor rejected *a priori* as an appropriate strategy but is subjected to a conjunctural and contextual assessment of its viability. Separate organizing, then, is not an ahistorical or static principle but one negotiated and re-negotiated in historical circumstances.

Student concerns that this approach may suffer from a lack of "foundational" principles opens up a discussion about the complexity of political ethics and the problems with foundationalism. Ann Ferguson (1998) argues for an ethico-politics called a "modified empowerment paradigm," especially for Northern feminist researchers whose "reliance on universalist code ethics allows them to abstract from their own privileged position as constructors of knowledge" (104).

Even though feminist materialist ethics rejects a universalist and fixed approach to ethical values based on some unchanging "authentic" human nature, it does not follow that ethical values are entirely subjective or relative (98) .... Unlike the totally contextual ethics of Northern postmodern feminists,[6] however, the ethico-politics of such an approach insists on developing universal visions of social justice (for example, that women's rights are human rights), but doing so not by abstracting away local contexts (103).

Students come to see that contextual analysis forces them to make decisions about what constitutes an ethical political position, and simultaneously an appropriate strategy in each particular instance. Such a process demonstrably increases individual and collective agency.

Identity Politics Versus Strategic Alliances

Examining diversity, identity, and coalition politics through the study of women's organizing poses a challenge to the politics of victimization, the romanticized commitments to sisterhood often expressed by undergraduate women's studies students, and the strategic paralysis sometimes effected by identity politics.

Despite their acknowledgement of differences, by and large, my undergraduate students remain hopefully committed to the idea of unity and common cause among women. Many embrace sisterhood as an alternative to individualism and the consumerist promotion of bodily competition among women. Their study of organizing, however, brings them up against the limits of unproblematized essentialized notions of sisterhood. At the same time, the practice of women's organizing offers up alternative visions of working across difference and negotiating alliances, and helps students nuance their strategic thinking.

Such study highlights the relevance of postmodern theorizing about identity to effective coalition politics.

Theorizing the practices of diversity means recognizing, on the one hand, that gender, class, race, ability, and sexuality influence organizational strategies and political perspectives; on the other hand, these identities are not stable, mutually exclusive, or comparable in a hierarchy of oppression. Liberatory postmodern theories concerned with political strategy provide a lens for this discussion in their decentring of the search for coherence, linearity, and generality and their refocusing on specificity, locality, and multiplicity.

Students find the concept of fluid identities counter-intuitive to their commonsense and often-deeply internalized notions of essentialist personalities and universalized identities. This way of thinking is made accessible through the study of organizing which demonstrates that in strategic contexts, the meaning of identities is not fixed but relationally constituted and always negotiated. Identities are not fixed barriers to alliances nor do common identities guarantee alliances; rather alliances are negotiated in practice, always fraught yet always possible.

Writing about South African feminism, Amanda Kemp et al. uses the term "strategic alliances" to describe this process: "Black women understand that they need to make strategic alliances, recognizing that these alliances may be temporary and limited to particular common interests rather than built on assumed, ongoing sisterhood. Further, these interests are fluid, and struggle over their validity across class or race lines will help deepen our solidarity and strengthen our position" (1995, 143).

Undoubtedly the most successful text that I have found for working with these ideas is Cynthia Cockburn's remarkable *The Space between Us* (1998) in which she describes her involvement in three women's projects which have struggled to co-operate across conflict: in Northern Ireland, Israel/Palestine, and Bosnia/Hercegovina. This book combines a complex analysis of collective identities, nationalism, and democracy with the study of the practices of women's organizing.

She examines the often coercive and always essentializing nature of collective identities in nationalist struggles:

> Many (sometimes it seems most) identity processes are coercive. We are labelled, named, known by identities that confine us, regulate us and reduce our complexity. The subtleties in our sense of self are difficult to convey in the terms available to us. We often feel misunderstood and misrepresented. And these processes are the more painful because they exploit our irreducible need to belong, our happiness in belonging (216).

The struggle of these women's groups around coerced identities makes understandable the notion that an individual's sense of self is "a production, which is never complete, always in process" (Cockburn 1998 quoting Stuart Hall, 212). Cockburn's study emphasizes that

> collective identities, such as gender and national identities, no matter in how essentialist a form they are dressed by politically interested parties, actually [are] lived by individuals as changeable and unpredictable. And the way they take shape and change is relational. In other words, there is no thinkable specification of selfhood that does not have reference to other people, known or imagined (212).

In these three conflict-ridden situations alliances are built through negotiation and are not based on abstract identity positionings. The women struggle with what Cockburn calls the "non-closure on identity":

> They do not essentialize identities and therefore do not predict what might flow from them. They are unusually willing to wait and see, to believe there may be many ways of living, for example, a Protestant identity .... [T]hey avoid ascribing thoughts or motivations or qualities to others on the basis of their ethnic or national label .... Likewise [they] will avoid ascribing collective guilt: you are not to be held accountable for everything done in your name. As the Medici women like to say ... "You judge people by what they do, not what they are" (225).

Identities as relational reveals the shifting realities of privilege and discrimination, highlights the importance of context and resists absolutes. The move away from absolutes shifts attention to processes rather than categories. Rather than race and gender, "racialization" and "genderization" capture the way in which the meanings of these identities are constantly being reshaped as a result of context, history, and struggle. Racialization is a process of defining the Other and simultaneously defining a dominant group. It makes visible political, social, and historical processes and rejects the significance of the inherently biological.[7]

Understanding identity "as something complex, ambiguous and shifting" (Cockburn 1998, 213) helps students to recognize the limits of essentialized notions of sisterhood and simultaneously highlights another strategic dilemma. In 1990 Ann Snitow talked about

> the common divide between the need to build the identity "woman" and give it a solid political meaning and the need to tear down the very category "woman" and dismantle its all-too-solid history .... [T]hough a constant choosing of sides is tactically unavoidable, feminists—and indeed most women—live in a complex relationship to this central feminist divide. From moment to moment we perform subtle psychological and social negotiations about how gendered we

choose to be. This tension—between needing to act as women and needing an identity not overdetermined by gender—is as old as Western feminism (9–10).

Linda Alcoff suggested combining "the concept of identity politics with a conception of the subject as positionality":

> We can conceive of the subject as nonessentialized and emergent from a historical experience and yet retain our political ability to take gender as an important point of departure. Thus we can say at one and the same time that gender is not natural, biological, universal, ahistorical, or essential and yet still claim that gender is relevant because we are taking gender as a position from which to act politically (1988, 433).

It is in organizing contexts that the tension between the non-essentialized subject and the significance of gender identities plays itself out strategically.[8] Undoubtedly, identity can be a powerful political tool: "gender" can mobilize even as gender is constituted relationally and contextually, and understood as a process. Cockburn grapples with these tensions. She seeks to understand how the women's groups "get around and above the immobilizing contradiction: between a dangerous belief in universal sisterhood and a relativist stress on difference that dooms us to division and fragmentation."[9] She draws on the notion of transversal politics articulated by Nira Yuval-Davis: "In 'transversal politics,' perceived unity, and homogeneity are replaced by dialogues which give recognition to the specific positionings of those who participate in them as well as to the 'unfinished knowledge' that each such situated positioning can offer .... The boundaries of a transversal

dialogue are determined by the message rather than the messenger" (Yuval-Davis quoted in Cockburn 1998, 9).

Cockburn argues finally for agonistic democracy which "breaks with the comfortable and dangerous illusion of 'community' and the politics of communitarianism, that assumes consensus is (must be) possible. Instead it settles for the difficult reality of unavoidable, unending, careful, respectful struggle" (216). This understanding of unavoidable respectful struggle not only offers students a vision of what is possible in troubled times but also underscores the ongoing agency involved in these negotiations.

Through the study of political practice, students can then make sense of Judith Butler's complex argument:

> The deconstruction of identity is not the deconstruction of politics; rather, it establishes as political the very terms through which identity is articulated. This kind of a critique brings into question the foundationalist frame in which feminism as an identity politics has been articulated. The internal paradox of this foundationalism is that it presumes, fixes, and constrains the very "subjects" that it hopes to represent and liberate (quoted in Martin 1992, 102).

Butler (1992) explains:

> We may be tempted to think that to assume the subject in advance is necessary to safeguard the agency of the subject. But to claim that subject is constituted is not to claim that it is determined; on the contrary, rather the constituted character of the subject is the very precondition of its agency (12) .... Paradoxically, it may be that only through releasing the category of women from a fixed referent that something like "agency" becomes possible (16).

In sharp contrast to my experience teaching these debates in a feminist theory class, in a course on organizing they are vivid and relevant. In this context, students simultaneously critique essentialized notions of sisterhood, reject "common experience" or "shared victimization" as the premises of unity, and embrace negotiated solidarities that recognize both diversities and the instability of identities. Solidarity is demonstrably built through struggle. Context, negotiation, and political agency become the central concepts.

International, Transnational, and Global Women's Organizing

Undoubtedly students find most exciting the new initiatives in international and transnational women's organizing. In these arenas, women are working strategically and often successfully across identity, region, and political differences. The teaching challenge is to deal with this material in ways that do not reinscribe a reconstituted conception of sisterhood, but facilitate students shifting from "romantic sisterhood" to "strategic sisterhood" (Agarwal, quoted in Tohidi 1996, 30).

Situating such organizing in its historical context is one useful strategy. Leila Rupp (1998) recounts the history of three first wave organizations: the International Council of Women founded in 1888, which by 1925, had 36 million members through National Councils of Women; the International Alliance of Women founded in 1904 to fight for suffrage; and the Women's International League for Peace and Freedom founded in 1915 (see also Stienstra 1994). Not surprisingly, the majority of the participants were elite white Christian women. Ruth Rosen (1998, 3) points out that this similarity of background "allowed them to forge unity out of the diversity of their national differences (and served to exclude women of other races and religions)." Examining these first wave international women's organizations highlights exclusionary organizational and political practices which can emerge from a unity based on homogeneity of class, race, and religious identities, despite differences in nationality.

It also shifts students' perceptions of "international relations." Despite the fact that women have been organizing at the international level for more than a century, like so much herstory, it is not commonly recognized. Too often, the international arena has been masculinized as a result of limited scholarly and media focus on state politics, foreign diplomacy, and military conflicts.

Disaggregating the concepts of international, transnational, local, and global also provides a foundation for an alternative paradigm to romantic sisterhood. To fully engage with these concepts is beyond the scope of this essay so here I will focus on two arguments: the need to reject the language of global feminism, and the value of differentiating between transnational and international organizing.

In the first instance, the language of "global feminism" is highly problematic. Inderpal Grewal and Caren Kaplan (1994) argue that

> "[G]lobal feminism" has stood for a kind of Western cultural imperialism ... [and] has elided the diversity of women's agency in favour of a universalised Western model of women's liberation that celebrates individuality and modernity. Anti-imperialist movements have legitimately decried this form of "feminist" globalizing (1994, 17).

Global feminism, then, asserts the commonality of women in an international arena. It is part of a western master narrative and assumes alliances among women rather than pro-actively building links cognizant of differences.[10]

Transnational organizing is an alternative formulation. It recognizes that the structures of global capitalism, corporate rule, and religious fundamentalism are affecting women everywhere but in structurally asymmetrical ways. As a result, alliances are possible and necessary. But they will only be successful if local differences are kept in focus, and if the gaze on difference refuses to construct exotic subjects—that is, it is not a western gaze. Transnational feminist solidarities are a new way of building alliances based on agency rather than shared victimization. They graphically challenge the argument that alliances are not possible because of difference but they also go well beyond simply recognizing difference.

Grewal and Kaplan recognize the imperative to

address the concerns of women around the world in the historicized particularity of their relationship to multiple patriarchies as well as to international economic hegemonies .... We need to articulate the relationship of gender to scattered hegemonies such as global economic structures, patriarchal nationalisms, "authentic" forms of tradition, local structures of domination, and legal-juridical oppression (17).

Such new cross-border alliances are emerging from increasingly shared economic realities, despite the divergent and asymmetrical ways in which women in the North, South, and East experience restructuring. Writing about the 1995 Beijing Conference, Charlotte Bunch, Maflika Dutt, and Swana Fried emphasize this point:

Women from North America and Western Europe discussed economic restructuring with its cutbacks in social services and health care in ways that echoed the devastation of structural adjustment policies described by women from the Third World. And the new voices of women from Eastern Europe and the former Soviet Union ... also reported their negative experiences in the transition to market economies .... [W]omen from all regions saw international economic and trade policies as placing increasing burdens on them (1996, 9).

Ana Isla, Angela Miles, and Sheila Molloy (1996, 116) note the "broad consensus among those lobbying in Beijing that the current global system is flawed at its deepest level."[11] The remarkable NGO [Non-Governmental Organizations] Beijing declaration, written over "three days of intensive consultation by participants from every region of the world" (118) was a collective response to the mainstreaming strategy of the Platform for Action, the main UN [United Nations] document, which excluded most clauses relevant to economic justice and the macro socio-economic context. (For a copy of the text, see Christiansen-Ruffman 1996.)

An emphasis on the leadership of women from the South needs to be at the centre of the study of such organizing in order to counteract the tendency of students to see Third World women as victims of "underdevelopment" and "barbaric" patriarchal practices such as genital surgeries.

Women from the economic South have played a major role in developing feminist understanding of the deeply negative aspects of the global economy and the "growth" and "development" pursued as an unquestioned good in its name. But feminists from the economic North increasingly share this understanding (Isla, Miles, and Molloy 1996, 116).

In her struggle to globalize her curriculum, Michiko Hase, a foreign-born woman of colour teaching in the US, explores American students' attitudes to Third World women. She identifies "American students' sense of superiority, mixed with their missionary attitude (they have to 'rescue' 'poor Third World sisters' from oppressive local cultures), their voyeurism, and their binary world view of 'us' versus 'them'" (2001, 95). Hase has a two-pronged strategy: to emphasize the "ways in which the US government, US-led international institutions, and US corporations might create or contribute to the 'plight' of Third World women and ways in which they, the students, might be benefiting from US hegemony in the global economy" (102) and to highlight the "agency and activism of Third World women" (90). In my view this emphasis on agency is critical.[12]

Second, although the meanings of these terms are contested, and invariably the boundaries between them are permeable, differentiating transnational from international organizing helps make visible forms of women's organizing that might be otherwise subsumed. I see the international as a supra-national arena, that is, an arena in which nations come together in formal structures representing "national" interests (often mis-represented as homogenous). It operates through and in international organizations and agencies such as the United Nations. Women organizing in the international arena do so both from inside and outside these structures. They attempt to alter the policies and practices of international organizations such as the UN (Reanda 1999), and may try to use these policies as levers to make change in their own national arenas (Roberts 1996).

In contrast, the transnational does not operate through the structures of nations, and those involved do not see themselves as representing nations, although of course, since they are always "nationalized" (as they are also racialized, classed, and gendered) the boundaries between nations do not disappear. Rather, transnational organizing maintains the local and the particular in the transnational context and thus resists the tendency to the national homogenization of the international arena. The local-transnational relation allows the development of a working agenda even as it is understood that women are differentially affected by similar processes, of globalization, for example.[13] The goal is to transform the local through transnational contact and, in some cases, to have an impact on the international arena. The emphasis on the local in transnational organizing also provides a basis to reject the language of global feminism.

Distinguishing between international and transnational is important because it makes visible organizing that is often erased by the focus on formal structures like the UN. It problematizes the relationship between international and transnational organizing rather than taking it for granted.

International and transnational initiatives not only help to refine students' understandings of working across difference, they also offer a unique and somewhat optimist entry into the study of global political economy. The globalization of capital and the growing permeability of national boundaries as a result of regional integration treaties like North American Free Trade Agreement (NAFTA) and the European Union (EU) are negatively impacting on workers around the world. Political and economic re-organization has meant deregulation, increasingly hostile neo-liberal states, "global" employers, wage competition across national boundaries, and increasing corporate rule. The dismantling and redefinition of the welfare state in the industrialized countries, and the introduction of structural adjustment programs (SAPS) in the developing countries have resulted in privatization of public services and decreased state funding to services like health, education, and family benefits, programs on which women depend and where they have often worked (often in better paid unionized positions).

These changes have politicized women and brought them to the forefront of resistance. They are also creating the basis for women to organize internationally and transnationally. Considering globalization through the lens of women's organizing challenges the resignation generated by such large-scale processes, and increases students' sense of the potential for agency and resistance, even in these difficult times.

Conclusion

Women's organizing as a subject of study is a gateway to a new approach for Women's Studies. The focus on women's organizing privileges agency and provides a new way to work with students around the complex intersections of theory, practice, and experience. It can enhance the relevance of Women's Studies and encourage students to redefine themselves as political actors. Finally, such an approach inspires students, a not-insignificant achievement in the current context where equity gains are under serious attack and demoralization is often the norm.

Notes

1. I am grateful to those who commented on an earlier draft of the Atlantis paper: Harriet Friedmann, Meg Luxton, Kathryn McPherson, Marilyn Porter, and Alissa Trotz. This version has minor revisions.

2. There are also many inspiring, provocative, and revelatory films made about women's organizing which offer an important medium for deepening student understanding of women's organizing. My experience has been that films offer a vehicle to radicalize women about possibility, politics, and agency. Here is a partial list of films I have used with great success over the years.

    Winds of Change (1999, 55 mins)
    Sweating for a T-shirt (1998, 23 mins)
    Fury for the Sound: The Women at Clayoquot (1997, 86 mins)
    Threads of Hope (1996, 51 mins)
    Women's March against Poverty (1996, 51 mins)
    Beyond Beijing (1996, 42 mins)
    Ballot Measure 9 (1995, 72 mins)
    The Vienna Tribunal (1994, 48 mins)
    Keepers of the Fire (1994, 55 mins)
    The Voice of Women (1992, 52 mins)
    Rising up Strong (1981/updated 1992, 90 mins [2 parts])
    Sisters in the Struggle (1991, 50 mins)
    You Have Struck a Rock (1981, 28 mins)
    Willmar 8 (1980, 55 mins)
    Wives' Tale (1980, 73 mins)
    With Babies and Banners (1978, 45 mins)
    Union Maids (1977, 45 mins)

3. The frame of women's organizing has been central both in my scholarship and in my teaching, and is grounded in my activist experience in the Canadian women's movement and the movement of union women. As a scholar, I was driven originally by the desire to document and make visible women's organizing during the early second wave women's movement. This led to *Union Sisters* (1983), co-edited with Lynda Yanz. Later my interest shifted to theorizing the practice of women's organizing and to *Feminist Organizing for Change* (1988), co-authored with Nancy Adamson and Margaret McPhail and *Women's Organizing and Public Policy in Sweden and Canada* (1999), co-edited with Mona Eliasson.

4. On this issue, Joan Scott says: "[S]ubjects have agency. They are not unified, autonomous individual exercising free will, but rather subjects whose agency is created through situations and statuses conferred on them. Being a subject means being 'subject to definite conditions of existence ....' These conditions enable choices, although they are not unlimited" (1992: 34).

5. Guida West and Rhoda Blumberg (1990) have developed a typology about women and social protest that students find useful. They identify four types of protest activities in which women are involved: struggles to attack problems that directly threaten their economic survival and that of their families and children; nationalist or racial/ethnic issues in either groups demanding liberation or equality, or in countermovements demanding protection against erosion of status quo (KKK, anti-busing etc); movements that

address humanistic/nurturing issues such as peace, environment, public education, prison reform in which their collective actions in the public male sphere are justified as an extension of their nurturing responsibilities within the domestic sphere, and which may encompass national or global "families"; and finally organizing on behalf of their own rights as women and for various groups of women (battered women, older women, child brides, etc).

6. Ferguson continues: "We must also reject the relativism of poststructuralist critics who would leave us with a participatory democratic politics so pluralistic and contextualized that it lacks any generalizable base for solidarity politics" (104).

7. Although undoubtedly "race" as corporeality remains a part of the lived experience of many people (Barot and Bird 2001), the concept of "racialization" is very useful in resisting biologistic racism. Robert Miles, a key proponent of this usage, uses the concept of racialization "to refer to those instances where social relations between people have been structured by the signification of human biological characteristics in such a way as to define and construct differentiated social collectivities. The concept therefore refers to a process of categorisation, a representational process of defining an Other (usually, but not exclusively) somatically" (quoted in Barot and Bird 2001, 610). Similarly, I think that "genderization" has similar value as a concept.

8. Sandra Gabriele (1997) comments on her experience as a practicum student working for Women's Action Coalition of Nova Scotia (WAC), an umbrella organization of grassroots women's groups. Where once she would have rejected an organization like WAC, which purported to "speak for all its member women," she came to recognize that "political alliances can be formed across bodily, geographic, racial and sexual orientations according to common political agendas. These alliances are always partial, always temporary, but always politically potent. By allowing for such fluidity we create space for local alliances and coalition building in political activism" (123–4).

9. Shane Phelan (1993: 786) emphasizes the need to resist "the temptations to cloak crucial differences with the cloak of universality and to deny generalities for fear of essentialism."

10. Despite the fact that Valentine Moghadam (2000) is writing about transnational feminist networks, she still makes some problematic assumptions about global feminism. Global feminism "is predicated upon the notion that notwithstanding cultural, class and ideological differences among the women of the world, there is a commonality in the forms of women's disadvantage and the forms of women's organizations worldwide" (62). It seems to me that the language of transnational organizing can offer a paradigm to problematize "commonalities."

11. Nayereh Tohidi (1996, 30) finds a sharp contrast between Beijing and the previous three world conferences on women, the key factor being the "relatively stronger sense of commonality and solidarity and much less political tension or ideological division. Apparently, the increasing international dialogue between women of the world, and the stronger voice of women from the 'Third World' as well as women of colour in the 'First World' in recent decades, has somewhat succeeded in bridging the conceptual gap between western feminists and women's groups from the developing countries. Women of the global North and South … came closer together not only because of a better appreciation of their differences in economic, socio-political, and cultural priorities, but also because today, many First World and Second World women are finding more common ground with Third World women on economic issues …. Confronted with the adverse implications of globalization, 'romantic sisterhood' is giving way to 'strategic sisterhood'" (Agarwal 2).

Moghadam (2000) also notes the shift. "In the 1970s, clashes occurred among nationally or regionally framed feminisms, mainly due to disagreements between Western feminists, who tended to emphasize women's need for legal equality and sexual autonomy, and Third World feminists, who tended to emphasize imperialism and underdevelopment as obstacles to women's advancement. These arguments were especially noticeable at the First UN Conference on Women, which took place in Mexico City in 1975, and especially at the second conference, which took place in Copenhagen in 1980. During the decade of the 1980s, however, a shift took place .... Feminists from the North came to appreciate the relevance of economic conditions and foreign policies to women's lives, while feminists from the South came to recognize the pertinence of 'body politics.' The Nairobi conference in 1985 seems to have been the turning point" (61).

12. This essay is part of larger text I am writing titled "Privileging Agency: A Strategy for Women's Studies in Troubled Times."

13. In her work on "transnational feminist networks" Moghadam (2000) examines professionalized organizations that work across national boundaries. For her, the TFNs (transnational feminist networks) supersede nationalist orientations and have universalistic objectives. TFNs consist "of active and autonomous local/national women's groups ... that transcend localisms or nationalisms. Their discourses and objectives are not particularistic but are universalistic. As such, these TFNs are situated in the tradition of progressive modernist politics, rather than in any new wave of postmodernist or identity politics" (77). For Moghadam, "TFNs acknowledge the diversity of women's experiences and the salience of class, ethnic and other differences, but do not appear to give difference the theoretical status or absolute character that postmodernists do" (77).

References

Adamson, Nancy, Linda Briskin, and Margaret McPhail. *Feminist Organizing for Change: The Contemporary Women's Movement in Canada.* Toronto: Oxford University Press, 1988.

Alcoff, Linda. "Cultural Feminism Versus Post-Structuralism: The Identity Crisis in Feminist Theory." *Signs* 13, 3 (1988): 405–36.

Barot, Rohit, and John Bird. "Racialization: The Genealogy and Critique of a Concept." *Ethnic and Racial Studies* 24, 4 (July 2001): 601–18.

Briskin, Linda. "Using Groundrules to Negotiate Power in the Classroom." In *Centring on the Margins: The Evaded Curriculum.* Proceedings of the Second Bi-annual Canadian Association for the Study of Women and Education (CASWE) International Institute, Ottawa, 1998, pp. 25–32, 49, 80.

_____. "Unions and Women's Organizing in Canada and Sweden." In Linda Briskin and Mona Eliasson, eds., *Women's Organizing and Public Policy in Canada and Sweden.* Montreal: McGill-Queen's University Press, 1999, pp. 147–83.

_____. "Autonomy, Diversity and Integration: Union Women's Separate Organizing in North America and Western Europe in the Context of Restructuring and Globalization." *Women's Studies International Forum* 22 (1999a): 543–54.

Bunch, C., M. Dutt, and S. Fried. "Beijing '95: A Global Referendum on the Human Rights of Women." *Canadian Woman Studies/les cahiers de la femme* 16, 3 (Summer 1996): 7–12.

Butler, Judith. "Contingent Foundations: Feminism and the Question of 'Postmodernism.'" In Judith Butler and Joan Scott, eds., *Feminists Theorize the Political.* New York: Routledge, 1992, pp. 3–21.

Christiansen-Ruffman, Linda. "Pages from Beijing: A Woman's Creed and the NGO Declaration." *Canadian Woman Studies/les cahiers de la femme* 16, 3 (Summer 1996): 35–43.

Cockburn, Cynthia. *The Space between Us: Negotiating Gender and National Identities in Conflict.* London: Zed, 1998.

Day, Shelagh. "Women's Sexual Autonomy: Universality, Sexual Rights, and Sexual Orientation at the Beijing Conference."

Canadian Woman Studies/les cahiers de la femme 16, 3 (Summer 1996): 46–54.

Ferguson, Ann. "Resisting the Veil of Privilege: Building Bridge Identities as an Ethico-Politics of Global Feminism." *Hypatia* 13, 3 (Summer 1998): 95–113.

Gabriele, Sandra. "Giving Feminist Theory a Heartbeat: Field-Based Learning and the Academy." *Atlantis* 22 (1997): 122–25.

Grewal, Inderpal, and Caren Kaplan. "Transnational Feminist Practices and Questions of Postmodernity." In Inderpal Grewal and Caren Kaplan, eds., *Scattered Hegemonies*. University of Minnesota Press, 1994, pp. 1–33.

Hase, Michiko. "Student Resistance and Nationalism in the Classroom: Some Reflections on Globalizing the Curriculum." *Feminist Teacher* 13, 2 (2001): 90–107.

Hayden, Dolores. *Redesigning the American Dream: The Future of Housing, Work and Family Life.* New York: Norton, 1984.

Isla, Ana, Angela Miles, and Sheila Molloy. "Stabilization/Structural Adjustment/Restructuring: Canadian Feminist Issues in a Global Framework." *Canadian Woman Studies/les cahiers de la femme* 16, 3 (Summer 1996): 116–21.

Jhabvala, Ruth. "Self-Employed Women's Association: Organising Women by Struggle and Development." In Swasti Mitter and Sheila Rowbotham, eds., *Dignity and Daily Bread: New Forms of Economic Organising among Poor Women in the Third World and the First.* New York: Routledge, 1994, pp. 114–38.

Kelly, Liz, Jill Radford, and Joan Scanlon. "Feminism, Feminisms: Fighting Back for Women's Liberation." In Karen Atkinson, Sarah Oerton, and Gill Plain, eds., *Feminisms on Edge: Politics, Discourse and National Identities.* Fairwater: Cardiff Academic Press, 2000, pp. 9–23.

Kemp, Amanda, et al. "The Dawn of a New Day: Redefining South African Feminism." In Amrita Basu, ed., *The Challenge of Local Feminisms: Women's Movements in Global Perspective.* Boulder: Westview Press, 1995, pp. 131–62.

Krauss, Celene. "Challenging Power: Toxic Waste Protests and the Politicization of White, Working Class Women." In Nancy Naples, ed., *Community Activism and Feminist Politics.* New York: Routledge, 1998, pp. 129–50.

Martin, Biddy. "Sexual Practices and Changing Lesbian Identities." In Michèle Barrett and Anne Phillips, eds., *Destabilizing Theory.* Stanford University Press, 1992, pp. 93–119.

Moghadam, Valentine. "Transnational Feminist Networks: Collective Action in an Era of Globalization." *International Sociology* 15, 1 (March 2000): 57–85.

Phelan, Shane. "(Be)Coming Out: Lesbian Identity and Politics." *Signs* 18, 4 (1993): 765–90.

Piercy, Marge. *Woman on the Edge of Time.* New York: Fawcett Crest, 1976.

Reanda, Laura. "Engendering the United Nations: The Changing International Agenda." *The European Journal of Women's Studies* 6 (1999): 49–68.

Roberts, Barbara. "Taking Them at Their Word: Canadian Government's Accountability for Women's Equality." *Canadian Woman Studies/les cahiers de la femme* 16, 3 (Summer 1996): 25–29.

Rosen, Ruth. "Thinking Globally, Acting Globally: Review of *Worlds of Women* by Leila Rupp." *Women's Review of Books* (June 1998): 1, 3–4.

Rowbotham, Sheila, and Swasti Mitter, eds. *Dignity and Daily Bread: New Forms of Economic Organizing among Poor Women in the Third World and the First.* London: Routledge, 1994.

Rupp, Leila. *Worlds of Women: The Making of an International Women's Movement.* Princeton: Princeton University Press, 1998.

Scott, Joan. "Experience." In Judith Butler and Joan Scott, eds., *Feminists Theorize the Political.* New York: Routledge, 1992, pp. 22–40.

Shohat, Ella. "Area Studies, Transnationalism and the Feminist Production of Knowledge." *Signs* 26, 4 (2001): 1269–72.

Snitow, Ann. "A Gender Diary." In Marianne Hirsch and Evelyn Keller, eds., *Conflicts in Feminism.* New York: Routledge, 1990, pp. 9–43.

Stienstra, Deborah. *Women's Movements and International Organizations.* Houndmills, UK: St. Martins Press, 1994.

Swerdlow, Amy. "Pure Milk, Not Poison: Women Strike for Peace." In Adrienne Harris and Ynestra King, eds., *Rocking the Ship of State: Toward a Feminist Peace Politics*. Boulder: Westview Press, 1989, pp. 225–37.

Tax, Meredith. *The Rising of the Women*. New York: Monthly Review Press, 1980.

Taylor, Barbara. *Eve and the New Jerusalem. Socialism and Feminism in the Nineteenth Century*. London: Virago, 1983.

Tohidi, Nayereh. "'Fundamentalist' Backlash and Muslim Women in the Beijing Conference: New Challenges for International Women's Movements." *Canadian Woman Studies/les cahiers de la femme* 16, 3 (Summer 1996): 30–34.

West, Guida, and Rhoda Blumberg. "Reconstructing Social Protest from a Feminist Perspective." In Guida West and Rhoda Blumberg, eds., *Women and Social Protest*. New York: Oxford, 1990, pp. 3–35.

Wharton, Amy. "Structure and Agency in Socialist Feminist Theory." *Gender and Society* 5, 3 (1991): 375–89.

Inclusive Pedagogy in the Women's Studies Classroom: Teaching the Kimberly Nixon Case

Viviane Namaste with Georgia Sitara

Introduction

This [essay] addresses pedagogical questions with respect to the Kimberly Nixon case, a situation in which a male-to-female transsexual was excluded from the volunteer counselling programme of Vancouver Rape Relief. We examine different feminist interpretations of these events, and remark that the discussion to date is primarily concerned with the identities of transsexual women.

We argue that the Nixon case is useful in the classroom not in a consideration of gender and identity, but rather in terms of other issues important to feminist politics. In our view, teachers can use the Nixon case to open up significant issues in feminist studies. We address five such issues: different definitions of "experience" within feminist theory and politics; implicit appeals to universalism within feminist discourse; false analogies established between race and gender by both pro-transsexual and anti-transsexual feminists; contradictions with respect to feminist definitions of and appeals to the state in the Nixon case; and a certain feminist appeal to "protecting" women's interests.

Throughout the essay, we suggest strategies for orienting the classroom discussion of the Nixon case,

which move the questions beyond a narrow consideration of identity.

This essay takes up questions of teaching and pedagogy in women's studies classrooms, with a particular case study on addressing transsexual and transgendered issues therein. Through a study of the Kimberly Nixon case, in which a male-to-female transsexual was denied the right to train as a volunteer counsellor at Vancouver Rape Relief, we want to provide some reflection, offer some pointers, and raise some critical questions about how to begin to address these issues.

We feel the need to intervene in this debate because, in many ways, the Nixon case is coming to stand in as a litmus test for the relations between (non-transsexual) feminists and transsexuals in Canada. There is more and more discussion of this case in the context of different English Canadian women's studies classrooms, and the case has been taken up in recent academic work.[1] The case is also examined in the English-language popular media, from the *National Post* to the feminist magazine *Herizons*.[2] In this regard, one of the objectives of this essay is to provide an overview of this case and the debates as a useful resource for teachers and students.

We are equally concerned with how this debate is framed within the teaching context, a discussion which focuses on whether or not transsexual women are women. We find this focus limited insofar as it understands the issue exclusively as a question of identity. Our observations of discussion of the Nixon case indicate that the case is used to raise the question, "Who is a woman?" It offers an opportunity for teachers to introduce the different ways in which sex and gender can be defined, broaching questions of genitals, chromosomes, social role, psychological identity, and biological determinism. We do think these questions are important, and need to be addressed in the context of women's studies. Yet we think this focus on identity can obscure other critical issues raised by the Nixon case. A second objective of this essay, then, is to encourage ways of teaching about transsexuality that move the debate beyond that of identity.

Thirdly, we believe that the Nixon case raises central questions about an inclusive vision of feminism, particularly with respect to race. The Nixon case provides an occasion to think through how an appeal to "woman's experience" made by some feminists is an appeal to the experiences of certain white women. We hope to offer some reflection on how teachers can help students understand the limitations of such a universalist position. Our third objective of this essay centres on learning from the history of imperialism in feminism, as well as taking seriously a commitment to diversity and inclusivity in feminist scholarship and politics.

Fourthly, we are interested in thinking about these issues in relation to questions of the state. We are particularly invested in these questions because the discussion of the Nixon case to date has not, in our opinion, adequately incorporated this matter into its analysis. We will draw on different historical examples to raise questions about the complicated relations between feminist politics and state formation, and to suggest how a critical teacher can use the Nixon case as a way to bring these questions out in the classroom. Our fourth

objective of this essay is to have teachers reflect on the definitions of the state deployed by feminist groups like Vancouver Rape Relief.

Finally, we want to reflect on a feminist appeal to "protecting" the autonomy of (non-transsexual) women's groups. Historically, the notion of "protection" has been invoked under the banner of "women's rights" in a deeply conservative manner, supporting the work of imperialism and calling on the state to enforce a particular practice of morality. In this regard, we want to interrogate the argument made by some feminists that the Nixon case is important with respect to protecting women's interests.

This essay seeks to offer reflection and stimulate further thought and dialogue on these issues. We do not offer a detailed exposition or analysis of the Nixon case in its entirety. Nor do we simply take a position with respect to the Nixon debate. Rather, we raise questions for teachers to take up in their work of critical pedagogy.

Background and an Overview of Some of the Main Arguments

Kimberly Nixon is a male-to-female transsexual woman who volunteered for a training programme of the Vancouver Rape Relief and Women's Shelter (VRR) in 1995. Upon discovery of her transsexuality, Nixon was excluded from the programme. She filed a complaint with the British Columbia Human Rights Commission, arguing that she was a victim of discrimination because of her transsexual status. The BC Human Rights Tribunal on the case commenced in December 2000 and concluded in February 2001. In January 2002, the Tribunal found in favour of Nixon, awarding her $7500 in damages, the highest damage award in the Tribunal's history. In June 2002, VRR filed an appeal with the BC Supreme Court. At the time of writing this essay, the case is ongoing.

There are a variety of different arguments outlined in this case.[3] In the first instance, Nixon maintains that she was subject to discriminatory treatment as a transsexual woman, and that VRR was in violation of human rights legislation with respect to sex. VRR, in its defence, contends that the particular circumstances of the VRR volunteer training programme are not covered by the existing Human Rights Code. Since the training programme is volunteer and unpaid, it cannot be considered under the rubric of employment.[4] Moreover, the unique programme of VRR cannot be considered as a service, insofar as Nixon was not denied access to *receiving* a service, but was rather denied access to training to provide a service.[5] VRR maintains that existing human rights legislation protects individuals who receive services, but not those who provide them. As such, there is no legal precedent for a finding of discrimination.

Even if the volunteer training programme is to be considered as a protected ground under the rubric of employment or services with respect to human rights legislation, VRR argues that exclusion of Nixon from the programme does not constitute discrimination since she does not have the life experience of living as a woman. VRR maintains that this is a *bona fide* requirement for participation in the volunteer training programme. Indeed, this position is central to VRR's defence. They contend that only women who have the life experience of being raised and living as women are in a position to counsel women victims of rape and domestic violence. This appeal to "life experience" is at the core of their argument.

VRR argues that the Nixon case raises fundamental questions about minority groups in society defining their membership. They appeal to legislation, which allows for members of minority groups to organize amongst themselves—freedom of association (Section 41 of the BC Human Rights Code). Freedom of association contends that disadvantaged groups have the legal right to exclude members who do not share their characteristics without it constituting discrimination, in an attempt for collective mobilization and social change. In other words, Mennonites can organize together and exclude non-Mennonites if the aim of their organizing is to improve their social conditions. This position outlines the difference between *distinction* and that of *discrimination*. VRR uses this framework to argue that the Code's use of the term "sex" ought also to be applied in this regard: (non-transsexual) women have the right to organize amongst themselves to promote (non-transsexual) women's interests without such a distinction constituting discrimination.[6] For VRR, non-transsexual women have the right to define who is a woman, and therefore who can participate in their training programme.

VRR's position raises a variety of questions, and some feminists have seen in this case an important case concerning the autonomy of women's organizing. Judy Rebick, former president of the National Action Committee on the Status of Women, for instance, testified at the Tribunal and declared,

> The issue at stake is whether or not a women's group has the right to decide who its members are .... there's no question that transgendered people suffer from discrimination, they suffer a great deal. So of course, in your heart as a feminist you want to be on their side in every fight but you can't because there's a conflict of rights. It goes to the heart of what the women's movement is and what feminism is. It's a very important discussion and a difficult one![7]

Rebick's comments help situate the importance of the Nixon case for the women's studies classroom. This situation is perceived by many non-transsexual feminists, such as Rebick, as fundamental to the autonomy of the women's liberation movement. VRR also takes this position, and links it to the notion of protection. They argue that human rights legislation needs to protect (non-transsexual) women's rights to define who is a woman. In a response to Mary-Woo Sims, former chief commissioner of the BC Human Rights Commission, they write,

> Human rights advance with each advance in the equality and liberation of women. We believe that it is critical to protect women's right to assess the significance of life experience and determine with whom and how we will be organized in order to protect and nurture the potential of the women's liberation movement.[8]

Having provided some background information and an overview of some of the main arguments, we turn our attention now to the pedagogical opportunities opened up by the Nixon case. Our comments address several different questions that a critical teacher can take up with students: different definitions of "experience" in feminist theory and politics; diversity and inclusivity within feminist thinking and politics; faulty analogies between race and gender made by both anti-transsexual and pro-transsexual feminists; definitions of the state implicit in the appeal to the law made by VRR's defence; and an invocation of the notion of "protection" as linked to "women's rights." We conclude with some general comments on pedagogical approaches to these matters.

Different Definitions of "Experience"

VRR's defence is premised on the assumption that transsexual women cannot counsel victims of sexual assault and/or domestic violence because they do not share a common experience of being raised as girls. This appeal to "life experience" thus functions as the mitigating difference between women who are transsexual and those who are not.

Such an invocation of "experience" allows the critical teacher to present a variety of different ways in which feminist theorists and thinkers have defined the notion of "experience." This type of pedagogy would be especially pertinent at the introductory level, as a way of offering students an overview of different feminist positions on the same issue. It would also lend itself quite well to teaching feminist theory, since it provides an occasion for students to think through different paradigms in feminist thought. In this regard, teachers can use the Nixon case as a way to introduce, or to revisit, some fundamental traditions within feminist thought.

How do feminists influenced by standpoint theory rely on the notion of "experience"? How is "experience" defined and used by radical feminists? What do poststructuralist feminists say about the notion of "experience"? What are the different underlying assumptions about knowledge and being of each of these positions? What are their epistemological and ontological foundations? Having provided such an overview, teachers can encourage students to situate VRR's response in relation to particular traditions of feminist thought. The objective of such an exercise is not so much to have them debate the merits of VRR's position, but rather to be able to think theoretically: to understand the claims about knowledge and being which underlie their position and to be able to situate these claims within a history of feminist scholarship.

Having introduced some basic theoretical traditions in feminist thought, a critical pedagogue can also encourage students to reflect on the relations between theory and practice, knowledge and action. What forms of political action become possible, or impossible, based on a particular way of understanding the world? If women are understood to be non-rational, as they were by many Enlightenment thinkers, how could they even make a claim to desire access to education? If transsexual women are understood, *a priori*, to be other than women, how can they make a claim to equal access to the public sphere as women?

The Nixon case allows students to understand that the work of doing "theory" is deeply political, since it determines what forms of political action are possible in various traditions of (feminist) thought. Furthermore, the case illustrates quite well that political work is always informed by a particular theoretical perspective. Politics contain specific assumptions about knowledge, being, and the social world. Pedagogically, then, the Nixon case helps the women's studies instructor to demonstrate that thinking theoretically can help illuminate a specific political issue. These relations between theory and politics, knowledge and action, are central to the work of teaching in the women's studies classroom.

Diversity

VRR argues that Nixon cannot counsel women victims of sexual assault and/or domestic violence because she does not share the experience of living as a woman since birth. Such an experience is necessary, according to VRR, in order to establish rapport and build trust between volunteer counsellors and clients. Indeed, one of the witnesses called in their defence contended that she would not want her daughter to be counselled by Nixon.[9] Within this discourse, the shared "lifelong" experience of women is understood as a necessary precondition to successful counselling.

Yet interestingly, such a criterion of "experience" is only invoked with regards to transsexual women as volunteers. There is no similar appeal to the common "experience" of volunteers with other kinds of differences. VRR does not require, for instance, that its volunteers have lived for their entire lives as prostitutes in order to effectively counsel clients who are prostitutes. Nor does VRR demand that volunteers have been physically disabled since birth as a precondition to counselling women who are physically disabled and who have been sexually assaulted. Presumably, it is only the difference of transsexuality that seems to matter to VRR.

Fortunately, the decision of the BC Human Rights Tribunal recognized the discriminatory nature of treating transsexual women differently. Commenting on VRR's argument that volunteers need to have the life-long experience of living as a woman, Heather MacNaughton writes,

> I accept that there may be some basis for that argument. However, it assumes that all the women who access Rape Relief for services, and who provide services, have a homogenous common life experience. Rape Relief is prepared to make that assumption about all other women who apply to them without making any inquiry about it, and without having in place a policy that makes it necessary. The only criteria they have in place for their volunteer trainees is that they accept the four basic principles on which Rape Relief operates, and that they are not men. Ms. Nixon accepted the four basic principles and is not a man.[10]

VRR's exception with respect to transsexuals is significant, and it speaks to the implicit assumptions about violence advocated by VRR. Indeed, VRR is quite explicit in its conception of violence as one perpetrated by men against women.

> Rape Relief deals with all forms of male violence against women. Rape Relief was especially interested in overriding Social Services' delivery categories around incest, wife assault, and rape. Rape Relief thought the political similarity was more important. The political similarity is that it's men who are attacking women and women as a group need to resist.[11]

This position establishes an immediate connection amongst women as victims of male violence. It is based on this perceived connection of womanhood—defined as the common experience of living under sexism—that allows VRR to make its claim as to rapport and trust that only a non-transsexual woman as service provider or as volunteer can establish with another non-transsexual woman as client.

This argument places priority on sex above other differences such as race and class. Yet such a position actively ignores a rich history of debates within feminist scholarship and activism with respect to race and class differences. Women of colour have criticized the ways in which this type of discourse appeals to a universal experience of "womanhood," which effaces differences within and across cultures, which forces women of colour to locate their political commitments primarily in terms of sex (not race), and which quietly bypasses the history of imperialism and oppression enacted by white women.[12]

Yet when we examine the complexities of violence against women, it becomes increasingly problematic to make such claims to universalism. Consider a variety of different experiences of violence against women in the Canadian context: that of a South Asian immigrant women, living in Canada having been sponsored by her legal husband who abuses her; the Native woman in Vancouver who works as a street prostitute and is beaten by a client; or the young white woman who injects heroin daily and who is beaten by a drug dealer for non-payment of debts. All of these situations reflect complicated dynamics and social relations which cannot be subsumed into a universal "experience" of "violence against women." Furthermore, the skills required to intervene in these situations demand much more than a simplistic appeal to "a life-long experience of living as a woman" as the VRR position implicitly maintains. These scenarios demand knowledge of different cultures, familiarity with street prostitution, and/or an awareness of harm reduction strategies when working with intravenous drug users. Establishing meaningful rapport and trust with such clients is hampered when white women hold racist assumptions about Native women, when women do not respect the work of prostitution in the short or the long term, or when middle-class women do not accept that some women use drugs intravenously. Clearly, an appeal to the life-long experience of living as a woman is an insufficient ground for solidarity.

VRR maintains that as an organization, it adopts an anti-racist position. Yet its conception of violence is one which cannot account for the different ways in which violence is organized. The organization's implicit appeal to a "sisterhood" established through the life-long experience of living as a woman effectively requires that violence be understood primarily in terms of gender—which is to say, the violence of men against women: "it's men who are attacking women and women as a group need to resist."[13] We would question this understanding of anti-racism, to the extent that VRR's position in the Nixon case requires a virtual erasure of the specificity of violence in different racial and ethnic contexts.

One of the limitations of this argument is that it highlights questions of sex and gender while downplaying those of race. Significantly, however, it also supports an underlying assumption about the nature of women. By understanding violence as something perpetrated by men against women, this position effectively precludes the possibility of women who enact violence against other women. One of the concrete results of this belief is that it makes it extremely difficult for feminists to respond adequately to violence perpetrated against women by women. Indeed, the whole question of violence within the lesbian community raises this issue to the forefront. Historically, feminist advocates of support services for women victims of violence have expressed a great deal of difficulty in acknowledging the reality of violence against women by women, to say nothing of organizing to provide these women with appropriate services.[14]

VRR's appeal to the trust and rapport established between women as victims of violence and non-transsexual volunteers emerges from this simplistic conception of violence. It necessarily ignores the violence that women enact against other women. Indeed, if some women can abuse other women, this means that women as victims of violence and as service providers or as volunteer counsellors do not, *a priori*, share any essential connection, regardless of the fact that they may have been raised since birth as girls and women. Furthermore, when we position women as victims of violence it makes it difficult to analyze the violence that women perpetrate on their own children.

We think that a critical pedagogue can help students to think through these issues. Teachers can ask their students how the position of VRR addresses the diversity amongst women, including the varied articulations of violence in different class and race contexts. Students can be encouraged to think about the function of universalism—the appeal to a common bond between (non-transsexual) women that is at the core of VRR's argument. How does this universalist appeal work to exclude transsexuals? What are its assumptions about the essentially good, moral nature of women? How does this appeal to morality relate to the work of early feminists in Canada, who appealed to the moral nature of Anglo-Saxon women and whose politics was marked by overt racism and imperialism?[15] In what ways does this position force feminists to place a priority on matters of sex, downplaying questions of race and class? How have feminist theories and politics made use of universalism in the past? Has this use of universalism been critiqued by some feminists and, if so, how?

Analogies of Race and Gender

In the previous section, we have outlined how the position of VRR works with a universalist conception of women and violence that effaces the complexity of violence as it is organized and manifested in different cultural, ethnic, and class contexts. We also suggested some particular strategies for teachers to help students better understand these issues. One of our central arguments was that VRR's position demands an understanding of violence primarily in terms of gender, downplaying questions of race and class.

Yet VRR is not the only party to engage in such a tactic—which is to say, one which situates the Nixon debate primarily with respect to violence against white women. Indeed, some supporters of Nixon make an analogy between race and gender, which also effaces the realities of non-white people. In a community forum on the Nixon case published in *Herizons*, Dodie Goldney, a non-transsexual woman who self-identifies as a "radical lesbian feminist woman," writes,

> I can do nothing but wholeheartedly embrace trans-gendered women as my sisters. I am also a white woman and I embrace women of colour as my sisters. To me, the issues are similar. To say that a woman might not feel comfortable receiving counselling or support from a trans-gendered woman is similar, to me, to saying that a white woman might not feel comfortable receiving counselling from a woman of colour, or that a heterosexual woman might not feel comfortable receiving counselling from a lesbian.[16]

This position is also articulated by the lawyer for Nixon. In a press release issued after the Tribunal rendered its verdict in favour of Nixon, Barbara Findlay writes,

> The decision will make it clear that it is no more acceptable to say that they (members of a women's organization) cannot imagine working in a rape crisis centre with a transsexual woman, than it would be to say that they cannot imagine

working in a rape crisis centre with a woman of colour, a lesbian, or a woman with a disability.[17]

The statements of both Goldney and Findlay establish a similarity between gender and race. While they are clearly in support of Nixon's struggle, and of equal access for transsexual women in women's organizations, they mobilize this support by invoking the similarity of transsexual women providing services with women of colour providing services. In this discourse, *gender is like race*.

We suggested earlier that critical teachers can use the Nixon case to raise important questions of diversity and inclusion in feminist politics. While it is necessary to think through the ways in which the position of VRR privileges gender over race, it is equally important to unpack the false analogies of race and gender established by supporters of Nixon.

Not all transsexuals are white. This statement shows the limitations of the argument put forward by Goldney and Findlay. Through their analogy, they implicitly suggest that all transsexuals are white. Of course, this type of reasoning and comparison needs to be interrogated, and the critical teacher can help students in such an exercise. We believe it is particularly important to do so given the general context of the discussion of the Nixon case—which is to say, the case is about violence against women, about the work done in a woman's service organization, and about the city of Vancouver. Non-white transsexuals make up a significant proportion of the transsexual population in Vancouver, particularly when one considers street prostitutes. To make an analogy between race and gender, as Goldney and Findlay do, effectively erases the realities of the Native, Philippina, and other non-white transsexuals who live and work in Vancouver.

Analogies between race and gender are sometimes deployed by white feminists in an attempt to undermine the possibility of transsexuality. Marisa Swangha

addresses this issue in taking up the white feminist statement "A man wanting to be a woman is like a white person wanting to be Black." As Swangha elegantly argues, this statement evacuates the realities of non-white transsexuals. In her words,

I have many problems with this ignorant racist statement. First: It implies that *all* transsexuals are white, that *all* transsexuals are MTF (male to female) and that being a woman is like being Black. But most of all it negates the millions of lives of transsexual/transgendered peoples of FIRST NATIONS, AFRIKAN and ASIAN descent, who are the world MAJORITY of transsexuals.

An Afrikan/Asian/Native "man wanting to be" an Afrikan/Asian/Native woman is not "like a white person wanting to be black," it is like a "man" of a certain colour wanting to be a woman of the same colour as "he" already is. GENDER is not like RACE.[18]

Swangha's intervention addresses the consequences of establishing a false analogy between gender and race. While her critical inquiry helps us to un-do the racism of an anti-transsexual discourse advocated by some white feminists, it can also assist us in thinking through the limitations of a pro-transsexual discourse advocated by some white allies and white supporters of transsexuals.

In this regard, the Nixon case offers an excellent pedagogical opportunity to help students think through the dangers of analogies between race and gender too often made by liberal thinkers. We suggest that teachers have students list some of the arguments put forward in support of Nixon, drawing on the discussion published in *Herizons* and the press release issued by Findlay. Having outlined some of these arguments, teachers can help students think about the invocation of "race" in certain positions. What is the connection put forward between gender and race? How is this invocation of race connected to the lives of non-white transsexuals in Vancouver? Having asked these questions, teachers can use the reflections offered by Swangha to assist students in understanding the limitations of these supposedly "progressive" positions.

We believe that this type of teaching—helping students to understand the limitations of making analogies between race and gender—is a fundamental aspect of anti-racist pedagogy in the women's studies classroom.

Appeal to the Law

The Nixon case is further useful from a pedagogical perspective given the appeal of feminists—both Nixon and VRR—to the terms of the law.

Nixon makes her case by arguing that she suffered discrimination as a transsexual woman. Interestingly, the response of VRR to this allegation also invokes the law. In their early defence—before the case arrived to the BC Human Rights Tribunal—they made an argument before the BC Supreme Court that the Human Rights Code did not explicitly protect transsexual and/or transgendered people.[19] Since the Code did not set out such formal protection, VRR argued, they could not be found to be in violation of the existing legislation. The BC Supreme Court rejected this argument, and found that the use of the term "sex" did include transsexuals in British Columbia.

In their defence at the Tribunal, VRR also made several arguments which maintained that the organization did not discriminate. In the first instance, they contended that the situation involved an individual who was to work as a volunteer counsellor. This particular circumstance was not covered under existing human rights legislation, they argued, which limited its scope to either the category "employment" or that of "services." VRR maintained that since Nixon was neither an employee of the organization, nor a recipient of services, the group could

not be found in breach of human rights legislation in BC. They maintained that Nixon was denied access to training to provide a service, but that this cannot be confused with receiving a service or with employment. The Tribunal disagreed with this position, basing its decision on some previous human rights cases in British Columbia with respect to volunteer labour.[20]

We wish to highlight here the strategy adopted by VRR with respect to the law and the state. In the first instance, they maintained that since the existing law does not include transsexuals, groups like VRR which exclude (male to female) transsexuals are not engaging in a discriminatory practice. This position thus understands that "discrimination" can only be what is set forth in the law. Importantly, such a strategy places the burden onto marginalized peoples to ensure that their specific differences are incorporated into human rights law. It shifts the responsibility away from institutions and organizations who do not need to prove that they did not discriminate in treating an individual differently based on a particular characteristic. Moreover, such a strategy opposes the practice of human rights law, which is always to be interpreted in an open manner in the interests of ensuring equal access to all citizens. The Tribunal judgement included a statement on precisely this purpose and function of human rights law: it "must be interpreted broadly and purposively."[21] In this regard, we find that the strategy chosen by VRR is a deeply conservative move which is detrimental not only to transsexuals, but to all marginalized peoples whose difference is not explicitly named in existing human rights legislation.[22]

It is perhaps useful to move into the hypothetical for a moment. If the courts had found that existing human rights legislation in BC does not include transsexuals under the protected ground of "sex," then the Nixon case would have been dismissed. But could we see such a judgement as liberatory? The Tribunal decision clearly states that VRR discriminated by making assumptions about Nixon based on the knowledge that she had lived some of her life as a man. If the case never made it to the Tribunal level in the event that the ground of "sex" was not understood to include transsexuals, does this mean that such discrimination did not take place? Or alternatively, if it was found that the particular context of volunteer work was not covered under existing human rights legislation, would such a finding have meant that there was no discrimination? We ask these questions as examples of inquiries teachers can raise with students in an effort to help them think through critically the function served by such an appeal to the law.

Moreover, this recourse to the law is further ironic given a strong feminist critique of the ways in which the law has not historically represented the interests of women. The struggle for the vote represents perhaps the most predictable example of such injustice.[23] An additional example is that of section 12.1(b) of the Indian Act, which denied Native status to women who married a non-Native man, as well as to their children.[24] Native men who married a non-Native woman, however, retained their status as Natives and bestowed it on their wives and children. Aboriginal women and some white feminists have used this case to show how the law is explicitly sexist in its application, treating Native men and women differently. This section of the Indian Act was only changed after intense lobbying efforts. Indeed, the legal change only occurred after the case was brought to the United Nations Human Rights Courts—in other words, after Canada had been embarrassed internationally. Feminists cite these examples of the history of the law in Canada to argue that the law has not served well the interests of women. More radically, some feminists contend that the law actively organizes oppressions of race and of gender.[25]

Given this historical background, in which feminists have been deeply critical of the law, what does it mean now that VRR appeals to the terms of the law in its defence? Is it possible that the law has been clearly discriminatory in an historical sense, but that the possibility of such discrimination no longer exists?

We see in VRR's appeal to the law a position which is entirely uncritical of the state and how it works, a position here mobilized under the name of "feminism." And we find it problematic that VRR adopts such a statist position with respect to this human rights case when their mission is clearly critical of the state. In their summary of the key evidence, VRR argues that the organization was established to move beyond the limitations of the state's services with respect to violence.[26]

This contradiction offers a wonderful pedagogical opportunity for teachers. Instructors can raise the obvious question with respect to VRR's defence: how is it that the organization can critique the functioning of the state with respect to its conception of violence against women, and use this critique as a foundation for the need of VRR's services, yet at the same time appeal to the terms of the state and its laws in order to argue that the organization has not discriminated against Kimberly Nixon? Can these two elements of their position be reconciled? What is the theory of the state which underlies them? Are there different feminist understandings of and appeals to the state? If so, which (feminist) tradition does VRR invoke in its defence? These questions lend themselves particularly well to discussions about women and politics, women and the law, and women and the state. In this regard, the Nixon case is useful not for discussion about who is or who is not a woman. Rather, the Nixon case allows teachers to introduce different theories of the state—including feminist theories—and to discuss how these different theories inform political action.

Protection

The final issue we would like to address is an appeal made by VRR to "protecting" the interests of women. Indeed, certain feminists (such as Judy Rebick) see in the Nixon case a fundamental struggle over the autonomy of women's groups. VRR's press release announcing an appeal of the Tribunal decision makes this perfectly clear. Suzanne Jay of VRR states, "we are fighting this case as a test case on the protection of women's rights to women-only organizing."[27] And as we cited earlier, the organization's response to Mary-Woo Sims, former Chief Commissioner of the BC Human Rights Commission, also appealed to this notion of "protection":

> Human rights advance with each advance in the equality and liberation of women. We believe that it is critical to protect women's right to assess the significance of life experience and determine with whom and how we will protect and nurture the potential of the women's liberation movement.[28]

The position of VRR establishes a crucial link between the autonomy of women's groups, women's rights, and this notion of "protection." Their argument opens up a pedagogical opportunity for teachers to better understand the function, and consequences, of such an appeal to "protection." Here, we believe it is important to understand these issues historically, learning from some of the ways in which feminists have mobilized support through an appeal to "protection," and thinking critically about some of the ways in which the concrete organizing efforts of such feminists have failed, in point of fact, to improve the social conditions of women.

Several examples illustrate the dangers implicit in a feminist appeal to protection. One such case is labour legislation, justified through this notion of "protection," which applied to women only and which established maximum hours of work, minimum wages, and/or mandatory breaks. Some feminists have argued that such legislation has been used to deny women promotion and advancement, effectively maintaining them at the bottom of a social hierarchy while ostensibly "protecting" their interests.[29] In this regard, an appeal to "protection" can serve a deeply conservative function.

A second example comes from the controversial field of pornography and censorship in Canada. In the early 1990s, the Supreme Court of Canada heard a case with respect to obscenity legislation. Some feminists, such as LEAF, the Women's Legal Education and Action Fund, maintained that pornography needed to be banned in order to protect women's interests. In the Butler decision on this matter, the state accepted this argument, despite the fact that none of the expert testimony in the trial at hand testified to a clear link between representations of violence and acts of violence. Interestingly, one of the first applications of the law since the Butler decision was enforced against lesbian pornography. Anti-censorship feminists have argued, then, that this application tells us of the danger in appealing to "protection."[30] While some feminists argued that women needed to be "protected" from sexually explicit representations, it is interesting that the Canadian state's first act of "protection" was directed against culture created by and for lesbians. This historical example warns of the danger in appealing to "protection" of women's interests, for it can too easily serve the needs of a moralist state uninterested and hostile to sexual diversity in Canada.

We offer these two historical examples, then, as an important reminder to teachers that we should not take a feminist appeal to "protection" at face value. Once we consider the deeply conservative political work which occurs in the name of protection, it is necessary to rethink the equation made between "women's rights" and "human rights" as proposed by VRR. We do not accept the claim that "human rights advance with each advance in the equality and liberation of women."

Indeed, critical scholars have shown us that the history of a struggle for "women's rights" in Canada is also a history of imperialism.[31] Feminists such as Nellie McClung and Emily Murphy held deeply racist beliefs, and their projects of social reform were intimately linked to colonialism and a settler society. Emily Murphy, for instance, is often hailed as one of the feminist leaders instrumental in getting women the vote in Canada. She was also active in matters of social reform such as drug policies and drug laws. In her book *The Black Candle*, Murphy argues that it is important to combat the trafficking in drugs because it weakens the nation. Together with a declining birth rate, Murphy contends that this factor will be the downfall of the British Empire.[32] Elsewhere in the book she writes of how white female addicts are enslaved to the negro and Chinese men who corrupt them through drugs.[33] In this regard, the political work of feminists like Murphy and McClung with respect to "women's rights" was carried out in service to the British Empire. These limitations of their political organizing challenge the assertion made by VRR that "human rights advance with each advance in the equality and liberation of women." In point of fact, the historical evidence in Canada shows that efforts to advance the legal equality of women had detrimental consequences for human rights more broadly.

We believe it is important for students and teachers to learn from this history. Careful reflection in this regard cautions us against making faulty equations between the advancement of "women's rights" and those of "human rights." Indeed, the task of the critical scholar includes understanding how an appeal to "women's rights" has been instrumental in the work of imperialism as well as in the functioning of a moralist state.

Teachers in the women's studies classroom can help students learn from the history of a feminist appeal to "protection." Given this history, what does it mean when VRR invokes the notion with respect to the Nixon case? Can we trust this appeal to "protecting" women's interests to be other than a conservative move, and if so, on what basis? How have feminists in the past linked the autonomy of women to the notion of protection? Does the position advocated by VRR differ from this history?

The Nixon case allows teachers to present the history of imperialism in feminism, a discussion particularly suited to courses on the history of women in Canada, as well as courses in feminist thought and anti-racism. Furthermore, it creates an opportunity for teachers to help students think about fundamental concepts used to advance a political agenda—in this instance, the notion of "protection." Such pedagogy is particularly useful in courses on feminist theory, although of course it can be usefully applied in any women's studies classroom.

Conclusion

In recent years, the Kimberly Nixon case is discussed more and more within university-based feminist circles. Frequently, analysis of the case limits itself to questions of identity. Is Nixon a woman? How do we define who is a woman? Can transsexual women be active members of (non-transsexual) women's groups?

Our reflections on the Nixon case seek to move teachers and students beyond this narrow framework. We have argued that the Nixon case is pedagogically useful and important not with respect to identity ("who is a woman?"), but rather in relation to some fundamental questions of feminist history, theory, and politics. The case allows teachers to introduce different theoretical traditions of feminist thought and how they define the concept of "experience." It creates an opportunity for teachers in the women's studies classroom to help their students think about an appeal to a universal women's experience, as well as the attending race and class biases of such an argument. The Nixon case can also help students to reflect on analogies made between race and gender within a liberal framework and the limitations therein. Furthermore, the case lends itself well to discussion on women and politics, since different positions with respect to the Nixon case embody different definitions of the state. Finally, the Nixon case provides an occasion for the critical teacher to facilitate learning with respect to an invocation of "protecting" women's rights, understanding how this notion of protection has been deployed in a conservative manner historically.

These reflections offer different ways to refocus the debate. We believe that it is necessary and productive to reorient how feminists think about the Nixon case in order to offer a broader conception of justice. In this regard, we take issue with Judy Rebick's statement at the Tribunal that

> The issue at stake is whether or not a women's group has the right to decide who its members are .... there's no question that transgendered people suffer from discrimination, they suffer a great deal. So of course, in your heart as a feminist you want to be on their side in every fight but you can't because there's a conflict of rights. It goes to the heart of what the women's movement is and what feminism is.[34]

Rebick's comments illustrate the implications of understanding the Nixon case exclusively with respect to identity. When the debate is framed as a matter of whether or not transsexual women are women, it becomes possible to advance the somewhat incredulous argument that there exists a "conflict of rights" between transsexual women and non-transsexual women.

Yet before we accept the terms set out by Rebick, we think it useful to reflect on how she can establish a "conflict of rights" between marginalized peoples. How is it that she can understand the oppression of people within a framework of conflict and competing interests? How does she reconcile this position with feminism's commitment to understanding the links among oppression? What are the social, political, and institutional conditions which produce divisive thinking like that of Rebick? Can feminists advocate a programme of justice which appeals to competing rights?

How have feminists resisted this type of analysis, and how have they adopted it?

We hope that this essay helps both teachers and students think critically about the Nixon case, in ways that move beyond the identity-based frame of reference advocated by Rebick. Analysis of the Nixon case, which moves beyond identity, can assist feminists in the development of truly inclusive conceptions and practices of justice.

Notes

1. Patricia Elliot, "Who Gets to Be a Woman? Feminism, Sexual Politics and Transsexual Trouble," presentation at "Transgender/Transsexual: Theory, Organizing, Cultural Production" Symposium, Graduate Programme in Women's Studies, York University, Toronto, November 29, 2002.

2. Ian Bailey, "Rebick Defends Rape Centre's Right to Reject Transsexual." *National Post,* December 19, 2000; Mary-Woo Sims, "Why Transgendered People Need Human Rights Protection," *Herizons,* Fall 2001: 19–21, 28; Vancouver Rape Relief, "Vancouver Rape Relief Responds to Mary-Woo Sims Remarks," *Herizons,* Fall 2001: 29; "Can a Transgendered Person Be 'One of Us,'" *Herizons,* Fall 2001: 22–23, 27.

3. We outline some of the main arguments here that are particularly relevant for the women' studies classroom. A detailed reading of the Tribunal transcripts, submissions to the Tribunal and the decision would, of course, offer additional arguments and evidence.

4. Christine Boyle, "Vancouver Rape Relief and Women's Shelter Legal Argument Part 1." Presented January 24–26, 2001. Available online at www.rapereliefshelter.bc.ca/issues/knixon_cboyle_argum.html.

5. Ibid.

6. Vancouver Rape Relief, "Nixon vs. Vancouver Rape Relief Society: Pending before the B.C. Human Rights Tribunal." January 2002. (Available online at www.rapereliefshelter.bc.ca/issues/knixon_outline.html.)

7. Cited in Ian Bailey, "Rebick Defends Rape Centre's Right to Reject Transsexual." *National Post,* December 19, 2000.

8. VRR, "Vancouver Rape Relief Responds to Mary-Woo Sims Remarks," *Herizons,* Fall 2001: 21.

9. Rape Relief's Summary of Key Evidence By Issue, Sections 63, 64. Presented January 24–26, 2001. Available online at www.rapereliefshelter.bc.ca/issues/knixon_summary.html.

10. Heather MacNaughton, Nixon v. Vancouver Rape Relief Society 2002 BCHRT1, S 202. Available online at www.bchrt.gov.bc.ca/nixon_v_vancouver_rape_relief_society_2002_bchrt_1.htm.

11. Rape Relief's Summary of Key Evidence By Issue, Section 8. Presented January 24–26, 2001. Available online at www.rapereliefshelter.bc.ca/issues/knixon_summary.html.

12. See, for instance, Audre Lorde, *A Burst of Light* (Ithaca, NY: Firebrand Books, 1988).

13. Rape Relief's Summary of Key Evidence By Issue, Section 8. Presented January 24–26, 2001. Available online at www.rapereliefshelter.bc.ca/issues/knixon_summary.html.

14. Kerry Lobel, ed., *Naming the Violence: Speaking Out against Lesbian Battering* (Seattle: Seal Press, 1986).

15. Carol Bacchi, *Liberation Deferred? The Ideas of the English Canadian Suffragists, 1877–1918* (Toronto: University of Toronto Press, 1983).

16. Goldney in "Can a Trans-gendered Person Be 'One of Us'?" *Herizons,* Fall 2001: 23.

17. Findlay, "Nixon Wins against Rape Relief," press release circulated via email January 17, 2002.

18. Swangha, "A Man Wanting to Be a Woman Is Like a White Person Wanting to Be Black." *Gendertrash* 3 (Winter 1995): 23–24. Emphasis in original.

19. Vancouver Rape Relief Society v. BC Human Rights Commission, 2000 BCSC 889. Cited in Heather MacNaughton, Nixon v. Vancouver Rape Relief Society 2002 BCHRT 1, S 3. Available online at www.bchrt.gov.bc.ca/nixon_v_vancouver_rape_relief_society_2002_bchrt_1.htm.

20. Heather MacNaughton, Nixon v. Vancouver Rape Relief Society 2002 BCHRT 1, Sections 47–73. Available online at www.bchrt.gov.bc.ca/nixon_v_vancouver_rape_relief_society_2002_bchrt_1.htm.

21. Heather MacNaughton, Nixon v. Vancouver Rape Relief Society 2002 BCHRT 1, S 52. Available online at www.bchrt.gov.bc.ca/nixon_v_vancouver_rape_relief_society_2002_bchrt_1.htm.

22. Cf. Findlay, "Nixon Wins against Rape Relief," press release circulated via email January 17, 2002.

23. Bacchi, *Liberation Deferred?*

24. Janet Stilman, *Enough Is Enough! Aboriginal Women Speak Out* (Toronto: Women's Press, 1987).

25. See, for instance, Sherene Razack, ed., *Race, Space, and the Law. Unmapping a White Settler Society* (Toronto: Between the Lines, 2002).

26. Rape Relief's Summary of Key Evidence by Issue. Presented January 24–26, 2001. Available online at www.rapereliefshelter.bc.ca/issues/knixon_summary.html.

27. "Vancouver Rape Relief Seeks BC Supreme Court of Appeal of Human Rights Decision in Women-Only Case," Press Release, June 24, 2002.

28. VRR, "Vancouver Rape Relief Responds to Mary-Woo Sims Remarks," *Herizons,* Fall 2001: 21.

29. See Allison Jaggar, *Feminist Politics and Human Nature* (Totawa, NJ: Rowman and Allanheld, 1983), 176.

30. A critical overview of the Butler decision and its effects is offered in Brenda Cossman, Shannon Bell, Lise Gotell, and Becki Ross, eds., *Bad Attitude/s on Trial: Pornography, Feminism and the Butler Decision* (Toronto: University of Toronto Press, 1997).

31. Bacchi, *Liberation Deferred?*

32. Emily Murphy, *The Black Candle* (Toronto: Thomas Allen, 1922), 46–47.

33. Ibid., 302–303.

34. Cited in Ian Bailey, "Rebick Defends Rape Centre's Right to Reject Transsexual." *National Post,* December 19, 2000.

Queer Pedagogies of the Closet: Teaching Ignorances in the Heteronormative Classroom

Jean Bobby Noble

A very meta-textual moment occurred recently on the Showcase hit television show *Queer As Folk,* a moment that has much to teach us about the stakes of identities, identity politics, and strangely enough, knowledge production and consumption in our classrooms. One of the *QAF* gay couples—Teddy and Emmitt—has recently purchased a new home away from the queer neighbourhood, Liberty Street, and deep into the belly of 21st century heteronormative suburban culture. Teddy, who still owns and operates a gay porn/jerk-off website at this point, and flamboyant, working class Emmitt, are invited to a neighbourhood *meet 'n greet* cocktail party with their new neighbours: middle aged, middle class, married, heterosexual couples of a variety of races and ethnicities. Fearing aggressive homophobia, or even worse, awkward silence, Teddy and Emmitt encounter instead a "progressive" and knowledgeable group of heterosexuals who are not only welcoming of their new gay neighbours, but also quite proudly recount what they think is "in" knowledge about gay life. Ted and Emmitt are introduced to their neighbours, who seem to go out of their (heterosexual) way, so to speak, to make them feel welcome. Comments such as "Thanks for coming, we know you boys have better things to do on a Friday night"; "Our favourite drama is that show,

Gay As Blazes—you know, gay people have the same problems that we do"; "I have a cousin who's a lesbian"; and "My brother is a tranny" have the opposite effect on Teddy and Emmitt, whose entire lives from gay Liberty Street have been quite easily consumed by folks who seemingly should not be so in the know. As *Queer As Folk* went to commercial, I sat spellbound, like Emmitt and Teddy, feeling caught in these epistemological and meta-textual headlights, wondering, queerly enough, whether being *out* of the closet really was worth all it promised, especially, as is evident not just with this episode but with big city Pride celebrations, all things gay now traffic amongst heteronormative cultures with ease and, dare I say it, ownership.

What is even more instructive about this *QAF* episode is the way it speaks to both the successes and failures of two simultaneous trajectories. The first trajectory has to be the success of gay, lesbian, bisexual, transgender/transsexual, two-spirit and queer (GLBTTQ) liberatory politics in the twentieth century.[1] On the eve of legal gay marriage in Canada, and begging the question of what *success* actually means (a long complicated question beyond the scope of this essay), the demarcation of a "gay demographic" by capitalism as both a consumer group and also target audience for shows like *QAF* surely bespeaks something like *success*. Part of what the latter might also mean is the inclusion of GLBTTQ epistemologies, should such a thing actually exist, into both post-secondary curriculum and agenda but also into, and indeed, as again a demographic for, academic publishing. [2]

But it is another trajectory that interests me more in this essay. While the inclusion of GLBTTQ and "sexuality studies" into postsecondary education as both curriculum and knowledge vis-à-vis publishing (read: codifying) practices certainly gestures toward *success*, these inclusions also mark sites of tremendous struggle and conflict for teachers working with these materials as *pedagogy* outside the context of identity-based programs. With respect to other critical scholarship, such as cultural studies—a sort of kissing cousin of GLBTTQ studies—Stuart Hall (1992) wrote of the dangers of institutionalization,

> My own feeling is that the explosion of cultural studies along with other forms of critical theory in the academy represents a moment of extraordinarily profound danger. Why? Well, it would be excessively vulgar to talk about such things as how many jobs there are, how much money there is around, and how much pressure that puts on people to do what they think of as critical political work and intellectual work of a critical kind, while also looking over their shoulders at the promotions stakes and the publication stakes, and so on. (285–86)

It's going to be my argument here that if we're not going to heed Hall's warning *against* the institutionalization of critical practices—a warning that certainly GLBTTQ studies must hear at the very least—then one of those profound dangers is the failure to elaborate a model of not just critical theory within queer studies but also, and perhaps more importantly, the

failure to institutionalize a model, and especially a practice, of counter-cultural pedagogies.[3] I want to elaborate such a model of counter-cultural pedagogy here. To that end, I suggest, any consideration of critical pedagogy and queer studies must return to Louis Althusser.

Of social formations, like the one under discussion here—that is, education—Althusser (2001) writes, "[…] a social formation which does not reproduce the conditions of production at the same time it is produced would not last a year … the ultimate condition of production is therefore the reproduction of the conditions of production" (1483). This is, then, precisely what ideology and ideological state apparatuses accomplish: not only do they produce the necessary subjects, but they also apprentice those subjects in what he calls the "know-how"—the value systems, the virtues—in other words, the cultures of these social formations that help to ensure their longevity. But, more significantly, of the educational apparatus he posits with some degree of alacrity: "no other ideological state apparatus has the obligatory (and not least, free) audience of the totality of the children in the capitalist social formation, 8 hours a day for 5 or 6 days out of 7 … in this concert of ISAs, one ideological state apparatus certainly has the dominant role although hardly anyone lends an ear to its music; it is so silent! This is the school" (1494).

He goes on, and again I quote at length:

> It [school] takes children from *every* class at infant-school age, and then for years, the years in which the child is most "vulnerable," squeezed between the family state apparatus and the educational state apparatus, it drums into them, *whether it uses new or old methods*, a certain amount of "know-how" wrapped in the ruling ideologies (French, arithmetic, natural history, the sciences, literature) or simply the ruling ideology in its pure state (ethics, civic instruction, philosophy). Somewhere around the age of 16,

a huge mass of children are ejected "into production"; these are the workers [...]. Another portion of scholastically adapted youth carries on: and, for better or worse, it goes somewhat further, until it falls by the wayside and fills the posts of small and middle technicians, white-collar workers, small and middle executives, petty bourgeois of all kinds. A last portion reaches the summit, either to fall into intellectual semi-employment, or to provide, as well as the "intellectuals of the collective labourer," the agents of exploitation (capitalists, managers), the agents of repression (soldiers, policemen, politicians, administrators, etc.) and the professional ideologists (priests of all sorts). Each mass ejection is practically provided with the ideology which suits the role it has to fulfill. Thus, the Church has been replaced today in its role as the dominant ISA by the school. (1485, emphasis added)

By implication then, any theory of critical pedagogy then has to base what we do inside the classroom on what the social and ideological functioning of educational institutions are; Foucault and others have certainly detailed the cultural and political work of knowledge regimes, but what about the ideological work of our post-secondary schools? It must be true then that if Althusser is right, our schools themselves produce students, among other things, as citizens in training; moreover (with the increasing intervention of our banking systems vis-à-vis on the names of buildings as well as on university governance boards but also into the student loan process and then offering student lines of credit once they got out of the student loan business) schools and postsecondary education is also producing young capitalist consumers. Nowhere do we see the perniciousness of this more than in the all too frequent student-cum-consumer claim that "I paid my money; I should get an

A." But most importantly, non-critical pedagogies reproduce themselves by reproducing educationalized subjects who then do the work of reproducing a demand for a continuance of the regime of knowledge itself.

Moreover, what of the trope Althusser uses? He argues that ISAs function as a "concert" but one where the instrument with the loudest ideological sway is the one we hear the least: "It is so silent!" These four words, complete with exclamation mark, remain to me something of a curiosity; on the one hand, Althusser seems to be saying, dare I say it, the obvious: that this is an ISA that is most naturalized and self-evident. But, if the most effective ISAs work through delimiting, overdetermining what we cannot hear, and cannot know, see, classify, define even, than might a strategy of resistance need to work similarly on—as, even— the same site?

The most curious thing to me in Althusser's reiterative, performative attribution of silence to ISAs, is its resonance with Eve Kosofsky Sedgwick's notion of ignorance. In a lovely essay called "The Privilege of Unknowing," Sedgwick (1990) similarly argues that ignorance is not the absence or opposite of knowledge but its silent co-creator. "Knowledge is not itself power," she writes, "although it is the magnetic field of power. Ignorance [in other words] and opacity collude or compete with it in mobilizing the flows of meaning" (24). Sedgwick uses an example of language to illustrate her point but this metaphor works on so many levels: if, for instance, a French Canadian knows English but an English speaking Canadian lacks French, it is the Francophone who must negotiate meanings through an acquired tongue while the *ignorant* Anglophone may dilate in his/her own mother language. In this instance, the terms of the exchange are delimited by the interlocutor's not mutual but *deficient* interpretative practices or knowledge. Any identity-based liberation movement knows this in its bones: that to achieve "equality" one must render difference (invisible and) knowable on the larger group's terms. These ignorance effects or epistemological asymmetries, Sedgwick argues, are harnessed, licensed, socially sanctioned, and regulated on a mass scale for what she calls striking enforcements of meaning making activities. They, in other words, are produced by and correspond to particulate knowledges and circulate not *as the absence of* but *as part of* particular regimes of truth. And like Althusser's concert, we often do not hear these silences functioning the way we should. "Inarguably," she concludes, "the power of our enemies over us is implicated, not in their command of knowledge, but precisely in their ignorance" (24). Sedgwick's argument is born out by the *Queer As Folk* anecdote at the opening of my essay. For many gay-positive and anti-homophobic heterosexual folks, the solution to heteronormative lacuna is merely the unselfconscious consumption of gay identities so that being *in the know* replaces being *out of the loop*. Pedagogically, this means simply filling in the details rather than troubling the ground of intelligibility itself. Instead, what this project calls for is an interrogation of the larger regime of truth overdetermining such epistemological gazes.

Conventional regimes of education, it seems to me, often attempt to implement similar remedies, equating ignorance and innocence. That is, we presume students come to us without knowledge, ignorant of a subject until the course that we've so carefully put together does its work to bring that innocence to an end. Content is key in that paradigm. They are, at that point, knowledgeable of Shakespeare, or Hitchcock, or whatever the course content has been. But how does this work with cultural studies? Does the same epistemological trajectory hold true? How can it when the meta-object of critical knowledge production—as I define it not just "the study of cultural objects" as content, but the process by which culture, knowledge, subjectivities, meaning, intelligibility, and so forth come into being at all—that we ourselves are not the originators of that regime but its byproduct? The obvious answer here is that pedagogies simply cannot work the same way.

I offer here then, two interdisciplinary models or trajectories as a way to begin developing critical queer studies pedagogies by re-mobilizing or harnessing such ignorance/silence effects in our critical classrooms: first, the concept of entrustment as part of a larger strategy of consciousness-raising (both of these I borrow from feminist critical pedagogies); second, the strategy of teaching ignorances, or teaching to un-know, rather than teaching knowledge (borrowed from both deconstruction and from queer theory).

Seems to me as though the concept of consciousness-raising might be a useful one to cultural studies. By consciousness-raising, I do not mean *upward mobility* and *feel good* individual empowerment vis-à-vis Oprah. I do mean teaching students/subjects to *recognize* the necessary interpellative mis-recognitions; I mean—with Patti Lather, Peter McLaren, Roger Simon, Henry Giroux and others—the need for critical pedagogy to be transformative with its subjects. If ideology necessitates that we misrecognize ourselves in the service of capitalism, and indeed, global capitalism and corporacracy (rule by corporations) then our pedagogies then must work toward decreasing distortions and mystifications in our culture's mythologies and narratives about itself. But they cannot do this—even in queer studies—if they remain duplicate the ideological work of post-secondary educational institutions while increasingly doing the bidding of capitalism.

Okay, so far so good. But how does this happen? Given that the pedagogical relation inside the classroom is one where the primary structure is not "equality," but rather is one of conscious, controlled, and self-conscious power imbalances, the rhetoric of "trust" in the classroom has to be replaced by the dynamic of "entrustment." Entrustment is a term I borrow from Teresa de Lauretis's introduction to the Milan Women's Bookstore Collective's historiography of Italian feminism, where a kind of mentorship occurred, as politics, between older and younger women in the feminist movement. The first is the symbolic practice of *affidamento* (or entrustment), in which one woman entrusts herself to another, as in a sisterhood, in acknowledgement of the disparity (intellectual, cultural, economic) between them. This entrustment provides an instrumental means toward self-affirmation and self-knowledge. This model was fascinating because it *required* power differences—albeit those mapped along the axes of age—to exist between its subjects for transformation to occur. Entrustment, as I want to use it in the classroom, requires a construction of knowledge as structure (more on that in a second) and not necessarily as content, as well as an understanding of power as manufactured consent in the face of unequal institutional power differences. We need to convince our students that the deconstructive program they are about to embark on is in their interest as much as it is painful. I, in other words, need to use our scripted scene of "learning" inside the classroom to deconstruct their misrecognitions of both themselves and the institutions we often ambivalently call home.

This program works best, though, when coupled with the interrogation and critical examination of that which appears as most self-evident, and that is with a deconstruction of the differences between "knowledge" and "ignorance." Enter deconstruction, through the work of Barbara Johnson. In an essay called "Teaching Ignorance," Johnson argues that one of the best pedagogical tools we have is the ability to mobilize the critical energy and intellectual upheaval of surprise (1987). What we need to teach in this line of thinking is not the repressive methods of telling our students what they should know; rather we need to teach students to be surprised by what they do not—perhaps can not ever—know. In other words, critical pedagogy must step away from a liberal humanist fantasy of teaching knowledge, and ground itself instead in the teaching of *ignorance*. I quote Johnson here: "If the deconstructive impulse [of critical thinking/cultural studies] is to retain its vital and subversive edge, we must become ignorant of it again

and again. It is only by forgetting what we know how to do, by setting aside the thoughts that have most changed us, that *those* thoughts and *that* knowledge can go on doing what a surprise encounter with otherness should do, that is, lay bare some hint of an ignorance one never knew one had" (16). In other words, we teach to un-know, to allow our students to become conscious of the fact that what they think of as knowledge is really a regime of received ideas, ideologies, prejudices and opinions, a way, as Johnson says, of not knowing that one does not know. So, if this is true, then the first thing that we need to do in our classroom is not think we can transmit knowledge, but rather we need to begin *suspending it*.

Our classroom work then becomes the critical de-familiarization of what has traditionally counted as "Knowledge." Clearly this agenda requires that students take risks, attempt to grapple with that which they *don't* know and *can't* yet think. In other words, in my experience "Learning" emerges out of that which confuses them, which frustrates them, which troubles them into an act of treachery against who they've been hailed as, not out of that which is easily reiterated and then "mastered." In this way, we can reconfigure the ways in which knowledge, not ignorance, becomes the obstacle of knowing.

I know this is the inverse opposite of what passes as common sense but I for one am particularly fond of inversion; but also, let me illustrate how this works through one quick example. In her other tremendously important work, *Epistemology of the Closet*, Sedgwick makes the argument that questions about subjectivity have been bound by a set of epistemological contradictions; Sedgwick is referring to what she calls the epistemologies or regimes of knowledge around homo/heterosexual definition, but I would argue that these generalize well to subject positions organized around trans-identities, sexuality, gender, class, and race as well: one the one hand, some questions of identity have been conservatively constructed as a minoritizing discourse (seeing that identity as an issue of active importance only for a small, distinct, relatively fixed group of people, for instance).

On the other hand, what we need to do instead is to re-theorize our subjectivities as universalizing discourses (an issue of continuing, determinative active importance in the lives of subjects across the spectrum of races or sexualities or genders). In other words, minoritizing discourses allow us to shift the burden of identity— whatever identities we are talking about here—to those always already marked as the Other versus a universalizing approach, which allows us to decentre and shift our gaze from those objectified by these discourses back on to the subject doing the gazing: folks with supposedly biologically secure identities, or to masculinity or to heterosexuality or on to whiteness, for instance.

This is, and I want to be clear about this, not shifting power back to these subjects, but shifting a destabilizing epistemological gaze back to argue that what we can best do in the classroom is facilitate a surprise encounter with these identities not as successfully naturalized identities

but with them as socially produced and socially reinforced imperatives, fictions we need to become "ignorant" of. Thus, my strategy is to always discursively *mark* unmarked silences within regimes of truth (identities such as heterosexuality, whiteness, and masculinity), interrogate *their* social and historical construction, examine how they are *systemically* located and positioned as something we are ignorant of. Second, the long term goal is to always critically de-familarize both *what* we read, *who* we read as, and *how* we read, eventually, to make the familiar (the known) strange, the unfamiliar knowledge-able. To allow students to be surprised by what they don't know about their own subjectivities, to have a surprise encounter with an ignorance about themselves that they didn't even know they had ... so that ignorance becomes a kind of deconstructive pedagogically productive imperative. Instead of *know thyself* we might want to encourage our students to *know their ignorances*, as that is more often than not, the place where we find critical knowledges.

Notes

1. It is noteworthy that these terms are the subject of much contestation. The terrain I'm mapping with the index "GLBTTQ" is never as simple as this grouping of letters or words suggests. While none of these subject positions is reducible to the other by way of ontology, histories, and articulations through race, gender, class, nation, physically ability, and so on, I strategically group them here to situate them rhetorically in opposition to heteronormative affiliations. The work of troubling the seeming coherence of "GLBTTQ" is the work of queer pedagogies and sexuality studies scholarship.

2. Routledge was one of the first publishers to begin codifying the field of gay, lesbian, bisexual, transsexual, transgender studies with, among other things, *The Lesbian and Gay Studies Reader* (1993). These types of books, while

necessary, certainly both constitute a scholarly field of study but also misrepresent the degree to which these fields of study are "acceptable" academic practices within universities and funded as such through departments and tenure stream jobs.

3. Hall notes this in the same essay:

> [W]hen we talk about the institutional position of cultural studies, we often fail to talk about questions of teaching and pedagogy. We talk about intellectual practice as if it is the practice of intellectuals in the library reading the right canonical texts or consulting other intellectuals at conferences or something like that. But the ongoing work of an intellectual practice for most

of us, insofar as we get our material sustenance, our modes of reproduction, from doing our academic work, in indeed to teach. Before we invoke the great mass ranks out there, it might be quite important that our students are with us in the project. (1992: 290)

References

Abelove, Henry, Barale, Michèle Aina, and Halperin, David M., eds. *The Lesbian and Gay Studies Reader.* New York: Routledge, 1993.

Althusser, Louis. "Ideology and Ideological State Apparatuses." *The Norton Anthology of Theory and Criticism.* Vincent B. Leitch, General Editor. New York: W.W. Norton, 2001. 1483–1509.

Britzman, P. Deborah. *Lost Subjects, Contested Objects: Toward a Psychoanalytic Inquiry of Learning.* Albany: SUNY Press, 1998.

Foucault, Michel. *The Order of Things: An Archaeology of the Human Sciences.* London: Tavistock Publishers, 1970.

_____. *The Archaeology of Knowledge and the Discourse on Language.* A.M. Sheridan Smith, Trans. New York: Pantheon, 1972.

Giroux, Henry. *Border Crossings: Cultural Workers and the Politics of Education.* New York: Routledge, 1992.

Hall, Stuart. "Cultural Studies and Its Theoretical Legacies," *Cultural Studies.* Lawrence Grossberg et al., Eds. New York: Routledge, 1992. 277–294.

Johnson, Barbara. *A World of Difference.* Baltimore and London: The Johns Hopkins University Press, 1987.

Lather, Patti. *Getting Smart: Feminist Research and Pedagogy With/in the Postmodern.* New York: Routledge, 1991.

McLaren, Peter. *Critical Pedagogy and Predatory Culture: Oppositional Politics in a Postmodern Era.* London: Routledge, 1995.

Milan Women's Bookstore Collective. *Sexual Difference: A Theory of Social-Symbolic Practice.* Bloomington: Indiana University Press, 1990.

Simon, Roger. *Teaching against the Grain: Texts for a Pedagogy of Possibility.* New York: Bergin and Garvey, 1992.

Sedgwick, Eve Kosofsky. *Epistemology of the Closet.* Berkeley: University of California Press, 1990.

_____. "Privilege of Unknowing," *Tendencies.* Durham: Duke University Press, 1993.

SECTION SEVEN

POPULAR CULTURE

Discovering the Spark

Janice Acoose

... fenced in and forced to give up everything that had meaning to [our] life ... But under the long snows of despair the little spark of our ancient beliefs and pride kept glowing, just barely sometimes, waiting for a warm wind to blow that spark into a flame again.

—Mary Crow Dog, *Lakota Woman*

In much of anglophone canadian fiction, Indigenous women are misrepresented in images that perpetuate racist and sexist stereotypes. Stereotypic images of Indian princesses, squaw drudges, suffering helpless victims, tawny temptresses, or loose squaws falsify our realities and suggest in a subliminal way that those stereotypic images are us. As a consequence, those images foster cultural attitudes that encourage sexual, physical, verbal, or psychological violence against Indigenous women. Stereotypic images also function as sentinels that guard and protect the white eurocanadian-christian-patriarchy (and now to a limited extent the same kind of matriarchy) against any threatening disturbances that might upset the status quo.

Throughout what can only be described as the overwhelmingly brutal history of Indigenous-white relations, the power held by Indigenous women constantly threatened the foundational ideology. Previous to those relations, our roles were constructed in woman-centred cultures which encouraged balance and respect for all things animate and inanimate in the environment. According to Paula Gunn Allen, the colonizing powers thought that, as long as women held such power, the imperialistic attempts to conquer Indigenous peoples throughout the continent were doomed to fail.[1] Therefore, the weccp structure—represented throughout history by white-christian-male colonial government officials, missionaries, and merchants—attempted to usurp women's power, although it may not always have been consciously or in visibly apparent ways. Throughout the struggles that resulted, we have survived and demonstrated autonomy through courageous acts of self-government and self-determination. In 1971 and 1977 respectively, Jeannette Corbiere-Lavell (Anishnabe) and Sandra Lovelace (Maliseet) prompted radical alterations to the Indian Act by mounting legal challenges to its discriminatory policies against "Indian" women. Prior to the efforts of these women and the subsequent 1985 Canadian Charter of Rights and Freedoms, "Indian" women, as defined by the Indian Act, who married non-"Indian" men lost their legal rights as "Indians" and thus became "non-status Indians," while "non-Indian" women who married "Indian" men became legal "Indian" women. In 1990, Kanine' Keha: Ka (Mohawk) women bravely defended the people and their ancestral lands, maintained peace, and participated in ongoing negotiations during the stand-off with the Canadian army at Oka, Quebec. In 1991 and again in 1994, the Assembly of First Nations' newly elected national chief, Ovide Mercredi, was not officially recognized until a council of women Elders raised him up into office. Despite these obvious manifestations of Indigenous women's vital role within our communities and larger society, the english-canadian patriarchy, and now the Indigenous patriarchy, continue to misrepresent and diminish our lives.

In "Our World: According to Ossennontion and Skonaganleh: ra," Ossennontion/Marlyn Kane (former president of the Native Women's Association of Canada) explains how women's roles are continually effaced.[2] In order to understand ideological differences between Indigenous peoples and non-Indigenous peoples, she maintains, all the old so-called truths about women must be re-examined. She explains that in her culture women have always had a central role as keepers of culture, values, and beliefs. But, more than keepers of culture, we also exercised political autonomy over our bodies, relations with others, and in the social, political, economic, and spiritual realms. Over the years, however, women have had to struggle against christian patriarchy imposed through church dogma, educational indoctrination tied to christianity which encourages specific gender roles, laws which discriminated against women, and legislation which allowed our children to be taken away and placed in residential schools.

In these schools, english-canadian literature institutionalizes the settler's ideology through language, which Emma LaRocque appropriately describes as "an ideological onion whose stinging layers of racism and sexism must be peeled away."[3] She also insists that literature is powerfully political because "its linguistic and ideological transmission is too often defined and determined by those in power."[4] In order to maintain power, the english-canadian patriarchy perpetuates stereotypical representations of Indigenous women. These representations subsequently function as ideological constructs which encourage justification of gender and cultural imbalance. To understand how this process works and reverse its effects, we must attempt to deconstruct and decolonize english-canadian literature. In doing so, readers will also help liberate Indigenous women from such false images as those of the Indian princess, the easy squaw, and the suffering helpless victim. Until such time, these images will continue to imprison us in racist and sexist stereotypes and therefore, as Patricia Albers explains, obscure fundamental realities about women's status and roles.[5]

In canada, the roots of english-canadian literature are nourished by centuries of christian ideology that justifies and sanctions a white-male rule premised on the central hierarchy of god-king-man-boy. Deconstructing and decolonizing literary traditions firmly planted in the age-old power structure requires both subverting the racist and sexist assumptions carried by colonial and patriarchal discourse in english, and re-naming and re-defining people and places based on the Indigenous peoples' own ideological context. In many respects, re-naming and re-defining the original peoples will be the most challenging because our languages have been violently suppressed and our cultures traumatized by close to five hundred years of physical, emotional, and spiritual coercion. Recognizing that language can and does shape our experiences, it is vitally important that Indigenous women appropriate the english language in order to represent our experiences. Anthologist Connie Fife reinforces this idea. She writes: "We [Aboriginal women] have found that the written word does not have to be wrapped in the thoughts of the colonizers, but rather can convey the resilience of our survival."[6] As this anthology reflects, more and more Indigenous women are not only surviving but encouraging and preserving our ways, ironically, some through the use of the colonizer's language. Others, however, reject the colonizer's language entirely and write only in their own language. Still others rely on both languages, english and their own Indigenous language, to reach wider audiences. As an educator, I feel it is important to use both languages. It is important to write in our own languages because we need to preserve the languages and cultures. But, it is also important to use english because we must know this language and by knowing it free ourselves from the oppression associated with ignorance.

As Indigenous peoples, our mythologies encourage the belief that our original ancestors' bodies were created from specific lands within the areas now known as north america. While distinguished by many different cultures, we share ideological assumptions about our relationship to the land, in ways analogous to those by which capitalism or socialism unites specific peoples. The Independent Commission of International Humanitarian Issues recognized that Indigenous peoples throughout the world share a world view which encourages a custodial concept of the land, as well as of the natural resources.[7] The formation of the World Council of Indigenous Peoples in 1975 institutionalized this common ideology.

This peculiar way of being and relating to the earth, this ideology, transmits what our Cree Elders refer to in ceremony as a Kah' Ki Yaw Ni Wahkomakanak (all our relations) philosophy. It is important to note here that in most Indigenous cultures Elders recite a similar invocation prior to and during spiritual ceremonies. In the introduction to *All My Relations* Thomas King explains that the idea of "all my relations" reminds us about who we are, not only within ourselves but in connection to our family, relatives, all human beings, the animals, plants, animate and inanimate forms, and everything that can be imagined. According to King, this philosophy also encourages Indigenous peoples to respectfully acknowledge responsibilities to those to whom we are connected and to live our lives in a harmonious and moral

way. This philosophy, albeit not always visible in every Indigenous person's life, is nevertheless constant in our spiritual lives, ceremonies, rituals, and pre-christian languages.

Within the pre-christian language systems, particularly among the Plains Nehiowin and the Nicowin cultures, the phrase Kah' Ki Yaw Ni Wahkomakanak expresses a way of life that embodies a non-hierarchical association between Elders, women, men, and children. Tomson Highway, who grew up on his Cree father's trapline in northwestern Manitoba, maintains that one of the most distinguishing differences between white european-rooted cultures and Indigenous cultures in north america is that within most Indigenous languages there is no reference to gender. He reinforces this idea by referring to Indigenous mythologies in which the central hero figure is not exclusively female or male, or can be both simultaneously. Highway indirectly refers to the philosophical "all my relations" way of living by expressing the connectedness of all "Indians" through his usage of the pronoun "our."[8]

This connectedness or unity among all forms of life within the environment essentially describes the philosophical aspect of living together as relations and it is a fundamental premise of much contemporary Indigenous peoples' writing. In the literature, this philosophy or way of life is symbolized by a circle. Paula Gunn Allen explains that her mother's teachings that "'Life is a circle, and everything has its place in it'" nourished *The Sacred Hoop*. Similarly, the anthology of "Native" women of western canada appropriately titled *Writing the Circle* implies that "Natives" can heal themselves by writing themselves back into the "circle of life" or empowering themselves by returning to an "all my relations" way of life. Emma LaRocque's preface to this anthology draws attention to "Indians [who] acknowledged and practised a host of distinctions, yet maintained a functional connectedness between parts."[9] Thomas King's previously cited text identifies the contemporary "Native" writers' source of inspiration as a way of life that incorporates living together as relations. Beatrice Medicine and Patricia Albers' *The Hidden Half: Studies of Plains Indian Women* offers unique information about Plains "Indian" Women, whose existence is marked as half of the population, who are women, but who in a patriarchal culture are hidden in the androcentric term "Indian." Kerrie Charnley's "Concepts of Anger, Identity and Power and the Vision in the Writings and Voices of First Nations Women" affirms that within "First Nations" there are many diverse and ever-changing cultures but makes clear that the term *First Nations* also expresses an "Indian" world view in which things are whole, co-operative, and balanced.[10]

Examining the processes which led up to changes to the so-called Native's way of life, Algerian psychiatrist Frantz Fanon focusses on the colonizing process used by european imperial powers. Although his theorizing is based primarily on african experience, it is useful in and relevant to the north american context. According to Fanon's usage, the word *native* appears to be synonymous with colonized Indigenous peoples. He suggests that the european colonizer used a divide-and-conquer strategy of disempowering the "native" to establish and maintain control. Here it is important to rely on his own words, which speak astutely of that process. He writes: "Europe has multiplied divisions and opposing groups ... fashioned classes and sometimes even racial prejudices ... and endeavoured by every means to bring about and intensify the stratification of colonized societies."[11] After strategically disconnecting the "native" from his or her source of power, the colonizer constructs an image of the "native as a sort of quintessence of evil ... [who] is insensible to ethics; ... the enemy of values ... the absolute evil," an image that serves imperialist purposes. While Fanon's study is useful in relation to the colonized and colonizer, it does have limitations. Educated within a european patriarchal tradition, Fanon produced a study that lacks a gender specific analysis.

Patricia Albers's woman-centred study cites writers such as John Ewer, Robert Berkhofer Jr., and John Price, who write about images and the "Indian," and she argues in her account of Plains "Indian" women that "for most Americans and Europeans, the Plains Indian is the quintessential symbol of "Indianness."[12] Moreover, in relation to the Plains Indians, the image that most predominantly appears in popular stereotyping is that of men. She insists that it is "the male-dominated universe of native diplomacy, warfare, and hunting that has captured the attention of national image makers."[13] According to Albers, this male-dominated eurocentric view of the "Indian" or the "Native" has almost totally effaced from history the lives of Indigenous women.

In the twentieth-century historical context, Indigenous women's lives were effaced in very profound ways through the residential school system and by christian missionaries. The residential schools and missionaries conspired to remove women's vital influences from the spiritual, political, economic, and social realms of Indigenous peoples' lives. Tomson Highway's *Dry Lips Oughta Move to Kapuskasing* offers a glimpse into this complex and misunderstood area. Employing the crucifix as the symbol of christianity, and Nanabush/Patsy Pegahmahgahbow as the symbolic representation of "Indian" spirituality, he attempts to communicate christianity's brutal rape of Indigenous peoples' spirituality. Compared to the rape scene in Highway's play, which is extremely brutal, but quick, and committed by a young boy suffering from fetal alcohol syndrome, white colonialists' attempts to impose christianity on Indigenous peoples, our families, communities, and nations, were much more prolonged and much more torturously coercive. For example, during the early contact period, many Indigenous peoples' immune systems were weakened by new diseases sometimes thoughtlessly and in other cases ignorantly spread by explorers and missionaries. As one can conjecture by perusing R.G. Thwaites's *Jesuit Relations and Allied Documents,*[14] the missionaries as coercive agents took advantage of spiritually and physically weakened individuals by offering them relief through baptism into the faith. Reading through Thwaites's collection of correspondence between the missionaries and their home office, one might assume that christianization had succeeded. Particularly, readers are encouraged to believe that large numbers abandoned their own spiritual/medicine people, who were seemingly helpless against the dreaded diseases, and that the subsequent transition to a white-christian-patriarchal rule was inevitable. Eleanor Leacock makes it clear, however, that there are significant contradictions in the interpretations of primary sources. Leacock compares "European observers who did not know personally the people about whom they were writing," and who thus wrote about "Indian" women as slaves, to "a man who knew the Montagnais-Naskapi well and recognized that women controlled their own work and made decisions accordingly."[15] Priscilla Buffalohead suggests that much of what was written from the mid-seventeenth to the early twentieth century by french, british, and american colonists too often perpetuated biased and contradictory images of Indigenous women.[16] Buffalohead's article encourages the construction of positive images of Indigenous women by calling attention to dynamic and resourceful women. Thus, while most white and some Indigenous male scholars would assert that christian missionaries successfully usurped power from women in Indigenous societies, a re-visiting of the old texts with an understanding of the women-centred way of living together as relations might enhance the reader's understanding of women's roles and status in Indigenous societies in a way that less informed readings could not.

Eurocanadian literature, in its representation of Indigenous life, takes much of its inspiration from many of these early euro-patriarchally-centred primary sources and therefore imprisons women in images that perpetuate white-eurocanadian-patriarchal stereotypes. Fanon explains that the "Native" is often reduced to animalistic forms in order to justify imperialist practices and the colonizers' consequential treatment of Natives. According to Fanon's analysis of colonialism, the colonists must erase all Indigenous traditions and cultures, replacing "Native" languages with their own.[17] Within the colonizers' cultural context, images like the romantic Indian princess, the easy squaw, and the hopeless, suffering victim are constructed to distort the reality of Indigenous women and justify social, political, economic, and spiritual oppression. There have been numerous attempts to suppress Indigenous women's voices and indeed many would argue that Indigenous women have been silent. In *Talking Back* bell hooks argues that when one contextualizes discussions like this within feminist circles, silence is often misinterpreted as the appropriate response of women or as a sign of "woman's submission to patriarchal authority."[18] She suggests, however, that there are some crucial differences between what may have taken place in the homes of women from WASP backgrounds in the United States and Canada and what took place in black (and diverse ethnic) communities. Specifically, she points out that black women (and I would add here, Indigenous women) have not been silent. Reinforcing this point, Gretchen Bataille insists that "Indian" women have not been silent, although commentators have assumed the inferiority of all women and therefore included the american "Indian" woman.[19]

Emma LaRocque points out that publishers "influenced by uncomprehending critics and audiences ... controlled the type of material that was published," and hence male writers like Harold Cardinal, Howard Adams, George Manual, Duke Redbird, Wilfred Pelletier, or Waubageshig were privileged over Indigenous women writers who in the late 1960s and early 1970s were struggling to make their voices heard.[20] The suppression of their voices is also reflected in the manipulative controls and labels that define what is or is not literature. As a result (until very recently), Indigenous women were excluded from the privileged ranks of writers of literature by the white literary establishment which did not accept them as authors of their own realities. Until very recently, Indigenous women were thought of as not only voiceless but also illiterate, the worst of the oppressed, and in some cases, not worth mentioning.

Instead of encouraging Indigenous women to articulate their experiences through the written word, publishers encouraged others to write about and for them. Instead of listening to and hearing the voices of early writers like Emma LaRocque, Beatrice Culleton, Lee Maracle, and Maria Campbell, the white literary establishment dismissed Indigenous women, and the strong autonomous images of surviving women were compromised by images constructed in relation to the white ideal. In terms of this white ideal, as Howard Adams's *Prison of Grass* reflects, the "Flowing golden hair ... [the] lovely white face ... pale skin, thin lips, and gorgeous big blue *eyes*" became the standard for goodness, virtue, and beauty, while "all native girls became undesirable" and associated with oppression.[21] This "white ideal," as Adams describes it, is symptomatic of the colonial mind and personality so clearly delineated by Frantz Fanon. Thus, Indigenous women were reduced to characters in fiction like Margaret Laurence's "vaguely embarrassing"[22] and "drunk and disorderly"[23] Metis, Piquette Tonnerre in "The Loons,"[24] or William Patrick Kinsella's whore, Linda Star in "Linda Star," who grosses "never less than $100 a day."[25] Even though, as Emma LaRocque insists, people like herself, Maria Campbell, Lee Maracle, and Beatrice Culleton were producing literature and offering more positive images based on their reality as Indigenous women struggling against and surviving rape, beatings, alcohol and drug addictions, economic and political oppression, their writings were dismissed as "biased" and "bitter." LaRocque points out that "our anger, legitimate as it was and is, was exaggerated as 'militant' and used as an excuse not to hear us. There was little comprehension of an articulate anger reflecting an awakening and a call to liberation."[26]

Another method used to suppress the voices of Indigenous women, as Bataille's discussion reveals, is to use one person's life as representative of a whole culture. For example, while Maria Campbell's autobiographical *Halfbreed*[27] established a new literary trend by revising and redefining Indigenous women's experiences, it was not accepted or defined as good literature. LaRocque maintains that it was instead reduced to "grist for social workers."[28] One could argue that Campbell's book feeds into the stereotypical representations of the easy squaw, and even the helpless suffering victim. If her text is read through white-eurocanadian patriarchal glasses, its images may satisfy ideological prejudices about Indigenous women. However, I maintain that if Campbell's text is re-examined from the perspective encouraged by Rich, "of looking back, of seeing with fresh eyes, of entering an old text from a new critical direction,"[29] one may come to understand her text in a different way. In Hartmut Lutz's *Contemporary Challenges: Conversations with Contemporary Canadian Native Writers*,[30] Jeannette Armstrong, Beth Cuthand, Lenore Keeshig-Tobias, Beatrice Culleton, and Emma LaRocque refer to *Halfbreed* as a prompt, which encouraged other Indigenous women to speak out. In order to appreciate Campbell's text, however, one must understand Indigenous women's vital role previous to white-european-christian impositions.

As a result of cultural impositions and ideological constructs, the reality is that Indigenous women's cultural roots may have been weakened, but we have nevertheless survived. In recent years our voices have been talking back through texts like Lee Maracle's *Bobby Lee: Indian Rebel, I Am Woman, Sojourner's Truth*; Marie Annharte Baker's *Being on the Moon*; Jeannette Armstrong's *Slash*; Louise Erdrich's *Love Medicine, The Beet Queen,* and *Tracks*; Mary Crow Dog's *Lakota Woman* (co-authored by Richard Erdoes); Agnes Grant's *Our Bit of Truth*; the contemporary western canadian

"Native" women's anthology *Writing the Circle*; Louise Halfe's *Bear Bones & Feathers*; Beth Cuthand's *Voices in the Waterfall*, and editor Connie Fife's *The Colour of Resistance: A Contemporary Collection of Writing by Aboriginal Women*.[31]

This essay maintains that, prior to the imposition of christianity, Indigenous cultures revolved around women. As such, our voices have kept alive the sanctity and universal power of Mother Earth through which all things flow. Not exclusively academics, or even writers, we speak from familial lineages that encompass thousands of years of survival. Unfortunately, our ways of being, seeing, and doing were intruded upon by extremely powerful imperialistic forces and colonial agents. Eurocanadian literature, as an institution of colonialism, perpetuates stereotypical images of Indigenous women which distort our realities, fragment our lives, and diminish our status. Readers must therefore attempt to understand these stereotypical images in the context of colonialism, be aware of their own ideological assumptions, understand how those assumptions encourage cultural attitudes towards Indigenous women, and approach texts (particularly in relation to images of Indigenous women) in a critical manner.

Notes

1. Paula Gunn Allen, *The Sacred Hoop: Recovering the Feminine in American Indian Traditions* (Boston: Beacon Press, 1986), 3.

2. Osennontion and Skonaganleh:ra, "Our World: According to Osennontion and Skonaganleh:ra," in *Canadian Women's Studies/les cahiers de la femme* (Downsview, Ontario: York University Press, 1989), 7–19.

3. Emma LaRocque, preface to *Writing the Circle: Native Women of Western Canada*, eds. Jaenne Perreault and Sylvia Vance (Edmonton: NeWest Publishers, 1990), xx.

4. Ibid., xvi.

5. Patricia Albers, "New Perspectives on Plains Indian Women," introduction to *The Hidden Half: Studies of Plains Indian Women* (Lanham: University Press of America, 1983), 8.

6. Connie Fife, ed., *The Colour of Resistance: A Contemporary Collection of Writing by Aboriginal Women* (Toronto: Sister Vision Press, 1993), 2.

7. Staff Kihi, et al. *Independent Commission on International Humanitarian Issues, Indigenous Peoples: A Global Quest for Justice* (London: Zed Books, 1987).

8. Tomson Highway, "Note on Nanabush," preface to *Dry Lips Oughta Move to Kapuskasing* (Saskatoon: Fifth House Publishing, 1990)

9. LaRocque, xx.

10. Kerrie Charnley, "Concepts of Anger, Identity and Power and the Vision in the Writings and Voices of First Nations Women," in *Gatherings: the En 'Owkin Journal of First North American Peoples* 1 (1990): 18.

11. Frantz Fanon, *The Wretched of the Earth* (New York: Grove Press, 1963), 11.

12. Albers, 1.

13. Ibid., 2.

14. R.G. Thwaites, *Jesuit Relations and Allied Documents*, 73 vols. (New York: Pageant Books, 1959).

15. Eleanor Leacock, "Montagnais Women and the Jesuit Program for Colonization," in *Myths of Male Dominance: Collected Articles on Women Cross-Culturally* (New York: Monthly Review Press, 1981), 45.

16. Priscilla Buffalohead, "Farmers, Warriors, Traders: A Fresh Look at Ojibway Women," *Minnesota History* 48 (1983): 236–44.

17. Franz Fanon, *The Wretched of the Earth* (New York: Grove Press, 1963), 15.

18. bell hooks, *Talking Back: Thinking Feminist. Thinking Black* (Toronto: Between the Lines, 1988), 6.

19. Gretchen Bataille, "Transformation of Tradition: Autobiographical Works by American Indian Women," in

Studies in American Literature (New York: Modern Language Association of America, 1983), 85.

20. Emma LaRocque, preface to *Writing the Circle: Native Women of Western Canada*, eds. Jaenne Perreault and Sylvia Vance (Edmonton: NeWest Publishers, 1990), xxiii.

21. Howard Adams, *Prison of Grass: Canada from a Native Point of View* (Saskatoon: Fifth House Publishers, 1975), 142.

22. Margaret Laurence, "The Loons," in *A Bird in the House* (Toronto: McClelland and Stewart, 1985), 97.

23. Ibid., 106.

24. Ibid.

25. William Patrick Kinsella, "Linda Star," in *Dance Me Outside* (Ottawa: Oberon Press, 1977).

26. LaRocque, xvii.

27. Maria Campbell, *Halfbreed* (Toronto: McClelland and Stewart, 1973).

28. LaRocque, xviii.

29. Rich, "When the Dead Awaken: Writing as Re-Vision," in *On Secrets, Lies and Silence: Selected Prose 1966-1978* (New York: W.W. Norton, 1979), 33–49.

30. Hartmut Lutz, ed., *Contemporary Challenges: Conversations with Contemporary Canadian Native Writers* (Saskatoon: Fifth House Publishers, 1991).

31. Lee Maracle, *Bobby Lee: Indian Rebel* (Toronto: Women's Press, 1990), *I Am Woman* (North Vancouver: Write-on Press Publishers, 1988), and *Sojourner's Truth and Other Stories* (Vancouver: Press Gang Publishers, 1990); Marie Annharte Baker, *Being on the Moon* (Winlaw: Polestar Press, 1990); Jeannette Armstrong, *Slash* (Penticton: Theytus Books, 1988); Louise Erdrich, *Love Medicine* (Toronto: Bantam Books, 1984), *The Beet Queen* (Toronto: Bantam Books, 1986), and *Tracks* (New York: Harper and Row, 1988); Mary Crow Dog and Richard Erdoes, *Lakota Woman* (New York: HarperCollins, 1990); Agnes Grant, ed., *Our Bit of Truth: An Anthology of Canadian Native Literature* (Winnipeg: Pemmican Publications, 1990); Jeanne Perreault and Sylvia Vance, eds., *Writing the Circle: Native Women of Western Canada* (Edmonton: NeWest Publishers, 1990); Louise Halfe, *Bear Bones & Feathers* (Regina: Coteau Books, 1994); and Connie Fife, ed., *The Colour of Resistance: A Contemporary Collection of Writing by Aboriginal Women* (Toronto: Sister Vision Press), 1993.

Black Woman Rage

Motion (Wendy Brathwaite)

Black Woman rage makes us take to the stages
Up front at rallies
Leading black families
Black woman rage is a thing of beauty
Doing our duty,
making our roles
Suffering in silence, giving the bad eye
Calling on God,
dealing with spirits
Jah-Jah takes over as riddims move hips
Cusses come from full brown female lips
Black woman rage is a sight to behold
Working the fields
suns beat on bent backs
Black songs rise with density of deep sound
Deep pasts seep to all who have the ear—
Can you understand the meaning
of Rage ... Black ... Woman ... Song?
Sad, true, throaty, tired
Awakened
As we stretch to the heights of creation
Leggo our hand in the offending face
Stay in our place? What place?
When we just be all over ...
Never removed as we feed the masses

with milk, poems and minds
Full breasts and asses
Queen Nzinga looks on
as we swing our small axes
through the forests of fearsome shadows
that mean us no good
We learn to run from home-grown licks
Give 2 snaps up
and stand akimbo
as only Raging Black Women could.
We beat the drums to call on the sisters
to pass on the secrets that only mothers know.
two hundred and forty days of
two heart-beats, two sighs,
two souls, two-fold life-form multiply
with the powers of Yin and Yang
One moment kisses to heal the sting of her strong hand
Raging, Woman Black—
back to the basics of the Motherland ...
Speak your story, speak
sister songs
and weep if you will
at the rage that kept us frozen, still
under humping weights
that pinned us in darkened places
Rage that kept us from killing our rapists
In order to maintain we paralyzed ourselves instead
They left us for dead
They *thought* we were
dead
But we don't die,
we ...
grow, laugh, spread, cry
Daughters of the cotton and cane
cannot wither and die.

Credo of a Passionate Skeptic

Adrienne Rich

Recently I collected a number of my prose writings for a forthcoming volume. Rereading them, it struck me that for some readers, the earlier pieces might seem to belong to a bygone era—twenty to thirty years ago. I chose to include them as background, indicating certain directions in my thinking. A burgeoning women's movement in the 1970s and early 1980s incited and provided the occasions for them, created their ecology. But, as I suggested in "Notes toward a Politics of Location," my thinking was unable to fulfill itself within feminism alone.

Our senses are currently whip-driven by a feverish new pace of technological change. The activities that mark us as human, though, don't begin, exist in, or end by such a calculus. They pulse, fade out, and pulse again in human tissue, human nerves, and in the elemental humus of memory, dreams, and art, where there are no bygone eras. They are in us, they can speak to us, they can teach us if we desire it.

In fact, for Westerners to look back on 1900 is to come full face upon ourselves in 2000, still trying to grapple with the hectic power of capitalism and technology, the displacement of the social will into the accumulation of money and things. "Thus" (Karl Marx in 1844) "all physical and intellectual senses (are) replaced by the simple alienation of all these senses, the sense of having." We have been here all along.

But retrospection can also remind us how one period's necessary strategies can mutate into the monsters of a later time. The accurate feminist perceptions that women's lives, historically or individually, were mostly unrecorded and that the personal is political are cases in point. Feminism has depended heavily on the concrete testimony of individual women, a testimony that was meant to accumulate toward collective understanding and practice. In "When We Dead Awaken," I borrowed my title from Ibsen's last play, written in 1900. Certainly the issues Ibsen had dramatized were very much alive. I "used myself" to illustrate a woman writer's journey, rather tentatively. In 1971 this still seemed a questionable, even illegitimate, approach, especially in a paper to be given at an academic convention.

Soon thereafter, personal narrative was becoming valued as the true coin of feminist expression. At the same time, in every zone of public life, personal and private solutions were being marketed by a profit-driven corporate system, while collective action and even collective realities were mocked at best and at worst rendered historically sterile.

By the late 1990s, in mainstream American public discourse, personal anecdote was replacing critical argument, true confessions were foregrounding the discussion of ideas. A feminism that sought to engage race and colonialism, the global monoculture of United States corporate and military interests, the specific locations and agencies of women within all this was being countered by the marketing of a United States model of female—or feminine—self-involvement and self-improvement, devoid of political context or content.

Still, those early essays suggest the terrain where I started: a time of imaginative and intellectual ferment, when many kinds of transformations seemed possible. "Women and Honor" belongs to a period when there was in the air a theoretical code of ethical responsibility among women: a precarious solidarity of gender. Within that ethic—which I shared—I was trying to criticize the deceptions we practiced on each other and ourselves. Published at a time of vigorous feminist small-press pamphleteering, "Women and Honor" seemed, for a while, usable. Today, the parts that most interest me are the descriptions of how lying can disrupt the internal balance of the one who accepts the lie, and the difficulties of constructing an honorable life. I believe these stretch beyond gender to other hoped-for pacts, comradeships, and conversations, including those between the citizen and her government. (I do not believe that truth-telling exists in a bubble, sealed off from the desire for justice.)

Looking back on her own earlier writings, Susan Sontag has remarked: "Now the very idea of the serious (and the honorable) seems quaint, 'unrealistic,' to most people." Like other serious and vibrant movements, feminism was to be countered by cultural patterns unforeseen before the 1980s: a growing middle-class self-absorption and indifference both to ideas and to the larger social order, along with the compression of media power and resources into fewer and fewer hands, during and beyond the Reagan years.

It interests me that in "Women and Honor," that poetically terse piece of writing, I first invoked the name of Marx—to dismiss Marxism "for women." I was of course echoing the standard anti-Marxism of the postwar American cultural and political mainstream. But, as I indicate in "Raya Dunayevskaya's Marx," written more than a decade later, this anti-Marxism, uncriticized and uninvestigated, was present also in the women's movement. Marxism was tainted there, both by garden-variety anticommunism and by the fear that class would erase gender once again, when gender was just beginning to be understood as a political category.

Sometime around 1980 I felt impelled to go back and read what I had dismissed or felt threatened by: I had to find out what Marx, along the way of his own development, had actually written. I began working my way through those writings, in the assorted translations and editions available to me, an autodidact and an outsider, not an academic or post-Marx Marxist. There were passages that whetted my hunger; others I traversed laboriously and in intellectual fatigue. I understood that I was sometimes overhearing early nineteenth-century German philosophical diatribes I could just as well skip.

What kept me going was the sense of being in the company of a great geographer of the human condition, and specifically, a sense of recognition: how profit-driven economic relations filter into zones of thought and feeling. Marx's depiction of early nineteenth-century capitalism and its dehumanizing effect on the social landscape rang truer than ever at the century's end.

Along with that flare of recognition came profound respect and empathy for Marx's restless vision of human capacities and the nature of their frustration. I found no blueprint for a future utopia but a skilled diagnosis of skewed and disfigured human relationships. I found a Marx who would have been revolted by Stalinism, by the expropriation of his ideas in the name of tyranny, by the expropriation of his name: "I am not a Marxist," he said. In the feminism I had embraced, as in the social field where it was rooted, there was a salient dialectic: racism as destructive presence, race as great social teacher. Time and again racial actualities pushed against the "primary oppression" of gender; time and again the lesson was forgotten. I came to realize that we were afraid: that a focus on class (read Marxism) might blot out a focus on gender and race; that gender (feminism) might blot out race and class; that you could look at history and see the big eraser wiping out each successive lesson of justice, so that collective knowledge could not accumulate. For the pressing motif of this excessive society was and is: There is not enough (space, livelihood, validation) for all.

I'm not sure that I could have read Marx with so much patience and appetite had I not participated in the inevitable shortcomings of the feminist movement in the United States. Though some feminists (mostly women of color) insisted on intersections of race, class, and gender, emphasis was more often laid on women's individual class identifications and how they negotiated them, or on poverty and welfare, than on how class, poverty and the need for welfare are produced and perpetuated in the first place. (Both kinds of work, of course, are necessary.) Elsewhere, movement was being parochialized into "women's culture." Meanwhile, the expansion of capitalism's force field, the impoverishment of women within it, and the steep concentration of wealth were all brutally accelerating.

We can think of second-wave feminism as a splinter off the radical movements of United States history, especially the Depression-driven movements of the 1930s and 1940s, movements always under fire, repressed in the 1950s, resurgent in new forms in the 1960s, and by the 1970s, again being deliberately defused and isolated. Above all, the political groupings of African Americans were under hostile surveillance. Earlier, Malcolm X and Martin Luther King Jr.—both leaders with large constituencies—had been murdered just as each was unscrolling a map on which race and class intersected in a shared landscape. The blotting of those maps was accomplished by violence, persecution, censorship, and propaganda. The energy, hopefulness, brains, and passion of a women's movement erupting in the United States at such a time was no match for these political

circumstances. The important legacies of that movement reside not in the names of a few women starring in the media, but in the many lifesaving, stubbornly ongoing grass-roots organizations it had the power to ignite. I still believe what I wrote in 1971: A change in the concept of sexual identity is essential if we are not to see the old political order reassert itself in every new revolution.

What prose I wrote in the 1990s was fired by a hope of bringing together ideas that had been forcibly severed from each other or thrown into competition: such as the making of literature and public education. Sometimes I felt ideas that attracted me mutually repelling each other. Or I felt the shortcomings of my own language pitted against a lethargic liberalism or a despicable rhetoric of "spin." Sometimes it all seemed mere Sisyphean effort, pushing uphill and futureless a rock bearing sweaty handprints of so many others.

But Sisyphus is not, finally, a useful image. You don't roll some unitary boulder of language or justice uphill; you try with others to assist in cutting and laying many stones, designing a foundation. One of the stonecutter-architects I met was Muriel Rukeyser, whose work I had begun reading in depth in the 1980s. Through her prose Rukeyser had engaged me intellectually; her poetry, however, in its range and daring, held me first and last. "Her Vision" is a tribute to the mentorship of her work. Another was Raya Dunayevskaya, who wrote vividly and trenchantly of the concrete revolutionary lives of women, and whose fusion of Marx's humanism with contemporary feminisms expanded my sense of the possibilities of both.

I was also undertaking a kind of research into poetics, both as writing and as reading. I had always worked fairly instinctually and independently as a poet, distrusting groups and manifestos, which I found mostly unuseful in their exclusive male compadreship; I trusted their poetry more than their bondings. (I have had to reckon in and out of gender to do my work.) But it seemed to me that an accumulating incoherence and disruption of public language and images in the late twentieth century was something poets had to reckon with, not just for our own work. I had explored this challenge in my 1993 book, *What Is Found There: Notebooks on Poetry and Politics*. I was looking for poetics and practice that could resist degraded media and a mass entertainment culture, both of them much more pervasive and powerful than earlier in the century.

There was nothing new about this; artists have long made art against the commodity culture. And innovative or transgressive art has itself been commodified, yet has dialectically frictioned new forms and imaginings into existence. One of the questions that pursued me is whether, and how, innovative or so-called avant-garde poetics are necessarily or even potentially revolutionary: Do they simply embrace a language so deracinated that it is privy in its rebellions only to a few? The question is not unreasonable given the decidedly antibourgeois, anticonformist claims of avant-garde tradition. The obverse question is inescapable: Can a radical social imagination clothe itself in a language worn thin by usage or debased by marketing, promotion, and the will to power? In order to meet that will to power, must we choose between the nonreferential and the paraphrasable?

I believe in the necessity for a poetic language untethered from the compromised language of state and media. Yet how, I have wondered, can poetry persist as a ligatory art rather than as an echo chamber of fragmentation and alienation? Can the language of poetry become too abstract (some might say elitist) even as it tries to claim what Octavio Paz has called "the other voice"? Is there a way of writing on the edge? Of course I think there is, and has been; I test my own work from that likelihood. "Language," I find in Marx, "is the presence of the community." In a 1979 essay by Gary Snyder: "The community and its poetry are not two."

Are writers, poets, artists, thinking people still merely gnashing away at the problems of the early twentieth century? But this is not "mere." These primal, unsilenced questions pursue us, wherever we are trying to live conscientiously in the time we have. A new century, even a new technology, doesn't of itself produce newness. It is live human beings, looking in all directions, who will do this.

For more than fifty years I have been writing, tearing, up, revising poems, studying poets from every culture and century available to me. I have been a poet of the oppositional imagination, meaning that I don't think my only argument is with myself. My work is for people who want to imagine and claim wider horizons and carry on about them into the night, rather than rehearse the landlocked details of personal quandaries or the price for which the house next door just sold.

At times in the past decade and a half I have felt like a stranger in my own country. I seem not to speak the official language. I believe many others feel like this, not just as poets or intellectuals but as citizens—accountable yet excluded from power. I began as an American optimist, albeit a critical one, formed by our racial legacy and by the Vietnam War. In both these cases it was necessary to look hard truths in the face in order to change horrible realities. I believed, with many others, that my country's historical aquifers were flowing in that direction of democratic change. I became an American skeptic, not as to the long search for justice and dignity, which is part of all human history, but in the light of my nation's leading role in demoralizing and destabilizing that search, here at home and around the world. Perhaps just such a passionate skepticism, neither cynical nor nihilistic, is the ground for continuing.

Review of *Diving into the Wreck*

Margaret Atwood

This is Adrienne Rich's seventh book of poems, and it is an extraordinary one. When I first heard the author read from it, I felt as though the top of my head was being attacked, sometimes with an ice pick, sometimes with a blunter instrument: a hatchet or a hammer. The predominant emotions seemed to be anger and hatred, and these are certainly present; but when I read the poems later, they evoked a far more subtle reaction. *Diving into the Wreck* is one of those rare books that forces you to decide not just what you think about it, but what you think about yourself. It is a book that takes risks, and it forces the reader to take them also.

If Adrienne Rich were not a good poet, it would be easy to classify her as just another vocal Women's Libber, substituting polemic for poetry, simplistic messages for complex meanings. But she is a good poet, and her book is not a manifesto, though it subsumes manifestoes; nor is it a proclamation, though it makes proclamations. It is instead a book of explorations, of travels. The wreck she is diving into, in the very strong title poem, is the wreck of obsolete myths, particularly myths about men and women. She is journeying to something that is already in the past, in order to discover for herself the reality behind the myth, "the wreck and not the story of the wreck/the thing itself and not the myth." What she finds is part treasure and part corpse, and she also finds that she herself is part of it, a "half-destroyed instrument." As explorer she is detached; she carries a knife to cut her way in, cut structures apart; a camera to record; and the book of myths itself, a book which has hitherto had no place for explorers like herself.

This quest—the quest for something beyond myths, for the truths about men and women, about the "I" and the "You," the He and the She, or more generally (in the references to wars and persecutions of various kinds) about the powerless and the powerful—is presented throughout the book through a sharp, clear style and through metaphors which become their own myths. At their most successful the poems move like dreams, simultaneously revealing and alluding, disguising and concealing. The truth, it seems, is not just what you find when you open a door: it is itself a door, which the poet is always on the verge of going through.

The landscapes are diverse. The first poem, "Trying to Talk with a Man," occurs in a desert, a desert which is not only deprivation and sterility, the place where everything except the essentials has been discarded, but the place where bombs are tested. The "I" and the "You" have given up all the frivolities of their previous lives, "suicide notes" as well as "love-letters," in order to undertake the risk of changing the desert; but it becomes clear that the "scenery" is already "condemned," that the bombs are not external threats but internal ones. The poet realizes that they are deceiving themselves, "talking of the danger/as if it were not ourselves/as if we were testing anything else."

Like the wreck, the desert is already in the past, beyond salvation though not beyond understanding, as in the landscape of "Waking in the Dark":

> The tragedy of sex
> lies around us, a woodlot
> the axes are sharpened for.
>
> ....
>
> Nothing will save this. I am alone,
> kicking the last rotting logs
> with their strange smell of life, not death,
> wondering what on earth it all might have
>   become.

Given her view that the wreck, the desert, the woodlot cannot be redeemed, the task of the woman, the She, the powerless, is to concentrate not on fitting into the landscape but on redeeming herself, creating a new landscape, getting herself born:

> your mother dead and you unborn
> your two hands grasping your head
> drawing it down against the blade of life
> your nerves the nerves of a midwife
> learning her trade

("The Mirror in Which
Two Are Seen As One")

The difficulty of doing this (the poet is, after all, still surrounded by the old condemned landscape and "the evidence of damage" it has caused) is one of the major concerns of the book. Trying to see clearly and to record what has been seen—the rapes, the wars, the murders, the various kinds of violation and mutilation—is half of the poet's effort; for this she requires a third eye, an eye that can see pain with "clarity." The other half is to respond, and the response is anger; but it is a "visionary anger," which hopefully will precede the ability to love.

These poems convince me most often when they are true to themselves as structures of words and images, when they resist the temptation to sloganize, when they don't preach at me. "The words are purposes./The words are maps," Rich says, and I like them better when they are maps (though Rich would probably say the two depend on each other and I would probably agree). I respond less fully to poems like "Rape" and references to the Vietnam War—though their truth is undeniable— than I do to poems such as "From a Survivor" and "August" with its terrifying final image:

> His mind is too simple, I cannot go on
> sharing his nightmares
>
> My own are becoming clearer, they open
> into prehistory
>
> which looks like a village lit with blood
> where all the fathers are crying: My son is mine!

It is not enough to state the truth; it must be imaged, imagined, and when Rich does this she is irresistible. When she does this she is also most characteristically herself. You feel about her best images, her best myths, that nobody else writes quite like this.

Not a Moral Issue

Catharine A. MacKinnon

Pornosec, the subsection of the Fiction Department which turned out cheap pornography for distribution among the proles ... nicknamed Muck House by the people who worked in it ... produce[d] booklets in sealed packets with titles like *Spanking Stories* or *One Night in a Girls' School*, to be bought furtively by proletarian youths who were under the impression that they were buying something illegal.

—George Orwell,
Nineteen Eighty-four (1949)

A critique of pornography[1] is to feminism what its defense is to male supremacy. Central to the institutionalization of male dominance, pornography cannot be reformed or suppressed or banned. It can only be changed. The legal doctrine of obscenity, the state's closest approximation to addressing the pornography question, has made the First Amendment[2] into a barrier to this process. This is partly because the pornographers' lawyers have persuasively presented First Amendment absolutism,[3] their advocacy position, as a legal fact, which it never has been. But they have gotten away with this (to the extent they have)

in part because the abstractness of obscenity as a concept, situated within an equally abstract approach to freedom of speech embodied in First Amendment doctrine, has made the indistinguishability of the pornographers' speech from everyone else's speech, their freedom from our freedom, appear credible, appealing, necessary, inevitable, *principled*.[4] To expose the absence of a critique of gender[5] in this area of law is to expose both the enforced silence of women and the limits of liberalism.

This brief preliminary commentary focuses on the obscenity standard in order to explore some of the larger implications of a feminist critique of pornography for First Amendment theory. This is the argument. Obscenity law is concerned with morality, specifically morals from the male point of view, meaning the standpoint of male dominance. The feminist critique of pornography is politics, specifically politics from women's point of view meaning the standpoint of the subordination of women to men.[6] Morality here means good and evil; politics means power and powerlessness. Obscenity is a moral idea; pornography is a political practice. Obscenity is abstract; pornography is concrete. The two concepts represent two entirely different things. Nudity, explicitness, excess of candor, arousal or excitement, prurience, unnaturalness—these qualities bother obscenity law when sex is depicted or portrayed. Abortion, birth control information, and treatments for "restoring sexual virility" (whose, do you suppose?) have also been included.[7] Sex forced on real women so that it can be sold at a profit to be forced on other real women; women's bodies trussed and maimed and raped and made into things to be hurt and obtained and accessed, and this presented as the nature of women; the coercion that is visible and the coercion that has become invisible—this and more bothers feminists about pornography. Obscenity as such probably does little harm;[8] pornography causes attitudes and behaviors of violence and discrimination that define the treatment and status of half of the population.[9] To make the legal and philosophical consequences of this distinction clear, I will describe the feminist critique of pornography, criticize the law of obscenity in terms of it, then discuss the criticism that pornography "dehumanizes" women to distinguish the male morality of liberalism and obscenity law from a feminist political critique of pornography.[10]

This inquiry is part of a larger project that attempts to account for gender inequality in the socially constructed relationship between power—the political—on the one hand and the knowledge of truth and reality—the epistemological—on the other.[11] For example, the candid description Justice Stewart once offered of his obscenity standard, "I know it when I see it,"[12] becomes even more revealing than it is usually understood to be if taken as a statement that connects epistemology with power. If I ask, from the point of view of women's experiences, does he know what I know when I see what I see, I find that I doubt it, given what's on the newsstands. How does his point of view keep what is there, there? To liberal critics, his admission exposed the obscenity standard's relativity, its partiality, its insufficient abstractness. Not to be emptily universal, to leave your concreteness showing, is a sin among men. Their problem with Justice Stewart's formulation is that it

implies that anything, capriciously, could be suppressed. They are only right by half. My problem is more the other half: the meaning of what his view permits, which, as it turns out, is anything but capricious. In fact, it is entirely systematic and determinate. To me, his statement is precisely descriptively accurate; its candor is why it has drawn so much criticism.[13] Justice Stewart got in so much trouble because he said out loud what is actually done all the time; in so doing, he both *did it* and gave it the stature of doctrine, even if only dictum. That is, the obscenity standard—in this it is not unique—*is* built on what the male standpoint sees. My point is: *so is pornography*. In this way the law of obscenity reproduces the pornographic point of view on women on the level of Constitutional jurisprudence.

Pornography, in the feminist view, is a form of forced sex, a practice sexual politics, an institution of gender inequality. In this perspective, pornography is not harmless fantasy or a corrupt and confused misrepresentation of an otherwise natural and healthy sexuality. Along with the rape and prostitution in which it participates, pornography institutionalizes the sexuality of male supremacy, which fuses the erotization of dominance and submission with the social construction of male and female.[14] Gender is sexual. Pornography constitutes the meaning of that sexuality. Men treat women as who they see women as being. Pornography constructs who that is. Men's power over women means that the way men see women defines who women can be. Pornography is that way.

In pornography, women desire dispossession and cruelty. Men, permitted to put words (and other things) in women's mouths, create scenes in which women desperately want to be bound, battered, tortured, humiliated, and killed. Or merely taken and used. This is erotic to the male point of view. Subjection itself, with self-determination ecstatically relinquished, is the content of women's sexual desire and desirability. Women are there to be violated and possessed, men to violate and possess them, either on screen or by camera or pen, on behalf of the viewer.

One can be for or against this pornography without getting beyond liberalism. The critical yet formally liberal view of Susan Griffin, for example, conceptualizes eroticism as natural and healthy but corrupted and confused by "the pornographic mind."[15] Pornography distorts Eros, which pre-exists and persists, despite male culture's pornographic "revenge" upon it. Eros is, unaccountably, *still there*. Pornography mis-takes it, mis-images it, mis-represents it. There is no critique of *reality* here, only objections to how it is seen; no critique of that reality that pornography imposes on women's real lives, those lives that are so seamlessly *consistent* with the pornography that pornography can be credibly defended by saying it is only a mirror of reality.

Contrast this view with the feminist analysis of Andrea Dworkin, in which sexuality itself is a social construct, gendered to the ground. Male dominance here is not an artificial overlay upon an underlying inalterable substratum of uncorrupted essential sexual being. Sexuality free of male dominance will require *change*, not reconceptualization, transcendence, or excavation. Pornography is not imagery in some relation to a reality elsewhere constructed. It is not a distortion, reflection, projection, expression, fantasy, representation, or symbol either. It is sexual reality. Dworkin's *Pornography: Men Possessing Women*[16] presents a sexual theory of gender inequality of which pornography is a core constitutive practice. The way pornography produces its meaning constructs and defines men and women as such. Gender is what gender means.[17] It has no basis in anything other than the social reality its hegemony constructs. The process that gives sexuality its male supremacist meaning is therefore the process through which gender inequality becomes socially real.

In this analysis the liberal defense of pornography as human sexual liberation, as derepression—whether by feminists, lawyers, or neo-Freudians[18]—is a defense not only of force and sexual terrorism, but of the subordination of women. Sexual liberation in the liberal sense frees male sexual aggression in the feminist sense. What looks like love and romance in the liberal view looks a lot like hatred and torture in the feminist view. Pleasure and eroticism become violation: Desire appears as lust for dominance and submission. The vulnerability of women's projected sexual availability—that acting we are allowed: asking to be acted upon—is victimization. Play conforms to scripted roles, fantasy expresses ideology— is not exempt from it—and admiration of natural physical beauty become objectification.

The experience of the (overwhelmingly) male audiences who consume pornography[19] is therefore not fantasy or simulation or catharsis[20] but sexual reality: the level of reality on which sex itself largely operates. To understand this, one does not have to notice that pornography models are real women to whom something real is being done,[21] nor does one have to inquire into the systematic infliction of pornographic sexuality upon women,[22] although it helps. The aesthetic of pornography itself, the *way* it provides what those who consume it want, is itself the evidence. When uncensored explicit—that is, the most pornographic— pornography tells all, all means what a distanced detached observer would report about who did what to whom. This is the turn-on. Why does observing sex objectively presented cause the male viewer to experience his own sexuality? Because his eroticism is, socially, a watched thing.

If objectivity is the epistemological stance of which objectification is the social process,[23] the way a perceptual posture is embodied as a social form of power, the most sexually potent depictions and descriptions *would* be the most objective blow-by-blow re-presentations. Pornography participates in its audience's eroticism because it creates an accessible sexual object, the possession and consumption of which *is* female sexuality.

In this sense, sex in life is no less mediated than it is in art. Men *have sex* with their *image* of a woman. Escalating explicitness, "exceeding the bounds of candor,"[24] is the aesthetic of pornography not because the materials depict objectified sex but because they create the experience of a sexuality that is itself objectified. It is not that life and art imitate each other; in sexuality they *are* each other.

The law of obscenity,[25] the state's primary approach[26] to its version of the pornography question, has literally nothing in common with this feminist critique. Their obscenity is not our pornography. One commentator has said, "Obscenity is not suppressed primarily for the protection of others. Much of it is suppressed for the purity of the 'community.' Obscenity, at bottom, is not a crime. Obscenity is a sin."[27] This is, on one level, literally accurate. Men are turned on by obscenity, including its suppression, the same way they are by sin. Animated by morality from the male standpoint, in which violation—of women and rules—is eroticized, obscenity law can be seen to proceed according to the interest of male power, robed in gender-neutral good and evil.

Morality in its specifically liberal form (although, as with most dimensions of male dominance, the distinction between left and right is more formal than substantive) revolves around a set of parallel distinctions that can be consistently traced through obscenity law. Even though the approach this law takes to the problem it envisions has shifted over time, its fundamental norms remain consistent: public is opposed to private, in parallel with ethics and morality, and factual is opposed to valued determinations. Under male supremacy, these distinctions are gender-based: female is private, moral, valued, subjective; male is public, ethical, factual, objective.[28] If such gendered concepts are constructs of the male experience, imposed from the male standpoint on society as a whole, liberal morality expresses male supremacist politics. That is, discourse conducted in terms of good and evil that does not expose the gendered foundations of these concepts proceeds oblivious to—and serves to disguise—the position of power that underlies, and is furthered by, that discourse.

For example, obscenity law proposes to control what and how sex can be publicly shown. In practice, its standard centers upon the same features feminism identifies as key to male sexuality: the erect penis and penetration.[29] Historically, obscenity law was vexed by restricting such portrayals while protecting great literature. (Nobody considered protecting women.) Having solved this by exempting works of perceived value from obscenity restrictions,[30] the subsequent relaxation—some might say collapse—of obscenity restrictions in the last decade reveals a significant shift. The old private rules have become the new public rules. The old law governing pornography was that it would be publicly repudiated while being privately consumed and actualized: do anything to women with impunity in private behind a veil of public denial and civility. Now pornography is publicly celebrated.[31] This victory for Freudian derepression theory probably did not alter the actual treatment of women all that much. Women were sex and still are sex. Greater efforts of brutality have become necessary to eroticize the tabooed—each taboo being a hierarchy in disguise—since the frontier of the tabooed keeps vanishing as one crosses it. Put another way, more and more violence has become necessary to keep the progressively desensitized consumer aroused to the illusion that sex is (and he is) daring and dangerous. Making sex with the powerless "not allowed" is a way of defining "getting it" as an act of power, an assertion of hierarchy. In addition, pornography has become ubiquitous. Sexual terrorism has become democratized. Crucially, pornography has become truly available to women for the first time in history. Show me an atrocity to women, I'll show it to you eroticized in the pornography. This central mechanism of sexual subordination, this means of systematizing the definition of women as a sexual class, has now become available to its victims for scrutiny and analysis as an open public system, not just as a private secret abuse.[32] Hopefully, this was a mistake.

Re-examining the law of obscenity in light of the feminist critique of pornography that has become possible, it becomes clear that male morality sees as good that which maintains its power and sees as evil that which undermines or qualifies it or questions its absoluteness. Differences in the law over time—such as the liberalization of obscenity doctrine—reflect either changes in the group of men in power or shifts in their perceptions of the best strategy for maintaining male supremacy— probably some of both. But it must be made to work. The outcome, descriptively analyzed, is that obscenity law prohibits what it sees as immoral, which from a feminist standpoint tends to be relatively harmless, while protecting what it sees as moral, which from a feminist standpoint is often that which is damaging to women. So it, too, is politics, only covertly so. What male morality finds evil, meaning threatening to its power, feminist politics tends to find comparatively harmless. What feminist politics identifies as central in our subordination— the erotization of dominance and submission—male morality tends to find comparatively harmless or defends as affirmatively valuable, hence protected speech.

In 1973 obscenity under law came to mean that which "'the average person applying contemporary community standards' would find that, ... taken as a whole, appeals to the prurient interest ... [which] depicts or describes, in a patently offensive way, sexual conduct specifically defined by the applicable state law; and [which], taken as a whole, lacks serious literary, artistic, political, or scientific value."[33] Feminism doubts whether the average person, gender-neutral, exists; has more questions about the content and process of definition of community standards than about deviations from them; wonders why prurience counts but powerlessness doesn't; why sensibilities are better protected from offense than women are from exploitation; defines sexuality, hence its violation and expropriation, more broadly than does any state law and wonders why a body of law that can't in practice tell rape from intercourse should be entrusted with telling pornography from anything less. The law of obscenity says that intercourse on street corners is not legitimized by the fact that the persons are "simultaneously engaged in a valid political dialogue."[34] But, in a feminist light, one sees that the requirement that a work be considered "as a whole" legitimizes something very like that on the level of publications like *Playboy*.[35] Experimental evidence is beginning to support what victims have long known: legitimate settings diminish the injury perceived as done to the women whose trivialization and objectification it contextualizes.[36] Besides, if a woman is subjected, why should it matter that the work has other value?[37] Perhaps what redeems a work's value among men *enhances* its injury to women. Existing standards of literature, art, science, and politics are, in feminist light, remarkably consonant with pornography's mode, meaning, and message. Finally and foremost, a feminist approach reveals that although the content and dynamic of pornography are about women—about the sexuality of women, about women as sexuality—in the same way that the vast majority of "obscenities" refer specifically to women's bodies, our invisibility has been such that the law of obscenity has *never even considered pornography a women's issue*.[38]

*****

Notes

Many of the ideas in this essay were developed and refined in close collaboration with Andrea Dworkin. It is difficult at times to distinguish the contribution of each of us to a body of work that—through shared teaching, writing, speaking, organizing, and political action on every level—has been created together. I have tried to credit specific contributions that I am aware are distinctly hers. This text is mine; she does not necessarily agree with everything in it.

1. This speech as a whole is intended to communicate what I mean by pornography. The key work on the subject is Andrea Dworkin, *Pornography: Men Possessing Women* (1981). No definition can convey the meaning of a word as well as its use in context can. However, what Andrea Dworkin and I mean by pornography is rather well captured in our legal definition: "Pornography is the graphic sexually explicit subordination of women, whether in pictures or in words, that also includes one or more of the following: (i) women are presented dehumanized as sexual objects, things or commodities; or (ii) women are presented as sexual objects who enjoy pain or humiliation; or (iii) women are presented as sexual objects who experience sexual pleasure in being raped; or (iv) women are presented as sexual objects tied up or cut up or mutilated or bruised or physically hurt; or (v) women are presented in postures of sexual submission, servility or display; or (vi) women's body parts—including but not limited to vaginas, breasts, and buttocks—are exhibited, such that women are reduced to those parts; or (vii) women are presented as whores by nature; or (viii) women are presented being penetrated by objects or animals; or (ix) women are presented in scenarios of degradation, injury, torture, shown as filthy or inferior, bleeding, bruised, or hurt in a context that makes these conditions sexual." Pornography also includes "the use of men, children or transsexuals in the place of women." Pornography, thus defined, is discrimination on the basis of sex and, as such, a civil rights violation. This definition is a slightly modified version of the one passed by the Minneapolis City Council on December 30, 1983. Minneapolis, Minn., Ordinance amending tit. 7, chs. 139 and 141, Minneapolis Code of Ordinances Relating to Civil Rights (Dec. 30, 1983). The ordinance was vetoed by the mayor, reintroduced, passed again, and vetoed again in 1984. *See* "Francis Biddle's Sister" for subsequent developments.

2. "Congress shall make no law … abridging the freedom of speech, or of the press …." U.S. Const. amend. I.

3. Justice Black, at times joined by Justice Douglas, took the position that the Bill of Rights, including the First Amendment, was "absolute." Hugo Black, "The Bill of Rights," *New York University Law Review* 865, 867 (1960); Edmund Cahn, "Justice Black and First Amendment 'Absolutes': A Public Interview," 37 *New York University Law Review* 549 (1962). For a discussion, see Harry Kalvern, "Upon Rereading Mr. Justice Black on the First Amendment," 14 *UCLA Law Review* 428 (1967). For one exchange in the controversy surrounding the "absolute" approach to the First Amendment, as opposed to the "balancing" approach, see, e.g., W. Mendelson, "On the Meaning of the First Amendment: Absolutes in the Balance," 50 *California Law Review* 821 (1962); L. Frantz, "The First Amendment in the Balance," 71 *Yale Law Journal* 1424 (1962); Frantz, "Is the First Amendment Law?—A Reply to Professor Mendelson," 51 *California Law Review* 729 (1963); Mendelson, "The First Amendment and the Judicial Process: A Reply to Mr. Frantz," 17 *Vanderbilt Law Review* 479 (1964). In the pornography context, see e.g., Roth v. United States, 354 U.S. 47, 514 (1957) (Douglas, J., joined by Black, J., dissenting); Smith v. California, 361 U.S. 147, 155 (1959) (Black, J., concurring); Miller v. California, 413 U.S. 15, 37 (1973) (Douglas, J., dissenting). The purpose of this discourse is not to present a critique of absolutism as such, but rather to identify and criticize some widely and deeply shared implicit beliefs that underlie both the absolutist view and the more mainstream flexible approaches.

4. The history of obscenity law can be read as a failed attempt to make this separation, with the failure becoming ever more apparent from the *Redrup* decision forward. *Redrup v. New York*, 386 U.S. 767 (1967). For a summary of cases exemplifying such a trend, see the dissent by Justice Brennan in *Paris Adult Theatre I v. Slaton*, 413 U.S. 49, 73 (1973).

5. Much has been made of the distinction between sex and gender. Sex is thought the more biological, gender the more social. The relation of sexuality to each varies. See, e.g., Robert Stoller, *Sex and Gender* 9–10 (1974). Since I think that that the importance of biology to the condition of women is the social meaning attributed to it, biology *is* its social meaning for purposes of analyzing the inequality of the sexes, a political condition. I therefore tend to use sex and gender relatively interchangeably.

6. The sense in which I mean women's perspective as different from men's is like that of Virginia Woolf's reference to "the difference of view, the difference of standard" in her "George Eliot," 1 *Collected Essays* 204 (1966). Neither of us uses the notion of a gender difference to refer to something biological or natural or transcendental or existential. Perspective parallels standards because the social experience of gender is confined by gender. See Catharine A. MacKinnon, *Sexual Harassment of Working Women* 107–41 (1979), and the articles mentioned in note 11, below; Virginia Woolf, *Three Guineas* (1938); see also Andrea Dworkin, "The Root Cause," in *Our Blood: Essays and Discourses on Sexual Politics* 96 (1976). I do not refer to the gender difference here descriptively, leaving its roots and implications unspecified, so they could be biological, existential, transcendental, in any sense inherent, or social but necessary. I mean "point of view" as a view, hence a standard, that is imposed on women by force of sex inequality, which is a political concept, not a biological attribute; it is a status socially conferred upon a person because of a condition of birth. As I use "male," it has nothing whatever to do with inherency, preexistence, nature, inevitability, or body as such. Because it is in the interest of men to be male in the system we live under (male being powerful as well as human), they seldom question its rewards or even see it as a status at all.

7. Criminal Code, Can. Rev. Stat. chap. C-34, § 159(2)(c) and (d) (1970). *People v. Sanger*, 222 N.Y. 192, 118 N.E. 637 (1918).

8. *The Report of the Commission on Obscenity and Pornography* (1970) (majority report). The accuracy of the commission's findings is called into question by: (1) widespread criticism of the commission's methodology from a variety of perspectives, e.g., L/ Sunderland, *Obscenity— The Court, the Congress and the President's Commission* (1975); Edward Donnerstein, "Pornography Commission Revisited: Aggression—Erotica and Violence Against Women," 39 *Journal of Personality and Social Psychology* 269 (1980); Ann Garry, "Pornography and Respect for Women," 4 *Social Theory and Practice* 395 (Summer 1978); Irene Diamond, "Pornography and Repression," 5 *Signs: A Journal of Women in Culture and Society* 686 (1980); Victor Cline, "Another View: Pornography Effects, the State of the Art," in *Where Do You Draw the Line?* (V.B. Cline ed. 1982); (2) the commission's tendency to minimize the significance of its own findings, e.g., those by Donald Mosher on the differential effects of exposure by gender; and (3) the design of the commission's research. The commission did not focus on questions about gender, did its best to eliminate "violence" from its materials (so as not to overlap with the Violence Commission), and propounded unscientific theories such as Puritan guilt to explain women's negative responses to the materials.

Further scientific causality is unnecessary to legally validate an obscenity regulation: "But, it is argued, there is no scientific data which conclusively demonstrate that exposure to obscene materials adversely effects men and women or their society. It is [urged] that, absent such a demonstration, any kind of state regulation is 'impermissible.' *We reject this argument*. It is not for us to resolve empirical uncertainties underlying state legislation, save in the exceptional case where that legislation plainly impinges upon rights protected by the Constitution itself .... Although there is no conclusive proof of a connection between antisocial behavior and obscene material, the legislature of Georgia could quite reasonably determine that such a connection does or might exist." Paris Adult Theatre I v. Slaton, 413 U.S. 49, 60–61 (1973) (Burger J., for the majority) (emphasis added); see also Roth v. U.S., 354 U.S. 476, 501 (1957).

9. Some of the harm of pornography to women, as defined in note 1 above, and as discussed in this talk, has been documented in empirical studies. Recent studies have found that exposure to pornography increases the willingness of normal men to aggress against women under laboratory conditions; makes both women and men substantially less able to perceive accounts of rape as accounts of rape; makes normal men more closely resemble convicted rapists psychologically; increases attitudinal measures that are known to correlate with rape, such as hostility toward women, propensity to rape, condoning rape, and predictions that one would rape or force sex on a woman if one knew one would not get caught; and produces other attitude changes in men, such as increasing the extent of their trivialization, dehumanization, and objectification of women. Diana E.H. Russell, "Pornography and Violence: What Does the New Research Say?" in Lederer, note 8 above, at 216; Neil M. Malamuth and Edward Donnerstein (eds.), *Pornography and Sexual Aggression* (1984); Dolph Zillman, *The Connection between Sex and Aggression* (1984); J.V.P. Check, N. Malamuth, and R. Stille, "Hostility to Women Scale" (1983) (unpublished manuscript); Edward Donnerstein, "Pornography: Its Effects on Violence against Women: A Field Experiment," 15 *Journal of Research in Personality* 436 (1981); Neil M. Malamuth, "Rape Proclivities among Males," 37 *Journal of Sex Research* 226 (1980); Mosher, "Sex Callousness towards Women," in 8 *Technical Report of the Commission on Obscenity and Pornography* 313 (1971); Dolph Zillman and J. Bryant, "Effects of Massive Exposure to Pornography," in Malamuth and Donnerstein, eds., *Pornography and Sexual Aggression* (1984).

10. The following are illustrative, not exhaustive, of the body of work I term the "feminist critique of pornography."

Andrea Dworkin, note 1 above; Dorchen Leidholdt, "Where Pornography Meets Fascism," *Win*, Mar. 15, 1983, at 18; George Steiner, "Night Words," in *The Case Against Pornography* 227 (D. Holbrook ed. 1973); Susan Brownmiller, *Against Our Will: Men, Women and Rape* 394 (1975); Robin Morgan, "Pornography and Rape: Theory and Practice," in *Going Too Far* 165 (Robin Morgan ed. 1977); Kathleen Barry, *Female Sexual Slavery* (1979); *Against Sado-Masochism: A Radical Feminist Analysis* (R.R. Linden, D.R. Pagano, D.E.H. Russell, and S.L. Star eds. 1982), especially chapters by Ti-Grace Atkinson, Judy Butler, Andrea Dworkin, Alice Walker, John Stoltenberg, Audre Lorde, and Susan Leigh Star; Alice Walker "Coming Apart," in Lederer, *Take Back the Night*, note 8 above, and other articles in that volume with the exception of the legal ones; Gore Vidal, "Women's Liberation Meets the Miller-Mailer-Manson Man," in *Homage to Daniel Shays: Collected Essays 1952–1972* 389 (1972); Linda Lovelace and Michael McGrady, *Ordeal* (1980). Works basic to the perspective taken here are Kate Millett, *Sexual Politics* (1969) and Florence Rush, *The Best Kept Secret: Sexual Abuse of Children* (1980). "Violent Pornography: Degradation of Women versus Right of Free Speech," 8 *New York University Review of Law and Social Change* 181 (1978) contains both feminist and nonfeminist arguments.

11. For more extensive discussions of this subject, see my prior work, especially "Feminism, Marxism, Method and the State: An Agenda for Theory," 7 *Signs: Journal of Women in Culture and Society* 515 (1982) [hereinafter cited as *Signs I*]; "Feminism, Marxism, Method and the State: Toward Feminist Jurisprudence," 8 *Signs: Journal of Women in Culture and Society* 635 (1983) [hereinafter cited as *Signs II*].

12. Jacobellis v. Ohio, 378 U.S. 184, 197 (1964) (Stewart, J., concurring).

13. Justice Stewart is said to have complained that this single line was more quoted and more remembered than anything he ever said.

14. See *Signs I*, note 11 above.

15. Susan Griffin, *Pornography and Silence: Culture's Revenge against Nature* 2–4, 251–65 (1981).

16. Dworkin, note 1 above.

17. *See also* Dworkin, note 6 above.

18. The position that pornography is sex—that whatever you think of sex you think of pornography—underlies nearly every treatment of the subject. In particular, nearly every nonfeminist treatment proceeds on the implicit or explicit assumption, argument, criticism, or suspicion that pornography is sexually liberating in some way, a position unifying an otherwise diverse literature. *See* e.g., D.H. Lawrence, "Pornography and Obscenity," in his *Sex, Literature and Censorship* 64 (1959); Hugh Hefner, "The Playboy Philosophy," *Playboy*, December 1962, at 73, and *Playboy*, February 1963, at 43; Henry Miller, "Obscenity and the Law of Reflection," in his *Remember to Remember* 274, 286 (1947); Deirdre English, "The Politics of Porn: Can Feminists Walk the Line?" *Mother Jones*, Apr. 1980, at 20; Jean Bethke Elshtain, "The Victim Syndrome: A Troubling Turn in Feminism," *The Progressive*, June 1982, at 42. To choose an example at random: "In opposition to the Victorian view that narrowly defines proper sexual function in a rigid way that is analogous to ideas of excremental regularity and moderation, pornography builds a model of plastic variety and joyful excess in sexuality. In opposition to the sorrowing Catholic dismissal of sexuality as an unfortunate and spirituality superficial concomitant of propagation, pornography affords the alternative idea of the independent status of sexuality as a profound and shattering ecstasy." David Richards, "Free Speech and Obscenity Law: Toward a Moral Theory of the First Amendment," 123 *University of Pennsylvania Law Review* 45, 81 (1974) (footnotes omitted). *See also* F. Schauer, "Response: Pornography and the First Amendment," 40 *University of Pittsburgh Law Review* 605, 616 (1979).

19. Spending time around adult bookstores, attending pornographic movies, and talking with pornographers (who, like all smart pimps, do some form of market research), as well as analyzing the pornography itself in sex gender terms, all confirm that pornography is for men. That women may attend or otherwise consume it does not make it any less for men, any more than the observation that mostly men consume pornography means that pornography does not harm women. *See* Martha Langelan, "The Political Economy of Pornography," *Aegis: Magazine on Ending Violence Against Women*, Autumn 1981, at 5; J. Cook, "The X-Rated Economy," *Forbes*, Sept. 18, 1978, at 60. Personal observation reveals that most women tend to avoid pornography as much as possible—which is not very much, as it turns out.

20. The "fantasy" and "catharsis" hypotheses, together, assert that pornography cathects sexuality on the level of fantasy fulfillment. The work of Edward Donnerstein, particularly, shows that the opposite is true. The more pornography is viewed, the *more* pornography—and the more brutal pornography—is both wanted and required for sexual arousal. What occurs is not catharsis, but desensitization, requiring progressively more potent stimulation. *See* works cited note 9 above; Murray Strauss, "Leveling, Civility, and Violence in the Family," 36 *Journal of Marriage & the Family* 13 (1974).

21. Lovelace and McGrady, note 10 above, provides an account by one coerced pornography model. *See also* Andrea Dworkin, "Pornography's 'Exquisite Volunteers,'" *Ms.*, March 1981, at 65.

22. However, for one such inquiry, *see* Russell, note 9 above, at 228: a random sample of 930 San Francisco households found that 10 percent of women had at least once "been upset by anyone trying to get you to do what they'd seen in pornographic pictures, movies or books." Obviously, this figure could only include those who knew that the pornography was the source of the sex, so this finding is conservative. *See also* Diana E.H. Russell, *Rape in Marriage* 27–41 (1983) (discussing the database). The hearings Andrea Dworkin and I held for the Minneapolis City Council on the ordinance cited in note 1 produced many accounts of the use of pornography to force sex on women and children. *Public Hearings on Ordinances to Add Pornography to Discrimination Against Women*,

Committee on Government Operations, City Council, Minneapolis, Minn., Dec. 12–13, 1983. (Hereinafter cited as *Hearings*.)

23. See *Signs I*; See also Susan Sontag, "The Pornographic Imagination," 34 *Partisan Review* 181 (1977).

24. "Explicitness" of accounts is a central issue in both obscenity adjudications and audience access standards adopted voluntarily by self-regulated industries or by boards of censor. See, e.g., Grove Press v. Christenberry, 175 F. Supp. 488, 489 (S.D.N.Y. 1959) (discussion of "candor" and "realism"); Grove Press v. Christenberry, 276 F.2d 433, 438 (2d Cir. 1960) ("directness"); Mitchum v. State, 251 So.2d 298, 302 (Fla. Dist. Ct. App. 1971) ("show it all"); Kaplan v. California, 413 U.S. 115, 118 (1973). How *much* sex the depiction shows is implicitly thereby correlated with how *sexual* (that is, how sexually arousing to the male) the material is. See, e.g., Memoirs v. Massachusetts, 383 U.S. 413, 460 (1966) (White, J. dissenting); Richard Heffner, "What G, PG, R, and X Really Means," 126 *Cong. Rec.* 172 (daily ed. Dec. 8, 1980); *Report of the Committee on Obscenity and Film Censorship* (the Williams Report) (1981). Andrea Dworkin brilliantly gives the reader the experience of this aesthetic in her account of the pornography. Dworkin, note 1 above, at 25–47.

25. To the body of law ably encompassed and footnoted by William Lockhart and Robert McClure, "Literature, the Law of Obscenity and the Constitution," 38 *Minnesota Law Review* 5 (1960), I add only the most important cases since then: Staney v. Georgia, 394 U.S. 557 (1969); U.S. v. Reidel, 402 U.S. 351 (1970); Miller v. California, 413 U.S. 15 (1973); Paris Adult Theatre I v. Slaton, 413 U.S. 49 (1973); Hamling v. U.S., 418 U.S. 87 (1973); Jenkins v. Georgia, 418 U.S. 153 (1973); U.S. v. 12 200-Ft. Reels of Super 8 mm Film, 413 U.S. 123 (1973); Erzoznik v. City of Jacksonville, 422 U.S. 205 (1975); Splawn v. California, 431 U.S. 595 (1976); Ward v. Illinois, 431 U.S. 767 (1976); Lovisi v. Slayton, 539 F.2d 349 (4ᵗʰ Cir. 1976). *See also* New York v. Ferber, 458 U.S. 747 (1982).

26. For a discussion of the role of the law of privacy in supporting the existence of pornography, see Ruth Colker, "Pornography and Privacy: Towards the Development of a Group Based Theory for Sex Based Intrusions of Privacy," 1 *Law and Inequality: A Journal of Theory and Practice* 191 (1983).

27. Louis Henkin, "Morals and the Constitution: The Sin of Obscenity," 63 *Columbia Law Review* 391, 395 (1963).

28. These parallels are discussed more fully in *Signs II*. It may seem odd to denominate "moral" as *female* here, since this essay discusses male morality. Under male supremacy, men define things; I am describing that. Men define women *as* "moral." This is the male view of women. My analysis, a feminist critique of the male standpoint, terms "moral" the concept that pornography is about good and evil. This is *my* analysis of *them*, as contrasted with their attributions to women.

29. A reading of case law supports the reports in Robert Woodward and Scott Armstrong, *The Brethren* 194 (1979), to the effect that this is a "bottom line" criterion for at least some justices. The interesting question becomes why the tactics of male supremacy would change from keeping the penis hidden covertly glorified, to having it everywhere on display, overtly glorified. This suggests at least that a major shift from private terrorism to public terrorism has occurred. What used to be perceived as a danger to male power, the exposure of the penis, has now become a strategy in maintaining it.

30. One possible reading of Lockhart and McClure, note 25 above, is that this was their agenda, and that their approach was substantially adopted in the third prong of the *Miller* doctrine. For the law's leading attempt to grapple with this issue, see Memoirs v. Massachusetts, 383 U.S. 413 (1966), *overruled in part*, Miller v. California, 413 U.S. 15 (1973). See also U.S. v. Ulysses, 5 F. Supp. 182 (S.D.N.Y. 1933), *aff'd* 72 F.2d 705 (2d Cir. 1934).

31. Andrea Dworkin and I developed this analysis in our class "Pornography" at the University of Minnesota Law School, Fall 1983. See also Dworkin, "Why So-Called Radical Men Love and Need Pornography," in Lederer, note 8 above, at 141 (the issue of pornography is an issue of sexual access to women, hence involves a fight among men).

32. Those termed "fathers" and "sons" in Dworkin's article, note 31 above, we came to call "the old boys," whose strategy for male dominance involves keeping pornography and the abuse of women private, and "the new boys," whose strategy for male dominance involves making pornography and the abuse of women public. In my view Freud and the popularization of his repression hypothesis figure centrally in "the new boys" approach and success. To conclude, as some have, that women have benefited from the public availability of pornography and hence should be grateful for and have a stake in its continuing availability is to say that the merits of open condoned oppression relative to covert condoned oppression warrant its continuation. This reasoning obscures the possibility of *ending* the oppression. The benefit of pornography's open availability, it seems to me, is that women can know who and what we are dealing with in order to end it. How, is the question.

33. Miller v. California, 413 U.S. 15, 24 (1973).

34. Paris Adult Theatre I v. Slaton, 413 U.S. 49, 67 (1973). See also Miller v. California, 413 U.S. 15, 25 n.7 ("A quotation from Voltaire in the flyleaf of a book will not constitutionally redeem an otherwise obscene publication," quoting Kois v. Wisconsin, 408 U.S. 229, 231 [1972]).

35. Penthouse International v. McAuliffe, 610 F.2d 1353, 1362-73 (5th Cir. 1980). For a study in enforcement, see Coble v. City of Birmingham, 389 So.2d 527 (Ala. Ct. App. 1980).

36. Malamuth and Spinner, note 9 above (" … the portrayal of sexual aggression within such 'legitimate' magazines such as *Playboy* and *Penthouse* may have a greater impact than similar portrayals in hard-core pornography"); Neil M. Malamuth and Edward Donnerstein, "The Effects of Aggressive-Pornographic Mass Media Stimuli," 15 *Advances in Experimental Social Psychology* 103, 130 (1982).

37. Some courts, under the obscenity rubric, seem to have understood that the quality of artistry does not undo the damage. People v. Mature Enterprises, 343 N.Y.S.2d 911, 925 n.14 (N.Y. Sup. 1973) ("This court will not adopt a rule of law which states that obscenity is suppressible but that well-written or technically well produced obscenity is not," quoting, in part, People v. Fritch, 13 N.Y.2d 119, 126, 243 N.Y.S.2d 1, 7, 192 N.E.2d 713 [1963]). More to the point of my argument here is Justice O'Connor's observation that "[t]he compelling interests identified in today's opinion … suggest that the Constitution might in fact permit New York to ban knowing distribution of works depicting minors engaged in explicit sexual conduct, regardless of the social value of the depictions. For example, a 12-year-old child photographed while masturbating surely suffers the same psychological harm whether the community labels the photograph 'edifying' or 'tasteless.' The audience's appreciation of the depiction is simply irrelevant to New York's asserted interest in protecting children from psychological, emotional, and mental harm." New York v. Ferber, 458 U.S. 747, 774–75 (1982) (concurring). Put another way, how does it make a harmed child *not harmed* that what was produced by harming him is great art?

38. Women typically get mentioned in obscenity law only in the phrase, "women and men," used as a synonym for "people." At the same time, exactly who the victim of pornography is, has long been a great mystery. The few references to "exploitation" in obscenity litigation do not evoke a woman victim. For example, one reference to "a system of commercial exploitation of people with sadomasochistic sexual aberrations" concerned the customers of women dominatrixes, all of whom were men. State v. Von Clef, 102 N.J. Super. 104, 245 A. 2d 495, 505 (1968). The children at issue in *Ferber* were boys. Similarly, Justice Frankfurter invoked the "sordid exploitation of man's nature and impulses" in discussing his conception of pornography in Kingsley Pictures Corp.v. Regents, 360 U.S. 684, 692 (1958).

Uses of the Erotic: The Erotic As Power

Audre Lorde

There are many kinds of power, used and unused, acknowledged or otherwise. The erotic is a resource within each of us that lies in a deeply female and spiritual plane, firmly rooted in the power of our unexpressed or unrecognized feeling. In order to perpetuate itself, every oppression must corrupt or distort those various sources of power within the culture of the oppressed that can provide energy for change. For women, this has meant a suppression of the erotic as a considered source of power and information within our lives.

We have been taught to suspect this resource, vilified, abused, and devalued within western society. On the one hand, the superficially erotic has been encouraged as a sign of female inferiority; on the other hand, women have been made to suffer and to feel both contemptible and suspect by virtue of its existence.

It is a short step from there to the false belief that only by the suppression of the erotic within our lives and consciousness can women be truly strong. But that strength is illusory, for it is fashioned within the context of male models of power.

As women, we have come to distrust that power which rises from our deepest and nonrational knowledge. We have been warned against it all our lives by the male world, which values this depth of feeling enough to keep women around in order to exercise it in the service of men, but which fears this same depth too much to examine the possibilities of it within themselves. So women are maintained at a distant/inferior position to be psychically milked, much the same way ants maintain colonies of aphids to provide a life-giving substance for their masters.

But the erotic offers a well of replenishing and provocative force to the woman who does not fear its revelation, nor succumb to the belief that sensation is enough.

The erotic has often been misnamed by men and used against women. It has been made into the confused, the trivial, the psychotic, the plasticized sensation. For this reason, we have often turned away from the exploration and consideration of the erotic as a source of power and information, confusing it with its opposite, the pornographic. But pornography is a direct denial of the power of the erotic, for it represents the suppression of true feeling. Pornography emphasizes sensation without feeling.

The erotic is a measure between the beginnings of our sense of self and the chaos of our strongest feelings. It is an internal sense of satisfaction to which, once we

– 411 –

have experienced it, we know we can aspire. For having experienced the fullness of this depth of feeling and recognizing its power, in honor and self-respect we can require no less of ourselves.

It is never easy to demand the most from ourselves, from our lives, from our work. To encourage excellence is to go beyond the encouraged mediocrity of our society is to encourage excellence. But giving in to the fear of feeling and working to capacity is a luxury only the unintentional can afford, and the unintentional are those who do not wish to guide their own destinies.

This internal requirement toward excellence which we learn from the erotic must not be misconstrued as demanding the impossible from ourselves nor from others. Such a demand incapacitates everyone in the process. For the erotic is not a question only of what we do; it is a question of how acutely and fully we can feel in the doing. Once we know the extent to which we are capable of feeling that sense of satisfaction and completion, we can then observe which of our various life endeavors bring us closest to that fullness.

The aim of each thing which we do is to make our lives and the lives of our children richer and more possible. Within the celebration of the erotic in all our endeavors, my work becomes a conscious decision—a longed-for bed which I enter gratefully and from which I rise up empowered.

Of course, women so empowered are dangerous. So we are taught to separate the erotic demand from most vital areas of our lives other than sex. And the lack of concern for the erotic root and satisfactions of our work is felt in our disaffection from so much of what we do. For instance, how often do we truly love our work even at its most difficult?

The principal horror of any system which defines the good in terms of profit rather than in terms of human need, or which defines human need to the exclusion of the psychic and emotional components of that need—

the principal horror of such a system is that it robs our work of its erotic value, its erotic power, and life appeal and fulfillment. Such a system reduces work to a travesty of necessities, a duty by which we earn bread or oblivion for ourselves and those we love. But this is tantamount to blinding a painter and then telling her to improve her work, and to enjoy the act of painting. It is not only next to impossible, it is also profoundly cruel.

As women, we need to examine the ways in which our world can be truly different. I am speaking here of the necessity for reassessing the quality of all the aspects of our lives and of our work, and of how we move toward and through them.

The very word *erotic* comes from the Greek word *eros*, the personification of love in all its aspects—born of Chaos, and personifying creative power and harmony. When I speak of the erotic, then, I speak of it as an assertion of the lifeforce of women; of that creative energy empowered, the knowledge and use of which we are now reclaiming in our language, our history, our dancing, our loving, our work, our lives.

There are frequent attempts to equate pornography and eroticism, two diametrically opposed uses of the sexual. Because of these attempts, it has become fashionable to separate the spiritual (psychic and emotional) from the political, to see them as contradictory or antithetical. "What do you mean, a poetic revolutionary, a meditating gunrunner?" In the same way, we have attempted to separate the spiritual and the erotic, thereby reducing the spiritual to a world of flattened affect, a world of the ascetic who aspires to feel nothing. But nothing is farther from the truth. For the ascetic position is one of the highest fear, the gravest immobility. The severe abstinence of the ascetic becomes the ruling obsession. And it is one not of self-discipline but of self-abnegation.

The dichotomy between the spiritual and the political is also false, resulting from an incomplete attention to our erotic knowledge. For the bridge which connects them is formed by the erotic—the sensual—those physical, emotional, and psychic expressions of what is deepest and strongest and richest within each of us, being shared: the passions of love, in its deepest meanings.

Beyond the superficial, the considered phrase, "It feels right to me," acknowledges the strength of the erotic into a true knowledge, for what that means is the first and most powerful guiding light toward any understanding. And understanding is a handmaiden which can only wait upon, or clarify, that knowledge, deeply born. The erotic is the nurturer or nursemaid of all our deepest knowledge.

The erotic functions for me in several ways, and the first is in providing the power which comes from sharing deeply any pursuit with another person. The sharing of joy, whether physical, emotional, psychic, or intellectual, forms a bridge between the sharers, which can be the basis for understanding much of what is not shared between them, and lessens the threat of their difference.

Another important way in which the erotic connection functions is the open and fearless underlining of my capacity for joy. In the way my body stretches to music and opens into response, hearkening to its deepest rhythms, so every level upon which I sense also opens to the erotically satisfying experience, whether it is dancing, building a bookcase, writing a poem, examining an idea.

That self-connection shared is a measure of the joy which I know myself to be capable of feeling, a reminder of my capacity for feeling. And that deep and irreplaceable knowledge of my capacity for joy comes to demand from all of my life that it be lived within the knowledge that such satisfaction is possible, and does not have to be called *marriage*, nor *god*, nor *an afterlife*.

This is one reason why the erotic is so feared, and so often relegated to the bedroom alone, when it is recognized at all. For once we begin to feel deeply all the aspects of our lives, we begin to demand from ourselves and from our life-pursuits that they feel in accordance with that joy which we know ourselves to be capable of. Our erotic knowledge empowers us, becomes a lens through which we scrutinize all aspects of our existence, forcing us to evaluate those aspects honestly in terms of their relative meaning within our lives. And this is a grave responsibility, projected from within each of us, not to settle for the convenient, the shoddy, the conventionally expected, nor the merely safe.

During World War II, we bought sealed plastic packets of white, uncolored margarine, with a tiny, intense pellet of yellow coloring perched like a topaz just inside the clear skin of the bag. We would leave the margarine out for a while to soften, and then we would pinch the little pellet to break it inside the bag, releasing the rich yellowness into the soft pale mass of margarine. Then taking it carefully between our fingers, we would knead it gently back and forth, over and over, until the color had spread throughout the whole pound bag of margarine, thoroughly coloring it.

I find the erotic such a kernel within myself. When released from its intense and constrained pellet, it flows through and colors my life with a kind of energy that heightens and sensitizes and strengthens all my experience.

We have been raised to fear the *yes* within ourselves, our deepest cravings. But, once recognized, those which do not enhance our future lose their power and can be altered. The fear of our desires keeps them suspect and indiscriminately powerful, for to suppress any truth is to give it strength beyond endurance. The fear that we cannot grow beyond whatever distortions we may find within ourselves keeps us docile and loyal and obedient, externally defined, and leads us to accept many facets of our oppression as women.

When we live outside ourselves, and by that I mean on external directives only rather than from our internal knowledge and needs when we live away from those erotic guides from within ourselves, then our lives are limited by external and alien forms, and we conform to the needs of a structure that is not based on human need, let alone an individual's. But when we begin to live from within outward, in touch with the power of the erotic within ourselves, and allowing that power to inform and illuminate our actions upon the world around us, then we begin to be responsible to ourselves in the deepest sense. For as we begin to recognize our deepest feelings, we begin to give up, of necessity, being satisfied with suffering and self-negation, and with the numbness which so often seems like their only alternative in our society. Our acts against oppression become integral with self, motivated and empowered from within.

In touch with the erotic, I become less willing to accept powerlessness, or those other supplied states of being which are not native to me, such as resignation, despair, self-effacement, depression, self-denial.

And yes, there is a hierarchy. There is a difference between painting a back fence and writing a poem, but only one of quantity. And there is, for me, no difference between writing a good poem and moving into sunlight against the body of a woman I love.

This brings me to the last consideration of the erotic. To share the power of each other's feelings is different from using another's feelings as we would use a kleenex. When we look the other way from our experience, erotic or otherwise, we use rather than share the feelings of those others who participate in the experience with us. And use without consent of the used is abuse.

In order to be utilized, our erotic feelings must be recognized. The need for sharing deep feeling is a human need. But within the european-american tradition, this need is satisfied by certain proscribed erotic comings-together. These occasions are almost always characterized by a simultaneous looking away, a pretense of calling them something else, whether a religion, a fit, mob violence, or even playing doctor. And this misnaming of the need and the deed give rise to that distortion which results in pornography and obscenity—the abuse of feeling.

When we look away from the importance of the erotic in the development and sustenance of our power, or when we look away from ourselves as we satisfy our erotic needs in concert with others, we use each other as objects of satisfaction rather than share our joy in the satisfying, rather than make connection with our similarities and our differences. To refuse to be conscious of what we are feeling at any time, however comfortable that might seem, is to deny a large part of the experience, and to allow ourselves to be reduced to the pornographic, the abused, and the absurd.

The erotic cannot be felt secondhand. As a Black lesbian feminist, I have a particular feeling, knowledge, and understanding for those sisters with whom I have danced hard, played, or even fought. This deep participation has often been the forerunner for joint concerted actions not possible before.

But this erotic charge is not easily shared by women who continue to operate under an exclusively european-american male tradition. I know it was not available to me when I was trying to adapt my consciousness to this mode of living and sensation.

Only now, I find more and more women-identified women brave enough to risk sharing the erotic's electrical charge without having to look away, and without distorting the enormously powerful and creative nature of that exchange. Recognizing the power of the erotic within our lives can give us the energy to pursue genuine change within our world, rather than merely settling for a shift of characters in the same weary drama.

For not only do we touch our most profoundly creative source, but we do that which is female and self-affirming in the face of a racist, patriarchal, and anti-erotic society.

Mama's Got the Blues

Angela Davis

> Trust no man, trust no man, no further than your eyes can see
> I said, trust no man, no further than your eyes can see
> He'll tell you that he loves you and swear it is true
> The very next minute he'll turn his back on you
> Ah, trust no man, no further than your eyes can see.
> —"Trust No Man"[1]

Classic blues comprised an important elaboration of black working-class social consciousness. Gertrude Rainey's and Bessie Smith's songs constituted historical preparation for social protest. They also foreshadowed a brand of protest that refused to privilege racism over sexism, or the conventional public realm over the private as the preeminent domain of power. Because women's blues were not ideologically structured by the assumptions that defined the prominent black women's organizations of the era as middle class, they could issue more direct and audacious challenges to male dominance. It is important, I think, to understand women's blues as a working-class form that anticipates the politicalization of the "personal" through the dynamic of "consciousness-raising," a phenomenon associated with the women's movement of the last three decades.

Studies of feminist dimensions in African-American women's historical activism tend to focus on individuals and organizations solidly anchored in the developing black middle class. Paula Giddings points out that while the mission of the black women's club movement was fundamentally anti-racist, it shared certain class assumptions with the white women's movement it criticized:

> The Black women's club movement did have a number of things in common with the White club movement …. [T]he membership of both organizations consisted mostly of middle-class educated women who were steeped in the Protestant ethic. Neither group questioned the superiority of middle-class values or way of life, or had any romantic notions of the inherent nobility of the poor, uneducated masses; education and material progress were values that Black and White women shared. Both also

believed in the importance of the home and the woman's moral influence within it. Black and White women saw the family as a microcosm and cornerstone of society.[2]

When the National Association of Colored Women was founded in 1896, it chose for its motto "Lifting as We Climb." This motto called upon the most educated, most moral, and most affluent African-American women to recognize the extent to which the dominant culture's racist perceptions linked them with the least educated, most immoral, and most impoverished black women. Mary Church Terrell described this cross-class relationship as a determination "to come into the closest possible touch with the masses of our women, through whom the womanhood of our people is always judged." More explicitly, "[s]elf-preservation demands that [educated black women] go among the lowly, illiterate and even the vicious, to whom they are bound by ties of race and sex ... to reclaim them."[3] While this posture was certainly admirable and helped to produce a distinguished tradition of progressive activism among black middle-class women from the NACW to the National Council of Negro Women and similar organizations today, what was and remains problematic is the premise that middle-class women embody a standard their poorer sisters should be encouraged to emulate.

The black women's club movement was especially concerned with the notion of "defending our name" against pervasive charges of immorality and sexual promiscuity.[4] Given the extent to which representations of black inferiority emanating from the dominant culture were bound up with notions of racial hypersexualization— the deployment of the myth of the black rapist to justify lynching is the most obvious example—it is hard to imagine that women like Fannie Barrier Williams, Ida B. Wells, and Mary Church Terrell could have been as effective as they were without defending the sexual purity of their sisters. Yet, in the process of defending black women's moral integrity and sexual purity, they almost

entirely denied sexual agency. As I emphasized in the first chapter [of *Blues Legacies and Black Feminism*], sexuality was one of the few realms in which masses of African-American women could exercise autonomy—and thus tangibly distinguish their contemporary status from the history of enslavement. Denial of sexual agency was in an important respect the denial of freedom for working-class black women.

The women about whom Gertrude Rainey and Bessie Smith sing are precisely those who were perceived by the club women as in need of salvation. Yet, middle-class women were not the only black women who engaged in community-building. I want to suggest that women's blues provided a cultural space for community-building among working-class black women, and that it was a space in which the coercions of bourgeois notions of sexual purity and "true womanhood" were absent.

During the period following World War I, large numbers of black people left the South or moved from rural areas into southern cities and thus into new job markets. At the same time, a distinctly post-slavery music culture was widely disseminated, thus accelerating and complicating the development of a postslavery working-class consciousness. Yet, blues scholars working within the discipline of musicology are rarely concerned with the ideological implications of the blues, and historians studying the African-American past rarely turn to blues history. In the few works that attempt to probe blues history for insights about the development of black cultural consciousness, masculinist bias almost inevitably leads to a failure to take seriously the efforts of women blues musicians and the female reception of their work. As a consequence, the central part played by women both in the blues and in the history of African-American cultural consciousness is often ignored.

Perhaps women's blues history has been so readily marginalized because the most frequently recurring themes of women's blues music revolve around male lovers and the plethora of problems posed by heterosexual relationships complicated by expressions of autonomous female sexuality. As I have attempted to point out, these love themes have complex social implications. Moreover, it is usually left unremarked that these songs provide a rich and complex backdrop for working-class women's lives, reflecting how they dealt with and experienced each other. Blues lyrics often construct these intragender relationships as antagonistic, as negotiations of encounters between competitors and rivals. At the same time, there are songs that highlight friendship, sisterhood, love, and solidarity between women. These range from Gertrude Rainey's "Prove It on Me Blues"[5]—and other songs recorded by women of that era celebrating sexual love between women—to songs such as Bessie Smith's "A Good Man Is Hard to Find," presenting advice to women on how to conduct themselves within their heterosexual relationships.[6]

[...] the abundance of themes revolving around love and sexuality in women's blues indicate the extent to which, for African Americans during the decades following emancipation, sexual love was experienced as physical and spiritual evidence—and the blues as aesthetic evidence—of freedom. From this historical vantage point, competition and rivalry in love may be seen as evidence of the historical construction of black working-class individuality. Although sexual rivalries no doubt existed among the emergent black middle class, ideological prohibitions required women either to be silent or to engage in a "proper" way of speaking about such matters.

As slave music suggests, the conditions for physical and spiritual survival during slavery (as well as the survival of transmuted African ancestral cultures) defined the value of the individual as subordinate to the community. The abolition of slavery, while it did not bring economic and political freedom, created a backdrop for new kinds of relationships between black individuals and thus for a different valuation of the individual in general. The new African Americans—women and men alike—came to perceive their individual selves not only as welded together within the community, but as different from and in opposition to one another as well. For working-class women and men, the blues both allowed and furnished cultural representations of this new individuality.

Blues portraits of women in competition with each other for sexual partners—as "vicious" as they may have appeared to women like Mary Church Terrell—revealed working-class women as capable of exercising some measure of agency in choosing their partners. This is not to deny the problematic aspects of blues constructions of female jealously and rivalry, sometimes to the point of violence. On the contrary, while representations of female sexual agency no doubt played a progressive role by encouraging assertiveness and independence among black women, these representations simultaneously legitimized a tradition of real and often murderous violence between women. As African-American women forged a continuum of independent womanhood—in contradiction to the prevailing ideology of women's place—they also affirmed, in frequently exaggerated forms, sexist models of women's conduct. While this contradictory character of the emergence of black female working-class individuality is far from inconsequential—and I will later identify some of the ways these contradictions are manifested in blues performances—I want to emphasize, for the moment, the importance of women's blues as a site for the independent elaboration and affirmation of subjectivity and community for women of the black working class. Through the blues, black women were able to autonomously work out—as audiences and performers—a working-class model of womanhood. This model of womanhood was based in part on a collective historical memory of what had been previously required of women to cope with slavery. But more important, it revealed that black women and men, the blues audience, could respond to the vastly different circumstances of the post-slavery era with notions of gender and sexuality that were, to a certain extent, ideologically independent of the middle-class cult of "true womanhood." In this sense, as Hazel Carby has pointed out, the blues was a privileged site in which women were free to assert themselves publicly as sexual beings.

Beginning with W.E.B. Du Bois's essay in *Darkwater*, many studies have emphasized the extent to which black working-class women's relative economic independence summoned various modes of female consciousness that emphasized strength, resilience, and autonomy.[7] However, such arguments often assume a strictly causal relationship between the economic conditions of slavery—which inflicted responsibilities for production on women that were equal to those placed on men—and the gendered consciousness among working-class black women that privileged independence.[8] I want to emphasize women's blues as an important cultural mediator for this gendered consciousness that transformed collective memories of slavery as it worked with a new social construction of love and sexuality. The blues provided a space where women could express themselves in new ways, a space in which they sometimes affirmed the dominant middle-class ideology but also could deviate from it.

I begin with the most complicated expressions of women's independence and assertiveness, in which an independent sense of women's strength was interwoven with themes of female rivalry over a male lover. "Rough and Tumble Blues," composed and recorded by Gertrude "Ma" Rainey, presents a powerful, fighting, rough-and-tumble woman, who boasts about her assertiveness and power. Her boasts, however, are directed at the women— Mama Tree Top Tall and Miss Shorty Toad—who have their eyes on her man. Her power is established partly by virtue of her ability to support the man financially— evidenced by the fact that she has bought him a "struttin' suit." The final verse of this song proclaims:

> I got rough and killed three women 'fore the
>   police got the news
> I got rough and killed three women 'fore police
>   got the news

'Cause mama's on the warpath with those rough
    and tumble blues.[9]

A similar song, "Wringing and Twisting Blues," composed by Paul Carter and also recorded by Rainey, announces the protagonist's desire to poison the woman for whom her lover left her:

> But if I know that woman that caused my heart
>   to moan
> I'd cook a special dinner, invite her to my home
> ....
> If she eats what's on my table, she will be
>   graveyard bound
> I'll be right there to tell her, when they put her
>   in the ground
> "You're the cause of me having those wringin'
>   and a-twistin' blues."[10]

There are comparable images of female violence directed against other women in Bessie Smith's songs:

> But if I find that gal
> That tried to steal my pal
> I'll get her told, just you wait and see.[11]

Or, in more aggressive terms:

> St. Louis gal, I'm gonna handle you, I said
>   manhandle you
> ....
> Your life won't be worth a dime
> You stole my pal, St. Louis gal
>
> I'm goin' a-huntin', root-dooti-doot
> You know just what I'm gonna shoot
> You stole my pal, St. Louis gal.[12]

Such representations of jealousy and violence need not be taken literally. However, we should keep in mind the current discourse on racialized violence that merges real violence and representations of violence. Critiques of gangsta rap, for example, argue for a rather simple and mechanical relation between cultural images and material reality. Of course, the murders of rappers Tupac Shakur and Biggie Smalls within six months of one another in late 1996 and early 1997 tended to affirm this. But, with respect to the role of violence in Rainey's and Smith's work, I am arguing that these performed lyrics provide a glimpse of a kind of working-class women's community-building that, rather than advocating violence, proclaims women's complexity by refusing to deny or downplay female antagonism. The jealousy and competitiveness that was so openly expressed in the blues surely also characterized middle-class women's relations with each other. Remaining unnamed and unacknowledged, these antagonisms must have had vast political consequences about which we could not even begin to speculate today.

Jealousy and rivalry, as they defined female blues subjects' attitudes toward other women, do not always erupt into actual or imagined violence as in the songs cited above. Often, there is simply suspicion, as in Bessie Smith's "Empty Bed Blues":

> Lord, he's got that sweet somethin', and I told my gal friend Lou
> He's got that sweet somethin', and I told my gal friend Lou
> From the way she's ravin', she must have gone and tried it too.

"Empty Bed Blues, Part II" concludes with a word of advice offered to other women:

> When you get good lovin', never go and spread the news
> Yeah, it will double cross you and leave you with them empty bed blues.[13]

In a similar vein, "He's Got Me Goin'"—a song replete with erotic imagery—reveals a subject so utterly captivated by her lover that she fears other women may hear about him and try to attract his attentions:

> 'Fraid to advertise my man, simply scared to death
> These gals'll hear about him and try him for they self.[14]

Unmitigated jealousy, however, is not always the posture assumed by jealous blues subjects. The blues never remain fixed on one perspective, but rather different songs—sometimes the same song—explore experiences from various vantage points. This feature of the blues, the aesthetic incorporation of several perspectives and dimensions, may be interpreted as reflective of West African philosophical outlooks and representational strategies. Beneath the apparent simplicity and straightforwardness of the blues, complex visions—reflecting the complexity with which reality is perceived—can always be uncovered. This is another way in which the blues are located on an African cultural continuum.[15]

Some songs describe the woman succumbing to feelings of jealousy. In other songs, jealousy is named and acknowledged—even celebrated as an important subject and a powerful blues theme. Still other songs reveal a critical attitude toward jealousy, pointing to its potential destructiveness. Within the body of Gertrude Rainey's work, all three of these attitudes are evident. In "Sleep Talking Blues," the protagonist warns her man of the disastrous consequences of calling another woman's name in his sleep:

> When you talk in your sleep, be sure your mama's not awake
> When you talk in your sleep, be sure your mama's not awake

You call another woman's name, you'll think
   you wake up in a earthquake.[16]

In "Jealous Hearted Blues"—one of Lovie Austin's
compositions—jealousy is repeatedly named, as the
jealous woman acknowledges the extent to which she
has been overcome by this emotion. The following chorus
is repeated four times:

Yes I'm jealous, jealous, jealous hearted me
Lord, I'm just jealous, jealous as I can be.

Indeed, the protagonist is so utterly driven by her jealousy
that she announces this measure:

Gonna buy me a bulldog to watch him while I
   sleep
To keep my man from making his midnight
   creep.[17]

Finally, in "Jealousy Blues," an analytical and implicitly
critical posture is assumed. This song focuses on the
catastrophic potential of jealousy for relationships and
for one's psychological well-being, as well as on its violence
and its material consequences:

If all the world is evil, all the world is evil, oh
   jealousy is the worst of all
It'll make you mad and lonely, your sweet love
   will feel so pale
It'll steal your loving daddy, have many folks in
   jail.[18]

The most complicated evocation of jealousy can be
found in "My Man Blues," a song written by Bessie Smith
and performed as a duet with Clara Smith, who was
known during the period as the Empress's most serious
musical rival. The piece is about competition for the
attentions of a man who each woman insists belongs to
her. There are powerful resonances in this song: the

actual competitive relationship between the two Smiths
as entertainers; the rivalry in general between women;
and a troubled but unmistakable reconciliation:

Bessie: Clara, who was that man I saw you with
         the other day?
Clara: Bessie, that was my smooth black
         daddy that we call Charlie Gray.
Bessie: Don't you know that's my man? Yes,
         that's a fact.
Clara: I ain't seen your name printed up and
         down his back.
Bessie: You better let him be.
Clara: What, old gal? Because you ain't talkin'
         to me.
Bessie: That's my man, I want him for my own.
Clara: [Spoken] No! No! [Sung] He's my sweet
         daddy.
         You'd better leave that man alone.
Bessie: See that suit he got on? I bought it last
         week.
Clara: I been buyin' his clothes for five years,
         for that is my black sheik.

[Charlie whistles]
[spoken]
Bessie: Is that you, honey?
Charlie: 'Tain't nobody but—who's back there?
Clara: It sounds like Charlie.
Bessie: It 'tis my man, sweet papa Charlie
         Gray.
Clara: Your man? How do you git that way?
Bessie: Now, look here, honey. I been had that
         man for sumpteen years.
Clara: Child, don't you know I'll turn your
         damper down?
Bessie: Yes, Clara, and I'll cut you every way
         but loose!
Clara: Well, you might as well be get it fixed.
Bessie: Well, then.

[sung]

Bessie: I guess we got to have him on co-
          operation plan.
          I guess we got to have him on co-
          operation plan.
[spoken]
Clara: Bessie!
Bessie: Clara!
[sung]
Both: Ain't nothin' different 'bout all those
          other two-time men.
[spoken]
Bessie: How 'bout it?
Clara: Suits me.
Bessie: Suits me too.
Clara: Well, then.[19]

Edward Brooks has called this humorous song "a fascinating document ... which completely dispels the doubts of some commentators about Bessie Smith's supremacy over her nearest rival."[20] With respect to the content of the song, the women apparently are equal competitors for the love of the same man. That this rivalry is presented in broadly comic terms encourages in the audience a critical attitude toward such conduct on the part of women. What is most striking about this song is its resolution: the two women agree to share the man over whom they have been engaging in a verbal duel. Bessie proposes to Clara, "I guess we got to have him, on co-operation plan." Her suggestion seems to imply how futile it is for them to be so consumed by jealousy that they constantly are at loggerheads with one another. At this point in the song, their focus on the male lover is displaced by their mutual acknowledgment of each other: each calls the other's name. And, in the final moments of the song, they sing together for the first time, agreeing that, since most other men would be as unfaithful as the one over whom they have been battling, they may as well act on Bessie's suggestion. The reconciliation with which the piece concludes, as comically as it may be formulated, alludes to a possibility of sisterhood and solidarity that is forged in and through struggles around sexuality.

The concluding posture of "My Man Blues" is especially interesting for the way it provides an imagined alternative to the notions of women's community-building on which middle-class black club women relied. From their vantage point, women could only come together in defense of sexual purity. In other words, sexuality could only play a role in community-building as an object of ideological protest and cleansing. Of course, the kind of political work the club women set out to do would have been impossible had they not denied the sexually motivated antagonisms so central in blues discourse. In light of the emergence of sexuality in recent decades as an important arena of political struggle, it is important, nevertheless, to understand the blues as a form that did allow explicit articulations and explorations of sexual politics.

There are far more songs of advice among women's blues recordings than there are songs of female competition. One of the principal modes of community-building in women's blues is that of sharing experiences for the purpose of instructing women how to conduct their lives. Many of the songs that describe the difficulties of romantic partnerships are pedagogical in character. In some instances, the instruction warns women to beware of the powers of seduction some men possess, as in the following stanza from Bessie Smith's "Lookin' for My Man Blues":

> He's a red hot papa, melt hearts as cold as ice
> He's a red hot papa, melt hearts as cold as ice
> Girls, if he ever love you once, you bound to
> love him twice.[21]

Or, as in Ma Rainey's "Trust No Man," women are instructed to "[t]rust no man, no further than your eyes can see."[22]

There are also songs that advise women how to avoid triangular entanglements—and how to keep other women from eyeing their men. In Bessie Smith's "Keep It to Yourself," there is an underlying perception of other women as competitors and rivals. However, the instruction seeks to avoid active rivalry over men:

> If your man is nice and sweet, servin' you lots of
>   young pigmeat
> Oh, yeah, keep it to yourself
> ....
> If your man is full of action, givin' you a lots of
>   satisfaction
> Oh, yeah, keep it to yourself
> ....
> If he tries to treat you right, give you lovin' every
>   night
> Oh, yeah, keep it to yourself
> [line #]
> He don't fall for no one, he don't call for no
>   one
> He don't give nobody his L-O-V-E, 'cause it's
>   yours
> With your man you've got the best go, don't
>   broadcast it on nobody's radio
> Oh, yeah, keep it to yourself.[23]

There is an interesting dialectic here between the individual woman and the larger female community. While women are clearly perceived as antagonists—as potential intruders into others' relationships—they are also viewed as possessing common fears and common interests. They are located both outside and inside a community of women. This aesthetic community of women emerges in its most developed form when blues women share stories about abusive partners or advise their sisters how to conduct themselves in relation to such men. Daphne Duval Harrison points out in her pioneering study of the classic blues singers that "[a]dvice to other women is a staple among women's blues themes, especially on how to handle your men."[24] Much of this advice seems to accept male supremacy without overtly challenging it,

but it also displays unmistakable oppositional attitudes in its rejection of sexual passivity as a defining characteristic of womanhood.

A process similar to the consciousness-raising strategies associated with the 1960s women's liberation movement unfolds in these songs, which are conversations among women about male behavior in which the traditional call-and-response structure of West African-based music takes on a new feminist meaning. Consciousness-raising groups affirmed the most dramatic insight of the early women's liberation movement: the personal is political. Individual women shared personal experiences with the aim of rendering explicit the underlying politics shaping women's lives. Because of the complicated racial politics of the 1960s, which defined the women's movement as white, and because of its emphasis on personal micropolitics (often seen as a retreat from the macropolitics of race), black women generally found it difficult to identify with the strategy of consciousness-raising. In retrospect, however, it is possible to detect ways in which the sharing of personal relationships in blues culture prefigured consciousness-raising and its insights about the social construction of individual experience. Seen in this light, the blues women can be understood as being responsible for the dissemination of attitudes toward male supremacy that had decidedly feminist implications.

That the blues is a highly "personal" aesthetic form in no way diminishes its important social and political dimensions. Lawrence Levine has pointed out that

> [t]he blues was the most highly personalized, indeed, the first almost completely personalized music that Afro-Americans developed. It was the first important form of Afro-American music in the United States to lack the kind of antiphony that had marked other black musical forms. The call and response form remained, but in blues it was the singer who responded to himself or herself either verbally or on an accompanying

instrument. In all these respects blues was the most typically American music Afro-Americans had yet created and represented a major degree of acculturation to the individualized ethos of the larger society .... [25]

Levine is certainly accurate in his emphasis on the personal and personalizing dimensions of the blues, but he fails to recognize a more complicated persistence of the call-and-response form. The blues in performance creates space for spontaneous audience response in a manner that is similar to religious testifying. Just as the sermon lacks vitality when no response is forthcoming from the congregation, so the blues performance falls flat without the anticipated affirmations of the audience. It was this invitation to respond that rendered women's blues such a powerful site for the construction of working-class consciousness and one of the only arenas in which working-class black women could become aware of the deeply social character of their personal experiences.

The contemporary blues woman Koko Taylor has pointed out that the songs she writes and performs do not always reflect her own individual experiences. Yet, as she insists, she knows that among the women in her audiences, some will certainly identify with the situation she constructs:

> Now when I write a song, I'm thinking about people in general, everyday living. Just look around, you know. Say, for instance, like when I wrote this tune "Baby Please Don't Dog Me." You know what I'm saying. I'm thinking about, O.K., here is some woman begging and she's pleading, Baby please don't dog me, when you know that you're doing wrong yourself .... Now that shoe might not fit my feet. That shoe might not fit your feet. But that shoe do fit somebody's feet. It's some woman out there is really thinking, she really feels the way that I'm singing about, what I'm talking about in this song. It's some

woman somewhere really feels this way. These are the words she would like to say. [26]

Call-and-response persists in women's blues through the construction of fictional subjects who assert their sexuality in a variety of ways. Such subjects permit a vast array of individual women to locate themselves within a blues community without having to abstract themselves from their personal lives. Rainey and Smith sang songs about women who had numerous male lovers, women angry about male sexual behavior, and women who loved women. Moreover, individual women were able to respond to and comment on the problems of other women without having to reveal the autobiographical sources of their authority and wisdom.

"The widespread use of the call-and-response discourse mode among African-Americans," black feminist sociologist Patricia Hill Collins points out,

> illustrates the importance placed on dialogue. Composed of spontaneous verbal and nonverbal interaction between speaker and listener in which all of the speaker's statements, or "calls," are punctuated by expressions, or "responses," from the listener, this Black discourse mode pervades African American culture. The fundamental requirement of this interactive network is active participation of all individuals. For ideas to be tested and validated, everyone in the group must participate. [27]

Collins defines call-and-response discourse as an essential dimension of the "Afrocentric feminist epistemology" she proposes. While she invokes black women musicians like Billie Holiday and Aretha Franklin in her discussion of yet another dimension of this alternative epistemology, the ethic of caring, she does not discuss the musical roots of call-and-response discourse. Such a discussion—particularly in relation to blues women like Bessie Smith—would render her compelling argument even more powerful. Collins is concerned with the possibility of knowledge production that suppresses neither the individual at the expense of the general welfare, nor feelings at the expense of rational thought. The participatory character of the blues affirms women's community without negating individual feelings.

Without the assumption of such an imagined community, the advice song in women's blues simply could not work. Gertrude Rainey's "Trust No Man," composed by Lillian Hardaway Henderson, is one of the finest examples of the advice song:

> I want all you women to listen to me
> Don't trust your man no further than your eyes
>   can see
> I trusted mine with my best friend
> But that was the bad part in the end
>
> Trust no man, trust no man, no further than
>   your eyes can see
> I said trust no man, no further than your eyes
>   can see
> He'll tell you that he loves you and swear it is
>   true
> The very next minute he'll turn his back on you
> Ah, trust no man, no further than your eyes
>   can see.[28]

Singing "I want all you women to listen to me" in the first verse of the song, Rainey constructs an audience, an imagined community of women. It is clear on the recording that Rainey is inviting response—even to this mechanical reproduction of her live performance. Her advice is framed and delivered in such a way that any woman listening can discover a way to identify with her admonition. The appeal is so powerful that it is easy to imagine the responses that came forth during her live performances. As if to preclude any doubt as to the invitation to respond, Rainey included spoken words in the second chorus: "Say! Take Ma Rainey's advice! Don't

trust *no* man. I mean, not even your own man!" She concludes this spoken session with the words: "Just don't trust nobody! You see where it got me, don't you? He sure will leave you."

Bessie Smith's "Safety Mama" is a song of advice that counsels women to take strong stands with the men with whom they are involved, and to take measures to guarantee their own economic independence:

> Let me tell you how and what one no-good man
>   done to me
> He caught me pretty, young, and wild, after that
>   he let me be
>
> He'd taken advantage of my youth, and that you
>   understand
> So wait awhile, I'll show you, child, just how to
>   treat a no-good man
>
> Make him stay at home, wash and iron
> Tell all the neighbors he done lost his mind
>
> Give your house rent shake on Saturday night
> Monday morning you'll hold collectors good and
>   tight.[29]

This song's domestic imagery—and the gender reversal—have already been discussed in the first chapter [of *Blues Legacies and Black Feminism*]. What is also striking about "Safety Mama" is that it emphatically counsels women to find ways of supporting themselves financially. Certainly, black women were compelled to work for a living, but for many decades following the abolition of slavery, the jobs that were available to them were limited to domestic work. "Safety Mama" suggests that rather than rely on their men—and perhaps also to avoid the perpetual servitude to which so many working black women were condemned—they organize rent parties in order to acquire funds to meet their landlords' demands.

By the 1920s these "house rent shakes" had developed into a community institution in the urban North, aiding men and women alike to raise the money necessary to "hold collectors good and tight." The imagined women's community in this song is one that refuses to place women in sexual and economic subordination to men. It affirms working-class women's independence. Again, it is possible to envision the enthusiastic responses that came from Smith's female audiences.

Another advice song recorded by Bessie Smith—also previously discussed—is "Pinchback Blues." It proposes to arm women with the power to resist men who attempt to use sexual attractiveness to exploit women. As in "Safety Mama" and Rainey's "Trust No Man," "Pinchback" opens with an evocation of a female community. "Girls," Smith states in the spoken introduction, "I wanna tell you about these sweet men. These men goin' 'round here tryin' to play cute. I'm hard on you, boys, yes sir." She then proceeds to narrate an experience of having been lured into a relationship that led to marriage with a "sweet man" who then refused to get a job to support either his female partner or himself:

> I fell in love with a sweet man once, he said he
>   loved me too
> He said if I'd run away with him what nice things
>   he would do
>
> I'd travel around from town to town, how happy
>   I would feel
> But don't you know, he would not work ...

Universalizing the lesson drawn from these experiences, Smith offers direct advice to her female audience:

> ... girls, take this tip from me
> Get a workin' man when you marry, and let all
>   these sweet men be
> ....

> There's one thing about this married life that
>   these young girls have got to know
> If a sweet man enter your front gate, turn out
>   your lights and lock your door.[30]

The admonition "get a working man" is even more than a sound bit of advice to a woman who wishes to acquire a measure of material security. It suggests an identification with workers—and by extension, the values and perhaps also the collective consciousness associated with the working class. Women are urged to seek out solid working men and to learn how to resist the temptations of parasitic men who try to dazzle with their good looks and smooth talk.

It is interesting that Bessie Smith's appearance in the 1929 motion picture St. Louis Blues[31]—the only extant recording of her image on film—was in the role of a woman who did not take the advice offered in "Pinchback Blues." In this film, which incorporates an overabundance of racist and sexist stereotypes, the character she plays is abused and exploited by a handsome, light-skinned, disloyal, crapshooting man who has obviously attached himself to her for the sole purpose of taking her money. "Bessie," the character she plays in the film, has bought clothes for "Jimmy" (played by Jimmy Mordecai), allowed him to live in the hotel room she is renting, and provided him with money. He, in turn, is involved with a thin, light-skinned woman (played by Isabel Washington) who fits a Eurocentric definition of feminine beauty.

The plot of this film, superficially constructed around Bessie Smith's performance of W.C. Handy's "St. Louis Blues," is based on Jimmy's taunting abandonment of Bessie, who is so utterly mesmerized by him that she pleads with him to stay even as she lies on the floor after being battered by him. When the scoundrel returns—the setting for this scene is a luxurious Harlem nightclub—she experiences a momentary exhilaration. However, she is soon overcome with despair once more because, as it turns out, Jimmy's romantic invitation to dance is simply a ploy to steal the money she has hidden in her garter. The film concludes with the pinchback, Jimmy, in a posture of triumph, and the victimized woman, Bessie, in a state of paralyzing depression.

The choice of Bessie Smith for the part in the film has been attributed to W.C. Handy, who, as a collaborator on the film, suggested to the director, Dudley Murphy, that she be cast in the leading role. "She had made the definitive version of the title tune," Chris Albertson has pointed out, and her powerful voice was one of the few that could be heard over the projected accompaniment of a forty-two-voice mixed choir, jazz band, and strings.[32] It is not difficult to understand Smith's decision to make this film. During the late twenties, the popularity of blues had begun to wane and many leading blues singers— Alberta Hunter and Ethel Waters included—increasingly began to sing Tin Pan Alley products and to seek roles in musicals. Smith had starred in a Broadway production that had flopped, and she, like other black women entertainers, was eager to break into the revolutionary medium of talking pictures. But black singers who had been able to exercise a certain measure of autonomy and control over their music found that the new medium used and abused their talents at the whims of producers and directors.

St. Louis Blues deserves criticism not only for its exploitation of racist stereotypes but for its violation of the spirit of the blues. Its direct translation of blues images into a visual and linear narrative violates blues discourse, which is always complicated, contextualized, and informed by that which is unspoken as well as by that which is named. *St. Louis Blues*, the film, flagrantly disregards the spirit of women's blues by leaving the victimized woman with no recourse. In the film, the response is amputated from the call. Although the advice song "Pinchback Blues" evokes a male figure who bears a striking resemblance to the character of Jimmy in the film, "Pinchback" warns women to stay away from such con men. In other women's blues that allude to these

men, even when the criticism is not open and direct, the female subjects are never left in a state of absolute despair. Such a posture violates the spirit of women's blues. It is precisely the presence of an imagined community of supportive women that rescues them from the existential agony that Smith portrays at the end of *St. Louis Blues*.

There are also a number of advice songs that suggest how women should conduct themselves in relationships with men who are worthy partners. A cover Bessie Smith recorded of Alberta Hunter's "A Good Man Is Hard to Find" is a typical woman-to-woman advice blues of this kind. It eventually became a standard. This song is unique in that it does not evoke an individual's experiences but rather is directed, in its entirety, to the female audience, articulating their collective experiences with their sexual partners. The persisting problems women encounter in their relationships are named: the unfaithful male lover whose actions provoke tumultuous feelings of jealousy in his female partner, as well as fantasies (if not realities) of violent assault. The main advice in this song is that if a woman does find a man who is loyal, respectful, and sensitive, she should know how to reciprocate:

> Lord, a good man is hard to find, you always
>   get another kind
> Yes, and when you think that he's your pal
> You look and find him fooling 'round some old
>   gal
> Then you rave, you are crazed, you want to see
>   him down in his grave
>
> So if your man is nice, take my advice
> Hug him in the morning, kiss him at night
> Give him plenty lovin', treat your good man right
> 'Cause a good man nowadays sho' is hard to
>   find.[33]

There is a series of songs among the recordings of Gertrude Rainey and Bessie Smith in which the woman who is experiencing difficulties in love shares her problems and her feelings with other women. These songs implicitly emphasize the dialectical relation between the female subject and the community of women within which this individuality is imagined. In an aesthetic realm, these songs construct a women's community in which individual women are able to locate themselves on a jagged continuum of group experiences. They encourage intimacy and familiarity between women. They contextualize particular events in the personal histories of the songs' subjects—often actions by their male partners that have wrought havoc in their lives—as stories they are sharing with their girlfriends. These girlfriends console them by implicitly confirming similar events in their own histories, thus providing emotional support and enabling women to confront such disruptive moments with attitudes that move from victimization to agency. Ma Rainey, for example, begins "Jelly Bean Blues" by asking, "Did you ever wake up with your good man on your mind?"[34] The song then proceeds to describe the subject's state of mind in the aftermath of her lover's desertion. The initial question establishes a relationship of intimacy and familiarity with her female audience.

Bessie Smith's version of Rainey's composition "Moonshine Blues" makes a few minor but significant changes, including the substitution in one stanza of "girls" for "lord." Smith thus explicitly conjures up a supportive female community. In Rainey's rendition:

> I feel like screamin', I feel like cryin'
> Lord, I been mistreated, folks, and don't mind dyin'.[35]

In Smith's version:

> Girls, I feel like screamin', I feel like cryin'
> I been mistreated, and I don't mind dyin'.[36]

Of course, Rainey, following the traditional patterns of blues discourse, is announcing her plight, publicizing her private woes, and thus, in this stanza, invokes her entire community—the folks—while directing her feelings of despair to the Lord. Smith, on the other hand, seeks solace not in the Lord but rather from the girls.

In "You Don't Understand," recorded by Bessie Smith in 1929, a collective female presence is invoked in the first line. The subject realizes that it is futile to try to persuade the man she loves to return to her: "Here I am, girls of mine, pleading but it's all in vain."[37] The entire text, with the exception of the opening phrase, is directed to the unresponsive man. Ma Rainey's "Titanic Man Blues" begins with a similar invocation: "Everybody fall in line, going to tell you 'bout that man of mine." From the story that follows, it is obvious that she is addressing herself to women. After this opening phrase, the female figure in the song proceeds to direct her comments to a lover she plans to leave, ending each verse with this statement: "It's the last time, Titanic, fare thee well."[38] It is as if she invites a community of women to be present at a ritualistic shunning. Invoking the presence of sympathetic women summons up the courage the woman needs in order to eject this man from her life.

Bessie Smith's "I Used to Be Your Sweet Mama" is one of the most stunning examples of sharing among women for the purpose of summoning up the emotional strength necessary to challenge male supremacy in personal relationships:

> All you women understand
> What it is to be in love with a two-time man
> The next time he calls me sweet mama in his lovin' way
> This is what I'm going to say
>
> "I used to be your sweet mama, sweet papa
> But now I'm just as sour as can be."

Again, this song anticipates the 1960s strategy of consciousness-raising. Affirming that the women in her listening audience have a common understanding of disloyal lovers, the protagonist creates, on the basis of that collective experience, a rehearsal space. One easily can imagine the testifying that punctuated Bessie Smith's performances of this song. She must have received enthusiastic shouts of encouragement from the women in her audiences as she sang, "This is what I'm going to say," and certainly as she informed her audience what she would tell "sweet papa":

"So don't come stallin' around my way expectin'
    any love from me
You had your chance and proved unfaithful
So now I'm gonna be real mean and hateful
I used to be your sweet mama, sweet papa
But now I'm just as sour as can be."

I ain't gonna let no man worry me sick
Or turn this hair of mine gray
Soon as I catch him at his two-time tricks
I'm gonna tell him to be on his way
To the world I scream, "No man can treat me
    mean
And expect my love all the time."
When he roams away, he'd better stay
If he comes back he'll find

"You've had your chance and proved unfaithful
So now I'm gonna be real mean and hateful
I used to be your sweet mama, sweet papa
But now I'm just as sour as can be."[39]

Notes

Such songs as this and Rainey's "Trust No Man," in part because they evoked enthusiastic, testifying responses from their female audiences, would have been considered distasteful by middle-class club women. Formally educated women assumed that such cultural expressions tended to confirm the dominant culture's association of black women with sexual license and immorality. As the club women went about their work of "defending our name," they disassociated themselves from working-class women's blues culture, and assumed the missionary role of introducing "true womanhood" to their less fortunate sisters. In fact, they were defending the name of the female contingent of the black bourgeoisie. It did not occur to them then—and may not be obvious to us today—that this women's blues community was in fact defending the name of its own members. And while the club women achieved great victories in the historical struggles they undertook against racism, and forcefully affirmed black women's equality in the process, the ideological terrain on which they operated was infused with assumptions about the inherent inferiority of poor—and especially sexually assertive—women. In hindsight, the production, performance, and reception of women's blues during the decade of the twenties reveal that black women's names could be defended by working-class as well as middle-class women. Women's blues also demonstrate that working-class women's names could be defended not only in the face of the dominant white culture but in the face of male assertions of dominance in black communities as well.

1. Gertrude "Ma" Rainey, "Trust No Man," Paramount 12395, Aug. 1926. Reissued on *Ma Rainey*, Milestone M47021, 1974.

2. Paula Giddings, *When and Where I Enter*, New York: William Morrow, 1984, p. 95.

3. Mary Church Terrell, "What Role Is the Educated Negro Woman to Play in the Uplifting of Her Race?" quoted in Giddings, p. 98.

4. This theme of the Black women's club movement was first formulated by Fannie Barrier Williams in an address she

gave at a worldwide gathering of women during the 1893 World Columbian Exposition:

> I regret the necessity of speaking to the question of the moral progress of our women because the morality of our home life has been commented on so despairingly and meanly that we are placed in the unfortunate position of being defenders of our name ... While I duly appreciate the offensiveness of all references to American slavery, it is unavoidable to charge to that system every moral imperfection that mars that character of the colored American. The whole life and power of slavery depended upon an enforced degradation of everything human in the slaves. The slave code recognized only animal distinctions between the sexes and ruthlessly ignored those ordinary separations of the sexes that belong to the social state. It is a great wonder that two centuries of such demoralization did not work a complete extinction of all the moral instincts.

The Present Status and Intellectual Progress of Colored Women (Chicago, 1893), quoted in Eleanor Flexner, *Century of Struggle: The Woman's Rights Movement in the United States* (New York: Atheneum, 1974), pp. 187–88.

5. Gertrude "Ma" Rainey. "Prove It on Me Blues," Paramount 12668, June 1928. Reissued on *Ma Rainey*, Milestone M-47021, 1974.

6. Bessie Smith, "A Good Man Is Hard to Find," Columbia 14250-D, Sept. 27, 1927. Reissued on *The Empress*, Columbia CG 30818, 1972.

7. W.E.B. Du Bois, *Darkwater: Voices from within the Veil* (New York: Harcourt, Brace, and Howe, 1920). See Patricia Hill Collins's account of the epistemological implications of this discourse in *Black Feminist Thought*.

8. See Angela Y. Davis, *Women, Race, and Class*, chap. 1, New York: Random House, 1981.

9. Gertrude "Ma" Rainey, "Rough and Tumble Blues," Paramount 112311, 1926. Reissued on *The Immortal Ma Rainey*, Milestone MLP-2001, 1966.

10. Gertrude "Ma" Rainey, "Wringing and Twisting Blues," Paramount 12338, Dec. 1925. Reissued on *The Immortal Ma Rainey*, Milestone MLP-2001, 1966. In another verse, the means of poisoning the rival are detailed:

> I had some green cucumbers, some half done
> 	tripe and greens,
> Some buttermilk and codfish, some sour kidney
> 	beans.

These images from black culinary culture reflect a number of myths as well as realities — regarding dangerous foods: unripe cucumbers, uncooked pork, milk and fish (considered a deadly combination), and beans gone bad.

11. Bessie Smith, "Any Woman's Blues," Columbia 13001-D, Oct. 16, 1923. Reissued on *Any Woman's Blues*, Columbia G 30126, 1972.

12. Bessie Smith, "St. Louis Gal," Columbia 13005-D, Sept. 34, 1923. Reissued on *Any Woman's Blues*, Columbia G 30126, 1972.

13. Bessie Smith, "Empty Bed Blues," Columbia 14312-D, Mar. 20, 1928. Reissued on *Any Woman's Blues*, Columbia G 30126, 1972.

14. Bessie Smith, "He's Got Me Goin'," Columbia 14464-D, Aug. 20, 1929. Reissued on *Any Woman's Blues*, Columbia G 30126, 1972.

15. As an aside, this makes for an interesting contribution to the debate on modernism and African-American culture, especially considering the similarities between the techniques associated with Cubism in the visual arts and the blues perspective. See Houston Baker's *Modernism and the Harlem Renaissance* (Chicago and London: University of Chicago Press, 1987).

16. Gertrude "Ma" Rainey, "Sleep Talking Blues," Paramount 12760, Sept. 1928. Reissued on *Ma Rainey*, Milestone M-47021, 1974.

17. Gertrude "Ma" Rainey, "Jealous Hearted Blues," Paramount 12252, Dec. 1925. Reissued on *Ma Rainey*, Milestone M-47021, 1974.

18. Gertrude "Ma" Rainey, "Jealousy Blues," Paramount 12364, March 1926. Reissued on *Oh My Babe Blues*, Biograph BLP-12011, n.d..

19. Bessie Smith, "My Man Blues," Columbia 14098-D, Sept. 1925. Reissued on *Nobody's Blues but Mine*, Columbia CG 31093, 1972.

20. Brooks, *The Bessie Smith Companion*, p. 95.

21. Bessie Smith, "Lookin' for My Man Blues," Columbia 14569-D, Sept. 28, 1927. Reissued on *The Empress*, Columbia CG 30818, 1972.

22. Rainey, "Trust No Man."

23. Bessie Smith, "Keep It to Yourself," Columbia 14516-D Mar. 27, 1930. Reissued on *Any Woman's Blues*, Columbia G 30126-1972.

24. Harrison, *Black Pearls*, New Brunswick, NJ: Rutgers University Press, 1990, p. 110.

25. Levine, *Black Culture and Black Consciousness*. Oxford: Oxford University Press, 1975, p. 221.

26. Koko Taylor in *Wild Women Don't Have the Blues*, Dir. Christine Dall, Calliope Film Resources, 1989, videocassette.

27. Patricia Hill Collins, *Black Feminist Thought: Knowledge, Consciousness, and the Politics of Empowerment*. Boston: Unwin Hyman, p. 213.

28. Rainey, "Trust No Man."

29. Bessie Smith, "Safety Mama," Columbia 14634-D, Nov. 20, 1931. Reissued on *The World's Greatest Blues Singer*, Columbia CG 33, 1972.

30. Bessie Smith, "Pinchback Blues," Columbia 14025-D, Apr. 5, 1924. Reissued on *Empty Bed Blues*, Columbia CG 30450, 1972.

31. *St. Louis Blues,* dir. Dudley Murphy, Gramercy Studio of RCA Photophone, presented by Radio Pictures, 1929. W.C. Handy coauthored the script for this film, the release of which occasioned a protest by the NAACP.

32. Chris Albertson, *Bessie*, New York: Stein and Day, p. 159.

33. Bessie Smith, "A Good Man Is Hard to Find."

34. Gertrude "Ma" Rainey, "Jelly Bean Blues," Paramount 12238, Feb. 1927. Reissued on *Ma Rainey*, Milestone M-47021, 1974.

35. Gertrude "Ma" Rainey, "Moonshine Blues," Paramount 12063, Dec. 1927. Reissued on *Ma Rainey*, Milestone M-47021, 1974.

36. Bessie Smith, "Moonshine Blues," Columbia 14018-D, Apr. 19, 1924. Reissued on *Empty Bed Blues*, Columbia CG 30450, 1972.

37. Bessie Smith, "You Don't Understand," Columbia 14487-D, Oct. 11, 1929. Reissued on *Any Woman's Blues*, Columbia G 30126, 1972.

38. Gertrude "Ma" Rainey, "Titanic Man Blues," Paramount 12374, Jan. 1926. Reissued on *Blues the World Forgot*, Biograph BLP-12001, n.d.

39. Bessie Smith, "I Used to Be Your Sweet Mama," Columbia 1492-D, Feb. 9, 1928. Reissued on *Empty Bed Blues*, Columbia CG 30450, 1972.

SECTION EIGHT

PRAXIS—
SOCIAL CHANGE

All for a Decent House

As told to Janet Silman

On August 31, 1977, the headline "Women Occupy Band Office—Want Indian Act Changes" appeared above a story in the Saint John *Telegraph-Journal*. This was only the beginning of virtually daily media coverage Tobique women received over the next several months as the demonstration against the housing practices of the local band administration developed into a lengthy siege. What follows is the account of that year by several of the women who were centrally involved.

Here we witness outbreaks of violence. The violence seems to be "horizontal," in other words, of women who identify with the band administration fight the women who have risen up against it. Soon the entire reserve becomes polarized into those who side with the women occupying the band office and those who side with the chief and his administration. As new crises arise virtually on a daily basis, the protesters collectively develop strategies to deal with them. For example, Glenna Perley recalls that they made the decision never to respond to taunts and name-calling. However provoked, "We never answered back. That was our policy." They always discussed situations at length before taking particular actions.

The women occupying the band office were dealing both with the immediate pressures and problems on the reserve and at the same time seeking assistance outside Tobique. They sought help at the district Indian Affairs office in Fredericton, the Union of New Brunswick Indians, the regional Indian Affairs office in Amherst, Nova Scotia, the National Indian Brotherhood (the national status Indian organization, now renamed the Assembly of First Nations), the national Department of Indian Affairs in Ottawa, the Human Rights Commissions in New Brunswick and Ottawa.

While seeking help further and further afield, and usually "getting the run around," a picture was coming into focus. The women were gaining an understanding of the bureaucracies and organizations which make up the Native Indian political reality in Canada. They were coming to see the enormous government bureaucracy of Indian Affairs which lay behind the local chief and council. They began to see more clearly the Indian Act, that piece of legislation which regulates almost every aspect of reserve life. In struggling to get some assistance for women's housing, they broadened their horizon to see the world which lies beyond the reserve, yet has an immense impact upon it. Here the women share their unique perspective on that world.

After Eva (Gookum) Saulis introduces the discussion, she leaves most of the story to "the younger women" to tell. During the occupation, however, she was a prominent spokeswoman. Sandra Lovelace Sappier became involved early in the occupation, but since much of her own story is of lobbying for change outside the reserve, more of her personal account is in Chapters Four and Five, where she also explains how she was persuaded to be the test case for the Tobique women's challenge of section 12(1)(b) of the Indian Act.

Gookum: After my daughter Elaine got kicked out of her home that spring of 1977, me and Glenna went around talking to other women who had been evicted by their husbands. We'd get statements from them telling what happened. Then we'd get a lawyer from Grand Falls to write those up in a document and send it to Indian Affairs in Ottawa. One woman really cried when she was writing up hers. We didn't get to all of them, but we got five to sign statements.

Also, we had petitions circulating around the reserve calling for property rights for women. The issue didn't include non-status yet—we were against the Indian Act giving sole property rights to men. By May most of the voting members on the reserve had signed the petition and we sent it to Warren Allmand (then minister of Indian Affairs) early in June, but he never acknowledged that petition.

Caroline: When I was going through the House of Commons a couple of years ago I met Warren Allmand in the hallway, I asked him about those petitions and he said he never received any. So either the bureaucrats kept them away from him or the guy was lying. After that, whenever we wanted to get something to a minister, we sent somebody to deliver it personally; we found out it stops at a certain level if you don't.

Gookum: In July we went down to the Indian Affairs building in Fredericton. Glenna said we should go and protest right there and we did.

Juanita: We demonstrated over housing conditions all that one day. Even the women who had housing weren't getting repairs, and if you were a single mother, you weren't getting anything. The administration would stuff you in a house only because you moved in there anyway. Then they'd never repair it. That demonstration was just before my son got so sick.

Gookum: The Indian Affairs superintendent told us it was "an internal matter" and the best thing to do was for us to apply pressure on the chief and council up here. But we kept demonstrating outside with our placards and signs until finally he promised to meet with us and the chief and council in two weeks. He never did.

Bet-te: That's when they said, "We don't want to get involved."

Gookum: We never got a reply from the minister of Indian Affairs until November when they got a lot of pressure from white women's groups, and we'd sent those petitions in the spring.

Glenna: That Indian Affairs official in Fredericton wasn't any help, he just did what the chief wanted. It was a waste of time when we went down there. *Empty promises.* Same with the human rights commissioner. We went to him, but he said he was provincial and we would have to go to the federal.

Caroline: When I went to Gordon Fairweather, the federal human rights office was so new they were still opening boxes. They said they couldn't help us, either, because the Indian Act didn't come under their charter. By the end of August we were so frustrated—band officials wouldn't even make a *pretence* of listening to our grievances—we decided to demonstrate in front of the band office.

Glenna: That very first day it was me, Juanita, Marjorie, Linda Bear, and one other woman. Eva (Gookum) didn't show up, but she said, "You're doing right and I hope you get something done." A lot of women said they weren't able to be there, walking back and forth all day, but they encouraged us to keep it up, said things like, "We went this far; we might as well keep on!"

We had all kinds of placards and signs up, "Fed. Govt. Supports Mismanagement of Band Money," "Did We Hear Someone Say, 'The Chief Represents the People?'" "We Need Help Now, Not Next Year." The very first day of protesting up here the staff would open the doors or windows and call us names, but we just laughed. I'd just look at them and think, you don't know how you look; you should be on this side and look at yourselves!

Then we had enough supporters that we split into two groups, with some people going down to protest—Gordon Fairweather was in Fredericton—while others stayed right here in front of the band office.

Caroline: Actually I didn't know anything about the protest until the demonstration in Fredericton. We were living in Fredericton—Dan and I were both in university. We weren't too in touch with what was happening up on the reserve; were mostly involved at the university. The only reason I got involved was Glenna phoned me up to call the newspapers. I certainly wasn't going to say to Glenna, "That's your business!" (laughter) Glenna needed somebody to go to the media and talk about what going on so that they would contact the women.

Glenna: You also got the students together. We got you working!

Karen: In Fredericton we had signs, too, and walked around the old Indian Affairs building. That's when we got the students supporting us—the Indian students in university there. My sister, Barbara, was in Old Town or Seybyick, Maine, but she heard about it and came right up.

Bet-te: Barbara called me and made me aware of what was going on. I was working for the non-status organization but I told her I would take the afternoon off work and go picket with them. That was the day of the protest in Fredericton. Then that weekend the women called and said they needed help here, so I came up. We were all outside the band office and the people inside were acting like it was a big joke. Here we were protesting for better conditions to live in and they were ridiculing us, making snide remarks.

Glenna: For the first few days we were just outside, picketing back and forth. We'd go up there from morning to night, then go home. One of the guys from the Union (New Brunswick Union of Indians) was up, and actually it was his idea to go in. He said, "Girls, you aren't going to accomplish anything out here. Why don't you move right in? But don't tell anyone who suggested it!" We said, "That is a good idea," and went right in.

Bet-te: By then we had a lot of supporters—even white people on the reserve backing us—but it didn't seem to be doing any good; the chief and his administration wouldn't talk to us. Some of us were pretty radical at that time and we all got together and went in. We didn't really move in; we were just going to sit there until we got a meeting with the chief and council. That's actually how the occupation started. Never once did we tell them we were going to throw them out. The kids were *always* with us—well, where are you going to put your kids? You're not going to have a babysitter for all that time, so they were all there!

We all sat in the reception area and said, "No, we're not leaving." So they just left us there; like they'd come in the morning to work and we'd still be there. After a while they moved out—couldn't take it, I guess—but all we were trying to do was get a meeting with the chief. He still wouldn't meet or fix up houses for the women. He'd say, "We'll listen if you move out of here," and we'd say, "No way. We know you're not going to listen." He was just trying to fool us into giving up.

Glenna: Really we went in mainly to try and talk to the chief. While we'd been on the outside, we would take turns going in to try and get a meeting with him. Either he wouldn't even reply or he'd say, "I don't have to talk to you." When we went in with all the kids, the people inside didn't say anything and we didn't say anything. We just sat down and they ignored us.

*****

So then the cops came in and told us, "The chief sent us over. You have to leave." We said, "We're not leaving. He won't talk to us, he won't help us, so we're not leaving." The cop said, "Okay, good enough," and went downtown to Perth-Andover and got the other cops, the RCMP.

The Mounties came to talk to us and we told them the same thing; that it was our building too and we weren't touching anything. So we moved our blankets and sleeping bags in. The kids were having fun—it was still a picnic to them. In the evenings after work a lot of people would come over to encourage us. The elders would tell us not to leave, say things like, "Don't leave ... don't let them chase you out. This is our building, too, now."

Caroline: The longer we were at it, we couldn't get out of it even if we wanted to.

Glenna: No, we were getting too much support, and other things we hadn't even known about started coming out. Like the way the administration had treated veterans or certain individuals—telling them there was no money when we found out there was.

Karen: A lot of reserve residents cooked meals and sent them over. Some stayed nights while others went back and forth to their homes. I remember coming home and talking to my husband, Carl. I was kind of reluctant to get involved at first because he was a band constable and I thought I wasn't supposed to get involved in reserve politics, but I did anyway. I was excited; I thought, wow, something is finally happening!

Glenna: When you think of it, how did we dare do this? (laughter)

Karen: It was great. It was brave!

Glenna: It was a really good feeling when all of a sudden we *knew* they were afraid of us because what we were saying was true. We didn't have to be afraid of anything. At first the chief said we were lying.

Karen: But do you think women with the responsibility of kids would do something like that for nothing? We had a good reason.

Glenna: Then they wanted to put us in jail. We didn't care. We said, "If some of us go to jail, other supporters will come and take our place." Early in September we were served with an injunction from the chief ordering us off the premises. It went to court because the sheriff in Woodstock wouldn't or couldn't enforce it until the court ordered him to. I think it was Dannie who got us a lawyer from Fredericton through the Human Rights Commission. We got a lot of threats, a lot of harassment. First it was mainly name-calling—they called us "the troublemakers." Gookum wanted to answer them back— she would have, too. (laughter) But I said, "Let's just ignore them. It's not important what they say; what's important is what we're doing. We don't need to waste our time on name-calling or answering back." After that, no matter what we were called, we never answered back. That was our policy.

Caroline: But they tried to intimidate people; they threatened people. The situation got more volatile as the occupation continued.

Glenna: Yes, our kids took a lot. When they'd get on the school bus, the opposition's kids would call them names, and they had to take all that; "Your mother's a troublemaker, a protester," things like that. One time someone almost ran my daughter, Kim, down with a car. It was deliberate.

Caroline: We called the RCMP and they couldn't do anything. There were one or two witnesses and they still couldn't do anything—at least that's what they claimed.

Bet-te: We were "the shit-disturbers, radicals, white-washed, women's lib ... You don't know what you want ... You don't have no rights anyway ... 'The Liberated Woman.'" They thought that was a big put-down to us, but we never considered ourselves "liberated women"; we were just women who needed decent homes.

Glenna: At first we went in there for the women mostly, but when our story came out in the papers, the war veterans came and brought their problems, too. There are a lot of veterans here and most of them supported us. They told us they were on fixed incomes, the ones who were pensioned off. The administration wouldn't repair the houses they got after the war—said they weren't band-owned.

Karen: The same things were happening to the elderly. Some got their heating paid for and others didn't. Some got help and others who really needed it didn't get any. It was really nice to see the elderly come and visit us.

Glenna: We had them write out their complaints and we would put them aside. We collected a whole bunch of them and a long time after, when the welfare officer came back, he said, "You have a better system than we have!" We had all the elderly, the widows, women with kids who were living alone—separated and single mothers—non-status, all filed separately. Those people started to come in and support us.

Gookum: It was the band administration we were going after—what they were not doing. In one paper I saw the statement, "These women don't know what they want"—they want Indian rights for Indian women and they want this and that. I told my husband, "The veterans should get together and speak up for themselves." It happened so many times that when people needed something, they would come to the Tobique women. The women had more guts, I guess. (laughter)

Karen: We got a lot of press. We never thought too much about going to the media at the very beginning, but when our story came out in the papers it had such a big impact—we got a lot of phone calls and reaction—we thought it was good.

Glenna: After that first day of the occupation, the telephone never stopped ringing and we knew we were getting a lot of support, even from as far away as Nova Scotia. Before that, the press didn't even know where Tobique Reserve was. There were so many calls coming in. I took some and Gookum took some.

You learn things as you go along. When I first started, I trusted the press, I trusted everyone. (laughs) But the press were pretty good to us all the way.

Of course, the reporters talked to the chief too. One time he told them, "Maybe you'd like to hear the other side," and he sent them to interview his sister-in-law and he thought she'd support him, but she said exactly the same things we were saying. It was funny. (laughter) Then another time the objectors were throwing rocks at a reporter because he had a camera. They threw the reporters out of a meeting, but it was good for us; the opposition really showed their true colours.

Bet-te: I couldn't believe that night not long after the occupation started when you got kicked out of your house, Mom.

YC: I got evicted because I believed so strongly in what the women were fighting for. Somebody even came and busted the big picture window at that place. My landlord blamed it on the women and threw me out. Why would the women come and throw a rock when I'm supporting them?

Bet-te: That's around the time the violence really started. Some of us couldn't go outside without being attacked after dark. The opposition kept coming around to the band office at night, so finally we got a spotlight in the back so we could see if someone was breaking in. We all took turns standing watch, because there were times they'd throw rocks, and some were threatening us with guns. They'd say they were going to come in with guns to get us out of there.

People were getting beaten up on the street; and even little kids threatened, like Glenna's and Juanita's. But then Juanita stopped protesting and she wouldn't have anything to do with us for a while. I don't know what happened; I don't know why her family made the switch, but all the time people were trying to turn our supporters against us. Rumours and accusations were flying around constantly.

Glenna: I'd get calls—somebody telling me that they were going to burn my place down. Rocks were thrown at the window of the band office and at our cars.

One good thing on our side was that none of us drank in there, and most of our supporters never drank. See, that was a major difference between us and the opposition. We had a ruling about no drinking or drugs in there right from the beginning.

Karen: Some of the people outside were drunk. We took the threats seriously—you wouldn't know what they would do when they were drunk. When they were sober they wouldn't say anything.

Bet-te: What I remember most vividly from those times was the violent things people tried to do to us because they wanted us out of there. It was mostly the chiefs' supporters. Rocks being thrown at the windows, flying glass just missing the kids and frightening them. But we never retaliated. We just stayed; we wouldn't leave. Actually most of the community was helping us out, bringing us food, and a lot of the guys were protecting us—they'd keep watch at night.

The occupation wasn't only hard on us; it was hard on the other reserve residents, too. Everybody was tense. You would go to bed at night and you wouldn't know what was going to happen by morning because the opposition kept coming and throwing rocks at the windows. People would be beat up.

When it got really bad we had guns in the band office. We weren't going to let the objectors beat us up; we were going to protect our kids. We told the RCMP that we had guns and they told us we shouldn't have them. But it wasn't their kids; it was our kids. One of the reserve constables told us, "You can keep the guns as long as you don't leave them out in sight."

Bet-te: We never showed those guns around, but the opposition knew we had them. They saw us taking them in.

YC: Some of them other women were *big*, coming after little old things like me. We had to protect our kids. I'd have used them if I had to, and they knew that. Big women.

Bet-te: Didn't scare me, though, because Mom always said, "The bigger they are, the harder they fall." We were getting threats—"We're going to kill your kids." The kids couldn't go to school because they were being harassed constantly.

YC: We took turns staying up all night—one of us downstairs looking out and one upstairs looking out. Gee, we had some hard times, especially weekends. During the week it was kind of quiet, but weekends was when they drank.

Caroline: It was like a "banana republic"—that's what Suzette Couture called it in that film [a CBC television dramatization based on the Tobique women's story].

Bet-te: Remember that time an ex-supporter and her whole family turned on us? It got even rougher then. We didn't participate with them too much when they went on the chief's side. Remember those opposition women lurking around in the bushes one night, trying not to be noticed? All the time we saw their cigarette butts sticking up. (laughter) Too bad we didn't have buckshot.

At Wounded Knee they had a chief who used some of the same tactics as the chief used against us here. Except with us nobody got killed—luckily. The chief had his goon squads here, but we had too much media behind us and they didn't dare do anything to the media.

But AIM (American Indian Movement) was ready to come in. Me and Barbara (Perley) kept after Glenna, "Tell AIM to come in so they can scare the shit out of these people; show them we've got protection and people believe in what we're doing." But we got talked out of it because people would have been really threatened by it. I can see Glenna's reasoning now, but at the time some of the situations got really violent and we weren't initiating *any* of them. Threats flying around and you knew they

could be carried out. We were always walking on eggshells.

Glenna: We never wanted to hurt anyone. We just wanted people to know what was happening; that we were being hurt. I talked to one of the AIM leaders and I think I kind of insulted him when I said we didn't want guns up here. It was bad then, but we didn't want our people to get hurt. It would always be the innocent that would get hurt.

Karen: A lot of people were afraid because AIM is associated with being violent and guns, shooting.

*****

Glenna: We had some individuals at Indian Affairs helping us. If they thought it was information we should know, they'd make sure we found out about it.

Caroline: Well, they wouldn't *volunteer* information; we had to dig it out of them. Some would give us what was *safe* to give. Often it actually was public information everybody could have access to, but the history of this reserve was that everything was kept such a secret from the people, we didn't know any of it. Then we started finding ways to get it.

Karen: Wasn't it when we didn't get any satisfactory results from Indian Affairs that we tried other women's groups and other people to apply some pressure?

Glenna: Yes, because the press kept asking us if we were getting any results. We tried the Union (New Brunswick Union of Indians), other chiefs. They didn't want to get involved, said it was an internal matter.

Karen: We tried to get help so many places. First locally with the band council. The councillors said they couldn't do anything, that *everything* was up to the chief. Then the other chiefs said, "We don't want to stick our nose into another chief's business." We got the same thing from the Union, and from Indian Affairs in Fredericton and in Amherst (the regional office for the Maritimes, situated in Nova Scotia).

Glenna: The National Indian Brotherhood said, "We can't get involved." Amherst Indian Affairs officials came up and had a meeting with us. They kept sending telegrams to Ottawa and federal Indian Affairs would say, "It is an internal matter. We already gave Tobique money and the chief and council can do whatever they want with that money."

Karen: After a while those Indian Affairs people just stopped talking to us, too.

Caroline: I came to the conclusion a long time ago that a whole lot of problems could be solved to everybody's satisfaction if government leaders would listen to women like us, but it seems they never do—most are men and chauvinistic themselves.

Sandra: I had gone to the band office before and asked for a house for myself and my child. I'd had to pitch a tent, because I couldn't find any place to stay. They'd told me I had no rights; that I was non-status. At the time I'd never heard of "non-status"—the Indian agent had always hid it from the women. Then the women occupying the band office approached me, "We heard you couldn't get help because you are non-status." I said, "Yes." I was living in that tent with my son, and it was getting really cold at nights.

So when they asked me if I would move into the band office and protest with them, I thought about it and said, "Yes." I remember the chief saying, "Squaws are trying to get us out of the band office." When the cops came to try and get us out, we blockaded ourselves right in. That was when Dan and Caroline Ennis approached me about taking my case to the United Nations.

Karen: Caroline and Dan asked Sandra to sign that complaint, and they got the lawyer Donald Fleming to take the case, but actually it was Glenna that came up with the idea.

Glenna: I was at the trailer one time and a number of us were talking about the non-status issue. That's when I mentioned the idea of going to the United Nations; said, "Why do we always just go to the Human Rights? What about the UN?" After that, Danny went to find out. Noel Kinsella (chairperson of the New Brunswick Human Rights Commission) helped us too, because he already had come up to see us a lot of times, over various complaints.

We had to have just one person to sign that petition for the UN, and actually we had one woman before Sandra, but she ended up not wanting to do it. Then we convinced Sandra, so after that, it was always Sandra we'd have talk to the reporters about non-status.

Sandra: I decided to do it, said to Dan and Caroline, "Yes, if it will help the non-status women." Most of us were so angry because the white women were getting all the jobs on the reserve. Meanwhile the Indian women were being treated like dirt. I told the administration I'd take any job; I was tired of being on welfare. I had my name in there, but … nothing. We had a lot to protest about.

Karen: It seemed that no Indian groups cared or gave a damn about non-status women until our protest started.

YC: I know why the chief was so much against the non-status women. The reason was because he'd been benefitting all them years by using our names and collecting from them.

Bet-te: Maybe that's what frightened him, because we were asking for an investigation of the records. He didn't want the records to go out. He was scared of us there, for awhile, when he knew he couldn't buck us. But he wasn't about to give, either. That was the attitude of a lot of the men.

*****

Glenna: And the men were mad. I remember this one old lady from a Micmac reserve who had a house the administration there wouldn't complete. It needed steps and the way it was, she couldn't live in it.

Karen: This cute little old woman, and they wouldn't help her. She had arthritis and high blood pressure. Somebody at the assembly kept telling her to get up and speak at the microphone. Finally I think she did and she did get interviewed by the media. After that she got some repairs done on her house, but it wasn't very good work.

Glenna: She was telling me the same thing happened there as here—even worse, I guess. Every night before a band election, there would be big parties at different houses, and the band would pay for the drinks and everything. She told me, "Everybody sees it, but nobody will do anything. I am the only one here." And she must have been in her eighties.

We had a lot of outsiders, including younger men and teenage boys, Indian students, who were supporting us. I didn't even know them, but they'd come up weekends.

There was an election coming up here at the beginning of October, so we wanted to get a chief in who was for the women. Vaughn Nicholas was a councillor who we thought would make a good chief, and we talked him into running. At the time he was the only one who had a chance to win. We campaigned really hard for him. Most of the councillors always tried to help us, but it was the chief and the band manager that put blocks in their way. I remember one time I went into the band manager's office and said to him, "You weren't brought us like this. I know your mother didn't raise you

to go around hurting people." He kept on saying, "I have to do my job or I'll get fired." I finally said, "But you're working along with them." He didn't say anything, just put his head down. But I don't think there was a time we went in there and called them names. I know I didn't.

Caroline: Some of those people, I could feel the hate coming off them. I never felt that from him when he was on the other side, though. His wife, yes, but not him.

YC: Then the chief ordered the Power Commission to cut off our power—no electricity, so no heat, no hot water. Bet-te brought her little wood stove in and that's what we cooked on. Raymond Nicholas and his boys hooked it up for us. We had light for a while when he started an emergency battery, but it ran out. After that we used kerosene lamps.

Bet-te: The men who supported us openly, like Raymond and Ramo, my brothers and a lot of the other younger guys, took a lot of ridicule and teasing from the other guys—"the women's libbers." But they stood by us.

Glenna: The men, like my uncles and their sons, would bring us wood *every* day, and the women would bring pots of food. By then the Voice of Women from Fredericton was sending us donations of money, blankets, clothing. To the kids it was like camping out. They had fun till we were attacked.

Bet-te: It was pretty damn cold, but we were all moved in there and we stayed. For one thing, many of us had no place else to live. We stayed all through potato picking season, and some of us worked out in the fields—we had to earn some money. The band office became home.

YC: We never done anything right away, not until we gathered together and talked it all out amongst ourselves first.

Bet-te: We always made our decisions together, even if it took time. The chief was getting his staff to come and take out files, then put the blame on *us* for their going missing. So every time they came in to take out stuff, we'd make them sign a piece of paper and record what they took and the date. For a time, we wouldn't let them take anything out.

One good thing, though, was that they couldn't cut our phones off, because they were connected to the fire hall next door.

Glenna: We ran up a big bill, called Ottawa, everywheres. We got so desperate towards the end, we were going to call the Russians. (laughter) The women are saying now, we should have tried it—scared old Canada. You see, we don't consider ourselves Canadians or Americans.

We had the phones, so people could call us, too. Also, the fire siren worked. The men supporting us said to let them know if the opposition *ever* came and touched the women or kids. We decided that, if we ever really needed help, we would turn the siren on. We used it a few times. The first time we had to sound the siren, initially there were some women outside throwing rocks; then we saw some guys coming, too, and there were quite a few. It was at night and they were all partying and drunk.

Caroline: There was that great big crowd standing around, throwing rocks and threatening to burn the band office down ....

Glenna: It wasn't *that* big ... the people were big though. (laughter)

Caroline: Was that first time when *we* called up the RCMP because the objectors were threatening to burn the building down? They didn't *ever* show up and we had to call Ottawa the next day to complain about the detachment. So the next time we called them they *really* showed up—in about four police cars.

That might have been one of the times we got served with an injunction ordering us out. There were rumours of an RCMP riot squad coming in, and we were given an hour to leave, or we'd be "forcibly ejected." We barricaded the doors and windows and contacted the media— whoever we could reach—politicians, Indian Affairs; called the minister in Ottawa and told him any violence would be on their hands; they could have done something before it reached a crisis point. We gathered a whole lot of our supporters inside, plus some reporters, and the riot squad backed off. We never found out what stopped them, likely a combination of outside pressure, publicity, and uncertainty about legalities around the Indian Act.

Glenna: Finally that injunction got thrown out of court because the chief had applied for it without going to the whole council—it wasn't signed by enough of the councillors.

Over the next few years we went to court several times—we always seemed to be getting served papers. The first time, one of our supporters advised us we couldn't get thrown out because the band owned the building, so we just threw the papers up in the air and wouldn't listen!

Caroline: We also knew that the injunction couldn't be issued without permission from the minister of Indian Affairs. That was in the Indian Act; and also the Act states that band property belongs to all band members. Actually our lawyer did advise us to leave, but we decided to take our chances and stay on.

As I remember, first a judge issued the injunction, which we defied, then later in September we got served with another one. But we were determined to stay because that was one of the issues; office space had been expanded with funds that were supposed to be for repairing older homes on the reserve. So one reason women were living in the band office was because that's where money for their homes had been spent.

Before the occupation, usually the reserve didn't get involved in anything they thought was the business of chief and council, but all that changed with the occupation—then people had to get involved. Everybody split into two opposite factions, and things just got more and more volatile.

Glenna: Even the priest got involved! He wrote a letter to the minister of Indian Affairs supporting us, then he got a lot of criticism over it. The objectors kept telling him all kinds of bad things were going on with us in the band office, that we were drinking. It turned into a big controversy on the reserve because some people wanted the priest to continue his support and some wanted him to mind his business. He was kind of caught in the middle, and I remember him being really upset over it.

After he got into trouble like that, he wouldn't support us openly any more, but by then he had written his letter to the minister, so I didn't care. (laughs) One Sunday there, he'd really praised the women in church; said, "This is the first time it *ever* happened on any reserve that women got up and helped themselves." It's a wonder he's still here! (laughter) […]

*****

Karen: The election was really a win for the women. We were so glad we had tears in our eyes. Oh, God. I was up there counting votes—a scrutineer—and as soon as I knew Vaughn was going to win, both Sandra and I had tears coming down our eyes.

Glenna: I'm too nervous; I can't go up there. Even that election I had to come up here and wait alone in my house. Then as soon as I found out, I came right down and, as I was coming in, I met the chief going out. He had his head down, and I heard he didn't want to shake hands with Vaughn ... the falling of an empire.

That night everyone was down celebrating at the party at Gookum's old house. We were going to take turns watching the band office, but Cheryl (Bear) had said, "I'll stay with the kids, but come and check up on us once in a while." I had my car and Gookum said, "We should go and check up on Cheryl."

There was a car right behind us and I didn't know who it was, but it followed us right up to the band office, so I thought it was Karen or Caroline. When we got out, the door was locked and I was knocking on the door. I had parked right near the door, so I got there first and Gookum had come around the back of the car.

Then somebody grabbed my jacket. I turned around and said, "Get your ...." They'd been drinking and were trying to fight us, swearing at us. I grabbed hold of the railings and kicked back. By that time the person had given up on Gookum and come back at me, so I had to fight two of them. I hung onto the porch and was kicking to keep them off me till Cheryl opened the door. I don't know what she was doing in there, but it seemed like it took her ages to open that damn door.

When Cheryl did open the door, they started to come in. There were four women by then but I only remember the two who were beating *me* up. The wood stove was right there and it was hot. I had a chance to push one of them right onto that stove, but I remembered I couldn't stand smoke. I thought, I'll hurt myself if I knock that stove pipe off. And the kids were in there. I just hung onto the woman fighting me.

While somebody was pounding me on the back I was thinking, they're not going to get me on the floor, and they didn't.

Cheryl: There were two of the women fighting me while the other two were fighting Glenna, but we managed to turn the tables. One of the women attacking me let go and I ended up on top of the other one. Glenna was doing pretty good too. (laughter)

Karen: Somebody came running to Carl's mother's house which is where I was. She was out of breath and said, "There's trouble at the band office." I remember

Caroline and I started running. God, Caroline could really run, but I couldn't.

Bet-te: That election night I was partying up at Gookum's old house with everybody. Not all of us were drinking, but we were all having a good time, celebrating the win. I didn't want to stay much longer, so I started heading up the street. Edward, Barbara Perley's son, was in his teens then and he was walking up with me. I told him I was going to check in on the band office. As we were walking past the school, one of the objectors, who was night watchman there, started shouting obscenities at us over the outside loudspeakers. Then he came outside and, God, he had one of those blackjacks you hit people with. He tried to go after young Edward, and we hadn't said or done a thing to him.

When I got to the band office, they were still fighting and I grabbed one of the women and pinned her up against a corner. That's when the reserve cops arrived and started to get them out of there.

Caroline: By then a big crowd had gathered outside the band office. The whole damn reserve was there and it almost turned into a riot. That was scary when the chief lost. All his supporters knew they'd lost and they blamed the women.

*****

Karen: The opposition thought that just because Vaughn got in as chief that the women would leave the band office, but we didn't.

Glenna: Since he was my cousin, I'd been the one to tell him, even before he got in, that if we didn't get help, we wouldn't leave. I said, "It's not going to solve anything, just you getting in." He was very understanding and I said, "It might hurt you, but we have to keep on protesting until we get some help." It was before the election I told him that, and he said he would still support us, even if it

meant him losing the election. We had thought his supporting the women might hurt his campaign, but I guess it helped.

Karen: Then things weren't any better after Vaughn got in because he had difficulty administering the band after having taken over from the old chief. So he got hassled by some of his own supporters, with them saying, "When are you going to do things? When are things going to start looking up?" Well, he tried.

Bet-te: Then some of the old council was still there—some of the old chief's councillors. Also, the old chief had influence down at Indian Affairs in Fredericton, so they all were working against the new chief. Vaughn was getting threats and it was a strain on his family.

Juanita: I remember coming all the way from the hospital in Saint John just to vote for the new chief, thinking there would be a big change!

They were building houses galore for men, and there was my sister, Marjorie, living in that dingy trailer with her floor caving in from rot. I told her, "There's no need of this. We're going to move you into that new house next to your trailer." She was scared, said, "I don't want anybody to have any bad feelings for me." I said, "Well, cripes, you had better do something to force their hand." So we went in and occupied that house.

I went up to see the chief, Vaughn, for some reason, and he was talking on the phone with his back towards me. He was telling the owner of that house, "We're going to kick her out of there in the morning. We're going to take the RCMP over and drag them out if necessary. We had a band council meeting last night and signed a band council resolution giving you a certificate of possession for it."

I just sat there watching him and thought, this is the s.o.b. I supported and he has the same attitude toward women as every other chief has had. I said to him, "You son of a bitch. If you had opposition before, mister, you don't know what opposition is. You're going to know it now," and I left.

The women here, the same women that were supposedly fighting for women's rights, wouldn't come and support my sister; they wouldn't even sign a petition for her. It just so happened that there were a group of Indians here from other reserves, and I told them what the administration was going to do the next morning. They stood guard all night with us, and when we saw the police cruiser coming in the morning we had blockades at the doors. They said, "We only want to talk," so they came in and, after first threatening my sister, they promised to build her a house if she moved out.

She moved out and they did build her a house, but it took that much. I don't know how many times she had tried to get one before. She had five children and was on the road, living from house to house, sometimes in a basement, for eight years. By the time she got that house her youngest was twelve years old.

From Trash to Treasure: Housewife Activists and the Environmental Justice Movement[*]

Harriet G. Rosenberg

Studying Mobilization: Deep Background

It is not communism that is radical, it is capitalism.

—Bertolt Brecht
(Cited in Wolf, *Peasant Wars of the Twentieth Century*)

In the last decade, hundreds of popular protests have been led by North American housewives, who have mobilized politically in response to community exposures to toxic wastes.[1] The most famous of these protests has been the case of Love Canal; but whether well known or locally contained, the majority of the protests have been organized, staffed, and led by working-class women and women of color.

Disempowered housewives, like peasant insurgents studied by Eric R. Wolf (1969), often find that their mobilization may begin with a conservative stance: a defense of children, family, and home. But for many this initial position has led to radical critiques of state and society and an undertaking of political actions of which they never dreamed themselves capable. To understand this pathway to mobilization, one needs a conception of politics that is not confined to or defined by the electoral process. Coming of age with the literature on patron-client relationships, friendships, coalition formation, and alliance patterns, I have looked for systems of human activity that are socially and culturally more intricate and historically deeper than can be disclosed by analyses of voting patterns or political parties.

In writing *Peasant Wars of the Twentieth Century* (1969), Wolf combined historical and political economy analyses to make the case that peasants calculated and executed strategic decisions, formed alliances, and ultimately picked up arms based on logical assessments of opportunities and constraints. This insight was an important intellectual liberation at a time when many theorists, hampered by racist and anti-peasant

* Versions of this essay were given at the Women and Development Seminar and the Department of Anthropology Seminar in the Fall of 1990 (University of British Columbia), the American Anthropological Association Meetings (Chicago) 28 November 1990, the Health and Society Speakers Series (York University) April 1991, and the Department of Anthropology Seminar (University of Connecticut, Storrs) May 1991.

stereotypes, were struggling to explain how peasants in Vietnam could be besting the United States militarily and ideologically.

Wolf's typology of mobilization in *Peasant Wars* argued that strategic/structural positioning and historically contingent opportunities opened to middle peasants arenas of maneuverability closed to under-resourced poor peasants and ideologically constrained rich peasants. Thus, he not only disagreed with the concept that peasants were incapable of authentic action and must be led by outsiders, he also disputed the notion that it is the most oppressed who mobilize. This was both a subtle and respectful position to take: it was neither dismissive nor triumphalist. This analytic framework applies to housewife activists as well.

The concept of "housewife activist" is popularly viewed today with the same sense of contradiction and implausibility with which peasant insurgency was viewed twenty-five years ago. Thus I am arguing here that housewife mobilization, based on the powerful ideology of maternalist child-protection, has situated housewives in a structurally analogous position to middle peasant insurgents. Women act not only because they feel themselves to be grievously wronged, but also because they have a strategic base that validates support, credibility, and the potential to form important alliances across race, class, ethnic, and gender boundaries.

To pursue this kind of analysis, I draw inspiration from Eric Wolf's methods, which lead us to trace relationships from the local to the global level and to expose connections between seemingly unrelated events (1982). On the informal level, we have learned from him respect for the data, respect for the people, and respect for the struggle.

History

Ill fares the land, to hastening ills a prey,
Where wealth accumulates, and men decay.
—Oliver Goldsmith, "The Deserted Village"

The history of the rise and expansion of industrial capitalism is also the history of the spread of industrial pollution of the environment of the worker and working-class families. The evils of environmental destruction became a theme for early anti-capitalist sentiments enshrined in pastoralist literature and also gave rise to an elitist natural science-based social movement incorporating themes of nature as moral guide, romanticized ruralism, anti-urbanism, and managerial conservation of soil and forest as economic and spiritual resources. Concern for the health impacts of industrial pollution on humans was largely absent from early ecological theory (Bramwell 1989).

However, environmental health was of concern both to states and to working-class radicals. Elites feared the spread of epidemic disease from working-class neighborhoods, and activists struggled against the poor quality of life and lowered life expectancy of workers and their families. The British state sponsored numerous statistical expeditions concerned with disease and mortality rates in the poor districts of industrial towns, the most famous of which was Sir Edwin Chadwick's surveys in the early 1840s. Chadwick's public health solutions were the now familiar technological response of managing pollution as a postproduction phenomenon through the development of sewerage and water purification (Finer 1955; Ridgeway 1970).

Later in the century when imperial dreams were construed as being threatened by high infant mortality rates, public health expanded into public hygiene campaigns that targeted working-class mothers. These activities were usually framed in the discourse of economic rationality rather than a moral appeal to child-rescue. For example, a London medical officer of health presented his profession's mission in these decidedly unsentimental terms:

> Over-production lessens, under-production enhances the value of commodities. Considering the life of an infant as a commodity, its money

value must be greater than 35 years ago. It is of concern to the nation that a sufficient number of children should be produced to more than make good the losses by death; hence the importance of preserving infant life is even greater now than it was before the decline of the birth rate. (Alexander Blyth 1907, cited in Davin 1978, 11)

Like previous state interventions these campaigns did not link capitalist production practices to health outcomes (Davin 1978). The most famous radical critique of the health impacts of capitalist practices was Friedrich Engels's survey of English industrial towns in 1844. Engels held the industrial bourgeoisie and the state directly responsible for the noxious practices of capitalism. He used the terminology of the workingmens' associations, "social murder," to signify the intensity of the crisis he was observing (Engels 1975 [1845], 394).

However, this signification did not become a basis for oppositional mobilization, in part because public health bureaucratic interventions were able to defuse crisis construction (Davin 1978; Enzensberger 1982; Ridgeway 1970).[2] Recent dramatic environmental health disasters, like Love Canal, have once again raised the possibilities of a social movement based on a radical analysis, which links industrial capitalist practices and state regulatory complicity to health crises. Crisis construction has been facilitated by the credibility of apocalyptic language within mainstream environmentalism, a social movement constituted, for the most part, by white, urban, well-educated supporters. Hans Magnus Enzensberger has argued that when the middle class fears for its future, then imagery and ideology are universalized—for the end of class privilege is truly the end of the world (1982, 191–194).

Although middle-class mobilization has enhanced the respectability of environmental concerns, it has, in the main, not been truly universal, since it has not dealt successfully with cross-class issues. Robert Bullard (1990)

notes that this elitism has estranged the movement from poor and minority peoples in the United States who are concerned about environmental issues, but who are uncomfortable with and feel unwelcomed by mainstream organizations. He describes three categories of elitism: (1) compositional elitism (environmentalists come from privileged backgrounds); (2) ideological elitism (environmental reforms appear to be self-interested); and (3) impact elitism (environmental reforms frequently operate in a jobs-versus-the-environment mode that discounts the issues of poverty and social justice for workers and poor people). Unlike mainstream organizations, grassroots groups dealing with specific community-based health and environmental problems have successfully organized cross-class and inter-ethnic alliances.

Toxic Treasure

> Thinking of making money? Hazardous toxic waste is a billion-dollar-a-year business. No experience necessary. No equipment necessary. No educational requirements. Think of your financial future and call now for exciting details.
> —Advertisement in the
> *International Herald Tribune*
> (cited in Center for Investigative Reporting and Moyers, *Global Dumping Ground*)

In the last thirty years, waste disposal has developed into one of the most profitable industries in the world. It is dominated by two US transnationals (Waste Management Inc. [WMI], and Browning-Ferris Industries [BFI]) and Laidlaw Environmental, a Canadian corporation. The largest is WMI. Today these private companies and smaller independents have turned waste disposal into a virtual private utility in many parts of North America. The history of this industry is a compressed version of the history of capitalist development. It begins with small independent haulers and ends with vertically and horizontally integrated North American monopolies and "garbage imperialism" overseas (Center for Investigative Reporting [CIR] and Moyers 1990; Russell 1989).

Privatized waste disposal began with horse and buggy operations at the turn of the century. In the 1950s and 1960s in the northeastern United States and Florida, much of private garbage collection was in the hands of various organized crime families who set prices, allocated territories, and handled "grievances" when haulers attempted to steal customers or customers attempted to switch to other companies. These "property rights" arrangements were enforced by bribes, threats, beatings, arson, and murder (Block and Scarpitti 1985).

Private firms also handled industrial toxic waste disposal. Since they had no pretensions at technological skills, and since landfills were virtually unregulated, disposal was a haphazard affair. They dumped in municipal landfills, down sewers, along roadsides, in abandoned gravel pits, in farmers' fields, abandoned warehouses, or abandoned coal mines. They mixed toxic liquid wastes with oil and sold it to rural municipalities to spread on dusty roads or they mixed it with fuel oil and sold it in cities (Brown 1981; Block and Scarpitti 1985; CIR and Moyers 1990; Freudenberg 1984; Jackson et al. 1982).

One technique revealed to an Associated Press reporter involved the filling of a tanker truck with hazardous liquid waste, waiting for rain or snowy weather, and then driving along a highway with the tanker valve open. It takes about sixty miles to get rid of 6,800 gallons of cargo, a driver reported. "The only way I can get caught is if the windshield wipers or the tires of the car behind me start melting" (Block and Scarpitti 1985, 61–62).[3]

Manufacturers, who generated toxic wastes, tended to dispose of the wastes themselves. Hooker Chemical in Niagara Falls, New York, for example, dumped toxic wastes for over a decade into the Love Canal and then sold the site to the Niagara Falls school board for $1.

Working-class housing and an elementary school were built over an estimated 43 million pounds of chemicals, many of which were known to be hazardous to human health. The deed of sale included a disclaimer that Hooker could not be held legally responsible for any adverse health outcomes (Levine 1982, 11).

Between the mid-1960s and mid-1970s the garbage industry changed rapidly. Environmental consciousness raised regulatory questions and governments in Canada and the United States responded with a variety of laws and the creation of agencies and ministries at various levels of government. The efficacy of these state actions has raised political controversies, but the legislation had a galvanizing effect on the garbage industry.

As an environmentally configured discourse emerged, names like Ace Scavenger Service disappeared and companies like Waste Management Inc. were born. Garbage was no longer dumped—waste was managed. Men with serious expressions, hard hats, or space-age protective gear appeared in company literature, trade journals, and popular media signifying that science had taken charge of garbage. Waste disposal became an engineering problem of risk assessment best left to the professionals. Profits skyrocketed.[4]

This alchemist's dream was accompanied by a rapid consolidation of the garbage business from about 12,000 private haulers, dump operators, and recyclers in North America in the 1960s to a few giant agglomerations today (Crooks 1982, 7). From the very beginning the industry has been riddled with anti-trust suits, environmental violations, and criminal prosecutions.[5]

Race, Class, and Noxious Sites

The results of these disposal practices has been the creation of a North American landscape covered with hundreds of thousands of contaminated sites. Approximately 275 million metric tons of hazardous wastes are produced annually in the United States, of which 90 percent is estimated to be improperly disposed (Edelstein 1988, 3). It is also estimated that there are 600,000 contaminated sites in the United States, of which 888 fall under the Superfund cleanup program.[6] Another 19,000 sites are under review (Edelstein 1988).[7]

Given past disposal practices and current industry and government siting strategies, working-class people or poor rural dwellers, and especially black, Hispanic, and Native peoples, are most likely to be exposed to noxious sites or have new waste disposal facilities located in their neighborhoods.

One report commissioned by the State of California to assess potential political opposition to incinerator sitings speaks to issues of class by concluding that

> middle and upper socioeconomic strata possess better resources to effectuate their opposition. Middle and higher socioeconomic strata neighborhoods should not fall within one-mile and five-mile radii of the proposed site. (Cerrell Associates 1984, 42–43)

Activists have mobilized with their own investigation of waste and siting patterns. The United Church of Christ commissioned a study on race and toxics which reported that three out of every five black and Hispanic Americans live in a community with uncontrolled toxic sites and that race, not hydrogeology, is the best predictor of waste siting (Commission for Racial Justice 1987; Bullard 1990).

For people in exposed communities, environmental politics has become an additional dimension of struggles against racism and poverty. Poor communities often find themselves torn between economic and health concerns. In Emelle, Alabama, for example, where WMI runs the world's largest dumpsite in a poor, predominantly black community, the county receives $2 million a year from the company, which it uses for basic social services including road, fire, ambulance, library, law enforcement, and school equipment (Bullard 1990, 69–73; Collette

1988, 13). The local mayor has expressed his frustration with this seemingly insoluble contradiction in saying "[We are] like dope addicts. We can't live with the poisons they're putting into the ground, but we can't live without the money" (Collette 1988, 13).

Mobilization against toxic waste disposal has led to wide-ranging political analyses and coalitions that cut across class, race, and gender lines. In Emelle, Alabama, where race politics and economics have been described as typical of "Old South" apartheid-like relationships, a small but growing segment of the local community has forged alliances across race and class lines and developed analyses that encompass social justice and environmental goals (Bullard 1990, 73). The multiplicity of issues and the intersection of interests that toxics mobilization addresses is described by one activist this way:

> People don't get all the connections. They say the environment is over here, the civil rights group is over there, the women's group is over there, and the other groups are here. Actually all of them are one group and the issues we fight become null and void if we have no clean water to drink, no clean air to breathe and nothing to eat. They say, "Now Miss Tucker, what you really need to do is go back to food stamps and welfare. Environmental issues are not your problem." And I say to him, "Toxic wastes, they don't know that I'm black." (Cora Tucker, keynote speaker at the 1987 conference, "Women in Toxic Organizing," cited in Zeff, Love, and Stults 1989, 5)

Maternalist Mobilization and Corporate Countermobilization

Although concerns about social justice, nature conservation, and fairness in risk distribution are all part of the language of toxics mobilization, it is the discourse of motherhood and child-protection that has become central in attracting women to the movement and legitimating their sustained involvement. For many women activists it seems inconceivable that their vision of child-protection would not be greeted with an immediate suppression of potential dangers. The language of risk-benefit analysis is not meaningful to them, not because they do not understand statistics (as their opponents often contend) but because for them maternalism is a much more powerful ideology than science.

Maternalist discourse has had a complex history in Western capitalist ideology. For the last one hundred and fifty years varieties of state maternalism and familism have emerged to justify state intervention into the family (e.g., compulsory education, residential schools for Native children, public health campaigns, criminalization of birth control and abortion, etc.) or to justify withdrawal of social services that are supposedly better performed in the family (daycare). These policies have been associated with the endless production of maternal devotion imagery (Bridenthal, Grossman, and Kaplan 1984; Davin 1978).

The child-saving movement and its ideology of child-protection at the turn of the nineteenth century has been the underpinning for the development of innumerable middle-class professions including psychology, teaching, pediatrics, nursing, children's literature, public health, home economics, and social work (Nasaw 1985; Sutherland 1976; Zelizer 1985). Although the movement itself had many contradictory impulses, which at times seemed more inclined to punish than protect, it has become a dominant force in the sacrilization of the child, which has virtually replaced the utilitarian child as essentialist ideology (Zelizer 1985). Children are no longer construed as workers or future soldiers (Davin 1978), nor in polite society should children be viewed in economic terms. In the course of the twentieth century, the construction of the priceless, sentimentalized, vulnerable child (Zelizer 1985) has produced a focus for the

multibillion-dollar cartoon, toy, movie, and television industry. Indeed, it is difficult to think of a stronger cultural icon.

Child-protection is completely naturalized for parent activists. As a mother with Concerned Citizens of South Central Los Angeles, a poor community with 78 percent unemployment, said in explaining her opposition to the siting of a solid waste incinerator:

> People's jobs were threatened, ministers were threatened ... but I said, "I'm not going to be intimidated." My child's health comes first, ... that's more important than a job. In the 1950s the city banned small incinerators in the yard and yet they want to build a big incinerator ... the Council is going to build something in my community which might kill my child ... I don't need a scientist to tell me that's wrong. (Charlotte Bullock, cited in Hamilton 1990, 217)

Maternalist ideology is an enormous source of mobilizing energy and has been met with a variety of corporate counterstrategies. The oldest counterstrategy to maternalist mobilization by state and corporate officials has been to label women "hysterical housewives" and dismiss their epidemiological data as "housewife statistics" (Brown and Mikkelson 1990; Gibbs 1982; Levine 1982; Rosenberg 1990b). A more recent and much more subtle corporate engagement of maternalist discourse has been to express direct concern for children. In doing so the companies avoid addressing emotionally charged health issues directly and concentrate on educational campaigns urging children and housewives to reduce litter, create less solid waste, and encourage recycling (Rosenberg 1990b, 131).

This strategy bears a striking similarity to nineteenth-century sanitary education campaigns (Davin 1978). In both cases the individual mother is exhorted to accept personal responsibility for a crisis that she is said to be able to ameliorate through private practices within her household. And in both cases, a radical critique of the structural determinates of crisis are vitiated by an appeal to maternalist duty.

These environmental education campaigns also serve to transform corporate images: polluters become environmentalists. The techno-eco modernist ("ecocratic") gesture within environmentalism (Sachs 1990) permits waste generators and disposers to speak with credibility as experienced ecomanagers, sharing their know-how with the public in such matters as solid waste management or recycling. Such companies also reinforce their self-representation as environmentalists by donating to mainstream nature conservationist organizations and by sitting on their boards of directors.[8]

An example of reputation metamorphosis is encapsulated in a contest sponsored by WMI, through its Recycle America program. The "From Trash to Treasure" contest aimed at getting "our kids involved in cleaning up the mess around us." Contestants were invited to submit works of art using paper, aluminum, plastic, and "lots of imagination" in their efforts to demonstrate the possibilities of recycling. First prize was an all-expense paid trip to Disney World (*Ladies Home Journal* 1989, 188).

A quick deconstruction of this tactic reveals mystification of corporate responsibility in "mess" production; the desirability of the amelioration of "messes" by individual solutions (which require lots of privatized "imagination"); and the quick reward of escape into fantasy, which is not identified as yet another corporate mess.

Corporations dislike housewife activists because women do not see child health as a negotiable category. "We must not compromise our children's futures by cutting deals with polluters and regulators," urges Lois Gibbs, Love Canal housewife activist and founder of the Citizen's Clearinghouse for Hazardous Waste (CCHW). She insists that grassroots activists name names and hold government and corporations directly responsible for their actions.

In public, industry assessments of grassroots mobilization express dismay at their wrongheaded naivete:

Grassroots local groups, many of them misinformed, wield increasingly disruptive power. "... [They] are concerned about the value of their homes and the health of their children. That means they are relentless. In general, unlike mainstream environmental groups, they are not interested in compromise or mediation." (Stephenson, environmental public relations consultant, cited in Kilpatrick 1990, 54–55)

In private, companies express much stronger fears about grassroots radicalism:

CCHW is one of the most radical coalitions operating under the environmentalist banner. They have ties into labor, the communist party and all manner of folk .... In October, at their grassroots convention, they developed the attached agenda which if accomplished, in total, would restructure U.S. society into something unrecognizable and probably unworkable. It's a tour de force of public policy issues to be affecting business in years to come. (Internal memo from Clyde Greenert, 14 Nov. 1989, to other Union Carbide executives reviewing CCHW Grassroots Convention; cited in Mueller 1990, 18)

This private analysis has led to corporate strategies of intimidation. One significant technique has been "SLAPP" (Strategic Lawsuits against Popular Participation). This tactic targeted local groups and researchers with multimillion-dollar suits based on industry claims that they have been libeled by local activists. When successful, such suits have caused fear among grassroots groups as they assess their meager funds in comparison to large corporations, have dispersed energies away from environmental health issues, and ultimately may have caused some local groups to fall apart. The effectiveness of this tactic has subsided as it became identified as malicious prosecution and local communities began launching countersuits against corporations.

Given the links that some corporations may still have or have had to organized crime, some activists also fear physical attack. One informant told me that she always paused anxiously before putting her key into her ignition after a meeting because she feared that her car was wired to a bomb.

The newest corporate countermobilization has been to sponsor local groups that mimic grassroots groups in organizational style and public self-presentation. These industry-financed groups have targeted job development and job security. They appeal to local citizenry on the issue that has been called "the weakest link" of the environmental justice movement (*Everyone's Backyard* 1991, 1). The collision between child-protection discourse and the imperatives of employment is one of many contradictions that housewife activists face.

Contradictions of Maternalist Ideology

Although maternalism is manipulated by corporate/state strategies, it also has its own internal contradictions that constrain mobilization. Complex processes of stigmatization occur in communities exposed to toxic wastes, where parents blame themselves for their children's present or potential health problems and are paralyzed into inaction (Brown and Mikkelson 1990; Edelstein 1988; Levine 1982; Madisso 1985). Sometimes their activism is delegitimated by the view that they are manipulators who are attempting to construct and then exploit a crisis situation to their own material advantage. Thus activists in Legler, New Jersey, reported being told,

"There's nothing wrong with your water, you're only out for the money" (Edelstein 1988, 114). And mothers at Love Canal were accused of "trying to make a bundle" from the government (Levine 1982, 185).

Visible disasters like floods or hurricanes produce community consensus and mutual support with relative ease; however, toxic crises are invisible and require agreement on an analytic framework that relates events in the distant past to health outcomes in the present and the future (Vyner 1988, 1–26). Parent activists, who might also be caring for sick children, are often also required to address forces of dissensus within the community.

Nonbelievers in the crisis (often nonparents or older residents, or those more geographically distant from the exposed area) may attack activists because of declining real estate values as a result of negative publicity. Thus activists who represent themselves as protecting the family are frequently attacked for undermining financial, social, and emotional investments in the home and turning the home from sanctuary into trap (Rosenberg 1990*b*).

The struggle to mobilize and to sustain mobilization is also played out within the family. Children and husbands may resent the time and energies that women put into antitoxics activism. Preserving familist ideology, in theory, often results, in practice, in long absences from the home, unprepared meals, undone laundry, and kitchens turned into offices. When women become active publicly, their husbands may resent their new confidence and skills. A United States support group for toxics activists (CCHW) has found these tensions so widespread that it has prepared educational material on managing household stresses as a result of activism, which suggests that women involve their children and husbands as much as possible.

A Mothers of East Los Angeles (MELA) activist analyzed the transformation in her marital relations (and her husband's political education) this way:

My husband doesn't like getting involved, but he takes me because he knows I like it. Sometimes we would have two or three meetings a week. And my husband would say, "Why are you doing so much? It is really getting out of hand." But he is very supportive. Once he gets there, he enjoys it and starts arguing too. See, it is just that he is not used to it. He couldn't believe things happen the way they do. He was in the Navy for twenty years and they brainwashed him to believe that none of the politicians could do wrong. So he has come a long way. Now he comes home and parks out front and asks me, "Well, where are we going tonight?" (Erlinda Robles, cited in Pardo 1990, 4)

In other households, tensions are not resolved this easily and the outcome has been separation and divorce (Gibbs 1982; Madisso 1985).

Maternalist essentialism is also the underpinning of a very different social movement: New Right antifeminism. Based on similar initial constructions of defense of home and child-protection, New Right women have mobilized around a different view of crisis, seeing feminism and abortion as the biggest threats to the family. For many women the maternalist child-protection mission seems at complete odds to the pro-abortion position. When these positions intersect, the contradictions embedded in maternalist ideology emerge and environmental health mobilization may fall apart.

In 1981, for example, a United States group attempted to bring together women, workers, and environmentalists in the "Coalition for the Reproductive Rights of Workers." The coalition ultimately disintegrated, in large part because the right to reproductive protection position could not be reconciled with the abortion rights position (Freudenberg 1984, 222).

The discourses of toxics mobilization and abortion can in fact intersect but configure in yet another way. In Italy, the Seveso disaster in 1976[9] coincided with a national debate on the decriminalization of abortion. The town of Seveso had been exposed to dioxins and when pregnant women were offered the option of legal abortion, those holding anti-abortion positions argued that the health hazards of exposure were being exaggerated in order to grant legitimacy to the abortion cause (Reich 1981, 105–112). Although state health officials tried to prove that dioxins were dangerous, a majority of community members mobilized around the position that "it's all an invention of the politicians" (Reich 1981, 105), supported their priests in the reoccupation of their homes, and narrowly avoided armed clashes with the police who were trying to keep them out.

Children's health was seen to be adversely affected by the exposure to toxic chemicals, but this observation did not become a central mobilizing focus. On the contrary, unlike residents of Love Canal, residents of Seveso fought overwhelmingly for repatriation and against environmental health crisis construction.

Finally, there is another possible interpretation of exposure to toxics. If the connection between exposure and negative fetal and child health is taken as a given, it may not always be industry and government who are deemed responsible for negative health outcomes. Women may find themselves being held responsible for mutagenesis and teratogenesis. Mothers may be labeled abusers and their fetuses may be seen as appropriate recipients of biogenetic and legal interventions. As Lin Nelson (1990) points out, women's bodies have already been defined as hazardous environments in some workplace "fetal rights" legislation. Thus the logic of prenatal rights discourse could produce litigation, based on the following argument:

Once a pregnant woman has abandoned her right to abort and has decided to carry her fetus to term, she incurs a "conditional prospective liability" for negligent acts toward her fetus ....

These acts could be considered negligent fetal abuse resulting in an injured child .... Withholding of necessary prenatal care, improper nutrition, *exposure to mutagens and teratogans, or even exposure to the mother's defective intrauterine environment* ... could all result in an injured infant who might claim that his right to be born physically and mentally sound had been invaded. (Attorney Margery Shaw, cited in Nelson 1990, 187. Emphasis added.)

These clashing discourses mediate the possibilities of alliances with pro- and anti-abortion groups, fetal rights groups, and disabled rights groups. The collision of competing "rights" under capitalism offers no easy predictor of alliances and can fracture coalitions based on maternalist essentialism.

The Environmental Justice Movement

For many women the experience of toxics activism is transformative. Said one Mother of East L.A.:

You should have seen how timid we were the first time we went to a public hearing. Now, forget it, I walk right up and make myself heard and that's what you have to do. (Aurora Castillo, cited in Pardo 1990, 6)

At present these transcendent experiences operate on the local level to educate and mobilize other potential activists and to establish information sharing and support links with other similar groups. This decentralized pattern is in the process of transforming itself into a broad-based social movement. A CCHW grassroots organizing conference has urged women to commit their housewife skills to a professional career as community organizers (Zeff, Love, and Stults 1989).

In the United States activists situate this movement in the tradition of the civil rights movement, the labor movement, and the women's movement (Zeff, Love, and Stults 1989) and distance themselves from mainstream environmentalism. The humanist social justice-based radicalism of the environmental justice movement often puts it in opposition to biocentered tendencies in mainstream environmentalism.

The following summary of a story, told by Lois Gibbs, illustrates these differences (Edelstein 1988, 167).

The scene is a hazardous waste site hearing in Louisiana several years ago. The group opposed to the siting has set up an aquarium filled with contaminated drinking water from their wells. They loudly announce their plan to place fish into the tank, claiming that these fish will be dead by the time the hearing is over. Environment officials and traditional environmentalists instantly protest, but the audience begins to chant "Kill the fish."[10]

Gibbs interpreted the chanting to mean that animal protection should be secondary to child protection and human protection: "If we have to kill the fish to make the point, we'll do it. We're sacrificing our children" (Edelstein 1988). Her view is congruent with critiques of mainstream environmentalism and Deep Ecology, which argue that they mask race, class, and gendered interests by claiming a spurious universalism (Bradford 1989*a*, 1989*b*; Enzensberger 1982).

For toxics activists and victims, the environment is not a "teacher" or "moral guide" (Devall and Sessions 1985) that can reveal new lifeways through contemplation and meditation. Rather it is a ticking time bomb, carelessly and ruthlessly set in place by the practices of state and capital. For them the lesson of nature is social and political and already inscribed in the bodies of their children.

Notes

A special thanks to the following for their sustaining interest and support: Alan Block, Julie Cruikshank, Richard Lee, Richard Rosenberg, Irene Silverblatt, Mary Vise, and members of the Frankel-Lambert Action Committee (FLAC).

1. A note on terminology: In the United States many activists organizing against residential toxic waste exposure have designated their mobilization as a struggle for "environmental justice" (CCHW) or "environmental equity" (Bullard 1990), or the toxics movement, or toxics environmentalism to distinguish it from mainstream environmentalism. These terms are not current in Canada.

2. Later in the nineteenth century, Ibsen's play *Enemy of the People* (1882) used the device of an environmental health disaster (poisoning of town baths by factory effluent) as a vehicle with which to critique middle-class corruption. The play resonated with strong anti-state and anti-capitalist sentiments when performed during the late nineteenth and early twentieth centuries (Ibsen 1966, 12–14).

3. In August 1978, waste oil contaminated with PCBs was disposed of this way along a rural highway in central North Carolina (Freudenberg 1984, 182–183). When a landfill site was selected for the contaminated soil, in 1982, in a predominantly African-American community, local grassroots groups and national civil rights leaders began organizing protests. Ultimately 414 activists were arrested, marking the first time in the United States that anyone had been jailed for trying to halt a toxic waste landfill (Bullard 1990, 35–38).

4. Big profits were being made in all forms of garbage disposal, but the biggest profits were being made in the high-tech specialty of hazardous waste disposal. As of August 1990, Chemical Waste Management, a subsidiary of WMI, was charging its customers in Emelle, Alabama, $112 a ton; the site normally handles 800,000 tons a year (Kemesis 1990, 40). The United States "hazwaste" market is currently valued at about $32 billion (Rotman 1990). WMI as of 1986 reported gross revenues of over $2 billion (Moody's *Handbook of Common Stocks* 1987). Its executives are among the highest paid in the United States: its president earned over $14 million in 1987 (Citizen's Clearing House 1988, 4).

5. For example, WMI has faced countless charges of fraud, bribery, price-fixing, illegal dumping, and unsafe practices. Between 1982 and 1987 WMI paid over $30 million in fines for violations of environmental regulations but it has been estimated that it took the company only six days to earn the revenues to pay these fines (Vallette 1987, 7). WMI regularly makes political donations to officeholders in the United States (Vallette 1987) and Canada (Rosenberg 1990a).

6. Inventories of the number of contaminated sites have not been undertaken on a national level in Canada, but in southern Ontario alone, it is estimated that there may be between 2,000 and 3,000 unrecorded sites (interview with Environment Canada official, October 1990, Jackson et al. 1982, 18).

7. In addition there are 400,000 municipal landfills in the United States, which may have received unregulated toxic wastes, hundreds of thousands of deep well injection sites, and 300,000 leaking underground storage tanks threatening groundwater (Edelstein 1988).

8. In 1987–1988, WMI disclosed donations to environmental groups, which included the National Wildlife Federation, the National Audubon Society, the Natural Resources Defense Council, and the Sierra Club of California (*Action Bulletin* 1989, 9). In 1987, WMI's Chief Executive Officer joined the Board of Directors of the National Wildlife Federation. Over the years, WMI has hired people from various mainstream environmental groups, including the former director of the Environmental Defense Fund, who currently runs WMI's Public Relations Department (Collette 1988).

9. In July of 1976, a toxic plume of contaminated gas escaped the Swiss-owned ICMESA factory that produced industrial perfumes and pharmaceutical chemicals and settled over the northern Italian community of Seveso. Pregnant women came under close observation by public health authorities.

Women, on an individual choice basis, were offered the opportunity to have abortions. This was the first time legal abortions were permitted in Italy (Reich 1981, 73–139).

10. Pardo (1990, 4) describes a similar narrative told to her by a Mother of East L.A. about the placement of an oil pipeline through the center of their community.

References

Action Bulletin (1989). San Francisco: Sierra Club Publications. 9.

Block, Alan A., and Frank R. Scarpitti (1985). *Poisoning for Profit: The Mafia and Toxic Waste in America.* New York: Morrow.

Bradford, George (1989a). "Return of the Son of Deep Ecology: The Ethics of Permanent Crisis and the Permanent Crisis in Ethics," *Fifth Estate* 24(Spring):5–38.

Bramwell, Anna (1989). *Ecology in the Twentieth Century: A History.* New Haven: Yale University Press.

Bridenthal, Renate, Atina Grossman, and Marian Kaplan, eds. (1984). *When Biology Became Destiny: Women in Weimar and Nazi Germany.* New York: Monthly Review Press.

Brown, Michael H. (1981). *Laying Waste: The Poisoning of America by Toxic Chemicals.* New York: Pocket Books.

Brown, Phil, and Edwin J. Mikkelsen (1990). *No Safe Place: Toxic Waste, Leukemia, and Community Action.* Berkeley, Los Angeles, London: University of California Press.

Bullard, Robert D. (1990). *Dumping in Dixie: Race, Class and Environmental Quality.* Boulder: Westview Press.

Center for Investigative Reporting (CIR) and Bill Moyers (1990). *Global Dumping Ground: The International Traffic in Hazardous Waste.* Washington: Seven Locks Press.

Cerrell Associates (1984). *Political Difficulties Facing Waste to Energy Conversion Plant Siting.* Los Angeles: California Waste Management Board.

Citizen's Clearing House for Hazardous Wastes (1988). *Action Bulletin,* no. 19(July).

Collette, Will (1988). *Waste Management, Inc.: A Corporate Profile.* Arlington, VA: Citizen's Clearinghouse for Hazardous Wastes.

Commission for Racial Justice (1987). Washington, DC.

Crooks, Harold (1982). *Dirty Business: The Inside Story of the Garbage Agglomerates.* Toronto: Lorimer.

Davin, Anna (1978). "Imperialism and Motherhood," *History Workshop,* no. 5(Spring): 9–66.

Devall, Bill, and George Sessions (1985). *Deep Ecology.* Salt Lake City: G.M. Smith.

Edelstein, Michael R. (1988). *Contaminated Communities: The Social and Psychological Impacts of Residential Toxic Exposure.* Boulder: Westview Press.

Engels, Friedrich (1975). *Marx and Engels Collected Works.* Vol. 4, *The Condition of the Working Class in England: From Personal Observation and Authentic Sources.* London: Lawrence and Wishart. (Orig. 1845).

Enzensberger, Hans Magnus (1982). "A Critique of Political Economy." In his *Critical Essays,* ed. Reinhold Grimm, 186–223. New York: Continuum.

Everyone's Backyard (1991). "Editorial," 9(1 October).

Finer, Samuel E. (1955). *The Life and Times of Sir Edwin Chadwick.* London: Methuen.

Freudenberg, Nicholas (1984). *Not in Our Backyards: Community Action for Health and the Environment.* New York: Monthly Review Press.

Gibbs, Lois M. (1982). *Love Canal: My Story.* Albany: State University of New York Press.

Hamilton, Cynthia (1990). "Women, Home and the Community: The Struggle in an Urban Environment." In *Reweaving the World: The Emergence of Ecofeminism,* ed. I. Diamond and G. Orenstein, 215–222. San Francisco: Sierra Club Books.

Ibsen, Henrik (1966). *Ghosts and Three Other Plays by Henrik Ibsen.* Trans. Michael Meyer. Garden City: Anchor Books.

Jackson, John, Phil Weller, and the Waterloo Public Interest Research Group (1982). *Chemical Nightmare: The*

Unnecessary Legacy of Toxic Wastes. Toronto: Between the Lines.

Kemesis, Paul (1990). "Court Nixes Alabama Waste Ban," *Chemical Week* (22 August):40.

Kilpatrick, David (1990). "Environmentalism: The New Crusade," *Fortune* 121, no. 4(12 February):44–55.

Ladies Home Journal (1989). New York: Ladies Home Journal.

Levine, Adeline (1982). *Love Canal: Science, Politics and People.* Lexington: Heath.

Madisso, Urmass (1984). *An Annotated Bibliography of the Literature on the Social and Psychological Effects of Exposure to Hazardous Substances.* Ottawa: Environment Canada, Inland Waters Directorate.

_____. (1985). *A Synthesis of Social and Psychological Effects of Exposure to Hazardous Substances.* Ottawa: Environment

Canada, Inland Waters Directorate.

Moody's Investors Service (1987). *Handbook of Common Stocks.* Vol. 4. New York: Moody's Investors Service Publications.

Mueller, P.S. (1990). "Corporate Corner: Carbide Apologizes to CCHW for McCarthyite Smear," *Everyone's Backyard* 8(June):18.

Nasaw, David (1985). *Children of the City: At Work and at Play.* Garden City: Anchor Press/Doubleday.

Nelson, Lin (1990). "The Place of Women in Polluted Places." In *Reweaving the World: The Emergence of Ecofeminism,* ed. I. Diamond and G. Orenstein, 173–188. San Francisco: Sierra Club Books.

Pardo, Mary (1990). "Mexican American Women Grassroots Community Activists: 'Mothers of East Los Angeles,'" *Frontiers* 11(1):1–7.

Reich, Michael (1981). "Toxic Politics: A Comparative Study of Public and Private Responses to Chemical Disasters in the United States, Italy and Japan." Ph.D. diss., Yale University.

Ridgeway, James (1970). *The Politics of Ecology.* New York: Dutton.

Rosenberg, Harriet G. (1988). *A Negotiated World: Three Centuries of Change in a French Alpine Community.* Toronto: University of Toronto Press.

_____. (1990a). "The Home is the Workplace: Stress, Hazards and Pollutants in the Household," In *Through the Kitchen Window: The Politics of Home and Family,* ed. M. Luxton, H. Rosenberg, and S. Arat-Koc, 57–80. Toronto: Garamond Press.

_____. (1990b). "The Kitchen and the Multinational Corporation." In *Through the Kitchen Window: The Politics of Home and Family,* ed. M. Luxton, H. Rosenberg, and S. Arat-Koc, 123–150. Toronto: Garamond Press.

Russell, Dick (1989). "Exporting Cancer," *New Internationalist,* no. 198 (August):10–11.

Sachs, Wolfgang (1990). "The Age of Ecology." Transcript of Canadian Broadcasting Corporation Radio Broadcast, "Ideas" Series, 18 June.

Sutherland, Neil (1976). *Children in English-Canadian Society: Framing the Twentieth Century Consensus.* Toronto: University of Toronto Press.

Vallette, Jim (1987). *Waste Management, Inc.* Washington: The Greenpeace Report.

Vyner, Henry M. (1988). *Invisible Trauma: The Psychosocial Effects of Invisible Environmental Contaminants.* Lexington: Lexington Books.

Wolf, Eric R. (1969). *Peasant Wars of the Twentieth Century.* New York: Harper and Row.

_____. (1982). *Europe and the People without History.* Berkeley: University of California Press.

Zeff, Robin Lee, Marsha Love, and Karen Stults (1989). *Empowering Ourselves: Women and Toxics Organizing.* Arlington, VA: Citizen's Clearinghouse for Hazardous Wastes.

Zelizer, Viviana (1985). *Pricing the Priceless Child: The Changing Social Value of Children.* New York: Basic Books.

Emerging from the Shadows: Women with Disabilities Organize

Diane Driedger

Women with disabilities experience discrimination because they are women and because they are disabled. In developing countries, women with disabilities face triple jeopardy: discrimination due to disability, gender, and developing world status. Many developing world governments argue that it is difficult to make education, training, and employment available to the general population, let alone to disabled people, who have more needs and who are usually seen as non-productive citizens. Disabled persons are thus forced into roles which deviate from the adult social norm—the roles of perpetual child; patient or invalid; curse or blessing from God. Although these roles vary according to disability and culture, they serve to disaffect disabled persons from the rights and privileges of most citizens. Although women with disabilities have faced discrimination throughout the ages, there has been some positive change since World War II. In wave after wave of social movements, oppressed people have discovered their own histories and challenged injustices. It has been important for marginalized, disadvantaged, and colonized people to confront their histories of oppression, to throw off society's view of them as different, and society's tendency to decide for them.

The Roots of the Disabled People's Movement[1]

Disabled people have experienced oppression for centuries—they have been locked away in asylums and family attics or considered fit only for domestic work in the family home. In short, they have been shut out of the mainstream of life the world over. However, after World War II, life began to change for people with disabilities.

In the West, improved rehabilitation techniques were developed for injured veterans. People with spinal cord injuries began to live longer. Casualties from other wars increased the ranks of young disabled people and the polio epidemics of the 1950s produced survivors, many of whom were also young people. Improved technical aids such as portable respirators and electric wheelchairs meant that disabled people were much more mobile and able to live independently in the community. In all, there were more disabled young people living more productive lives.

At the same time, the second half of the twentieth century saw the rise of the rehabilitation professions. Doctors, physiotherapists, nurses, and social workers were trained to deal with the lives of disabled persons.

By classifying them as sick, they tended to medicalize all aspects of life for disabled persons. Because society in general excuses sick people from participating in everyday life, this became another reason to exclude people with disabilities and to deny them responsibility for their lives.

In the 1960s and 1970s, liberation movements swept the developing world. Countries emerged from colonialism in Africa, Asia, and the Caribbean. Many people became disabled as a result of liberation and other civil and cross-border wars. Liberation movements in developing countries, and civil rights movements in North America and other parts of the developed world, set the stage for the rise of the disabled people's movement.

Organizations of Disabled Persons in North America

In the early 1970s in the United States, people with disabilities began to organize for their rights. The American Coalition of Citizens with Disabilities (ACCD) was organized nationally in the 1970s but closed down in 1983. Currently, disability groups with many purposes have started up across the country, particularly on the east and west coasts. Today, there are many Independent Living Centres (ILCs) throughout the United States that provide services and individual advocacy.

There are also two large training-oriented groups on the west coast of the United States. World Institute on Disability (WID) works with countries such as Japan, El Salvador, and Russia, conducting research and training on international disability issues. Mobility International (MI) USA, which has focused in part on women with disabilities, brings people with disabilities from around the world to Oregon for training in leadership, self-esteem, and organizational development. As well, it facilitates exchange trips to other countries for American disabled people. Another group, Disability International

(DI) USA, has been organizing since 1992 and has recently become a member of Disabled Peoples' International (DPI).

Not long after the disability movement started in the United States, people began to organize in Canada. Provincial groups were formed in Alberta, Saskatchewan, and Manitoba from 1972–74. These were "cross-disability" groups (meaning that they were open to people of various physical and mental disabilities) made up entirely of disabled people speaking for the rights of disabled people, and founded on the premise that uniting people with various disabilities gave them a stronger voice. These provincial groups formed a national organization in 1976 and soon other provinces across Canada became members. This organization was called the Coalition of Provincial Organizations of the Handicapped (COPOH). (In 1994, it changed its name to the Council of Canadians with Disabilities, or CCD, and that is the name I will use for the rest of this essay).

Disabled Peoples' International

The first international organization to focus on the issues of people with various disabilities was called Rehabilitation International (RI). Composed mostly of non-disabled professionals who work in the areas of disability and disabled persons, it was formed in 1922 and holds a World Congress every four years to discuss matters related to rehabilitation and disabled persons.

In 1980, the World Congress of RI was held in Winnipeg, Manitoba, Canada. At that time, the Swedish delegation brought forward a resolution calling for people with disabilities to have equal representation in the decision-making process within RI. The RI Delegate Assembly turned them down. At the same congress, the Council of Canadians with Disabilities organized after-hours meetings. Several hundred people with disabilities attended each meeting, including about fifty disabled Canadians. (CCD had raised the money for them to attend the congress.) Fired up by the rejection of the Swedish resolution, disabled people decided to form their own international organization composed entirely of disabled people. The mandate of the new organization would be to promote the full participation and equality of people with disabilities all over the world, and to have "a voice of our own."

A steering committee, chaired by Henry Enns of Winnipeg, Canada, was struck to network, plan, and fundraise for the founding congress of the new organization. Held in 1981 in Singapore, it included representatives of national disability organizations from around the world. The organization had originally been given the name World Coalition of People with Disablities, but by the time the founding meeting was held, the organization had a new name: Disabled Peoples' International (DPI).

Disabled Women Excluded

In many countries, women with disabilities were involved in local and national disability organizations and fledgling international organizations. And, like women's experience in other groups and in society, they tended to be in supporting roles or were often given token positions within the executive.

In the early years of forming disability organizations, women with disabilities generally saw themselves as disabled first and as women second. In Canada, women's issues were not considered serious issues by disabled men in the 1970s and early 1980s. Only when women brought up "important" issues such as transportation, accessibility, or housing were they listened to. Few women held leadership positions and they often felt patronized and laughed at.

At the same time as women with disabilities were struggling within disabled persons' organizations in Canada, they found that they also did not feel welcome within the women's movement—they were not seen as "women," only as "different" and "disabled." In general, many women with disabilities did not even identify themselves as "women" because of the attitudes they had absorbed from society and the women's movement.

As the second wave of feminism swept North America and Europe in the 1960s and 1970s, issues important to women with disabilities were clearly not a priority. In addition, many women with disabilities found themselves physically isolated from the women's movement. The chronic underfunding of feminist organizations, coupled with insensitivity to disability issues, has meant and continues to mean that women's events, women's shelters, and the offices of women's organizations are inaccessible, that sign language interpretation is not provided, and that hotlines lack Telephone Devices for the Deaf (TDDs).

Women with disabilities, confronted by barriers within disability and feminist groups, decided to organize for their own interests. This has translated into pushing through women's agendas within disability organizations and starting groups specifically for women with disabilities.

Canadian Women with Disabilities Organize

In Canada, women with disabilities have worked to increase the number of women in leadership positions within the Council of Canadians with Disabilities and to ensure that their issues are addressed by CCD. Thanks to the efforts of a small number of disabled Canadian feminists, the CCD national conference passed a resolution in 1981 calling for equal representation of women in leadership positions and affirmative action policies to make that happen. In 1983, CCD resolved to study women's issues (although CCD's first discussion paper on disabled women was not published until 1987).

In 1985, resolutions were passed that called for a workshop on women's issues at the next conference and for an investigation of women's participation within CCD structure. By the mid- to late 1980s, gender parity was fairly well integrated into CCD. In 1986, Irene Feika was elected as the first female Chair of CCD (a position she held until 1990). Another woman, Francine Arsenault, was the Chair of CCD from 1992–96.

Like the Canadian disabled people's movement ten years before, the disabled women's movement also had its birth in Western Canada. Grassroots women in Saskatchewan held a women's conference in 1984 that eventually led to the formation of the first provincial DisAbled Women's Network (DAWN). Around the same time, a small number of disabled and non-disabled feminists in Manitoba worked together to fight the abuse faced by one disabled woman in that province. Ultimately, they took on other issues facing women with disabilities, calling themselves the Consulting Committee on the Status of Women with Disabilities (CCSWD).

Nineteen eighty-five was an important year in Canadian disabled women's organizing. Women with disabilities organized a "Women with Disabilities Networking Meeting" in June. It was attended by delegates from across Canada. A steering committee was struck to set up a national organization called DisAbled Women's Network (DAWN) Canada. Delegates agreed to return home and start their own groups of disabled women. That year, local groups were founded in Toronto, Montreal, and Ottawa, and provincial groups formed in Prince Edward Island and Nova Scotia. British Columbia founded its group in 1986. In March 1987, the founding national meeting of DAWN Canada was held in Winnipeg.

Since then, DAWN Canada has researched the concerns of disabled women and has published position papers on issues such as self-image, employment, parenting, and violence. These issues—especially violence against women with disabilities—have been traditionally overlooked by both the women's and the disabled

persons' movements. In recent years, DAWN Canada has worked with both women's organizations and the disabled people's movement. As a result, Canada's largest feminist organization, the National Action Committee on the Status of Women (NAC), now holds its meetings in accessible locations, has an accessible office, and actively looks for ways to support its disabled sisters around the country.

DAWN Canada has also joined with CCD to work together on issues of broad social policy and has worked with another group of disabled persons, the Canadian Disability Rights Council (CDRC), to make sure that disabled women's rights are protected under the Charter of Rights and Freedoms. (This is a part of the Canadian constitution that prohibits discrimination on many grounds, including disability.) Recently, DAWN and CDRC have published a series of papers on the implications of new reproductive technologies for women and disabled persons.

Despite this progress, the women's and disabled persons' communities in Canada still need to do more work to ensure recognition of the importance of disabled women's issues. And the same struggle is faced by women with disabilities around the globe.

Disabled Women in other Countries

While organizations of disabled persons have sprung up in over 100 countries since 1945, women have been poorly represented—or not represented at all—in decision-making positions. As in Canada, women's issues have not been seen as important by the greater disabled persons' or women's movements. At the national level, very few separate disabled women's organizations exist At present, women have formed their own groups only in Australia, Canada, and Uganda and are working on becoming a separate group in Trinidad and Tobago.

In Australia, women with disabilities have been very active within the disability movement for years. They formed their own organization in 1995—it is separate from the greater disabled persons' group, but still retains membership in that group. Women with Disabilities Australia (WDA) has a newsletter and funding from the Australian government for its office.

The Disabled Women's Network of Trinidad and Tobago (DAWN T and T) was formed in 1992 and, since then, has held numerous training workshops on self-esteem, educational enhancement, and health maintenance. Violence and employment are issues that DAWN T and T intends to focus on in the coming years. (See my article with Kathleen Guy [...] for more information about DAWN T and T.)

The Uganda Disabled Women's Association (UDWA), formed around 1986, is also involved in self-help. In support of its goal to contribute to the well-being of disabled women in Uganda, the group operates a craft store to sell its own products and has managed its own revolving loan fund since 1991. The group is proud to state that "... many who were beggars are no longer so and are thus contributing to national development. Incomes received from this form of employment breathe life into the ... beneficiaries by improving their standards of living and rendering them more responsible and self-supporting."[2]

Disabled women have also addressed under-representation in the disabled persons' movement by forming caucuses within those organizations. Although traditional views regarding women have made gains difficult, the caucuses provide disabled women with the opportunity to formulate their own ideas first and then present them to the greater membership for action. There are women's caucuses in organizations in countries such as: Cambodia, Costa Rica, Dominica, El Salvador, Jamaica, Malaysia, Mauritius, South Africa, St. Lucia, and Zimbabwe.

Women with Disabilities in DPI

Within Disabled Peoples' International (DPI), women with disabilities have spoken up and pointed out that very few women are leaders in local, national, or international organizations. At the 1983 DPI World Council Meeting, a resolution calling for more representation for women was not acted upon. In 1984 in Jamaica, women with disabilities met separately at a DPI symposium on development and again asked for equal representation. Again, no action was taken.

Nineteen eighty-five became a watershed year for women with disabilities within DPI. At the DPI World Congress in the Bahamas that year, DAWN Canada organized three meetings for women with disabilities. Strong leadership from the Australian delegation, Dr. Fatima Shah of Pakistan and DAWN Canada, along with lots of hard work, led to the presentation of a resolution at the main DPI meeting that called for fifty percent representation by women in decision-making. The resolution passed.

Since then, DPI has created a Women's Committee with representation from all the regions. DPI has held leadership training seminars for disabled women in different parts of the world and, in 1985, created a Deputy Chair position to look at the inclusion of underrepresented groups in DPI—including women, deaf persons and people with mental disabilities.

Although the representation of women in DPI has increased at all levels since 1985, there is still much progress needed before equality can be reached. DPI's World Council is about one-third women. Of DPI's five Regional Councils, only two have equal representation for women and men: Africa and the North American and the Caribbean region. In the other three regions (Latin America, Asia/Pacific, and Europe), the representation for women is thirty percent or lower.

International Networks of Women with Disabilities

Several international disabled women's networks have formed in the last decade. In 1985, even as women were challenging DPI to include disabled women in decision-making, women with disabilities were mobilizing on their own.

Like the conference in Beijing ten years later, the World Conference to Review the Achievements of the United Nations Decade for Women, held in Nairobi, Kenya, in July 1985, was inaccessible. At a workshop about barriers to women with disabilities, disabled women from fourteen countries decided to form their own organization, called Disabled Women's International (DWI). The final report from the Nairobi conference called on governments to provide opportunities for disabled women to participate in all aspects of life.

The intention behind the formation of DWI was to facilitate information sharing among women with disabilities in different countries. Delegates to the Nairobi conference went home and encouraged others to join. DWI published one information-sharing newsletter annually for the first few years, but, due to a lack of funding, little else has been accomplished.

Partially as a result of DWI's inaction, and because no DWI women attended the August 1990 United Nations Meeting of Disabled Women in Vienna, the World Coalition of Women with Disabilities (WCWD) was founded. WCWD's mandate was to advocate for the concerns of disabled women in the disabled and women's movements. DAWN Canada, chaired by Pat Israel at that time, was the driving force behind WCWD and, in 1992, organized WCWD meeting of disabled women to coincide with a disability conference called Independence '92. Since then, however, DAWN Canada's leadership has focused on national issues and WCWD is no longer an active organization.

In September 1995, one day prior to the Fourth World Conference on Women in Beijing, China, an International Symposium on Women with Disabilities was held at the conference site. The symposium was organized by Disabled Peoples' International, the World Blind Union, Mobility International USA and the World Federation of the Deaf. Over two hundred women with disabilities attended. Although woefully inaccessible (as described in detail in E. Catherine Boldt's article "We Want Access *Now!*"[3]), the symposium and the Fourth World Conference on Women provided a tremendous opportunity for women with disabilities to network and to flex political muscles in the international media.

Although women with disabilities know that they have a long way to go before they will truly have equality of opportunity comparable to that of non-disabled persons, they are beginning to enjoy the fruits of their efforts the world over.

Issues Facing Women with Disabilities

Worldwide, women with disabilities are emerging from the shadows to establish women's caucuses, self-help organizations, and income-generating ventures. Nonetheless, poverty and limited opportunities continue to define their status around the world. As women with disabilities organize, they must confront the problems of access, housing, and transportation that are faced by every disabled person. These barriers, coupled with the unique challenges faced by women with disabilities— negative attitudes, lack of role models, lack of education, and many forms of violence—prevent them from taking their rightful place in society.

Women with no Place in Society

By and large, women with disabilities lack the opportunities to fill positive societal roles. The image of a disabled woman does not flash to mind when words like colleague, doctor, engineer, wife, mother, and friend are spoken. Given that there are few positive role models for women with disabilities, they are left to feel invisible and without goals. Myths about disability lead to profound social, political, and economic consequences for women.

Attitudes form a huge barrier to the education and employment of people with disabilities. There is a widespread perception that if you have some sort of physical disability, you cannot think or work. People who are mentally handicapped face the perception that they cannot learn or work at all. The prevailing attitude is that disabled persons are recipients, not contributors.

These attitudes are magnified towards women with disabilities. Prejudices regarding the competency of women and their ability to measure up to men exist to varying degrees in countries around the world. Women with disabilities are often overprotected in the home and their families do not view their education as a priority. On the other hand, some families in the developing world see women with disabilities as houseworkers and want to keep them at home.

The lack of role models and negative attitudes about disability have the greatest consequences for women in developing countries. The roles of wife and mother are often the most important roles assigned to women— they give women societal status. If a woman is unable to participate in this role, she is seen as a non-person.

To quote Dr. Fatima Shah, a blind leader from Pakistan, "... always conscious of her lack of a place in the social order, she [the blind woman] is gradually brainwashed into accepting herself as a non-person with no rights or privileges to claim, no duties or functions to perform, no aim in life to achieve, no aptitudes to consult or fulfill."[4]

The Struggle for Education and Employment

The vast majority of the world's 500 million disabled people are illiterate, and disabled women are less likely to be literate than disabled men. Most of the 350 million disabled people living in developing countries have no formal education.[5] To begin with, physical barriers to transportation and schools prevent disabled children from getting an education. Moreover, the attitudes of families who want to keep their disabled daughters at home to do chores inhibit disabled women's education. In those developing countries where there are opportunities for basic education or training, disabled boys—not girls—usually receive them. Zohra Rajah, a mobility impaired leader from Mauritius and formerly a Deputy Chair of DPI, has remarked, "In many societies it is difficult to convince people that able-bodied women need to be educated; for disabled women it is worse. Due to traditional role perceptions, disabled women are given less encouragement to continue with education."[6]

In developed countries, education is often affordable and more women are literate, but people who are disabled still face barriers to access and success in publicly funded schools. Governments and communities are slow to remove the barriers which impede disabled people's success in the education system.

There is a general lack of support and encouragement for women with disabilities in every sphere of life, and nowhere is this more blatant than in the workforce and opportunities for training. In some developing countries, the traditional training of both women and men with disabilities tends to over-emphasize the acquisition of the simplest craft skills, regardless of the individual's educational level or interest. There is nothing wrong with training in craft skills, but disabled people want the opportunity to follow their vocational interests and to have access to the highest-paying jobs.

Systemic barriers in society also present significant obstacles to securing employment. These barriers include inaccessible public transportation, offices with stairs, office equipment at the wrong height, and lack of TDDs. Job positions which require ongoing expenses, such as sign language interpretation for a deaf employee, are even harder to obtain.

Finding employment is among the greatest challenges for disabled women globally. Those who find employment are often ghettoized in the lowest-paying jobs—for instance, they may work as street vendors selling fruit or administrative clerks. Because disabled people have difficulty finding employment, many disabled persons' organizations in the developing world are starting their own businesses. In Soweto, South Africa, disabled people started the Self-Help Factory, which specializes in electronics, because it was impossible to get accessible transportation to mainstream employment. In Trinidad and Tobago, the Disabled Women's Network is starting several businesses and training its members for the jobs.

Violence against Disabled Women

Many disabled women live in situations characterized by a high degree of economic and social dependency, whether they live with relatives or in an institutional setting where services are provided by paid caregivers. Unfortunately, their lack of power leaves them more vulnerable than usual to violence.

Common forms of abuse encountered by women with disabilities can include: "… criminal acts such as assault and sexual assault or negligence (not washing, feeding or toileting an individual); human rights violations (such as sexual harassment); verbal taunting; degrading, humiliating behavior; rough handling; or isolation through silence. Abuse can take place once, or it can happen on an on-going basis."[7]

Some disabled women require assistance with many of the activities of daily living. Because more people have access to the intimate aspects of their daily lives, either in their familial homes or in the institutions where they reside, these women are more vulnerable to assault. Considering the isolation and anonymity of women with disabilities in the community, the potential for both emotional and physical abuse is high. It has been estimated that having a disability doubles an individual's likelihood of being assaulted. Few statistics exist to substantiate the issue of abuse of women with disabilities in developing countries, but Canadian figures speak boldly about the magnitude of the violence. In a 1989 survey of women with disabilities, 40 percent of the women had been raped, abused, or assaulted; 64 percent had been verbally abused. Girls with disabilities have even less chance of escaping violence. Women with multiple disabilities are multiply abused,[8] and moreover, women with disabilities have little access to services for victims of violence. There is little to indicate that the situation for women with disabilities has changed in Canada since 1989, or is any better in developing countries.

Consider the circumstances: Disabled women are often trapped in the home with their abusers, and women's crisis services tend to be both attitudinally and architecturally inaccessible. In many developing countries, there are no shelters for battered women at all. Women with disabilities are also likely to have fewer people to turn to for help and fewer resources to create services to help escape or recover from violence.

While disabled women in developed and developing countries confront abuse daily, this problem has received scant attention from policy makers and service providers, despite pressure to confront the problem from disabled feminists in developed countries.

Seen as Non-Sexual

Because society often views women with disabilities as asexual, many do not receive appropriate sex education from their parents. It is assumed that disabled women will not attract men because they are undesirable. Disabled survivors of assault report that no one believed that they had been assaulted. The typical response to their claims was a callous, "Who would want to rape a disabled woman?"

Women with disabilities are also discouraged from marrying by their families and communities. In some countries, families reinforce society's view of disabled persons as undesirable by hiding disabled girls in their homes. They believe that having a disabled family member could ruin the marriage opportunities for the whole family.

Women everywhere feel pressure to conform to the perfect body-beautiful images with which they are bombarded. Those pressures are magnified for women with disabilities. As a result, women with disabilities experience low self-esteem and a sense that they are unattractive. Society's image of disability, and the woman's own ideas about her body, lead to a self-defeating circle of misconceptions. The consequences of this mythology are devastating. Lack of information has resulted in sexual abuse—sometimes because the woman doesn't know she has the right to say "no"—unwanted pregnancies and sexually transmitted diseases. The concerns of women with disabilities are ignored when services are created to improve sex education and reproductive health, provide child care, and offer services such as rape crisis centres.

Violence in our Communities

Societies the world over do not value women, and they especially do not value women with disabilities. This has led to a range of violent acts against women. In many developing countries, women with disabilities are harassed when they appear in public. This harassment can vary from name-calling to physical attack. Many women with disabilities have been considered to be outcasts because their disability cannot be cured, or have been treated as specimens in teaching hospitals. The message in many cultures is clear: Disabled women should not be visible—in the street, in jobs around their communities, or even in their homes.

During times of war, the obstacles to survival are greatly increased for people with disabilities. Disabled people are often left behind when their fellow citizens are fleeing war zones. Disabled refugees are not always welcome. Because women are often considered the spoils of war and subjected to rape and other degradations, women with disabilities are even more vulnerable to this kind of assault.

Finally, genital mutilation—or female circumcision, as it is sometimes called—affects some 75 million women. While the highest incidence of genital mutilation occurs in Africa and the Middle East, cases have been reported in Australia, Brazil, Pakistan, England, and Russia. These practices are sanctioned by a variety of religions using a range of justifications such as encouraging cleanliness, preventing promiscuity, ensuring female virginity at marriage, and preventing women from finding sex pleasurable. These procedures often have a disabling affect upon women, resulting in physical illness and permanent physical or mental disability.

Genital mutilation has much in common with many other forms of women's oppression. Like the involuntary sterilization of mentally disabled women, which still occurs in parts of the developed world, genital mutilation is an example of how little control women exercise over their own bodies.

Conclusion

Globally, women with disabilities are continuing to organize to promote improvements in their economic and social status. They have worked within the disability movement and the women's movement to demand room for themselves and their issues. They started their own groups and committees in order to focus on their own concerns.

Today, they are much more aware of the extra barriers faced by women with disabilities. They are working at the community level to make a difference for women. In many countries, disabled women are coming together for the first time to discuss problems and to strategize for change. They are working with the disability movement and women's organizations to remove the barriers to their full participation in society. Around the world, they are making connections, working together, learning from each other, and supporting each other in their efforts to take their place within their societies and communities and homes—a place where women with disabilities have as many choices and opportunities as everyone else.

Notes

1. The historical information provided in this essay is based on research presented in Driedger, Diane, "Discovering Disabled Women's History," in *The More We Get Together: Women and Disability*, Houston Stewart, Beth Percival and Elizabeth R. Epperley, eds. (Charlottetown, Canada: Gynergy Books, 1992), pp. 81–93. Some of this research was also published in: *Resources for Feminist Research/ Documentation sur la recherche feministe* (Vol. 20, Nos. 1 & 2, Spring/Summer 1991); and, with April D'Aubin, in *Canadian Women's Studies* (Vol. 12, No. 1, Fall 1991); *Match News* (Spring 1991); *Women's Education des femmes* (Vol. 8, No. 3/4, Winter 1991); and *Healthsharing* (Winter/Spring 1992).

2. Boldt, E. Catherine, "We Want Access *Now!*" in *Across Borders: Women with Disabilities Working Together*, Diane Driedger, Irene Feika, and Eileen Girón Batres, eds. (Charlottetown: Gynergy Books, 1996), pp. 150–160.

3. *Uganda Disabled Women's Association Newsletter*, Jan/ Feb 1995, p. 7.

4. Shah, Dr. Fatima, "The Blind Woman and Her Family and Participation in the Community (Rural)," in *Women, Development and Disability*, Ann Gajersld-Cauley (ed.), (Winnipeg, Canada: Coalition of Provincial Organizations of the Handicapped, 1989), p. 20.

5. Fricke, Yutta, "International Year for Literacy: Education for All?" *Vox Nostral* (1990), p. 6.

6. Rajah, Zohra, "Thoughts on Women and Disability," *Vox Nostral* (1989), p. 10.

7. McPherson, Cathy, *Responding to the Abuse of People with Disabilities* (Toronto, Canada: Advocacy Resource Centre for the Handicapped, 1990), p. 1.

8. Ridington, Jillian, *Beating the "Odds": Violence and Women with Disabilities* (Vancouver: DAWN Canada, 1989), p. 1.

Reformulating the Feminist Perspective: Giving Voice to Women with Disabilities

Neita Kay Israelite and Karen Swartz

This essay focuses on women with disabilities, a significant and growing segment of Canadian society. According to Statistics Canada (2001), 3.6 million Canadians—12.4% of the population—have disabilities, and more than 50% of them are women. The rate of disability increases with age. Of children from birth to age 14, 3.3% have a disability; amongst working age adults aged 15 to 64, 9.9% have a disability. This figure rises to 40.5% for Canadians over the age of 65, and more than 50% for those over the age of 75 (Government of Canada, 2002). With more people living longer, and the tendency of women to outlive men, we can expect the number of disabled women to continue to grow.

Persons with disabilities demonstrate relatively high rates of unemployment and low rates of work-related earnings in comparison to those without disabilities. Not surprisingly, women with disabilities have even higher rates of unemployment and lower earnings than their male counterparts (Bunch and Crawford, 1998; Fawcett, 1996). Women with disabilities in Ontario demonstrate exceptionally low rates of workforce participation, and nearly one-third live in poverty.

Despite the growing number of women with disabilities and the challenges they face, disabled women constitute a group that is typically marginalized by the mainstream feminist movement (as well as the masculinist disability movement). As Barbara Cassidy, Robina Lord, and Nancy Mandell point out (1998), feminist analyses of women's oppression tend to take white middle-class women as the norm. Those who differ from this norm with regard to their physical, sensory, or mental status— i.e., women with disabilities—as well as those who differ with regard to factors such as race, class, or ethnicity, are often "left out without anyone noticing they are absent" (Cassidy, Lord, and Mandell, 1998, p. 33).

Our essay begins with an overview of the two major models of disability: the medical model and the social model. Next, we review feminist debates on two critical concerns regarding the social model: (1) its exclusion of the subjective experience of people with disabilities, and (2) its exclusion of discourses on the body and the reality of impairment. Finally, we take up critiques of mainstream feminism by feminist disability theorists.

Throughout this essay, we use personal accounts of women with disabilities to illuminate critical aspects of our discussion. Most of the narratives were collected by second author Karen Swartz (2003) in her participatory qualitative research study of the life transitions of university women with disabilities. These accounts are augmented by narratives of women and girls with disabilities gathered by first author Neita Israelite and her colleagues in several qualitative research projects (Israelite, 2003; Israelite, Karambatsos, Pullan, and Symanzik, 2000; Israelite, Swartz, Huynh, and Tocco, 2004.

The disability field is currently split regarding the use of "disability-first" versus "person-first" terminology (Marks, 1999). Disability-first (i.e., disabled women) is preferred by some women as it acknowledges the community and culture of disabled people and the primacy of disability in their lives; person-first (i.e., women with disabilities) is preferred by other women as it acknowledges the primacy of their personhood. We use both terms in recognition of both points of view.

Models of Disability

Two major theoretical positions inform attitudes and beliefs about disability: the traditional medical model, and the social model.

The Medical Model

The medical model assumes that differences from the norm in terms of physical, sensory, or mental capabilities produce a defective member of society. This model holds that any difficulties people with disabilities experience are due to problems within the individual, and not because of environmental, societal, physical, or attitudinal barriers within the larger society. For instance, it is assumed that women with physical disabilities will have problems with public transit because they cannot climb stairs, that women who are deaf will have parenting problems because they cannot hear their children's voices, and that women with visual impairments will have problems with employment because they cannot read work manuals.

A critical dimension of the medical model is the notion of power. Considering disability as a defect within the individual allows those who are not disabled to take charge. This gives rise to a patriarchal-like set of dynamics in which power is held by, and transferred through, nondisabled people, who are often doctors, allied health professionals, clinicians, or educators. Their professional dominance has led to the medicalization of disability—the extension of the power and influence of medicine such that it "dominates the daily lives and experiences of many disabled people" (French and Swain, 2001, p. 738). One byproduct of this form of social control is labelling, a "medical discourse of diagnosis of impairment" (Swain and Cameron, 1999, p. 77), in which the impairment, nature of the remediation, or the individual's assistive devices become a description of her identity. In a study of attitudes toward university students with disabilities (Israelite et al., 2000), a disabled woman complained about nondisabled peers who identify people with disabilities in terms of their assistive devices:

> One of the things that I consistently state when I speak in public is that I am not my machine .... And I'm sure it can be said ... whether that machine happens to be a computer or a wheelchair or a hearing aid. If you can't see the person, then you haven't seen me.

Some disabled people internalize medicalized identities to such an extent that they even refer to themselves in terms of a medical definition rather than "an affirming self-definition" (Marks, 1999, p. 69). In interviews with hard-of-hearing high school students (Israelite, 2003), one young woman with congenital (from birth) hearing loss called herself a "hearing aid" student; another with recently acquired loss said, "Now I am a 'hearing impaired.'"

The Social Model

In contrast to the medical model, the social model views disability as a social identity. It holds that the "problem" of disability is inherent not to the individual, but rather to the social structure. In social model theory, the following distinction is made between impairment and disability:

> Impairment is the functional limitation within the individual caused by physical, mental, or sensory impairment. Disability is the loss or limitation of opportunities to take part in the normal life of a community on an equal level with others due to physical and social barriers. (Barnes, 1991, p. 2)

Therefore, the cause of disability is not impairment per se, but society's failure to provide appropriate services and to adequately ensure that the needs of people with disabilities are fully taken into account. Disability, from this perspective, is constructed as all the things that impose restrictions on people with disabilities, such as individual prejudice, institutional discrimination, inequitable legislation, and restrictive school and work environments. Participants in a study of school-to-work transitions (Israelite et al., 2004) were disabled by a range of restrictions in the workplace. For instance, when a woman with a physical impairment approached a potential place of employment for a job application, she discovered that the human resources building was not wheelchair accessible.

> I went into the human resources building to pick up an application and I couldn't get in because I got stuck. I had to go all the way around to the back and come through, and I just knew that it didn't feel right. If you can't get into the human resources building to get an application, you know, it already discourages you by thinking, "Why would they want me when they wouldn't even let me in?"

Another woman in the study felt that prospective employers seriously underestimated the abilities of disabled people:

> They think, they assume, the job is too big for you. They underestimate you. And they have no faith in you or confidence. And you tell them you can do it successfully ... But generally they'll tell you, "Oh, you can't do it."

The attitudes this woman describes exemplify some of the taken-for-granted or commonly held beliefs that people without disabilities hold about those with disabilities. In our culture, physical, sensory, and mental impairments are often considered to have far-reaching effects on ability. Although such beliefs may be unconscious, they nevertheless strongly influence behaviour and expectations.

Taken-for-granted beliefs play a large part in widespread assumptions of dysfunction regarding the sexuality of disabled women, such as the myth that they are unfit as sexual partners. The women in Karen Swartz's study (2003, p. 21; 22), for example, said that, as they were growing up, they got the constant message from non-disabled peers that they were undesirable.

> What I found in high school, a lot of times, was when you try to pursue somebody you're interested in, they wouldn't even look at you twice. There was that perception of, "Oh, you have a disability, part of your body is broken, so therefore you're a not sexual being."

Taken-for-granted beliefs also contribute to marginalization, a process that relegates women who "fall out of the scope of what is currently defined as socially acceptable" (Rauscher and McClintock, 1997, p. 198) to the outer margins of economic and social power and the cultural life of a society, leading to their exclusion from a range of social, cultural, and economic experiences that are part of the everyday lives of non-disabled women. One woman in Karen Swartz's (2003, p. 29) study discussed how society's preoccupation with external beauty, exemplified by media portrayals, hampered her self-perceptions and marginalized her with regard to peer interaction.

> The mass media portrays women to be beautiful: "You must be a skinny model; you must be this, that and the other." And I did not fit that model and it was very hard to take. There was that perception of, "You're not attractive you know … I don't want to be seen around with you because my friends are going to reject me."

Since its original conception in Britain more than two decades ago, the social model has had a profound influence on the lives of people with disabilities. At the theoretical level, this model demonstrates "how the previously taken-for-granted, naturalistic category 'disability' is in reality an artificial and exclusionary social construction that penalizes those people who do not conform to mainstream expectations of appearance, behaviour, and/or economic performance" (Tregaskis, 2002, p. 457).

At the personal level, the social model has "liberated individual disabled people from the burden of personal tragedy, the oppression of individual inadequacies" (Morris, 1996, p. 12) by helping them understand that it is an impaired society, not their impaired bodies, that is responsible for the discrimination, marginalization, and exclusion they face.

Feminist Critiques of the Social Model

Although the social model has been beneficial to disabled people in both theory and praxis, it has been criticized

for its failure to address the complexity of factors that shape the production of disability. Some prominent feminist debates deal with the exclusion of the subjective experience of people with disabilities from many social model accounts as well as the exclusion of discussions of the body and the reality of impairment.

Subjective Experience and Social Model Theory

Feminists with disabilities such as Susan Wendell (1996), Jenny Morris (1996), and Carol Thomas (1999) have put forward accounts of disability in which personal narratives play an important role. Given the inequitable power differentials that characterize relations between women with and without disabilities, these women emphasize the necessity of foregrounding the individual experiences of disabled women as a vehicle for understanding their collective oppressions (Tregaskis, 2002). Other writers (e.g., Sheldon, 1999) argue that such analyses are too individualized and prioritize subjective experiences of disability over more theoretical explanations. Our position, however, is in line with Carol Thomas, who points out that "by taking the personal experiences of disabled women as their starting point and writing themselves into their own analyses, disabled feminist writers … are thus building upon well-established practices among feminist writers more generally" (1999, p. 70). Giving voice to the personal narratives of women with disabilities is also an important way of increasing the general public's sense of social responsibility while informing and clarifying social model theory.

The Body, Impairment, and Social Model Theory

Recent critiques of the social model focus on the exclusion of discussions of the body and impairment from many social model accounts. Many feminist disability theorists (e.g., Crow, 1996; French, 1994; Morris, 1991; Thomas,

1999; Wendell, 1996) and some masculinist disability theorists (e.g., Abberley, 1987; Hughes, 1999; Hughes and Paterson, 1997; Paterson and Hughes, 1999) take issue with the social model because it neither connects with the embodied experience nor the pain associated with impairment. Some theorists (e.g., Wendell, 1996; French, 1994) argue that the only way for the social model to move forward is to integrate the experience of impairment—the pain and the real limitations—with the experience of disability. Susan Wendell, who has an acquired physical disability, writes that disabled feminists should be discussing "how to live with the suffering body, with that which cannot be noticed without pain, and that which cannot be celebrated without ambivalence" (1996, p. 179). Wendell's comments took on heightened meaning to us after receiving the following note from a disabled graduate student who we had asked to share her experience of pain for this essay.

I am so sorry that it has taken me so long to get back to you. I have been in bed for the last few weeks as the pain in my back has been so severe I could not get out of bed. I have found it too painful to sit or stand for any length of time, therefore doing what you asked was out of the question.

Sally French, who has a visual impairment, points out that it is her actual lack of visual acuity, and not some barrier created by a sighted society, that prevents her from recognizing people and reading nonverbal cues in social situations (1993).

While I agree with the basic tenets of [the social] model and consider it to be the most important way forward for disabled people, I believe that some of the most profound problems experienced by people with certain impairments are difficult, if not impossible, to solve by social manipulation. (1993, p. 17)

Social model proponents such as Michael Oliver (1996) point out that the original goal of the social model, when it was proposed more than 20 years ago, was to eradicate what they identify as the "true causes" of disability: societal discrimination and prejudice. The fact that these causes still permeate the lives of women with disabilities is exemplified by their reaction to workplace prejudice and discrimination in our study of school-to-work transitions (Israelite et al., 2004, p. 20):

"It gets right to the core of your identity. You begin to question, 'What is my role in this world.'"

"I thought, 'Oh my God, this is what it's like out there. Oh my God, how am I going to find a job?'"

Some disability scholars are calling for an updated version of the social model, one that acknowledges the relevance of bodily experience to the lives of disabled people. They argue that by not incorporating impairment, the social model concedes the body to medicine, thus giving tacit permission for it to be understood in terms of the medical model (Hughes and Paterson, 1997). Bill Hughes and Kevin Paterson (1997) assert that there is a need to wrest control of the impairment discourse from the medical profession and to establish the impaired body as an integral part of what it means to be disabled. This would entail, in part, "tackling the very real repulsion that society feels for the impaired body" (Tregaskis, 2002, p. 464). This repulsion was something that most of the participants in Karen Swartz's (2003, p. 27) study had not only experienced, but also internalized, to a significant extent. One woman explained:

What you stare at in the mirror is not just something that is going to go away. You're not going to wake up from a dream. This is reality.

Impairment theory provides an explanation that, in keeping with the social model, places the responsibility for "the problem of repulsion" on non-disabled people. Claire Tregaskis (2002) explains that, "in reality, it is the non-disabled gaze which creates abnormality, and that actually it is the gaze that is disfigured, not the [disabled] 'other' who is being gazed at" (p. 463). This point is clearly illustrated in the comments of two women in Karen Swartz's (2003, p. 27) study:

> The only time I saw myself as disabled was when … someone said, "Oh what happened to you." [I would reply] "Oh what do you mean what happened to me? Oh yeah. Oh God. Oh you're talking about that."

> [You have to] realize what you are feeling isn't you. It is the images that somebody else has transferred on to you.

Marion Corker (1999) notes that incorporation of impairment theory into the social model could result in the maintenance and reproduction of essentialist distinctions between impaired and non-impaired bodies and disabled and non-disabled individuals. Despite the relevance of this criticism, we agree with theorists who posit that, through the development of a sociology of impairment, the disabled body has the potential to become a site of resistance to societally imposed ideas and practices in an emerging politics of identity (e.g., Giddens, 1991; Hughes and Paterson, 1997). As Carol Gill (2001) has stated:

> By honoring subjectivity and remaining closer to the experience of disabled persons in their research, disability studies scholars cannot escape the realizations that bodies matter. Whether grappling with pain and the unwanted limitations of impairment or reveling in the carnal

expression of cultural aesthetic subversion, the disability experience is undeniably embodied. (p. 369)

Disability Theorists Critique Feminist Theory

Many women with disabilities write that they feel marginalized within the feminist movement. Their experience is that mainstream feminist theories tend to privilege "the functional capabilities and social roles characteristic of 'normal' women" (Kittay, Schriempf, Silvers, and Wendell, 2001, p. viii), often not taking women with disabilities into account. Feminist disability scholars share in the marginalization. Carol Thomas cites the cases of Jenny Morris (1991, 1996) and Susan Wendell (1996), both of whom have acquired disabilities. These scholars were accepted as feminist thinkers and writers until they became disabled; after that, they, too, found themselves marginalized from feminist scholarship.

According to feminist scholars Fine and Asch (1988):

> Women with disabilities traditionally have been ignored not only by those concerned about disability but also by those examining women's experiences. Even the feminist scholars to whom we owe great intellectual and political debts have perpetuated this neglect. The popular view of women with disabilities has been one mixed with repugnance. Perceiving disabled women as childlike, helpless, and victimized, nondisabled women have severed them from the sisterhood in an effort to advance more powerful, competent, and appealing female icons. As one feminist academic said to the non-disabled co-author of this essay: "Why study women with disabilities? They reinforce traditional stereotypes of women being dependent, passive and needy." (p. 3-4)

Several of Karen Swartz's (2003) participants said that, during their childhood, doctors, teachers, counselors, and even some family members encouraged them, through both implicit and explicit messages, to be passive and dependent rather than strong and independent. They were dismayed when they got to university to find that such attitudes still predominated. One woman sought out courses in Women's Studies in the hopes of finding answers to her questions about the oppression of disabled women. She was dismayed to find that even a course on the history of women did not address this issue:

> I won't take a women's history course because it doesn't cover disabled women. You can't tell me that disabled women didn't exist .... I think we need to make professors more aware and almost demand that it get put on the curriculum. I mean if they can study women's issues, gay issues, African/American issues. We are part of society and we deserve to be studied. (p. 37)

Feminist disability scholars agree with this student's assessment of university programs and have proposed ways of infusing disability issues into the postsecondary curriculum and making the experience of disabled women more central to teaching and research in Women's Studies (e.g., Garland-Thomson 2002; Linton, 1997). Rosemary Garland-Thomson (2002) argues for the positioning of feminist disability studies as a field of academic study and the inclusion of feminist disability theory as a major subgenre of feminist theory. Garland-Thomson is but one of many feminist scholars calling for the inclusion of the ability/disability binary as a category of analysis alongside gender, race, age, and social class in feminist analyses of oppression.

The salience of feminist denial of the significance of disability was brought home to us during a graduate class on qualitative research taught by Neita Israelite. Karen Swartz and one of her research participants, a disabled woman of colour, made a presentation on the participatory methodology Karen used in her study. Some class members, who were women of colour and self-stated feminists, questioned the participant relentlessly, not about her perspectives on the research method, but rather about the fact that she had identified disability as her primary category of affiliation. These women insisted that race and gender had to be more important than any physical impairment. They would not accept the participant's explanation that, in her life, she had experienced discrimination primarily because of her disability and never because of her race. Even today, the participant still recalls how unsettling it was for her to be treated so disrespectfully by women she expected to be her sisters. And we still recall this incident because it resonates so vividly with our reading of current feminist scholarship when it comes to disability.

Unlike race and ethnicity, disability is a fluid category. Some women are born with disabilities; others acquire them. Some are disabled for some portion of their lives, others for their whole lives. Virtually all women can expect to become disabled if they live long enough. Within the disability movement, masculinist disability scholars have been too slow to acknowledge the gendered nature of disability. Within the feminist movement, non-disabled feminist scholars have been too slow to acknowledge the importance of the disability to identity construction and feminist analyses of oppression. Sadly, what Marion Blackwell-Stratton, Mary Lou Breslin, Arlean Mayerson, and Susan Bailey stated in 1988 still holds true: "For the disabled feminist, neither the disability movement nor the women's movement fully addresses her concerns" (p. 307).

As Garland-Thomson so aptly states:

> Disability—like gender—is a concept that pervades all aspects of culture: its structuring

institutions, social identities, cultural practices, political positions, historical communities, and the shared human experience of embodiment

.... To understand how disability operates is to understand what it means to be fully human. (2002, p. 4)

References

Abberley, P. (1987). "The Concept of Oppression and the Development of a Social Theory of Disability." *Disability, Handicap and Society*, 2, 5–20.

Barnes, C. (1991). *Disabled People in Britain and Discrimination: A Case for Anti-discrimination Legislation*. London: Hurst.

Blackwell-Stratton, M.; Breslin, M., Mayerson, A., and Bailey, S. (1988). "Smashing Icons: Disabled Women and the Disability and Women's Movements." In M. Fine and A. Asch (Eds.), *Women with Disabilities: Essays in Psychology, Culture and Politics* (pp. 306–332). Philadelphia: Temple University Press.

Bunch, M., & Crawford, C. (1998, June). *Persons with Disabilities: Literature Review of the Factors Affecting Employment and Labor Force Transitions*. Hull: Human Resources Development Canada. Retrieved June 19, 2003 from www.hrdc-drhc.gc.ca/sp-ps/arb-dgra/publications/research/disability.shtml.

Cassidy, B., Lord, R., and Mandell, N. (1998). "Silenced and Forgotten Women: Race, Poverty and Disability." In N. Mandell (Ed.), *Feminist Issues: Race, Class and Sexuality* (2nd ed.) (pp. 27–54). Toronto: Prentice-Hall.

Corker, M. (1999). "Differences, Conflations, and Foundations. The Limits to "Accurate" Representation of Disabled People's Experience?" *Disability and Society*, 14, 627–642.

Crow, L. (1996). "Including All of Our Lives: Renewing the Social Model of Disability." In J. Morris (Ed.), *Encounters with Strangers: Feminism and Disability* (pp. 206–226). London: Women's Press.

Fawcett, G. (1996). *Living with Disability in Canada: An Economic Portrait*. Hull: Office for Disability Issues, Human Resources Development Canada.

French, S. (1993). "Disability, Impairment, or Something in Between." In J. Swain, V. Finkelstein, S. French, & M. Oliver (Eds.), *Disabling Barriers, Enabling Environments*. Buckingham: Open University Press.

French, S. (1994). *On Equal Terms: Working with Disabled People*. Oxford: Butterworth-Heinemann.

French, S., and Swain, J. (2001). "The Relationship between Disabled People and Health and Welfare Professionals." In G. Albrecht, K. Seelman, and M. Bury (Eds.), *Handbook of Disability Studies* (pp. 734–753). Thousand Oaks: Sage.

Garland-Thomson, R. (2002). "Integrating Disability Theory, Transforming Feminist Theory." *Feminist Disability Studies* [Special issue] [Electronic version]. *NWSA Journal*, 14 (3), 1–32.

Giddens, A. (1991). *Modernity and Self-Identity: Self and Society in the Late Modern Age*. Oxford: Polity Press.

Gill, C. (2001). "Divided Understandings: The Social Experience of Disability." In G. Albrecht, K. Seelman, and M. Bury (Eds.), *Handbook of Disability Studies* (pp. 351–372). Thousand Oaks: Sage.

Government of Canada (2002). "Advancing the Inclusion of Persons with Disabilities." Hull: Human Resources Development Canada. Retrieved March 12, 2004, from www.hrdc-drhc.gc.ca/bcph-odi.

Hughes, B. (1999). "The Construction of Impairment: Modernity and the Aesthetic of Oppression." *Disability and Society*, 14, 155–172.

Hughes, B., and Paterson, K. (1997). "The Social Model of Disability and the Disappearing Body: Towards a Sociology of Impairment." *Disability & Society*, 12, 325–340.

Israelite, N. (2003). "Identity Construction of Hard-of-Hearing Adolescents." Unpublished raw data.

Israelite, N., Karambatsos, S., Pullan, J., and Symanzik, A. (2000, June). "Attitudes of University Students toward Students with Disabilities." Paper presented at the annual meeting of the Society for Disability Studies, Chicago, IL.

Israelite, N., Swartz, K., Huynh, J., and Tocco, A. (2004). "Postsecondary Students and Graduates with Disabilities: The School-to-Work Transition." Forthcoming.

Kittay, E., Schriempf, A., Silvers, A., and Wendell, S. (2001). "Introduction." *Feminism and Disability* [Special issue] [Electronic version]. *Hypatia*, 16 (4), vii–xii.

Linton, S. (1997). "Claiming Disability: Knowledge and Identity." New York: New York University Press, p. 94.

Marks, D. (1999). *Disability: Controversial Debates and Conversations*. London: Routledge.

Morris, J. (1991). *Pride against Prejudice: Transforming Attitudes to Disability*. London: Women's Press.

Morris, J. (1996). "Introduction." In J. Morris (Ed.), *Encounters with Strangers: Feminism and Disability* (pp. 1–16). London: The Women's Press Ltd.

Oliver, M. (1996). *Understanding Disability: From Theory to Practice*. New York: St. Martin's Press.

Paterson, K., and Hughes, B. (1999). "Disability Studies and Phenomenology: The Carnal Politics of Everyday Life." *Disability and Society*, 14, 597–610.

Rauscher, L., and McClintock, J. (1997). "Ableism Curriculum Design." In M. Adams, L.A. Bell, and Griffen, P. (Eds.), *Teaching for Diversity and Social Justice* (pp. 198–231). New York: Routledge.

Sheldon, A. (1999). "Personal and Perplexing: Feminist Disability Politics Evaluated." *Disability and Society*, 14, 643–657.

Swain, J. and Cameron, C. (1999). "Unless Otherwise Stated: Discourses of Labeling and Coming Out." In M. Corker and S. French (Eds.), *Disability Discourse* (pp. 68–78). Buckingham: Open University Press.

Swartz, K. (2003). "Life Transitions of Student with Disabilities Revisited: A Feminist Approach." Unpublished manuscript. York University, Toronto, Canada.

Thomas, C. (1999). *Female Forms: Experiencing and Understanding Disability*. Buckingham: Open University Press.

Tregaskis, C. (2002). "Social Model Theory: The Story so far." *Disability and Society*, 17, 457–470.

Wendell, S. (1996). *The Rejected Body: Feminist Philosophical Reflections on Disability*. New York: Routledge.

Identity, Community, and Same-Sex Marriage

Joanne Cohen

Who are we and where are we headed as twenty-first century queer Jews? I am anything but certain. In this fragmentary political memoir, I wish to explore this uncertainty and demonstrate the importance of working with our memories of alienation and remembering our experiences of estrangement. I hope this work might somehow reflect and inform diverse efforts to integrate queer and Jewish identities, to work creatively with personal and political history, and to build enduring, warm, vibrant, and viable communities and relationships. In particular, I'd like to raise some disquieting questions and practical/political concerns posed by endorsing same-sex unions (as affirmed by the CCAR, the Central Conference of American Rabbis) as a contemporary model for queer Jewish community development and identity integration. I argue against exclusively assimilationist or isolationist strategies in advocating diverse queer participation and ongoing struggle in mainstream Jewish life.

I hope this essay will stimulate intelligent discussion, shatter complacency in some quarters, and pointedly question the informal positive consensus that has developed around same-sex union ceremonies and the marriage model [....]

*****

Like many queer Jews, I have struggled, not altogether unsuccessfully, with issues of queer and Jewish identity and community, ethics, power, equality, and resistance in virtually every aspect of my life for as long as I can remember. From the time I was a precocious Hebrew dayschool tomboy wearing blue jeans under my school uniform skirt and successfully arguing with my rabbi teachers, I have yearned for equal and equitable participation in Jewish and secular life.

In our perpetual seats in our small town Orthodox synagogue, I would regularly amaze my mother at my ability to find our place, to the word, in the Hebrew prayers the moment we walked in, without a page number being announced. I wish I could find my place as easily now in my own queer Jewish identity, relationships, and community, but I can't, and not for lack of trying.

I am viewed publicly as an accomplished adult, who helped build an internet community of diverse queer Jewish women, has appeared on television, spoken publicly, and published articles on queer Jewish identity. I am active, respected, and openly queer in a large mainstream Conservative synagogue, close to my family, and have demonstrated cultural literacy and competence in diverse social, academic, and professional settings. Despite this, I am personally, practically, philosophically, and politically about as far as one could get from being a role model or poster-child for completely proud, positive, enduringly integrated queer Jewish identity. [...]

*****

I have begun to accept that whatever our compensatory accomplishments as individuals, no single person's skills and experience could possibly achieve a permanent and positive integration of queer Jewish identity, however fervently many of us may have tried. Even the couple or family unit is an insufficient base for identity formation, without a framework of culture, history, and community. None of us can possibly do this alone, nor should we try to do so in isolation, either as individuals, or as queer Jews in insular communities.

To affirm proud queer and Jewish marginal identities in an historical and cultural context of genocide, anti-semitism, homophobia, and anti-religious secularism requires that we repeatedly deal with internal and external moments of conflict, oppression, doubt, resistance, and self-loathing. My personal and academic experiences would suggest that our struggles with alienation, identity integration, and community formation are likely to be inherently ongoing. Every historic triumph and personal success should be viewed provisionally, requiring extensive rethinking as new developments and understandings emerge. The imperfect personal and communal means available may sometimes be insufficient for us to form enduringly integrated queer Jewish identities, relationships, and communities. Perhaps provisional, imperfect, and somewhat compartmentalized moments of integrated identity may be more reasonable goals.

*****

Once we join queer or Jewish communities to develop our identities, we may experience unanticipated and powerful conflicts inside and outside ourselves. We may experience moments of integration and later disappointment when we realize that, despite our fervent hopes, no solution is likely to be permanent or perfect. Our work to overcome alienation and integrate our queer Jewish identities will likely never be complete. We may need to compromise on some of our most ideal hopes, to prevent naïve setbacks we can ill afford, and recognize that no solution and no community is likely to serve all our needs all the time.

*****

Like many single people, I have often felt alienated in queer and Jewish communal settings that overwhelmingly and simplistically celebrate monogamy and the family, both queer and conventional. I have experienced the pleasures of home, family, shared culture, and holiday celebrations with Jewish lovers, only to experience the losses of those relationships so profoundly that it became too painful to participate in queer or Jewish communal life for a time. I have looked around at my surrounding queer and Jewish communities and wondered whether I could really identify with these people who seem both reassuringly familiar and disconcertingly different, and who sometimes demonstrate the negatively stereotyped behaviors I have sometimes feared and disliked in myself. I have found the complacent sanctimony of some Jewish religious communities and the apparently dissolute nihilism of some queer settings less than fulfilling. At times I have been perplexed by my own sexuality and gender expression—as both sacrament and sacrilege it is sometimes haunting and disturbing at its most raw and vulnerable. As a postmodern intellectual and queer feminist, I have sometimes felt completely absurd as I tried to fit my experience into various Jewish, feminist, or queer cultural models and rituals. And, as a 30-

something single person facing a widely acknowledged postmodern decline of public life, I am still seeking admirable models of successful queer Jewish aging.

I believe we need to explore, document, and share our moments of disillusionment, doubt, conflict, confusion, loneliness, and alienation as much as our celebratory moments if we're going to be honest about our needs, experiences, and our real challenges as queer Jews. And yes, the reality of our break-ups needs to be considered whenever we think about forming healthy queer Jewish communities and identities.

In writing this piece, I learned that my own reluctance, anguish, and struggles to confront, understand, and share my imperfect experiences are symptomatic of the problems many of us face. We try to reconcile histories of persecution, stigmatized and stereotyped identities as queers and Jews, self-hatred and pride, pain, conflict, ambivalence, and personal experiences of pain, loss, and trauma.

These *personal* struggles as a single queer Jew helped me remember old lessons from political theory and my early Jewish education, paradoxically demonstrating how much our *community* development may depend on each of us remembering and sharing our painful experiences of estrangement and alienation. The Jewish tradition teaches us to befriend and remember the stranger, because we were strangers in the land of Egypt (Exodus 23:9, Deuteronomy 10:19). This fundamental awareness of the pain of alienation, estrangement, and exile underlies many valuable Jewish and secular ethical teachings on identity and community obligation, inspiring diverse charitable works, acts of decency, and struggles against oppression. Our ability to befriend and empathize with others, especially those who are socially distant from us, may be the very foundation for ethical community development.

In short, Blanche Dubois was right. From the time we were Israelite strangers in Egypt, and throughout our frequently precarious historical experiences as queers and as Jews, our very survival has often depended on the "kindness of strangers." Because we know what it means to be different, displaced, vilified, struggling, violated, and oppressed, we are expected to learn empathy, and not to impose needless suffering on others. Even when we rejoice at our personal and communal successes, we are taught to remember those who are different, alone, and struggling, and to demonstrate friendship, hospitality, decency, and solidarity. The Exodus from Egypt marks not only the historical beginning of ethical Jewish identity and nationhood, but is also a liberatory lesson recalled daily in Jewish religious practice.

Many of us have been estranged and vilified as queers within our own families and Jewish communities, and have faced anti-semitism in secular contexts. By remembering estrangement in our personal and community experiences, both Jewish and secular, we might learn to be kinder, to ourselves and each other, and to build more livable communities, within and beyond our immediate personal relationship networks.

If we remind the mainstream Jewish community of this key teaching, we might assert a powerful religious and ethical claim for better treatment of queers and all of us who are oppressed in our communities. Far too many contemporary Jewish communities often overemphasize material prosperity and private family relationships, at the expense of recalling our origins as an ethical community. As well, as Jews in secular queer communities, we might proudly reclaim our Jewish origins and inform our secular activism by remembering alienation.

When the Central Conference of American Rabbis (CCAR) of the US Reform movement announced its willingness to perform and recognize Jewish same-sex union ceremonies, many of my friends rejoiced. They believed this to be a clear signal that at long last, queer Jews were beginning to be more fully accepted in Jewish life. Although this is an important symbolic historical milestone, I tend to regard this development far more cautiously.

The challenges of integrating our queer and Jewish identities are so great, and our historic pain of exclusion is so deep, it would not be surprising for us to leap at each new theory or cultural development, hoping for it to resolve our long-standing fragmentation. While it would be a welcome respite from our usual anxieties, failing to consider the implications of the CCAR decision could lead us to dangerously alienating disappointments that we can ill afford. We need to be realistic and inclusive of our diversity as queer Jews.

There are a number of theological and practical limitations posed by CCAR's decision to allow same-sex unions, however much it presents a valuable statement of acceptance and affirmation of Jewish same-sex relationships. First, from a traditional Jewish perspective, which includes many queer Jews and their families and communities, the CCAR decision is not based in religious law (halacha), and would not be regarded as theologically valid religious practice, however well intentioned.

Second, the CCAR decision has been affirmed even in the absence of correlative civil recognition of these ceremonies. Currently, most civil authorities legally recognize traditional religious marriage ceremonies across denominations. Such would not be the case with a same-sex ceremony, where civil recognition of same-sex marriage does not yet exist in most jurisdictions. Thus, the CCAR ceremony would lack secular legal validity.

Third, even if one were to assume that these unions were valid in religious and civil law, given the realities of serial monogamy and relationship break ups in both heterosexual and same-sex Jewish relationships, would it not have been prudent to develop a Jewish same-sex divorce ceremony at the same time? Note that the traditional Jewish wedding includes the reading of the ketubah, or marriage contract, which includes a statement of the parties' respective responsibilities, should the relationship dissolve. Could the absence of a same-sex Jewish divorce ceremony create a queer religious status similar to that of agunot, Jewish women who have obtained civil, but not religious, divorces from their

husbands? Most contracts include conditions for their dissolution. The CCAR ceremony may require further development to avoid imposing unintentional religious legal disabilities on queer Jewish couples.

Fourth, however creative and well intentioned CCAR's development of a same-sex union ceremony, it would be helpful to learn how CCAR explains this innovation in relation to the historic prohibitions of Jewish same-sex marriages and lesbianism implied by Leviticus 18:3. Traditional Jewish authorities interpreted this biblical passage, which forbids following the practices of the land of Egypt, to prohibit not only lesbian sexuality, but also same-sex marriages.[1] How has CCAR acknowledged its departure from these traditional religious and cultural prohibitions?

Fifth, considering the theological innovation involved in celebrating same-sex relationships, it would be helpful for CCAR to respond more fully to traditional biblical prohibitions of male homosexual behavior (Leviticus 18:22, 20:13), as well as prohibitions of taking on appurtenances of the opposite sex (Deuteronomy 22:5). To have greater influence across Jewish denominations, and to avoid worsening doctrinal schisms (including within the Reform movement), it would be helpful for CCAR to provide some coherent theological definition of its same-sex union ceremony in relation to traditional Jewish practice.

What are the religious and legal assumptions of dependence and economic support underlying the CCAR decision? My suspicion is that CCAR's development of the same-sex union ceremony was well intentioned as a courageous symbolic statement and affirmative service to Jewish same-sex couples seeking religious and cultural recognition of their relationships, but that many of the practical and religious implications require further consideration.

As well, there are pressing practical issues to consider when we imagine diverse queer Jews seeking to affirm their relationships through a CCAR ceremony. Whether we are secular, of other liberal denominations, or traditional Jews, laypeople and rabbis alike cannot easily change their enduring theological commitments to accommodate contemporary political developments. Many queer Jews would be unable to affiliate with the Reform movement, even temporarily, to gain access to a same-sex union ceremony. Those of us who are single or in non-monogamous or interfaith partnerships would not be included in a CCAR ceremony. Given the anticipated controversy, it would not be surprising for some Reform rabbis to be reluctant to officiate at the unions of couples who are not temple members or who are unable to affirm a commitment to Reform theology and practice. Thus, many queer Jews would not be easily served by this innovation.

As has already occurred in the mainstream Reform community's backlash against the CCAR decision, some Reform and feminist rabbis have already refused to officiate at same-sex union ceremonies for anyone, anticipating congregational and community resistance. Note that the CCAR decision is not a binding directive on Reform rabbis, but is a theological statement affirming the legitimacy of these ceremonies. Regardless of its theological status, the real practical decisions on allowing same-sex unions would likely be made locally by senior rabbis, synagogue boards, and ritual committees who are often socially and religiously conservative. Thus, due to career and political considerations, many well-intentioned Reform rabbis may be unable to officiate at these ceremonies, even for queer Reform couples who are members of their congregations.

Considering general Jewish and queer political interests, it might be helpful to ensure that the pioneering couples for whom these ceremonies would be performed have likely prospects of enduring relationships. Imagine the negative repercussions if a happy couple were to break up a year or two later after the strain brought by their unanticipated prominence and celebrity in the congregation and wider community. Thus, willing Reform rabbis might be especially selective about choosing "suitable" couples for whom they would be willing to perform same-sex unions, perhaps requiring years of personal acquaintance and "pre-marital" classes and counseling. It will likely be quite some time before any queer Jewish couple breaks a glass under a *huppa*, with a rabbi officiating, at least in Canada.

Contemporary Canadian legal developments might also make couples reconsider organizing their relationships on the marriage model. Currently, cohabiting same-sex partners are deemed legally equivalent to common-law spouses, with the requisite requirement to divide jointly held property and negotiate income-equalization payments through legal processes on the dissolution of the relationship. Cohabiting same-sex partners are required to report their status on tax returns, census forms, and applications for social benefits. These developments could have an ironic chilling effect on our ability to form and dissolve diverse same-sex relationships freely, particularly if there are economic disparities between the partners. As well, law has perverse effects, often punishing the very marginal communities it seeks to protect. Given a history of disproportionate policing and monitoring of queers and social activists, many of us are concerned about registering our partnerships with government agencies who have historically persecuted us or that have troubling histories of misusing personal information. Informal blacklisting and inappropriate disclosure are not unreasonable concerns.

Far from being an easy answer to our problems of exclusion as queer Jews, the CCAR decision presents many practical issues needing further consideration. Our initial jubilation rapidly leads to the realization that this innovation far from resolves our fragmentation as queer Jews. The CCAR decision would not include traditional Jews, those in interfaith partnerships, those in nonmonogamous relationships, and those who are uncoupled. Even same-sex Reform couples could encounter alienating difficulties in seeking to affirm their relationships. Rather than "widening the parameters of queer Jewish belonging," as some have argued, the practical implications could tragically raise and then deny expectations, ironically narrowing opportunities for inclusion.

The prospect of religious same-sex unions makes me uneasy, much as I would want to support diverse relationship options. I am troubled by attempts to legitimize our relationships in a religious framework that has historically vilified queer sexuality and gender-bending behavior, limiting sexuality to monogamous and mainly procreative heterosexual marriage and property relationships. While pioneering theologians have affirmed ethical same-sex sexuality, many queer Jews cannot help but remain conflicted by the vehement disapproval of our sexuality and gender expression in the Jewish tradition that makes up a key part of our identities. I suspect many of us engage in a kind of double-minded denial when we want to function sexually, or make uneasy compromises in our own minds, communities, and bedrooms. We need to talk more about this in safe ways that do not assume that those struggling with these issues are foolish dupes of traditional religious thinking, or that the sexual adventurers among us are inherently morally unfit.

As much as I value diversity and choice, I question what values are potentially affirmed by endorsing CCAR's religiously sanctioned model of marital monogamy as a template for queer Jewish relationships. Sanctification implies exclusion—to hallow something is to render other things profane. Might our support for religious same-sex marriage inadvertently imply that those who are ethically nonmonogamous, who date outside our faith, who pursue monogamy outside of "marriage," or who remain uncoupled are inherently less morally worthy? Would we be reasserting a kind of monogamous "missionary position" for politically and religiously legitimate queer Jewish sexuality? Considering the privatizing and alienating effects of family-centered celebrations (queer and straight) in many congregations, how might celebrating an individual couple's relationship necessarily contribute to affirming community values, and

reconnecting with those who are estranged within the community? Recalling our historic exclusion as queers by virtue of our distinctly non-missionary, non-procreative sexuality and non-traditional gender behaviors, and reiterating the value of remembering our own and others' estrangement, I'd suggest that we think carefully before endorsing religiously sanctioned monogamy as a moral ideal for ethical queer Jewish relationships.

While some political compromise, discretion, and respect for our surrounding communities is required for our integration and ethical participation in Jewish life, I would advocate a moderate course between outright assimilationism and outright isolationism. Overemphasizing traditional marriage models and private family ceremonies may lead both queer Jews and mainstream Jewish communities to neglect the needs of those outside these models. Because every new legal recognition of queer rights and coupled status is often accompanied by regressive policing and persecution of less well-protected sexual minorities and queer sites, queer Jews cannot afford to forget our powerful queer antecedents or the strangers among us. Given the lessons of the Holocaust on the irrelevance of assimilation, many of us would find any approach to community building and identity formation that would seem to separate "good queer Jewish sexuality" from "bad queer Jewish sexuality" to be highly questionable.

In the same way that assimilated and parochial Jews alike have contributed to a vibrant Jewish culture, pride in our diverse queer community requires that all of us contribute to advancing wider awareness and acceptance, from closeted middle-class professionals to "in-your-face" sexual libertines and social activists. As queer Jews, we need to celebrate our diverse sexualities and religious beliefs, even when these sexualities and beliefs are troubling, and when we may be disturbed by elements of Jewish religious culture, by the apparent nihilism of some queer settings, or by the overwhelming tendency in both settings to privilege personal relationships above the principle of community.

As diverse queer Jews, our challenges are too complex to be resolved by a single denomination, religious ceremony, or relationship model. One of the greatest hurdles preventing us from taking our places in diverse mainstream Jewish communities is a rightful fear of homophobia. Traditional Jewish social prohibitions of homosexuality and non-traditional gender expression continue to be invoked even by non-observant Jewish families and communities, because these challenge enduring Jewish cultural values emphasizing marriage, family, children, cultural transmission, and continuity. The social sanctions we face may range from raised eyebrows to casual social ostracism to being utterly disowned by one's family and community. Aside from other factors encouraging secular assimilation, this *"naches* machine" of the mainstream Jewish community (which seeks gratification through its children's marriages, offspring, and professional attainments) has presented negative pressures leading many Jews to leave Judaism, a cultural loss the community can no longer afford.

Gradually, the mainstream Jewish community has begun to learn about the needless trauma and fragmentation caused by obstinately enforcing traditional Jewish values of heterosexuality, marital monogamy, and procreation at all costs. The attendant informal social controls are powerful, enduring, and potentially devastating. In the last five years, I have informally counselled two young queer university students who were coming out in non-observant Jewish middle-class families. As I once was, they were being threatened with forced psychotherapy and economic dislocation by their well-meaning Jewish parents who were working with the best of anguished intentions. Thankfully, there were community resources, including a queer Jewish coming-out group, to which I could direct my young friends for support. However much institutional recognition may improve, serious risks still remain for queer youth in many mainstream communities.

Every secular and religious struggle queer people have undertaken, with the attendant media coverage, has improved awareness, as has coming out in diverse contexts. It is no longer unusual to hear of Jewish coming-out groups, Jewish Parents and Friends of Lesbians and Gays, or Jewish AIDS committees meeting at mainstream synagogues and Jewish community centers. One increasingly sees same-sex couples attending mainstream Jewish weddings, funerals, and other family functions. Even in Orthodox settings, one Jewish ex-lover and I were informally acknowledged as a couple by family, friends, and community members, even though no words to that effect were explicitly spoken.

The rise of queer Jewish congregations across North America, and their gradual acceptance, despite vehement resistance, in local and international Jewish federations has been extremely important in fostering greater awareness of our needs as queer Jews. One also cannot underestimate the importance of arts, literature, liturgy, cultural events, and local and virtual communities reflecting our life interests and providing information, social support, and networking opportunities for many gay and lesbian Jews, secular to religious.

Despite the importance of gay and lesbian congregations, I believe it's now time for those of us who can to stop working in isolation and to come out in our mainstream Jewish communities, preferably with support networks in place. For too long, the mainstream Jewish community has been able to ignore our needs through outright homophobia or by capitalizing on our retreat to insular queer Jewish communities. Despite the personal challenges, we need to return and claim our rightful places in our mainstream communities, as committed Jews and visible queers who are respectful but no longer self-annihilating through absence or assimilation. This is especially important in a time when mainstream Jewish identities and communities have never been more fragile and fragmented. Rather than justifiably criticizing homophobia from outside the mainstream, we might best achieve recognition by showing the courage to become involved and share some communal responsibilities. In joining, but not assimilating, we might powerfully demonstrate that those of us who are single, queer, or in alternative families may have as great a need for and commitment to Jewish community and cultural continuity as those in traditional families.

I took my own advice to heart, after years of involvement in a traditional alternative synagogue, and affiliated with one of North America's largest and most affluent Conservative congregations. My choice included careful consideration of my theological commitments, political and learning opportunities, my family's needs, proximity to my home, and genuine affection for the congregation. I have been moved by the warmth, respect, and encouragement I have received from most congregants, simply for being myself—a discreet, respectful, but openly queer, articulate, educated, and active contributor to ritual and study. I have support from the rabbinate and lay leadership, and have been asked to help develop anti-homophobia teaching materials. My involvement has provided an unanticipated and deep source of identity and community in an otherwise anonymous city. While being visible brings moments of self-consciousness, I believe more of us should try this, providing we do so sincerely, responsibly, and honestly, in ways consistent with our convictions. As mainstream Jewish communities learn to deal with queer Jews as diverse real people, with lives, families, and moments of mourning and celebration similar to their own, the less likely they may be to oppress us unthinkingly. Our presence makes a difference.

*****

In a time when programmatic progressive, queer, and feminist politics are largely in decline, and in which many of us have already retreated from public life, it might be helpful to revisit the alienation and fear many of us have experienced. We might consider relearning the simple friendship, empathy, and support for diversity many of us first found in the gay and lesbian community. Remember the stranger. Let me know how it goes.

Note

1. See Rebecca Alpert, *Like Bread on the Seder Plate: Jewish Lesbians and the Transformation of Tradition* (New York: Columbia, 1997), who cites *Sifra Ahare Mot*, Genesis Rabbah 26:6 and Leviticus Rabbah 23:9.

Equal Marriage for Same-Sex Couples

Beverly Smith

[The following is the complete text prepared by Beverly Smith for her April 2 testimony in Edmonton (Alberta) at parliament's travelling Justice and Human Rights Committee marriage hearings. The actual presentation was abbreviated to fit within the time allotted.]

My name is Beverley Smith and I am a women's rights activist and school teacher in Calgary. I have worked for many years to address equality issues and though I am not gay, I have given much thought to movements for equal rights. I would like to speak to you today about equal rights for same-sex marriage.

The issue of same-sex marriage is clouded by emotion and most people have already taken a stand on it and are simply seeking a chance to express the opinion. I must admit that I have changed my thinking on it over the years so openness to reassess is something I value.

I would like to address the issue in terms of what it is about, which is the right to marry, and also in terms of what it is not about—which often gets in the way of the discussion.

Legal Commitment

First of all—this is mainly about two adults who want to take on the legal responsibility of marriage, who want to express publicly a commitment to each other for life, and who want this commitment to be one they are socially obliged to live up to. It is about a legal designation to recognize a promise they want to make. I am married and I made the promise, which I took very seriously, even in tears, "in sickness, and in health, for better or for worse, as long as we both shall live."

Mine is a heterosexual marriage, and traditional, but the vows we made were acts of courage for no one knows what lies ahead. Our vows simply said that what we will face, we will face together, come what may. Same-sex couples are asking if they could make that same vow to each other. I do not see that as threatening.

Financial Commitment

Second, this is about money, not sex. In the law marriage is the union of a man and a woman but actually, physical union is not the determiner of it. Whether or not a couple is sexually active is not grounds for divorce and if the couple is still living under the same roof and eating and shopping together it is deemed they are still married, even if they sleep separately. So the law does not in fact define marriage based on sexual activity. The law does, however, require certain financial consequences of marriage. Some may think that wanting to be married means you are seeking some financial advantage but actually in present law, marriage is more penalized than rewarded financially. Yet gays want it. I do not see that as threatening.

A couple that is dating and living together is taxed quite differently from a married couple. Marriage creates an obligation for spousal support, even after the marriage ends. There is a sharing of standard of living and some legal responsibility for joint debts. The married couple can only deduct costs of one residence, not two, and only costs of childcare off the lower-earning spouse, not both being able to claim costs as single parents.

So what we are seeing is that marriage is both a legal commitment and a financial arrangement, both of which are somewhat onerous in fact, at least serious and certainly rarely convenient. And we are here seeing that some gay couples want into this arrangement. I do not see that as threatening.

The Sexual Fixation of Opponents to Equality

I would like to address other things that often are cited as relevant to the discussion, which I think are not at the core of the matter at all.

First, this is not about the revulsion some feel to the idea of gay sex. Revulsion is a strong sentiment, probably undeniable, but truth be told most of us disagree on what is appealing in sexual attractiveness of others anyway, and most children express a revulsion at the idea of their own parents having sex. It is not about revulsion.

Second this is not about opening up the floodgates to other types of marriage such as polygamy. Polygamy historically has been a tradition in some cultures where the will of one of the parties, usually the woman, was completely discounted. We are not talking about forcing anyone here. We are talking about two adults who want to make a public commitment, voluntarily and exclusively to each other.

The Spiritual Message Is One of Love

Third, this is not about religion. I am a member of a mainstream church and have been all my life. And I am a student of the Bible. The message I get from that book is summarized in the entreaty "Love one another." If we are Christian and often those who object to gay marriage are, we must recognize that Jesus summarized his philosophy many times in one word. "The greatest of these is love." I find it hard to see how love between two people of the same sex is against that entreaty for the entreaty had no gender to it.

I think it is important to remember that Jesus had 12 male disciples one of whom was referred to as "the disciple Jesus loved." I am not suggesting Jesus was gay, but I am suggesting that Jesus loved all people, male and female, and what we are talking about here is love and commitment. "For this reason shall a man leave his parents and cleave unto his wife and the two shall become one flesh" is cited. But let us look at the intent here—the intensity of the commitment to the new person and the self-sacrifice involved in it. There are also passages in the Bible that speak against any marriage, where the apostle Paul wanted men to not marry because marriage was a sign of weakness. So I think that for me at least the Bible shows a number of personal views of how best to have a religious life, with the focus being on the goal itself—living a life of service to others and of love to others. Some interpret this within marriage and some not. But the Bible does not actually take sides in that regard.

Nurture

Fourth, this is not about corrupting youth. I am a school teacher and I can assure you that in the schools where I teach it is not cool to be gay. I do whatever I can to discourage gay-bashing, kids insulting each other by calling each other gay, but I can assure you that there is no danger from what I have seen that treating gays with dignity will make people want to be gay. I am pleased to say that over the 30 years that I have been working with children, something wonderful has been happening though in the classroom about equality of minority groups. Many of the classes I teach have students from different races and cultures and the climate for them is much more accepting than it was when I was in school in the fifties. Our school literature has changed to remove insulting references to those of different skin color and different language and do you know what? Kids accept this equality very easily. The Russian child and the Polish child and the African child really do play together very well and barely notice each other's difference. And that is the wave of the future. We can make it so for gays too.

Nature

This is also not about going against nature. The argument that only heterosexual relationships are natural is biologically supported by many but not all animal species. And I think that those who are strongly heterosexual can rest secure knowing that they are indeed right—that most people are drawn to a person of the opposite sex and that is their nature to be so drawn. You can't go against your nature in how you feel. But by the same token, we should admit that a very small minority of people do not have that same biological urge apparently, and for them it is natural to feel drawn to someone of the same sex. I am not part of that drive, and I don't feel it personally, but I can admit that for them it does exist.

The fact that it is so very natural for most of us to feel differently may console us because the minority's attractions pose no threat to us—they can't change our nature just as we are unlikely to change theirs. So this is not about convincing people to become gay, about making youth gay, about changing fundamental natures of a person—because if we believe these attractions we feel are natural and ingrained, so they are. And we need not fear.

Some may fear that children would be shocked at having gay parents or seeing gay sex, but let's remember that it is offensive to have any kids see the sex act and we should not assume gays would expose children to it any more than heterosexual parents do. Private acts will remain private acts and were they not, there are other areas of the law that deal with them.

Tradition

And last, this is not a threat to tradition. Just as it is wrong to hold onto any idea just because it is old, for if that were true we would never have tried using an airplane, it is also wrong to reject any idea just because it is old. We need not endorse a new idea as a fad. There are some tried and true values we must never leave. But if I serve my family Chinese pork at a family dinner, that is a departure from turkey, but it maintains the tradition of the family dinner. When we speak of marriage, let's be aware of the intent of what is worth upholding and surely it is commitment, permanence, and love. And that is not threatened by gay marriage.

One of my children observed to me an irony some years ago and I thought about it and pass it along now because I have come to believe it also. Gay marriage endorses tradition. Gays simply want in. They want to be part of our tradition of the burden, the cost, the financial responsibility, the public promise of a lifetime commitment to someone else. They are not rejecting tradition. They are endorsing it.

Nowadays many young people are hesitant to make the marriage commitment and rates of common-law unions are skyrocketing. Many marriages end in divorce, as many as one in three by latest statistics. For many of us in the heterosexual community, it is sad to see the lack of permanent commitment people feel able to make in this troubled world. And I find it kind of heartening to see this one small group wanting to take that risk, to express a promise of forever being by each other's side, through all life's struggles. Gays want to be part of what anchors society when they want into marriage.

Democratic Equality and Freedom

Finally, in a democracy, we have the opportunity to do what is fair, to treat well not just those who agree with us but those who don't. We defend not just the right of people to act as we do but their right to act differently and where no one is harmed to have the freedom to practice their beliefs, their religion, their political views. This is not about us agreeing with their ideas. It is about our defending their right to have them.

Canada has a tradition of being one of the first off the mark to extend equal rights to others. We gave women the vote way before many other nations. We have a health care system that is the envy of most nations since we ensure the poor do not suffer illness more severely because of their poverty. Canada is the right place to ask for openness to defining what love and commitment are—to allowing that small group of gays who want it, to also make a marriage commitment to each other.

2000 Good Reasons to March

Fédération des femmes du Québec 1999

The idea to hold a world march of women in the year 2000 was born out of the experience of the Women's March against Poverty that took place in Quebec in 1995. This march, initiated by the Fédération des femmes du Québec (FFQ), was hugely successful. Fifteen thousand people greeted the 850 women who marched for ten days to win nine demands related to economic justice. The entire Quebec women's movement mobilized for the march as did many other segments of the population. The presence of women from countries of the South in that march reminded us of the importance of global solidarity-building.

The Beijing Conference later that year proved that women everywhere are struggling for equality, development, and peace more than ever before. It was in Beijing that we made our first proposal to organize an international women's march. The International Preparatory Meeting for the World March was held in Montreal, Quebec, Canada, on October 16–18, 1998; 140 delegates from 65 countries adopted the platform of world demands stated here and developed a plan of action for the World March of Women in the Year 2000.

The World March of Women in the Year 2000 is an action to improve women's living conditions. More precisely, the specific demands centre on the issues of poverty and violence against women. The international meeting held in October 1998 was only one of countless initiatives from civil society where women reaffirmed their determination to eradicate poverty and violence against women, with the conviction that this change must come from a large-scale mobilization of women around the world.

We Are Counting on the Presence of Thousands, Hopefully Millions, of Women in the Streets in the Year 2000!

We, the women of the world, are marching against the poverty that crushes four billion people on our planet, most of whom are women.

We are also marching to protest violence against women because this is a fundamental negation of human rights.

Against neoliberal capitalism that turns human beings, especially women, into an increasingly disposable, interchangeable, and exploitable commodity. Against the subordination of individual and collective rights to the dictates of financial markets. Against the progressive disappearance of political power in the face of rising economic power.

Against the complicit silence of international financial institutions that sprang up after the Second World War (International Monetary Fund, World Bank, World Trade Organization) and other international and regional institutions: they perpetuate the exploitation of peoples by imposing structural adjustment programs in the South, deficit fighting and social program cutbacks in the North, and by concocting trade and other kinds of agreements such as the Multinational Agreement on Investment.

Against patriarchal ideology, still largely dominant today, under which violence against women continues to be a universal fact of life: spousal violence, sexual abuse, genital mutilation, homophobic and racist attacks, systematic rape in wartime, etc.

Against all wars. Against threats to the planet's survival and to a healthy environment.

Against all forms of violence against women, adolescent girls, and children. Against all forms of violence perpetrated against the most vulnerable women in society.

We are marching against poverty and for sharing of wealth, against violence against women, and for the control and respect of our bodies.

What Kind of a World Do We Live in?

We live in a world where, at the turn of the millennium, profound disparities still exist between North and South, rich and poor, women and men, human beings and Nature.

We live in a world where unrestricted globalization of markets, coupled with unbridled speculation, are giving rise to extreme poverty. A total of 1.3 billion people, of whom 70 percent are women and children, live in abject poverty. It is a world that is hungry, a world where the richest 20 percent possess 83 percent of the planet's revenue.

We live in a world where the State is neglecting its responsibilities and obligations due to the dictatorship of the market. It is a world where institutions such as the World Bank and the International Monetary Fund impose their rules on governments through structural adjustment policies.

We live in a world where discrimination against women is the main source of gender inequality. It is a world where, since time immemorial, women have contributed to humanity's development without their work being truly acknowledged. Thus although women actually supply two-thirds of work hours, they only receive one-tenth of world revenue. Since the earliest times, the economy, no matter what kind, has been largely based on women's work, whether paid or unpaid, visible or invisible.

We live in a world where violence against women continues to be a universal reality. Conjugal violence, sexual aggression, genital mutilation, rape in wartime are the plight of thousands of women. Racism and homophobia add to the bleak picture.

What Kind of World Do We Want to Live in?

Women from all over the world are marching so that in the third millennium, their fundamental freedoms, indissociable from their human rights and undeniably universal in nature, are implemented once and for all. They are determined in their belief that all human rights are interdependent and that the values of equality, justice, peace, and solidarity will predominate.

Women from all over the world are marching in the knowledge that they have a responsibility to participate in political, economic, cultural, and social life.

Women from all over the world are marching against all forms of violence and discrimination to which they are subjected.

Women from all over the world are marching to consolidate actions, based on principles of cooperation and sharing, aimed at instituting crucial changes.

Women are marching in affirmation of their desire to live in a better world.

Our Demands

Central to the purpose of the World March are the demands to end poverty and violence against women (drafted at the International Preparatory Meeting in October, 1998).

TO ELIMINATE POVERTY WE DEMAND:

1. That all States adopt a legal framework and strategies aimed at eliminating poverty.

    States must implement national anti-poverty policies, programs, action plans and projects including specific measures to eliminate women's poverty and to ensure their economic and social independence through the exercise of their right to:

    - Education;
    - Employment, with statutory protection for work in the home and in the informal sectors of the economy;
    - Pay equity and equality at the national and international levels;
    - Association and unionization;
    - Property and control of safe water;
    - Decent housing;
    - Health care and social protection;
    - Culture;
    - Life-long income security;
    - Natural and economic resources (credit, property, vocational training, technologies);

    - Full citizenship, including in particular recognition of civil identity and access to relevant documents (identity card); and
    - Minimum social wage.

    States must guarantee, as a fundamental right, the production and distribution of food to ensure food security for their populations.

    States must develop incentives to promote the sharing of family responsibilities (education and care of children and domestic tasks) and provide concrete support to families such as daycare adapted to parents' work schedules, community kitchens, programs to assist children with their school work, etc.

    States must promote women's access to decision-making positions. They must make provisions to ensure women's equal participation in decision-making political bodies.

    States must ratify and observe the labour standards of the International Labour Office (ILO). They must enforce observance of national labour standards in free trade zones.

    States and international organizations should take measures to counter and prevent corruption.

    All acts, pieces of legislation, regulations, and positions taken by governments will be assessed in the light of indicators such as the human poverty index (HPI), introduced in the Human Development Report 1997; the human development index (HDI), put forth by the United Nations Development Program; the gender-related development index (including an indicator on the representation of women in positions of power) discussed in the Human Development Report 1995, and Convention 169 of the International Labour Organization particularly as it concerns Indigenous and tribal peoples' rights.

2. The urgent implementation of measures such as:

- The Tobin tax. [In 1972, to stem rising speculation, James Tobin, economist and advisor to President Kennedy of the USA, proposed that a small tax of 0.1 percent to 0.5 percent be imposed on each speculative transaction. The World March has chosen to target the Tobin Tax in particular for its immediate impact on speculation, because this tax would generate a significant world fund, and because it is an attainable objective in the short term.] Revenue from the tax would be paid into a special fund:
- Earmarked for social development;
- Managed democratically by the international community as a whole;
- According to criteria respecting fundamental human rights and democracy;
- With equal representation of women and men; and
- To which women (who represent 70 percent of the 1.3 billion people living in extreme poverty) would have preferred access;
- Investment of 0.7 percent of the rich countries' Gross National Product (GNP) in aid for developing countries;
- Adequate financing and democratization of United Nations programs that are essential to defend women's and children's fundamental rights; for example, UNIFEM (UN women's program), UNDP (United Nations Development Program), and UNICEF (program for children);
- An end to structural adjustment programs;

- An end to cutbacks in social budgets and public services; and
- Rejection of the proposed Multilateral Agreement on Investment (MAI).

3. Cancellation of the debt of all Third World countries, taking into account the principles of responsibility, transparency of information, and accountability.

We demand the immediate cancellation of the debt of the 53 poorest countries on the planet, in support of the objectives of the Jubilee 2000 campaign.

In the longer term, we demand cancellation of the debt of all Third World countries and the setting up of a mechanism to monitor debt write-off, ensuring that this money is employed to eliminate poverty and further the well-being of people most affected by structural adjustment programs, the majority of whom are women and girls.

4. The implementation of the 20/20 formula between donor countries and the recipients of international aid. (In this scheme, 20 percent of the sum contributed by the donor country must be allocated to social development and 20 percent of the receiving government's spending must be used for social programs.)

5. A non-monolithic world political organization, with authority over the economy and egalitarian and democratic representation of all countries on earth and equal representation of women and men. This organization must have real decision-making power and authority to act in order to implement a world economic system that is fair, participatory, and where solidarity plays a key role. The following measures must be instituted immediately:

- A World Council for Economic and Financial Security, which would be in charge of redefining the rules for a new international financial system based on the fair and equitable distribution of the planet's wealth. It would also focus on increasing the well-being, based on social justice, of the world population, particularly women, who make up over half that population. Gender parity should be observed in the composition of the Council's membership. Membership should also be comprised of representatives of the civil society (for example, NGOs, unions, etc.), and should reflect parity of representation between countries from the North and South;

- Any ratification of trade conventions and agreements should be subordinated to individual and collective fundamental human rights. Trade should be subordinated to human rights, not the other way around;
- The elimination of tax havens;
- The end of banking secrecy;
- Redistribution of wealth by the seven richest countries; and
- A protocol to ensure application of the International Covenant on Economic, Social and Cultural Rights.

6. That the embargoes and blockades—principally affecting women and children—imposed by the major powers on many countries, be lifted.

TO ELIMINATE ALL FORMS OF VIOLENCE AGAINST WOMEN, WE DEMAND:

1. That governments claiming to be defenders of human rights condemn any authority—political, religious, economic or cultural—that controls women and girls, and denounce any regime that violates their fundamental rights.

2. That States recognize, in their statutes and actions, that all forms of violence against women are violations of fundamental human rights and cannot be justified by any custom, religion, cultural practice, or political power. Therefore, all states must recognize a woman's right to determine her own destiny, and to exercise control over her body and reproductive functions.

3. That States implement action plans, effective policies, and programs equipped with adequate financial and other means to end all forms of violence against women. States should take all possible steps to end patriarchal values and sensitize the society towards democratization of the family structure.

These action plans must include the following elements in particular: prevention; public education; punishment; "treatment" for attackers; research and statistics on all forms of violence against women; assistance and protection for victims; campaigns against pornography, procuring, and sexual assault, including child rape; non-sexist education; end to the process of homogenization of culture and the commodification of women in media to suit the needs of the market; easier access to the criminal justice system; and training programs for judges and police.

4. That the United Nations bring extraordinary pressure to bear on member states to ratify without reservation and implement the conventions and covenants relating to the rights of women and children, in particular, the International Covenant on Civil and Political Rights, the Convention on the Elimination of All Forms of Discrimination against Women, the

Convention on the Rights of the Child, the International Convention on the Elimination of All Forms of Racial Discrimination, the International Convention on the Protection of the Rights of All Migrant Workers and their Families.

That the United Nations pressure governments to respect human rights and resolve conflicts.

That States harmonize their national laws with these international human rights instruments as well as the Universal Declaration of Human Rights, the Declaration on the Elimination of Violence against Women, the Cairo and Vienna Declarations, and the Beijing Declaration and Platform for Action.

5. That, as soon as possible, protocols be adopted (and implementation mechanisms be established):

- To the International Convention on the Elimination of All Forms of Discrimination Against Women; and
- To the Convention on the Rights of the Child.

These protocols will enable individuals and groups to bring complaints against their governments. They are a means to apply international pressure on governments to force them to implement the rights set out in these covenants and conventions. Provision must be made for appropriate sanctions against non-compliant States.

6. That mechanisms be established to implement the 1949 Convention for the Suppression of the Traffic in Persons and of the Exploitation of the Prostitution of Others, taking into account recent relevant documents such as the two resolutions of the United Nations General Assembly (1996) concerning trafficking in women and girls and violence against migrant women.

7. That States recognize the jurisdiction of the International Criminal Court and conform in particular to the provisions defining rape and sexual abuse as war crimes and crimes against humanity.

That the United Nations end all forms of intervention, aggression, and military occupation.

8. That all States adopt and implement disarmament policies with respect to conventional, nuclear, and biological weapons. That all countries ratify the Convention against Land Mines.

9. That the right to asylum for women victims of sexist discrimination and persecution and sexual violence be adopted as soon possible. Also, that the United Nations assure the right of refugees to return to their homeland.

The next two demands were supported by the majority of women present at the meeting on the condition of a country-by-country adoption process. Some delegates were not in a position to be able to commit to defending publicly these demands in their country. They remain an integral part of the World March of Women in the year 2000.

10. That, based on the principle of equality of all persons, the United Nations and States of the international community recognize formally that a person's sexual orientation should not bar them from the full exercise of the rights set out in the following international instruments: the Universal Declaration of Human Rights, the International Covenant on Civil and Political Rights, the International Covenant on Economic, Social, and Cultural Rights, and the International Convention on the Elimination of All Forms of Discrimination against Women.

11. That the right to asylum for victims of discrimination and persecution based on sexual orientation be adopted as soon as possible.

The Next Steps

The World March of Women in the Year 2000 is about women gathering from around the globe to fight poverty and violence against women. Since the very beginning, women from many countries have helped to organize the World March and many more are taking part in their own countries. There will be as many ways of mobilizing on the national scale as there are countries participating in the March. Each will bear the stamp of its own traditions and day-to-day reality, the richness of its own history and culture, and the array of its own concerns.

Three levels of action have been proposed for the March. First, there will be an action demonstrating women's mass support of the overall demands, signified by signing support cards. On March 8, 2000, the awareness and support card campaigns will be launched.

Secondly, women's movements in each country will organize national actions that will present demands reflecting their realities and priorities. National coalitions made up of different groups in the women's movement in each country will coordinate the local and national activities having to do with their priorities. Some coalitions may decide to take up as national demands some of the world demands that are most important in their context. Other coalitions will concentrate on existing demands of the women's movement in their country in relation to poverty and violence against women.

Finally, a world demonstration or rally will be held. On October 17, 2000, International Day for the Eradication of Poverty, women from the participating countries will meet in front of the United Nations after having marched, rallied, or demonstrated in their respective country. In some countries, women will choose to have a big national rally. Others will organize a relay march from one end of the country to the other, or simultaneous one-day marches in many cities and towns. Together with marches and rallies, others will hold awareness-raising workshops, popular theatre, training sessions, school contests, photo or art exhibitions, or activities in streets and markets. Women's imagination and creativity know no bounds!

What we want is to stimulate a vast movement of grassroots women's groups so that the march becomes a gesture of affirmation by the women of the world. What we want is to promote equality between men and women. What we want is to highlight the common demands and initiatives issuing from the global women's movement relating to the issues of poverty and violence against women. What we want is to force governments, decision-makers, and individuals the world over to institute the changes necessary for improving the status of women and women's quality of life. And what we want is to enter the new millennium by demonstrating women's ongoing determination to change the world.

We are certain that our international mobilization and pooling of ideas and analyses will generate world political pressure that cannot be ignored. It will be strong enough to initiate radical changes that are indispensable to the well-being of the world's population. This is how women will march forth into the new millennium: They will put the world back on track through sharing, peace, and formal equality and they will proclaim that women more than ever will be players in fostering major change.

Note

For further information or to get involved, contact: Marche mondiale des femmes en l'an 2000/World March of Women in the Year 2000/Marcha mundial de las mujeres en el año 2000, 110 rue Ste-Thérèse, #307, Montréal, Québec, Canada H2Y 1E6; phone: 514-395-1196; fax: 514-395-1224; e-mail: marche2000@ffq.qc.ca; website: www.ffq.qc.ca.

Women's Experiences with Mandatory Charging for Wife Assault in Ontario, Canada: A Case against the Prosecution

Tammy C. Landau[1]

The criminalization of wife assault, through the policy of mandatory charging and prosecution of appropriate cases, has been the primary state response to this particular form of violence against women in Canada for over a decade.[2] It emerged at a time of increasing pressure to recognize first, the severity and amount of violence perpetrated against women by their male partners, and second, that the agents of the criminal justice system (primarily the police but including Crown prosecutors and other criminal justice workers) ignored women who called on them for protection in what were often long-term, abusive relationships. Most, if not all, provinces in Canada have formally adopted criminalization strategies to prevent and reduce violence against women by their male partners through punishment and deterrence. The details of how the policy is implemented is continually evolving, and varies across locations. In general, however, the policy centres around mandatory charging in all cases of wife assault and the reduction in case attrition in the prosecution process (Prairie Research Associates 1994; Ursel 1994). These are achieved through policy directives aimed at the police and Crown prosecutors ("Crowns"). Police discretion in charging is removed in cases where there are reasonable and probable grounds to believe an assault has taken place, and Crowns are discouraged from dropping, staying, or withdrawing these charges through guidelines developed specifically for dealing with wife assault.

While the formal policy is limited to law enforcement and prosecution, the strategy nevertheless has significant, direct repercussions for assaulted women who come to the attention of the police. By removing any influence of the women over charging decisions, the policy is, in part, an attempt to relieve women of the moral responsibility for the criminal prosecution of their spouses, and to protect them from any intimidation or retaliation from their spouses which may follow. Additional strategies are therefore employed to "encourage" the full participation of victims as witnesses, through, for example, establishing Victim/Witness Assistance Programs. Nevertheless, the proportion of women who refuse to co-operate in providing evidence against their spouse is high, and is seen by police and Crowns as the primary cause of case attrition (Roberts 1996).[3] For many women who still refuse to testify, coercive legal measures, such as the issuing of bench warrants or subpoenas, may be, and have been, used.

Evaluating Mandatory Charging

There have been a number of evaluations of the mandatory charging policy in Canada (see, for example, Gill and Landau 1996, 1998; Prairie Research Associates 1994; Roberts 1996; Ursel 1994). A main component of most studies is a cross-sectional analysis of wife assault cases prosecuted under the policy, combined with data from interviews with the main players in the prosecution process, particularly police officers, Crown prosecutors and community workers. Some (e.g., Roberts 1996) include interviews with assaulted women who may or may not have had direct experience with the prosecution process. However, in most studies, pre- and post-charge measures with respect to the occurrence and recurrence of violence are lacking or based on unreliable data, so conclusions cannot generally be drawn about the extent to which mandatory charging is "working" to prevent or reduce violence against women. These studies might, therefore, be best characterized as "operational" evaluations, in that they provide valuable data on the nature of the cases processed under the policy, and the social context and consequences of prosecuting wife assault. Interview data are also extremely valuable in identifying strengths and weaknesses of the current policy, from very different perspectives.

Data from previous studies suggest that support for the mandatory charging policy is strong, although a number of concerns have been identified (e.g., Gill and Landau 1998; Prairie Research Associates 1994; Roberts 1996). According to Crowns, the apparent increase in the number of wife assault cases has led to significant delays at each point in the process, and undermines successful prosecution. The police in particular feel that their efforts in laying the foundation for prosecution through charging are undermined by the high proportion of charges which continue to be dropped or stayed. In spite of various tactics to encourage or coerce

co-operation, the number of victims who are unwilling to co-operate in the prosecution of their spouses remains high.

Feminist critiques of criminal law (MacLeod 1995b; Martin and Mosher 1995; Snider 1995; Valverde 1995) and, most importantly, studies which have included women who have themselves been victims of wife assault (Erez and Belknap 1998; Gill and Landau 1998; Busch et al. 1995; Martin and Mosher 1995; Roberts 1996; Rodgers 1994) have raised significant questions about the value of an aggressive criminal justice response. Martin and Mosher (1995) have noted the additional harms experienced by many women as a direct result of criminal justice intervention: loss of economic security, increased institutional surveillance and intervention, and destruction of their family and community. Erez and Belknap (1998) have pointed out "the problematic use of adversarial proceedings when parties are simultaneously family members and assailants" (p. 263). Others have identified the unique language, informational and social barriers to using the criminal justice system experienced by Aboriginal, ethnocultural, and immigrant women (Currie 1995; Godin 1994; Roberts 1996; Sy and Choldin 1994). Community-oriented responses which better reflect the cultural and social values of the women are often preferred, but not possible under rigid mandatory charging policies.

Nevertheless, the criminalization strategy for wife assault in Canada has been continually strengthened and expanded, in spite of emerging evidence of these various problems. Why this is the case warrants serious consideration. This essay explores the hypothesis that the needs and interests of women/victims are seen as barriers to the smooth and successful prosecution of wife assault cases, while aggressive criminal justice responses prioritize the bureaucratic, professional, and structural imperatives of the administration of justice and its agents.

The Current Study

The data presented here are from an operational evaluation of the mandatory charging policy in Ontario, Canada (Gill and Landau 1996, 1998). There were two separate phases to the evaluation. The first involved the collection of data from a random sample of 661 files from four communities in Ontario in which charges were laid against a male for a crime of violence against a female victim who was either his partner or former partner. Communities in Ontario were chosen to represent a range of large, medium, and small communities, and communities with French language, Aboriginal, and ethnically diverse populations. A wide range of data on social and demographic characteristics of both the victim and the accused were collected. While there is a degree of unreliability in most types of data, a number of variables in the original data collection instrument were excessively so, either in their social construction or in the inconsistency in the extent to which they were recorded by police. For example, assignments of "race," or "ethnicity" are generally problematic, but even more so when done by law enforcement or correctional workers (Commission on Systemic Racism in the Ontario Criminal Justice System 1995). Immigration or employment status for both the victim and the accused, and criminal justice variables such as previous calls to the police, are inconsistently recorded. Our focus has, therefore, been limited to the context of the assault and more routine criminal justice factors, which have greater reliability and validity.

The second phase of the evaluation involved interviews with police officers, Crown prosecutors, judges, probation officers, victim/witness program workers, and women whose current or former partners had been charged with offences of violence against them. Only data from the interviews with women/victims are presented here, for a number of reasons. Firstly, the interviews with women were more systematic and structured to provide feedback on specific dimensions of mandatory charging. Secondly, the complexities of and difficulties in accessing an appropriate sample of women/ victims of wife assault for research purposes make the data highly valuable. Finally, as Snider (1995, p. 244) states, "in this area, the effect on the women the legislation is aimed at empowering—the battered or assaulted woman—must be the prime, if not the only, criterion for evaluating the success or failure of law reform."

The interview data are based on the responses of 94 women whose cases had gone through the courts in one of the four research communities between 1994 and 1997. Most of the interviews were carried out in person, either at the local Victim/Witness Assistance Program office or in a convenient public place (such as a coffee shop). A small number were carried out over the telephone. All women were paid $25 to cover the costs of transportation, parking, and child care. Interviews ranged from 25 minutes to one hour in length. While women were asked about their experiences at various points in the criminal justice system, the data presented here focus on the women's views and experiences as they relate specifically to the mandatory charging policy. In a number of the tables, responses which fell into the "other" category are large. This is the result of the broad range of responses often given by the women, as well as the large number of responses which did not necessarily directly address the question as asked.

Phase I: Results from the File Review

The Social Context of Wife Assault

In over two-thirds of the cases the accused and victim were living together in a spousal relationship: in an additional 25% the victim and accused were former partners but were separated at the time of the occurrence.

Overall, the files indicate that more than half of the victims had experienced previous violence at the hands of this accused: in 11% of cases there had been previous convictions for assault on this victim, and in 27% of the cases the women indicated that they had experienced violence by this accused but the police were not called. These data are likely to underestimate the extent of previous violence experienced by the women in this sample.

In 55% of the cases there was a witness to the assault, most frequently a child (28% of the time), or neighbours/friends of the victim, and/or accused (15% of the time). Nevertheless, in 75% of the cases it was the victim who contacted the police. One-third of incidents resulted in no physical injury to the victim—i.e., the victim indicated to the police that she had received no lasting injuries, or the police noted that, at the time they attended the incident, there were no visible injuries, such as redness or swelling. Stated differently, in almost 67% of cases there were injuries to the woman. While most were relatively minor (slap marks, bruising, swelling), 7% involved significant injury such as significant loss of blood, missing teeth, or serious bruising.

In the vast majority of cases (87%) the victim remained in the home after the incident was reported to the police, and in most cases the children remained with her.

The Criminal Justice Context of Wife Assault

Eighty percent of primary charges laid in the file review sample were for simple assault and an additional 6% were for assault with a weapon. Just under 5% were for criminal harassment, a relatively new offence under the Criminal Code of Canada. A very small percentage (2%) were charges for various types of breaches (e.g., recognizance, probation orders, conditions of peace bonds) (Table 1).

In almost 20% of the cases, all charges against the accused were dropped (Table 2): in an additional 15% of cases, all charges were dropped in exchange for entering into a peace bond with the victim. In one-third of cases,

Table 1
Primary Charge

	Frequency	Percent
Assault	526	79.6
Assault with a weapon	42	6.4
Aggravated assault	3	0.5
Sexual assault	9	1.4
Sexual assault with a weapon	1	0.2
Breach of probation	2	0.3
Breach of peace bond	2	0.3
Breach of recognizance	10	1.5
Criminal harassment	30	4.5
Uttering threats	22	3.3
Missing	14	2.1
Total	661	100.0

Table 2
Charge Outcome

	Frequency	Percent
All charges dropped	127	19.2
All charges dropped, peace bond	101	15.3
Accused pled guilty to primary charge, other charges dropped	220	33.3
Primary charge dropped, accused pled guilty to assault	64	9.7
Found guilty on all charges	19	2.9
Accused pled guilty to all charges	28	4.2
Found not guilty on all charges	49	7.4
Other outcomes	53	8
Total	661	100

the accused pleaded guilty to the main charge and all other charges against him were withdrawn.

Half of all accused who were convicted received terms of probation for one year, and an additional 23% received terms of probation of 1–2 years; just over 20% received jail terms of relatively short (less than 6 months) duration.

Phase II—Results of Interviews with Women

Decisions to Call the Police

Seventy percent of women contacted the police themselves. Women said that they decided to contact the police because they were afraid for their lives (22%), they wanted police to stop the assault (13%), they were concerned about harm to the children (8%), or because that time was worse than other times.

We asked the women what they were hoping the police would do once they arrived (Table 3): 30% stated that they were hoping the police would remove their spouse from the house, 17% stated that they wanted the police to stop the assault, 16% stated that they wanted the police to talk to him or to warn him, and 15% stated that they wanted the police to lay charges.

Views of Mandatory Charging

We asked women a number of very specific questions about their views and experiences with the mandatory charging policy. The results indicate that the women's views of the policy are complex. When asked specifically whether they wanted the police to lay charges in their case, 60% said that they did. Women identified many reasons in support of charging: it would teach him not to do it again (14%), it is a crime to assault someone (6%) and he had done it before (3%) (Table 4). Conversely, 40% of women did not want charges laid. The most frequent reasons given were that charging was not on their minds when they called the police—stopping the

Table 3
Responses to "What were you hoping the police would do?"

	Frequency	Percent
Stop the assault	16	17.4
Remove him from the house	28	30.4
Talk to him/warn him	15	16.3
Charge him	14	15.2
Help me get out safely	2	2.2
Other	30	32.6

Note: Column percentages add up to more than 100% because more than one response was possible.

Table 4
Responses to "Did you want the police to lay charges? Why/Why not?"

	Frequency	Percent
No, I wanted the violence to stop	4	4.3
No, I wanted him warned	3	3.2
No, I didn't want him to go to jail	1	1.1
Yes, what he did was a crime/to teach him not to do it again	21	22.3
He's done it before	5	5.3
Yes, so I'll be protected/this time was the worst	8	5.3
Other	55	58.5
Total	94	100

violence was, or it was the first time, or it was not that serious or it was a personal or family matter.

Questions were also asked about the women's knowledge of the mandatory charging policy. Even though every one of these cases would have been affected by the policy, almost 40% of the women did not know that the police were required to lay charges, even if the woman was against it. Indeed, 32% of the women reported that they asked to have the charges dropped, even though 80% of women reported that they agreed with the charges that were laid. Nevertheless, 80% of women agreed with the policy of the police to lay charges against the wishes of other women: 35% believed that the woman may be too scared to go through with the prosecution, and 15% believed that she will be pressured by the man or his family to drop them (Table 5).

Table 5
Responses to the question "Did you know that the police are given official orders to arrest a husband/boyfriend and to lay charges if there is any sign that an assault has taken place, even if you tell them you don't want him to be arrested or charged? Do you feel this is right?"

	Frequency	Percent
All charges dropped	127	19.2
No, it should be the woman's choice	4	4.3
No, it depends on the situation	2	2.1
No, charging doesn't change anything	1	1.1
Yes, it's a crime/men have to learn	11	11.7
Yes, it's the only way to stop it	2	2.1
Yes, women may be too scared to go through with charging	33	35.1
Yes, women might be pressured into dropping charges	14	14.9
Other	27	28.7
Total	94	100

Open-Ended Questions

In the open-ended questions of the interview, the women shared personal experiences that also reflected the nature of the policy and the extent to which it can, or does, meet their needs. Once they made the decision to call the police, women felt they had little, if any, control over the direction of the case. This was clearly what some women needed during such a traumatic experience:

> "Women aren't in the right state of mind to make that decision (to charge) ... they have other things on their minds. The law does the thinking for you."

> "Women can't think straight under that kind of trauma."

> "[Women] need to have someone to step in and take charge—emotionally abused women aren't in a state to do that."

> "There needs to be a way to take responsibility off the woman to prove it, to go through charging."

At the same time, women spoke about the anxiety and uncertainty that the prosecution of their spouses created for them. For example, when asked what she remembered most about her experience with the process, one woman stated that she remembered "feeling lost in a sea with the waves washing me around." Indeed, for many women, this was a highly disempowering experience, which heightened their anxiety:

> "It removes the flexibility to look at the context. The woman has no say in why she called and what she wants done. It increases feelings of powerlessness."

"Many women are so abused they can't do it on their own. But other women have enough power to make their own decision."

"They should have listened to me more—show a little respect and consideration for me ... they didn't ever asked me (about issuing a no-contact order), they just did it anyway."

When asked what could have made the experience better for her, one woman replied: "Stop making me a victim again ... if the system could just give women a little more power, women would have the confidence to get out."

Indeed, women have competing and complex concerns which often transcend the episodes of violence they experience at the hands of their spouse. The financial and emotional dependence of many on their abusive partners was clear. One woman expressed her feelings about the prospect of her partner going to prison:

"The court system made me angry towards them—he didn't deserve a long jail sentence. It wouldn't have helped and would have done more harm—I would have lost child support."

Women often mentioned that the need to keep the family together and protect their children outweighed the need for formal criminal justice intervention:

"I wanted him to get counselling, not detox, which would have taken him away from the family."

"The restraining order was not necessary ... it was more unsettling for us—we needed to talk."

"The Crown wanted to send him away, I wanted him at home. They over-reacted."

One woman said that the thing she remembers most about her experience with the prosecution process was the police taking her husband away in handcuffs, with her daughter looking on. Clearly, many wanted to work together on changes in their relationship that would put an end to the violence and keep the family intact. Criminal prosecution is seen as a strong threat to these ends.

Regardless of whether individual women wanted their spouse charged, women expressed dissatisfaction that the justice system was not sensitive to their needs, experiences, and wishes. One woman most remembered "the pathetic way in which I was treated by the Crown—I felt abused by him." Another spoke of "the horror, humiliation and degradation of the courtroom—for both of us—I hated it." Feelings of being "revictimized" by the prosecution process also emerged:

"The Crown was mad at me, actually made me cry. It was like I was being victimized again, with nobody on my side because I didn't want my husband to go to jail."

"I felt the system wasn't on my side—I thought they would be when they found someone who really wanted to charge."

At the same time, things which seem to be trivial and easily accomplished would have, for many women, made a significant difference: "listening to them" by, for example, not charging or dropping charges, including alcohol/anger management as part of conditions, or perhaps just having someone sit with them in court for support.

The most frequent and consistent feedback from women was the need for more information about the court process, trial dates, release dates for the accused, and, incredibly, court outcomes. "Some information from someone would have made a difference—I felt like a victim again." A few women stated that they learned of the outcome in court either from the accused himself (who they were both estranged from and terrified of), or his family. Another learned during the interview for the current research that the charges of assault against her husband were withdrawn. It may be that, in such situations, no amount of information is sufficient, or that it is such a distressful time that the complexities of the legal system cannot be easily absorbed. Nevertheless, women are clearly identifying limited information and knowledge about their case as an important source of anxiety during the prosecution process.

Not surprisingly, the high proportion of cases in which charges were stayed or dropped later in the prosecution process left many women angry, frustrated, and embittered. This was true for those women who wanted charges laid, but even more devastating for women who asked, sometimes begged, to have the charges dropped but were ignored. They felt that they were coerced into the process, abandoned, and finally blamed for having initiated the whole process by calling in the police. One woman most remembered "being made to feel that I had done something wrong," even though her husband was convicted and sent to jail. Another remembered "being put on the stand and raked over the coals by (the lawyer of the accused), looking like it was my fault, like I did something wrong."

> "The Crown didn't want me to drop the charges—she almost yelled at me .... 'It's women like you ....' I felt insulted, abused, like I had done something wrong, encouraged him ...."

In the context of an abusive partnership, a failed prosecution was a personal and quite public failure for them.

Without doubt, many women reported positive experiences and recollections. They often occurred in the context of the response of individual police officers or certain Crown Attorneys. One woman reported that she most remembered "little tiny bits of humanity," like how well the Crown treated her son. Another stated that, "with some help from the system, I discovered I could be stronger." Again, however, many others left with feelings of bitterness over having made that first call:

> "I did everything the police asked me, but they did nothing in return for me."

> "They make such a big deal about violence against women and then they don't do very much. That upsets me."

> "(Calling the police) is not worth it—it left a bad taste in my mouth the first time."

Discussion

The file data support findings from previous research on wife assault in Canada, particularly with respect to the relatively high incidence of previous violence by the same partner and the seriousness of much of this violence. For example, the Violence against Women Survey found that in two-thirds of cases the violence had occurred on more than one occasion and that 10% resulted in what the women characterized as serious violence (Rodgers 1994).

At the same time, the reasons given by the women in the Violence against Women Survey for not calling the police set them apart in significant ways from those included in this study. Women reported that they did not report the violence they experienced at the hands of their abusive partners for a variety of reasons: 52% said the incident was too minor and 10% stated that they didn't want or need help. Only 9% of women reported that they were afraid of their partner.

The same cannot easily be said about the violence experienced by the women interviewed for the research reported here, where the violence was likely to be of a more immediate threat to the women. In our sample, the women made the pivotal decision of calling the police for protection, reflecting the critical role of police in providing primary security in high risk situations (Landau 1996). In most cases, they did not do so with the intent of having their partners charged and prosecuted to the fullest extent permitted by the law. Many women go to great lengths to end this process, which they often experience as disempowering and destructive in itself. Clearly, women have mixed feelings about the extent to which they support using the justice system to deal with the violence they experience at the hands of their partners. This research, supported by other woman-focussed research (Erez and Belknap 1998) clearly underlines the importance of both choice and viable options for assaulted women.

The extent to which the needs and interests of many women are unmet or perhaps even compromised by the policy is increasingly documented and has been discussed above (Erez and Belknap 1998; Currie 1995; MacLeod 1995a, 1995b; Martin and Mosher 1995; Snider 1995; Sy and Choldin 1994). The work of critical feminists such as Martin and Mosher (1995), Snider (1995), and others has shown the problematic nature of the policy in reducing violence against women. MacLeod (1995b) points out that the strategy not only reduces options for the Crown, but also for women who have experienced violence by their spouse: it disempowers, even patronizes women, by taking decision-making power out of their hands while others take action in their best interests. Nevertheless, there is a strong commitment to the policy as the primary social and political response to wife assault in Canada. In fact, evaluations generally result in recommendations to expand the strategy, and suggest only minor tinkering with the fundamental structure of the policy. Indeed, Ontario has strengthened its policy by establishing specialized "Domestic Violence Courts" more rigorously to prosecute and convict men accused of wife assault. In order to understand better

why it is that the views of women themselves have had such a limited impact on the essential direction of the strategy, consideration must be given to the bureaucratic, structural, and political imperatives of administration of justice and its agents in prosecuting cases of wife assault in Canada.

Bureaucratic and Professional Considerations
Bureaucratic and professional considerations are those which meet the needs of the administration of justice and/or its agents, such as the police and Crown (for example, Ericson and Baranek 1982). In the context of mandatory charging and prosecution for wife assault, the needs and interests of many women compromise the smooth administration of justice or successful prosecution of cases which keep the strategy alive. However, this is largely the result of an undue emphasis on the victim-cum-witness as at the foundation of prosecutorial success. For example, Crown prosecutors in at least one study (Prairie Research Associates 1994) identified an unwilling victim as the most significant barrier to a successful prosecution. Women are seen as unwilling to testify, not out of fear of retaliation by the accused, or out of financial dependence, but because they want to reconcile with him. In informal discussions for the research reported here, police officers often revealed similar beliefs, and expressed frustration, even disgust, at women who call police for protection then refuse to appear as witnesses in court. "[B]attered women have been uniquely singled out by system's agents as 'problematic' victim/witnesses" (Erez and Belknap 1998, p. 252). In the context of spousal assault, this is extremely worrying. It takes on the aura of victim blaming—not simply for tolerating spousal violence in an ongoing situation, but also for undermining the whole prosecution process and the material and institutional resources that have been committed to the strategy. An atmosphere of intolerance, paternalism, and punitiveness has developed towards women who refuse to co-operate in the prosecution of their spouses. As

Erez and Belknap (1998) note, "there has not been a significant change in the sexist and victim-blaming attitudes of legal agents who serve domestic violence victims" (p. 252).

This emphasis on the women as the cause of unsuccessful prosecutions serves to insulate the police and Crown from their own professional limitations, shortcomings, or lack of commitment to reducing violence against women. For example, police investigations are often less than thorough. In the first phase of our study, we found that police very rarely documented independent, material evidence of an assault (Gill and Landau 1996; see also Erez and Belknap 1998). In the vast majority of cases, the only evidence in the file was the statement taken from the victim, even though there were witnesses to the assault in over 50% of the cases. Photographs of injuries could have been taken, or the actual weapons used in an assault could have been seized. In fact, police officers from Toronto who have begun to videotape victim/witness statements admit they rarely hand the video over to the Crown because of the costs involved (Gill and Landau 1998).

Lack of preparation of cases by the Crown goes hand in hand with police activity and preparation. Most Crowns only see the file on the day of the trial, and attempt to meet with the victim just before the case is to be heard. Indeed, fewer than 30% of the women in our study met with the Crown before their case came to court, and almost 60% reported that they met with the Crown for the first time on the day of the trial. While Crowns have the authority to request additional evidence from the police, they do so rarely and then only in very serious cases. This lack of rigour in investigations by police and preparation by the Crown is neither new nor unacknowledged in evaluations. However, these matters never elicit the rage or blame for unsuccessful prosecutions that women do who hesitate to participate in the criminal prosecution of their spouses.

Many police and Crown will cite the need to "cover themselves" from legal, professional, and civil liability through the laying of charges against the wishes of women. This is an extremely lame argument: the data indicate that charging practices vary considerably across jurisdictions (Gill and Landau 1996; Roberts 1996), and the number of cases in which police are not laying charges remains high. For example, Rodgers (1994) found that police arrested or charged in only 28% of cases in which they were called in to respond to wife assault (see also Roberts 1996). Indeed, police, with the support of many Crowns and some members of the judiciary, are requesting a loosening of the mandatory charging policy to allow them to exercise their discretion not to charge in more "minor" cases or where there is no independent evidence of an assault. Erez and Belknap (1998) found that 71% of their sample reported that some criminal justice processing agent tried to convince them to drop their complaint. Clearly, discretionary decisions of this type leave officers, and women, vulnerable to the repercussions of escalating violence.

Structural Barriers

In addition to the professional and bureaucratic barriers, there are significant structural barriers to meeting the needs of women, since they are located outside the formal machinery of justice. The clients of the criminal justice system are the police, Crown, and judiciary. The emphasis in the prosecution process is on the accused—it is naive at best to think that criminal prosecution can be sensitive to the needs and experiences of women as victims. Victim Witness Assistance Programs are important, but are limited to providing information to witnesses. They do not, and cannot, change the essential role of victims in the courts. Nor can information alone meet the social, economic, and emotional needs of assaulted women. As Snider (1995) notes, "[t]he institutional arm of punishment, criminal justice systems, consist of a subset of bodies and practices that were never designed to provide remedies, or to offer alternatives to the victimized."

Political and Symbolic Considerations

Perhaps the most untenable are the political considerations behind the mandatory charging policy. Aggressive criminal justice responses give the appearance of confronting violence against women. However, the commitment to prevent and reduce violence against women is questionable when funding for shelters, training and education, daycare, social assistance, and legal aid has been decimated by these same governments. Redirecting even a fraction of the material, financial, and human resources which are funnelled into the criminal justice system would instill a modicum of confidence in the commitment to reducing violence against women.

A strong philosophical commitment to the perceived deterrent and symbolic effects of criminalizing behaviours first, through legislation, then through the use of the criminal justice system, is apparent. The limited deterrent effect of the law has been quite clearly established (Canadian Sentencing Commission 1986). At the same time, the symbolic values of criminalization are not as easy to measure or to dismiss. But they must be accepted as symbolic, and weighed against the repercussions they may have for women (Snider 1995). Criminalization emerged in the light of clear evidence that assaulted women were not being heard, or even believed, when they tried to use the justice system to protect them from abusive partners. We have come a very long way from those days in mobilizing the machinery of justice against abusive men. But we are faced again with the challenge of listening to the voices of those very women. A policy that was meant to empower them has, in fact, silenced them and has disempowered them, arguably to an even greater degree. As Erez and Belknap (1998) state, "[i]nappropriate or inadequate system's responses may cause battered women a deeper despair than the abuse itself. Negative comments or discouraging attitudes by criminal processing agents underline victims' powerlessness and helplessness" (p. 263). To date, there is no strong empirical evidence to show that the mandatory charging policy has reduced spousal violence against women. In fact, the Violence against Women Survey in Canada (Rodgers 1994) has shown that the violence continued in over 50% of the cases in which the police were called. As it currently stands, the policy sends out clear messages to women that, in spite of their fears, concerns, and efforts, they are still alone in their battle as assaulted women. We must ask ourselves why that is, and whose interests are now, or still, being served.

Notes

1. I would like to express my deepest gratitude to the women who shared their personal experiences with me, and Marlene Thompson and the staff at the Victim/Witness Assistance Programs in Ontario who facilitated this research. Members of the project committee from the Ministry of the Attorney General of Ontario, the Ministry of the Solicitor-General of Ontario, the Department of Justice, Canada, and the Ontario Women's Directorate facilitated the broader evaluation. I would also like to thank Mary Condon, Myrna Dawson, Mary Easton, and Vappu Tyyskä for their valuable feedback on earlier drafts of this essay.

2. See Roberts (1996) for an historical overview of the development and expansion of the policy in Canada.

3. Many assert that the attrition rate in cases of wife assault is greater than in other types of criminal cases, although this is difficult to assess. However, the Manitoba Tracking Study (Prairie Research Associates 1994) found that 21% of cases where police were dispatched resulted in charges, 12% resulted in conviction, and 4% resulted in incarceration. The Canadian Centre for Justice Statistics (Du Wors 1997) reported that, in 1996, 22% of criminal incidents resulted in charges, 15% resulted in convictions, and 4% resulted in incarceration.

References

Busch, R., Neville R., and Lapsley, H. (1995). "The Gap: Battered Women's Experience of the Justice System in New Zealand." *Canadian Journal of Women and the Law* 8, 190.

Canadian Sentencing Commission. (1986). *Sentencing Reform: A Canadian Approach*. Ottawa: Minister of Supply and Services Canada.

Commission on Systemic Racism in the Ontario Criminal Justice System. (1995). *Report*. Toronto: Ministry of the Attorney General.

Currie, J. (1995). *Ethnocultural, Minority Women, Spousal Assault and Barriers to Accessing and Problems in Using the Justice System: A Review of the Literature*. Ottawa: Department of Justice, Canada, Research, Statistics and Evaluation Directorate.

Du Wors, R. (1997). "The Justice Data Factfinder." *Juristat* 17:13.

Erez, E., and Belknap, J. (1998). "In Their Own Words: Battered Women's Assessment of the Criminal Processing System's Response." *Violence and Victims*, 13:3, 251.

Ericson, R.V., and Baranek, P.M. (1982). *The Ordering of Justice*. Toronto: University of Toronto Press.

Gill, R., and Landau, T. (1996). *A Review of the Criminalization of Wife Assault in Ontario*. Toronto: Ministry of the Attorney General of Ontario. Unpublished.

Gill, R., and Landau, T. (1998). *A Review of the Criminalization of Wife Assault in Ontario: Final Report*. Toronto: Ministry of the Attorney General of Ontario. Unpublished.

Godin, J. (1994). *More Than a Crime: A Report on the Lack of Public Legal Information Materials for Immigrant Women Who Are Subject to Wife Assault*. Ottawa: Department of Justice, Canada, Research and Statistics Directorate.

Landau, T. (1996). "Policing and Security in Four Remote Aboriginal Communities: A Challenge to Coercive Models of Police Work." *Canadian Journal of Criminology* 38:1, 1.

MacLeod, L. (1995a). "Expanding the Dialogue: Report of a Workshop to Explore the Criminal Justice System Response to Violence against Women." In M. Valverde, L. MacLeod, and K. Johnson (Eds.), *Wife Assault and the Canadian Criminal Justice System*. Toronto: Centre of Criminology, University of Toronto.

MacLeod, L. (1995b). "Policy Decisions and Prosecutorial Dilemmas: The Unanticipated Consequences of Good Intentions." In M. Valverde, L. MacLeod, and K. Johnson (Eds.), *Wife Assault and the Canadian Criminal Justice System*. Toronto: Centre of Criminology, University of Toronto.

Martin, D.L., and Mosher, J.E. (1995). "Unkept Promises: Experiences of Immigrant Women with the Neo-Criminalization of Wife Abuse." *Canadian Journal of Women and the Law* 8, 3.

Prairie Research Associates. (1994). *Manitoba Spouse Abuse Tracking Project: Final Report, Volume I*. Ottawa: Department of Justice Canada, Research and Statistics Directorate.

Roberts, T. (1996). *Spousal Assault and Mandatory Charging in the Yukon: Experiences, Perspectives and Alternatives*. Ottawa: Department of Justice Canada, Research and Statistics Section.

Rodgers, K. (1994). "Wife Assault: The Findings of a National Survey." *Juristat* 14:9.

Snider, L. (1995). "Feminism, Punishment and the Potential of Empowerment." In M. Valverde, L. MacLeod, and K. Johnson (Eds.), *Wife Assault and the Canadian Criminal Justice System*. Toronto: Centre of Criminology, University of Toronto.

Sy, S.S., and Choldin, S. (1994). *Legal Information and Wife Abuse in Immigrant Families*. Ottawa: Department of Justice Canada, Research and Statistics Directorate.

Ursel, E.J. (1994). "The Winnipeg Family Violence Court." *Juristat* 14:12.

Ursel, E.J, and Brickey, S, (1996). "The Potential of Legal Reform Reconsidered: An Examination of Manitoba's Zero-Tolerance Policy on Family Violence." In T. O'Reilly-Fleming (Ed.), *Post Critical Criminology*. Scarborough: Prentice-Hall.

Valverde, M. (1995). "Introduction." In M. Valverde, L. MacLeod, and K. Johnson (Eds.), *Wife Assault and the Canadian Criminal Justice System*. Toronto: Centre of Criminology, University of Toronto.

Women Hackers: A Report from the Mission to Locate Subversive Women on the Net

Cornelia Sollfrank

*****

Hacking and Cyberfeminism

My research shows that few women are active in the field of hacking. Not just in the commercial development of technology, but also in alternative fields, and in the technological underground. No matter what area of application and no matter what the objective, gender differentiation is still maintained. Of all the technological spheres, however, it is in the hacker scene that we find the fewest women. Hacking is seen as a purely male domain, and in that sense is a clearly gendered space.

The point at which I started to deal with the subject of women hackers is the importance of the work hackers do, their function in society, and the persistence in seeing the practice as a gendered site. I think it is significant that the deconstruction of the all-pervasive power of technology, from a cyberfeminist point of view, has first to be combined with a gender-specific deconstruction of power. This is because technology is still primarily associated with maleness.

Although the handling of technology has traditionally been male-associated, industrial machinery, scientific projects, and computer languages are often symbolized by female names. So the intersection between femininity and technology can be located where such attributes as technical competence, power, and control over technology and the construction of machines are introduced. As Heidi Schelhowe, a German computer scientist, points out in her paper "Computer in der Informationsgesellschaft: Technologie mit neuem Gesicht—und altem Geschlecht?", it is the task of gender studies in technical sciences to deconstruct the category of "technology" in the way that gender and sex are being deconstructed by the social and human sciences. Technology has traditionally been perceived as something that is based on abstraction, logical thinking, and reason—all characteristics that traditionally have male connotations—whereas femininity has been associated with nature, emotion, mysticism, and intuition. Although abstraction has been posited as the antithesis of a nature-related and physical femininity, however, one might argue that abstract thought is something that is basically independent of physical conditions, and also of gender.

Yet the simple presence of more women would not necessarily change the resulting products. The demand for a higher proportion of women in technology implies a desire to question traditional assumptions and to raise consciousness regarding technology-implicated power structures. Software development and the required competencies have to be redefined. The new and yet ungendered fields would then offer fresh opportunities for women.

In the same way that Schelhowe argues on behalf of computer science, I would like to argue for the hacker scene that it is imperative to deconstruct technology in the described way and to stop closing our eyes to the fact that "the hacker" is a white male. Although hackers represent a danger for the closed knowledge and power systems, they paradoxically simultaneously these systems in the sense that only white males embody the new illegal knowledge.

While this opinion contains a generalisation about men and women and refers to the biological sex of a person, it also relates to the social construct of gender. Girls and boys are socialized differently, and thus develop differing preferences. It is necessary to face this fact and the resulting conflicts in order to bridge the gap between social and political realities and wishful cyberfeminist thinking.

I am not assuming that women and technology necessarily have as special and as close a relationship as some cyberfeminists might argue. My clitoris does not have a direct line to the Matrix—unfortunately. Such rhetoric mystifies technology and misrepresents the daily life of the female computer worker. I would suggest that most women prefer to spend their lives doing other things than programming fanatically or exploring the depths of the net. And even within the cyberfeminist community,

there are fewer computer professionals and nerds than there are men.

Women seem to prefer to undertake politically engaged work in a purely cultural environment and on a non-technological level. They are not actively influencing the development of hardware and software, and are therefore surrendering any chance to share the related power. The question is: can cultural/aesthetic practice alone sufficiently affect technological development, or will women finally have to get their hands dirty with technology? We have to ask ourselves such questions as "How deep do we have to get into technology in order to be able to handle it consciously and influence technological developments?"; "What prevents us from just going for it?"; and "Does cyberfeminism necessarily require technical competence, or is it sufficient to theorize about technology and to focus on the social, cultural, and political aspects of new technologies?"

We are living in a mental climate full of contradictions. Utopian theories promise a post-humanist age that is marked by gender- and body-obsolescence. On the other hand, the individual is still part of the power structures constituted by capital, race, and gender. We have to bear with this contradiction, try to attenuate the power and the explosive force of the new utopias, and build new social realities with it.

*****

Note

For another interesting discussion on the work that some women hackers are doing to protect children from child pornographers who use the internet as their point of contact, see "Hacker Women Are Few But Strong," by Sascha Segan, which, at the time of going to press, could be read at www.dvara.net/HK/fewbutstrong.asp

SECTION NINE

GLOBALISM

Lee-Anne Broadhead
The Gender Dimension to the Search for Global Justice
-519-

Naila Kabeer
Gender Equality and Human Development
Outcomes: Enhancing Capabilities
-525-

Maria Mies and Vandana Shiva
Ecofeminism
-537-

The Gender Dimension to the Search for Global Justice

Lee-Anne Broadhead

" I suppose this is going to be the new industry, is it?" queried one of my colleagues when he caught a glimpse of the *Canadian Woman Studies'* call for papers sitting on the table. He laughed at the notion that globalization would have anything to do specifically with women.

Academics and activists who spend their time working on the importance of a gendered approach to political inquiry might well be hurt by the biting remarks. For my part, however, there is something more worrying about these callous, off-hand comments: the profound ignorance they reveal about the importance of gender issues in the modern world order. If the educated men of the academy can so easily dismiss the disproportionately heavy costs of the neo-liberal agenda borne by women, then much less progress has been made than I had previously believed to be the case. These comments also point to the wisdom of the *CWS/cf's* editorial board in its decision to dedicate an issue to an in-depth exploration of the way in which globalization affects women.

It is indeed time to re-state (even yell from the rooftops) the importance of a gendered approach that can serve to highlight the false promises of the New Right, an agenda implemented through market de-regulation, privatization, and a dramatic reduction in social spending.

To begin, it is important that we take a close look at the language of *globalization*. The word is bandied about in common parlance as though it identifies a self-evident phenomenon. Indeed, the discourse surrounding globalization—with its air of inevitability—serves to mystify the operation of the international marketplace and encourage the belief that the direction of international economic policies and the myriad "free" trade arrangements are not a matter of choice or the outcome of ideologically driven policy but are, rather, the result of inexorable forces outside our control. This belief was neatly summed up by Bill Clinton's depiction of globalization as a "great tide, inexorably wearing away at the established order of things." Aside from the fact that this "tide" might well be experienced as a tidal wave by people around the world, why on earth is it inevitable? What makes it so?

Concepts are important, and to have such an obviously contestable one as this accepted by the media and many pundits as some sort of divine "given" is deeply troubling. It is clearly time to examine the presuppositions of "globalization" in a manner allowing the purposes and perspectives of its adherents to be drawn into the spotlight.

For the media, bureaucrats, and politicians who use it, "globalization" describes a new world order in which advancements in communications technology bring states closer together, with the resulting benefits shared and transnationalized.

If we look behind the policies presented as the necessary accompaniments to the phenomenon, we can begin to see what is actually being supported: a set of policies aimed at the elimination of the role of the state as a force for mediating the harsh excesses of the marketplace. Globalization, it seems, can be regarded as both the cause and the effect of neo-liberal orthodoxy to the extent that the international economic structures establish policies which encourage (and sometimes force) states to take specific steps in order to play by the rules of free market competition, foregoing policies designed to ameliorate the negative social and environmental effects of social competition. The unwillingness or inability of states to resist this pressure lead to the very "reality" of a transnationalized economy, which is presented as the reason for undertaking policy objectives in the first place. The circular logic is curiously simplistic—and, of course, convenient—as a tool for the invocation of economic harmonization as a self-evident good.

At the domestic level we can witness the various privatization projects, the elimination of health, environmental, and social regulations and standards previously deemed important and the acceptance of rules dictating these (and other) policies articulated by the institutions which oversee the world economic system, notably, the World Bank, the International Monetary Fund (IMF), the World Trade Organization (WTO). The subordination of national economic decision-making to the dictates of economic efficiency and a rules-based system constructed with a view to facilitating the interests of transnational corporations is the main ingredient in this particular recipe. Despite increasingly energetic

protests on the streets and many articulate critiques of the ideological underpinnings of the project, governments around the world continue to advance the neo-liberal project which serves to *create* the conditions, which are then described as inevitable.

So, there it is: the flimsy veil ripped from the claims of inevitability. Globalization stands revealed as nothing more than a concept to justify the transformation of the international economic system into one in which economic deregulation serves the interests of international capital. So why a need for a gendered approach?

First and foremost, it seems to me, looking at the international economic order through gendered lenses assists with the important goal of exposing the illogic of the system in a concrete manner. The claims that the structures of this new "global" system are providing the "people of the world" with higher environmental, social, economic, and human rights standards are obviously arguable. How better to contest such blatant fallacies than through an examination of the costs paid by those who bear the brunt of the dislocation produced by the rush to "harmonize economies" and "globalize" the marketplace?

Let's return for a moment to those pillars of the post-war economic construction upon which the "inevitable" was built. Presented as the institutional mechanisms by which peace and prosperity can be furthered, a close examination of the impact their policies has had—especially, but of course not solely on women— reveals a startling picture of the costs of "progress."

For the IMF and World Bank, the central task is to bring the world's various economies into line with the neo-liberal orthodoxy which is the foundation of "globalization." In order to qualify for loans and other forms of economic aid, these economic institutions attempt to "adjust" the economic operation of member countries in order that they can fulfill certain requirements. Through the much-despised Structural Adjustment Programs (SAPS), the IMF and World Bank established rigid economic programs for participating countries. Any government can, of course, refuse to "restructure" in accordance with the proposed plan, but to do so is to commit economic suicide in the international marketplace.

What, one might ask, does this have to do with women? Unfortunately, a great deal. Although the declared aim of SAPS is the stabilization of developing economies, one of their central features is the imposition of harsh economic measures, particularly the demand for reductions in government spending on social welfare. Having little to do with the long-term development needs of the people in the target countries, the advocates of the SAPS demonstrated instead a clear-headed interest in ensuring that developing economies promote private sector operations and market liberalization. Encouraging foreign investment was to be a central component of the overall structure as was celebrating the inevitably low costs of resources to be sold on the international market.

Benefiting those able to take advantage of the deregulated and open economy, the poorest people in the affected societies have paid a heavy price indeed as agricultural and other subsidies were removed to ensure "global competitiveness."

Aside from the environmental costs associated with these policies (stemming, for instance from the degradation of land which inevitably results from the vast increase in exports of raw materials required to fulfill the IMF's dictate of increased commodity exports), a great deal of evidence has been gathered over the years to demonstrate that women (and, as a result, children) are hardest hit by the austerity policies which governments commit to in an effort to meet the standards set by the programs established by international bureaucrats thousands of miles away.[1]

Women's unpaid work inevitably increases when governments diminish their role in the provision of social services. Often toiling outside the "economy" as it is defined by the policy wonks at international economic institutions, women's role is constantly diminished by the calculations of what a society is "worth." Aside from the very obvious point that women are rarely asked for their opinions about how to create the conditions for a more just and harmonious society, it is also worth mentioning that the notion of what makes a society "prosperous" is being dictated in the crassest of terms. The efforts on the part of women around the world to articulate their vision of an alternative global order are consistently and resolutely marginalized by the international media and virtually silenced by those to whom such original thinking is directed. Witness, for example, the lack of coverage of the concrete suggestions emerging from the Fourth United Nations Conference for Women held in Beijing in 1995. The silencing of women's visions—based on the lived experiences of those struggling to envisage a better world for all—is, alas, a theme all too evident in the world around us.

It should also be noted that it is not solely in the developing world that gender inequality is being exacerbated as a result of the institutionalization and globalization of neo-liberal economic policies. The evidence is clear in the developed world (including Canada): women's work load dramatically increases as governments rush to absolve themselves of any role in the provision of social goods (especially in areas of health, education, and social policy) while, at the same time, the gender bias of economic austerity programs means that more women than men are negatively affected by the so-called restructuring of economies.[2] The costs of these misguided and unbalanced policy decisions take a toll on society as a whole.

Another central spoke on the wheel of globalization is the (so-called) "freeing" of trade undertaken by the WTO and, once again, the gender lenses help us to see more clearly the true costs involved. Space does not permit an extended consideration of the many social ills resulting from this supposedly progressive and beneficial activity, but it is essential to at least point out that the corporate rules which are being embedded in the international trade agreements serve multinational interests and not those of the people who are displaced by the logical outcome of them.

Take, for example, the current quest for establishing intellectual property rights. We are living in an age where patent laws are seeking to own and quantify every living organism and to market it for profit. The corporate worldview embodied in—and furthered by—the WTO and its view of ownership and property is distressingly short-sighted. When a corporate executive can attempt to convince Indian farmers to buy into this narrow worldview by proclaiming that "we bring Indian farmers smart technologies, which prevent bees from usurping the pollen," (qtd. in Shiva 16) the major gulf between the corporate perspective and a traditional worldview based on true sustainability and an inclusive view of nature becomes evident. It is the women's and farmers' movements in India that have attempted to resist the seed patent laws threatening biodiversity with their corporate double-speak and quest for profits from all of nature. It is, as Vandana Shiva argues, the worldview of Indian women—an ecological worldview based on a belief in the interrelationship of species—that is necessary to counter the dangerous path of the trade proponents and their corporate allies.

There have, of course, been numerous strategies developed to challenge governments acceding to the neo-liberal orthodoxy and the destructive ideas of profit and control embedded therein, but international efforts to liberalize trade and investment have continued apace. Those who protest are declared to be "isolationist" (when, in fact, it is they who are often the true internationalists) or intent on policies denying the fruits of progress to the masses. These charges may be ridiculous but, even in an age of global communications and access to wide-ranging ideas, it remains extraordinarily easy to sideline or silence views running counter to the dominant worldview.

As a further corrective to the view of those who would heap derision upon a gendered approach to the international realm, it is instructive to reflect on the most obvious example of the persecution and marginalization of women in the global order today. I mean, of course, the treatment of women in Afghanistan—not just by the Taliban, and before them the Northern Alliance, but also by the western media and governments.

The Revolutionary Association of the Women of Afghanistan (RAWA) struggled through the nightmarish years of Taliban rule to draw the world's attention to its struggle to create the conditions for a just order within that country. Their attempts largely fell on deaf ears. The international community roused itself briefly in its attempt to save Buddhist statues threatened, and ultimately destroyed by the Taliban, then fell once more into silent complicity with, or indifference to, the regime's brutal war against women. The cynical, hypocritical claim on the part of the Bush Administration, and many other governments quickly falling into line with Washington's "crusade against evil," is that the coalition is attempting to rid Afghanistan of the Taliban in part to liberate the country's women. RAWA's opposition to the bombing campaign (described as a "vast aggression on our country") is not played alongside the tapes of bin Laden for a simple reason: the women of Afghanistan take the view that violence is not the way to rid the world, and their war-ruined country, of injustice and oppression. RAWA's vision of an alternative global order is unacceptable to those determined to bring all countries into the western orbit. Alternative visions of lasting peace and prosperity are, once again, silenced in order that the dominant perspective on global power relations can remain privileged and unchallenged.

Those who dismiss a gendered approach will doubtless continue to see power in the international system in an artificially constructed and constricting manner, never seeking to use all the critical tools at their disposal to understand the enormous costs incurred by some in the interests of others. The price of this ignorance is great—not just for women, but for the whole of humanity.

[Lee-Anne Broadhead is Assistant Professor in the Department of Politics, Government and Public Administration at the University College of Cape Breton. Her book, *International Environmental Politics: The Limits of Green Diplomacy* is forthcoming from Lynne Rienner Press.]

Notes

1. See, for instance, Gladwin; Pearson; Sparr; Ashfar and C. Dennis; Elson; Cornia, Jolly, and Stewart.

2. For an overview of the gender inequalities inherent in "globalization," see Krause and Jacobs; Cohen *et al*.

References

Ashfar H., and C. Dennis. Eds. *Women and Adjustment Policies in the Third World*, London: Macmillan, 1992.

Clinton, Bill. "Remarks by the President to the 52nd Session of the United Nations General Assembly." New York, 22 September 1997.

Cohen, M. Girffen, L. Ritchie, M. Swenarchuck, and L. Vosko. "Globalization: Some Implications and Strategies for Women." Paper prepared for the National Action Committee on the Status of Women. Revised April 2000. Online. Date accessed; January 2002. www3.sympatico.ca /truegrowth/womenstrat1.html.

Cornia, G., R. Jolly, and F. Stewart. Eds. *Adjustment with a Human Face*. Oxford: Oxford University Press, 1987.

Elson, D. "Structural Adjustments: Its Effect on Women." Eds. T. Wallace and C. March. *Changing Perceptions: Writings on Gender and Development*. Oxford: Oxfam, 1991.

Gladwin, C. *Structural Adjustment and African Women Farmers*. Gainsville: University of Florida Press, 1991.

Jacobs, S. "Globalisation, States and Women's Agency: Possibilities and Pitfalls." Eds. Jacobs, R. Jacobson and J. Marchbank. *States of Conflict: Gender, Violence and Resistance*. London: Zed Books, 2000.

Krause, J. "Gender Inequalities and Feminist Politics in a Global Perspective." Eds. E. Kofman and G. Youngs. *Globalization: Theory and Practice*. London: Pinter, 1996.

Pearson, R. "Gender Matters in Development." Eds. T. Allen and A. Thomas. *Poverty and Development in the 1990s*. Oxford: Oxford University Press, 1992.

Sparr, P. *Mortgaging Women's Lives: Feminist Critiques of Structural Adjustment*. London: Zed Books, 1994.

Tsikata, Dzodzi. "Effects of Structural Adjustment on Women and the Poor." Date Accessed: 15 Dec. 2001. Online. www.earthsummit2002.org/wcaucus.

Shiva, V. *Stolen Harvest: The Hijacking of the Global Food Supply*. Cambridge, MA: South End Press, 2000.

Revolutionary Association of the Women of Afghanistan (RAWA). "Statement on the US Strikes on Afghanistan." Online. Date Accessed: 15 December 2001. www.RAWA.false.net/us-strikes.htm

Gender Equality and Human Development Outcomes: Enhancing Capabilities

Naila Kabeer

*****

Eliminating the gender gap in human capabilities depends [many] kinds of factors. However, it also depends on the value attached to girls and women in the family, which in turn reflects their value in the wider society. This is only partly a question of economic value. It is also bound up with social values. Improvements in maternal mortality, for example, will also depend on the kind of nourishment and care that women have received in the course of their lives. Poverty eradication is thus as much a question of values as of resources and the value attached to gender equality is central to its achievement.

*****

Gender Inequality and Human Development: The Equity Rationale

*****

Gender Inequality and Basic Well-being

The form and severity of gender inequalities in basic needs are not uniform across the world. Nor are they related in a systematic way to the regional distribution of poverty. Instead, they seem to be connected to regional variations in women's economic activity, itself a reflection of differences in kinship and gender relations. The most extreme forms of gender inequality—those whose life-threatening consequences for women and girls are evident in excess rates of female mortality—are found in regions of extreme patriarchy, where women's economic options are most limited.

*****

Gender Inequality and Child Survival: The Evidence from South Asia

Extreme forms of gender inequality of a life threatening kind have a long history in South Asia. Overall, women have had a lower life expectancy than men, unlike most other parts of the world. Analysis of age-specific mortality rates suggested that girls and women died in larger numbers than boys and men until the age of 35. Declining rates of maternal mortality, however, have meant that excess levels of female mortality are now largely found among the under-fives.

There is considerable variation in the distribution of this excess female mortality within the region. For example, using juvenile sex ratios (JSRs) from 1961/71, one study noted that it was largely concentrated in Pakistan and the north-west plains of India. The Himalayan zones of India and Nepal, the eastern and southern states of India and Bangladesh reported more balanced JSRs. Other analysis suggests that gender inequalities in life expectancy in India also reflected socioeconomic differentials associated with caste, giving rise to a "perverse" positive relationship between property and inequality.

This intersection between region, social status, and gender discrimination persists and continues to confound any straightforward relationship between gender inequality and poverty in the country. Research in 2000 confirmed that highly masculine sex ratios were concentrated in the north-west, with more favourable ratios in the northern and south-eastern states. The pattern for the scheduled castes was similarly differentiated by region, with evidence of gender discrimination greater in the north. By contrast, ratios for the scheduled tribes, the poorest social groups in the country, were the most balanced. Micro-level studies from within the different sub-regions confirm this "perverse" pattern.

In terms of nutrition, studies from rural Punjab in northern India generally reported that gender disparities in nutrition among children were greater among landowning than landless households. Excess levels of female mortality there also tended to be much greater for higher order female births. The fact that first-born daughters were more likely to survive suggested that parents used the "lethal neglect" of daughters to achieve their preferred number and gender composition of children. Moreover, while *absolute* levels of mortality were lower among the propertied classes, excess levels of female mortality were higher. In addition, it was also higher among educated mothers.

Studies from southern and central India, on the other hand, reported little evidence of gender disparity among the better off or the poor. Within these more egalitarian kinship regimes, the relationship between gender inequality and poverty takes the more conventional inverse relationship. For instance, unexpectedly heavy rainfall in rural India, which increased income, was likely to improve girls' survival chances relative to boys in the first two years, thereby closing the gender gap in mortality. In rural south India, parents gave more weight to health-related outcomes for boys than girls during the lean season.

In rural Bangladesh, one study found that the literacy of mothers had a positive effect on the nutritional status of boys. Another, using data from the mid-1970s, found that boys benefited more than girls from an improvement in household resources, although this did raise the

The "Prosperity" or "Sanskritisation" Effect

The northern states of India with the highest per capita incomes in 1981 reported some of the lowest sex ratios (around 870 women to 1,000 men). This can be compared to 1,032 in Kerala and 977 in Tamil Nadu, both southern states with lower per capita incomes. Nationally, sex ratios have declined further from 933 women per 1,000 men in 1981 to 927 in 1991, despite the fact of declining poverty. In addition, "masculine" sex ratios have begun to spread to the lower castes as well as to the southern states. This increase in gender inequality reflects what has been called a "prosperity" or "sanskritisation" effect. Across India, upward mobility and increased prosperity have led to the emulation of the practices of the northern propertied castes who have traditionally reported the most severe forms of gender discrimination. The seclusion of women, resistance to widow remarriage, increased kin and village exogamy, and a rise in the practice and value of dowry—all traditionally associated with the propertied castes of the north—are spreading throughout the country as the poorest groups imitate those better off.

nutritional status of all children. Discrimination against girl children appeared to be one aspect of household responses to economic crisis, so that excess female mortality in the under-five age group increased during the 1974 famine.

It is generally believed in the field of development studies that economic growth and increasing prosperity are likely to lead to a decline in gender discrimination, at least at the level of basic survival. Also, life expectancy and child survival do improve with growth. However, the "perverse" relationship between poverty and gender discrimination shown in some of these studies gives room for pause. And more recent evidence from South Asia provides further confirmation that gender discrimination does not necessarily disappear with economic growth or poverty reduction (see box).

Gender Inequality and the Quantity-Quality Trade-off

Demographic transition leading to lower levels of fertility has now occurred in many parts of the developing world and is ongoing in others. Family size in East and South-East Asia has halved. This transition is also underway in other parts of Asia as well as in Latin America. The least evidence of demographic change at the regional level is in sub-Saharan Africa.

Economists suggest that one of the factors behind demographic transitions is the "quantity-quality" trade off: the reduction in numbers of children as more resources are invested in each child. Studies from South-East Asia suggest that fertility decline has been accompanied by increased investment in the education of girls as well as boys. This has led to a closing of the gender gap in education—and its elimination at primary level—in countries such as the Philippines, Thailand, and Vietnam. In Latin America and the Caribbean too, there is little evidence of discrimination against girls.

In countries characterised by extreme patriarchy, on the other hand, there is troubling evidence that parents have achieved the reduction in the "quantity" of children

through a strategy of sex-selective investments in child "quality." In some parts of India, this has taken the form of sex-selective investments in children's education. Even more alarming, however, is evidence that fertility decline there has been accompanied by sex-selective investment in child survival. The relative chances of survival among female children has gone down so that the worsening of the JSR has been more marked than the sex ratio at all ages. Discrimination against girl children allows parents to simultaneously reduce their fertility rates and achieve the desired sex composition of children. These practices are now in evidence in the southern states of India, particularly in Tamil Nadu, where fertility decline has been most rapid. Even Kerala, long held up as a model of gender egalitarianism, appears to be achieving further fertility decline through a widening of gender disparities in child survival—though it continues to have higher levels of absolute welfare for girls and boys than the rest of the country.

Gender-discriminatory practices have also extended to the pre-natal stage so as to influence the sex composition of *births* as well as of surviving children. Amniocentesis and ultrasound screening technologies are increasingly used to detect the sex of the foetus and then the females are aborted. This is shown by a marked shift in sex ratios at birth in north and north-west India and urban areas of central India and supported by various smaller scale studies and reports.

These practices are not confined to South Asia, although they have been more extensively researched there. The Republic of Korea, along with China, has the highest male-to-female birth ratios in the world: around 113.6 males per 100 females in 1988. Because measures to identify the sex of a child, followed by sex-selective abortion, tend to be resorted to after the first birth, birth ratios become more male dominated for higher order births. Between 1985 and 1987, the sex ratio was more than 130 males to 100 females for third births and the estimate in 1988 was 199 for fourth births. However, it is probably in China—with its a rigidly enforced one-child policy and deeply entrenched preference for sons—that the most devastating consequences on the survival and well-being of girl children have occurred (see box).

East Asian economies all experienced very high rates of economic growth and remarkable declines in poverty in the 1980s. Indeed, they were the basis for the labour-intensive growth strategies advanced in the 1990 *World Development Report* (WDR). These findings are a reminder that neither economic growth nor rising rates of female labour force participation necessarily eradicate gender inequality. Sex-selective investments in the human capabilities of children cannot be explained in this case in terms of differential employment opportunities. Instead the reason can be found in the social values and practices that reflect the patriarchal ordering of social relations. The state could potentially take action to undermine these values and practices, but this has not occurred. From gender inequalities in citizenship rights entrenched in the constitutions of Bangladesh, India, and Pakistan—all three of which recognise religious law in the arena of personal life—to China's one-child policy and its tragic consequences, the state has been a force for greater inequality.

Gender Inequalities, Work Burdens, and Nutrition

Elsewhere in the world, gender discrimination rarely takes the systematically life-threatening form that it takes in regions of extreme patriarchy. Moreover, it is generally related to poverty and tends to be greater among poor households and communities. Studies from South-East Asia, for example, reveal weak evidence of gender bias in well-being in the household. A study in Indonesia found little evidence of discrimination against girls in choice of health treatment and standardised child weights, but mild malnourishment among girls and higher birth-order children. Data from some of the poorer rural provinces in the Philippines found mild gender discrimination in favour of husbands, who received more of their protein requirements compared to wives and children. Among

Gender Discrimination and Sex Ratios in China

It is evident in China that the "lethal neglect" of infant girls is a factor in achieving desired sex composition of children. The "normal" sex ratio among infant deaths is around 130 boys to 100 girls. The substantially lower rates here, particularly in rural areas, of around 114 during the 1980s suggest substantial neglect of infant girls. The Chinese estimates are comparable to Pakistan (118) and Tunisia (115), both characterised by extreme forms of patriarchy, but much lower than Malaysia and the Philippines (128) in South-East Asia. Moreover, there is also evidence of pre-natal discrimination in China. Studies show that the sex ratio of births went from around 105 boys per 100 girls for all birth order combined in the 1970s (before the introduction of the one-child policy) to around 114 in the 1980s to even higher levels of 153 in 1993. Sex ratios of reported births increased between 1988 and 1993 from 133 for the first birth to 172 for the second to 1,100 for the third.

children, boys and lower birth orders were relatively favoured. Evidence from Vietnam does not show significant gender inequalities in basic nutrition and health care. Early analysis of nutritional data from 94 Latin American villages, however, indicated that girls aged 0–4 were 87 percent of their expected weight/age measurements while boys were 90 percent.

Studies from sub-Saharan Africa show high levels of infant and child mortality but little evidence of differences suggesting gender bias. A report from the Subcommittee on Nutrition of the UN Administrative Committee on Coordination (ACC/SCN) estimated that around 20 percent of African women were undernourished, compared to 60 percent in South Asia. However, there

Levels of Maternal Mortality

While estimates of maternal mortality need to be treated with caution because of the absence of accurate data, a report by the World Health Organization (WHO) gives some idea of the magnitude of the problem in sub-Saharan Africa, particularly in West Africa. Figures of 1,750–2,900 per 100,000 births are reported for Mali and 500–1500 for Ghana. In contrast, in Asia they vary between 600 for Bangladesh and 900 for Papua New Guinea on the high side, and around 10–50 for China and 9–42 for the Republic of Korea. Sub-Saharan Africa accounts for 20 percent of the world's births but 40 percent of its maternal deaths. These high levels of maternal mortality partly reflect the overall poverty of the region but also the lack of basic services. West Africa performed more poorly in translating its per capita GNP into human development outcomes than other regions with similar levels of per capita GNP.

is evidence of rising excess female mortality in recent years. Demographic and Health Surveys (DHSs) from the early 1990s report excess death rates among girls in the 0–5 age group in 9 out of 14 countries, while UN estimates suggest a decline in the ratio of women to men in most regions of Africa except the south. Inequalities in health care, rather than nutritional bias, probably explain this deterioration. In addition, there are high levels of maternal mortality (see box).

However, along with overall levels of poverty, high rates of maternal mortality in this region also show the effects on women's well-being of their survival strategies at the lower end of the income scale. The value given to labour in otherwise resource-poor agrarian economies, which lack well-developed markets and basic health services, has resulted in high levels of both fertility and

child mortality that are mutually reinforcing. The intersection of women's long working hours in production and reproduction combined with their high rates of fertility takes its toll on their physical well-being. This is compounded by the risks of childbirth.

While women work longer hours than men in most parts of the world [...] it was in sub-Saharan Africa that the concept of women's "time poverty" first emerged and where it continues to have the greatest resonance. For example, women's excessive workload was identified by both women and men in one poverty assessment based in Guinea as a major factor in their disadvantage.

Long working hours in energy-intensive forms of work also have implications for women's nutritional status. The most common nutritional deficiencies among females are iron-deficiency anaemia and protein-energy malnutrition. Variations in the severity of female nutritional deprivation draw attention to: (a) life cycle factors; (b) the poverty of their households; and (c) aspects of their wider environment. It is at its most severe among women in the reproductive age group, often reducing energy among mothers for any activities beyond those essential for basic survival. It also has a regional dimension. Along with high percentages of low birth weight infants (a reflection of mothers' nutritional status) and high rates of maternal mortality, nutritional anaemia is also much higher among women from West Africa than the rest of the continent.

Women's nutritional status also has a seasonal dimension, reflecting fluctuations in their workloads during the agricultural cycle. The period of greatest nutritional stress for rural women is the "lean months" of the pre-harvest period when household stocks and energy intake are low but the energy demands of agricultural work tend to be highest. Heavy work during pregnancy can lead to premature labour and, without increased caloric intake, to low birth-weight babies.

Finally, and not surprisingly, women's nutritional deficiency has a poverty dimension. The main cause is household food insecurity due to unreliable food availability and very low incomes. The interaction between female nutritional deprivation and the heavy demands on their labour leads to high rates of miscarriage. In fact, "reasonably adequate" birth weights reported in sub-Saharan Africa may reflect the fact that the most malnourished foetuses, infants, and mothers simply do not survive.

Micro-level studies confirm not only that women from lower income households tend to be at a greater nutritional disadvantage than those in better off households but also that they often pay part of the price of household attempts to cope with crisis. A study from Côte d'Ivoire found no significant difference between the body mass index (BMI) of males and females but noted that women's nutritional status was more likely than men's to be affected by fluctuations in household income and per capita expenditure. In Zimbabwe, the drought of the early 1990s was found to have significantly decreased women's BMI but not men's. In situations of severe shortage in Cameroon, women coped by going hungry for the whole day while men were more likely to migrate.

It would appear, therefore, that while households' coping strategies in times of economic hardship and crises generally include cutting back on food consumption, women bear the brunt of this strategy far more than men. The link between poverty and female ill-being is also supported by evidence from the Gambia that an increase in overall household income—the result of increased productivity of rice production due to improved technology—led to improvement in the nutritional status of women and children and a reduction in seasonal fluctuations of women's weight.

Gender Inequality and Hazardous Livelihoods

Another strategy adopted by households, particularly in times of crisis, is to resort to exploitative or hazardous forms of livelihoods. This is likely to have adverse effects on the well-being and also self-worth of members. For both men and women, there are certain forms of work that are more physically exhausting, worse for their health or more degrading. For example, rickshaw-pulling in South Asia, an extremely energy-consuming and almost entirely male occupation, is associated with tuberculosis (TB). Since these forms of work are avoided by those who can afford it, involvement in them is often an indicator of poverty.

Prostitution is one response to crisis more frequently adopted by women and girls than men and boys. In parts of South-East Asia, where tourism is a major source of foreign exchange, "export-orientation" has been associated with the rise of a female-dominated "hospitality industry" in which sex work plays an important role. Remittances from daughters who have entered prostitution represent the sole source of income for many poor rural households in the region.

While prostitution has traditionally been associated with a variety of sexually transmitted infections (STIs), the spread of AIDS has introduced a potentially fatal risk to what has always been a hazardous form of livelihood. Moreover, it is not only those who supply sexual services who are at risk but also those who "demand" and, through them, the wider population. While this demand is not necessarily confined to any particular section of the population, it does appear to be higher in certain areas and among certain occupational groups (see box).

The highest rates of HIV/AIDS are currently found in sub-Saharan Africa, which accounts for 79 percent of people living with the disease and 81 percent of deaths associated with the epidemic, massively outweighing its share of the global population (10%). However, AIDS is spreading rapidly in other parts of the world, particularly in Asia.

While AIDS clearly poses risks for all sections of the population, it also has certain gender-specific aspects. As in the case with most STIs, women are at greater biological risk than men of contracting the HIV virus from each sexual intercourse. Forced sex increases this risk

Men Most at Risk of HIV/AIDS

Along with sex workers and "single women," the Poverty Reduction Strategy Paper (PRSP) in Burkina Faso identified truckers and the military as most at risk of HIV/AIDS infection. In India, surveys also suggest that truck drivers are one of the largest causes of transmission of the virus. One survey in Calcutta found that over 5 percent of truck drivers had HIV. More than 90 percent visited at least one prostitute a week, they had an average of 200 sexual encounters a year, and 68 percent had never used a condom. They appeared to be the main channels through which HIV migrated from urban to rural areas as new transportation networks connect outlying areas with cities. Men more likely to visit sex workers are non-skilled and low-skilled workers in manufacturing industries located in urban areas; workers in various types of transportation industries such as rickshaw drivers, taxi drivers, and bus drivers; construction workers; and traders and customers in periodic markets in both urban and rural areas.

because micro-lesions make it easier for the virus to enter the bloodstream. Social beliefs that younger women are either free of or able to "cure" AIDS has made them a particularly vulnerable group in Africa. Women under 25 represent the fastest growing group with AIDS in the region, accounting for nearly 30 percent of all female cases. In Burkina Faso, where 7 percent of the population is affected by the epidemic, the incidence among girls aged 19–24 is four or five times higher than boys of the same age. It has been found that circumcision provides men with some degree of protection from STIs and HIV, which partly explains the low incidence in West Africa.

In addition, however, the spread of AIDS is related to wider gender inequalities in income, wealth,and economic opportunity. In contrast to, for example, South Asia where sex is viewed as either acceptable (marriage) or unacceptable (prostitution), there is a continuum of possible sexual relationships between these two extremes in other regions of the world. Women may exchange sex for money, goods, or services as part of their survival strategy, and on a transient or permanent basis. Studies from Zimbabwe and South Africa have pointed out that the decision by women to sell sex is usually in response to economic need. Poverty, along with peer pressure, leads young schoolgirls to get involved in sexual relationships with fellow students and teachers in schools and "sugar daddies" outside. They need money for basic necessities such as uniforms, books, fees, and bus fare as well as to participate in the social life of the school. Whenever sex is part of an economic exchange, women's ability to protect themselves from STIs is limited.

Gender Inequality and Family Well-Being: The Instrumental Rationale

As well as an end goal of development, gender equality can also be seen as a route to achieving other human development goals. There are a number of links between women's well-being, agency, and resources, on the one hand, and a variety of demographic and welfare outcomes on the other. Some of these links work through biological synergies. One example noted above is that between a mother's nutritional status and the birth weight of her baby. Gender discrimination in access to food and health care explains why South Asia has the highest rates of low birth weight babies in the world. Nutritionally deprived women are likely to give birth to low-weight babies whose chances of survival are severely limited. While these links are biological, they reflect social processes. Moreover, there are other synergies where the social causalities are even clearer. They provide a rationale for investing in gender equality on the grounds of what might be called "welfare instrumentalism."

Gender, Resources, and Children's Well-Being: The Social Connections

Some of these links work through improvements in women's education and many relate to demographic outcomes. One of the most widely documented findings, and one that appears to hold true across much of the world, is an inverse relationship between mother's schooling and child mortality, particularly in lower-income countries (see box).

A variety of explanations have been put forward for these findings. Education:

Mothers' Schooling and Child Mortality
DHS data from 25 developing countries suggest that, other things being equal, 1–3 years of maternal schooling reduce child mortality by 15 percent while an equivalent level of paternal schooling achieves a 6 per cent reduction. Despite some of the highest rates of infant mortality in the world, the relationship also applies in Africa. Analysis of 1975–1985 data for 13 African countries showed that a 10 percent increase in female literacy rates reduced child mortality by 10 percent but that changes in male literacy has little influence. In addition, there is broad-based evidence of a link between women's education and fertility rates. Again, the relationship is stronger than with fathers' education. While the effect is generally evident at primary school levels, it comes into operation somewhat later at secondary levels of education in sub-Saharan Africa.

(a) delays women's age of marriage and hence age of first birth;

(b) eases their access to contraception and to health services as well as their ability to use both more effectively; and

(c) improves their treatment by health providers.

There is considerable empirical evidence for this interpretation. In Kenya, for example, women were able to understand the instructions for administering oral rehydration salts after four or more years of schooling. Education in Nigeria was seen to increase women's capacity to deal with the outside world, including the world of health service providers. In rural areas, uneducated women preferred not to deliver in hospitals because of the treatment they received at the hands of nurses, a treatment not meted out to more educated women.

Several studies show that mothers' education consistently affects the chances that:

- women will attend antenatal clinics;
- births will be attended by trained medical personnel;
- complete immunisation of children will take place; and
- sick children will receive timely and effective medical care.

This effect is particularly strong in poorer areas where proper health services are not available. In such cases, education puts women at an advantage in accessing available services.

Gender, Resources, and Family Welfare: Preferences and Priorities

In addition, there is evidence to suggest that women may use resources at their disposal differently to men. Brazilian data, for example, indicated that unearned income in the hands of mothers had a far greater effect on family health than income in the hands of fathers. For child survival, the effect was 20 times larger. The effect of maternal education was also larger than that of paternal education. Women were slightly more likely to use unearned income in favour of daughters while men were slightly more likely to favour sons.

A study in Côte d'Ivoire reported that raising women's share of household income reduced household expenditure on alcohol and cigarettes but increased spending on food. An increase in male share of income increased expenditure on alcohol and cigarettes but also on clothing for children and adults. In Rwanda, holding income constant, members of female-headed households consumed 377 more calories per adult equivalent per day than male-headed households. This difference was greatest among lower income households. In the Gambia, the share of cereal production under women's control added 322 more calories per adult equivalent per day to household energy consumption. In Kenya and Malawi, moderate to severe levels of malnutrition were much lower among children in female-headed households, whether *de jure* or *de facto*, than children in male-headed households. In fact, children in *de facto* female-headed households received a higher proportion of total household calories than did children from other household groups.

Similar "welfare" effects in relation to children are reported for the rural Philippines, where male household heads were found to be favoured in nutritional allocation. Increased wages for husbands and fathers had a positive effect on share of calories allocated to themselves and their spouses but a negative effect on children's share. However, an increase in the wages of wives and mothers had a significant positive impact on their own and their children's relative share of household calories and a negative effect on husbands' share.

The evidence of a link between women's access to resources or capacity to exercise agency and family welfare in South Asia has varied over time, location, and level of analysis. However, an analysis that controlled for differences in "gender regimes" across the subcontinent showed that variations in child mortality could be explained by variations in female literacy and labour force participation. Female literacy was associated with lower levels of under-five mortality while female literacy together with labour force participation reduced mortality rates of female children and led to a closing of the gender gap.

Gender, Resources, and Family Welfare in Bangladesh

In urban Bangladesh, an increase in the percentage of women working in manufacturing employment has been accompanied by a decline in the number of child labourers per urban household. The desire to educate children or younger siblings was a widely cited reason why women entered the factories. Evidence from rural areas suggests that access to micro-credit has also led to improvements in educational levels, particularly of girls. Detailed analysis of 1995 data from two districts found that:

- while the education of both mother and father increased the likelihood of children going to school, the effect of mother's schooling was statistically higher;
- only the mother's education reduced the likelihood of children working; and
- women's access to loans significantly increased the likelihood of children going to school while men's access to loans had no such effect. In fact, a 10 percent increase in female credit increased the probability of a child going to school by 10–11 percent and decreased the probability of full time work among children by 10%.

On the other hand, in those regions in India that practise extreme forms of gender discrimination, women are likely to share the values of the wider community. Here female education is not necessarily associated with a benevolent effect. For example, a study in rural Punjab reported that female education increased the likelihood of excess female mortality among daughters.

While evidence on education from India is complicated by the interactions between class, caste, and gender, that from neighbouring Muslim countries appears less ambiguous. Studies from Bangladesh and Pakistan suggest that the educational levels of both parents have played an important role in increasing the likelihood of children's education. However, women's education levels were far more important than that of their spouse. A separate study using household data from Pakistan also found that mothers' education was more powerfully associated than that of fathers with the likelihood of children going to school, but also of *girls* going to school. In Bangladesh, growing employment opportunities for women appears to be translating into higher levels of children's education—as well as on reducing the gender gap in education (see box).

Altruism or Interests? Explaining the "Welfare" Effect

Attempts to explain these findings have varied between those who emphasise gender-differentiated *preferences* and those who suggest they might reflect gender differentiated *interests*. The former tend to emphasise socialisation processes by which women acquire a more "connected" sense of self and pursue more altruistic forms of behaviour while men define themselves in more "separative" terms and display more self-interested forms of behaviour. This interpretation is supported by findings from a wide range of contexts that men are likely to retain a greater percentage of their income for personal use while women tend to spend a greater percentage of their income on collective welfare.

On the other hand, it has also been pointed out that women's fortunes are more closely bound up with the fortune of their families and children (particularly their sons in South Asia). Women tend to live longer in most parts of the world and will be reliant on their children for support in old age. Older men are also far more able to marry younger wives, particularly in polygamous marriages. The ideology of maternal altruism may thus merely disguise self-interested forms of behaviour (investments in family as a form of "social capital") or distract attention from non-altruistic forms of discrimination against daughters.

Alternatively, of course, both explanations might be true. Gender differences in upbringing and socialisation play a role in shaping values and preferences and also experiences. The close physical bonding that occurs between mothers and children in the first years of the child's life and the very direct care and emotional support that mothers provide are all likely to make their bond with their children a special one. And women's domestic responsibilities means that they are more likely to hear a child crying from hunger than men who work away from the household. At the same time, inequalities in access to independent resources mean that women have a greater stake in nurturing their family networks and thus discriminating in ways that are likely to secure their status in the family. As those directly responsible for the care and welfare of infants, excess forms of female mortality must at least partly reflect women's agency. The finding from some places that educated mothers meant higher levels of excess female mortality among daughters, particularly those born later, suggests that education can increase women's effective agency in lethal, as well as benevolent, ways.

Nevertheless, these findings help show how patterns of behaviour at the micro-level, including improvements in women's access to education and employment, translate into discernible trends at the macro-level. These trends include demographic transition and the formation of human capital and human capabilities. They provide some of the micro-foundations for the macroeconomic models [that explore] the implications for the social distribution of income on the human capital dimensions of economic growth.

Conclusion

These various findings underscore the fact that the connection between women's productive and reproductive work is critical for their families (particularly their children) and for themselves. This is partly historical and entrenched in the deep structures of their societies. In regions where women have been denied an economically visible and socially acknowledged role in production, and have been confined to an economically devalued and socially invisible role in the domestic arena and reproductive work, they and their daughters have had shorter life expectancies, poorer health status, and more circumscribed life choices than both men and boys in their own cultures and women and girls elsewhere. Such patterns persist into the present.

The issue of poverty is also crucial. Poorer women are far more likely than women from better-off households to experience conflicting demands on their time from these two sets of responsibilities. Their attempts to balance them can lead to a variety of adverse outcomes, including:

- longer working hours than men in their families;
- greater fatigue and nutritional deprivation; and
- withdrawal of children, especially daughters, from school in order to relieve their mothers from domestic chores.

On the other hand, the positive synergies that have been identified between different aspects of human development can be built on. This means addressing gender inequality in access to resources, including time, within the household and various welfare failures, including gender inequalities in welfare distribution and the inter-generational transmission of poverty.

Ecofeminism

Maria Mies and Vandana Shiva

Ecofeminism

Ecofeminism, "a new term for an ancient wisdom"[1] grew out of various social movements—the feminist, peace, and the ecology movements—in the late 1970s and early 1980s. Though the term was first used by Francoise D'Eaubonne,[2] it became popular only in the context of numerous protests and activities against environmental destruction, sparked off initially by recurring ecological disasters. The meltdown at Three Mile Island prompted large numbers of women in the USA to come together in the first ecofeminist conference—"Women and Life on Earth: A Conference on Eco-Feminism in the Eighties"—in March 1980, at Amherst. At this conference the connections between feminism, militarization, healing, and ecology were explored. As Ynestra King, one of the Conference organizers, wrote:

> Ecofeminism is about connectedness and wholeness of theory and practice. It asserts the special strength and integrity of every living thing. For us the snail darter is to be considered side by side with a community's need for water, the porpoise side by side with appetite for tuna, and the creatures it may fall on with Skylab. We are

a woman-identified movement and we believe we have a special work to do in these imperilled times. We see the devastation of the earth and her beings by the corporate warriors, and the threat of nuclear annihilation by the military warriors, as feminist concerns. It is the same masculinist mentality which would deny us our right to our own bodies and our own sexuality, and which depends on multiple systems of dominance and state power to have its way.[3]

Wherever women acted against the ecological destruction or/and the threat of atomic annihilation, they immediately became aware of the connection between patriarchal violence against women, other people and nature, and that:

> In defying this patriarchy we are loyal to future generations and to life and this planet itself. We have a deep and particular understanding of this both through our natures and our experience as women.[4]

The "corporate and military warriors" aggression against the environment was perceived almost physically as an aggression against our female body. This is expressed by many women who participated in these movements. Thus, women in Switzerland who demonstrated against the Seveso poisoning wrote:

> We should think of controlling our bodies in a more global way, as it is not only men and doctors who behave aggressively towards our bodies, but also the multinationals! What more aggression against the body of women, against the children than that of La Roche-Givaudan at Seveso? From 10 July 18 1976, their entire lives have been taken over by the "accident" and the effects are going to last for a long time.[5]

On the night of 2–3 December 1984, 40 tons of toxic gas are released from a Union Carbide pesticides plant in Bhopal, India; 3,000 people died during the disaster and of the 400,000 other who were exposed, many have since died, and the suffering continues. Women have been those most severely affected but also most persistent in their demand for justice. The Bhopal Gas Peedit Mahila Udyog Sangathan has continued to remind the Government of India, Union Carbide, and the world that they still suffer, and that no amount of money can restore the lives and health of the victims. As Hamidabi, a Muslim woman from one of the poor *bastis* which were worst hit in the disaster said, "We will not stop our fight till the fire in our hearts goes quiet—this fire started with 3,000 funeral pyres—and it will not die till we have justice." Or, as the women of Sicily who protested against the stationing of nuclear missiles in their country stated:

> Our "no" to war coincides with our struggle for liberation. Never have we seen so clearly the connection between nuclear escalation and the culture of the musclemen; between the violence of war and the violence of rape. Such in fact is

the historical memory that women have of war ... But it is also our daily experience in "peacetime" and in this respect women are perpetually at war ... It is no coincidence that the gruesome game of war—in which the greater part of the male sex seems to delight—passes through the same stages as the traditional sexual relationship: aggression, conquest, possession, control. Of a woman or land, it makes little difference.[6]

The women who were a driving force in movements against the construction of nuclear power plants in Germany were not all committed feminists, but to them also the connection between technology, war against nature, against women, and future generations was clear. The peasant women who actively protested against the proposed construction of a nuclear power plant at Whyl in South-West Germany also saw the connection between technology, the profit-oriented growth mania of the industrial system, and the exploitation of the "Third World."[7] This connection was also most clearly spelt out by a Russian woman after the Chernobyl catastrophe in 1986: "Men never think of life. They only want to conquer nature and the enemy."

The Chernobyl disaster in particular provoked a spontaneous expression of women's outrage and resistance against this war technology and the general industrial warrior system. The illusion that atomic technology was malevolent when used in bombs but benevolent when used to generate electricity for the North's domestic appliances was dispelled. Many women too, also understood that their consumerist lifestyle was also very much part of this system of war against nature, women, foreign peoples, and future generations.

The new developments in biotechnology, genetic engineering, and reproductive technology have made women acutely conscious of the gender bias of science and technology and that science's whole paradigm is characteristically patriarchal, anti-nature, and colonial and aims to dispossess women of their generative capacity as it does the productive capacities of nature. The founding of the Feminist International Network of Resistance to Genetic and Reproductive Engineering (fiNRRAFE) in 1984 was followed by a number of important congresses: 1985 in Sweden and in Bonn, 1988 in Bangladesh, and 1991 in Brazil. This movement reached far beyond the narrowly defined women's or feminist movement. In Germany women from trade unions, churches, and universities, rural and urban women, workers, or housewives mobilized against these technologies for women, but also for animals, plants, for agriculture in the Third World as well as in the industrialized North. They understood that the liberation of women cannot be achieved in isolation, but only as part of a larger struggle for the preservation of life on this planet.

This movement also facilitates the creation of new connections and networks. An African woman at the Bangladesh congress, on hearing of these technologies exclaimed: "If that is progress, we do not want it. Keep it!"

"Spiritual" or "Political" Ecofeminism?

As women in various movements—ecology, peace, feminist, and especially health—rediscovered the interdependence and connectedness of everything, they also rediscovered what was called the spiritual dimension of life—the realization of this interconnectedness was itself sometimes called spirituality. Capitalist and Marxist materialism, both of which saw the achievement of human happiness as basically conditional on the expansion of material goods' production, denied or denigrated this dimension. Feminists also began to realize the significance of the "witch hunts" at the beginning of our modern era in so far as patriarchal science and technology was developed only after these women (the witches) had been murdered and, concomitantly, their knowledge, wisdom, and close relationship with nature had been destroyed.[8] The desire to recover, to regenerate this wisdom as a means to liberate women and nature from patriarchal destruction also motivated this turning towards spirituality. The term "spiritual" is ambiguous, it means different things to different people. For some it means a kind of religion, but not one based upon the continuation of the patriarchal, monotheistic religions of Christianity, Judaism, or Islam, all of which are arguably hostile to women and to nature vis-à-vis their basic warrior traditions. Hence some tried to revive or recreate a goddess-based religion; spirituality was defined as the Goddess.

Some call it the female principle, inhabiting and permeating all things—this spirituality is understood in a less "spiritual," that is, less idealistic way. Although the spirit was female, it was not apart from the material world, but seen as the life force in everything and in every human being: it was indeed the connecting principle. Spirituality in these more material terms was akin to magic rather than to religion as it is commonly understood.[9] This interpretation of spirituality is also spelt out in the writings of Starhawk,[10] for whom spirituality is largely identical to women's sensuality, their sexual energy, their most precious life force, which links them to each other, to other life forms and the elements. It is the energy that enables women to love and to celebrate life. This sensual or sexual spirituality, rather than "other-worldly," is centred on and thus abolishes the opposition between spirit and matter, transcendence and immanence. There is only immanence, but this immanence is not inert, passive matter devoid of subjectivity, life and spirit. The spirit is inherent in everything and particularly our sensuous experience, because we ourselves with our bodies cannot separate the material from the spiritual. The spiritual is the love without which no life can blossom, it is this magic which is contained within everything. The rediscovered ancient wisdom consisted of the old magic insight into the existence of these all-embracing connections and that through these, powerless women could therefore influence powerful men. This at least informed the thinking of the women who, in 1980, surrounded the Pentagon with their rituals and who formulated the first ecofeminist manifesto.[11]

The ecological relevance of this emphasis on "spirituality" lies in the rediscovery of the sacredness of life, according to which life on earth can be preserved only if people again begin to perceive all life forms as sacred and respect them as such. This quality is not located in an other-worldly deity, in a transcendence, but in everyday life, in our work, the things that surround us, in our immanence. And from time to time there should be celebrations of this sacredness in rituals, in dance and song.

This celebration of our dependence on Mother Earth is quite contrary to the attitude promoted by Francis Bacon and his followers, the fathers of modern science and technology. For then this dependence was an outrage, a mockery of man's right to freedom on his own terms and therefore had forcefully and violently to be abolished. Western rationality, the West's paradigm of science and concept of freedom are all based on overcoming and transcending this dependence, on the subordination of nature to the (male) will, and the disenchantment of all her forces. Spirituality in this context endeavours to "heal Mother Earth" and to re-enchant the world. This means to undo the process of disenchantment, which Max Weber saw as the inevitable outcome of the European rationalization process.

Ecofeminists in the USA seemingly put greater emphasis on the "spiritual" than do those in Europe. For example, in Germany particularly since the early 1980s this tendency has often been criticized as escapism, as signifying a withdrawal from the political sphere into some kind of dream world, divorced from reality, and

thus leaving power in the hands of men. But the "spiritual" feminists argue that theirs is the politics of everyday life, the transformation of fundamental relationships, even if that takes place only in small communities. They consider that this politics is much more effective than countering the power games of men with similar games. In Germany, too, this debate has to be seen against the background of the emergence of the Greens, who participated in parliamentary politics since 1978. Many feminists joined the Green Party, less out of ecological than feminist concerns. The Greens, however, were keen to integrate these concerns too into their programmes and politics. The critique of the "spiritual" stand within the ecofeminist movement is voiced mainly by men and women from the left. Many women, particularly those who combine their critique of capitalism with a critique of patriarchy and still cling to some kind of "materialist" concept of history, do not easily accept spiritual ecofeminism, because it is obvious that capitalism can also co-opt the "spiritual" feminists critique of "materialism."

This, indeed, is already happening. The New Age and esoteric movement have created a new market for esoterica, meditation, yoga, magic, alternative health practices, most of which are fragments taken out of the context of oriental, probably Chinese and Indian, cultures. Now, after the material resources of the colonies have been looted, their spiritual and cultural resources are being transformed into commodities for the world market.

This interest in things spiritual is a manifestation of Western patriarchal capitalist civilization's deep crisis. While in the West the spiritual aspects of life (always segregated from the "material" world), have more and more been eroded, people now look towards the "East," towards pre-industrial traditions in the search for what has been destroyed in their own culture.

This search obviously stems from a deep human need for wholeness, but the fragmented and commodified way in which it takes place is to be criticized. Those interested in oriental spiritualism rarely know, or care to know, how people in, for example, India, live or even the socio-economic and political contexts from these which fragments—such as yoga or tai-chi—have been taken. It is a kind of luxury spirituality. It is, as Saral Sarkar put it,[12] the idealist icing on top of the material cake of the West's standard of living. Such luxury spiritualism cannot overcome the dichotomies between spirit and matter, economics and culture, because as long as it fails to integrate this search for wholeness into a critique of the existing exploitative world system and a search for a better society, it can be co-opted and neutralized.

For Third World women who fight for the conservation of their survival base, this spiritual icing-on-the-cake, the divorce of the spiritual from the material, is incomprehensible for them, the term Mother Earth does not need to be qualified by inverted commas, because they regard the earth as a living being which guarantees their own and all their fellow creatures' survival. They respect and celebrate Earth's sacredness and resist its transformation into dead, raw material for industrialism and commodity production. It follows, therefore, that they also respect both the diversity and the limits of nature, which cannot be violated if they want to survive. It is this kind of materialism, this kind of immanence rooted in the everyday subsistence production of most of the world's women which is the basis of our ecofeminist position. This materialism is neither commodified capitalist nor mechanical Marxist materialism, both of which are based on the same concept of humanity's relationship to nature. But the ecofeminist spirituality as we understand it is not to be confused with a kind of other-worldly spirituality, that simply wants "food without sweat,"[13] not caring where it comes from or whose sweat it involves.

*****

Notes

1. Diamond, I., and G.F. Orenstein, *Recovering the World: The Emergence of Ecofeminism*. Sierra Club Books, San Francisco, 1990. Op cit.

2. D'Eaubonne, F., "Feminism or Death," in Elaine Marks and Isabelle de Courtivron (eds.), *New French Feminisms, an Anthology*. Amherst University Press, Amherst, 1980.

3. King, Y., "The Eco-Feminist Perspective," in L. Caldecott and S. Leland (eds.), *Reclaiming the Earth: Women Speak out for Life on Earth*. The Women's Press, London, 1983, p. 10.

4. Ibid., p. 11.

5. Howard-Gorden, F., "Seveso Is Everywhere," in Caldecott and Leland, op. cit., pp. 35–45.

6. Statement of Sicilian Women, quoted in Caldecott and Leland, op. cit., p. 126.

7. Gladitz, N., op cit. *Lieber heute aktiv als morgen radioaktiv,* Wagenbach, Berlin, 1976.

8. Merchant, C., *The Death of Nature: Women, Ecology and the Scientific Revolution*. Harper and Row, San Francisco, 1983.

9. Mies, M. TANTRA, Magie oder Spiritualitat? in beitraege zur.

10. Starhawk, 1982.

11. Caldecott and Leland, op. cit., p. 15.

12. Sarkar, S., Die Bewegung und ihre Strategie. Ein Beitrag zum notwendigen Klärungspronzb, in *Kommune,* Nr. Frankfurt, 1987.

13. Diamond, I. "Resisting the Logic of Control: Feminism, Fertility and the Living Earth," paper (unpublished), 1990.

Bibliography

Acoose, Janice. *Iskwewak—Hah' Ki Yaw Ni Wahkomakanak: Neither Indian Princesses nor Easy Squaws*. Toronto: Women's Press, 1995.

Anderson, Kim. "The Construction of a Negative Identity," *A Recognition of Being: Reconstructing Native Womanhood*. Toronto: Sumach Press, 2000.

Armstrong, Pat, and Hugh Armstrong. "Class Is a Feminist Issue," in Armstrong et al. (eds.), *Studies in Political Economy: Developments in Feminism,* 35–47. Toronto: Women's Press, 2003.

Atwood, Margaret. "Review of *Diving into the Wreck*," *The New York Times Book Review* (December 30, 1973), 1–2.

Bannerji, Himani. *Thinking Through: Essays on Feminism, Marxism and Anti-Racism*. Toronto: Women's Press, 1995.

Bobb-Smith, Yvonne. *I Know Who I Am: A Caribbean Woman's Identity in Canada*. Toronto: Women's Press, 2003.

Borowy, Jan, Shelly Gordon, and Gayle Lebans. "Are These Clothes Clean? The Campaign for Fair Wages and Working Conditions for Homeworkers," in Linda E. Carty (ed.), *And Still We Rise: Feminist Political Mobilizing in Contemporary Canada*, 209–330. Toronto: Women's Press, 1993.

Briskin, Linda. "Privileging Agency and Organizing: A New Approach for Women's Studies." Toronto: 2003.

Broadhead, Lee-Anne. "The Gender Dimension to the Search for Global Justice," *Canadian Woman Studies* 21/22:4/1 (Spring/Summer 2002), 90–99.

Bruckert, Chris. *Taking It Off, Putting It On: Women in the Strip Trade*. Toronto: Women's Press, 2002.

Cho, Margaret. "Crush Crash," in *I'm the One that I Want*, 132–139. New York: Ballantine Books, 2001.

Cruikshank, Margaret. "A Feminist's View of Gerontology and Women's Aging," in *Learning to Be Old: Gender, Culture and Aging*, 190–199. Lanham, MD: Rowman & Littlefield Publishers, 2003.

Davis, Angela. "Mama's Got the Blues," in *Blues Legacies and Black Feminism*, 42–65. New York: Random House, 1998.

de Beauvoir, Simone. "Myth and Reality," in *The Second Sex*, 282–292. New York: Random House.

Driedger, Diane. "Emerging from the Shadows: Women with Disabilities Organize," in Driedger et al. (eds.), *Across Borders: Women with Disabilities Working Together*, 10–25. Toronto: Women's Press, 1996.

Egan, Carolyn, and Linda Gardner. "Racism, Women's Health, and Reproductive Freedom," in Enakshi Dua and Angela Robertson (eds.), *Scratching the Surface: Canadian Anti-Racist Feminist Thought*, 295–307. Toronto: Women's Press, 1999.

Estés, Clarissa Pinkola. "The Howl: Resurrection of the Wild Woman," in *Women Who Run With the Wolves: Myths* and Stories of the Wild Woman, 25–38. New York: Ballantine Books, 1992.

Fausto-Sterling, Anne. "The Five Sexes Revisited," The Sciences (July/August 2000), 19–25.

Fédération des femmes du Québec. "2000 Good Reasons to March," in Somer Brodribb (ed.), Reclaiming the Future: Women's Strategies for the 21st Century, 273–283. Toronto: Women's Press, 1999.

Frankenberg, Ruth. "Growing Up White; Feminism, Racism and the Social Geography of Childhood," The Feminist Review 45, 51–84. London: Thomson Publishing, 1993.

Friedan, Betty. "The Crisis in Woman's Identity," in The Feminine Mystique, 69–79. New York: W.W. Norton & Company, 1963.

Glaser, Julie. "Eat and Disorder," in Elizabeth Ruth (ed.), Bent on Writing: Contemporary Queer Tales, 49–57. Toronto: Women's Press, 2002.

Goldman, Emma. "Marriage and Love," in Anarchism and Other Essays. New York: Mother Earth Publishing Association, 1917.

Gould, Lois. "X: A Fabulous Child's Story," in Blythe McVicker Clinchy and Julie K. Norem (eds.), The Gender and Psychology Reader, 523–530. New York: New York University Press, 1998.

Graham, Nancy. Afraid of the Day. Toronto: Women's Press, 2003.

Greer, Germaine. "The Middle Class Myth of Love and Marriage," in The Female Eunuch, 195–215. New York: McGraw Hill, 1971.

Handa, Amita. Of Silk Saris and Miniskirts: South Asian Girls Walk the Tightrope of Culture. Toronto: Women's Press, 2003.

hooks, bell. "Feminism: A Transformational Politic," in Talking Back: Thinking Feminist, Thinking Black, 19–27. Toronto: Between the Lines, 1988.

Israelite, Neita Kay, and Karen Swartz. "Reformulating the Feminist Perspective: Giving Voice to Women with Disabilities." Toronto: 2004.

Kabeer, Naila. "Gender Equality and Human Development Outcomes: Enhancing Capabilities," in Gender Mainstreaming in Poverty Eradication and the Millennium Development Goals, 147–167. London: The Commonwealth Secretariat, 2003.

Kinahan, Anne-Marie. "Women Who Run from the Wolves: Feminist Critique As Post-Feminism," Canadian Review of American Studies 31:2 (2001), 1–15.

Landau, Tammy. "Women's Experiences with Mandatory Charging for Wife Assault in Ontario, Canada: A Case Against the Prosecution," in Domestic Violence: Global Responses, 141–157. Oxford: AB Academic Publishers, 2000.

LeBesco, Kathleen. "Fat and Fabulous: Resisting Constructions of Female Body Ideals." Toronto: 2003.

Lorde, Audre. "Uses of the Erotic: The Erotic As Power," in Sister Outsider: Essays and Speeches, 53–59. Berkeley, CA: The Crossing Press, 1984.

Luxton, Meg. "Feminism As a Class Act: Working-Class Feminism and the Women's Movement in Canada," Labour / Le Travail 48 (2001), 63–88.

MacKinnon, Catherine A. "Not A Moral Issue," in Feminism Unmodified: Discourses on Life and Law, 169–185. Harvard University Press, 1987.

McIvor, Sharon Donna. "Self-Government and Aboriginal Women," in Enakshi Dua and Angela Robertson (eds.), Scratching the Surface: Canadian Anti-Racist Feminist Thought, 167–186. Toronto: Women's Press, 1999.

Mies, Maria, and Vandana Shiva. Ecofeminism. London: Zed Books, 1993.

Motion. Motion in Poetry. Toronto: Women's Press, 2002.

Muscio, Inga. "Blood and Cunts," in Cunt: A Declaration of Independence, 28–52. Seattle: Seal Press, 1998.

Namaste, Viviane, and Georgia Sitara. "Inclusive Pedagogy in the Women's Studies Classroom: Teaching the Kimberly Nixon Case." Toronto: 2004.

Noble, Jean Bobby. "Queer Pedagogies of the Closet." Toronto: 2004.

O'Reilly, Andrea. "Mothers, Daughters and Feminism Today: Empowerment, Agency, Narrative, and Motherline," in Canadian Woman Studies: An Introductory Reader, 495–504. Toronto: Inanna Publications, 1999.

Payette, Patricia. "The Feminist Wife? Notes from a Political Engagement," in *Jane Sexes It Up: True Confessions of Feminist Desire*, 139–167. New York: Four Walls Eight Windows, 2002.

Rankin, L. Pauline, and Jill Vickers. *Women's Movements and State Feminism: Integrating Diversity into Public Policy*. Available at www.swc-cfc.gc.ca/pubs/0662657756/200105_0662657756_e.pdf.

Rich, Adrienne. "Credo of a Passionate Skeptic," *LA Times Book Review* (March 11, 2001), 1.

Rosenberg, Harriet G. "From Trash to Treasure: Housewife Activists and the Environmental Justice Movement," in *Articulating Hidden Histories: Exploring the Influence of Eric R. Wolf*, 190–204. Berkeley, CA: University of California Press, 1995).

Sacks, Samantha. "Why Are You a Feminist?" in *Canadian Woman Studies: An Introductory Reader*, 15–17. Toronto: Inanna Publications, 1999.

Schneer, David, and Caryn Aviv. "Identity, Community and Same-Sex Marriage," in *Queer Jews*, 172–185. New York: Routledge Books, 2002.

Silman, Janet. *Enough Is Enough: Aboriginal Women Speak Out*. Toronto: Women's Press, 1997.

Silvera, Makeda. "Man Royals and Sodomites: Some Thoughts on the Invisibility of Afro Caribbean Lesbians," in *Piece of My Heart: A Lesbian of Colour Anthology*, 14–26. Toronto: Sister Vision Press, 1991.

Smith, Beverly. *Equal Marriage for Same-Sex Couples*. Available at www.samesexmarriage.ca.

Sollfrank, Cornelia. *Women Hackers*. Available at www.obn.org/hackers/text1.htm#cf.

Sontag, Susan. "The Double Standard of Aging," in Juanita Williams (ed.), *Psychology of Women: Selected Readings*. New York: Norton, 1979.

Steinem, Gloria. "Life Between the Lines," in *Outrageous Acts and Everyday Rebellions*, 1–26. New York: Holt, Rinehart and Winston, 1983.

Tamaki, Mariko. *True Lies: The Book of Bad Advice*. Toronto: Women's Press, 2002.

Walker, Alice. "Womanist / A Letter to the Editor of Ms.," in *In Search of Our Mothers' Gardens: Womanist Prose*, xi-xiii; 273–277. San Diego: Harcourt Brace Jovanovich, 1983.

Wolf, Naomi. "Nakedness, Pride and Shame," in *Promiscuities: The Secret Struggle For Womanhood*, 35–49. New York: Random House, 1998.

Copyright Acknowledgements

Recent titles by
Canadian Scholars' Press
and Women's Press

Afraid of the Day: A Daughter's Story
Nancy Graham

*And Still We Rise: Feminist Political
Mobilizing in Contemporary Canada*
Edited by Linda Carty

*Aversion and Desire:
Muslim Female Identity in the Diaspora*
Shahnaz Khan

*The Dark Side of the Nation: Essays on
Multiculturalism, Nationalism and Gender*
Himani Bannerji

*Feminism, Political Economy and the State:
Contested Terrain*
Edited by Pat Armstrong and
M. Patricia Connelly

*I Know Who I Am: A Caribbean
Woman's Identity in Canada*
Yvonne Bobb-Smith

Is Anyone Listening? Women, Work and Society
Merle Jacobs

*More Than a Labour of Love: Three Generations
of Women's Work in the Home*
Meg Luxton

*Mother Outlaws: Theories and Practices
of Empowered Mothering*
Edited by Andrea O'Reilly

*The Muslim Veil in North America:
Issues and Debates*
Sajida Alvi, Homa Hoodfar, Sheila McDonough

*Of Silk Saris and Mini-Skirts:
South Asian Girls Walk the Tightrope of Culture*
Amita Handa

*Out on the Field:
Gender, Sport and Sexualities*
Helen Lenskyj

*Politics and Poetics of Migration:
Narratives of Iranian Women from the Diaspora*
Parin Dossa

*Studies in Political Economy:
Developments in Feminism*
Edited by Pat Armstrong et al.

*Taking It Off, Putting It On:
Women in the Strip Trade*
Chris Bruckert

*Thinking Through: Essays on Feminism,
Marxism and Anti-Racism*
Himani Bannerji